Scott Foresman
ELL Handbook

Glenview, Illinois
Boston, Massachusetts
Chandler, Arizona
Upper Saddle River, New Jersey

ISBN-13: 978-0-328-47641-1
ISBN-10: 0-328-47641-2
7 8 9 10 V011 15 14 13

CC1

Contents

Part 1
English Language Learners: Professional Development Articles

Contents

Resources on Reading Street for English Language Learner Support

All the support you need for your ELL instruction.

The Teacher's Edition has ELL instructional strategies built into the lesson plans at point of use. The lessons provide guidance in using sheltered techniques and routines for teaching academic vocabulary, listening comprehension, phonics, vocabulary, reading comprehension, grammar and conventions, and writing.

Teacher's Edition

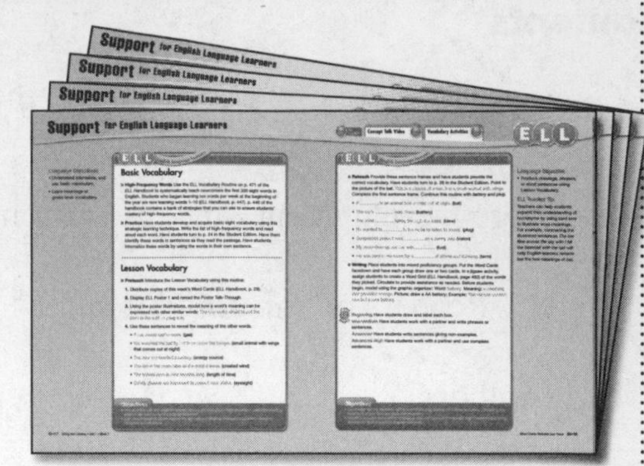

ELL Support pages

ELL Posters contain high-quality illustrations and five days of activities to support key oral vocabulary, selection vocabulary, and lesson concepts.

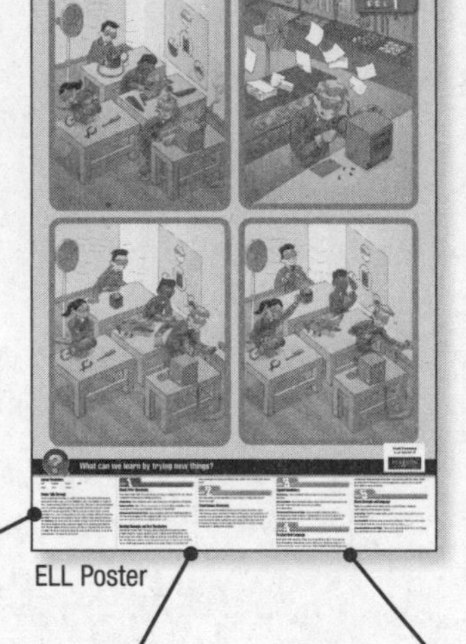
ELL Poster

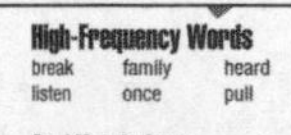

High-Frequency Words
break family heard
listen once pull

Oral Vocabulary
courageous hazard rescue

Poster Talk-Through
This **family's** cat is stuck in the tree. The family **heard** the cat meowing loudly. They came out to see what was wrong. The mother went back inside and called 911. Then she came out to wait for help with her family. Courageous firefighters came to rescue the cat. They started to work at **once**. They did not wait. Now one fireman **pulls** the cat from the tree as the branch is about to **break**! The family **listens** as the fireman talks gently to the cat. When they listen, they feel calm. Everything is going to be all right. The hazard is gone.

DAY 1

Check Prior Knowledge
Read the Poster Talk-Through aloud, pointing to images in the art. Check children's knowledge by asking questions.

Beginning Ask children to point to items they recognize on the poster and say what they are. Help them name items if necessary.

Intermediate Have children use short sentences to describe what is happening in the poster.

Advanced/Advanced High Ask children to describe the dangerous situation shown in the poster. Have them explain why it is dangerous.

Develop Concepts and Oral Vocabulary
Reread the Poster Talk-Through to introduce the Oral Vocabulary words. Give visual support by pointing to items on the poster that illustrate courageous, hazard, and rescue. Work with the class on a list of ideas that exemplify the words. Generate examples of hazards, ways to rescue something or someone, and courageous acts. Relate these concepts to the Question of the Week by asking children how they can help each other in dangerous situations.

DAY 2

Use the poster art and question to help children briefly discuss the lesson concept.

Teach High-Frequency Words
Share the Poster Talk-Through again, this time to introduce the tested High-Frequency Words. Label the poster with the High-Frequency Words. Then have the children, one at a time, act out one of the words for the others to guess.

DAY 3

Expand Vocabulary
Give the class examples of possible dangerous situations, such as: *Somebody gets hurt on the playground. Your friend is lost on a busy street.* As you name each situation, give pairs time to discuss and write down or sketch an appropriate way to help. Have pairs share their responses with the class at the end of the allotted time. Tell children that when there is real danger, they should tell an adult or call 911.

DAY 4

Produce Oral Language
Have the class pretend that they are in the poster scene. Have groups act out a television interview with the poster characters. Write *Who?*, *What?*, *When?*, *Where?*, *Why?*, and *How?* on the board to guide questions.

Beginning/Intermediate Have children act as reporters and ask simple questions of people on the scene.

Advanced/Advanced High Have them play the parts of family members or firefighters.

DAY 5

Check Concepts and Language
Read the Question of the Week aloud. Monitor children's understanding of the lesson concept.

Beginning Provide the children with this sentence prompt: *In a dangerous situation, we can help by ______.* Ask each child to come up with one or two ways to complete the sentence.

Intermediate Ask: *What are two things that we can do to help in dangerous situations?* Have children write a simple sentence for each response.

Advanced/Advanced High Have children write a very brief paragraph that answers the Question of the Week, *How can we help each other in dangerous situations?*

The ELL Handbook includes phonics and grammar transition lessons, comprehension skill practice, selection vocabulary word cards, study guides for ELL Readers, and multilingual selection summaries and vocabulary charts. Weekly planners provide daily instructional plans.

ELL Handbook

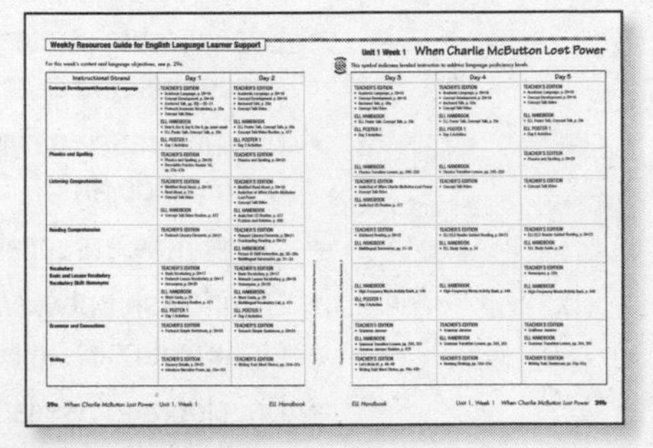

Weekly Planner

Instructional-level fiction and nonfiction books are provided for readers at all proficiency levels. The ELL, ELD, and Concept Literacy Readers relate to weekly concepts and offer students opportunities to read texts and practice target skills and strategies.

ELD/ELL Reader Teaching Guide

ELD Reader

ELL Reader

Concept Literacy Reader

Technology

Concept Talk Video

Use the Concept Talk Video to activate an engaging discussion about the weekly concept. Use the Concept Talk Video Routine found in the ELL Handbook to guide students' understanding.

AudioText CD

Use the AudioText CD and the AudioText CD Routine in this ELL Handbook to help students build fluency and comprehension and prepare for reading the main selection.

Grammar Jammer

Grammar Jammer provides additional practice with weekly grammar skills. For suggestions on how to use this learning tool, see the Grammar Jammer Routine in the ELL Handbook.

Language Development Student Outcomes

Language Learning Strategies	• Use prior knowledge and experiences to understand English. • Self-monitor oral or written language to recognize and correct errors or to seek help. • Use strategic learning techniques (such as concept mapping, drawing, memorizing, comparing, contrasting, or reviewing) to learn vocabulary. • Use learning strategies when speaking (request assistance, employ non-verbal cues, or use synonyms and descriptions in place of unknown English words). • Use and reuse newly acquired English words and expressions to improve proficiency and to build concepts. • Learn new essential language by using familiar or accessible language. • Distinguish between formal and informal English and use each language register in appropriate circumstances, in accord with grade-level expectations. • Develop and use language-learning strategies (such as looking for patterns in language or analyzing sayings and expressions), in accord with grade-level expectations.
Listening Skills	• Distinguish sounds and intonation patterns in English words and expressions with increasing clarity. • Distinguish phonetic sounds of English during word learning. • Learn English language structures, expressions, and vocabulary by listening to instruction and talking with peers and teachers. • Self-monitor for understanding of language during instruction and conversations, and seek clarification as needed. • Use visual resources, context, and familiar language to better understand unfamiliar spoken English. • Listen to a variety of media, paying attention to language meaning, to build concepts and acquire language. • Understand the meaning, main points, and important details of spoken language about familiar or unfamiliar topics. • Understand information and implied ideas in complex spoken language, in accord with grade-level expectations. • Demonstrate listening comprehension by following directions, responding to questions and requests, collaborating with peers, taking notes, or retelling and summarizing spoken messages.
Speaking Skills	• Produce phonetic sounds in newly acquired words and expressions in order to pronounce English words in an understandable manner. • Learn and use high-frequency English words to identify and describe people, places, animals, and objects. • Learn English vocabulary by retelling simple stories and information represented or supported by pictures. • Learn and use English words and expressions needed for classroom communication. • Speak using a variety of English grammatical structures, sentence lengths, sentence types, and connecting words with increasing accuracy and ease. • Speak using grade-appropriate content-area vocabulary in context to learn new English words and build academic language proficiency. • Share information interactively with peers and teachers. • Ask for and give information, using high-frequency, concrete words and expressions for basic communication and using abstract and content-based vocabulary during extended speaking assignments.

	• Express opinions, ideas, and feelings, ranging from using words and short phrases to participating in discussions about various grade-appropriate topics. • Explain, narrate, and describe with increasing specificity and detail as more English is acquired. • Adapt spoken language appropriately for formal and informal purposes. • Respond orally to information in print, electronic, audio, and visual media to build concepts and acquire language.
Reading Skills	• Learn relationships between sounds and letters in English, and decode words by recognizing sound-letter relationships and identifying cognates, affixes, roots, and base words. • Recognize the directionality of written English: left to right and top to bottom. • Develop basic English sight vocabulary. • Derive meaning of environmental print. • Comprehend English used routinely in grade-level texts. • Use before-reading strategies such as previewing graphic organizers and illustrations or learning topic-related vocabulary to enhance comprehension of written text. • Read adapted content-area material with a decreasing need for linguistic accommodations as more English is learned. • Use visual resources and context to read grade-appropriate text with understanding and to acquire vocabulary including academic language. • Use support from peers and teachers to read grade-appropriate text with understanding and to acquire vocabulary including academic language. • Demonstrate comprehension of increasingly complex grade-appropriate texts in English by participating in shared reading, retelling, or summarizing; responding to questions; and taking notes. • Read silently with increasing ease and comprehension for sustained periods. • Demonstrate English comprehension by employing and expanding basic reading skills (such as summarizing, understanding supporting ideas and details in text and graphic sources, and distinguishing main ideas from details) in accord with grade-level needs. • Demonstrate English comprehension by employing and expanding inferential skills (such as predicting, making connections between ideas, drawing conclusions from text and graphic sources, and finding supporting text evidence) in accord with grade-level needs. • Demonstrate English comprehension by employing and expanding analytical skills (such as evaluating written information and critically examining texts) in accord with grade-level needs.
Writing Skills	• Represent the sounds of the English language with letters when writing words in English. • Write using newly acquired basic English vocabulary and grade-level academic vocabulary. • Spell common English words with increasing accuracy, and use spelling patterns correctly as more English is acquired. • Edit writing for standard grammar and usage, including subject-verb agreement, pronoun agreement, and appropriate verb tenses, in accord with grade-level expectations as more English is acquired. • Use grammatical structures (such as verbs in different tenses, pronouns, possessive nouns, contractions, and negatives) correctly in writing, in accord with grade-level expectations. • Write using a variety of grade-appropriate sentence lengths, patterns, and connecting words to combine phrases, clauses, and sentences in increasingly accurate ways. • Narrate, describe, and explain with increasing detail to fulfill grade-appropriate writing needs as more English is acquired.

Grade 3 Readers on Reading Street

Every week there are a variety of readers to choose from to target instruction and meet the language development needs and reading levels of all learners. Every reader supports weekly grade-level concept development and the Question of the Week.

Leveled Readers

Weekly fiction and nonfiction readers are provided for students at the On-Level, Strategic Intervention, and Advanced levels.

On-Level

Strategic Intervention

Advanced

Build Concepts

The Concept Literacy Reader builds concepts and language.

Concept Literacy

Build Language

Scaffolded versions build vocabulary and comprehension skills each week at different proficiency levels.

ELD Reader

ELL Reader

Beginning • Intermediate
• Contains the same high-quality art as the ELL Reader.
• Text adapted for Beginning and Intermediate proficiency levels.
• High-frequency and concept words are emphasized.
• Graphic elements are simplified.
• Captions for photos are simple, then progress to either phrases or short sentences.

Intermediate • Advanced • Advanced High
• Contains the same high-quality art as the ELD Reader.
• Text adapted for Intermediate to Advanced High proficiency levels.
• Concept words that students need to know to understand the text are highlighted and defined.
• Graphic elements such as captions, diagrams, maps, flow charts, and signs are included.
• Captions for photos are complete sentences.

Scott Foresman ELL Authors

Elena Izquierdo, Ph.D.
Associate Professor
University of Texas at El Paso

Jim Cummins, Ph.D.
Professor
Department of Curriculum, Teaching and Learning
University of Toronto

Lily Wong Fillmore, Ph.D.
Professor Emerita
Graduate School of Education
University of California, Berkeley

Georgia Earnest García, Ph.D.
Professor
Language and Literacy Division
Department of Curriculum and Instruction
University of Illinois at Urbana-Champaign

George A. González, Ph.D.
Professor (Retired)
School of Education
University of Texas-Pan American, Edinburg

The Three Pillars of English Language Learning

Dr. Jim Cummins, the University of Toronto

In order to understand how English learners develop second-language literacy and reading comprehension, we must distinguish between three different aspects of language proficiency:

Conversational fluency This dimension of proficiency represents the ability to carry on a conversation in face-to-face situations. Most native speakers of English have developed conversational fluency by age 5. This fluency involves use of high-frequency words and simple grammatical constructions. English learners generally develop fluency in conversational English within a year or two of intensive exposure to the language in school or in their neighborhood environments.

Discrete language skills These skills reflect specific phonological, literacy, and grammatical knowledge that students can acquire in two ways— through direct instruction and through immersion in a literacy-rich and language-rich environment in home or in school. The discrete language skills acquired early include:

- knowledge of the letters of the alphabet
- knowledge of the sounds represented by individual letters and combinations of letters
- the ability to decode written words

Children can learn these specific language skills concurrently with their development of basic English vocabulary and conversational fluency.

Academic language proficiency This dimension of proficiency includes knowledge of the less frequent vocabulary of English as well as the ability to interpret and produce increasingly complex written language. As students progress through the grades, they encounter:

- far more low-frequency words, primarily from Greek and Latin sources
- complex syntax (for example, sentences in passive voice)
- abstract expressions

Acquiring academic language is challenging. Schools spend at least 12 years trying to teach all students the complex language associated with academic success. It is hardly surprising that research has repeatedly shown that English language learners, on average, require *at least* 5 years of exposure to academic English to catch up to native-speaker norms.

Effective instruction for English language learners is built on three fundamental pillars.

English Language Learners

Activate Prior Knowledge/ Build Background	Access Content	Extend Language

Activate Prior Knowledge/ Build Background

No learner is a blank slate. Each person's prior experience provides the foundation for interpreting new information. In reading, we construct meaning by bringing our prior knowledge of language and of the world to the text. The more we already know about the topic in the text, the more of the text we can understand. Our prior knowledge enables us to make inferences about the meaning of words and expressions that we may not have come across before. Furthermore, the more of the text we understand, the more new knowledge we can acquire. This expands our knowledge base (what cognitive psychologists call *schemata*, or underlying patterns of concepts). Such comprehension, in turn, enables us to understand even more concepts and vocabulary.

It is important to *activate* students' prior knowledge because students may not realize what they know about a particular topic or issue. Their knowledge may not facilitate learning unless that knowledge is brought to consciousness.

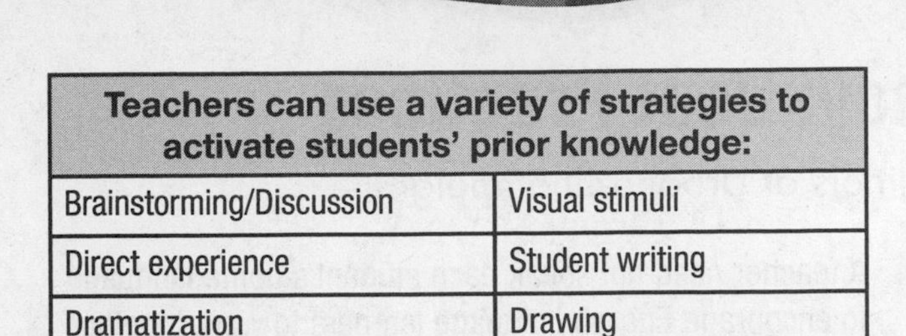

Teachers can use a variety of strategies to activate students' prior knowledge:	
Brainstorming/Discussion	Visual stimuli
Direct experience	Student writing
Dramatization	Drawing

When students don't already have knowledge about a topic, it is important to help them acquire that knowledge. For example, in order to comprehened texts such as *The Midnight Ride of Paul Revere,* students need to have background knowledge about the origin of the United States.

Access Content

How can teachers make complex academic English comprehensible for students who are still in the process of learning English?

We can *scaffold* students' learning by modifying the input itself. Here are a variety of ways of modifying the presentation of academic content to students so that they can more effectively gain access to the meaning.

Using visuals Visuals enable students to "see" the basic concepts we are trying to teach much more effectively than if we rely only on words. Among the visuals we can use are:

- pictures/diagrams
- vocabulary cards
- real objects
- graphic organizers
- maps

Dramatization/Acting out For beginning English learners, physical response, in which they follow commands such as "Turn around," can be highly effective. The meanings of words can be demonstrated through *gestures* and *pantomime.*

Language clarification This category of teaching methods includes language-oriented activities that clarify the meaning of new words and concepts. *Use of dictionaries,* either bilingual or English-only, is still the most direct method of getting access to meaning.

Making personal and cultural connections We should constantly search for ways to link academic content with what students already know or what is familiar to them from their family or cultural experiences. This not only validates children's sense of identity, but it also makes the learning more meaningful.

Extend Language

A systematic exploration of language is essential if students are to develop a curiosity about language and deepen their understanding of how words work. Students should become *language detectives* who investigate the mysteries of language and how it has been used throughout history to shape and change society.

Students also can explore the building blocks of language. A large percentage of the less frequently heard academic vocabulary of English derives from Latin and Greek roots. Word formation follows predictable patterns. These patterns are very similar in English and Spanish.

When students know rules or conventions of how words are formed, it gives them an edge in extending vocabulary. It helps them figure out the meanings of words and how to form different parts of speech from words. The exploration of language can focus on meaning, form, or use.

Focus on meaning Categories that can be explored within a focus on meaning include:

- home language equivalents or cognates
- synonyms, antonyms, and homonyms
- meanings of prefixes, roots, and suffixes

Focus on form Categories that can be explored within a focus on form include:

- word families
- grammatical patterns
- words with same prefixes, roots, or suffixes

Focus on use Categories that can be explored within a focus on use include:

- general uses
- idioms
- metaphorical use
- proverbs
- advertisements
- puns and jokes

The Three Pillars

- Activate Prior Knowledge/Build Background,
- Access Content,
- Extend Language,

establish a solid structure for the effective instruction of English language learners.

English Learners and Literacy: Best Practices

Dr. Georgia Earnest García, the University of Illinois at Urbana-Champaign

Like other children, English language learners come to school with much oral language knowledge and experience. Their knowledge and experience in languages other than English provide skills and world knowledge that teachers can build on.

Making literacy instruction comprehensible to English language learners is essential. Many of the teaching strategies developed for children who are proficient in English can be adapted for English learners, and many strategies from an English language learner curriculum are also useful in "mainstream" reading education.

Building on Children's Knowledge

It is vital to learn about each student's literacy development and proficiency in the home language. School personnel should ask parents:

- How many years of school instruction has the child received in the home language?
- Can the child read and write in that language?
- Can the child read in any other language?

Students can transfer aspects of home-language literacy to their English literacy development, such as phonological awareness and reading (or listening) comprehension strategies. If they already know key concepts and vocabulary in their home languages, then they can transfer that knowledge to English. For the vocabulary concepts they already know in their home languages, they only need to learn the English labels. Not all English learners automatically transfer what they have learned in the home language to their reading in English. Teachers can help facilitate relevant transfer by explicitly asking English learners to think about what they have learned about a topic in the home language.

A teacher need not speak each student's home language to encourage English language learners to work together and benefit from one another's knowledge. Students can communicate in their home languages and English, building the content knowledge, confidence, and English skills that they need to participate fully in learning. Devising activities in which students who share home languages can work together also allows a school to pool resources, such as bilingual dictionaries and other books, as well as home-language tutors or aides.

Sheltering Instruction in English

Often, beginning and intermediate English language learners may not understand what their classroom teachers say or read aloud in English. These students benefit when teachers shelter, or make comprehensible, their literacy instruction.

Sheltered techniques include using:

- consistent, simplified, clearly enunciated, and slower-paced oral language to explain literacy concepts or activities
- gestures, photos, illustrations, drawings, real objects, dramatization, and/or physical action to illustrate important concepts and vocabulary
- activities that integrate reading, writing, listening, and speaking, so students see, hear, read, and write new vocabulary, sentence structures, and content

When it is clear from students' actions and responses that they understand what is being said, teachers can vary their strategies. As students' comprehension expands, teachers can gradually curtail their use of adapted oral language and of gestures, illustrations, and dramatizations.

Adapting Literacy Activities

Teachers can use many instructional activities developed for native English speakers with English language learners. For example, teacher read-alouds, shared reading, and paired reading can allow an English learner to follow the text during a reading. Such techniques greatly improve students' learning skills and comprehension.

Similarly, interactive journal writing, in which the teacher and student take turns writing entries, allows students to explore topics and ask questions. It also allows teachers to engage in ongoing authentic assessment of student proficiency and to pinpoint areas of misunderstanding.

Small group instruction and discussion also are helpful. Beginning English language learners benefit from the repeated readings of predictable texts with illustrations, especially when the teacher has provided a brief preview of each text to introduce the topic of the story and preview new vocabulary.

Repeated reading aloud of such predictable, patterned, illustrated texts provides English language learners with multiple opportunities to match the text they read with the words they hear. When students participate in shared reading and echo the spoken text or read the words aloud chorally, anxiety about pronunciation or decoding errors is reduced. When teachers choose texts that are culturally familiar and ask English language learners personal questions related to the text, the result is a lower-risk learning environment and an increased opportunity for students to make accurate inferences.

Examples of Teaching Strategies

Before students read content material, provide them with hands-on or visual experience directly related to the content. Then have them use a graphic organizer to map what they have learned or seen about the topic. Let pairs or small groups of students brainstorm for words that are related to the concept. Then introduce other related words, including vocabulary from the reading. Illustrate new concepts or vocabulary with drawings, photographs, or artifacts that represent the concepts. The hands-on experience and graphic organizer that precede the reading help introduce students to new concepts. Students will thus be familiar with the selection's subject before they begin to read.

Semantic Mapping Working with graphic organizers can help teach vocabulary and concepts in subject areas.

For example, before a reading on the subject of baby animals, have students help you to complete a semantic map showing pictures of animals and the names of baby animals. Ask them to volunteer the names for animal babies in their home language and transcribe their responses. Then show students examples of the different forms of writing. Ask students to meet in small groups to identify the examples. They may do this in English or their home language. If they use the home language, the teacher needs to write the English labels on the board for each form of writing. Then students need to enter the words for the different forms of writing, with drawings or home language equivalents, into a vocabulary notebook.

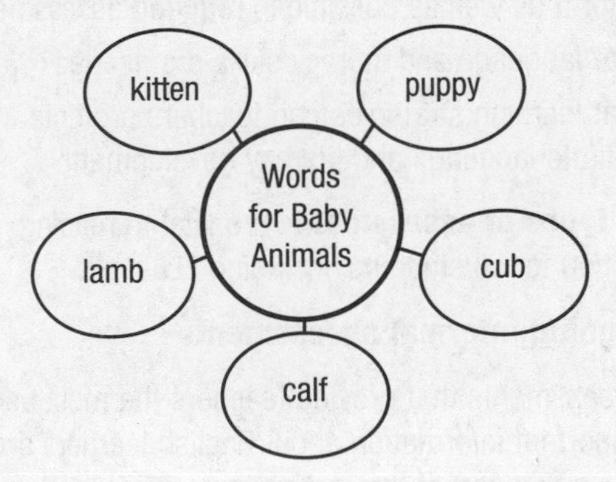

Summarizing After reading, students can dictate what they remember from their reading to the teacher. Students can then illustrate their summaries, and label the illustrations with vocabulary from the reading.

Preparing English Language Learners for Assessment

Dr. Lily Wong Fillmore, the University of California, Berkeley

Under federal and state law, all students—including English learners—must be assessed annually on their progress toward mastery of academic standards in reading, math, and science. Many questions arise when certain assessments are used with ELLs because their test scores are never easy to interpret when they are assessed in English. The most critical question is this: What do test scores mean when they are based on instruction and assessments given in a language students have not yet mastered? Although difficult to interpret, assessments are required of all students, so we must consider how to help ELLs perform as well as possible.

Addressed in this essay

- What can teachers do to fast-track their ELL students' mastery of the language and content needed to perform as well as possible in required assessments?
- What language and literacy skills are needed?
- What learning strategies can teachers promote to facilitate language and literacy development?

Three types of assessments are vital to reading instruction for all students, including ELLs.

1. Ongoing informal assessments

The assessments that provide teachers the most useful and important information about English learners are those used as part of the instructional process. How well do children understand the materials they are working with, and what needs adjustment or modification in instruction? These are built into these instructional materials and help teachers keep an ongoing record of student progress over time. Such assessments do not need to be elaborate. Asking children what they think is happening in a text can reveal how well they comprehend what they are reading. Asking children what they think words or phrases mean can show whether they are trying to make sense of text. These types of questions are highly useful to teachers since they allow them to monitor participation levels and help them discover who understands the materials and who needs more attention and support.

2. Diagnostic assessments

A second type of assessment that some ELLs may require is diagnostic, and it is needed when individuals are not making the progress expected of them. The school must determine where student problems lie (e.g., skill development, or perception or awareness of English sounds, vocabulary, or grammar) before teachers can provide the corrective help needed.

3. Standardized assessments

The type of assessments that causes teachers of ELLs the greatest concern are the standards-based tests of English Language Arts and content area tests (especially in Math). These state tests are required of all students and are recognized as "high stakes" tests for students and for schools. They are often used to evaluate the effectiveness of a curriculum, the teacher, or the instructional approach used.

What's involved in reading?

Reading skills are built on several types of knowledge: linguistic, symbolic, experiential, and strategic. Each is crucial and is linked with the others. *Language is fundamental;* it is the medium through which meaning—information, story, knowledge, poetry, and thought—is communicated from writer to reader. Unlike speech, what is communicated by written language is indirect and *encoded in symbols* that must be deciphered before access to meaning is possible.

But reading goes beyond mere decoding. Texts call for readers to apply what they know about how language is used to convey thought and ideas to interpret what they are reading. Having *experienced reading as a sense-making activity,* readers will seek meaning as they learn to read. This calls for *special strategies:* They look for meaning if they assume it is to be found in texts. If they do not know

the language in which the texts are written, they will recognize that learning the code is the key to unlocking meaning. They will pay attention to the language and ask: *What is this saying? What does this mean? How does this relate to what I already know about the way the language works?*

English learners have an easier time learning to read in English if they have already learned to read in their first language. Without question, a language barrier makes learning to read a more difficult task. But if students have already learned to read in their primary language, they know what is involved, what to expect, and thus they are in a better position to deal with learning to read in the new language in order to access meaning.

Can children learn to read in a language before they are fully proficient in that language?

Can they in fact learn the language through reading? *Yes, but only with ample instructional assistance that supports the development of both.* Ideally, reading instruction in English comes after ELLs have gained some familiarity with the sounds and patterns of spoken English. Children need to hear the sounds of the new language before they can connect symbols to those sounds. For example, in order for children to gain confidence relating the many vowel sounds of English to the five vowel symbols used to "spell them," they need help hearing them and differentiating them in words.

Similarly, many ELLs need help dealing with the ways consonants pile up at the beginning and at the ends of syllables and words in English, which may be quite different than the way consonants are used in their primary language. Most crucially, ELLs need help in connecting the words they are learning to decode from the text to their referents. Using pictures, demonstrations, diagrams, gestures, and enactments, teachers can help ELLs see how the words, phrases, and sentences in the reading selections have meaning that can be accessed through the language they are learning.

Helping ELLs become successful readers

The most important way to help ELLs perform well in mandated reading assessments is by giving them the instructional support they need to become successful readers. This involves help in:

- Learning English
- Discovering the purpose of reading
- Becoming active learners
- Gaining access to academic language

Learning English

The more proficient children are in the language they are reading, the more readily they learn to read. For ELLs, support for learning English is support for learning to read. The most effective kind of help comes in content-focused language instruction, where learners are engaged in grade-level-appropriate instructional activities and their participation is scaffolded and supported as needed.

The most effective activities provide ELLs ample opportunity to hear English and to use it productively in meaningful communication. Teachers play a vital role in creating a supportive classroom environment. ELLs must be able to participate to the extent possible (again, with as much support as needed) in discussions with classmates who are more proficient in English. Peers can offer practice and support, but only teachers can ensure that ELLs get access to the kind of language needed for literacy development.

Purpose of reading

The greatest dangers ELLs face in learning to read in English before they are proficient in that language is that the effort involved in decoding takes precedence in their minds over all else. Connections between words and referents, between words and structures, and between text and meaning are overlooked when children focus on sounding out, figuring out symbols, and figuring out sounds. This is especially likely to happen when there is too little emphasis placed on reading as a sense-making activity in instructional programs. If meaning—no matter how difficult it is to come by—is not constantly emphasized in reading instruction, children end up believing that decoding is reading, and that there is nothing missing when they read without understanding.

Decoding becomes an end in itself, and the real purpose of reading is lost. Unfortunately, this is the outcome for many ELLs, who even after having learned English do not perform well in reading assessments.

Literacy in English begins as deciphering for ELLs; they must first figure out how the code in which the text is written works. It is not until the reader engages in an interpretive process in which the thoughts, information, concepts, situations, and relations encoded in the texts are manifested as meanings that there is real reading. This is true for both ELLs and for native English speakers. ELLs, however, will need a lot of guidance and instructional support from teachers to do that. Once children have gained enough familiarity with English to participate even at a rudimentary level in discussions about reading selections and content, they begin to learn that the materials they are reading have something to say to them and that hearing what they have to say is the real purpose of learning to read.

Active readers

Helping children become active learners of English and users of the literacy skills they are acquiring is a key to their becoming successful students and performing well in the assessments they have to take. This is accomplished by encouraging children to take an active role in instructional activities, asking questions, seeking answers, and trying to make sense of what they are studying in school.

Both teachers and students can have many preconceived ideas about the roles they play as teachers and learners. Children sometimes come to school believing that learning is something that will be done to them, rather than something they must take an active role in doing. In their view, the role of the teacher is active and the role they play as learners is passive. When teachers share that belief, there is little likelihood of active or independent learning. Instruction is most effective when teachers are knowledgeable about the subject matter they are teaching, and they create a classroom environment in which learners can take an active role in discovering how things work, what things mean, and how to get and make sense of information.

Academic English

Teachers are aware that the language used in written texts is sufficiently different from everyday spoken language to constitute a barrier to children who are not already familiar with it. Academic English is not just another name for "standard English." It is, instead, the special forms of standard English used in academic discourse and in written texts. It makes use of grammatical constructions, words, and rhetorical conventions that are not often used in everyday spoken language.

Paradoxically, academic language is both a prerequisite for full literacy and the outcome of it. Some children arrive at school with a running start in acquiring it. Children who come from homes where family members engage in frequent discussions of books and ideas are already familiar with it, and thus have an advantage learning to read.

It should be noted that the language used at home does not have to be English for children to benefit from such experiences. Teachers can provide their students, irrespective of background, experiences with academic language by reading to them and discussing readings, instructional activities, and experiences. By drawing children into instructional conversations focused on the language they encounter in their school texts and other materials, teachers get children to notice language itself and to figure out how it works.

Supporting language and literacy development for ELLs

Teachers support language development by engaging children as active participants in making sense of the texts they are working on. They do it by drawing the English learners into discussions relating to the texts. Even relative newcomers are able to participate in these discussions as long as ample scaffolding is provided:

It says here, "Her teacher picked up the paper and studied it carefully."

Hector, what does the text tell us Vashti's teacher did first?

Yes, she picked up the paper first.

Take a look at the picture. Marta, can you show us which part of the sentence tells us what the teacher is doing?

Can you tell us what she is doing?

Yes! She is studying the paper carefully.

Teachers draw attention to words, phrases, and sentences, asking: "Let's see if we can figure out what that means!" By relating language to meaning, they help students gain access to meaning by demonstrating, referring to illustrations and diagrams, and paraphrasing in simpler language.

Instructional conversations about the texts they are reading are as essential for newcomers as they are for ELLs who have already gained some proficiency in English. It is vital to their literacy development to realize that what they are "reading" can be understood, even if its meaning is not immediately available to them as it would be to readers who are fully proficient in English. Without such help, ELLs sometimes come to believe that decoding without access to meaning is an empty exercise one does in school, and except for that, it has little relevance to their lives.

Teachers can help students discover how the language works and how to extract meaning from texts by considering how the language they encounter can convey information, ideas, stories, feelings, and images. This cannot wait until the learners are fully proficient in the language they are reading. It can enhance language development if done from the start, as soon as ELLs are introduced to English reading.

Strategies for supporting language and literacy development and preparing ELLs for assessment

The most effective support comes in the form of instructional conversations in which ELLs are drawn into discussions of reading selections and content. By hearing their teachers and other classmates discuss the materials they are reading, they gradually learn how the language works in texts and in conversation.

- Draw attention to the language used in reading selections and other text materials—words, phrases, and sentences—and relate them to meaning that is discussed and commented on, both locally and globally, to help ELLs learn how to get at meaning in texts.
- Provide students ample opportunity to use the language of texts in speaking (during discussions of the reading selections, for example) and in writing (in response to writing prompts).
- Teach English learners to be strategic readers by guiding them to assume that the text should make sense and that meaning can be accessed by figuring out what the words, phrases, and sentences mean.
- Teach students to ask questions about meaning as it unfolds in the text. Help them recognize that some parts of texts provide background knowledge while other parts reveal new information.
- Teach children how to relate new information presented in a text to what is already known. Train students to make inferences about meaning based on the words and phrases used in a text.
- Expect ELLs to make progress, and then ensure it by providing ample grade-level discussion of content. At the same time, recognize that it takes time to learn English, and that learners may differ in the amount and kind of help they need in order to make progress.
- Recognize that the most crucial kind of preparation for assessment is in helping children develop the ***language and literacy skills*** that are essential to successful performance in tests and for academic progress itself.
- Call children's attention to words, phrases, and constructions that often figure in text items. For example, words such as *both, not,* and *best* may not seem to be noteworthy, but their uses in test questions prove otherwise. ELLs need help in seeing how such words frame and constrain the ideas expressed in sentences in which they appear.
- Teach children the logic of test questions. Use released test items or models of test items (both of which are likely to be available online from your state department of education or district Web sites). Show children, for example, that the question, "Which of the following is NOT a sentence?" entails that all of the listed options except one *are* sentences.
- Teach children to read carefully. Children who are fully proficient in English may occasionally benefit

from test-taking strategies such as reading the test question and answer options first and then skimming the test passage to find information that will aid in the selection of the correct answer to the question. This tactic does not serve English learners well. They need to read and understand the passage carefully, and then consider how to answer the questions asked.

- Teach children when the text calls for activation of prior knowledge. All children have such knowledge, but English learners need help in deciding where it is called for and how they should bring what they already know to interpret the texts they are reading.
- Expand children's horizons by reading them texts that may be too difficult to handle on their own. Help them make sense of such materials by commenting on meaning, drawing attention to how language is used in them, and engaging children in discussions about aspects of the texts.

The texts that are read to children, and the ones they read themselves, provide reliable access to the academic language they need for literacy and for assessment, provided teachers call their attention to language and help children see how it works. Teachers do this by identifying interesting (not just new) phrases and commenting on them, inviting children to try using the phrases, and providing scaffolds as needed; they model the uses of language from texts in subsequent instructional activities; they encourage children to remember and keep records of words they learn from texts; they remind them when words and phrases encountered earlier show up again in different contexts.

The Concept of Transfer

Dr. Elena Izquierdo, the University of Texas at El Paso

Research continues to support the critical role of the child's first language (L1) in literacy development and its effect on literacy in (L2) English. Strong L1 literacy skills facilitate the transfer into English literacy, and students ultimately progress rapidly into learning in English. In reality, the concept of transfer refers to the child's facility in appropriating knowledge from one language to the other. Children do not know they know, but they know. They are constantly and indirectly, unconsciously and automatically, constructing the knowledge that is inherent in the contexts for which each of these languages can function. Reasearch by Jim Cummins has shown that the effective transfer of skills transpires as students develop their metalinguistic and metacognitive skills and as they engage in a contrastive analysis of the two languages.

Matters of transfer occur within essentials of language that are (1) common to L1 and L2; (2) similar, but not exact in both languages; and (3) specific to each language and not applicable to the other language. In essence, children develop a special awareness of language and its function; learn that some sounds are the same in both languages; and also learn that there are certain boundaries for specific sounds depending on the language.

Children who have developed an awareness for phonemes, phonics, vocabulary building, and reading comprehension skills, can transfer these skills to English. They develop an enhanced awareness of the relationship between their L1 and English, which leads them to successfully appropriate strategies of transfer in similar types of word recognition processing; searching for cognates; making reference to prior knowledge, inferencing, questioning, and monitoring. Facilitating these cognitive skills in children will support their success in English literacy and their learning in English.

English Language Learner Profiles

English Language Learners—ELLs—are a quickly growing population in U.S. schools. While some are children of recent immigrants, many more were born in the United States but have spoken other languages in their homes. ELLs may come to classrooms with knowledge of other places as well as diverse cultures and customs. As you work with ELLs, you will want to consider how proficient your students are and how you can make the academic content accessible. You will be integrating language and content instruction, most likely within the context of a classroom of students with many abilities and proficiencies. As you consider how to best meet the needs of ELLs in your classroom, think about their characteristics, patterns of development, and literacy challenges.

General Characteristics of English Language Learners

- ELLs have a first language—also called a home language, primary language, or native language—other than English and are in the process of acquiring English.
- Some ELLs have newly arrived in the United States, while others were born in the United States but have lived for many years in households where family members do not speak English.
- Some ELLs have already acquired and developed literacy skills in their native languages, while others have not learned the academic vocabulary and background knowledge necessary for continued success in school.
- ELLs vary in that some have primary languages that resemble English in word order, sound system, and in the patterns of forming words. Spanish, French, and Portuguese, for example, are languages that share alphabets and left-to-right directionality with English. Some words in English and Spanish are cognates. Some languages, such as Swahili or Vietnamese, do not have as much in common with English. For children who speak these languages, initial learning of English is more difficult.

Types of English Language Learners

- **Newly Arrived English Language Learners** may come with adequate or limited schooling. Those with adequate schooling will make steady academic progress, although they may have difficulty on standardized tests in English. Those with limited formal schooling may lack a sense of school culture and routines. Their limited literacy development may lead to poor academic achievement until both their background knowledge and English proficiency grow.
- **Long Term English Language Learners** have been in the United States for some time, but they have had limited exposure to English in their communities and little reason to learn or know English. As they begin to acquire English, they may lose proficiency in their native languages and have difficulty grasping new content.
- **Older English Language Learners** may be more capable of quickly learning academic concepts even though they have not developed the language proficiency of other students their age. Curriculum challenges will help these students bridge their academic gaps while they gain English proficiency. Provide scaffolds for instruction and organize collaborative activities to help these students gain success.

Literacy Challenges for ELLs

1. **Phonemic Awareness** ELLs may find it difficult to differentiate between certain phonemes in English. Some children may find it difficult to separate groups of phonemes into words.
2. **Phonics** ELLs need to be able to match sounds to letters and letters to sounds in order to read and write English successfully. They need to develop both oral vocabularies of frequently used words and written vocabularies of sight words.
3. **Vocabulary Development** Some ELLs are able to repeat, pronounce, decode, and produce words in English without really knowing what these words mean. ELLs need opportunities to link vocabulary words to meaning through routines, concrete objects, pictures and gestures, physical movement, and experiences. These students need multiple exposures to words through explanation, discussion, and repeated readings.
4. **Fluency** Fluent reading involves reading quickly, accurately, and expressively. This can be challenging for ELLs, who need many opportunities to listen and speak English before they can feel comfortable and successful with fluent reading. In large groups, ELLs may be reluctant to read orally. They need opportunities to listen and follow along with read-alouds.
5. **Comprehension** Help ELLs gain comprehension in reading by choosing reading materials with familiar topics, settings, and concepts. Use nonfiction materials, such as photographs and science experiments. Use anticipation guides and graphic organizers to prepare ELLs for reading and allow them to comprehend more of what they read.

Best Practices

Scaffolding instruction for ELLs allows them to access content while gaining proficiency in English. Most strategies that help ELLs access content and language are appropriate for struggling readers in your classroom whose native language is English, so these strategies can be used with the whole class. Some best practices for teaching ELLs include:

- using questioning techniques to elicit experiences that relate to students' native cultures;
- using visual aids, including photographs, graphic organizers, and real objects;
- linking learning to a physical response, such as raising hands, doing a "thumbs up," nodding, and moving to a different part of the room;
- actively engaging students in the lesson by including less teacher talk and down time and keeping students involved;
- using scaffolding techniques, such as think-alouds, paraphrasing, partnering, and reciprocal teaching; and
- building background with such activities as cloze sentences, creating word walls, and working with students to make personal dictionaries.

English language learners are generally divided into proficiency levels. The chart below describes what you might expect from students at each level, and it compares different proficiency levels used across the United States. It also includes teaching strategies for your classroom. *Reading Street* provides systematic leveled support to meet the needs of all students.

	LEVELS OF PROFICIENCY		BEHAVIORS	TEACHING STRATEGIES
I	Beginning		• may be unfamiliar with sounds, rhythms, or patterns in English • respond by pointing, gesturing, or drawing • can use simple yes/no responses or one- to two-word answers • read simple language that they have already heard • write labels, patterned sentences, or short cloze sentences	• provide opportunities for active listening and visuals • model language with songs and chants • pair students with more proficient speakers • ask yes/no questions; require responses of one or two words • use manipulatives and pictures • provide writing frames
II	Early Intermediate	Intermediate	• may understand more details in spoken English • use longer phrases and sentences with better grammar • write for a variety of purposes using models • can read independently after oral previews	• allow students to make personal connections with the material • structure group discussion time • ask open-ended questions and then model, expand, restate, and enrich student language • allow students opportunities to create language for a variety of purposes and audiences
III	Intermediate		• participate in discussions about academic content • can use higher-order language to describe or persuade • write narratives and expository text • use vocabulary with more accuracy and correctness	• use graphic organizers to prepare students for reading and to discuss selections • promote academic concepts and vocabulary with nonfictional texts, magazines, newspapers, and so on • conference with students about writing to point out areas of progress and areas for improvement
IV	Early Advanced	Advanced	• have a deeper understanding of everyday language, including idioms • use more extensive vocabulary and produce language with fewer grammatical errors • use standard forms when writing • produce writing about varied topics	• structure discussion for the group • provide reference materials for students and guide them with the research • introduce more variety of literary forms • provide opportunities for more variation in writing assignments
V	Advanced	Advanced High	• use more complex and varied grammatical structures and vocabulary • read texts appropriate for grade level • write about a variety of topics on grade level • begin to self-monitor and correct as they read and write	• provide opportunities for students to publish their writing for others to read • increase students' production of language through drama and music • continue to make strong links between content-area materials and literacy activities

Essentials of ELL Instruction in *Reading Street*

Imagine students from diverse language backgrounds communicating in English on the playground. It's easy to think that they are fluent English speakers, but they may still be at the beginning stage of using English for learning purposes. Research proves that it takes at least five years of exposure to academic English to catch up with native-speaker proficiency in school.

How Do English Language Learners Differ from Other Learners?

ELLs face challenges because they have not acquired academic English. Student's reading and language skills may seem deficient because their language experiences have lacked academic instruction. ELLs need targeted instruction to participate fully in reading/language arts lessons with their peers. Helping ELLs achieve academically is critically important because they must meet the same state and federal grade-level standards as other children. Their academic success depends on learning to read well, and this depends on rich language knowledge.

Academic Language is the language of the classroom. It's used for academic purposes, not social or personal ones.

Essentials of ELL Instruction

These five essential practices take into account language and academic needs of English language learners. They are incorporated into *Reading Street* as common-sense, everyday strategies that help you build an effective learning relationship between you and your ELL students.

Identify and Communicate Content Objectives and Language Objectives English language learners need instruction for the same grade-level skills and strategies as students whose first language is English. Deliver your instruction with clear, simple language. Provide extra support for academic vocabulary. Provide direct instruction for the academic language that students need to use to complete classroom tasks successfully.

Frontload the Lesson When new information arrives as a blur to ELL students, they are lost at the beginning of a lesson. Taking time to frontload, or preteach lesson elements, will bring them into mainstream instruction. Activating prior knowledge, building background, previewing, and setting a purpose for reading are frontloading methods that remove learning obstacles. Asking students to make personal connections helps them see relationships and gives you insight into their experiences and backgrounds.

Provide Comprehensible Input The instruction and content you present to ELL students may be unclear because of language barriers. Use visual supports, multimedia, examples of real items, and demonstrations to provide comprehensible instruction. Communicating with methods such as gestures, props, and dramatization can be an effective approach. Hands-on activities and multiple exposures to new concepts can lessen confusion.

Enable Language Production The listening, speaking, reading, and writing ELLs do for school is different from the language they use in everyday conversation. In school, ELLs need ample opportunities to demonstrate their use of English. Two critical methods for enabling student's English language production are direct instruction and modeling the use of a skill in a comprehensible way. Create scaffolds so that students can read and hear English language patterns and build on them to express their own thoughts. Paraphrasing, restatements, cloze sentences, writing prompts, and templated forms for note-taking are useful supports. Responding to student's strengths and needs by modifying instruction gives them opportunities to express themselves in an academic setting and gain proficiency in English.

Assess for Content and Language Understanding ELLs are required to achieve the same high standards as mainstream students. Keep in mind that children are at different stages for learning English language and literacy skills. Asking these questions frequently and using assessments will help you determine how to modify your instruction for different proficiency levels.

- Where are ELL students in their acquisition of English language proficiency?
- Where are they in their acquisition of literacy skills?

Just as for all students, you will rely on diagnostic, formative, and summative assessments for ELLs. Consistently integrate informal assessment into your lessons to target specific problem areas for learning, adapt your instruction, and intervene earlier rather than later.

You can modify both formal and informal assessments so that ELLs show their proficiency in literacy skills with a minimal amount of negative impact. These modifications include time extensions, use of bilingual dictionaries and glossaries, repeated readings of listening passages, use of dual-language assessments, and allowing written responses in the first language.

To meet ELLs at their own levels of English acquisition, teachers use instructional supports and tools. Through scaffolding and modifying instruction you can lead ELLs to achieve the same instructional goals that mainstream students do. The ELL strategies and supports in *Reading Street* have the five essential principles of ELL as their foundation. Use them throughout your instruction to modify or scaffold core instruction. With *Reading Street* ELL Leveled Support activities, you meet students where they are—from beginning to advanced levels of English proficiency.

Essentials of ELL Instruction in *Reading Street*

- Identify and Communicate Content Objectives and Language Objectives
- Frontload the Lesson
- Provide Comprehensible Input
- Enable Language Production
- Assess for Content and Language Understanding

Other English language learner resources include:

Student Edition The Student Edition builds every student's reading and language skills.

Teacher's Edition The Teacher's Edition has ELL instructional strategies built into the lesson plans. The ELL weekly lessons have pacing plans to help you carefully integrate instruction. The ELL Support lessons guide you in using sheltered techniques and routines for teaching concept development, academic vocabulary, listening comprehension, phonics, phonemic awareness, vocabulary, comprehension, and writing.

ELD/ELL Readers ELD/ELL Readers develop English learners' vocabulary and comprehension skills. Study guides support comprehension and provide writing and take-home activities.

ELL Posters ELL Posters contain high-quality illustrations and five days of activities supporting key oral vocabulary, selection vocabulary, and lesson concepts.

ELL Handbook The ELL Handbook supports teachers' professional development and the transition to advanced levels of English proficiency for all ELLs. The Handbook contains comprehension skill practice, selection vocabulary word cards, multilingual summaries of Student Edition literature, study guides for ELL Readers, and multilingual vocabulary charts. The English selection summaries and vocabulary charts are accompanied by translations in Spanish and in several other languages. The flexible bank of Phonics and Grammar Transition Lessons provides differentiated practice.

Ten Important Sentences The Ten Important Sentences reproducibles help students focus on comprehension while they expand their English proficiency.

English Language Proficiency-What, Why, and How
The next section, English Language Proficiency-What, Why, and How, provides ideas for how to use *Reading Street* across language proficiency levels and instructional strands. Using research from Dr. Jim Cummins, this section explains why and how *Reading Street* promotes literacy attainment for English language learners at all levels.

English Language Proficiency—What, Why, and How

Concept Development

"No learner is a blank slate. The more we know about the topic in the text, the more of the text we can understand."—Dr. Jim Cummins

Why

Organizing concept development around big question themes is essential for ELLs. Through the use of themes, it is easier to connect the curriculum to students' lives and backgrounds. Themes help to make sense of the curriculum because students know what the topic is, even if the instruction is in English. By learning more about the topic through concept development, students will increase their social and academic vocabulary production and be more engaged when reading the text.

How

Reading Street promotes literacy attainment through Concept Development activities in the core and ELL Support lessons that encourage literacy engagement. These activities activate prior knowledge and build background, scaffold meaning, affirm identity, and extend language.

Activate Prior Knowledge/Build Background

Frontload the Lesson Build background and scaffold meaning to prepare for the core Anchor Talk lesson. In a small group, use Preteach Concepts from the Concept Development section of the ELL Support pages and the Poster Talk Through to frontload the lesson.

Access Content

Provide Comprehensible Input Use the linguistically accommodated questions in the Concept Development section of the ELL Support pages to reach all language proficiency levels and make personal and cultural connections that validate identity and link academic content with what students already know.

Scaffold Meaning Give visual support that students need to access academic content with the photographs in the Let's Talk About section in the Student Edition, the Concept Map created during the week's discussion, the Concept Talk Video from the digital path, and the daily Poster Activities. The activities in the ELL Support pages for Concept Development and the ELL Support notes throughout the Teacher Edition give ideas to scaffold meaning for all language proficiency levels.

Extend Language

Enable Language Production Use the daily activities on the ELL Poster and the Anchored Talk questions in the core to build concept attainment and encourage oral language production. The Team-Talk Routine in the core instruction and the Poster Talk, Concept Talk activities from the *ELL Handbook* provide nonthreatening small group oral practice with social and academic vocabulary related to the concept. The Concept Literacy Reader builds both concepts and language.

	Student Behaviors	Teacher Behaviors	Examples
Beginning	• Actively listens • Responds nonverbally • Responds to simple commands • Answers in one- or two-word phrases • May not seek clarification Student can: point, move, choose, match, mime, draw.	• Use gestures, repetition, slower speech, visuals, and simple language. *Point to the __________.* *Find the __________.* *Is this a __________?*	How does city life compare to life in the country? Use the *Let's Talk About It* photographs in the Student Edition to activate prior knowledge and build background. *Point to the city. Find the picture of the country.* *Are they the same or different?* *Is this a building?* *Is this a farm?* *Where is the cow?*
Intermediate	• Actively listens with greater understanding • Needs processing time • Uses short phrases • Identifies people and objects • Begins to seek clarification Student can: name, list, say, tell, restate.	• Model correct responses. • Don't call attention to grammar errors. • Ask general questions to encourage production. • Ask questions for two-word responses. *Is this a ________ or a ________?* *What is this?*	*Is this a building or a farm?* *Is this the city or the country?* *What do you see in the city?* *What do you see in the country?* *Are they the same or different?*
Advanced	• Actively listens to longer questions and directions • Uses language more freely • Sometimes needs more processing time and depends on visuals • Will seek clarification Student can: describe, restate, compare, contrast.	• Ask open-ended questions to encourage language production. • Check comprehension frequently. *Why?* *How?* *Tell me about __________.* *Describe __________.*	*Describe the city.* *Tell me about the country.* *How are they the same?* *How are they different?*
Advanced High	• Understands longer, elaborated discussions • Occasionally needs more processing time • Understands details and information comparable to a native speaker • Rarely seeks clarification. • Produces a variety of sentence lengths Student can: explain, define, support, describe, summarize.	• Make lessons interactive and comprehensible. • Structure group discussions. *Describe/compare __________.* *How are these similar or different?* *What would happen if __________?* *What is your opinion of __________?*	*Compare the pictures of the city and country.* *How are they the same and different?* *Which place do you like better? Why?*

Listening Comprehension

"How can teachers make complex academic English comprehensible for children who are still in the process of learning English? We can scaffold students' learning by modifying the input itself." –Dr. Jim Cummins

Why

English language learners must be able to comprehend newly acquired language in all content areas. They must listen to a variety of speakers, including teachers and peers, along with understanding the language they hear in electronic media. In order for English language learners to meet grade-level learning expectations and have access to the core curriculum, all instruction delivered in English must be linguistically accommodated for all levels of English language proficiency.

How

Reading Street promotes literacy attainment with listening comprehension activities in the core lessons and ELL Support lessons that encourage literacy engagement. These activities activate prior knowledge, build background, scaffold meaning, affirm identity, and extend language.

Activate Prior Knowledge/Build Background

Each adapted Read Aloud in the Listening Comprehension section of the ELL Support pages covers the same concept and information as the Read Aloud in the core curriculum. Use it with a small group to build background and scaffold meaning before listening to the core Read Aloud. Each adapted Read Aloud has frontloading activities that build background to improve comprehension before listening to the selection. In the core Teacher Edition, ELL Notes give ideas for frontloading the regular Read Aloud at point of use.

Access Content

Provide Comprehensible Input For Beginning and Intermediate levels, use the grade-appropriate adapted Read Aloud in place of the regular Read Aloud until children no longer need the linguistic support and modification.

First Listening: Listen to Understand gives children a purpose for listening. The questions are designed to generate interest and help children get the gist of the adapted Read Aloud so that all proficiency levels can achieve success without cognitive overload.

Language Clarification Second Listening: Listen to Check Understanding allows children to clarify what they have heard. Once children have understood the main idea of the adapted Read Aloud, they can listen again on subsequent days to clarify understanding of important details of spoken language. The graphic organizers provide visual support for organizing information.

Extend Language

Enable Language Production Discussing the adapted Read Aloud in a small group setting provides a nonthreatening environment, lowering the affective filter and facilitating increased language production.

The *Sing with Me* Big Book, the Audiotext CD of the main reading selection, and the digital products provide more opportunities for listening practice throughout each week, building and reinforcing children's concept and language attainment.

	Student Behaviors	Teacher Behaviors	Examples
Beginning	• Needs accommodations to understand grade-appropriate stories • Responds non-verbally • Can follow one-step oral directions • Answers in one or two words • Can match oral statements to illustrations or objects Student can: point, move, choose, match, mime, draw, label.	• Use gestures, repetition, slower speech, visuals, and simple language. *Point to the ______.* *Find the ______.* *Is this a ______?*	In a small group, use the modified Read Aloud. Build background and scaffold comprehension by reviewing the concept or showing a visual. Read the text clearly. Stop at intervals to check for understanding and clarify language. Use gestures to scaffold meaning. Students may need to hear the text repeated multiple times.
Intermediate	• Actively listens with greater understanding • Uses short phrases • Understands simple directions • Identifies people and objects • Identifies key words and phrases • Begins to seek clarification Student can: name, list, say, tell, restate.	• Model correct responses. • Use visuals, gestures, and preteaching to preview topic-related vocabulary. • Don't call attention to errors. • Ask general questions to encourage production. • Ask questions that elicit two-word responses *Is this a ______ or a ______?* *What is this?*	In a small group, use the modified Read Aloud. Preview topic-related vocabulary and then read the text clearly. Stop at intervals to check for understanding and clarify language. Then use the Anchored Talk photographs to build vocabulary and concepts and to encourage discussion.
Advanced	• Actively listens to longer questions • Understands multistep directions • Understands main points and most important details • Will seek clarification • Uses language more freely Student can: describe, restate, compare, contrast.	• Ask open-ended questions to encourage language production. • Check comprehension frequently. • Give more time to process information and provide visual support as needed. *Why? How?* *Describe ______.*	In a small group, use the modified Read Aloud to prepare for listening to the oral reading in the core text. Then have partners restate some of the important points.
Advanced High	• Understands longer, elaborated discussions • Understands details and information comparable to a native speaker • Rarely seeks clarification • Produces a variety of sentence lengths Student can: explain, define, support, describe, summarize.	• Make lessons interactive and comprehensible. • Structure group discussions. • Give more processing time. *Describe/compare ______.* *How are these similar or different?* *What would happen if ______?* *What is your opinion of ______?*	In a small group, use the modified Read Aloud to prepare for listening to the oral reading in the core text. Then have students summarize the selection.

Phonics, Spelling, and Word Analysis

"A systematic exploration of language is essential if children are to develop a curiosity about language and deepen their understanding of how words work. Children should become language detectives who investigate the mysteries of language and how it has been used throughout history to shape and change society."— Dr. Jim Cummins

Why

Discrete language skills that English language learners need to develop second language literacy and comprehension include:

- knowledge of the letters of the alphabet
- knowledge of the sounds represented by individual letters and combinations of letters
- the ability to decode words
- knowledge of the rules and conventions of how words are formed

Students can learn these skills at the same time they are developing basic English vocabulary. While letter-sound correspondences in numerous languages are relatively simple, the relationships of letters to sounds in English can be complicated. The challenges of written English affect spelling, word recognition, comprehension of text, and confidence in language learning. *Reading Street* addresses these challenges in both the core curriculum and in the ELL Support pages.

How

Reading Street promotes literacy attainment through engaging phonics, spelling, and word analysis activities in the core lessons and ELL Support lessons. These activities activate prior knowledge and build background, scaffold meaning, affirm identity, and extend language.

Activate Prior Knowledge/Build Background

Frontload the Lesson Use the Phonics and Spelling and Word Analysis lessons in the ELL Support pages with a small group to preteach the skill before the core lesson. Then use the Reteach activities from the ELL Support pages to provide more practice and help students internalize language.

Affirm Identity Use the Transfer Skills Notes throughout the core Teacher Edition, on the ELL Support pages, and in the Phonics Transition Lessons in the *ELL Handbook,* to activate prior knowledge about a phonics or word analysis skill before the core lesson or for reteaching the skill to a small group to scaffold meaning.

Access Content

Provide Comprehensible Input Use the Sound-Spelling Cards and the Envision it! Words to Know from the Student Edition to provide visual support and scaffold meaning for the phonics and spelling lessons at all proficiency levels. Choose appropriate Phonics Transition Lessons and reproducible practice pages from the bank of lessons in the *ELL Handbook* to provide instruction on consonant sounds and blends, varying English vowel sounds, and other phonics challenges for all proficiency levels. The *Words! Vocabulary Handbook* in the Student Edition provides visual support for explaining the Word Analysis skill. Use it to preteach or reteach the skill. Use the leveled ideas in the Word Analysis section of the ELL Support pages to differentiate instruction and reach all students. The Word Analysis lessons focus on word endings, contractions, prefixes, suffixes, compound words, cognates, and other vocabulary builders.

Extend Language

Enable Language Production Guide small groups of students in exploring the rules and conventions of how words are formed using the leveled Word Analysis lessons from the ELL Support pages. When students learn the patterns of English word formation, students will become more engaged in literacy activities, and oral and written production will increase.

Focus on Meaning and Form Use the Word Analysis lessons from the ELL Support pages to teach home language equivalents, synonyms, antonyms, and the meaning of prefixes, roots, and suffixes. This knowledge engages students in figuring out meanings of new words, increasing their comprehension and language production.

	Student Behaviors	Teacher Behaviors	Examples
Beginning	• Actively listens and responds non-verbally • Can follow one-step oral directions • Answers in one- to two-word phrases • Uses high-frequency words, concrete words, and phrases Student can: point, move, choose, match, mime, draw label.	• Use gestures, repetition, slower speech, visuals, and simple language. *Point to the* ________. *Find the* ________. *Is this a* ________?	prefixes *un-* and *in-* Give students a piece of cloth and model the difference between *cover* and *uncover*. Use Student Edition *Words! Vocabulary Handbook* to provide more visual support for meaning. Have students draw pictures to show *lock / unlock* and *happy / unhappy*.
Intermediate	• Actively listens with greater understanding • Needs more processing time • Uses short phrases • Identifies people and objects • Begins to seek clarification if he or she doesn't understand Student can: name, list, say, tell, restate.	• Model correct responses. • Don't call attention to grammar errors. • Ask general questions to encourage production. • Ask questions that elicit two-word responses. *Is this a* ________ *or a* ________? *What is this?*	Use the Student Edition *Words! Vocabulary Handbook* to provide visual support for meaning. Ask questions about the picture to clarify meaning. Provide more practice using *in-* with words *expensive* and *inexpensive*. Use the handbook reproducible pages to provide more practice with prefixes.
Advanced	• Actively listens to longer questions and directions • Uses language more freely • Sometimes needs more processing time and depends on visuals • Will seek clarification Student can: describe, restate, compare, contrast.	• Ask open-ended questions to encourage language production. • Check comprehension frequently. *Why? How?* *Tell me about* ________.	Use the Student Edition *Words! Vocabulary Handbook* to provide visual support for meaning. *Tell me about the first picture. Compare it to the second picture. Look at the chart. What does the prefix un- mean? Where do we find prefixes?* Repeat with prefix *in-*.
Advanced High	• Understands longer, elaborated discussions • Occasionally needs more processing time • Understands details and information comparable to a native speaker • Rarely seeks clarification Student can: explain, define, support, describe, summarize.	• Make lessons interactive and comprehensible. • Structure group discussions. *Describe/compare* ________. *How are these similar or different?* *What would happen if* ________? *What is your opinion of* ________?	Use the Student Edition *Words! Vocabulary Handbook* to provide visual support for meaning. *Compare the two pictures. Look at the chart. What do the prefixes un- and in- mean? Explain what else you know about prefixes.* Write the words *lock, happy, complete,* and *action* on the board. Have pairs add the appropriate prefix and then write sentences using the words.

Vocabulary

"We should constantly search for ways to link academic content with what students already know or what is familiar to them from their family or cultural experiences. This not only validates children's sense of identity, but it also makes the learning more meaningful."— Dr. Jim Cummins

Why

Vocabulary development is critically important for English language learners, even more so than for their English-speaking peers. English learners need explicit instruction to acquire both social and academic language for literacy attainment. Research indicates that a broad knowledge of academic vocabulary is critical to student achievement and distinguishes students who experience academic success from those who struggle in school. Instruction in social and academic vocabulary should be explicit and systematic. Students need multiple exposures to new vocabulary through frequent listening, reading, writing, and oral language activities.

How

Reading Street promotes literacy attainment through interactive vocabulary activities in the core lessons and ELL Support pages that encourage literacy engagement. These activities activate prior knowledge and build background, scaffold meaning, affirm identity, and extend language.

Activate Prior Knowledge/Build Background

Frontload the Lesson The Concept Development activities from the ELL Support lessons, the Vocabulary Routines in the core and in the ELL Support pages, the ELL Poster, and the word cards from the *ELL Handbook* can be used to activate prior knowledge and build background for reading the selection.
Use them in a small group to preteach, practice, and reinforce the grade-level lesson vocabulary. By using and reusing the words in meaningful interactions, students will internalize the words and be more engaged in reading the selection.

Access Content

Provide Comprehensible Input The Vocabulary Activities in the ELL Support lessons provide ideas for giving visual, contextual, and linguistic support so students can access grade-level lesson vocabulary. The activities are designed so students reuse the vocabulary using different modalities to confirm and enhance understanding. Give visual support that students need to access academic content vocabulary with the Anchored Talk photos and illustrations in the Student Edition, the Poster illustrations, Envision It! Words to Know in the Student Edition, and the digital vocabulary activities.

Affirm Identity Multilingual vocabulary lists in the *ELL Handbook* translate the selection vocabulary words from English into Spanish, Chinese, Vietnamese, Hmong, and Korean. Use the lists to preview the words or to check understanding.

Language Clarification Throughout the core and ELL Support pages, there are a variety of ideas for teachers to use to help students clarify meaning of language. Ideas range from activities using bilingual and English dictionaries to leveled questioning examples. In the core Teacher Edition, helpful ELL notes are located at point of use. These notes give language transfer support and a variety of ideas to clarify meaning for students.

Extend Language

Enable Language Production Use the Concept Talk and Vocabulary Activities on the ELL Support pages and the daily activities on the ELL Poster for ideas to give repeated exposure to social and academic vocabulary to build concept and language attainment.

The leveled vocabulary activities in the ELL Support lessons and the reproducible word cards in the *ELL Handbook* actively engage students in producing and reusing grade-level vocabulary in different contexts through spoken and written communication so that vocabulary becomes internalized.

	Student Behaviors	Teacher Behaviors	Examples
Beginning	• Actively listens • Answers in one- to two-word phrases • Uses and reads some high-frequency words, concrete words, and phrases represented by pictures Student can: point, move, choose, match, mime, draw, label, copy.	• Activate prior knowledge. • Use gestures, repetition, slower speech, and visuals. • Preteach topic-related vocabulary. *Point to the ______.* *Find the ______.* *Is this a ______?*	Use a word grid or word cards to preteach vocabulary. Students can write the new word in the circle in the middle and then draw or find a picture to illustrate the meaning of the word. Students can point to the squares while the other students describe the card to the class.
Intermediate	• Actively listens with greater understanding • Uses short phrases • Understands simple directions • Identifies people and objects • Begins to seek clarification if he or she doesn't understand Student can: name, list, say, tell, restate.	• Model correct responses. • Use visuals, gestures, and preteaching to preview topic-related vocabulary. • Ask general questions to encourage production. • Ask questions that elicit two-word responses. *Is this a ______ or a ______?* *What is this?*	Students can write a synonym or antonym for the word. They can assist beginners with creating a visual of the word. When sharing with the class, these students can list the synonyms and antonyms.
Advanced	• Understands longer, more elaborate directions and conversations • Understands main points and most important details • Sometimes needs processing time; depends on more visuals • Will seek clarification Student can: describe, restate, compare, contrast.	• Ask open-ended questions to encourage language production. • Check comprehension frequently. • Give more time to process information. *Why?* *How?* *Tell me about ______.* *Describe ______.*	Students can write sentences with the word and identify cognates. They can describe their cards to the class when they are finished.
Advanced High	• May need more processing time • Understands details and information comparable to a native speaker • Rarely seeks clarification • Produces a variety of sentence lengths Student can: explain, define, support, describe, summarize.	• Make lessons interactive and comprehensible. • Structure group discussions. • Give extra processing time. *Describe/compare ______.* *How are these similar or different?* *What would happen if ______?* *What is your opinion of ______?*	Students can check the work of others and edit and revise the sentences so they are correct. They can describe the cards to the class when they are finished.

Reading Comprehension

"The more of the text we understand, the more new knowledge we can acquire. This expands our knowledge base, what cognitive psychologists call *schemata,* or underlying patterns of concepts. Such comprehension, in turn, enables us to understand even more concepts and vocabulary."— Dr. Jim Cummins

Why

English learners need guidance to become active readers who engage with texts on multiple levels before, during, and after reading. Comprehension instruction in *Reading Street* focuses on *metacognition*, a good reader's ability to independently reflect on the purpose of reading, select appropriate approaches to texts, ask questions as he or she reads, and actively resolve areas of confusion.

How

Core Comprehension Skill

Activate Prior Knowledge/Build Background

Frontload the Lesson Use the Preteach activities in the Guide Comprehension section of the ELL Support lessons with a small group to build background for the main Comprehension Skill. The Envision It! Visual Skills Handbook in the Student Edition and Envision It! Animations from the digital path provide visual support to fully engage students in the core skill instruction.

Access Content and Scaffold Meaning

Provide Comprehensible Input The leveled Reteach activities in the Guide Comprehension section of the ELL Support pages provide visual, contextual, and linguistic support for the grade-level Comprehension Skill. The interactive activities are designed so students reuse the academic vocabulary related to each Comprehension Skill using different modalities to enhance understanding. Topics range from basic reading skills, such as understanding supporting ideas and details in text, to expanded skills, such as making inferences.

Language Clarification The leveled support notes in the Reteach activities of the Guide Comprehension section of the ELL Support pages provide ideas for clarifying meaning for all proficiency levels.

Extend Language

Enable Language Production and Affirm Identity
The mini-lessons in the Guide Comprehension section of the ELL Support pages focus on the Comprehension Skill. Use them to encourage students to express ideas and participate in discussions using social and academic vocabulary.

Comprehension of Core Selection Sheltered Reading

Activate Prior Knowledge/Build Background

Frontload the Lesson Use the Before Reading activities in the Sheltered Reading section in the ELL Support pages for ideas to preview the text and set a purpose for reading. The Multilingual Summaries in the *ELL Handbook* activate prior knowledge, affirm identity, and build background before reading the main selection.

Access Content and Scaffold Meaning

Provide Comprehensible Input Use the Sheltered Reading questions and the graphic organizer on the ELL Support pages to guide comprehension and clarify understanding of the selection.

Extend Language

Enable Language Production The Sheltered Reading section on the ELL Support pages has questions that encourage students to use oral language during reading to demonstrate understanding. The Fluency and the After Reading sections have ideas for shared reading, summarizing, and organizing information for each selection.

ELD and ELL Readers

There is an ELD and an ELL Reader for each week of instruction. Each Reader has a topic that supports grade-level concept development, tying into the Question of the Week. The ELD Readers are written for Beginning and Intermediate language proficiency levels, and the ELL Readers are designed for Intermediate to Advanced High levels. The rich language and information, sentence patterns, repetition, and visual support will unlock new words for students and give them models for using English words, phrases, and sentence structures.

Activate Prior Knowledge/Build Background

Frontload the Lesson Use the Before Reading section in the ELL Support pages for the ELL and ELD Readers for ideas to preview the text and set a purpose for reading.

Access Content and Scaffold Meaning

Provide Comprehensible Input Use the During Reading Routine along with the sheltered questions in the ELL/ELD Reader Support pages and visuals in the Readers to build background, model, and guide comprehension.

Extend Language

Enable Language Production and Affirm Identity Use the Anchored Talk and Let's Write About It activities on the inside back cover of each ELL Reader to have students apply the lesson's target comprehension skill. The reproducible Study Guide found in the ELL Handbook supports students' comprehension and provides writing and take-home activities.

	Student Behaviors	Teacher Behaviors	Examples
Beginning	• Uses vocabulary that includes environmental print, some high-frequency and concrete words represented by pictures • Depends on visuals and prior knowledge • Able to apply comprehension skills when reading texts at his or her level • May recognize a few letter-sound relationships • Reads word by word	• Use gestures, repetition, slower speech, visuals, and simple language. • Assess prior knowledge, build background, and frontload extensively before reading text. • Make sure text is linguistically accommodated for level or provide teacher/peer support for grade-level text.	Use gestures to explain first, next, and last. Hold up one finger as you say *first* and put on a shoe. Hold up two fingers as you say *next* and tie the shoe. Hold up three fingers as you say *last* and take a step forward. Then use the Envision It! Visual Skills Handbook picture in the Student Edition to identify sequence words first, *next, and last.* Use the Picture It! activity from the *ELL Handbook* to practice and assess sequence.
Intermediate	• Reads some everyday oral language, knows literal meanings of common words, and uses routine academic language • Reads slowly and in short phrases and may need to re-read to clarify meaning • Can locate and classify information • Understands simple sentences but is dependent on visual cues, topic familiarity, prior knowledge, or pre-taught vocabulary • Can apply basic and higher-order thinking skills in texts that are linguistically accommodated	• Use gestures, repetition, slower speech, visuals, and simple language. • Assess prior knowledge, build background, and frontload extensively before reading text. • Make sure text is linguistically accommodated for level or provide support for grade-level text.	Use gestures to explain *first, next, and last.* As you tie your shoe, have students describe what you do first, next, and last. Then use the Envision It! Visual Skills Handbook in the Student Edition to have students identify sequence words *first, next,* and *last* and then describe the sequence in the pictures. Use the Picture It! activity from the *ELL Handbook* to practice and assess sequences.
Advanced	• Reads with greater ease • Uses a variety of comprehension strategies • Can understand words and phrases beyond their literal meanings • Able to apply basic and higher-order comprehension skills • Occasionally dependent on visuals and teacher/peer assistance with unfamiliar topics	• Frontload text and build background before reading. • Preteach unfamiliar concepts and related vocabulary. • Use visuals to clarify meanings of new topics. • Provide support for grade-level text.	Use the Envision It! Visual Skills Handbook in the Student Edition to preteach sequence. Students can describe what is happening in each picture and identify sequence words. After using the Routine to frontload the ELL Reader, guide students to find words that show sequence. Use the graphic organizer to fill in the sequence of events. Use the organizer to retell the sequence of events with a partner and then share with the class.
Advanced High	• Reads and understands vocabulary nearly comparable to native English-speaking peers • Can infer meaning, draw conclusions, and use context to infer meanings of new words • Can interpret information and find details that support main ideas	• Frontload text and build background before reading. • Preteach unfamiliar concepts and related vocabulary. • Use visuals to clarify meanings of new topics. • Provide support for grade-level text as needed.	Use the Envision It! Visual Skills Handbook in the Student Edition to preteach sequence. Students can describe what is happening in each picture and identify other sequence words they may know. After using the routine to frontload the ELL Reader, pairs can find words that show sequence. Use a graphic organizer to fill in the sequence of events and then retell the the story. Use the organizer if needed.

Conventions and Writing

"Writing helps solve problems, affirms students' identities, and generates linguistic feedback from teachers that can increase language awareness and academic language proficiency."— Dr. Jim Cummins

Why

Research shows that students acquire language most readily when they are fully involved in all learning activities in the classroom. Activities should integrate listening, speaking, reading, and writing, since these language skills develop interdependently. Teachers can facilitate language learning and literacy development by ensuring that students hear language in natural ways, in real and practical contexts, and write it in structured formats.

Each English language learner comes from a unique background of language, literacy, and culture. Because students are at varying levels of English proficiency, it is important that each student has challenging work, appropriate for his or her level of English proficiency and literacy. The conventions and writing lessons in the ELL Support pages of *Reading Street* provide the systematic instruction that students need at each language proficiency level to scaffold use of increasingly complex grammatical structures in content area writing.

How

Reading Street promotes literacy attainment through engaging Conventions and Writing activities in the core Teacher Edition and ELL Support lessons. These activities activate prior knowledge and build background, scaffold meaning, affirm identity, and extend language.

Activate Prior Knowledge/Build Background

Frontload the Lesson Use the Preteach activities in the Conventions and Writing sections of the ELL Support pages with a small group of students before the lesson to introduce the concepts. Each Conventions lesson contains a helpful chart to convey grammatical forms and has ideas for addressing the functions of the grammatical structure to students. The Writing section contains a simple model to use when guiding instruction for beginning and intermediate levels.

Affirm Identity Use the Language Transfer notes in the core Teacher Edition, the Language Transfer Charts in the *ELL Handbook*, and the ELL Handbook Grammar Transition Lessons to lead students in transferring knowledge from their home languages to English.

Access Content and Scaffold Meaning

Provide Comprehensible Input Use the leveled Conventions practice activities in the ELL Support pages for contextual and linguistic support for each grade-level grammar skill. The interactive activities are designed so students reuse the language related to each core convention using different modalities to enhance understanding. For more practice on a core skill, or to meet the needs of beginners and intermediate students, use the Grammar Transition bank of flexible activities in the *ELL Handbook* or the Grammar Jammer from the digital path during small group time. Use the leveled writing ideas and the simplified writing models in the ELL Support pages to scaffold meaning for all students.

Language Clarification The leveled support notes throughout the Teacher Edition pages and the Grammar Transition Lessons in the *ELL Handbook* contain ideas for clarifying meaning for all proficiency levels.

Extend Language

Enable Language Production The Conventions and Writing sections of the ELL Support pages have practice activities for students to actively use grammar and writing skills. The sentence frames and leveled writing prompts guide and encourage oral and written language production for all levels of English proficiency. Use the ELL Notes throughout the core Teacher Edition Language Arts pages for ideas to support all levels of English language learners in prewriting, editing, revising, and publishing writing pieces.

References for English Language Proficiency—What, Why, and How

Gottlieb, Margo, M. Elizabeth Cranley, and Andrea R. Oliver. (2007). *The WIDA English Language Proficiency Standards and Resource Guide, Pre-Kindergarten through Grade 12.* Board of Regents of the University of Wisconsin on behalf of the WIDA Consortium.

Peregoy, Suzanne F., and Owen F. Boyle (2008). *Reading, Writing, and Learning in ESL: A Resource Book for Teaching K–12 English Learners.* New York: Pearson.

	Student Behaviors	Teacher Behaviors	Examples
Beginning	• Can label, list, copy, use basic punctuation and capitalization • Uses some standard word order • Uses high-frequency words phrases and short sentences in present tense • May recognize a few letter-sound relationships • Responds to pictured events using words or phrases based on models	• Allow extra time for prewriting and build background before writing. • Use language experience stories. • Help students turn words and phrases into sentences. • Accept phonetic spelling, but show corrections. • Give a checklist for revising that has visual cues and help students use dictionaries or word walls.	Descriptive paragraph about a family member. Students can produce words or phrases about a family member using a drawing or photograph. Guide production of supporting details on a graphic organizer. Write out sentences and have students copy the sentences and read them to you or a partner.
Intermediate	• Communicates best when topics are familiar and concrete • Produces short phrases and simple sentences • May use simple future and past tenses inconsistently • Can compare and contrast • Can describe events, people, processes, and procedures with limited details	• Allow extra time for building background and prewriting. • Help students turn phrases into sentences. • Accept phonetic spelling, but show corrections. • Give a checklist for revising that has written cues and help students use dictionaries or word walls.	Students can write short sentences about a family member. Guide students to use a graphic organizer to add details. Have partners work together to write at least three interesting details describing the family member. Share their sentences with the class.
Advanced	• Can engage in grade-appropriate writing tasks with support • Can write phrases, sentences, and paragraphs with some errors • Can edit and revise using a checklist with a written description • Has a basic grasp of basic verb tenses, grammar features, sentence patterns, and cohesive devices • Provides increased detail and can summarize information from graphics and notes	• Allow extra time for prewriting. • Use brainstorming, concept mapping, peer conferencing, interviewing, and reading. • Help students with correct spelling, capitalization, and punctuation. • Clarify error correction by peers or teachers to make changes.	Use a graphic organizer to develop ideas and details about a family member. Students can develop a paragraph based on the Concept Map.
Advanced High	• Can express ideas in writing and engage meaningfully in grade-level writing assignments with minimal support • Writes comparable to native English speaker • Makes minor errors that rarely interfere with communication	• Use brainstorming, concept mapping, peer conferencing, interviewing, and reading. • Help students with correct spelling, capitalization, and punctuation if needed. • Clarify error correction by peers or teachers to make changes.	Use a graphic organizer to develop ideas about a family member. Students can develop a paragraph based on the concept map. Share the details they find most interesting.

ELL Language Development Routine

Hear It! **See It!** **Say It!** **Use It!**

Use this flexible routine with all levels of English language learners to guide their language development as they learn new basic and academic vocabulary, increase conceptual knowledge, and improve their reading comprehension. The following instructional sequence will encourage production and guide language development.

Start with choral work (Whole Group), and then move to partners or small groups, followed by "on your own" activities. Because choral, partner, and small group practice activities are nonthreatening, the affective filter is lowered, increasing language production.

Academic Vocabulary Routine

Hear It!

Model the word so that students can hear the correct pronunciation. Provide a student-friendly definition and relate it to something that students know, affirming their identity.

Display the word, and use a picture or pantomime to visually clarify meaning. Ask questions, and have students respond to show their understanding of the word.

Have students repeat the word chorally and then with a partner. Students will be able to use the word with more confidence and accuracy.

Engage students in activities that encourage language production. Have them create their own definitions and use the word multiple times orally and in writing to internalize vocabulary and concept knowledge.

ELL Use the Academic Vocabulary Routine

This example shows how to use the Academic Vocabulary Routine to pre-teach the word *noun*.

How to Teach the Word *Noun*

Hear It!	Say the word ***noun***. A ***noun** is a naming word for people, places, animals, or things.* Point to a desk. Say: *This is a desk. A desk is a thing, so the word* desk *is a **noun**.*
See It!	Write the word **noun** on the board and word wall. To clarify meaning, point to other items in the classroom. Ask: *What is this?* (a chair) *Is this a person?* (no) *Is this a place?* (no) *Is this a thing?* (yes) *So, the word* chair *must be a **noun**.*
Say It!	Have students repeat the word ***noun***. In pairs, have them say the word ***noun*** and the definition, *a **noun** is a naming word for people, places, animals, or things.*
Use It!	Have pairs work together to identify more **nouns** for people and things they see in the classroom. Then have them write and illustrate their own definition of **noun**. Pairs can then share their definitions orally with the class.

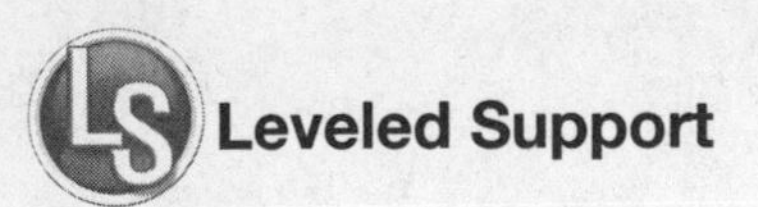

Leveled Support

Beginning Pair students with more proficient speakers or students who speak the same language. Use more gestures and repetition. Allow students to answer by pointing, gesturing, or giving one-word responses.

Intermediate Continue to use visuals and gestures. Model correct responses. Ask questions that elicit two-word responses.

Advanced Continue to provide visual support. Give students more time to process information. Questions can be more open-ended, but be sure to check comprehension frequently.

Advanced High Provide visual support as needed. Have students work with beginners who speak the same language to clarify meaning.

Contents

Professional Development

Introduction: How to Use This Book

Across the United States, teachers are welcoming increasing numbers of English language learners (ELLs) into their classrooms. English language learners make up the fastest growing K–12 student population in the United States.

While English language learners share many characteristics with other students, they need support and scaffolding specific to their needs. They represent a highly diverse population. They come from many home language backgrounds and cultures, and they have a wide range of prior educational and literacy experiences acquiring in their home languages.

This Handbook is designed to help you identify and support the needs of ELLs in your classroom. The strategies and activities will allow you to scaffold and support instruction so that all students can learn in ways that are comprehensible and meaningful, and in ways that promote their academic success and achievement.

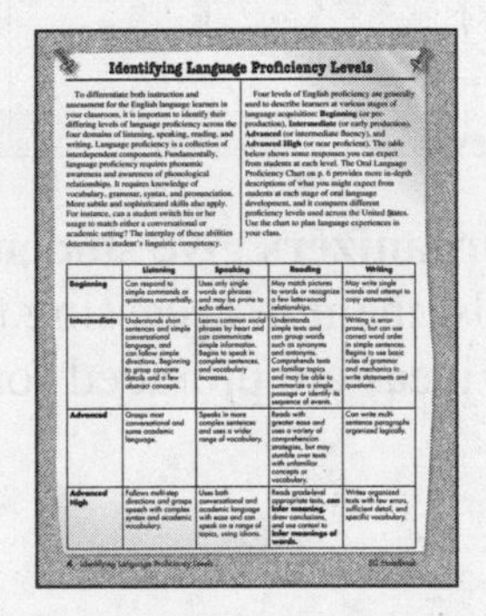
Identifying Language Proficiency Levels

Carefully crafted **professional development articles** assist you in understanding and planning for the unique needs of English language learners in your classroom.

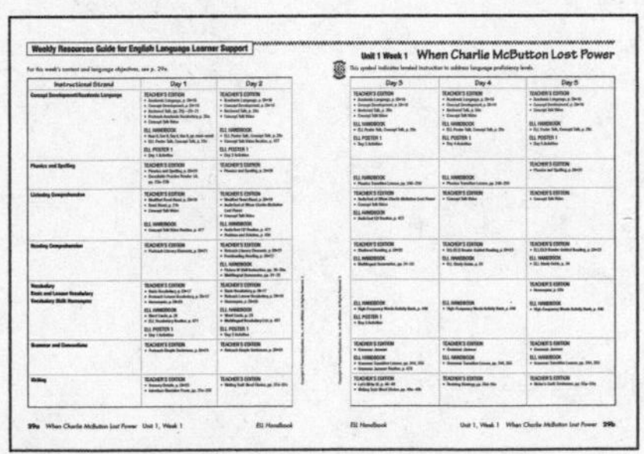
Weekly Resource Guide for English Language Learner Support

When Charlie McButton Lost Power

Weekly Planners outline all activities in a "week at a glance" format and include objectives for each instructional strand.

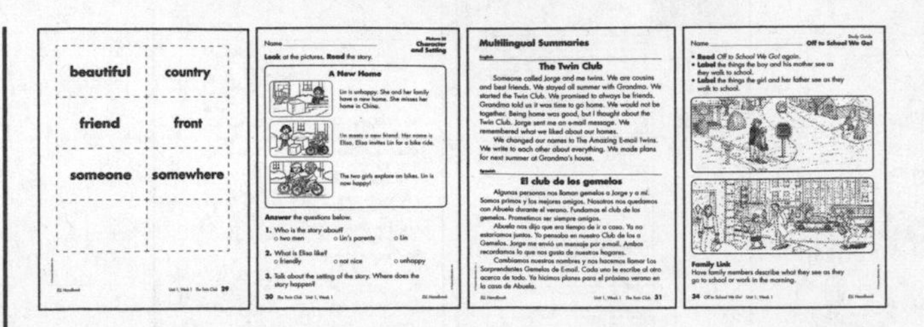
beautiful | country
friend | front
someone | somewhere

A New Home

Multilingual Summaries

The Twin Club

El club de los gemelos

Each reading selection is supported by a set of reproducibles. **Word Cards** allow students to use key vocabulary for speaking, writing, and content acquisition. Each **Picture It!** focuses on a reading comprehension skill with leveled instruction targeted to English language learners. **Multilingual Selection Summaries,** in English, Spanish, Chinese, Vietnamese, Korean, and Hmong, allow students to access selection content and share their reading with their families. **Study Guides** for ELL Readers allow you to assess comprehension of content and the use of key reading strategies. All of these resources provide access to core content material, each unit and week of the year. Detailed instructions for using these resources are provided in the ELL Support pages of the Teacher's Edition.

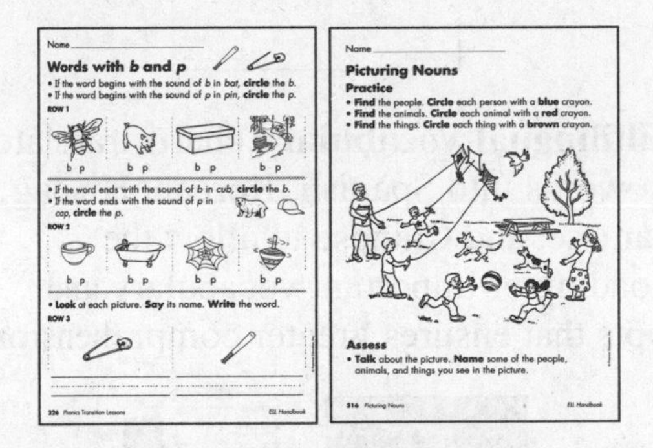
Words with b and p

Picturing Nouns

Phonics pages target instruction with consonants, vowels, and syllable patterns that may be challenging for English language learners. **Grammar** lessons supplement core instruction in speaking and writing. Use these lessons as students need additional support.

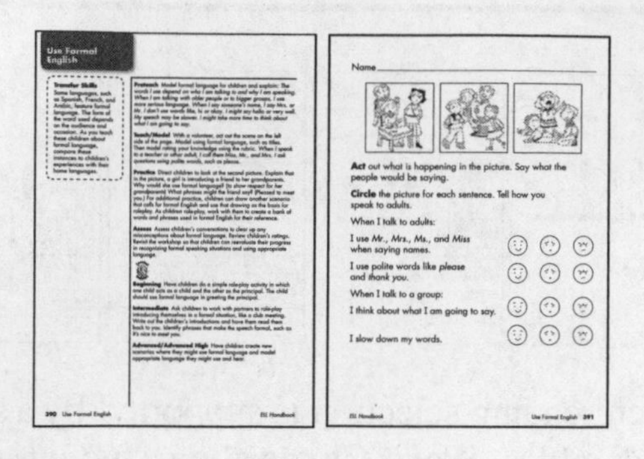

English Language Learner Workshops provide direct and explicit instruction in such topics as using transactional language, retelling or summarizing in English, asking for assistance, giving and following directions, and using formal and informal English. A teacher-driven lesson as well as a student worksheet is provided for a model/teach/practice/assess progression as students gradually master these skills.

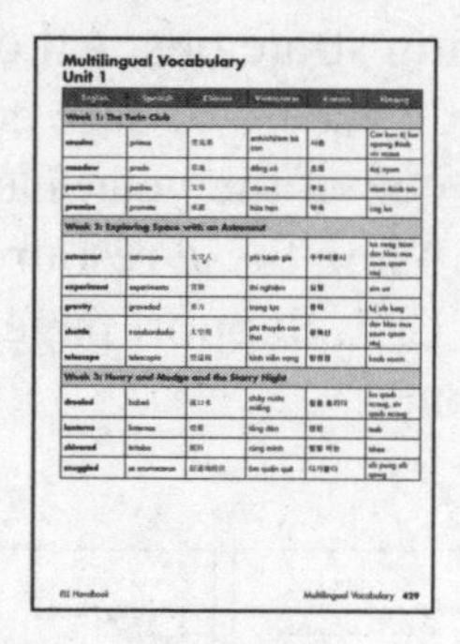

Multilingual Vocabulary charts translate the lesson words into Spanish, Korean, Hmong, Vietnamese, and Chinese to allow the frontloading of important vocabulary and concepts that ensures greater comprehension.

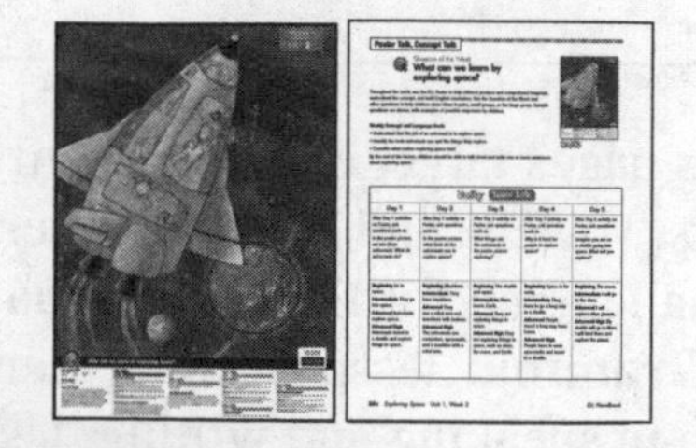

Poster Talk, Concept Talk leveled activities encourage language production using the poster visuals and vocabulary related to the weekly concept.

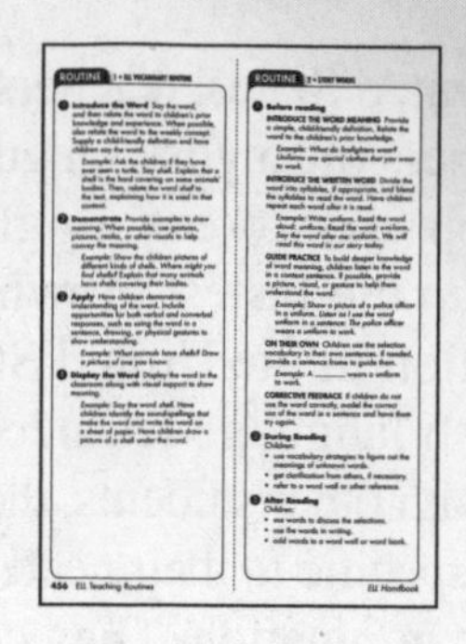

Teaching Routines for English language learners allow for a systematic approach to learning that yields results. Routines are tied to instruction, allowing students to master the skills needed to succeed.

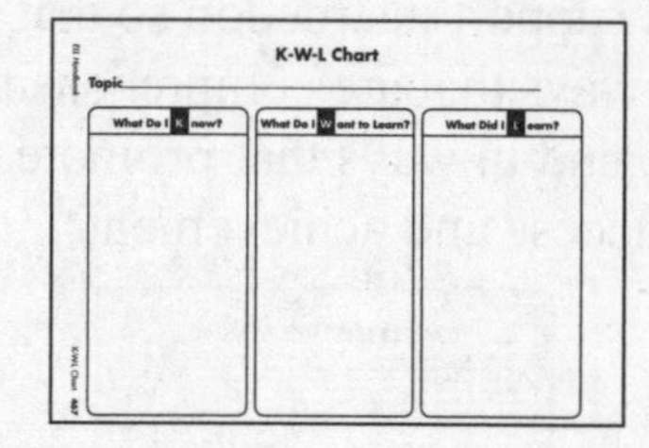

Graphic Organizers give students visual support to assist them in accessing the content. ELL teaching ideas are provided for each graphic organizer.

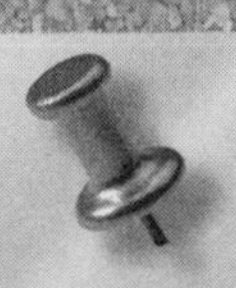

Identifying Language Proficiency Levels

To differentiate both instruction and assessment for the English language learners in your classroom, it is important to identify their various levels of language proficiency across the four domains of listening, speaking, reading, and writing. Language proficiency is a collection of interdependent components. Fundamentally, language proficiency requires phonemic awareness and awareness of phonological relationships. It requires knowledge of vocabulary, grammar, syntax, and pronunciation. More subtle and sophisticated skills also apply. For instance, can a student switch his or her usage to match either a conversational or academic setting? The interplay of these abilities determines a student's linguistic competency.

Four or five levels of English proficiency are generally used to describe learners at various stages of language acquisition: **Beginning** (or pre-production), **Intermediate** (or early production), **Advanced** (or intermediate fluency), and **Advanced High** (or near proficient). The table below shows some responses you can expect from students at each level. The Comparative Oral Language Proficiency Chart on p. 6 provides more in-depth descriptions of what you might expect from students at each stage of oral language development, and it compares different proficiency levels used across the United States. Use the chart to plan instruction for your class.

	Listening	Speaking	Reading	Writing
Beginning	Can respond to simple commands or questions nonverbally.	Uses only single words or phrases and may be prone to echo others.	May match pictures to words or recognize a few letter-sound relationships.	May write single words and attempt to copy statements.
Intermediate	Understands short sentences and simple conversational language and can follow simple directions. Beginning to grasp concrete details and a few abstract concepts.	Learns common social phrases by heart and can communicate simple information. Begins to speak in complete sentences, and vocabulary increases.	Understands simple texts and can group words such as synonyms and antonyms. Comprehends texts on familiar topics and may be able to summarize a simple passage or identify its sequence of events.	Writing is error-prone, but can use correct word order in simple sentences. Begins to use basic rules of grammar and mechanics to write statements and questions.
Advanced	Grasps most conversational and some academic language.	Speaks in more complex sentences and uses a wider range of vocabulary.	Reads with greater ease and uses a variety of comprehension strategies, but may stumble over texts with unfamiliar concepts or vocabulary.	Can write multi-sentence paragraphs organized logically.
Advanced High	Follows multi-step directions and grasps speech with complex syntax and academic vocabulary.	Uses both conversational and academic language with ease and can speak on a range of topics, using idioms.	Reads grade-level appropriate texts, can infer meaning, draw conclusions, and use context to infer meanings of words.	Writes organized texts with few errors, sufficient detail, and specific vocabulary.

How can you differentiate instruction for the different proficiency levels?

You can use a variety of instructional techniques, activities, and assessment tools to support English language learners at different levels of proficiency—all within the same lesson. For example, to teach sequence of events, you might choose to adapt your instruction as follows:

Teach/Model

Read a short passage to the whole class, showing pictures of each event in the story as you do so. When you have finished reading, review the events in the story. Model using sequence words.

- Use gestures to explain "first," "next," and "last" to students at the **Beginning** level. For example, hold up one finger as you say "first" and put on a shoe. Hold up two fingers as you say "next" and lace up the shoe. Hold up three fingers as you say "last" and take a step.
- Have students at the **Intermediate** level echo you as you say "first," "next," and "last" and then add a detail to each to make a phrase or short sentence.
- Have students at the **Advanced** level answer questions about sequence of events as you read aloud.
- Have students at the **Advanced High** level answer questions about the sequence of inferred events as you read aloud. (For example, "What must have happened before Jack slipped in the paint?" "The paint can fell.")

Practice

- After you read, have students at the **Beginning** level arrange the pictures in the story in the correct order.
- Have students at the **Intermediate** level answer the questions, "What happened first?" "What happened next?" "What happened last?"
- Have students at the **Advanced** level verbally describe the events in the story using sequence words.
- Have students at the **Advanced High** level write the sequence of events in the story using complete sentences.

Assess

- Have students at the **Beginning** level arrange a new series of pictures in the correct order.
- Have students at the **Intermediate** level look at a new series of pictures and then answer the questions, "What happened first?" "What happened next?" "What happened last?"
- Have students at the **Advanced** level read a new passage and then verbally describe its events using sequence words.
- Have students at the **Advanced High** level read a new passage and answer questions about the sequence of inferred events.

Comparative Oral Language Proficiency Chart

Levels of Proficiency	Level I Entering	Level II Beginning	Level III Developing	Level IV Expanding	Level V Bridging
	Beginning	Early Intermediate	Intermediate	Early Advanced	Advanced
	Beginning	**Intermediate**		**Advanced**	**Advanced High**
Characteristics of the English Language Learner	• Minimal comprehension • May be very shy • No verbal production • Non-English speaker • Silent period (10 hours to 3 months) • Uses gestures and actions to communicate	• Limited comprehension • Gives one- or two-word responses • May use two- or three-word phrases • Stage may last 6 months to 2 years	• Comprehension increases • Errors still occur in speech • Simple sentences • Stage may last 2 to 4 years	• Good comprehension • Sentences become more complex • Engages in conversation • Errors in speech are more complex	• Few errors in speech • Orally proficient • Near-native vocabulary • Uses complex sentences
What They Can Do: Performance Indicators	• Listen • Point • Illustrate • Match • Choose	• Name • List and group • Categorize • Label • Demonstrate	• Compare and contrast • Recall and retell • Summarize • Explain	• Higher-order thinking skills • Analyze, debate, justify	• All performance indicators
Instructional Ideas for Teachers	• Visual cues • Tape passages • Pair students • Total Physical Response activities • Concrete objects • Graphic organizers	• Short homework assignments • Short-answer quizzes • Open-ended sentences	• Graphs • Tables • Group discussions • Student-created books • Cloze activities	• Group panels • Paraphrasing • Defending and debating	• Lessons on writing mechanics • Free reading of appropriate books • Cooperative learning groups

What Reading Teachers Should Know About Language

Why do reading teachers need to know about the structure of language?

English language learners are entering U.S. classrooms in steadily increasing numbers. The demands on teachers are also surging. To communicate effectively with these students, teachers need to know how to make their instructional talk more comprehensible. All teachers need to better understand their students' attempts at written and spoken language. To improve students' literacy skills in English, teachers must understand how language works *in education.* What should we know about English and other languages? What truths about language help teachers as communicators, as guides, and as evaluators?

Knowledge about the structure of languages—and particularly of English—is vital not only to linguists and ELL teachers. Reading and content-area teachers, too, can make practical, everyday use of the concepts that are posed and explored by the following questions.

What are the basic units of language?

Spoken language consists of units of different sizes:

Phonemes

Phonemes are the individual sounds in a word that affect meaning. The word *cat* consists of these three phonemes: /k/ /a/ /t/.

Different languages use different sets of phonemes. English language learners may not be familiar with some English phonemes and may need help recognizing and producing these sounds.

Phonemes signal different word meanings. For example, the different vowel sounds in the words *hit* and *heat* indicate that these are two different words.

Morphemes

Morphemes are the smallest units of meaning in a language. Some morphemes are **free** (or independent) units. Words such as *dog, jump,* and *happy* are free morphemes. Other morphemes are **bound** (or attached), such as inflected endings, prefixes, and suffixes:

- the noun ending *-s* in *dogs*
- the verb ending *-ed* in *jumped*
- the prefix *un-* in *unhappy*
- the adjective ending *-er* in *happier*
- the suffix *-ness* in *happiness*

These bound morphemes add meaning and, in fact, form new words.

Words

A word consists of one or more morphemes. A word also can be defined as a meaningful group of morphemes. Native English speakers may pronounce words in ways that make it difficult for English language learners to hear word boundaries. For example, in conversation, an English speaker may ask, "Did you eat?"—but pronounce it like "Jeet?"

Some languages use bound morphemes (for example, word endings) to convey the meanings of certain functional English words such as the prepositions *in, on,* and *between.* English language learners may need explicit instruction in order to use these functional words correctly. On the other hand, an English word such as *in* may seem familiar to a Spanish speaker who uses the similar preposition *en.*

Phrases

A phrase is a group of words that have meaning together but do not include a subject and a predicate. Since some languages allow the subject or verb to be understood, students may believe that certain phrases in English are equivalent to sentences.

Sentences

A sentence is a meaningful group of words that includes a subject and a predicate. English language learners may understand the concept of sentences, but they may apply word order conventions from their home languages. They also may struggle with the dense sentence structures of academic English.

Discourses

Discourses include speeches, essays, and many other kinds of communication made up of sentences. One kind of discourse frequently heard in U.S. classrooms involves the teacher asking questions and students responding aloud. Depending on their home cultures, some English language learners may find the question-and-answer form of discourse unfamiliar.

Why do English language learners need to learn about basic units of language?

It helps teachers to understand that units, such as bound and free morphemes, words, phrases, and sentences or clauses, operate differently in different languages. For example:

- In Chinese, the past tense is not expressed with verb endings, but by separate words that indicate the time of the action (similar to *yesterday* and *already*).
- In Spanish, verb endings indicate the person and number of sentence subjects, so the subject may not be stated in some sentences.
- In Arabic, related words share three-consonant roots. Speakers form related verbs, nouns, and adjectives by applying fixed patterns to these roots and sometimes adding prefixes and suffixes.

English language learners are working mentally to determine how units of English work—as they also try to understand texts and acquire content knowledge.

What is academic English?

Academic English might be described as the language of teachers, literature, textbooks, and content areas, such as science and social studies. Unlike conversational English, academic English is language of a cognitively demanding register, or range. Academic English does not depend as much upon the gestures and circumstances of speech as conversational English does.

Academic English includes content-area vocabulary embedded in complex grammatical structures. It features words about abstract ideas. Understanding this language requires knowledge of content, as well as experience with written materials and classroom discussions. Many English language learners can carry on conversations in English with their native-English-speaking classmates. But they still struggle with reading and writing English—and even understanding their teachers in class. They have acquired social English skills used in personal communication, but they have not yet mastered the academic English used at their grade level.

How do English language learners learn vocabulary?

English language learners must learn much more than the selected vocabulary words in a lesson. They also must make sense of the other unfamiliar words in the lesson—and thousands of other words they continually encounter in school.

Knowing a word involves much more than hearing it and learning its definition. Students must learn how each word relates to its other forms. They gradually learn how it relates to other words and concepts. Knowledge of a word grows during many encounters.

Students learn words in meaningful groups more effectively than in unrelated lists. Look for opportunities to group words in meaningful ways. For example, as students learn the word *invite*, they also can learn *invited, uninvited, invitation, inviting,* and other words in this family.

What is "regular" to English language learners?

Proficient English speakers often take for granted irregularities in English that can puzzle younger and less fluent learners.

For example, a student who learns the plural forms *dogs, cats,* and *turtles* may wonder why *mouses, mooses,* and *childs* meet with disapproval. A student who masters these past tense forms—*jumped, walked,* and *stopped*—may try to use *throwed, catched,* or *taked.* In both cases, the child demonstrates an awareness of English conventions, and a teacher should acknowledge this in a positive way. The teacher also should gradually help each student master the many exceptions to the rules. Teachers who are aware of the principles of word formation in English can help students acquire vocabulary. English has many helpful patterns for new speakers, readers, and writers to learn. Savvy teachers break up the instruction into manageable chunks so that students are not overwhelmed by the many English word patterns they encounter.

What characteristics of written words might challenge English language learners?

- Written English is an alphabetic language, and letters represent sounds in words. Languages such as Chinese and Japanese are not alphabetic; written symbols can represent larger parts of words than just individual sounds. For students whose home languages are not alphabetic, learning the alphabetic system is an early and continuing challenge.
- The home languages of many English language learners—including Spanish, Vietnamese, Hmong, Haitian Creole, and others—are alphabetic. Yet the letter-sound correspondences in these languages are different from those of English. Students can use literacy skills they may have in their home languages, but much new learning is needed to master English.
- While letter-sound correspondences in numerous languages are relatively simple, the relationships of letters to sounds in English can be complicated. In Spanish, for example, the vowel *a* has one sound. In English, *a* can represent many different sounds.
- Even in related English words, the same letters can stand for different sounds. Consider *c* in the words *electric, electricity,* and *electrician.* The spellings of these words may challenge English language learners.
- The challenges of written English affect not only spelling but also word recognition, comprehension of text, and confidence in language learning.

Welcoming Newcomers to the Mainstream Classroom

The teacher's first concern when welcoming newcomers to the mainstream classroom must be to help each student learn the basic concepts and vocabulary needed to participate in school life.

Prepare

Learn as much as possible about your newcomer students in order to tailor instruction to their individual needs.

Find out from parents or other sources about educational practices in the student's home country or culture. For example, if the student is accustomed to memorizing and reciting material in a group, he or she may feel anxious about independent work or homework, particularly if the family is not able to help the child in English.

Newcomers who are acquiring English may experience identifiable stages of adjustment and adaptation.

- **A Silent Period** For a student quite new to an English-language environment, a "silent period" is normal. The student may be learning classroom routine and acquiring basic vocabulary by watching and listening.
- **Culture Shock** In this phase, newcomers may prefer to spend much of their time with family or friends from the home culture and to temporarily reject the new language and culture. Help children to cope with this phase by providing extra help and attention when possible. A bilingual friend or classroom aide can help to make the environment feel more navigable to the child and can help to alleviate any feeling of anxiety or sadness.

Getting Started in the Classroom

Before classes begin, you may wish to plan a small reception for newcomers. Invite the students' parents or other family members, and include someone who can translate.

- **Orient the newcomer to the classroom.** Have students help you to label the classroom and the objects in it with self-stick notes. Pronounce the name of each item as you do, and use the word in a short sentence. *"Desk. This is your desk."*
- **Show interest in and respect for each child's home culture.** Create opportunities for the class to learn more about the newcomer's home country and culture. Learn a few phrases in the student's home language. Correctly pronounce the student's name.
- **Demonstrate crucial skills.** Have students tour the school with older students who speak the same home language. Post seating charts and go through assigned textbooks with newcomers to help them understand what content is presented in each.
- **Try to provide a risk-free learning environment.** Create opportunities for students to practice speaking English in small groups or with a partner without worrying about errors they may make. Accept errors in speech without comment and model the correct phrasing.
- **Provide a "buddy."** A buddy system helps students feel more secure in their environment. Buddies need not speak the same home language, but pairing up buddies with the same home language can allow buddies to serve as tutors.
- **Include newcomers in classroom routines.** Assign newcomers their share of regular classroom chores. Such responsibilities can help them feel they are part of the group. Students can be shown how to successfully carry out routine tasks without using or needing extensive English.

Teaching Strategies

Educational strategies should assist students to learn in content areas at the same time that they acquire the new language. Remember that students' skills in the home language can be transferred to English learning. Encourage students to continue to speak and read in the home language.

- **Build on students' prior knowledge.** Newcomers often have knowledge bases that are much greater than their skill levels in English. Find ways to gauge students' familiarity with the topics of upcoming lessons. Regularly using visual aids, such as semantic maps, K-W-L charts, or time lines, can help you determine how much each student already knows or needs to learn about a topic.
- **Encourage students to use learning resources.** Teach students how to use a picture dictionary or a children's dictionary, and encourage them to use it frequently to find the words they need. Ask them to start their own word banks by listing frequently used vocabulary in a notebook. Provide bilingual dictionaries for extra support.
- **Use environmental print to teach.** Put up posters and other materials from periodicals and magazines. If possible, provide students with parallel texts about the same topic in English and in the home language.
- **Invite the families of newcomers to participate in school life.** Find ways to communicate information about homework and class projects in English and the home language. Make families aware that literacy skills in the home language can help students transfer those skills to English.
- **Build a support network.** Bilingual tutors or classroom aides can clarify assignments or lesson content for English language learners without disrupting the day's activities. Similarly, family members who volunteer to help in the classroom can greatly lessen students' anxiety levels.
- **Help students transfer their writing skills.** For English language learners who have developed any emergent writing skills in their home languages, build on these skills by occasionally having them write in both languages. Short sentences and picture labels written in a home language and English help students with writing and English acquisition.
- **Include culturally relevant assignments.** Try to find readings for students that refer to their home cultures. If writing skills are limited, encourage learners to show their understanding by talking about the stories and creating illustrations.

While it may take some time for English language learners to gain proficiency in academic English, newcomers need not feel like outsiders for very long.

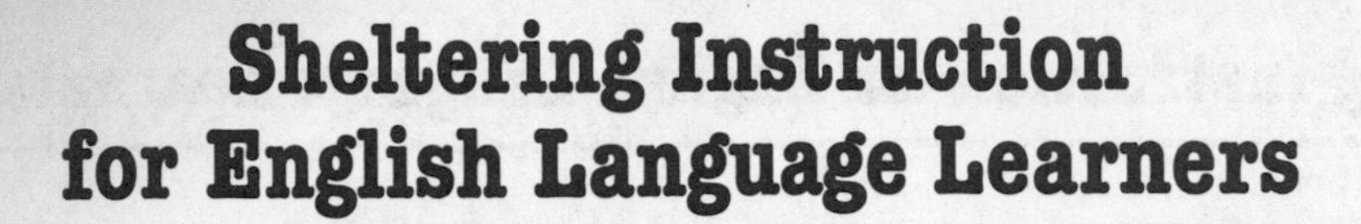

Sheltering Instruction for English Language Learners

What is sheltered instruction?

Sheltered instruction is a combination of strategies for teaching academic content to English language learners at the same time that they are developing proficiency in the English language. This approach to instruction is called *sheltered* because it offers a haven, or refuge, for students who must comprehend subject matter presented in a language they are still learning. Sheltered instruction supports English language learners who do not have grade-level academic vocabulary or the familiarity with the American school system that their English speaking classmates have. It provides extended English language support that English language learners receive as they learn subject-area concepts.

How does sheltered instruction help students and teachers?

Sheltered instruction offers practical, easy-to-implement strategies that teachers can use in a mainstream classroom to extend and scaffold instruction about the English language. Sheltered instruction helps English language learners find the keys they need to make sense of instruction in English about the concepts and processes they need to perform grade-level work in all subjects.

Teachers can help students build mental bridges to new concepts and learning in English by encouraging them to connect their prior knowledge—the diverse skills, experiences, language, and cultural knowledge that they bring to the classroom—to their new learning activities. Finding ways for students to draw on their home language, cultural background, and prior experience can facilitate each English language learner's ability to grasp and retain abstract ideas and grade-level vocabulary. Finding connections between what they are learning and what they already know in their home language can motivate students to read, write, listen, and speak in English. As comprehension and vocabulary increase, students can transfer more and more concepts from their home languages into English.

This knowledge transfer can work for teachers, too. As teachers tap into students' prior knowledge, the teachers will discover when they need to supply background about American events, customs, and idioms that may be new to English language learners. At the same time, they will be expanding their knowledge about English language learners' backgrounds and traditions.

Some Basics

1. Use Appropriate Speech (Comprehensible Input)

✓ **Enunciate.** Speak slowly and clearly, especially when introducing new content and vocabulary.

✓ **Provide wait time.** English language learners often need extra time to process questions in English and to formulate responses.

✓ **Explain and demonstrate the meanings of complex terms.** Use activities that help students practice speaking, hearing, writing, and reading key words and phrases.

Complex term	Activities to clarify meaning
weather	Write and say: weather Write and say: hot, cold Say: *The weather is hot today.* (Fan yourself to show you are hot.) Then say: *The weather is cold today.* (Hug yourself and shiver to show you are cold.) Have volunteers repeat each sentence with gestures. Then fan yourself and ask: *What is the weather like today?* (hot) Hug yourself and shiver and ask: *Is the weather hot or cold today?* (cold) Have partners take turns using gestures and asking and answering the questions. Start a wall chart of weather words with pictures.

✓ **Allow students to show comprehension at their levels of language proficiency.** Ask questions that can be answered with "yes" or "no," by choosing one of two words as the answer (*Is ice hot or cold?*), by pointing to a picture or object (*Point to the tree.*), or by following simple oral directions.

2. Develop Academic Concepts

✓ **Link concepts explicitly to students' prior knowledge and background.** For example, if you introduce a unit on weather, ask students to describe, illustrate, and share what they know about weather. Create and display a class chart that tells about weather in places where students have lived.

✓ **Use hands-on activities to build background for new information.** For example, introduce the idea of touch (The Five Senses) by having students touch objects with different textures and learn a word or words to describe how each object feels.

✓ **Use supplementary materials.** Picture books can clarify and support concept learning. Use picture books that show terms that are hard to explain, such as *covered wagons, rations,* or the *Pony Express.*

3. Emphasize and Develop Key Vocabulary

✓ **Repeat key words, phrases, and concepts, and have students practice using them.**

✓ **Provide feedback on students' language use.** Use gestures to indicate understanding, as well as supportive questions to prompt students to provide more details.

✓ **Make the development of proficiency in English an explicit goal in all of your teaching. To learn new academic vocabulary, students need to use it.** Provide situations that challenge students to push themselves to a higher level of proficiency.

4. Connect Written and Oral Language

✓ **Say and write new vocabulary.** When teaching new words or phrases, such as idioms, write the word or phrase where everyone can see it. Say it slowly as you point to it. Have students repeat the word or phrase. Use gestures, role play, or drawings to demonstrate what the word means. Have students practice saying, reading, and writing the word or phrase in sentences.

✓ **Use word and picture cards to explain vocabulary and content.**

✓ **Have students build personal word files.** Have them write a word on one side of a card and draw a picture to represent its meaning on the other side. The files can include target words for different content areas as well as words that students find interesting or important. Have students use the cards for sorting and categorizing activities (e.g., color words, animal names, weather words, math words, action words).

✓ **Provide letter and phoneme cards for phonics activities.** Pair English language learners with native English speakers to use cards in order to build and say words that contain target sounds and spelling patterns. Give English language learners extra time and support to hear, say, and practice sounds and to build words using those sounds.

5. Use Visuals, Dramatization, and Realia (Real Things)

✓ **Use picture walks to preview text, concepts, and vocabulary—and to build background knowledge.** Use pictures to introduce characters and the setting and to give a simple summary of a story. You can use this same strategy with nonfiction text, having students preview illustrations, captions, boldfaced words, and other text features.

- ✓ **Use realia and graphic organizers.** Whenever possible, show objects and pictures that will help students understand concepts and speak about them in English. Use graphic organizers, diagrams, drawings, charts, and maps to help students conceptualize abstract information.
- ✓ **Use Total Physical Response (TPR) for active learning, so that students can show comprehension through physical movement.** For example, have students hear and follow instructions: *Clap your hands for Carla. Go to the board and circle the noun in red.*
- ✓ **Use role play, drama, rhymes, songs, and movement.** All students need opportunities to be active learners. For English language learners, participating in a small group re-enactment of a story, for example, can allow them to show comprehension and personal responses beyond what their language abilities may allow them to express.

6. Ongoing Formal and Informal Assessment

- ✓ **Assess early to understand a student's language level and academic preparedness. Use your assessment to plan and guide instruction.**
- ✓ **Set personal goals for each student and monitor progress regularly.** A student who uses phrases might be pushed to say and write complete sentences. A student who uses simple sentences might be pushed to add clauses to the sentences.
- ✓ **Provide various ways to demonstrate knowledge, including acting, singing, retelling, demonstrating, and illustrating.**
- ✓ **Use a variety of formal assessments such as practice tests, real tests, and oral and written assessments.** Use multiple choice, cloze, and open-response formats to help students become familiar with various assessment formats.

Sheltered instruction provides English language learners with opportunities to understand and access content-area learning. Within this framework, teachers provide activities that integrate reading, writing, listening, and speaking. Teachers can address the range of cultural, linguistic, and literary experiences that English language learners bring to the classroom. Sheltered instruction provides English language learners with many opportunities to understand and access content-area learning. Within this kind of instruction, teachers support English language learners by providing activities that integrate reading, writing, listening, and speaking. Teachers use students' experiences and prior knowledge as the key to unlock doors to content and language learning.

Vocabulary Knowledge and Strategies

Knowing how to organize vocabulary instruction around a few key areas will go a long way toward ensuring that students achieve both language proficiency and overall academic success. The new vocabulary that you teach should be carefully selected. As you consider the vocabulary you will teach in your classroom, you'll need to be aware of both survival language and academic language.

Survival Language

Think of survival language as a useful toolkit for new English language learners—a practical store of words and phrases that can be used to navigate new environments and accomplish everyday tasks in the classroom and at home. Survival language not only involves teaching students labels for common objects, places, and people, but includes giving students instruction in how to understand and follow directions, ask for help, and function appropriately in social situations. While it is valuable to reinforce this type of vocabulary acquisition throughout the day, as spontaneous interactions with students arise, it is also important to offer structured and intentional instruction in survival language. Consider organizing related words and phrases under the heading of a topic such as "School," as in the following table.

People	Places	Objects	Phrases
principal teacher nurse student coach	cafeteria classroom bathroom library gym	desk chair chalkboard worksheet ruler	May I have...? Please show me.... I want to... What is a ...? I need help with....

Teachers Support Vocabulary Learning

English language learners come to school with a wide range of home language literacy, English language proficiency, and previous educational experiences. All of these factors impact their learning in English.

Teachers can use various strategies to support vocabulary development. Students need multiple exposures to words. Understanding deepens over time through gradually increased and varied experiences with the words.

English language learners need opportunities to learn vocabulary through activities that integrate reading, writing, speaking, and listening skills in the context of meaningful literacy experiences. Language learning is an exploration. Students have a curiosity about learning, and effective teachers nurture this quality through engaging and meaningful activities. Teachers can use what students already know to help them extract meaning from text by teaching them ways to learn and think about words.

Strategies for Exploring Words

Use these strategies to build vocabulary.

Related Words

Provide opportunities for English language learners to learn new words by grouping words that are related to a specific theme, quality, or activity. Help students classify English words in meaningful categories.

Use word walls, graphic organizers, and concept maps to group related words and create visual references that can be used in future lessons. Teachers can help students group and relate words in different ways, depending on what they can notice and understand, as well as how students will use the vocabulary.

Color names are one example of related words that can be the focus of a lesson.

✓ Write the word *colors* at the top of a wall chart.

✓ With colored markers, make a column of squares under the heading: red, blue, yellow, green.

✓ Point to the word *colors* and tell students they are going to learn the names of colors.

✓ Point to the first square and say, *This color is red.* Write *red* and repeat it clearly as you underline it with your finger.

✓ Show a familiar red object, such as a block, and say: *This is a red block. The color of this block is red. What color is this block?* (red)

Repeat this process with the other colors, making sure that students hear, say, and read each color name, and connect it to the color itself.

Have students create other sections in their personal word card files such as "family names," "numbers," "days and months," "weather," and "time."

Whenever you introduce a new topic or concept, take time to teach English language learners words they will need to understand the lesson. Keep in mind that they may need to learn some words and phrases in the lesson—including idioms and background references—that may already be common knowledge to native speakers. Encourage native speakers to act as resources for English language learners when they encounter a word, phrase, or concept that puzzles them.

Charts such as the one here can help students learn how words change form, depending on their function.

Naming Word	Describing Word	Action Word
rain	rainy	rain, rains, rained, raining
dance, dancer	dancing	dance, dances, danced, dancing
sleep, sleeper	sleepy	sleep, sleeps, slept, sleeping

<u>Cognates</u>

When students hear or see a word that looks or sounds similar to a word they know in their home language, encourage them to explore the connection. For example, a Russian speaker hearing the word *music* may recognize its connection to the Russian word *musika.* Many words that sound similar in two or more languages are cognates—they have the same or similar meaning in both languages. Record cognates on a wall chart and add to it during the year.

<u>Multiple-meaning Words</u>

Many English words have multiple meanings. Illustrating and creating examples of the ways words are used can build English language learners' experiences and understanding of the multiple meanings that words may have. Teachers can help students expand their understanding of multiple meanings by sharing sentences, definitions, and pictures that demonstrate the different meanings. For example, contrasting *The pitcher is full of water* with *The pitcher threw the ball,* with illustrations, will help English language learners remember the two meanings of *pitcher.*

Academic Language

Research indicates that acquiring a strong grasp of academic vocabulary is perhaps the most vital factor that distinguishes successful students from those who struggle in school. Becoming fluent in academic language will enable English language learners to understand and analyze texts, write clearly about their ideas, and comprehend subject-area material. Academic vocabulary differs from conversational English. It is the language of classroom discourse, and it is used to accomplish academic, not social or personal, purposes. Academic vocabulary also includes words, phrases, and sentence structures not commonly found in oral language but used frequently in academic texts such as textbooks, reports, essays, articles, and test materials. Instruction in academic vocabulary should be explicit and systematic. Give students multiple exposures to academic terms through frequent reading, writing, and oral language activities. Because academic vocabulary involves the use of language that is not commonly encountered in conversational contexts, English language learners need structured opportunities to practice this vocabulary in formal settings where teachers and peers are modeling the use of effective academic language.

Below is a partial list of types of academic vocabulary to which students should be exposed:

- **Transition words**
  therefore; thus; however; similarly; alternatively
- **Content-specific words**
  cell (science); *era* (social studies); *graph* (math)
- **Difficult verb and tense forms**
  was written by (passive voice); *have voted* (present perfect); *had ended* (past perfect)
- **The language of written instructions**
  compare; define; analyze; calculate; summarize

Home Language Activities

Teachers can use home language activities to help students reinforce their learning of the concepts and meanings of vocabulary and literacy activities. English language learners can participate in a variety of activities such as discussion, telling or reading stories, listening to songs and music, hearing radio or television weather or sports reports, and interviewing family members, and then use those experiences as topics for discussion and sharing in the classroom. Students can transfer their understanding of a word or concept from their home language to English when they have experiences that illustrate meaning. Teachers can find ways to use the home environment as an educational resource by planning activities that involve reading, writing, listening, and speaking about students' family histories, cultures, and experiences.

Technology

Teachers can use various forms of technology (computer, Internet, audio, video recording) to meet the specific and varied needs of English language learners.

For example, you might choose target words and have students use computers to find images that illustrate their meanings.

Creating and Adapting Strategies

A great deal of reading in English, listening to selections read aloud, and conversing in English will help learners acquire thousands of words per year if they are engaged in learning. Continue using the instructional strategies that work, adapt (or discontinue) the ones that are not effective, and try new approaches as needed.

References

August, Diane (Principal Investigator), and T. Shanahan (Panel Chair) (2006). *Developing Literacy in Second-Language Learners: Report of the National Literacy Panel on Language-Minority Children and Youth.* Mahwah, New Jersey: Lawrence Erlbaum Associates.

Blachowicz, Camille L. Z., and Peter Fisher. *Teaching Vocabulary in All Classrooms.* Upper Saddle River, NJ: Prentice Hall, 2002.

Vocabulary Development for Reading Success. Scott Foresman Professional Development Series, Module 6. Glenview, IL: Scott Foresman, 2004.

Effective Comprehension Instruction for English Language Learners

Clear and explicit comprehension instruction is a key component of successful English language development. Traditionally, the main purpose of comprehension instruction has been limited to having students answer assigned questions related to a passage they have read. As a result, what can and should be a complex, analytical process has been diminished by a narrow focus on products. A greater benefit to English language learners, as for all students, is guidance in becoming active readers who are engaged in texts on multiple levels before, during, and after reading.

Jim Cummins identifies conditions that promote engaging with literacy for English language learners and, in fact, for all students. To attain literacy, students must be fully engaged in their reading and writing. Students need to read a variety of texts that reflect children's cultures and languages. Teachers must use strategies that promote a deep understanding of the text. Through engaging students by activating prior knowledge, frontloading to build background, affirming identity, scaffolding the language, and extending language through various experiences, students move from engagement in literacy to achievement in literacy.

Comprehension instruction that will achieve this more sophisticated goal focuses on *metacognition*, the name we give to a good reader's ability to independently reflect on the purpose of reading, select appropriate approaches to texts, ask questions as he or she reads, and actively resolve areas of confusion. Metacognitive strategies such as predicting, questioning, self-monitoring, summarizing, and making inferences should be transferable from one type of text to another. For this reason it is important to introduce these strategies to students using a variety of fiction and nonfiction texts. The following comprehension instruction techniques will help you encourage literacy engagement and the development of metacognition in your students.

What Is Frontloading?

Imagine that you are teaching someone how to bake a cake. If you knew that your pupil had no experience in the kitchen, you would not jump right into the recipe and instructions. Instead, you would start by naming and explaining the key ingredients in the cake—the flour, sugar, baking powder, eggs, and so on. You would demonstrate how to use measuring cups. You might explain how baking differs from frying or boiling. In other words, you would anticipate the knowledge that your budding baker requires in order to be successful at this new task, and make sure to introduce that knowledge first. This is the essence of frontloading.

Frontloading for English language learners involves preteaching the vital vocabulary, background concepts, and sometimes the text structures that students need to know before they can understand an upcoming lesson. Prior to a lesson in which students will be reading a story from *Aesop's Fables*, for example, you might choose to frontload the following vocabulary using a graphic organizer.

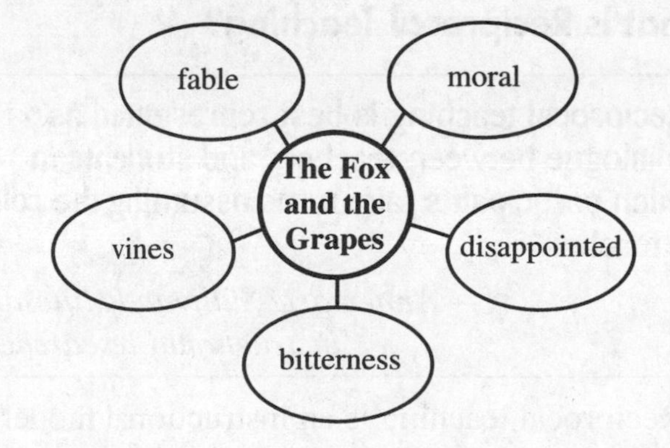

What Is Shared Reading?

Shared reading is reading that is rich with interactions between teacher and students. When using the shared reading model, the goal is to invite students to actively participate in the reading process. This is an excellent opportunity to encourage English language learners to use oral language in a relaxed and informal setting. Use an enlarged text as the central focus as you conduct a shared reading session, so that everyone in the group can clearly see the text. The basic elements of shared reading include:

✓ **Think Alouds:** Model making predictions, asking questions, and drawing conclusions about the text by thinking aloud as you read.

✓ **Guided Discussions:** Using open-ended questions, encourage students to respond to, analyze, and summarize the text.

✓ **Active Participation:** Students can contribute to the reading of the text by chorusing repetitive words or phrases or reading sight words that you point to.

✓ **Multiple Readings:** Return to the same text several times over a few days. Set a focus for each reading such as enjoyment, decoding, comprehension, or vocabulary.

What Is Reciprocal Teaching?

> **"Reciprocal teaching is best represented as a dialogue between teachers and students in which participants take turns assuming the role of teacher."**
>
> *— Annemarie Sullivan Palincsar, instructional researcher*

Reciprocal teaching is an instructional model that focuses on four key comprehension strategies: predicting, question generating, clarifying, and summarizing. First, you explain, discuss, and model the strategies. Then, while working in small groups, students gradually take responsibility for strategies while making their way through a text.

- **Predicting:** Make predictions about what an author will discuss next.
- **Question Generating:** Pose "teacher-like" questions about main ideas in the text.
- **Clarifying:** Notice potential areas of confusion and take steps to clarify them (e.g., reread, identify the definition of a word).
- **Summarizing:** Identify and recap the most important information.

Reciprocal teaching has proven to be of great help in developing the skills of English language learners. Although it can be used with a variety of text types, this technique is especially useful for deepening comprehension of expository text.

References

Cummins, Jim. *Reading Instruction and Reading Achievement Among EL Students* (Research Into Practice monograph). Glenview, IL: Pearson, 2009.

Drucker, M. J. "What Reading Teachers Should Know About ESL Learners." *The Reading Teacher,* 57(1) (2003), pp. 22–29.

Francis, D. J., et al. "Practical Guidelines for the Education of English Language Learners: Research-Based Recommendations for Instruction and Academic Interventions." Houston, TX: Center on Instruction, 2006.

Institute of Education Sciences, National Center for Educational Evaluation and Regional Assistance. "Effective Literacy and English Language Instruction for English Learners in the Elementary Grades." IES Practice Guide, 2007.

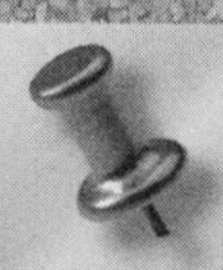

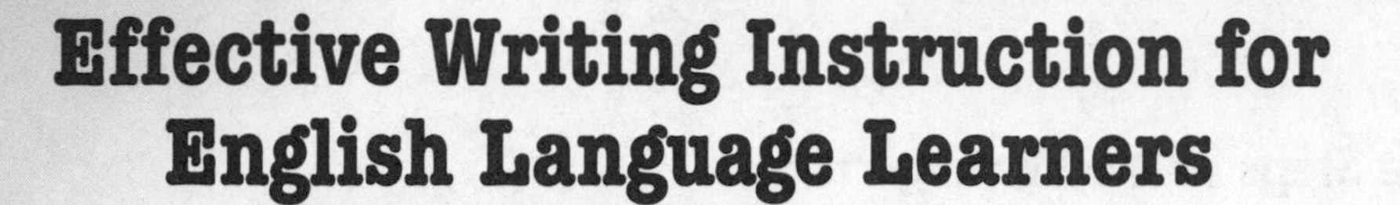

Effective Writing Instruction for English Language Learners

The Role of Writing in Language and Literacy Development

Research shows that students acquire language most readily when they are fully involved in all learning activities in the classroom. Classroom activities should integrate reading, writing, listening, and speaking, as these language skills develop interdependently. This approach supports English language development in the context of meaningful instructional content. That is, students will learn to write (in English) about real ideas and things.

Teachers can facilitate students' language learning and literacy development by ensuring that:

- students hear language in natural ways, in real and practical contexts—and write it in structured formats
- activities in which students participate regularly provide opportunities for listening and speaking so students can internalize the language
- opportunities for acquiring new vocabulary are always present in reading activities and environmental print, and are related to the content areas of the curriculum
- opportunities are always available for interesting conversations with English-speaking peers
- mistakes are accepted as part of learning
- students understand why they are being asked to complete various oral communication, reading, and writing tasks

English language learners who are already literate, or are emergent readers and writers in their home languages, no doubt have been influenced by their backgrounds and experiences with writing genres, writing styles, and cultural discourse. By learning more about the characteristics of English language learners' literacy experiences, teachers can recognize when students are transferring what they already know to their new, early literacy learning in English, and teachers can support these efforts. It is helpful to seek information about students in sensitive ways, appropriately respecting families' privacy and regarding home languages and cultures with respect.

Such efforts to find out students' strengths and needs are worthwhile. For example, teachers who compare spelling patterns between a home language and English will better understand the efforts students make to acquire and write English words. Teachers can point out the differences and similarities so that students can learn to compare the languages and develop metalinguistic understanding about how both languages work. This will help them sort out the ways they can use language in their writing.

ENGLISH	rose
SPANISH	rosa

Young English language learners also are emergent writers. For most children, the line between emergent writing and drawing (that is, art) is not a bold border. It helps learners to write in both words and pictures. Experts in English language learning advise, however, that English language learners who draw too often without writing any words are missing vital opportunities to practice writing in English. Encourage students to write about their pictures.

Scaffolding the Steps of the Writing Process

Writing, whether in a home language or especially in a new language, is the most difficult mode of language use to master (Collier and Ovando, 1998). Each English language learner has a unique background and set of experiences with language, literacy, and culture. Students access writing instruction at varying levels of English proficiency. It is important for teachers to provide each student with challenging work that is appropriate for his or her level of English proficiency and literacy.

By understanding the specific kinds of support English language learners need at each stage of the writing process, teachers can tailor their instruction to fit individual needs. The chart below provides suggestions to help you do this.

	Level I	Level II & III	Level IV & V
	Beginning (little experience in English)	**Intermediate** (conversational but not academic English)	**Advanced/ Advanced High** (gaining skills in academic English)
Prewrite	Allow extra time for prewriting. Use brainstorming. Have student draw or act out ideas. Map, or illustrate and label, words that the student needs.	Allow extra time for prewriting. Use brainstorming. Have student draw and label, or act out and describe, ideas. Help student learn and write the words he or she needs.	Allow extra time for prewriting. Use brainstorming, drawing, word mapping, and story mapping. Help student learn and write the words he or she needs.
Draft	Allow student to dictate, as appropriate. As skills emerge, student writes words and phrases. Accept phonetic invented spelling, but model correct spelling, capitalization, and punctuation.	Student writes words, phrases, and simple sentences. Help student turn phrases into sentences. Accept phonetic invented spelling, but show correct spelling, capitalization, and punctuation.	Student writes words, phrases, and simple sentences. Help student add details to sentences and create paragraphs. Accept phonetic invented spelling, but show correct spelling, capitalization, and punctuation.
Revise	With help, student revises work with the aid of a checklist that has visual clues about each task.	Student revises work with the aid of a checklist that has visual and written clues about each task. Help student incorporate written or oral commentary from teacher in revisions.	Student revises work with the aid of a checklist that has visual and written clues about each task—and asks for clarification. Help student incorporate written or oral comments from teacher in revisions.
Edit	Student sees teacher model how to correct errors and begins to correct errors.	Student corrects errors with help from the teacher.	Student corrects errors with help from the teacher and incorporates teacher's suggestions into writing.
Publish	Student creates final product of writing with teacher's guidance.	Student creates final product of writing with teacher's guidance.	Student creates final product of writing with teacher's guidance.

Effective Writing Instruction for English Language Learners, continued

Structured Writing

Teachers can use **structured writing** to scaffold writing instruction. Structured writing aids include writing/sentence frames and graphic organizers, which help students record and organize their ideas.

Writing Assignments for English Language Learners

There are various kinds of assignments and activities that encourage English language learners to use their background knowledge and previous experiences to connect with the writing process. Establishing a daily or weekly **routine** for these assignments and activities helps cue students about what to expect and provides extra support for participating in classroom instruction.

Teachers can compile a **writing portfolio** to show progress and to facilitate home communication and teacher/student dialogue about writing.

Writing Products

While there are varieties of authentic writing assignments that encourage students to write about their interests and experiences, there are specific genres with which students must become familiar in order to build an understanding of text structures that reflect district and state standards/ curriculum frameworks. The following examples suggest ways to approach each genre in relation to English language learners' needs.

Language Experience Approach
Students dictate stories to the teacher (or aide), who writes them down. Students then copy the words that the teacher wrote. In this way, reading and writing become processes directly related to children's experiences. They read and write to express themselves and communicate their experiences.

Dialogue Journals
Dialogue journals develop writing skills and provide authentic communication between a student and teacher. This writing is informal and may include pictures. It allows students to choose topics for writing. The teacher may suggest topics, but the choice is the writer's. The student writes as in conversation with the teacher. The teacher responds to the content of the writing, also in a conversational manner. Writing errors are not explicitly corrected, but the teacher's writing serves as a model (Collier and Ovando, 1998).

Home Literacy Activities
Home literacy activities encourage conversation between students and their families as they read together in their home language and/or in English. If parents are not literate, students can practice reading aloud and discussing stories with them. Teachers can plan activities such as interviewing family members in the home language and then sharing the responses with the class in English.

Students learning to write will benefit from writing in their home language as well as the new language, English. Bilingual parents, staff members, and students can help children write in home languages.

Rubrics to Evaluate Writing

Teachers can use school, district, state, or national standards for English language learners (which are aligned with English Language Arts standards) to create rubrics that adjust expectations for English language learners based on their individual English proficiency levels.

The sample rubric on the following page focuses on one of the traits of good writing: rules (or conventions) of English. It describes what English language learners at various levels (beginning, intermediate, advanced, and advanced high) would be expected to write. Teachers can develop similar evaluation forms that reflect the needs of the school, the grade, and the students involved. Other examples of traits of good writing may include Focus/Ideas, Order, Writer's Voice, Word Choice, and Sentences.

Traits of Good Writing: Rules (English Language Learners)

	Level	Capitalization	Punctuation	Sentence Structure and Grammar	Spelling
Beginning (little experience in English)	1	Uses capitalization when writing one's own name.	Adds a period to the end of a sentence and a question mark to the end of a question.	Begins to use some standard word order, with mostly inconsistent grammatical forms (for example, subject/verb agreement).	Produces some independent writing that includes inconsistent spelling.
Intermediate/ Advanced (conversational but not academic English)	2–4	Uses capitalization to begin sentences and proper nouns.	Produces independent writing that may include some inconsistent use of periods and question marks.	Uses standard word order but may use inconsistent grammatical forms.	Produces independent writing that includes some misspellings.
Advanced High (gaining skills in academic English)	5	Produces independent writing with consistent use of correct capitalization.	Produces independent writing with generally consistent use of correct punctuation.	Uses complete sentences and generally correct word order.	Produces independent writing with consistent use of correct spelling.

References

August, Diane (Principal Investigator), and T. Shanahan (Panel Chair) (2006). *Developing Literacy in Second-Language Learners: Report of the National Literacy Panel on Language-Minority Children and Youth.* Mahwah, New Jersey: Lawrence Erlbaum Associates.

Collier, V. P., and C. J. Ovando (1998). *Bilingual and ESL Classrooms: Teaching in Multicultural Contexts.* Boston, MA: McGraw Hill.

Echevarria, J.; M. Vogt; and D. Short (2004). *Making Content Comprehensible for English Learners: The SIOP Model.* Boston: Allyn & Bacon.

Fillmore, L. W., and C. E. Snow (2000). "*What Teachers Need to Know About Language.*" Washington, DC: ERIC Clearinghouse on Languages and Linguistics.

English Language Learners and Assessment

Assessment Needs of Diverse Learners

Because English language learners make up a dynamic group of learners who enter school with a wide range of linguistic, cultural, and learning experiences, it is important for teachers to learn about the unique background of each individual learner. Overall, assessment can provide important information about students' learning that can be used to plan appropriate and meaningful instruction. However, the kinds of assessment, the purposes for which they are used, and how the results are evaluated can directly impact how meaningful the assessments are (Cummins, 1981).

High-stakes Testing vs. Authentic Assessment

While so-called "high-stakes" testing has become increasingly influential, high-profile tests can be difficult for English language learners because they require proficiency in academic English, understanding of grade-level subject matter, and an understanding of cultural contexts. While high-stakes test results in the United States influence instructional decisions made in schools, these results often do not reflect what English language learners know. Consequently, the instructional decisions based on test results often do not reflect the specific learning needs of English language learners (Bielenberg and Fillmore, 2005).

It is important to find a variety of ways to assess English language learners that show what each learner is able to do. Focusing on what students already know—and what they are learning but have not mastered—helps teachers identify specific educational needs and enables educators to build their ongoing instruction upon all the resources, experiences, and abilities that English language learners bring to school. Authentic assessment, or ongoing classroom-based (often informal) assessment of students by teachers, allows students to show their strengths. Ongoing assessment also provides teachers with an accurate, dynamic picture of how to plan instruction and provide feedback in ways that meet the changing learning needs of each student (García, 1994).

Outcome-based/norm-referenced tests are different from ongoing authentic assessment because they evaluate, or make a judgment about, the performance of a student at a given time, while authentic assessment informs both teachers and students about day-to-day learning and provides feedback about how to proceed in order to meet the needs of individual learners.

English language learners must be taught test-taking strategies and must build background about the language and procedures of test taking. Use the suggestions below when preparing English language learners, who may not be experienced with the specialized language and implications of standardized tests. (Bielenberg and Fillmore, 2005):

- Point out text structures and conceptual references used in tests.
- Point out difficult language structures, and provide sufficient practice before the test.
- Preteach basic and content-area vocabulary.
- Build background and knowledge about test taking and procedural language.

Preteach Vocabulary and Question Types

- Make a T-chart to show examples of the question types students will find on tests. Explain what the structures mean and what they ask test-takers to do.
- Make a short list of test vocabulary, phrases, and instructions found on tests—such as *choose, write, fill in the circle, less than,* and *greater than.* Illustrate what these expressions ask students to do.

Example:

TEST DIRECTIONS	WHAT SHOULD I DO?
<u>Choose</u> the word that goes in the <u>blank</u>. **<u>Mark</u> your answer.** 1. Nancy rides her ____. O book O bike O store O gloves	• **Choose** = pick, decide on one • **Blank** = the line 1. Nancy rides her ____. • **Mark** = use pencil to fill in the circle

Example:

INSTRUCTIONS	WHAT SHOULD I DO?		
Find the **<u>sum</u>.**	Add numbers, + $10 + 1 = 11$		
Compare the numbers using **>** , **<** , or **=**	<	less than	$1 < 10$
	>	greater than	$9 > 2$
	=	equals	$3 = 3$

Reading Fluency and Comprehension Assessment

Authentic assessment focuses on teachers making informed decisions based on authentic literacy tasks within the classroom context that reflect individual student's progress and learning (García, 1994). Finding ways to help English language learners develop reading fluency means finding out if students really comprehend what they read, rather than just decode words.

Student's English language proficiency levels, the kinds of literacy and learning experiences students have had, and how familiar they are with the topic of the reading passage will affect how much they struggle with understanding what they read. Literature also can be challenging for English language learners because of the use of figurative language, including metaphors, similes, and symbolism. Check students' reading comprehension and understanding of concepts such as *setting, characters, plot, beginning, middle,* and *end.*

When assessing fluency and comprehension, it is helpful for teachers to learn how students' home literacy and languages affect their learning in English. English language learners may draw on what they already know; for example, an English language learner whose home language is Spanish may use Spanish spelling patterns and/or phonetics when reading or writing words in English. Recognizing the influence of the home language, and the student's reliance upon the literacy skills and strategies he or she knows in the home language, will help teachers not only assess more accurately, but know how to point out similarities and differences between English and the home language as a way to develop awareness about how different languages are related. This helps develop metalinguistic awareness, or thinking about how language works.

Teachers must ultimately use all they know about each student's English proficiency and literacy skills in order to:

- monitor progress
- organize students in groups for effective learning
- differentiate instruction

Assessing English language learners and learning about their cultural, linguistic, and learning experiences can help teachers plan instruction that is comprehensible and challenging.

Scaffolding High-stakes Testing

While "high-stakes" testing presents various challenges for English language learners, there are various test-taking strategies that teachers can use to support students in preparing for eventual mastery of standardized testing. Showing students ways in which they can recognize test formats and decode the questions of a test will help them figure out what each question is asking them to do.

Assessment Accommodations for English Language Learners

While English language learners need time to acquire the academic language necessary to be able to practice and perform well on standardized tests in English, there are some accommodations that may support their attempts at extracting meaning from test language, questions, and passages. Accommodations for English language learners may include the following:

- Provide English language learners with extra time to complete the test.
- Allow the use of a bilingual dictionary or a picture dictionary to clarify words that may hinder comprehension.
- Read the question aloud in some cases.

References

August, D., and K. Hakuta. *Improving Schooling for Language Minority Children: A Research Agenda.* Washington, DC: National Academy Press, 1997.

Bielenberg, B., and L. W. Fillmore. "The English They Need for the Test." *Educational Leadership,* 62(4) (2004/2005), pp. 45–49.

Cummins, J. "The Role of Primary Language Development in Promoting Educational Success for Language Minority Students." *Schooling and Language Minority Students: A Theoretical Framework.* Sacramento, CA: California Department of Education, 1981.

García, G. E. "Assessing the Literacy Development of Second Language Students: A Focus on Authentic Assessment" in K. Spangenbergk-Urbschat and R. Pritchard, eds. *Kids Come in All Languages: Reading Instruction for ESL Students,* pp. 180–205. Newark, DE: International Reading Association, 1994.

Scott Foresman Reading Street

Overview of Weekly Support for English Language Learners

The ELL Handbook provides weekly lesson materials to support English language learners with scaffolded and leveled comprehension and vocabulary instruction for language development. It builds on the Student Edition and on literacy instruction in the Teacher's Edition. Each strand contains a wide variety of activities that promote literacy attainment for your English language learners.

Weekly Planners offer a quick reference to the ELL Support materials for each lesson of the year.

Weekly Resources Guide for English Language Learner Support

Unit 2 Week 1 *Penguin Chick*

For this week's content and language objectives, see p. 59e.

This symbol indicates leveled instruction to address language proficiency levels.

Instructional Strand	Day 1	Day 2	Day 3	Day 4	Day 5
Concept Development/Academic Language	TEACHER'S EDITION • Academic Language, p. DI•16 • Concept Development, p. DI•16 • Anchored Talk, pp. 200j—200–201 • Preteach Academic Vocabulary, p. 205a • Concept Talk Video ELL HANDBOOK • Hear It, See It, Say It, Use It, pp. xxxvi–xxxvii • ELL Poster Talk, Concept Talk, p. 59c ELL POSTER 6 • Day 1 Activities	TEACHER'S EDITION • Academic Language, p. DI•16 • Concept Development, p. DI•16 • Anchored Talk, p. 206a • Concept Talk Video ELL HANDBOOK • ELL Poster Talk, Concept Talk, p. 59c • Concept Talk Video Routine, p. 477 ELL POSTER 6 • Day 2 Activities	TEACHER'S EDITION • Academic Language, p. DI•16 • Concept Development, p. DI•16 • Anchored Talk, p. 216a • Concept Talk Video ELL HANDBOOK • ELL Poster Talk, Concept Talk, p. 59c ELL POSTER 6 • Day 3 Activities	TEACHER'S EDITION • Academic Language, p. DI•16 • Concept Development, p. DI•16 • Anchored Talk, p. 226a • Concept Talk Video ELL HANDBOOK • ELL Poster Talk, Concept Talk, p. 59c ELL POSTER 6 • Day 4 Activities	TEACHER'S EDITION • Academic Language, p. DI•16 • Concept Development, p. DI•16 • Concept Talk Video ELL HANDBOOK • ELL Poster Talk, Concept Talk, p. 59c ELL POSTER 6 • Day 5 Activities
Phonics and Spelling	TEACHER'S EDITION • Phonics and Spelling, p. DI•20 • Decodable Practice Reader 6A, pp. 203a–203b	TEACHER'S EDITION • Phonics and Spelling, p. DI•20	ELL HANDBOOK • Phonics Transition Lesson, pp. 232, 236	ELL HANDBOOK • Phonics Transition Lesson, pp. 232, 236	TEACHER'S EDITION • Phonics and Spelling, p. DI•20
Listening Comprehension	TEACHER'S EDITION • Modified Read Aloud, p. DI•19 • Read Aloud, p. 201b • Concept Talk Video ELL HANDBOOK • Concept Talk Video Routine, p. 477	TEACHER'S EDITION • Modified Read Aloud, p. DI•19 • AudioText of *Penguin Chick* • Concept Talk Video ELL HANDBOOK • AudioText CD Routine, p. 477 • Main Idea, p. 487	TEACHER'S EDITION • AudioText of *Penguin Chick* • Concept Talk Video ELL HANDBOOK • AudioText CD Routine, p. 477	TEACHER'S EDITION • Concept Talk Video	TEACHER'S EDITION • Concept Talk Video
Reading Comprehension	TEACHER'S EDITION • Preteach Main Idea and Details, p. DI•21	TEACHER'S EDITION • Reteach Main Idea and Details, p. DI•21 • Frontloading Reading, p. DI•22 ELL HANDBOOK • Picture It! Skill Instruction, pp. 60–60a • Multilingual Summaries, pp. 61–63	TEACHER'S EDITION • Sheltered Reading, p. DI•22 ELL HANDBOOK • Multilingual Summaries, pp. 61–63	TEACHER'S EDITION • ELL/ELD Reader Guided Reading, p. DI•23 ELL HANDBOOK • ELL Study Guide, p. 64	TEACHER'S EDITION • ELL/ELD Reader Guided Reading, p. DI•23 ELL HANDBOOK • ELL Study Guide, p. 64
Vocabulary **Basic and Lesson Vocabulary** **Vocabulary Skill: Synonyms**	TEACHER'S EDITION • Basic Vocabulary, p. DI•17 • Preteach Lesson Vocabulary, p. DI•17 • Synonyms, p. DI•20 ELL HANDBOOK • Word Cards, p. 59 • ELL Vocabulary Routine, p. 471 ELL POSTER 6 • Day 1 Activities	TEACHER'S EDITION • Basic Vocabulary, p. DI•17 • Reteach Lesson Vocabulary, p. DI•18 • Synonyms, p. DI•20 ELL HANDBOOK • Word Cards, p. 59 • Multilingual Vocabulary List, p. 433 ELL POSTER 6 • Day 2 Activities	ELL HANDBOOK • High-Frequency Words Activity Bank, p. 446 ELL POSTER 6 • Day 3 Activities	ELL HANDBOOK • High-Frequency Words Activity Bank, p. 446	TEACHER'S EDITION • Synonyms, p. 231h ELL HANDBOOK • High-Frequency Words Activity Bank, p. 446
Grammar and Conventions	TEACHER'S EDITION • Preteach Common and Proper Nouns, p. DI•24	TEACHER'S EDITION • Reteach Common and Proper Nouns, p. DI•24	TEACHER'S EDITION • Grammar Jammer ELL HANDBOOK • Grammar Transition Lesson, pp. 314–315, 318–321 • Grammar Jammer Routine, p. 478	TEACHER'S EDITION • Grammar Jammer ELL HANDBOOK • Grammar Transition Lesson, pp. 314–315, 318–321	TEACHER'S EDITION • Grammar Jammer ELL HANDBOOK • Grammar Transition Lesson, pp. 314–315, 318–321
Writing	TEACHER'S EDITION • Writing Poems with Figurative Language, p. DI•25 • Introduce Poetry, pp. 205e–205f	TEACHER'S EDITION • Cinquain, pp. 215d–215e	TEACHER'S EDITION • Let's Write It!, p. 224–225 • Diamante, p. 225a • Writer's Craft: Figurative Language, p. 225b	TEACHER'S EDITION • Writer's Craft: Repetition, p. 231d	TEACHER'S EDITION • Editing and Presenting, pp. 231p–231q

59a *Penguin Chick* Unit 2, Week 1 — *ELL Handbook*

ELL Handbook — Unit 2, Week 1 *Penguin Chick* 59b

Weekly Planner

The daily Concept Development activities activate prior knowledge and build background, scaffold meaning, affirm identity, and develop and extend language.

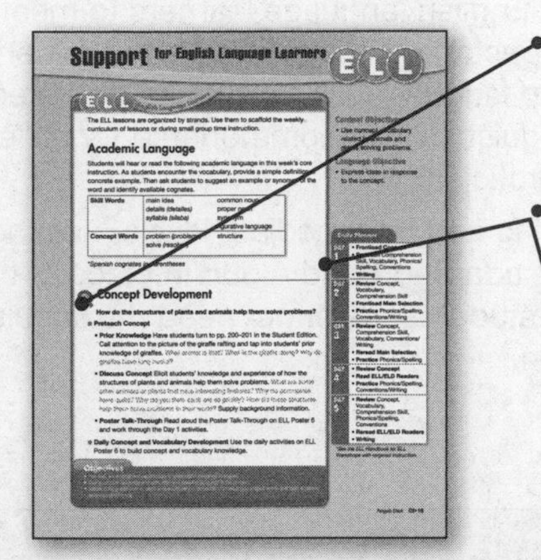
Support for English Language Learners
Academic Language
Concept Development
How do the structures of plants and animals help them solve problems?

- Use the linguistically accommodated questions to reach all language proficiency levels and make personal and cultural connections that validate identity and link academic content with what students already know.
- Use the Concept Development section and the Poster in a small group prior to the core lesson to build background and scaffold meaning.

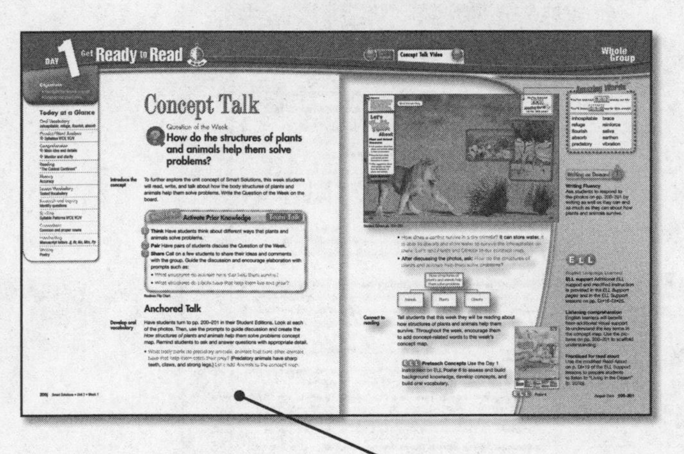
DAY 1 Get Ready to Read
Concept Talk
How do the structures of plants and animals help them solve problems?
Activate Prior Knowledge
Anchored Talk

- Use the daily activities on the ELL Poster and the Anchored Talk questions in the core lesson to build concept attainment and encourage oral language development and production.

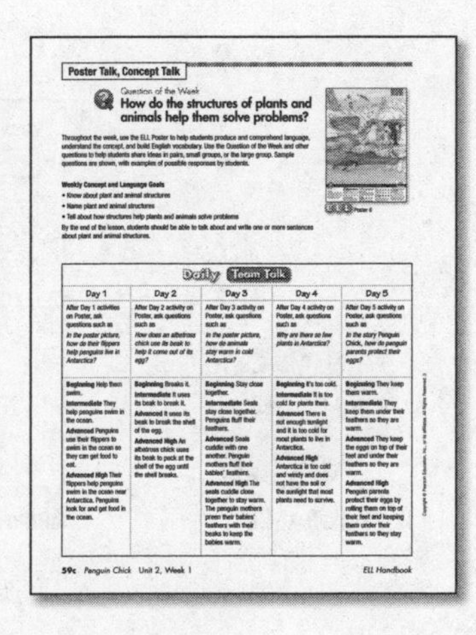
Poster Talk, Concept Talk
How do the structures of plants and animals help them solve problems?
Daily Team Talk

- Use the daily, leveled Poster Talk, Concept Talk in the ELL Handbook and the Team Talk activities in the core lesson to encourage oral language production.

Listening Comprehension

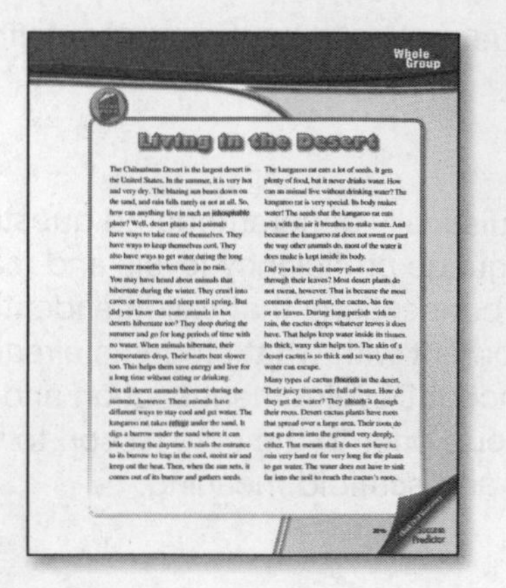

Living in the Desert

The adapted Read Aloud in the Listening Comprehension section of the ELL Support pages covers the same concept and information as the Read Aloud in the core curriculum.

In order for English language learners to meet grade-level learning expectations, have access to the core curriculum, and develop language, all instruction delivered in English must be linguistically accommodated for all levels of English language proficiency.

For Beginning and Intermediate levels, use the grade-appropriate adapted Read Aloud in place of the regular Read Aloud until students no longer need the linguistic support and modification.

- **First Listening: Listen to Understand** gives students a purpose for listening. The questions are designed to generate interest and help students understand the meaning of the adapted Read Aloud, so all proficiency levels can achieve success.
- **Second Listening: Listen to Check Understanding** Once students understand the main idea of the adapted Read Aloud, they can listen on subsequent days to clarify understanding of important details of spoken language.

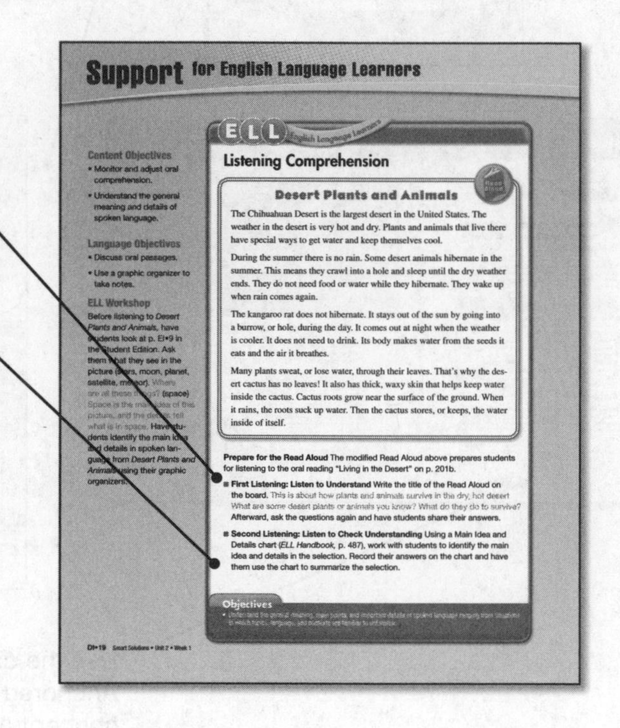

Support for English Language Learners

Content Objectives
- Monitor and adjust oral comprehension.
- Understand the general meaning and details of spoken language.

Language Objectives
- Discuss oral passages.
- Use a graphic organizer to take notes.

ELL Workshop
Before listening to *Desert Plants and Animals*, have students look at p. EI•9 in the Student Edition. Ask them what they see in the picture (stars, moon, planet, satellite, meteor). Where are all these things? (space) Space is the main idea of this picture, and the details tell what is in space. Have students identify the main idea and details in spoken language from *Desert Plants and Animals* using their graphic organizers.

ELL English Language Learners

Listening Comprehension

Desert Plants and Animals

The Chihuahuan Desert is the largest desert in the United States. The weather in the desert is very hot and dry. Plants and animals that live there have special ways to get water and keep themselves cool.

During the summer there is no rain. Some desert animals hibernate in the summer. This means they crawl into a hole and sleep until the dry weather ends. They do not need food or water while they hibernate. They wake up when rain comes again.

The kangaroo rat does not hibernate. It stays out of the sun by going into a burrow, or hole, during the day. It comes out at night when the weather is cooler. It does not need to drink. Its body makes water from the seeds it eats and the air it breathes.

Many plants sweat, or lose water, through their leaves. That's why the desert cactus has no leaves! It also has thick, waxy skin that helps keep water inside the cactus. Cactus roots grow near the surface of the ground. When it rains, the roots suck up water. Then the cactus stores, or keeps, the water inside of itself.

Prepare for the Read Aloud The modified Read Aloud above prepares students for listening to the oral reading "Living in the Desert" on p. 201b.

- **First Listening: Listen to Understand** Write the title of the Read Aloud on the board. This is about how plants and animals survive in the dry, hot desert. What are some desert plants or animals you know? What do they do to survive? Afterward, ask the questions again and have students share their answers.
- **Second Listening: Listen to Check Understanding** Using a Main Idea and Details chart (*ELL Handbook*, p. 487), work with students to identify the main idea and details in the selection. Record their answers on the chart and have them use the chart to summarize the selection.

Objectives

DI•19 Smart Solutions • Unit 2 • Week 1

Additional Products

Concept Talk Video

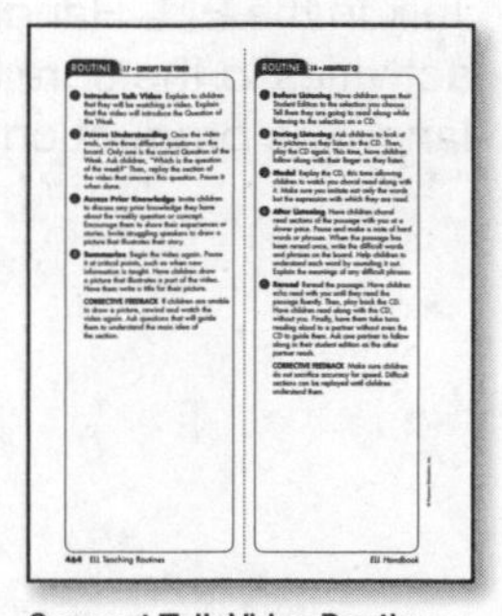

Concept Talk Video Routine

AudioText CD

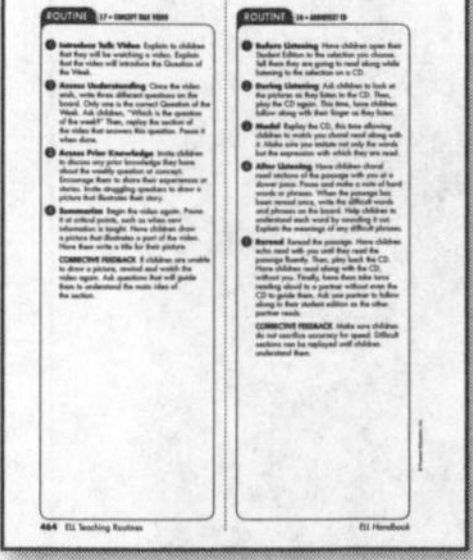

AudioText Routine

Discrete language skills that English language learners need include knowledge of the letters of the alphabet, familiarity with the sounds represented by letters, the ability to decode words, and the rules and conventions of how words are formed.

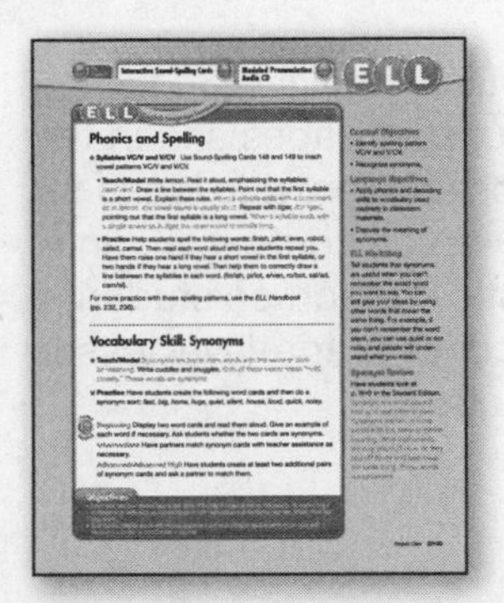

The Phonics support lessons work along with the core lessons to help students learn these skills at the same time they are developing basic English vocabulary.

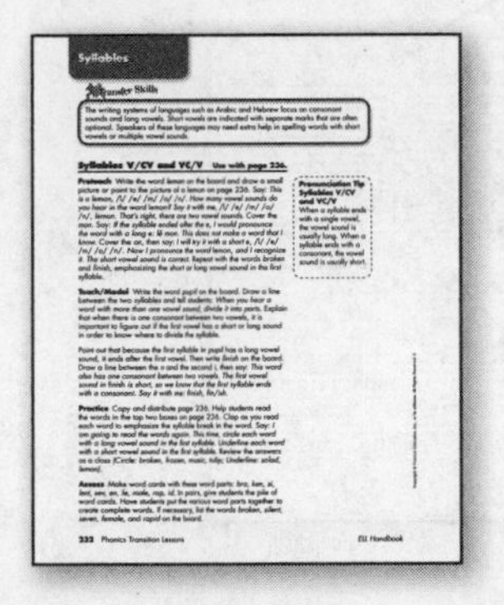

Language Transfer Notes activate prior knowledge about a phonics skill. Relating the skill being taught to the student's home language helps students build on what they already know and affirms their identities.

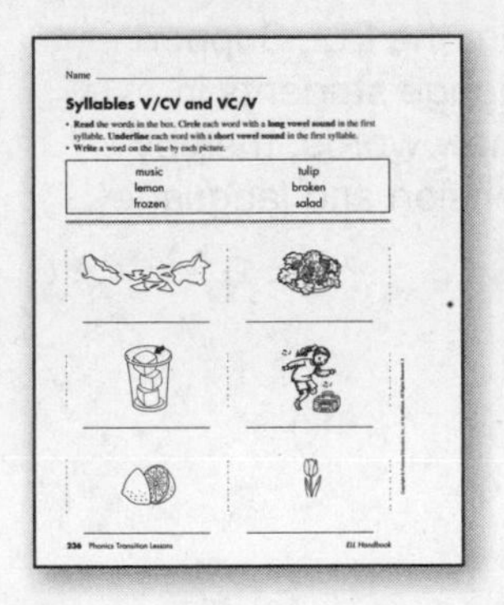

The flexible bank of Phonics Transition Lessons provides practice for developing and internalizing language at all proficiency levels. The practice pages provide visual support and context for the skills.

Additional Products

Modeled Pronunciation Audio CD

The Modeled Pronunciation Audio CD and routine offers additional practice with sound-spelling correspondence.

Vocabulary

English learners need explicit and systematic instruction to acquire both social and academic language for literacy attainment. Students need multiple exposures to new vocabulary through frequent listening, reading, writing, and oral language activities.

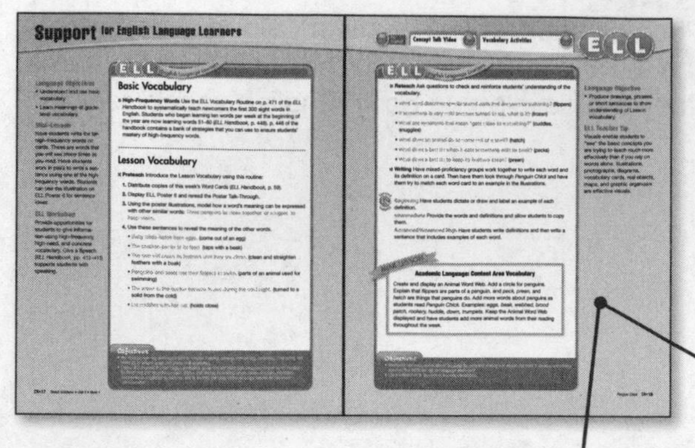

- Vocabulary activities in the ELL Support pages and in the core lessons provide ideas for giving visual, contextual, and linguistic support so students can access grade-level lesson vocabulary.

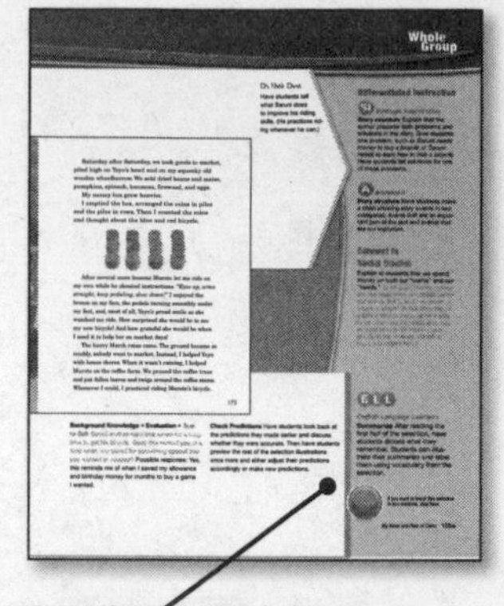

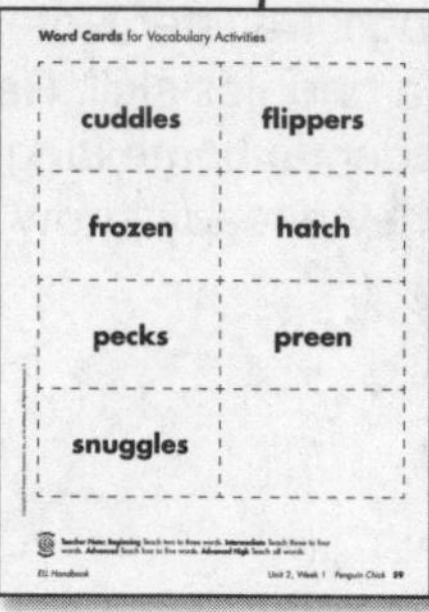

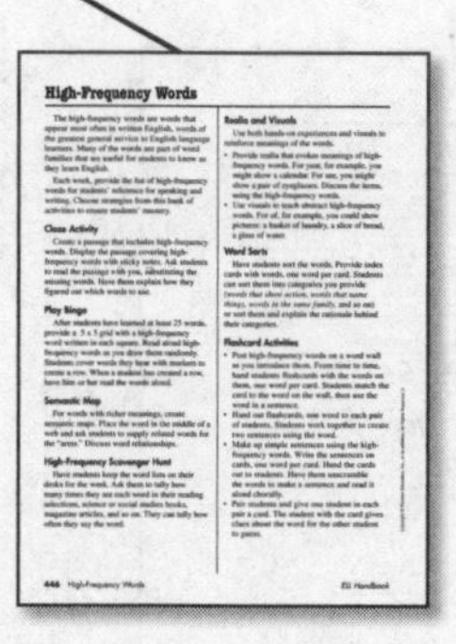

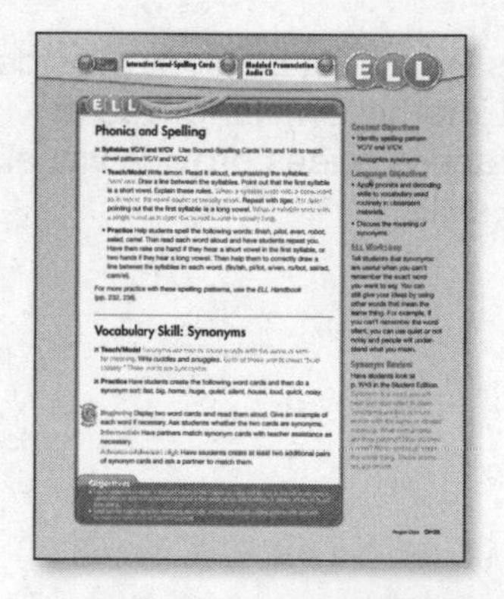

- Word Analysis lessons from the ELL Support and core lesson pages engage students in figuring out meanings of new words, thereby increasing their comprehension and language production.

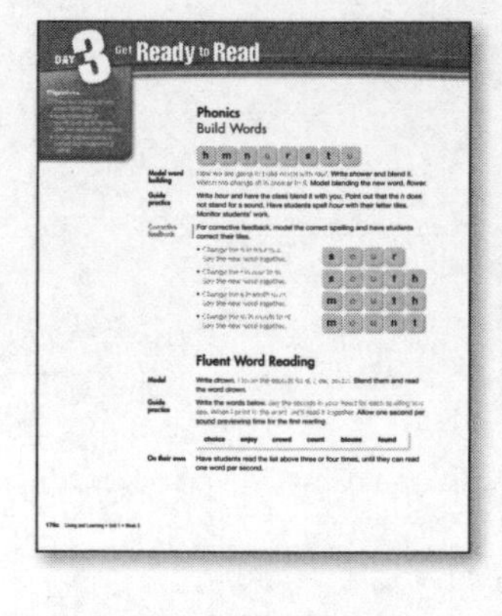

- Daily activities in the Poster increase oral and written production of newly acquired vocabulary.

- The Poster Talk, Concept Talk provides leveled support to meet the needs of all students.

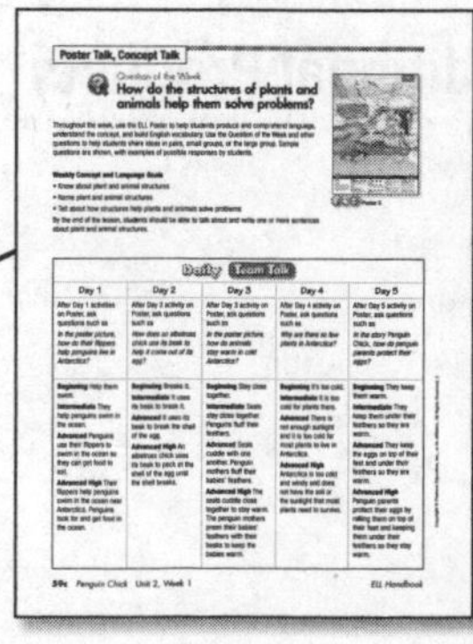

Engaging activities in the core lessons, the ELL Handbook, and the three Comprehension sections of the ELL Support lessons activate prior knowledge, build background, scaffold meaning, affirm identity, and develop and extend language.

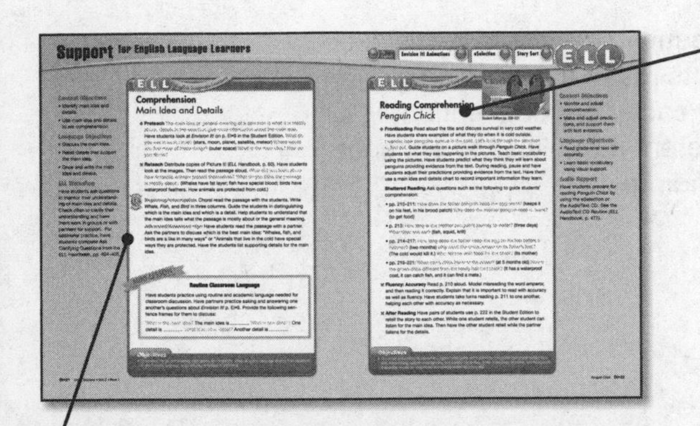

- Comprehension activities provide questions that encourage students to use oral language during reading to demonstrate understanding of text and to employ inferential skills.

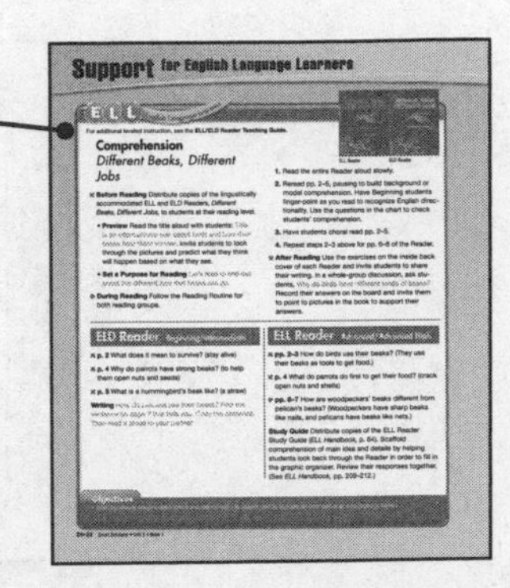

- The leveled notes in the ELL Support and Picture It! instruction pages provide ideas for differentiating instruction at all proficiency levels.

- The ELD Readers are written for Beginning and Intermediate language proficiency levels, and the ELL Readers are designed for Advanced to Advanced High levels, allowing you to meet the needs of a diverse classroom.

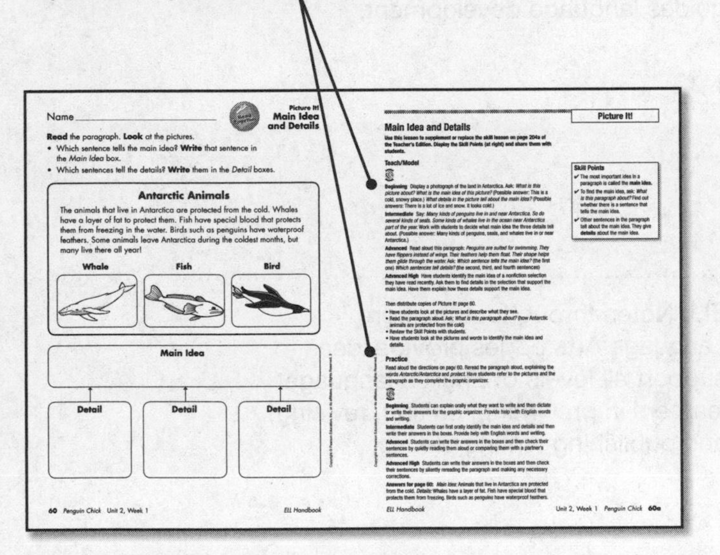

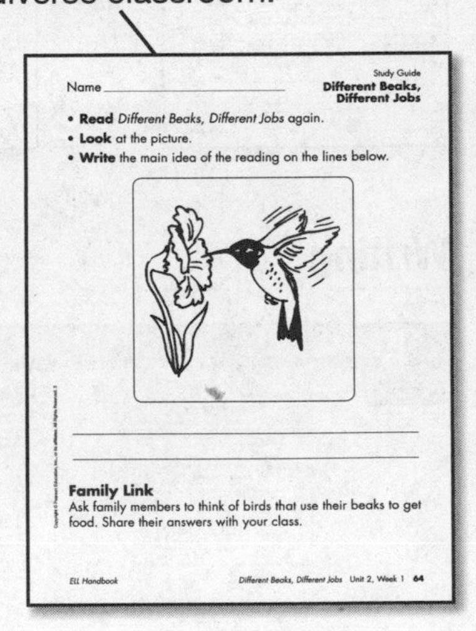

Additional Products

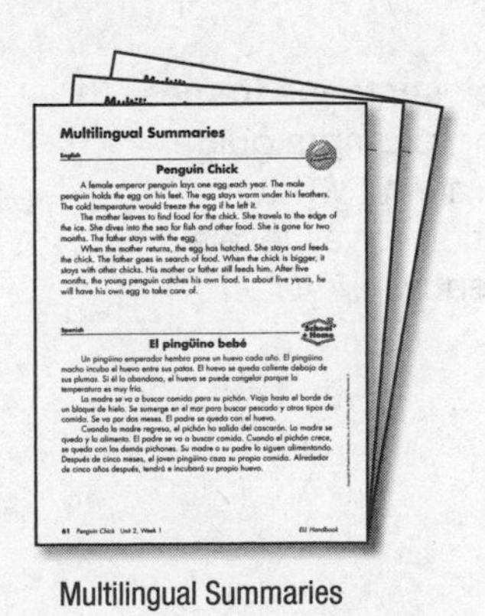

Multilingual Summaries

AudioText CD

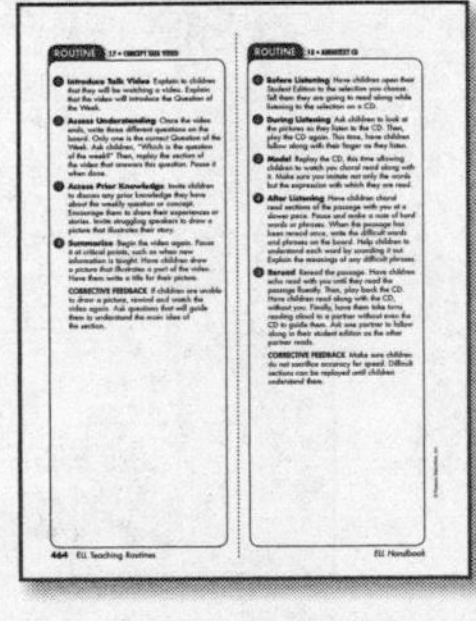

AudioText CD Routine

Language Arts

The Grammar and Conventions and Writing lessons provide the systematic instruction that students need at each language proficiency level to scaffold use of increasingly complex grammatical structures in content area reading and writing.

Grammar and Conventions

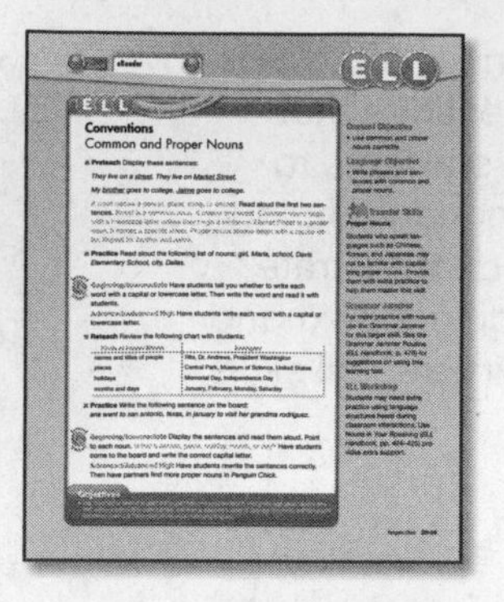

- The interactive activities are designed so students reuse the language related to each core convention, using different modalities to enhance understanding.

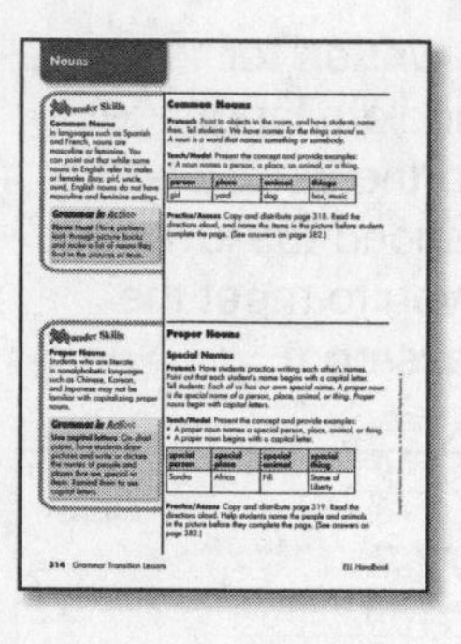

- The flexible bank of Grammar Transition Lessons leads students in transferring knowledge from their home languages to English and guides language development.

Writing

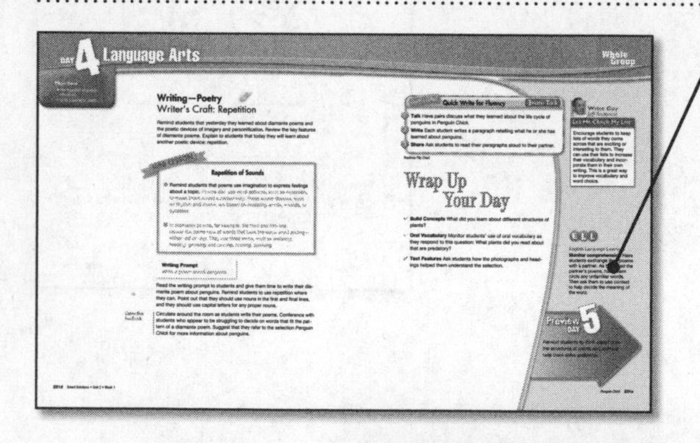

- ELL Notes throughout the core Language Arts pages provide ideas to support all levels of English language learners in prewriting, editing, revising, and publishing writing pieces.

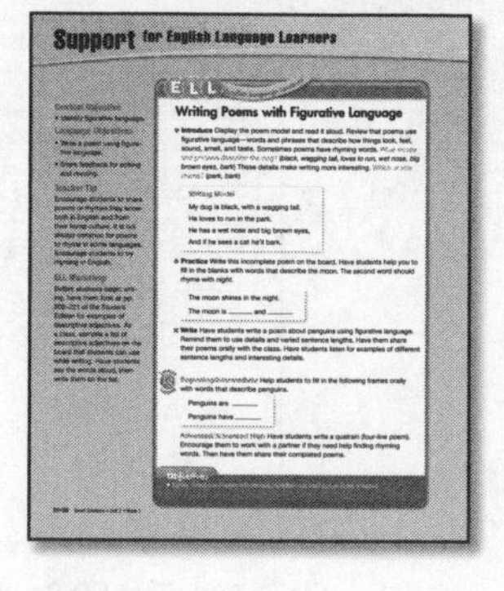

- The writing model, sentence frames, and leveled writing prompts guide and encourage oral and written language production for all levels of English proficiency.

Concept Talk Video

- Use the Concept Talk Video to activate an engaging discussion about the weekly concept. Use the Concept Talk Video Routine found in the ELL Handbook to guide students' understanding.

AudioText CD

- Students can build fluency and comprehension and prepare for reading the main selection by using the AudioText CD and the AudioText CD Routine.

Grammar Jammer

- Use the Grammar Jammer for additional practice with the target skill. For suggestions on how to use this learning tool, see the Grammar Jammer Routine in the ELL Handbook.

Concept Literacy Reader

- Use the Concept Literacy Reader for additional support to develop the weekly concept.

Sound Spelling Cards

- Provide visual support and scaffold meaning for the weekly phonics skill.

Part 2
English Language Support

Contents

Weekly Resources Guide for English Language Learner Support

For this week's content and language objectives, see p. 29e.

Instructional Strand	Day 1	Day 2
Concept Development/Academic Language	TEACHER'S EDITION • Academic Language, p. DI•16 • Concept Development, p. DI•16 • Anchored Talk, pp. 20j—20–21 • Preteach Academic Vocabulary, p. 25a • Concept Talk Video ELL HANDBOOK • Hear It, See It, Say It, Use It, pp. xxxvi–xxxvii • ELL Poster Talk, Concept Talk, p. 29c ELL POSTER 1 • Day 1 Activities	TEACHER'S EDITION • Academic Language, p. DI•16 • Concept Development, p. DI•16 • Anchored Talk, p. 26a • Concept Talk Video ELL HANDBOOK • ELL Poster Talk, Concept Talk, p. 29c • Concept Talk Video Routine, p. 477 ELL POSTER 1 • Day 2 Activities
Phonics and Spelling	TEACHER'S EDITION • Phonics and Spelling, p. DI•20 • Decodable Practice Reader 1A, pp. 23a–23b	TEACHER'S EDITION • Phonics and Spelling, p. DI•20
Listening Comprehension	TEACHER'S EDITION • Modified Read Aloud, p. DI•19 • Read Aloud, p. 21b • Concept Talk Video ELL HANDBOOK • Concept Talk Video Routine, p. 477	TEACHER'S EDITION • Modified Read Aloud, p. DI•19 • AudioText of *When Charlie McButton Lost Power* • Concept Talk Video ELL HANDBOOK • AudioText CD Routine, p. 477 • Problem and Solution, p. 490
Reading Comprehension	TEACHER'S EDITION • Preteach Literary Elements, p. DI•21	TEACHER'S EDITION • Reteach Literary Elements, p. DI•21 • Frontloading Reading, p. DI•22 ELL HANDBOOK • Picture It! Skill Instruction, pp. 30–30a • Multilingual Summaries, pp. 31–33
Vocabulary **Basic and Lesson Vocabulary** **Vocabulary Skill: Homonyms**	TEACHER'S EDITION • Basic Vocabulary, p. DI•17 • Preteach Lesson Vocabulary, p. DI•17 • Homonyms, p. DI•20 ELL HANDBOOK • Word Cards, p. 29 • ELL Vocabulary Routine, p. 471 ELL POSTER 1 • Day 1 Activities	TEACHER'S EDITION • Basic Vocabulary, p. DI•17 • Reteach Lesson Vocabulary, p. DI•18 • Homonyms, p. DI•20 ELL HANDBOOK • Word Cards, p. 29 • Multilingual Vocabulary List, p. 431 ELL POSTER 1 • Day 2 Activities
Grammar and Conventions	TEACHER'S EDITION • Preteach Simple Sentences, p. DI•24	TEACHER'S EDITION • Reteach Simple Sentences, p. DI•24
Writing	TEACHER'S EDITION • Sensory Details, p. DI•25 • Introduce Narrative Poem, pp. 25e–25f	TEACHER'S EDITION • Writing Trait: Word Choice, pp. 37d–37e

Unit 1 Week 1 When Charlie McButton Lost Power

This symbol indicates leveled instruction to address language proficiency levels.

Day 3	Day 4	Day 5
TEACHER'S EDITION • Academic Language, p. DI•16 • Concept Development, p. DI•16 • Anchored Talk, p. 38a • Concept Talk Video ELL HANDBOOK • ELL Poster Talk, Concept Talk, p. 29c ELL POSTER 1 • Day 3 Activities	TEACHER'S EDITION • Academic Language, p. DI•16 • Concept Development, p. DI•16 • Anchored Talk, p. 50a • Concept Talk Video ELL HANDBOOK • ELL Poster Talk, Concept Talk, p. 29c ELL POSTER 1 • Day 4 Activities	TEACHER'S EDITION • Academic Language, p. DI•16 • Concept Development, p. DI•16 • Concept Talk Video ELL HANDBOOK • ELL Poster Talk, Concept Talk, p. 29c ELL POSTER 1 • Day 5 Activities
ELL HANDBOOK • Phonics Transition Lesson, pp. 246–250	ELL HANDBOOK • Phonics Transition Lesson, pp. 246–250	TEACHER'S EDITION • Phonics and Spelling, p. DI•20
TEACHER'S EDITION • AudioText of *When Charlie McButton Lost Power* • Concept Talk Video ELL HANDBOOK • AudioText CD Routine, p. 477	TEACHER'S EDITION • Concept Talk Video	TEACHER'S EDITION • Concept Talk Video
TEACHER'S EDITION • Sheltered Reading, p. DI•22 ELL HANDBOOK • Multilingual Summaries, pp. 31–33	TEACHER'S EDITION • ELL/ELD Reader Guided Reading, p. DI•23 ELL HANDBOOK • ELL Study Guide, p. 34	TEACHER'S EDITION • ELL/ELD Reader Guided Reading, p. DI•23 ELL HANDBOOK • ELL Study Guide, p. 34
ELL HANDBOOK • High-Frequency Words Activity Bank, p. 446 ELL POSTER 1 • Day 3 Activities	ELL HANDBOOK • High-Frequency Words Activity Bank, p. 446	TEACHER'S EDITION • Homonyms, p. 55h ELL HANDBOOK • High-Frequency Words Activity Bank, p. 446
TEACHER'S EDITION • Grammar Jammer ELL HANDBOOK • Grammar Transition Lesson, pp. 344, 355 • Grammar Jammer Routine, p. 478	TEACHER'S EDITION • Grammar Jammer ELL HANDBOOK • Grammar Transition Lesson, pp. 344, 355	TEACHER'S EDITION • Grammar Jammer ELL HANDBOOK • Grammar Transition Lesson, pp. 344, 355
TEACHER'S EDITION • Let's Write It!, p. 48–49 • Writing Trait: Word Choice, pp. 49a–49b	TEACHER'S EDITION • Revising Strategy, pp. 55d–55e	TEACHER'S EDITION • Writer's Craft: Sentences, pp. 55p–55q

Poster Talk, Concept Talk

Question of the Week

What can we learn by trying new things?

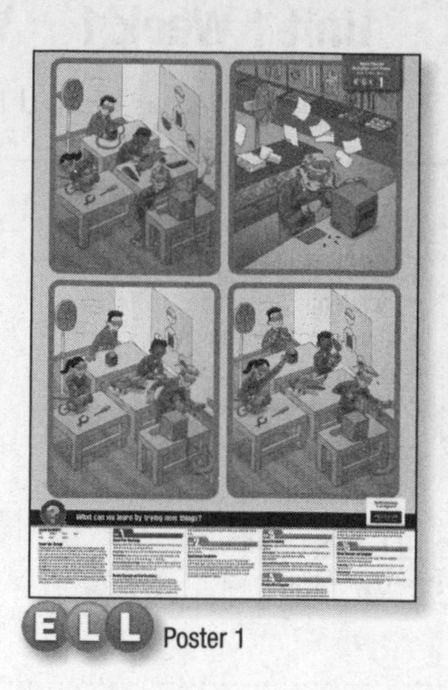
Poster 1

Throughout the week, use the ELL Poster to help students produce and comprehend language, understand the concept, and build English vocabulary. Use the Question of the Week and other questions to help students share ideas in pairs, small groups, or the large group. Sample questions are shown, with examples of possible responses by students.

Weekly Concept and Language Goals

- Discuss what people can learn by trying new things
- Identify new activities to try
- Tell about trying new things

By the end of the lesson, students should be able to talk about and write one or more sentences about trying new things.

Daily Team Talk

Day 1	Day 2	Day 3	Day 4	Day 5
After Day 1 activities on Poster, ask questions such as *In the poster picture, what new thing does the boy with the airplane try?*	After Day 2 activity on Poster, ask questions such as *In the poster picture, what new thing does the boy with the computer try?*	After Day 3 activity on Poster, ask questions such as *Do you think the students in the poster picture like to try new things? Why or why not?*	After Day 4 activity on Poster, ask questions such as *In the story* When Charlie McButton Lost Power, *how does Charlie McButton feel about trying new things?*	After Day 5 activity on Poster, ask questions such as *Tell about something new that you tried. What happened?*
Beginning Puts it together. **Intermediate** He puts the pieces of the airplane together. **Advanced** He puts all the pieces together to build an airplane. He also paints it. **Advanced High** The boy builds the airplane by putting the pieces together. He also paints the word *FLYER* on the side.	**Beginning** Fixing it. **Intermediate** He tries to fix the computer. **Advanced** First he can't fix the computer. Then he fixes it. **Advanced High** The boy tries to fix the computer. He uses tools to fix it.	**Beginning** Yes. They smile. **Intermediate** Yes, I do. They look happy at the end. **Advanced** Yes, I think they like to try new things. They look happy when they are done. **Advanced High** Yes, I think the students like to try new things. They clap and cheer when the boy fixes the computer.	**Beginning** It's fun. **Intermediate** He does not want to try new things, but then he does. **Advanced** Charlie does not want to try new things, but when he does, he has a lot of fun. **Advanced High** At first Charlie McButton is mad that he has to try new things, but in the end, he has fun trying new things.	**Beginning** Jumping rope. I like it. **Intermediate** I tried jumping rope. I had fun. **Advanced** I learned how to jump rope. I liked it. **Advanced High** Last week I learned how to jump rope. It was hard, but I had fun learning.

This Week's Materials

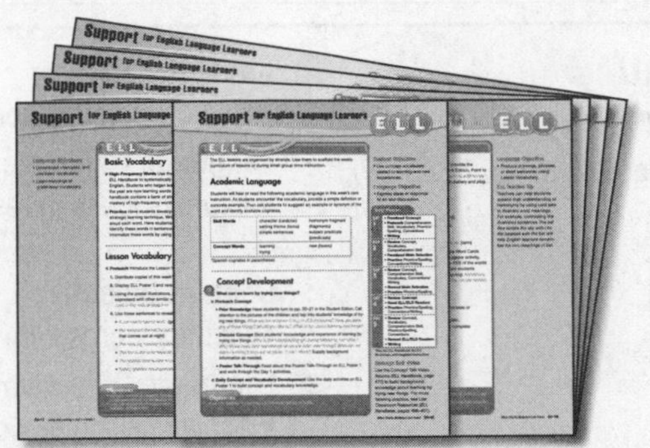

Teacher's Edition pages 20j–55q

See the support for English language learners throughout the lesson, including ELL strategies and scaffolded activities at points of use.

Teacher's Edition pages DI•16–DI•25

Differentiated Instruction for English language learners provides daily group activities that "frontload," or preteach, core instruction.

ELL Handbook pp. 29a–34

Find additional lesson materials that support the core lesson and the ELL instructional pages.

ELL Poster 1

ELL Reader 3.1.1

ELD Reader 3.1.1

Concept Literacy Reader

ELD, ELL Reader Teaching Guide

Concept Literacy Reader Teaching Guide

Technology

Online Teacher's Edition Use the digital version of the core Teacher's Edition for planning and instruction.

eReaders
This week's ELL and ELD Readers and Concept Literacy Reader are also available in digital format.

This Week's Content and Language Objectives by Strand

Concept Development/ Academic Language What can we learn by trying new things?	**Content Objective** • Use concept vocabulary related to learning and new experiences. **Language Objective** • Express ideas in response to art and discussion.
Phonics and Spelling Syllables VC/CV	**Content Objective** • Identify words with short vowel VC/CV pattern. **Language Objective** • Apply spelling in words pattern VC/CV.
Listening Comprehension Modified Read Aloud: "Gallagher Goat Tries New Food"	**Content Objective** • Monitor and adjust oral comprehension. **Language Objectives** • Discuss oral passages. • Use a graphic organizer to take notes.
Reading Comprehension Literary Elements	**Content Objectives** • Distinguish between the literary elements of character, setting, and theme. • Monitor and adjust comprehension. **Language Objectives** • Discuss character, setting, and theme. • Use literary elements to retell a reading. • Use literary elements to describe a favorite book or movie. • Read grade-level text accuracy.
Vocabulary Basic and Lesson Vocabulary	**Language Objectives** • Understand internalize, and use basic vocabulary. • Learn meanings of grade-level vocabulary. • Produce drawings, phrases, and short sentences to show understanding of Lesson Vocabulary.
Vocabulary Homonyms	**Content Objective** • Identify and define homonyms. **Language Objective** • Discuss the meaning of homonyms.
Grammar and Conventions Simple Sentences	**Content Objectives** • Identify simple sentences. • Use simple sentences correctly. **Language Objectives** • Speak using simple sentences. • Write simple sentences.
Writing Sensory Details	**Content Objective** • Identify sensory details in a text. **Language Objectives** • Write using sensory details. • Share feedback for editing and revising.

Word Cards for Vocabulary Activities

bat	**battery**
blew	**fuel**
plug	**term**
vision	

Teacher Note: Beginning Teach two to three words. **Intermediate** Teach three to four words. **Advanced** Teach four to five words. **Advanced High** Teach all words.

Name ______________________

Read Together

Look at the pictures. **Read** the story.

- What does Kwan do? **Write** it in the box.
- Where is Kwan? **Write** it in the box.
- What does Kwan learn from his visit? **Write** it in the box.

The Farmers' Market

Every Saturday, Kwan and his mom go to the farmers' market. Kwan likes the farmers' market. He can try different kinds of food here.

Today, he sees an avocado. The farmer gives a slice of avocado to Kwan.

"Yum, this is good," Kwan says. "Mom, let's buy some avocados!"

What Kwan Does	Where Kwan Is	What Kwan Learns

Character, Setting, and Theme

Use this lesson to supplement or replace the skill lesson on page 24a of the Teacher's Edition. Display the Skill Points (at right) and share them with students.

Skill Points

✔ A **character** is a person or animal who appears in a story.

✔ The **setting** is the time and place of a story.

✔ The **theme** is the big idea, or author's message.

Teach/Model

Review the fable "The Lion and the Mouse" with students.

Beginning Ask students to draw the characters in "The Lion and the Mouse." Have them add a background to their drawing to show the story's setting. Help students brainstorm sentences that tell what they think is the theme, or big idea, of the story.

Intermediate Ask: *Which character in "The Lion and the Mouse" is your favorite? Why?* List the characters on the board. Ask: *What words describe the setting of this story?* Record students' words. Say: *Draw a picture that shows the theme of the story.* Remind students to include the characters and setting in their pictures.

Advanced Have students write sentences describing characteristics of the characters and setting of "The Lion and the Mouse." Ask: *What is the theme of the story? How do the characters and setting help you identify the theme?*

Advanced High Pair students. Have one partner tell a favorite story. The other partner identifies the characters and setting of the story and offers a sentence about the theme. Then the partners trade roles.

Then distribute copies of Picture It! page 30.

- Have students look at the pictures and tell what is happening.
- Read the story aloud. Ask: *What happens in this story?* Have students identify the characters, setting, and theme.
- Review the Skill Points with students.
- Have students look at the pictures and words to identify the characters, setting, and theme.

Practice

Read aloud the directions on page 30. Reread or have volunteers reread the story aloud. Have students look at the pictures and the story as they write in the boxes.

Beginning Students can draw and explain their drawings orally before writing words or phrases in the boxes. Provide help with the English word *avocado,* a food with which students may be unfamiliar.

Intermediate Students can first draw or orally answer and then write their answers in the boxes. Provide help with the English word *avocado,* which Spanish speakers may confuse with *abogado* (advocate).

Advanced Students can write their answers in the boxes and then check them by comparing them with a partner's.

Advanced High Students can write their answers in the boxes and then check them by rereading the story and making any changes they think are necessary.

Answers for page 30: *What Kwan Does:* goes to the market with his mom; *Where Kwan Is:* at the farmers' market; *What Kwan Learns:* You won't know if you like something new unless you try it.

Multilingual Summaries

English

When Charlie McButton Lost Power

Charlie McButton likes computerized games. A lightning bolt strikes and his house loses electrical power. He cries for help. His mother tells him to find something else to play.

Charlie finds a toy that uses batteries. The battery is gone. He takes a battery from his sister's doll. His mother puts him in the time-out chair. Isabel Jane plays at his feet with all of her toys that use batteries. Charlie gets mad and makes his sister cry.

Charlie feels rotten. He finds Isabel Jane. They play hide-and-go-seek and build a fort. Charlie forgets to be bored without electricity. When the electricity comes back on, Charlie thinks about plugging in, but also about playing with Isabel Jane.

Spanish

Cuando Charlie McButton se quedó sin energía

A Charlie McButton le gustan los juegos de computadora. Un rayo cae sobre su casa y se queda sin energía eléctrica. Él grita pidiendo ayuda. Su madre le dice que busque algún otro juego.

Charlie encuentra un juguete que necesita baterías. La batería no funciona. Él saca una batería de la muñeca de su hermana. Su mamá lo castiga haciéndolo sentar en una silla. Isabel Jane juega a sus pies con todos sus otros juguetes que funcionan con baterías. Charlie se enoja y hace llorar a su hermana.

Charlie se siente fatal. Charlie encuentra a su hermana. Ellos juegan a las escondidas y construyen un fuerte. Charlie olvida que estaba aburrido sin la electricidad. Cuando regresa la electricidad, Charlie piensa en conectarse de nuevo, pero también quiere jugar con Isabel Jane.

Multilingual Summaries

Chinese

查理 麥克布頓家停電了

查理 麥克布頓喜歡玩電腦遊戲。天空劃過一道閃電，之後他家就停電了。 他大叫著要別人幫忙。 他的媽媽要他玩別的東西。

查理找到了一個電動玩具。 但電池卻不見了。 於是，他拿走了妹妹玩偶裡的電池。 他的媽媽罰他坐在思過椅上。 伊莎貝 珍在他身旁玩她的所有電動玩具。 查理很生氣，所以把妹妹弄哭了。

查理覺得自己錯了。 他找到了伊莎貝 珍。 他們一起玩捉迷藏，還蓋了一座碉堡。 查理忘記了沒電很無聊這件事。 來電後，查理想著要插上插頭，而且還想著要跟伊莎貝珍一起玩。

Vietnamese

Khi Charlie McButton Bị Cúp Điện

Charlie McButton thích các trò chơi vi tính. Sau một tiếng sét đánh thì nhà của em bị cúp điện. Em la cầu cứu. Mẹ em bảo phải tìm trò chơi khác để chơi.

Charlie tìm ra được một món đồ chơi chạy bằng pin. Cục pin thì đã mất. Em mới lấy cục pin từ con búp bê của em gái. Em bị mẹ phạt cho ngồi trên ghế. Isabel Jane chơi dưới chân em với tất cả đồ chơi chạy bằng pin. Charlie tức giận và chọc cho em gái khóc.

Charlie cảm thấy xấu hổ. Em tìm đến Isabel Jane. Chúng chơi trốn bắt và xây đồn lũy. Charlie không còn chán nữa khi không có điện. Khi điện có trở lại thì Charlie muốn xài đồ chơi điện, nhưng cũng muốn chơi với Isabel Jane.

Multilingual Summaries

Korean

찰리 맥버튼네 집에 전기가 나갔을 때

찰리 맥버튼은 컴퓨터 게임을 좋아한다. 어느날 번개가 쳐서 찰리네 집에 전기가 나간다. 그는 도와달라고 소리친다. 엄마는 찰리에게 다른 것을 하며 놀아보라고 말한다.

찰리는 건전지를 사용하는 장난감을 찾아낸다. 건전지가 다 닳아있다. 찰리는 여동생의 인형에서 건전지를 빼낸다. 찰리의 발치에서 이사벨 제인이 건전지를 사용하는 장난감을 몽땅 갖고 논다. 찰리는 화가 나서 동생을 울린다.

찰리가 이사벨 제인을 찾아냈다. 그들은 숨바꼭질을 하고 요새를 만들었다. 찰리는 전기가 없어서 지루했던 걸 잊었다. 다시 전기가 들어왔을 때, 찰리는 컴퓨터 게임에 접속하는 것을 생각하면서 이사벨 제인과 함께 노는 것에 대해서도 생각했다.

Hmong

Thaum Charlie McButton Tsis Muaj Ib Tib Phoo Lawm

Charlie McButton nyiam tua nkee ua si hauv computer. Lub tsheb loj muaj teeb thiab nws lub tsev tsis muaj fais fab lawm. Nws quaj kom pab. Nws qhia kom nws mus nriav lwm yam los ua si nrog.

Charlie mus nriav tau ib yam khoom ua si noj roj teeb. Lub roj teeb los tas lawm. Nws mus nyiag tau ib lub roj hauv nws tus muam tus me nyuam roj hmab los. Nws niam muab nws rau-txim rau ntawm lub rooj. Isabel Jane ua si nrog nws me nyuam roj hmab uas noj roj nrog txais ko taw. Charlie chim thiab ua rau nws tus muam quaj.

Charlie chim heev kawg. Nws pom Isabel Jane. Lawv ua si pos-tsiv-nraim thiab ua lub rooj. Charlie mas laj nyob kawg thaum tsis muaj fais fab lawm. Thaum uas fais fab rov qab tuaj lawm Charlie xav txog qhov ua ntxig kiag rau, tabsis mas nws tseem ua si nrog Isabel Jane.

Name ______________________________

The Spanish Club

- **Read** *The Spanish Club* again.
- **Draw** pictures to show what happens in the beginning, in the middle, and at the end of the story.
- **Write** words or a sentence to go with your pictures.

Pages	Picture	Words or Sentence
Beginning (pages 2–3)		
Middle (pages 4–5)		
End (pages 6–8)		

Family Link

Ask family members if they have studied another language. It could be on their own or by going to a language class.

Weekly Resources Guide for English Language Learner Support

For this week's content and language objectives, see p. 35e.

Instructional Strand	Day 1	Day 2
Concept Development/Academic Language	TEACHER'S EDITION • Academic Language, p. DI•41 • Concept Development, p. DI•41 • Anchored Talk, pp. 56j—56–57 • Preteach Academic Vocabulary, p. 61a • Concept Talk Video ELL HANDBOOK • Hear It, See It, Say It, Use It, pp. xxxvi–xxxvii • ELL Poster Talk, Concept Talk, p. 35c ELL POSTER 2 • Day 1 Activities	TEACHER'S EDITION • Academic Language, p. DI•41 • Concept Development, p. DI•41 • Anchored Talk, p. 62a • Concept Talk Video ELL HANDBOOK • ELL Poster Talk, Concept Talk, p. 35c • Concept Talk Video Routine, p. 477 ELL POSTER 2 • Day 2 Activities
Phonics and Spelling	TEACHER'S EDITION • Phonics and Spelling, p. DI•45 • Decodable Practice Reader 2A, pp. 59a–59b	TEACHER'S EDITION • Phonics and Spelling, p. DI•45
Listening Comprehension	TEACHER'S EDITION • Modified Read Aloud, p. DI•44 • Read Aloud, p. 57b • Concept Talk Video ELL HANDBOOK • Concept Talk Video Routine, p. 477	TEACHER'S EDITION • Modified Read Aloud, p. DI•44 • AudioText of *What About Me?* • Concept Talk Video ELL HANDBOOK • AudioText CD Routine, p. 477 • Story Map A, p. 483
Reading Comprehension	TEACHER'S EDITION • Preteach Sequence, p. DI•46	TEACHER'S EDITION • Reteach Sequence, p. DI•46 • Frontloading Reading, p. DI•47 ELL HANDBOOK • Picture It! Skill Instruction, pp. 36–36a • Multilingual Summaries, pp. 37–39
Vocabulary **Basic and Lesson Vocabulary** **Vocabulary Skill: Compound Words**	TEACHER'S EDITION • Basic Vocabulary, p. DI•42 • Preteach Lesson Vocabulary, p. DI•42 • Compound Words, p. DI•45 ELL HANDBOOK • Word Cards, p. 35 • ELL Vocabulary Routine, p. 471 ELL POSTER 2 • Day 1 Activities	TEACHER'S EDITION • Basic Vocabulary, p. DI•42 • Reteach Lesson Vocabulary, p. DI•43 • Compound Words, p. DI•45 ELL HANDBOOK • Word Cards, p. 35 • Multilingual Vocabulary List, p. 431 ELL POSTER 2 • Day 2 Activities
Grammar and Conventions	TEACHER'S EDITION • Preteach Subjects and Predicates, p. DI•49	TEACHER'S EDITION • Reteach Subjects and Predicates, p. DI•49
Writing	TEACHER'S EDITION • Correct Spelling and Punctuation, p. DI•50 • Introduce Fable, pp. 61e–61f	TEACHER'S EDITION • Writing Trait: Organization, pp. 71d–71e

Unit 1 Week 2 What About Me?

This symbol indicates leveled instruction to address language proficiency levels.

Day 3	Day 4	Day 5
TEACHER'S EDITION • Academic Language, p. DI•41 • Concept Development, p. DI•41 • Anchored Talk, p. 72a • Concept Talk Video ELL HANDBOOK • ELL Poster Talk, Concept Talk, p. 35c ELL POSTER 2 • Day 3 Activities	TEACHER'S EDITION • Academic Language, p. DI•41 • Concept Development, p. DI•41 • Anchored Talk, p. 82a • Concept Talk Video ELL HANDBOOK • ELL Poster Talk, Concept Talk, p. 35c ELL POSTER 2 • Day 4 Activities	TEACHER'S EDITION • Academic Language, p. DI•41 • Concept Development, p. DI•41 • Concept Talk Video ELL HANDBOOK • ELL Poster Talk, Concept Talk, p. 35c ELL POSTER 2 • Day 5 Activities
ELL HANDBOOK • Phonics Transition Lesson, pp. 268, 270	ELL HANDBOOK • Phonics Transition Lesson, pp. 268, 270	TEACHER'S EDITION • Phonics and Spelling, p. DI•45
TEACHER'S EDITION • AudioText of *What About Me?* • Concept Talk Video ELL HANDBOOK • AudioText CD Routine, p. 477	TEACHER'S EDITION • Concept Talk Video	TEACHER'S EDITION • Concept Talk Video
TEACHER'S EDITION • Sheltered Reading, p. DI•47 ELL HANDBOOK • Multilingual Summaries, pp. 37–39	TEACHER'S EDITION • ELL/ELD Reader Guided Reading, p. DI•48 ELL HANDBOOK • ELL Study Guide, p. 40	TEACHER'S EDITION • ELL/ELD Reader Guided Reading, p. DI•48 ELL HANDBOOK • ELL Study Guide, p. 40
ELL HANDBOOK • High-Frequency Words Activity Bank, p. 446 ELL POSTER 2 • Day 3 Activities	ELL HANDBOOK • High-Frequency Words Activity Bank, p. 446	TEACHER'S EDITION • Compound Words, p. 89h ELL HANDBOOK • High-Frequency Words Activity Bank, p. 446
TEACHER'S EDITION • Grammar Jammer ELL HANDBOOK • Grammar Transition Lesson, pp. 340, 348 • Grammar Jammer Routine, p. 478	TEACHER'S EDITION • Grammar Jammer ELL HANDBOOK • Grammar Transition Lesson, pp. 340, 348	TEACHER'S EDITION • Grammar Jammer ELL HANDBOOK • Grammar Transition Lesson, pp. 340, 348
TEACHER'S EDITION • Let's Write It!, p. 80–81 • Writing Trait: Conventions, pp. 81a–81b	TEACHER'S EDITION • Revising Strategy, pp. 89d–89e	TEACHER'S EDITION • Fable, pp. 89p–89q

Poster Talk, Concept Talk

Question of the Week

What can we learn by trading with one another?

ELL Poster 2

Throughout the week, use the ELL Poster to help students produce and comprehend language, understand the concept, and build English vocabulary. Use the Question of the Week and other questions to help students share ideas in pairs, small groups, or the large group. Sample questions are shown, with examples of possible responses by students.

Weekly Concept and Language Goals

- Explain the concept of trade
- Name things at the market
- Discuss buying and trading things at the market

By the end of the lesson, students should be able to talk about and write one or more sentences about trading.

Daily Team Talk

Day 1	Day 2	Day 3	Day 4	Day 5
After Day 1 activities on Poster, ask questions such as *In the poster picture, what are some things people are trading with one another?*	After Day 2 activity on Poster, ask questions such as *What do you think the woman sewing a shirt and the woman carrying a basket of eggs will do?*	After Day 3 activity on Poster, ask questions such as *Imagine the woman with the eggs does not want the shirt. What else can the woman with the shirt trade for the eggs?*	After Day 4 activity on Poster, ask questions such as *In the story* What About Me?, *what happens when people trade with one another?*	After Day 5 activity on Poster, ask questions such as *When your family goes to the grocery store or market, how do you trade for food?*
Beginning Food and clothes. **Intermediate** They trade vegetables, clothes, and chickens. **Advanced** People are trading vegetables, chickens, clothes, and carpets. **Advanced High** Some people are trading things they made, such as carpets, clothes, chairs, and baskets. Other people are trading things they grew, such as vegetables.	**Beginning** Trade things. **Intermediate** They will trade their things. **Advanced** The woman sewing a shirt will trade the shirt for eggs. **Advanced High** The women will trade the shirt and the basket of eggs. Each woman will get something she needs.	**Beginning** Money. **Intermediate** She can use money to get eggs. **Advanced** The woman with a shirt can trade money for the eggs. **Advanced High** The woman with a shirt can trade money for the eggs. Then the woman who had the eggs can trade the money for something she needs.	**Beginning** Get what they need. **Intermediate** The people get things they need. They are happy. **Advanced** When people trade things, they all get what they need. Then they are happy. **Advanced High** When people trade things with one another, each person gets something he or she needs. Everyone is happy.	**Beginning** With money. **Intermediate** We use money to trade for food. **Advanced** When we go to the market, we trade money for food. **Advanced High** My family trades money for food. We pick out the food we want. Then we give money to the grocery store for the food.

This Week's Materials

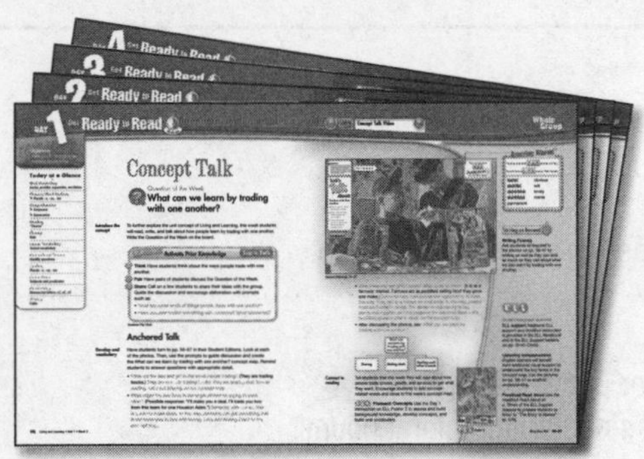
Teacher's Edition pages 56j–89q

See the support for English language learners throughout the lesson, including ELL strategies and scaffolded activities at points of use.

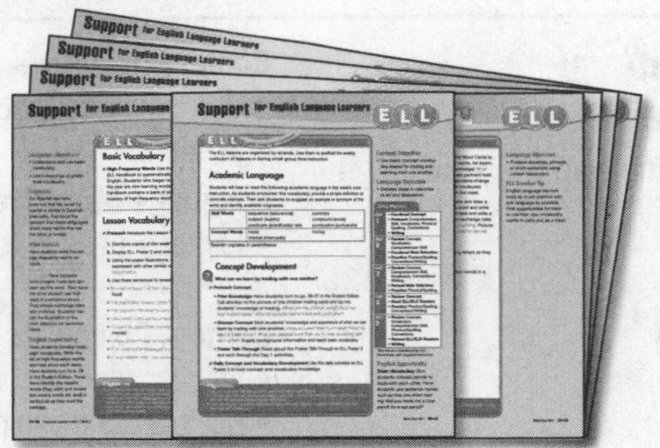
Teacher's Edition pages DI•41–DI•50

Differentiated Instruction for English language learners provides daily group activities that "frontload," or preteach, core instruction.

ELL Handbook pp. 35a–40

Find additional lesson materials that support the core lesson and the ELL instructional pages.

ELL Poster 2

ELL Reader 3.1.2

ELD Reader 3.1.2

Concept Literacy Reader

ELD, ELL Reader Teaching Guide

Concept Literacy Reader Teaching Guide

Technology

Online Teacher's Edition Use the digital version of the core Teacher's Edition for planning and instruction.

eReaders
This week's ELL and ELD Readers and Concept Literacy Reader are also available in digital format.

This Week's Content and Language Objectives by Strand

Concept Development/ Academic Language What can we learn by trading with one another?	**Content Objective** • Use concept vocabulary related to trading and learning from one another. **Language Objective** • Express ideas in response to art and discussion.
Phonics and Spelling Plurals *–s, -es, -ies*	**Content Objectives** • Identify spelling rules for plural endings. • Review the meaning of singular and plural nouns. **Language Objective** • Write plural forms for basic vocabulary.
Listening Comprehension Modified Read Aloud: "From Trading to Money"	**Content Objective** • Monitor and adjust oral comprehension. **Language Objectives** • Discuss oral passages. • Use a graphic organizer to take notes.
Reading Comprehension Sequence	**Content Objectives** • Identify sequence of events to aid comprehension. • Monitor and adjust comprehension. **Language Objectives** • Discuss words that signal a sequence of events. • Retell a sequence of events. • Summarize text using visual support. • Read grade-level text at an appropriate rate.
Vocabulary Basic and Lesson Vocabulary	**Language Objectives** • Understand and use basic vocabulary. • Learn meanings of grade-level vocabulary. • Produce drawings, phrases, and short sentences to show understanding of Lesson Vocabulary.
Vocabulary Compound Words	**Content Objective** • Identify and define words in compounds words. **Language Objective** • Discuss the meanings of compound words.
Grammar and Conventions Subjects and Predicates	**Content Objectives** • Identify subjects and predicates in sentences. • Correctly form sentences with subjects and predicates. **Language Objectives** • Speak using subjects and predicates in sentences. • Write sentences with subjects and predicates.
Writing Correct Spelling and Punctuation	**Content Objectives** • Identify accurate spelling of familiar words. • Identify correct punctuation in sentences. **Language Objective** • Write paragraphs, using accurate spelling of familiar words and correct punctuation.

Word Cards for Vocabulary Activities

carpenter	**carpetmaker**
knowledge	**marketplace**
merchant	**plenty**
straying	**thread**

Teacher Note: Beginning Teach three to four words. **Intermediate** Teach four to six words. **Advanced** Teach six to seven words. **Advanced High** Teach all words.

Name ______________________

Picture It!
Sequence

Look at the pictures. **Read** the story.

- What happens in the story? **Write** the events shown in the story.
- Be sure to write them in the order in which they happened.

Winter Friend

Albert is lonely. His best friend is on vacation. First, Albert reads a book.

Then he draws a picture.

"What should I do next?" asks Albert. "Go play outside," says Mom.

Albert has a new friend. He came *here* on vacation!

First ______________________

Then ______________________

Next ______________________

Last ______________________

Picture It!

Sequence

Use this lesson to supplement or replace the skill lesson on page 60a of the Teacher's Edition. Display the Skill Points (at right) and share them with students.

Skill Points

- ✔ **Sequence** is the order in which things happen.
- ✔ Look for clue words such as *first, then, next,* and *last.*
- ✔ Sometimes a story will not have clue words.

Teach/Model

Prepare picture cards showing a snowman being made in four simple steps.

Beginning Display the picture cards in order. Tell about the events in the story using the words *first, then, next,* and *last.* Then ask students to tell what happens first, then, next, and last as you point to each picture in the sequence.

Intermediate Display the picture cards in order. Ask students to tell the sequence using the words *first, then, next,* and *last.* Write their sentences on the board above the corresponding pictures.

Advanced Display the picture cards out of order. Ask students to arrange them in an order that makes sense. Have them tell about the events using the words *first, then, next,* and *last.* Ask students to use the picture cards to write sentences about the events.

Advanced High Pair students. Have partners make up a story that has a sequence of at least four events. Students can draw pictures or write sentences about the events. Have partners tell their story to the class using the words *first, then, next,* and *last.*

Then distribute copies of Picture It! page 36.

- Have students look at the pictures and tell what is happening.
- Read the story aloud. Ask: *What happens in this story?* Encourage students to use *first, then, next,* and *last.* Ask for clarification if they give answers without sequence words.
- Review the Skill Points with students.
- Have students look at the pictures and words to identify the sequence.

Practice

Read aloud the directions on page 36. Reread or have volunteers reread the story aloud. Have students look at the pictures and the text as they write about the story events in order.

Beginning Students can act out the events of the story in the correct sequence before writing sentences about the events. Provide help with English words and writing.

Intermediate Students can point to each picture in order and orally explain the event before they write about it on the lines. Provide help with English words and writing.

Advanced Students can write their answers on the lines and then check them by rereading them aloud or comparing them with a partner's answers.

Advanced High Students can write their answers on the lines and then check them by retelling the story in their own words, paying attention to the sequence.

Answers for page 36: *First:* Albert reads a book. *Then:* He draws a picture. *Next:* He goes outside. *Last:* He makes a new friend.

Multilingual Summaries

English

What About Me?

A boy wanted knowledge. He didn't know how to get it. He asked a wise man, a Grand Master. The Grand Master wanted a carpet for doing work.

The boy went to a carpetmaker, who wanted thread to make the carpet. The spinner needed goat hair to make thread. The goatkeeper wanted a pen to keep the goats in. The carpenter would not make a pen without a wife. The boy went to a matchmaker. She wanted knowledge too. She sent the boy away.

One day, the boy met a merchant. The merchant wanted his daughter to marry. The boy took her to the carpenter, who made the pen. The goat keeper gave the boy goats. The spinner made thread. The boy took thread to the carpetmaker. The boy took a carpet to the Grand Master. The Grand Master told the boy he already had knowledge.

Spanish

¿Y yo qué?

Un niño quería conocimiento. No sabía cómo conseguirlo. Le preguntó a un hombre sabio, a un Gran Maestro. El Gran Maestro le pidió una alfombra por su trabajo.

El niño fue a ver a un alfombrista. Él quería hilo para hacer la alfombra. El hilandero necesitaba pelos de cabra para hacer el hilo. El pastor de cabras quería un corral para poner allí sus animales. El carpintero no quería hacer un corral si no conseguía una esposa. El niño fue a ver a una casamentera. Ella también quería conocimiento y no quiso ayudar al niño.

Un día, el niño conoció a un comerciante. El comerciante quería casar a su hija. El niño se la presentó al carpintero. El carpintero hizo el corral. El pastor le dio al niño las cabras. El hilandero hizo el hilo. El niño le llevó el hilo al alfombrista. El niño le llevó la alfombra al Gran Maestro. El Gran Maestro le dijo al niño que ya tenía el conocimiento.

Multilingual Summaries

Chinese

我可以做什麼？

有個男孩想要得到知識，可是他不知道怎樣才能得到知識。他跑去問一個很聰明的人，大家都叫他大師。大師說他想要一張工作用的地毯。

男孩去找做地毯的工匠，工匠說要有線才能做地毯。紡紗工人說要有羊毛才能紡紗做線。牧羊人說要有圍欄才能讓山羊乖乖待著不亂跑。木匠說沒有太太就不想做圍欄。男孩去找了媒婆，媒婆說她也想要有知識，她幫不上忙只好送男孩走。

有一天，男孩見到一個商人，商人想要幫他女兒找丈夫。男孩就把商人的女兒帶給木匠，木匠有了太太就做了圍欄。牧羊人把羊帶給男孩。紡紗工人有了羊毛就紡紗做線。男孩把做好的線拿給地毯工匠。地毯做好後，男孩拿去送給大師。大師跟男孩說，他已經擁有知識了。

Vietnamese

School
+ Home

Còn Tôi Thì Sao?

Một cậu bé muốn có kiến thức. Cậu bé không biết làm cách nào để có được. Cậu đi hỏi người thông thái, một vị Đại Sĩ. Vị Đại Sĩ muốn có một tấm thảm để làm việc.

Cậu bé đi đến người thợ làm thảm, người này muốn có chỉ để làm thảm. Người quay chỉ cần có lông dê để làm chỉ. Người chăn dê muốn có một cái chuồng để giữ dê trong đó. Người thợ mộc không làm một cái chuồng nếu không được vợ. Cậu bé đi đến một người mai mối. Bà mai mối cũng muốn có kiến thức. Bà đuổi cậu bé đi nơi khác.

Đến ngày kia, cậu bé gặp một thương gia. Ông thương gia muốn gả chồng cho con gái. Cậu bé đưa cô gái đến người thợ mộc, ông này đóng cái chuồng. Người chăn dê đưa cho cậu bé mấy con dê. Người quay chỉ làm chỉ. Cậu bé mang chỉ đến người thợ làm thảm. Cậu bé mang tấm thảm đến vị Đại Sĩ. Vị Đại Sĩ bảo rằng cậu bé đã có được kiến thức.

Multilingual Summaries

Korean

나는 어떠한가?

지식을 얻고자 하는 한 소년이 있다. 이 소년은 지식을 어떻게 얻어야 하는지 몰라 현인인 그랜드 마스터에게 묻는다. 그랜드 마스터는 지식을 가르쳐 주는 일에 있어 카펫 하나를 갖고 싶어한다.

소년은 카펫 만들 실을 필요로 하는 카펫 만드는 사람에게 간다. 실 잣는 사람은 실을 만드는데 염소털이 필요하고 염소지기는 염소를 안에 잘 가둬 두도록 우리를 갖고 싶어한다. 목수는 아내 없이는 우리를 만들려 하지 않아 소년은 중매쟁이에게 갔는데 그녀 역시 지식을 얻고 싶어한다. 그녀는 소년을 멀리 보낸다.

어느 날 소년은 자신의 딸을 결혼시키고 싶어하는 한 상인을 만난다. 소년은 상인의 딸을 목수에게 데려가고 목수는 우리를 만든다. 염소지기는 소년에게 염소들을 주고 실 잣는 사람은 실을 만든다. 소년은 그 실을 카펫 만드는 사람에게 가져가고 다 만들어진 카펫을 그랜드 마스터에게 가져간다. 그랜드 마스터는 소년에게 그가 이미 지식을 얻었다고 말한다.

Hmong

Es kuv neb?

Muaj ib tug menyuam tus uas xav muaj lab lim tswvyim. Nws tsi paub yuav ua cas thiaj li tau. Nws hnug ib tug txiv neej txawj ntse, ib tug xib fwb. Tus xib fwb tau ib daim kas pev los ua hauj lwm.

Tus tub mus cuag ib tug neeg ua kas pev, uas xav tau xov los ua ib daim kas pev. Tus neeg uas xov yuav tsum tau plaub tshis los ua xov. Tus neeg zov tshis xav tau ib tug xaum los kaw cov tshis rau hauv. Tus kws ntoo tsis kam txua ib tug xaum yog tsis muaj riam. Tus tub mus cuag ib tug saub. Nws kuj xav tau lab lim tswvyim thiab. Nws kom tus tub khiav mus.

Muaj ib hnub, tus tub ntsib ib tug neeg muag khoom. Tus neeg muag khoom xav kom nws tus ntxhais yuav txiv. Tus tub cov nws mus rau tus kws ntoo, uas tau ua tus xaum. Tus neeg zov tshis muab tau ib cov tshis rau tus tub. Tus neeg ua xov ua tau xov. Tus tub nqa cov xov mus rau tus kws ntoo. Tus tub nqa daim kas pev mus rau tus xib fwb. Tus xib fwb qhia tus tub tias nws twb muaj lab lim tswvyim lawm.

Name ______________________ **It Started with Nails**

- **Read** *It Started with Nails* again.
- **Complete** the chart below. **Write** what Johannes did first and last. Then **write** whom he worked for. In the second column, use complete sentences.

Pages	Whom did Johannes work for?	What did he do?
3	wood merchant	
4–5		He fixed the roof.
6–7	saw merchant	

Family Link

Ask family members what tools they know how to use. How have they used them in the past?

Weekly Resources Guide for English Language Learner Support

For this week's content and language objectives, see p. 41e.

Instructional Strand	Day 1	Day 2
Concept Development/Academic Language	TEACHER'S EDITION • Academic Language, p. DI•66 • Concept Development, p. DI•66 • Anchored Talk, pp. 90j—90–91 • Preteach Academic Vocabulary, p. 95a • Concept Talk Video ELL HANDBOOK • Hear It, See It, Say It, Use It, pp. xxxvi–xxxvii • ELL Poster Talk, Concept Talk, p. 41c ELL POSTER 3 • Day 1 Activities	TEACHER'S EDITION • Academic Language, p. DI•66 • Concept Development, p. DI•66 • Anchored Talk, p. 96a • Concept Talk Video ELL HANDBOOK • ELL Poster Talk, Concept Talk, p. 41c • Concept Talk Video Routine, p. 477 ELL POSTER 3 • Day 2 Activities
Phonics and Spelling	TEACHER'S EDITION • Phonics and Spelling, p. DI•70 • Decodable Practice Reader 3A, pp. 93a–93b	TEACHER'S EDITION • Phonics and Spelling, p. DI•70
Listening Comprehension	TEACHER'S EDITION • Modified Read Aloud, p. DI•69 • Read Aloud, p. 91b • Concept Talk Video ELL HANDBOOK • Concept Talk Video Routine, p. 477	TEACHER'S EDITION • Modified Read Aloud, p. DI•69 • AudioText of *Kumak's Fish* • Concept Talk Video ELL HANDBOOK • AudioText CD Routine, p. 477 • Main Idea, p. 487
Reading Comprehension	TEACHER'S EDITION • Preteach Sequence, p. DI•71	TEACHER'S EDITION • Reteach Sequence, p. DI•71 • Frontloading Reading, p. DI•72 ELL HANDBOOK • Picture It! Skill Instruction, pp. 42–42a • Multilingual Summaries, pp. 43–45
Vocabulary **Basic and Lesson Vocabulary** **Vocabulary Skill: Unknown Words**	TEACHER'S EDITION • Basic Vocabulary, p. DI•67 • Preteach Lesson Vocabulary, p. DI•67 • Unknown Words, p. DI•70 ELL HANDBOOK • Word Cards, p. 41 • ELL Vocabulary Routine, p. 471 ELL POSTER 3 • Day 1 Activities	TEACHER'S EDITION • Basic Vocabulary, p. DI•67 • Reteach Lesson Vocabulary, p. DI•68 • Unknown Words, p. DI•70 ELL HANDBOOK • Word Cards, p. 41 • Multilingual Vocabulary List, pp. 431–432 ELL POSTER 3 • Day 2 Activities
Grammar and Conventions	TEACHER'S EDITION • Preteach Declarative and Interrogative Sentences, p. DI•74	TEACHER'S EDITION • Teach Declarative and Interrogative Sentences, p. DI•74
Writing	TEACHER'S EDITION • Correct Use of Commas, p. DI•75 • Introduce Thank-You Note, pp. 95e–95f	TEACHER'S EDITION • Writing Trait: Organization, pp. 105d–105e

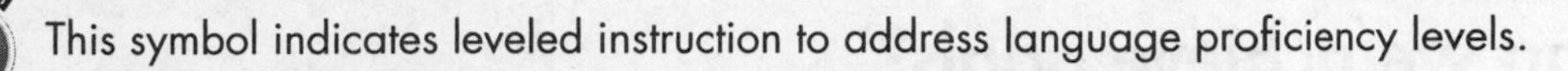

Unit 1 Week 3 Kumak's Fish

This symbol indicates leveled instruction to address language proficiency levels.

Day 3	Day 4	Day 5
TEACHER'S EDITION • Academic Language, p. DI•66 • Concept Development, p. DI•66 • Anchored Talk, p. 106a • Concept Talk Video **ELL HANDBOOK** • ELL Poster Talk, Concept Talk, p. 41c **ELL POSTER 3** • Day 3 Activities	**TEACHER'S EDITION** • Academic Language, p. DI•66 • Concept Development, p. DI•66 • Anchored Talk, p. 118a • Concept Talk Video **ELL HANDBOOK** • ELL Poster Talk, Concept Talk, p. 41c **ELL POSTER 3** • Day 4 Activities	**TEACHER'S EDITION** • Academic Language, p. DI•66 • Concept Development, p. DI•66 • Concept Talk Video **ELL HANDBOOK** • ELL Poster Talk, Concept Talk, p. 41c **ELL POSTER 3** • Day 5 Activities
ELL HANDBOOK • Phonics Transition Lesson, pp. 269, 271	**ELL HANDBOOK** • Phonics Transition Lesson, pp. 269, 271	**TEACHER'S EDITION** • Phonics and Spelling, p. DI•70
TEACHER'S EDITION • AudioText of *Kumak's Fish* • Concept Talk Video **ELL HANDBOOK** • AudioText CD Routine, p. 477	**TEACHER'S EDITION** • Concept Talk Video	**TEACHER'S EDITION** • Concept Talk Video
TEACHER'S EDITION • Sheltered Reading, p. DI•72 **ELL HANDBOOK** • Multilingual Summaries, pp. 43–45	**TEACHER'S EDITION** • ELL/ELD Reader Guided Reading, p. DI•73 **ELL HANDBOOK** • ELL Study Guide, p. 46	**TEACHER'S EDITION** • ELL/ELD Reader Guided Reading, p. DI•73 **ELL HANDBOOK** • ELL Study Guide, p. 46
ELL HANDBOOK • High-Frequency Words Activity Bank, p. 446 **ELL POSTER 3** • Day 3 Activities	**ELL HANDBOOK** • High-Frequency Words Activity Bank, p. 446	**TEACHER'S EDITION** • Unknown Words, p. 121h **ELL HANDBOOK** • High-Frequency Words Activity Bank, p. 446
TEACHER'S EDITION • Grammar Jammer **ELL HANDBOOK** • Grammar Transition Lesson, pp. 342, 352 • Grammar Jammer Routine, p. 478	**TEACHER'S EDITION** • Grammar Jammer **ELL HANDBOOK** • Grammar Transition Lesson, pp. 342, 352	**TEACHER'S EDITION** • Grammar Jammer **ELL HANDBOOK** • Grammar Transition Lesson, pp. 342, 352
TEACHER'S EDITION • Let's Write It!, p. 116–117 • Writer's Craft: Note/Tone, pp. 117a–117b	**TEACHER'S EDITION** • Revising Strategy, pp. 121d–121e	**TEACHER'S EDITION** • Pronoun Agreement, pp. 121p–121q

Poster Talk, Concept Talk

Question of the Week

How can we achieve goals?

ELL Poster 3

Throughout the week, use the ELL Poster to help students produce and comprehend language, understand the concept, and build English vocabulary. Use the Question of the Week and other questions to help students share ideas in pairs, small groups, or the large group. Sample questions are shown, with examples of possible responses by students.

Weekly Concept and Language Goals

- Describe what it means to reach a goal
- Identify personal goals and dreams
- Discuss goals and how to reach them

By the end of the lesson, students should be able to talk about and write one or more sentences about reaching goals.

Daily Team Talk

Day 1	Day 2	Day 3	Day 4	Day 5
After Day 1 activities on Poster, ask questions such as *In the poster picture, what goal does the man under the tree have?*	After Day 2 activity on Poster, ask questions such as *What does the woman with the camera do to reach her goal?*	After Day 3 activity on Poster, ask questions such as *What are some things the other people in the poster picture are using to help them reach their goals?*	After Day 4 activity on Poster, ask questions such as *What goal did the woman on top of the mountain have? Has she achieved her goal?*	After Day 5 activity on Poster, ask questions such as *What is one goal you have? How will you reach that goal?*
Beginning Wants a fish. **Intermediate** He wants to catch a fish. **Advanced** The man under the tree is fishing. He wants to catch a fish. **Advanced High** The man under the tree has a net and a box full of fishing gear. He is holding a fishing pole. His goal is to catch a fish from the lake.	**Beginning** Takes pictures. **Intermediate** She takes pictures of the lake. **Advanced** The woman sets up her camera to take pictures of the lake. **Advanced High** The woman wants pictures of the lake. She comes out on a beautiful day, and she brings her camera so she can take beautiful pictures.	**Beginning** The rope and the coat. **Intermediate** The man has a rope and the woman has a coat. **Advanced** One man has a rope to help him climb, and one woman has a coat to stay warm. **Advanced High** The man climbing the mountain uses a rope to help him climb. The woman on top of the mountain wears a coat to keep her warm.	**Beginning** She's on top. Yes. **Intermediate** Yes. She wanted to climb to the top. **Advanced** Yes. She wanted to climb to the top of the mountain, and she did it. **Advanced High** The woman's goal was to climb to the top of the mountain. She is standing on the top, so she has achieved her goal.	**Beginning** Good grades. Study. **Intermediate** I want to get good grades. I will study. **Advanced** My goal is to get good grades in school. I will study hard. **Advanced High** One goal I have is to get good grades in school. I plan to study an extra hour every night to reach my goal.

This Week's Materials

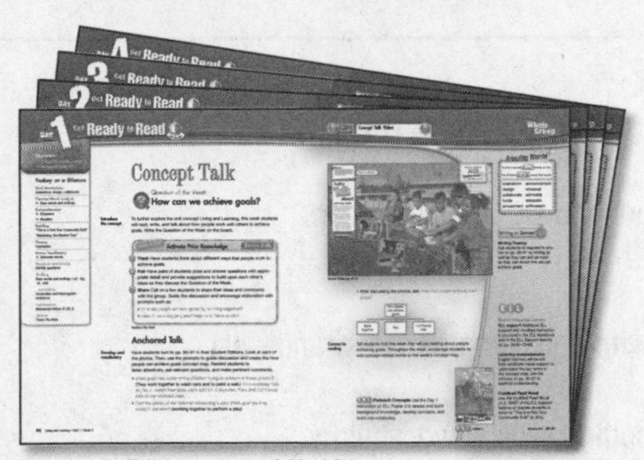
Teacher's Edition pages 90j–121q

See the support for English language learners throughout the lesson, including ELL strategies and scaffolded activities at points of use.

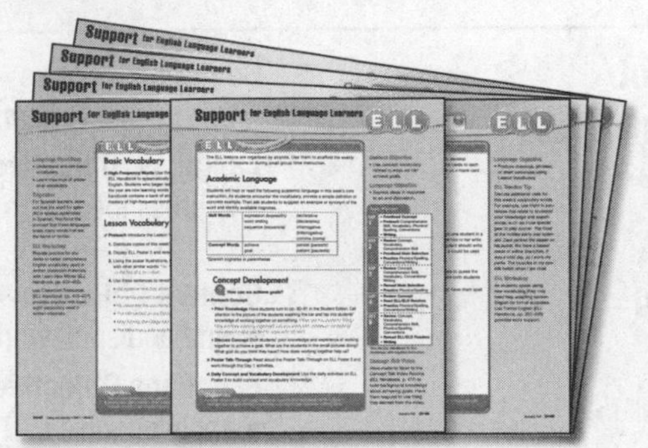
Teacher's Edition pages DI•66–DI•75

Differentiated Instruction for English language learners provides daily group activities that "frontload," or preteach, core instruction.

ELL Handbook pp. 41a–46

Find additional lesson materials that support the core lesson and the ELL instructional pages.

ELL Poster 3

ELL Reader 3.1.3

ELD Reader 3.1.3

Concept Literacy Reader

ELD, ELL Reader Teaching Guide

Concept Literacy Reader Teaching Guide

Technology

Online Teacher's Edition Use the digital version of the core Teacher's Edition for planning and instruction.

eReaders
This week's ELL and ELD Readers and Concept Literacy Reader are also available in digital format.

This Week's Content and Language Objectives by Strand

Concept Development/ Academic Language How can we achieve goals?	**Content Objective** • Use concept vocabulary related to ways we can achieve goals. **Language Objective** • Express ideas in response to art and discussion.
Phonics and Spelling Endings *–er* and *-est*	**Content Objective** • Find and spell words with ending patterns *–er* and *–est.* **Language Objective** • Apply phonics and decoding skills to vocabulary.
Listening Comprehension Modified Read Aloud: "Planning for a Community Park"	**Content Objective** • Monitor and adjust oral comprehension. **Language Objectives** • Discuss oral passages. • Use accessible language and learn essential language.
Reading Comprehension Sequence	**Content Objectives** • Identify sequence to aid comprehension. • Monitor and adjust comprehension. **Language Objectives** • Discuss evidence for sequence. • Retell a sequence based on a reading. • Summarize text using visual support. • Read grade-level text with expression.
Vocabulary Basic and Lesson Vocabulary	**Language Objectives** • Understand and use basic vocabulary. • Learn meanings of grade-level vocabulary. • Produce drawings, phrases, and short sentences to show understanding of Lesson Vocabulary.
Vocabulary Unknown Words	**Content Objective** • Identify unknown words in text. **Language Objective** • Discuss the meanings of unknown words.
Grammar and Conventions Declarative and Interrogative Sentences	**Content Objective** • Identify and use declarative and interrogative sentence patterns. **Language Objectives** • Speak using declarative and interrogative sentences. • Write declarative and interrogative sentence patterns.
Writing Correct Use of Commas	**Content Objectives** • Identify the use of commas. • Write using content-based grade-level vocabulary. **Language Objective** • Write paragraphs, using commas and content-based grade level vocabulary.

Word Cards for Vocabulary Activities

gear	**parka**
splendid	**twitch**
willow	**yanked**

Leveled Support

Teacher Note: Beginning Teach two to three words. **Intermediate** Teach three to four words. **Advanced** Teach four to five words. **Advanced High** Teach all words.

Name ______________________________

Picture It!
Sequence

Look at the pictures. **Read** the story.

- Pretend that you are Lucy. **List** the things you do in order.

Lucy's Gift to Her Mom

Lucy wants to buy a gift. She will make some money by doing small jobs. On Monday, she will walk the dog.

On Tuesday, she will mow the lawn.

On Wednesday, she will sell lemonade.

On Thursday, Lucy can buy her mom a gift!

Things To Do

1. ______________________________

2. ______________________________

3. ______________________________

4. ______________________________

Sequence

Use this lesson to supplement or replace the skill lesson on page 94a of the Teacher's Edition. Display the Skill Points (at right) and share them with students.

Skill Points

- ✔ **Sequence** is the order in which things happen.
- ✔ Look for clue words such as *first, next, then,* and *last.*
- ✔ Sometimes a story will not have clue words.

Teach/Model

Prepare four picture cards showing a pitcher of water, four lemons, a bowl of sugar, and a big spoon.

Beginning Display the picture cards in the above order and read aloud this story: *I'm making lemonade. I pour cold water into a pitcher. I cut and squeeze four lemons into the water. I add sugar. I stir with a spoon.* Ask: *What do I do first? Next? Then? Last?*

Intermediate Tell students the above story without showing them the picture cards. Display the picture cards out of order. Have students place them in the correct sequence. Ask them to explain how they know this is the correct sequence.

Advanced Display the picture cards in the correct sequence. Have students write sentences that tell a story based on the cards. Remind them to use the clue words *first, next, then,* and *last.* Have students read their sentences to the group.

Advanced High Have students draw pictures of events from familiar stories and share their pictures and stories with the group. Remind them to use words such as *first, next, then,* and *last* or phrases such as *last week* or *on Tuesday* to indicate sequence.

Then distribute copies of Picture It! page 42.

- Have students look at the pictures and tell what is happening.
- Read the story aloud. Ask: *What happens in this story?* Encourage students to use *first, next, then,* and *last.* Ask for clarification if they give answers without sequence words.
- Review the Skill Points with students.
- Have students look at the pictures and words to identify the sequence.

Practice

Read aloud the directions on page 42. Reread or have volunteers reread the story aloud. Have students look at the pictures and the text as they write their list of story events.

Beginning Students can point to the pictures and orally explain the events in sequence before writing about them in the list. Provide help with English words and writing.

Intermediate Students can first orally say the events in order and then write about the events in the list. Provide help with English words and writing.

Advanced Students can write their list and then check it by comparing their sequence of events with a partner's.

Advanced High Students can write their list and then orally tell what happens in the story using the words *first, next, then,* and *last.*

Answers for page 42: 1. walk the dog; 2. mow the lawn; 3. sell lemonade; 4. buy mom a gift

Multilingual Summaries

English

Kumak's Fish

It is spring. Kumak and his family say that it is a good day for fish. Kumak packs his family and Uncle Aglu's amazing hooking stick. Uncle Aglu tells Kumak to use the stick. Kumak's family digs their fishing holes and is patient.

Kumak's family catches fish. The stick begins to twitch and yanks Kumak towards the fishing hole. Kumak's family helps him pull the fish. Villagers help Kumak pull the fish. The stick twitches and pulls Kumak down the fishing hole. No one gives up. They hold on to each other and give one more pull.

Kumak comes out of the fishing hole with the hooking stick. There are hundreds of fish. There are enough fish for the entire village.

Spanish

Los peces de Kumak

Es primavera, Kumak y su familia piensan que es un buen día para pescar. Kumak prepara a su familia y lleva con él la increíble vara para pescar del tío Aglu. El tío Aglu le dijo a Kumak que la usara. La familia de Kumak cava un hoyo y se sientan pacientemente.

Y pican los peces. La vara comienza a sacudir a Kumak y lo tira a través del agujero para pescar. Su familia lo ayuda a halar el pez. También los aldeanos ayudan a subirlo. Nadie se da por vencido. Se agarran todos y dan un último tirón.

Kumak sale del agujero con la vara. Hay cientos de peces. Hay suficiente pescado para toda la aldea.

Multilingual Summaries

Chinese

庫麥克的魚

現在是春天。 庫麥克和他的家人覺得今天是釣魚的好日子。 庫麥克帶著家人和阿格魯叔叔超棒的釣魚鉤棒去釣魚。 阿格魯叔叔要庫麥克用他的鉤棒。 庫麥克的家人先挖好了釣魚洞，然後耐心等待。

庫麥克家人的鉤棒有魚上鉤了。 鉤棒開始猛烈抽動，並把庫麥克使勁往釣魚洞裡扯。 庫麥克的家人幫他把魚拉出來。 村裡的人也過來幫庫麥克把魚拉出來。 鉤棒抖動得很厲害，並把庫麥克拉進了釣魚洞。 但沒有人放棄。 他們合力再一次用力拉。

庫麥克連同鉤棒一起被拉出了釣魚洞。 他們釣到了數百隻魚， 全村的人都有魚吃了。

Vietnamese

Cá của Kumak

Bây giờ là mùa xuân. Kumak và gia đình thấy đây là một ngày tốt để đi câu. Kumak lấy cái que móc kỳ lạ của Chú Aglu và gia đình. Chú Aglu nói với Kumak dùng que cây. Gia đình Kumak đào lổ để câu cá và kiên nhẫn chờ.

Gia đình Kumak bắt được cá. Cái que bắt đầu giựt giựt và kéo Kumak về hướng lổ bắt cá. Gia đình Kumak giúp nó kéo cá lên. Người trong làng giúp Kumak kéo cá lên. Cái que cây giựt giựt và kéo Kumak xuống lổ câu cá. Không ai chịu thua. Họ giữ chặt lấy nhau và kéo thêm một lần nữa.

Kumak trồi lên khỏi lổ câu cá với cái que móc. Có cả trăm con cá. Có đủ cá cho cả làng dùng.

Multilingual Summaries

Korean

쿠막의 물고기

봄이다. 쿠막과 가족은 낚시하기에 좋은 날이라고 말한다. 쿠막은 가족들과 아글루 아저씨의 놀라운 낚시바늘을 챙긴다. 아글루 아저씨가 쿠막에게 그 낚시바늘을 쓰라고 말했다. 쿠막의 가족은 낚시구멍을 파내고 끈기 있게 기다렸다.

쿠막의 가족이 물고기를 낚았다. 낚싯대가 쿠막을 낚시구멍 쪽으로 홱 잡아당겼다. 쿠막의 가족이 물고기 끌어올리는 것을 도왔다. 마을 사람들도 물고기 끌어올리는 것을 도왔다. 낚싯대가 쿠막을 홱 잡아채서 낚시구멍으로 빠뜨렸다. 아무도 포기하지 않았다. 그들은 서로를 붙들고 마지막으로 한 번 더 잡아당겼다.

쿠막이 낚시바늘을 들고 낚시구멍을 빠져 나왔다. 거기에는 수백 마리의 물고기가 달려있었다. 그것은 마을 전체에도 충분한 양이었다.

Hmong

Kumak Tus Ntses

Nws txog lub caij ntuj tshiab. Kumak thiab nws tsev neeg hais tias yog hnub nyoog zoo mus nuv ntse. Kumak tu nra rau nws tsev neeg thiab nws tus txiv ntxawm Aglu tus pa nuv zoo tshaj. Txiv ntxawm Aglu qhia rau Kumak kom siv nws tus pa nuv ntses. Kumak tsev neeg mus khawb lawv cov qhov nuv ntses thiab ua siab ntev zov.

Kumak tsev neeg nuv tau ntses. Tus pa nuv ntses pib co thiab nws chua Kumak mus rau hauv lub qhov. Kumak tsev neeg pab nws rub tus ntses. Lub zos cov neeg los pab Kumak rub tus ntses. Tus pa nuv ntses tig thiab rub Kumak mus dua hauv lub qhov lawm. Tsis muaj ib tus neeg tso tseg li. Lawv ib tug tuav ib tug ib tug rub ib tug ib zaug tas ib zaug tuaj.

Kumak tawm hauv lub qhov nuv ntses los nrog nws tus pa nuv ntses. Nws muaj puas puas tus ntses. Nws tau ntses ntau txaus lub zos cov neeg noj tas nro.

Name ______________________

Time for the Team

- **Read** *Time for the Team* again.
- **Draw** pictures to show how Maria prepares for basketball team tryouts in the story.
- **Write** words or a sentence to go with each picture.

First (pages 2–4)

____

____

Next (page 5)

____

____

Then (page 6)

____

____

Last (pages 7–8)

____

Family Link

Ask family members if they have played on a sports team in school. How did they practice to make the team?

Weekly Resources Guide for English Language Learner Support

For this week's content and language objectives, see p. 47e.

Instructional Strand	Day 1	Day 2
Concept Development/Academic Language	TEACHER'S EDITION • Academic Language, p. DI•91 • Concept Development, p. DI•91 • Anchored Talk, pp. 122j—122–123 • Preteach Academic Vocabulary, p. 127a • Concept Talk Video ELL HANDBOOK • Hear It, See It, Say It, Use It, pp. xxxvi–xxxvii • ELL Poster Talk, Concept Talk, p. 47c ELL POSTER 4 • Day 1 Activities	TEACHER'S EDITION • Academic Language, p. DI•91 • Concept Development, p. DI•91 • Anchored Talk, p. 128a • Concept Talk Video ELL HANDBOOK • ELL Poster Talk, Concept Talk, p. 47c • Concept Talk Video Routine, p. 477 ELL POSTER 4 • Day 2 Activities
Phonics and Spelling	TEACHER'S EDITION • Phonics and Spelling, p. DI•95 • Decodable Practice Reader 4A, pp. 125a–125b	TEACHER'S EDITION • Phonics and Spelling, p. DI•95
Listening Comprehension	TEACHER'S EDITION • Modified Read Aloud, p. DI•94 • Read Aloud, p. 123b • Concept Talk Video ELL HANDBOOK • Concept Talk Video Routine, p. 477	TEACHER'S EDITION • Modified Read Aloud, p. DI•94 • AudioText of *Supermarket* • Concept Talk Video ELL HANDBOOK • AudioText CD Routine, p. 477 • T-Chart, p. 493
Reading Comprehension	TEACHER'S EDITION • Preteach Compare and Contrast, p. DI•96	TEACHER'S EDITION • Reteach Compare and Contrast, p. DI•96 • Frontloading Reading, p. DI•97 ELL HANDBOOK • Picture It! Skill Instruction, pp. 48–48a • Multilingual Summaries, pp. 49–51
Vocabulary **Basic and Lesson Vocabulary** **Vocabulary Skill: Multiple-Meaning Words**	TEACHER'S EDITION • Basic Vocabulary, p. DI•92 • Preteach Lesson Vocabulary, p. DI•92 • Multiple-Meaning Words, p. DI•95 ELL HANDBOOK • Word Cards, p. 47 • ELL Vocabulary Routine, p. 471 ELL POSTER 4 • Day 1 Activities	TEACHER'S EDITION • Basic Vocabulary, p. DI•92 • Reteach Lesson Vocabulary, p. DI•93 • Multiple-Meaning Words, p. DI•95 ELL HANDBOOK • Word Cards, p. 47 • Multilingual Vocabulary List, p. 432 ELL POSTER 4 • Day 2 Activities
Grammar and Conventions	TEACHER'S EDITION • Preteach Commands and Exclamations, p. DI•99	TEACHER'S EDITION • Reteach Commands and Exclamations, p. DI•99
Writing	TEACHER'S EDITION • Writer's Personality, p. DI•100 • Introduce Description, pp. 127e–127f	TEACHER'S EDITION • Writing Trait: Focus/Ideas, pp. 139d–139e

This symbol indicates leveled instruction to address language proficiency levels.

Day 3	Day 4	Day 5
TEACHER'S EDITION • Academic Language, p. DI•91 • Concept Development, p. DI•91 • Anchored Talk, p. 140a • Concept Talk Video **ELL HANDBOOK** • ELL Poster Talk, Concept Talk, p. 47c **ELL POSTER 4** • Day 3 Activities	**TEACHER'S EDITION** • Academic Language, p. DI•91 • Concept Development, p. DI•91 • Anchored Talk, p. 154a • Concept Talk Video **ELL HANDBOOK** • ELL Poster Talk, Concept Talk, p. 47c **ELL POSTER 4** • Day 4 Activities	**TEACHER'S EDITION** • Academic Language, p. DI•91 • Concept Development, p. DI•91 • Concept Talk Video **ELL HANDBOOK** • ELL Poster Talk, Concept Talk, p. 47c **ELL POSTER 4** • Day 5 Activities
ELL HANDBOOK • Phonics Transition Lesson, pp. 253–256	**ELL HANDBOOK** • Phonics Transition Lesson, pp. 253–256	**TEACHER'S EDITION** • Phonics and Spelling, p. DI•95
TEACHER'S EDITION • AudioText of *Supermarket* • Concept Talk Video **ELL HANDBOOK** • AudioText CD Routine, p. 477	**TEACHER'S EDITION** • Concept Talk Video	**TEACHER'S EDITION** • Concept Talk Video
TEACHER'S EDITION • Sheltered Reading, p. DI•97 **ELL HANDBOOK** • Multilingual Summaries, pp. 49–51	**TEACHER'S EDITION** • ELL/ELD Reader Guided Reading, p. DI•98 **ELL HANDBOOK** • ELL Study Guide, p. 52	**TEACHER'S EDITION** • ELL/ELD Reader Guided Reading, p. DI•98 **ELL HANDBOOK** • ELL Study Guide, p. 52
ELL HANDBOOK • High-Frequency Words Activity Bank, p. 446 **ELL POSTER 4** • Day 3 Activities	**ELL HANDBOOK** • High-Frequency Words Activity Bank, p. 446	**TEACHER'S EDITION** • Multiple-Meaning Words, p. 159h **ELL HANDBOOK** • High-Frequency Words Activity Bank, p. 446
TEACHER'S EDITION • Grammar Jammer **ELL HANDBOOK** • Grammar Transition Lesson, pp. 343, 353–354 • Grammar Jammer Routine, p. 478	**TEACHER'S EDITION** • Grammar Jammer **ELL HANDBOOK** • Grammar Transition Lesson, pp. 343, 353–354	**TEACHER'S EDITION** • Grammar Jammer **ELL HANDBOOK** • Grammar Transition Lesson, pp. 343, 353–354
TEACHER'S EDITION • Let's Write It!, p. 152–153 • Writing Trait: Voice, pp. 153a–153b	**TEACHER'S EDITION** • Revising Strategy, pp. 159d–159e	**TEACHER'S EDITION** • Imperative/Exclamatory Sentences, pp. 159p–159q

Poster Talk, Concept Talk

Question of the Week

How can we get what we want and need?

Poster 4

Throughout the week, use the ELL Poster to help students produce and comprehend language, understand the concept, and build English vocabulary. Use the Question of the Week and other questions to help students share ideas in pairs, small groups, or the large group. Sample questions are shown, with examples of possible responses by students.

Weekly Concept and Language Goals

- Understand the difference between needs and wants
- Identify things people need and want
- Explain how we get what we need and want

By the end of the lesson, students should be able to talk about and write one or more sentences about getting things we need and want.

Daily Team Talk

Day 1	Day 2	Day 3	Day 4	Day 5
After Day 1 activities on Poster, ask questions such as *What is one thing the poster picture shows that people need? Why is that a need, not a want?*	After Day 2 activity on Poster, ask questions such as *What is one thing the poster picture shows that people want? Why is that a want, not a need?*	After Day 3 activity on Poster, ask questions such as *The little boy in the poster picture wants a stuffed animal, but he does not have enough money to buy it. What can he do to get money to buy the stuffed animal?*	After Day 4 activity on Poster, ask questions such as *Think about the story* Supermarket. *Before there were stores and markets, how did people get the things they needed?*	After Day 5 activity on Poster, ask questions such as *What is one thing you want? What is one thing you need?*
Beginning We need food. **Intermediate** It has food. We need food to eat. **Advanced** The store sells food. People need to eat food to live. **Advanced High** The store sells food and people need food. Food is a need because people have to eat to live.	**Beginning** We want toys. **Intermediate** It has toys. We do not need toys. **Advanced** The store sells toys. Toys are fun, but people do not need them to live. **Advanced High** The store sells toys and people want toys. Toys are a want because people do not have to have them to live.	**Beginning** Do chores. **Intermediate** He can do chores at home. **Advanced** The boy can do chores at home to earn money. **Advanced High** The boy can earn money by doing extra chores at home. He might dust the furniture or rake leaves.	**Beginning** They grew things. **Intermediate** They grew food and traded for things. **Advanced** People grew their own food. They traded for things they needed. **Advanced High** Families grew the food they needed. Then they traded with other people to get the other things they needed.	**Beginning** A bike and a coat. **Intermediate** I want a new bike. I need a new coat. **Advanced** I want a faster bike to ride. I need a warmer coat for the winter. **Advanced High** I want a faster bike so I can keep up with my friends. I need a new coat that will keep me warm this winter.

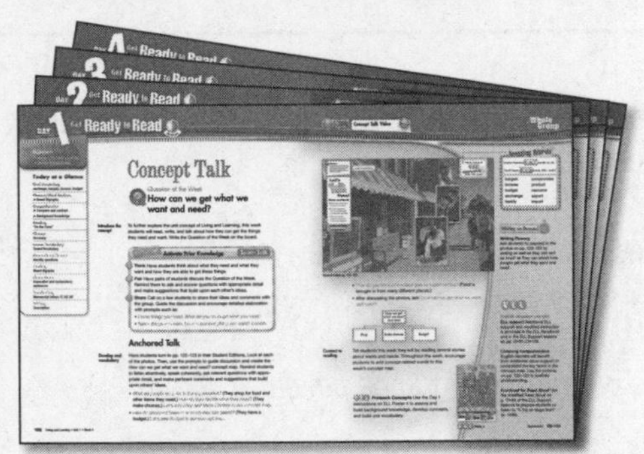

Teacher's Edition pages 122j–159q

See the support for English language learners throughout the lesson, including ELL strategies and scaffolded activities at points of use.

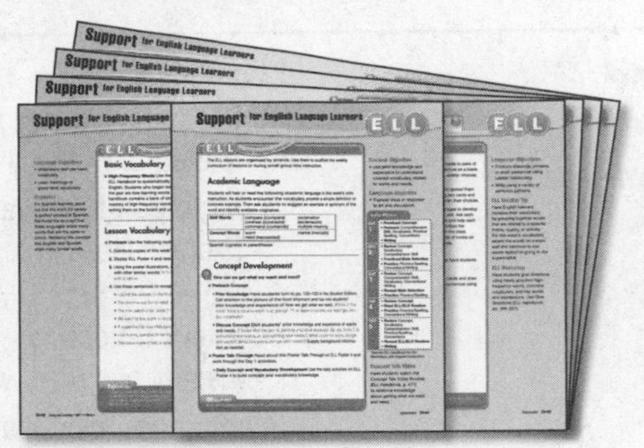

Teacher's Edition pages DI•91–DI•100

Differentiated Instruction for English language learners provides daily group activities that "frontload," or preteach, core instruction.

ELL Handbook pp. 47a–52

Find additional lesson materials that support the core lesson and the ELL instructional pages.

ELL Poster 4

ELL Reader 3.1.4

ELD Reader 3.1.4

Concept Literacy Reader

ELD, ELL Reader Teaching Guide

Concept Literacy Reader Teaching Guide

Technology

Online Teacher's Edition Use the digital version of the core Teacher's Edition for planning and instruction.

eReaders
This week's ELL and ELD Readers and Concept Literacy Reader are also available in digital format.

This Week's Content and Language Objectives by Strand

Concept Development/ Academic Language How can we get what we want and need?	**Content Objective** • Use prior knowledge and experience to understand concept vocabulary related to wants and needs. **Language Objective** • Express ideas in response to art and discussion.
Phonics and Spelling Vowel Digraphs	**Content Objective** • Identify and read words with vowel digraphs *ee, ea, ai, ay.* **Language Objective** • Read and write words with vowel digraphs *ee, ea, ai, ay.*
Listening Comprehension Modified Read Aloud: "Buy Only What You Need"	**Content Objective** • Monitor and adjust oral comprehension. **Language Objectives** • Discuss oral passages. • Use visual support to enhance understanding of spoken language.
Reading Comprehension Compare and Contrast	**Content Objectives** • Identify the difference between *compare* and *contrast.* • Monitor and adjust comprehension. **Language Objectives** • Compare and contrast a character in a reading. • Write comparisons and contrasts about a character in the reading. • Identify environmental print. • Read grade-level text with accuracy.
Vocabulary Basic and Lesson Vocabulary	**Language Objectives** • Understand and use basic vocabulary. • Learn meanings of grade-level vocabulary. • Produce drawings, phrases, and short sentences to show understanding of Lesson Vocabulary.
Vocabulary Multiple-Meaning Words	**Content Objective** • Identify words with multiple meanings. **Language Objective** • Use words with multiple meanings correctly.
Grammar and Conventions Commands and Exclamations	**Content Objectives** • Identify and use commands and exclamations. • Correctly write imperative and exclamatory sentences. **Language Objectives** • Speak using commands and exclamations. • Write imperative and exclamatory sentences.
Writing Writer's Personality	**Content Objective** • Identify writer's personality in a text. **Language Objective** • Write paragraphs with a strong voice.

Word Cards for Vocabulary Activities

laundry	**section**
shelves	**spoiled**
store	**thousands**
traded	**variety**

Teacher Note: Beginning Teach three to four words. **Intermediate** Teach four to six words. **Advanced** Teach six to seven words. **Advanced High** Teach all words.

Name ______________________

Picture It!
Compare and Contrast

Look at the pictures. **Read** the story. **Think** about what the pictures and words tell you. Then **answer** the questions below.

Apples for Sale

Anna lives in the country. There are many farms. Every week, she walks to an apple farm. She picks fresh apples from a tree and puts them in a sack. A farm worker puts the sack on a scale. She pays $1.00 for one pound of apples.

Henry lives in the city. There are many big buildings and stores. Every week, he takes a bus to the supermarket. He buys a different kind of apple each week. A store worker puts his apples on a scale. He pays $1.75 for one pound of apples.

1. How are Anna and Henry similar?

____

____

2. How are Anna and Henry different?

____

____

Compare and Contrast

Use this lesson to supplement or replace the skill lesson on page 126a of the Teacher's Edition. Display the Skill Points (at right) and share them with students.

Skill Points

✔ When we **compare,** we look for the ways things are alike.

✔ When we **contrast,** we look for the ways things are different.

Teach/Model

Beginning Display a ruler and a yardstick or two other classroom objects that have similarities and differences. Ask: *How are the ruler and the yardstick alike?* (Possible answer: We can use both to measure things.) *How are they different?* (Possible answer: One is short; the other is long.)

Intermediate Tell what you and a friend buy at the grocery store: *I buy milk, eggs, apples, and cereal. My friend buys bread, milk, cereal, and berries.* Have students draw pictures showing how the two sets of purchases are alike and different.

Advanced Tell a simple version of the story "The Country Mouse and the City Mouse." Say: *Tell how the two characters are alike.* Write students' answers on the board. Then have students contrast the two characters.

Advanced High Have students choose two favorite fairy tales or fables. Write the name of a main character in each story on the board. Have students suggest character traits to write under each name. Ask them to write sentences comparing and contrasting the characters.

Then distribute copies of Picture It! page 48.

- Have students look at the pictures and tell what is happening.
- Read the story aloud. Ask: *What happens in this story?* Have students tell how Anna and Henry are alike and different.
- Review the Skill Points with students.
- Have students look at the pictures and words to compare and contrast.

Practice

Read aloud the directions on page 48. Reread or have two volunteers reread the story aloud. Have students look at the pictures and the story as they answer the questions.

Beginning Students can point out and describe similarities and differences in the pictures and then write about the similarities and differences on the lines. Provide help with English words and writing.

Intermediate Students can first underline and circle similarities and differences in the text and then write them on the lines. Provide help with English words and writing.

Advanced Students can write their answers to the questions and then check them by comparing them with a partner's answers.

Advanced High Students can write their answers to the questions and then orally compare and contrast the two characters, pointing to evidence in the story.

Answers for page 48: 1. Both like apples. They buy them every week. 2. Anna lives in the country, and Henry lives in the city. Anna walks to a farm, and Henry takes the bus to a store. Anna pays less for her apples than Henry does.

Multilingual Summaries

English

Supermarket

The supermarket is a necessary place. Food at the supermarket comes from farms. Farmers grow the food, and workers harvest the fruits and vegetables. They pack everything in boxes. They load the boxes onto trucks. Trucks deliver the food to the supermarkets.

Before supermarkets, people grew their own food. They began trading with one another. Marketplaces turned into general stores and then grocery stores. Today we have supermarkets with a variety of fruits and vegetables. Supermarkets also have meat and fish. They also have a bakery and a dairy section.

Supermarkets have electronic scanners and cash registers. Baggers pack up the groceries. Groceries are moved from the farm or factories, to the supermarket, and then to your kitchen shelves.

Spanish

El supermercado

El supermercado es algo necesario. Los alimentos que están en los supermercados vienen de las granjas. Los granjeros siembran los alimentos y los trabajadores cosechan las frutas y los vegetales. Ellos empacan todo dentro de unas cajas. Suben las cajas a los camiones. Los camiones llevan los alimentos a los supermercados.

Antes de que existieran los supermercados, las personas sembraban sus propios alimentos. Las pequeñas tiendas se convirtieron en tiendas de abarrotes y luego en mercados. Hoy en día contamos con supermercados que ofrecen una variedad de frutas y vegetales. También en los supermercados se puede comprar carnes y pescados. Allí también hay panadería y sección de lácteos.

En los supermercados hay cajas registradoras con escáneres. Los empacadores empacan los víveres. Los víveres son trasladados desde las granjas o fábricas hasta los supermercados. Y luego a las despensas de sus cocinas.

Multilingual Summaries

Chinese

超級市場

超級市場是必不可缺的地方。 超級市場裡的食物來自農場。 農夫種植食物，而工人採收水果和蔬菜。他們把所有的東西都裝到箱子裡。 然後將箱子放到卡車上。 之後，卡車再把食物運送到超級市場。

還沒有超級市場的時候，人們都吃自己種的食物。 後來他們開始彼此進行交易。 市場變成了一般的商店，然後又變成了雜貨店。 現在，則出現了販賣各種水果和蔬菜的超級市場。 超級市場中也賣肉和魚， 還有麵包糕點和奶製品。

超級市場使用電子掃描器和收銀機。 裝袋工負責包裝食品雜貨。食品雜貨先從農場或工廠運到超級市場，然後再送到你家廚房的櫃子裡。

Vietnamese

Siêu Thị

Siêu thị là một nơi cần thiết. Thực phẩm tại siêu thị đến từ các nông trại. Nông dân trồng thực phẩm và các nhân công gặt hái trái cây và rau cải. Họ đóng tất cả vào thùng. Họ chất các thùng lên xe tải. Xe tải giao thực phẩm đến siêu thị.

Trước khi có siêu thị, người ta tự trồng thực phẩm. Họ bắt đầu trao đổi hàng hóa lẫn nhau. Các chợ trở thành tiệm tạp hóa và sau đó là tiệm bách hóa. Ngày nay siêu thị có trái cây và rau cải đủ loại khác nhau. Siêu thị cũng có thịt và cá. Chúng cũng có cả nơi bán bánh và bán sản phẩm bơ sữa.

Siêu thị cũng có máy quẹt và máy thu tiền điện tử. Người bỏ hàng sắp xếp thực phẩm vào bao. Thực phẩm di chuyển từ nông trại hay các nhà máy, rồi đến siêu thị, và sau đó đến các kệ ở nhà bếp của bạn.

Multilingual Summaries

Korean

슈퍼마켓

슈퍼마켓은 꼭 필요한 곳이다. 슈퍼마켓의 먹을 것들은 농장에서 온다. 농부가 농사를 지으면 일꾼들이 과일과 야채를 거두어들이고 상자에 담아 트럭에 싣는다. 트럭은 먹을 것들을 슈퍼마켓으로 배달한다.

슈퍼마켓이 없었을 때 사람들은 각자 먹을 것을 길렀다. 사람들은 서로 물물교환을 하기 시작했으며, 시장이 잡화점이 되고 식품점이 되었다. 요즘 슈퍼마켓에는 다양한 과일과 야채가 많다. 또한 고기와 생선도 있으며 빵과 유제품도 있다.

슈퍼마켓에는 전자 스캐너와 금전 등록기가 있다. 짐 싸주는 사람들이 식품을 담아준다. 식품은 농장이나 공장에서 슈퍼마켓으로 배달된 후 여러분의 부엌 선반으로 옮겨진다.

Hmong

Tsheej Kw

Tlub tsheej kw yogib qho chaw tseem ceeb. Khoom noj nyob hauv lub tsheej kw los tom teb los. Cov neeg ua teb cog tej khoom noj thiab ua hauj lwm di tej txiv ntoo thiab zaub. Lawv muab txhua yam tso hau thawv ntawv. Lawv muab cov khoom tso hauv tsheb loj tuaj. Tsheb loj xav cov khoom noj rau hauv cov tsheej kw.

Ua ntej thaum muaj tsheej kw, neeg nyias cog nyia li khoom noj. Lawv muab los sib pauv. Tej chaw muab khoom mam li mus ua kiab kws thiab mam li mus kws muag khoom. Niaj hnub no peb muaj tsheej kws muag ntau yam txiv ntoo thiab zaub. Tsheej kw muaj nqaij thiab muag ntses. Lawv muaj chav muag khob noom thiab mis nyuj.

Tsheej kws muaj lub cav electronic scanners thiab lub cav ntau nyiaj hu ua cash registers. Lawv muaj neeg ntim khoom tib si. Khoom noj mas tawm tom teb los rau hauv npaus li xav los rau rau hauv tsheej kws, thiab mus rau hauv nej lub txee rau khoom noj tom chaw ua mov.

Name ______________________ **Going to the Market**

- **Read** *Going to the Market* again.
- **Describe** the girls' shopping trip, in order. The first sentence is written for you.

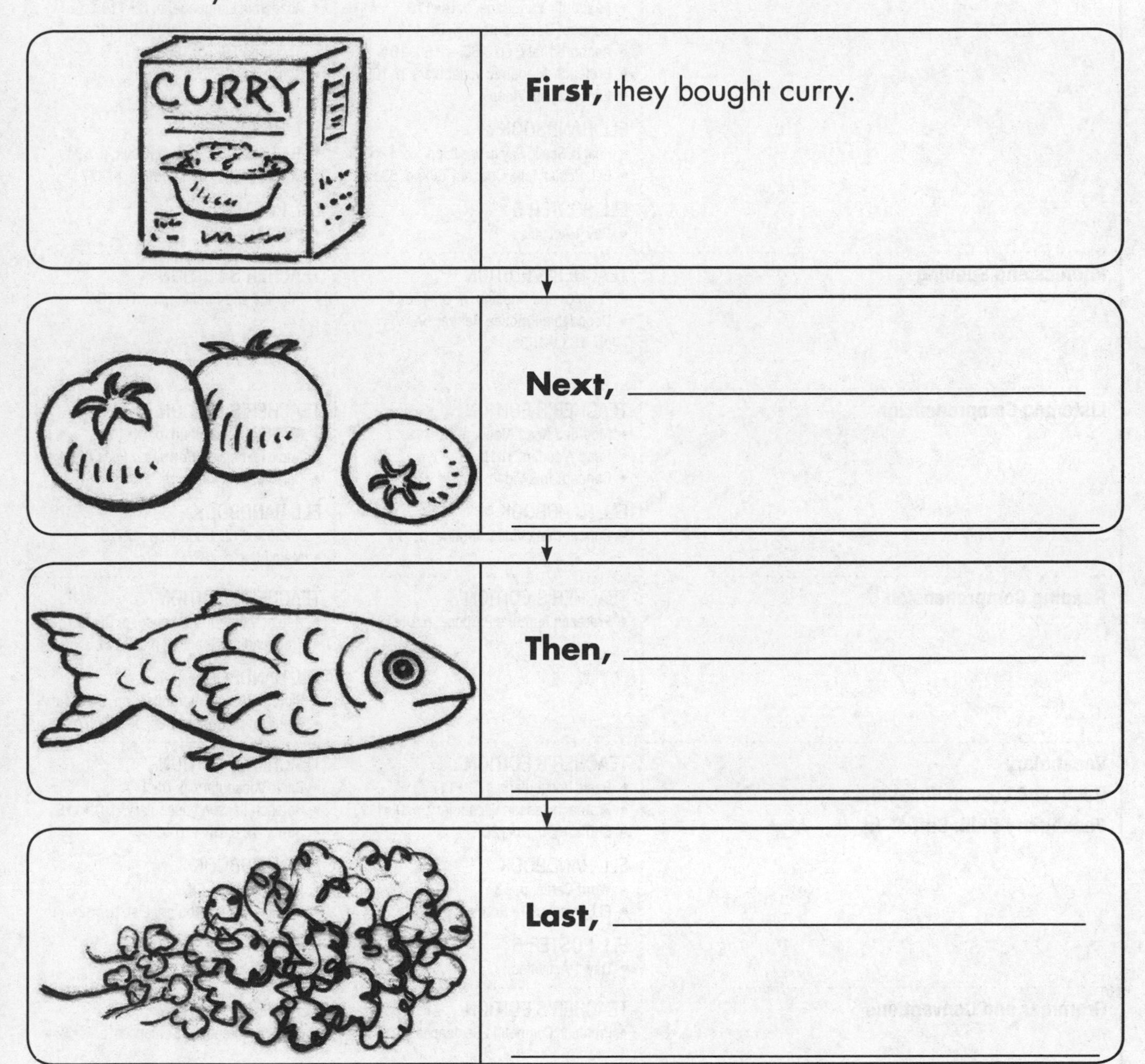

First, they bought curry.

Next, ______________________

Then, ______________________

Last, ______________________

Family Link

Ask family members to tell about their favorite market. It could be in their homeland or near where you live now.

Weekly Resources Guide for English Language Learner Support

For this week's content and language objectives, see p. 53e.

Instructional Strand	Day 1	Day 2
Concept Development/Academic Language	TEACHER'S EDITION • Academic Language, p. DI•116 • Concept Development, p. DI•116 • Anchored Talk, pp. 160j—160–161 • Preteach Academic Vocabulary, p. 165a • Concept Talk Video ELL HANDBOOK • Hear It, See It, Say It, Use It, pp. xxxvi–xxxvii • ELL Poster Talk, Concept Talk, p. 53c ELL POSTER 5 • Day 1 Activities	TEACHER'S EDITION • Academic Language, p. DI•116 • Concept Development, p. DI•116 • Anchored Talk, p. 166a • Concept Talk Video ELL HANDBOOK • ELL Poster Talk, Concept Talk, p. 53c • Concept Talk Video Routine, p. 477 ELL POSTER 5 • Day 2 Activities
Phonics and Spelling	TEACHER'S EDITION • Phonics and Spelling, p. DI•120 • Decodable Practice Reader 5A, pp. 163a–163b	TEACHER'S EDITION • Phonics and Spelling, p. DI•120
Listening Comprehension	TEACHER'S EDITION • Modified Read Aloud, p. DI•119 • Read Aloud, p. 161b • Concept Talk Video ELL HANDBOOK • Concept Talk Video Routine, p. 477	TEACHER'S EDITION • Modified Read Aloud, p. DI•119 • AudioText of *My Rows and Piles of Coins* • Concept Talk Video ELL HANDBOOK • AudioText CD Routine, p. 477 • Main Idea, p. 487
Reading Comprehension	TEACHER'S EDITION • Preteach Author's Purpose, p. DI•121	TEACHER'S EDITION • Reteach Author's Purpose, p. DI•121 • Frontloading Reading, p. DI•122 ELL HANDBOOK • Picture It! Skill Instruction, pp. 54–54a • Multilingual Summaries, pp. 55–57
Vocabulary **Basic and Lesson Vocabulary** **Vocabulary Skill: Suffix *-ly***	TEACHER'S EDITION • Basic Vocabulary, p. DI•117 • Preteach Lesson Vocabulary, p. DI•117 • Suffix *-ly*, p. DI•120 ELL HANDBOOK • Word Cards, p. 53 • ELL Vocabulary Routine, p. 471 ELL POSTER 5 • Day 1 Activities	TEACHER'S EDITION • Basic Vocabulary, p. DI•117 • Reteach Lesson Vocabulary, p. DI•118 • Suffix *-ly*, p. DI•120 ELL HANDBOOK • Word Cards, p. 53 • Multilingual Vocabulary List, p. 432 ELL POSTER 5 • Day 2 Activities
Grammar and Conventions	TEACHER'S EDITION • Preteach Compound Sentences, p. DI•124	TEACHER'S EDITION • Reteach Compound Sentences, p. DI•124
Writing	TEACHER'S EDITION • Sentence Variety, p. DI•125 • Writing for Tests: Realistic Fiction, pp. 165e–165f	TEACHER'S EDITION • Writing for Tests: Realistic Fiction, pp. 175d–175e

Unit 1 Week 5 My Rows and Piles of Coins

This symbol indicates leveled instruction to address language proficiency levels.

Day 3	Day 4	Day 5
TEACHER'S EDITION • Academic Language, p. DI•116 • Concept Development, p. DI•116 • Anchored Talk, p. 176a • Concept Talk Video ELL HANDBOOK • ELL Poster Talk, Concept Talk, p. 53c ELL POSTER 5 • Day 3 Activities	TEACHER'S EDITION • Academic Language, p. DI•116 • Concept Development, p. DI•116 • Anchored Talk, p. 188a • Concept Talk Video ELL HANDBOOK • ELL Poster Talk, Concept Talk, p. 53c ELL POSTER 5 • Day 4 Activities	TEACHER'S EDITION • Academic Language, p. DI•116 • Concept Development, p. DI•116 • Concept Talk Video ELL HANDBOOK • ELL Poster Talk, Concept Talk, p. 53c ELL POSTER 5 • Day 5 Activities
ELL HANDBOOK • Phonics Transition Lesson, pp. 260–261	ELL HANDBOOK • Phonics Transition Lesson, pp. 260–261	TEACHER'S EDITION • Phonics and Spelling, p. DI•120
TEACHER'S EDITION • AudioText of *My Rows and Piles of Coins* • Concept Talk Video ELL HANDBOOK • AudioText CD Routine, p. 477	TEACHER'S EDITION • Concept Talk Video	TEACHER'S EDITION • Concept Talk Video
TEACHER'S EDITION • Sheltered Reading, p. DI•122 ELL HANDBOOK • Multilingual Summaries, pp. 55–57	TEACHER'S EDITION • ELL/ELD Reader Guided Reading, p. DI•123 ELL HANDBOOK • ELL Study Guide, p. 58	TEACHER'S EDITION • ELL/ELD Reader Guided Reading, p. DI•123 ELL HANDBOOK • ELL Study Guide, p. 58
ELL HANDBOOK • High-Frequency Words Activity Bank, p. 446 ELL POSTER 5 • Day 3 Activities	ELL HANDBOOK • High-Frequency Words Activity Bank, p. 446	TEACHER'S EDITION • Prefixes and Suffixes, p. 193h ELL HANDBOOK • High-Frequency Words Activity Bank, p. 446
TEACHER'S EDITION • Grammar Jammer ELL HANDBOOK • Grammar Transition Lesson, pp. 344, 355, 379, 381 • Grammar Jammer Routine, p. 478	TEACHER'S EDITION • Grammar Jammer ELL HANDBOOK • Grammar Transition Lesson, pp. 344, 355, 379, 381	TEACHER'S EDITION • Grammar Jammer ELL HANDBOOK • Grammar Transition Lesson, pp. 344, 355, 379, 381
TEACHER'S EDITION • Let's Write It!, p. 186–187 • Writing for Tests: Evaluation, pp. 187a–187b	TEACHER'S EDITION • Writing for Tests: Realistic Fiction, p. 193d	TEACHER'S EDITION • Writing for Tests: Revising Strategy: Clarifying, pp. 193p–193q

Poster Talk, Concept Talk

Question of the Week

What do we need to know about saving and spending?

Poster 5

Throughout the week, use the ELL Poster to help students produce and comprehend language, understand the concept, and build English vocabulary. Use the Question of the Week and other questions to help students share ideas in pairs, small groups, or the large group. Sample questions are shown, with examples of possible responses by students.

Weekly Concept and Language Goals

- Share ideas about spending and saving
- Describe ways to save money
- Tell about earning, buying, and saving

By the end of the lesson, students should be able to talk about and write one or more sentences about spending and saving.

Daily Team Talk

Day 1	Day 2	Day 3	Day 4	Day 5
After Day 1 activities on Poster, ask questions such as *In the poster picture, what is one way a person is earning money?*	After Day 2 activity on Poster, ask questions such as *The man in the poster picture likes the glass he is holding. How can he get the glass?*	After Day 3 activity on Poster, ask questions such as *In the poster picture, the boy looking at the basketball does not have enough money to buy it. How can he save enough money?*	After Day 4 activity on Poster, ask questions such as *Why do you think the boy in the poster picture wants to earn money by selling his old toys and books?*	After Day 5 activity on Poster, ask questions such as *What is something you want to buy? How can you earn money to buy it?*
Beginning Selling things. **Intermediate** The woman sells food. **Advanced** The boy's neighbor sells vegetables she grew. **Advanced High** The boy's neighbor sells eggplants, tomatoes, and cucumbers she grew in her garden.	**Beginning** Buy it. **Intermediate** The man can buy the glass. **Advanced** The man can pay money to buy the glass from the people selling it. **Advanced High** The man can spend his money to get the glass. He pays the people money and buys the glass from them.	**Beginning** Work for it. **Intermediate** The boy can do work for money and save it. **Advanced** The boy can work for his family or neighbors and save the money he earns. **Advanced High** The boy can mow lawns or babysit to earn money. When he has saved enough money, he can buy the basketball.	**Beginning** Wants to save it. **Intermediate** He wants to earn money so he can buy something. **Advanced** The boy is earning money to buy something he really wants. **Advanced High** I think the boy wants to earn money so he can save up to buy something he really wants, such as a new skateboard.	**Beginning** A bat. I can work. **Intermediate** I want a new bat. I can help my neighbor. **Advanced** I want to buy a new bat. I can clean the yard to earn money. **Advanced High** I want to buy a new baseball bat. I can run errands for my mom or do other chores to earn enough money to buy the bat.

This Week's Materials

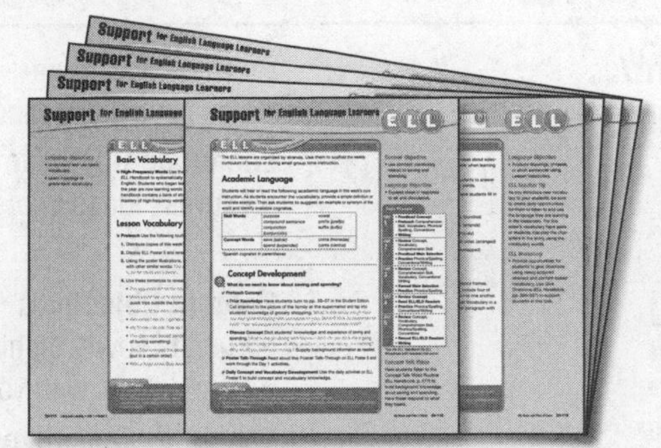

Teacher's Edition pages 160j–197a

See the support for English language learners throughout the lesson, including ELL strategies and scaffolded activities at points of use.

Teacher's Edition pages DI•116–DI•125

Differentiated Instruction for English language learners provides daily group activities that "frontload," or preteach, core instruction.

ELL Handbook pp. 53a–58

Find additional lesson materials that support the core lesson and the ELL instructional pages.

ELL Poster 5

ELL Reader 3.1.5

ELD Reader 3.1.5

Concept Literacy Reader

ELD, ELL Reader Teaching Guide

Concept Literacy Reader Teaching Guide

Technology

Online Teacher's Edition Use the digital version of the core Teacher's Edition for planning and instruction.

eReaders
This week's ELL and ELD Readers and Concept Literacy Reader are also available in digital format.

This Week's Content and Language Objectives by Strand

Concept Development/ Academic Language What do we need to know about saving and spending?	**Content Objective** • Use concept vocabulary related to saving and spending. **Language Objective** • Express ideas in response to art and discussion.
Phonics and Spelling Vowel Diphthongs	**Content Objectives** • Identify vowel diphthongs. • Read words with vowel diphthongs. **Language Objective** • Apply phonics and decoding skills to vocabulary.
Listening Comprehension Modified Read Aloud: "The Market"	**Content Objective** • Monitor and adjust oral comprehension. **Language Objectives** • Discuss oral passages. • Use a graphic organizer to take notes.
Reading Comprehension Author's Purpose	**Content Objectives** • Identify author's purpose. • Use author's purpose to aid comprehension. **Language Objectives** • Discuss evidence for an author's purpose. • Retell details that support an author's purpose. • Draw and write an author's purpose. • Read grade-level text with expression.
Vocabulary Basic and Lesson Vocabulary	**Language Objectives** • Understand and use basic vocabulary. • Learn meanings of grade-level vocabulary. • Produce drawings, phrases, and short sentences to show understanding of Lesson Vocabulary.
Vocabulary Suffix *–ly*	**Content Objective** • Identify words with the suffix *–ly*. **Language Objective** • Write with structure of suffix *-ly*.
Grammar and Conventions Compound Sentences	**Content Objectives** • Use conjunctions to make compound sentences. • Correctly write compound sentences. **Language Objectives** • Speak using conjunctions to make compound sentences. • Write compound sentences.
Writing Sentence Variety	**Content Objective** • Identify sentence variety in a text. **Language Objectives** • Write paragraphs using sentence variety. • Share feedback for editing and revising.

Word Cards for Vocabulary Activities

arranged	**bundles**
dangerously	**errands**
excitedly	**steady**
unwrapped	**wobbled**

Teacher Note: Beginning Teach three to four words. **Intermediate** Teach four to six words. **Advanced** Teach six to seven words. **Advanced High** Teach all words.

Name ______________________________

Read the story. **Look** at the pictures.

- **Read** each question. **Read** each of the answer choices.
- **Circle** the letter of the correct answer for each question.

Hard Work Pays Off

All fall Ant was very busy. He carried seeds to his home. It was hard work. He did not want to do it. He wanted to play with his friends. He needed to store food, though. Now winter is here. The snow is falling, and it is cold outside. There are no seeds outside. Ant is a smart bug. He is happy. He has enough food for the winter. He knows hard work makes a difference.

1. What is the author's purpose?
  a. to teach a lesson
  b. to inform the reader about ants
  c. to make the reader laugh
  d. to frighten the reader

2. How does the author meet this purpose?
  a. by giving facts
  b. by giving opinions
  c. by telling a story
  d. by writing about his emotions

Picture It!

Author's Purpose

Use this lesson to supplement or replace the skill lesson on page 164a of the Teacher's Edition. Display the Skill Points (at right) and share them with students.

Skill Points

- ✔ The **author's purpose** is the reason an author writes something.
- ✔ An author may write to entertain, to inform, to express ideas, or to persuade.
- ✔ Sometimes the title helps you predict the author's purpose.

Teach/Model

Beginning Display an article from the news section of a newspaper. Read aloud the title. Ask: *Did the author write this to inform or to entertain readers?* (to inform) Repeat this process with a comic from the newspaper as an example of writing to entertain.

Intermediate Display a photograph of an insect in a nonfiction children's book. Ask: *What is the author's purpose?* (to inform) *How do you know?* Repeat this process with an illustration of an insect in a children's fiction book. (to entertain)

Advanced Write these titles: *Save the Bees; All About Insects; Iggy Insect's Great Adventure.* Say: *These are the titles of books about bugs.* Briefly describe the contents of the books. Have students decide, based on the title and content description, whether the author's purpose for each book is to persuade, to inform, or to entertain.

Advanced High Have students write and illustrate a sentence about insects. Ask them to write for one of these purposes: to inform; to persuade; to entertain; to express feelings. Remind them that the style of their illustration as well as their writing must match their purpose. Have students identify the purposes of their classmates' sentences.

Then distribute copies of Picture It! page 54.

- Have students read the title and predict what the story might be about.
- Review the Skill Points with students.
- Read the story aloud. Ask: *What is the author's purpose? Why did the author write this story?*
- Have students look at the pictures and words to identify the author's purpose.

Practice

Read aloud the directions on page 54. Reread or chorally reread the story aloud. Have students look at the pictures and the story as they answer the questions.

Beginning Students can orally answer the questions and then point to the correct answers and mark them. Provide help with marking the correct choices.

Intermediate Students can first orally answer the questions and then mark their answers on the page.

Advanced Students can mark their answers and then check them by comparing and discussing answers with a partner.

Advanced High Students can mark their answers and then check them by rereading the story and pointing out the evidence that supports their answers.

Answers for page 54: 1. a; 2. c

Multilingual Summaries

English

My Rows and Piles of Coins

Saruni helped his mother every Saturday at the market. She gave him ten-cent coins each time. He was saving his money to buy a bicycle.

Saruni's father let him practice riding his bicycle. The bicycle was too big for Saruni. He often fell. He thought about how nice it would be to have his own bicycle. Each day after the market, Saruni counted his coins.

One day Saruni thought he had enough money to buy a bicycle. The man who sold bicycles laughed at Saruni because he did not have enough money for the bicycle. Saruni was disappointed.

The next day Saruni's father bought a motorbike. He gave Saruni his bicycle for being a good helper at the market. Saruni decided to save his money to buy a cart to help his mother bring things to market.

Spanish

Mis montones de monedas

Saruni ayudaba todos los sábados a su mamá en el mercado. Cada vez que la ayudaba, ella le daba monedas de diez centavos. Él estaba ahorrando su dinero para comprar una bicicleta.

El papá de Saruni lo dejaba practicar en su bicicleta. La bicicleta era muy grande para Saruni y él se caía a menudo. Él pensaba en lo bueno que sería tener su propia bicicleta. Todos los días, después de llegar del mercado, Saruni contaba sus monedas.

Un día, Saruni pensó que tenía suficiente dinero para comprar una bicicleta. El hombre que vendía bicicletas se rió porque él no tenía suficiente dinero para comprar una. Saruni estaba triste.

Al día siguiente, el papa de Saruni compró una motocicleta. Le regaló su bicicleta a Saruni por ser un buen ayudante en el mercado. Saruni decidió ahorrar su dinero y comprar un carrito para ayudar a su mamá a llevar las cosas al mercado.

Multilingual Summaries

Chinese

我的錢

沙路尼每個星期六都會去市場幫媽媽的忙，每次媽媽都會給他十分錢。他把錢存起來，因為他想買一輛腳踏車。

沙路尼的爸爸把腳踏車借給他練習騎，可是腳踏車太大了，害他經常摔車。他總是想，如果有自己的腳踏車不知道該有多好。每天從市場回來後，沙路尼都會算算他賺到的錢。

有一天，沙路尼覺得他存的錢夠了，所以就想去買一輛腳踏車，但是賣腳踏車的人笑沙路尼，因為他帶的錢根本不夠。沙路尼很失望。

第二天，沙路尼的爸爸買了一輛摩托車，所以就把腳踏車送給沙路尼，這樣去市場的話比較方便。 沙路尼決定再把錢存起來，這次他想買一輛運貨馬車，幫助媽媽運送東西到市場賣。

Vietnamese

Các Dãy và Cọc Tiền Bạc Cắc của Tôi

Saruni phụ giúp mẹ ở chợ vào mỗi Thứ Bảy. Mẹ cho cậu bé những đồng mười xu mỗi lần cậu giúp mẹ. Cậu bé để dành tiền để mua một chiếc xe đạp.

Ba của Saruni để cho cậu bé tập chạy xe đạp của ông. Chiếc xe đạp này quá lớn cho Saruni. Cậu bé thường bị ngã. Cậu mơ nghĩ đến lúc có riêng một chiếc xe đạp. Mỗi ngày sau buổi chợ, Saruni lại đếm những đồng tiền của mình.

Ngày kia Saruni nghĩ là mình đã có đủ tiền để mua một chiếc xe đạp. Người bán xe đạp cười nhạo Saruni vì cậu bé không có đủ tiền mua chiếc xe. Saruni thất vọng.

Hôm sau ba của Saruni mua một chiếc xe gắn máy. Ông cho Saruni chiếc xe đạp của ông vì cậu bé đã giúp việc giỏi ở chợ. Saruni quyết định để dành tiền mua một chiếc xe đẩy để giúp mẹ mang hàng ra chợ.

Multilingual Summaries

Korean

내 동전 더미들

사루니는 매주 토요일마다 시장에서 어머니를 도와드리고 그때마다 어머니한테 10센트짜리 동전을 받는다. 그는 그 돈을 자전거를 사기 위해 모아 둔다.

사루니의 아버지는 아들이 자신의 자전거를 타는 것을 내버려 둔다. 하지만 자전거가 너무 커서 사루니는 자주 넘어진다. 사루니는 자신의 자전거를 갖는다는 것이 얼마나 멋진 일일까에 대해서 생각하며 시장에 다녀올 때마다 받은 동전들을 세어본다.

어느 날 사루니는 자전거를 사기에 충분한 돈을 가지고 있다고 생각하지만 자전거 상인은 돈이 부족하다며 사루니를 비웃는다. 사루니는 이에 실망한다.

다음 날 사루니의 아버지는 오토바이를 산다. 그리고 사루니가 시장에서 아주 큰 도움이 된다며 아들에게 자전거를 준다. 이제 사루니는 어머니가 시장에 물건들을 옮길 때 도와줄 수레를 사기 위해 돈을 모으기로 결심한다.

Hmong

Kuv Tej Liaj Tej Pawg Npib

Saruni pab nws niam txhua hnub vas xyaum pem tab laj tshav puam. Nws muab kaum xees rau nws txhua zaus. Nws tseg nws cov nyiaj kom yuav tau ib lub tsheb kauj vab.

Saruni txiv cai nws xyaum caij nws txiv lub tsheb kauj vab. Lub tsheb kauj vab loj dhau rau Saruni. Nws ib sij poob ib lwm. Nws xav tias yuav ua cas zoo yog nws muaj nws ib lub tsheb kauj vab. Txhua txhua hnub tab laj tshav puam tag, nws suav nws cov npib.

Muaj ib hnub Saruni xav tias nws muaj nyiaj txaus yuav ib lub tsheb kauj vab. Tus txiv neej muag tsheb kauj vab hluag Saruni vim nws tsis muaj nyiaj txaus yuav lub tsheb kauj vab. Saruni tub siab.

Hnub tom qab Saruni txiv yuav tau ib lub tsheb maus taus. Nws muab nws lub tsheb kauj vab rau Saruni rau qhov nws yogi b tug tus pab ua hauj lwm zoo pem tab laj tshav puam. Saruni txiav txim siab tseg nws cov nyiaj kom yuav tau ib lub laub los pab nws niam nqa khoom mus rau pem tab laj tshav puam.

Name ___________________________

Money to Spend

- **Read** *Money to Spend* again.
- Pretend you have $5. **Draw** what you would buy from the store.
- **Write** a sentence about your choice.

____

____

Family Link

Ask family members what they would buy with $5.

Weekly Resources Guide for English Language Learner Support

For this week's content and language objectives, see p. 59e.

Instructional Strand	Day 1	Day 2
Concept Development/Academic Language	TEACHER'S EDITION • Academic Language, p. DI•16 • Concept Development, p. DI•16 • Anchored Talk, pp. 200j—200–201 • Preteach Academic Vocabulary, p. 205a • Concept Talk Video ELL HANDBOOK • Hear It, See It, Say It, Use It, pp. xxxvi–xxxvii • ELL Poster Talk, Concept Talk, p. 59c ELL POSTER 6 • Day 1 Activities	TEACHER'S EDITION • Academic Language, p. DI•16 • Concept Development, p. DI•16 • Anchored Talk, p. 206a • Concept Talk Video ELL HANDBOOK • ELL Poster Talk, Concept Talk, p. 59c • Concept Talk Video Routine, p. 477 ELL POSTER 6 • Day 2 Activities
Phonics and Spelling	TEACHER'S EDITION • Phonics and Spelling, p. DI•20 • Decodable Practice Reader 6A, pp. 203a–203b	TEACHER'S EDITION • Phonics and Spelling, p. DI•20
Listening Comprehension	TEACHER'S EDITION • Modified Read Aloud, p. DI•19 • Read Aloud, p. 201b • Concept Talk Video ELL HANDBOOK • Concept Talk Video Routine, p. 477	TEACHER'S EDITION • Modified Read Aloud, p. DI•19 • AudioText of *Penguin Chick* • Concept Talk Video ELL HANDBOOK • AudioText CD Routine, p. 477 • Main Idea, p. 487
Reading Comprehension	TEACHER'S EDITION • Preteach Main Idea and Details, p. DI•21	TEACHER'S EDITION • Reteach Main Idea and Details, p. DI•21 • Frontloading Reading, p. DI•22 ELL HANDBOOK • Picture It! Skill Instruction, pp. 60–60a • Multilingual Summaries, pp. 61–63
Vocabulary **Basic and Lesson Vocabulary** **Vocabulary Skill: Synonyms**	TEACHER'S EDITION • Basic Vocabulary, p. DI•17 • Preteach Lesson Vocabulary, p. DI•17 • Synonyms, p. DI•20 ELL HANDBOOK • Word Cards, p. 59 • ELL Vocabulary Routine, p. 471 ELL POSTER 6 • Day 1 Activities	TEACHER'S EDITION • Basic Vocabulary, p. DI•17 • Reteach Lesson Vocabulary, p. DI•18 • Synonyms, p. DI•20 ELL HANDBOOK • Word Cards, p. 59 • Multilingual Vocabulary List, p. 433 ELL POSTER 6 • Day 2 Activities
Grammar and Conventions	TEACHER'S EDITION • Preteach Common and Proper Nouns, p. DI•24	TEACHER'S EDITION • Reteach Common and Proper Nouns, p. DI•24
Writing	TEACHER'S EDITION • Writing Poems with Figurative Language, p. DI•25 • Introduce Poetry, pp. 205e–205f	TEACHER'S EDITION • Cinquain, pp. 215d–215e

This symbol indicates leveled instruction to address language proficiency levels.

Day 3	Day 4	Day 5
TEACHER'S EDITION • Academic Language, p. DI•16 • Concept Development, p. DI•16 • Anchored Talk, p. 216a • Concept Talk Video **ELL HANDBOOK** • ELL Poster Talk, Concept Talk, p. 59c **ELL POSTER 6** • Day 3 Activities	**TEACHER'S EDITION** • Academic Language, p. DI•16 • Concept Development, p. DI•16 • Anchored Talk, p. 226a • Concept Talk Video **ELL HANDBOOK** • ELL Poster Talk, Concept Talk, p. 59c **ELL POSTER 6** • Day 4 Activities	**TEACHER'S EDITION** • Academic Language, p. DI•16 • Concept Development, p. DI•16 • Concept Talk Video **ELL HANDBOOK** • ELL Poster Talk, Concept Talk, p. 59c **ELL POSTER 6** • Day 5 Activities
ELL HANDBOOK • Phonics Transition Lesson, pp. 232, 236	**ELL HANDBOOK** • Phonics Transition Lesson, pp. 232, 236	**TEACHER'S EDITION** • Phonics and Spelling, p. DI•20
TEACHER'S EDITION • AudioText of *Penguin Chick* • Concept Talk Video **ELL HANDBOOK** • AudioText CD Routine, p. 477	**TEACHER'S EDITION** • Concept Talk Video	**TEACHER'S EDITION** • Concept Talk Video
TEACHER'S EDITION • Sheltered Reading, p. DI•22 **ELL HANDBOOK** • Multilingual Summaries, pp. 61–63	**TEACHER'S EDITION** • ELL/ELD Reader Guided Reading, p. DI•23 **ELL HANDBOOK** • ELL Study Guide, p. 64	**TEACHER'S EDITION** • ELL/ELD Reader Guided Reading, p. DI•23 **ELL HANDBOOK** • ELL Study Guide, p. 64
ELL HANDBOOK • High-Frequency Words Activity Bank, p. 446 **ELL POSTER 6** • Day 3 Activities	**ELL HANDBOOK** • High-Frequency Words Activity Bank, p. 446	**TEACHER'S EDITION** • Synonyms, p. 231h **ELL HANDBOOK** • High-Frequency Words Activity Bank, p. 446
TEACHER'S EDITION • Grammar Jammer **ELL HANDBOOK** • Grammar Transition Lesson, pp. 314–315, 318–321 • Grammar Jammer Routine, p. 478	**TEACHER'S EDITION** • Grammar Jammer **ELL HANDBOOK** • Grammar Transition Lesson, pp. 314–315, 318–321	**TEACHER'S EDITION** • Grammar Jammer **ELL HANDBOOK** • Grammar Transition Lesson, pp. 314–315, 318–321
TEACHER'S EDITION • Let's Write It!, p. 224–225 • Diamante, p. 225a • Writer's Craft: Figurative Language, p. 225b	**TEACHER'S EDITION** • Writer's Craft: Repetition, p. 231d	**TEACHER'S EDITION** • Editing and Presenting, pp. 231p–231q

Poster Talk, Concept Talk

Question of the Week

How do the structures of plants and animals help them solve problems?

Poster 6

Throughout the week, use the ELL Poster to help students produce and comprehend language, understand the concept, and build English vocabulary. Use the Question of the Week and other questions to help students share ideas in pairs, small groups, or the large group. Sample questions are shown, with examples of possible responses by students.

Weekly Concept and Language Goals

- Describe animal structures
- Name animal structures
- Discuss ways structures help plants and animals solve problems

By the end of the lesson, students should be able to talk about and write one or more sentences about how plant and animal structures help them solve problems.

Daily Team Talk

Day 1	Day 2	Day 3	Day 4	Day 5
After Day 1 activities on Poster, ask questions such as *In the poster picture, how do the penguins' flippers help them live in Antarctica?*	After Day 2 activity on Poster, ask questions such as *How does an albatross chick use its beak to help it come out of its egg?*	After Day 3 activity on Poster, ask questions such as *In the poster picture, how do animals stay warm in cold Antarctica?*	After Day 4 activity on Poster, ask questions such as *Why are there so few plants in Antarctica?*	After Day 5 activity on Poster, ask questions such as *In the story* Penguin Chick, *how do penguin parents protect their eggs?*
Beginning Help them swim. **Intermediate** They help penguins swim in the ocean. **Advanced** Penguins use their flippers to swim in the ocean so they can get food to eat. **Advanced High** Penguins' flippers help them swim in the ocean. Penguins look for and find food in the ocean.	**Beginning** Breaks it. **Intermediate** It uses its beak to break it. **Advanced** It uses its beak to break the shell of the egg. **Advanced High** An albatross chick uses its beak to peck at the shell of the egg until the shell breaks.	**Beginning** Stay close together. **Intermediate** Seals stay close together. Penguins fluff their feathers. **Advanced** Seals cuddle with one another. Penguin mothers fluff their babies' feathers. **Advanced High** The seals cuddle close together to stay warm. The penguin mothers preen their babies' feathers with their beaks to keep the babies warm.	**Beginning** It's too cold. **Intermediate** It is too cold for plants there. **Advanced** There is not enough sunlight and it is too cold for most plants to live in Antarctica. **Advanced High** Antarctica is too cold and windy and does not have the soil or the sunlight that most plants need to survive.	**Beginning** They keep them warm. **Intermediate** They keep them under their feathers so they are warm. **Advanced** They keep the eggs on top of their feet and under their feathers so they are warm. **Advanced High** Penguin parents protect their eggs by rolling them on top of their feet and keeping them under their feathers so they stay warm.

This Week's Materials

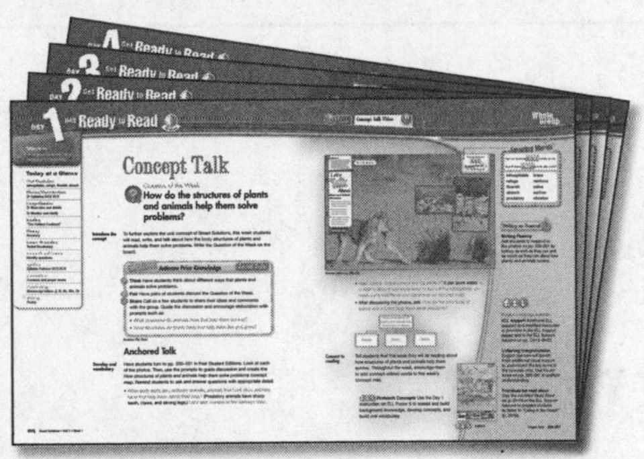
Teacher's Edition pages 200j–231q

See the support for English language learners throughout the lesson, including ELL strategies and scaffolded activities at points of use.

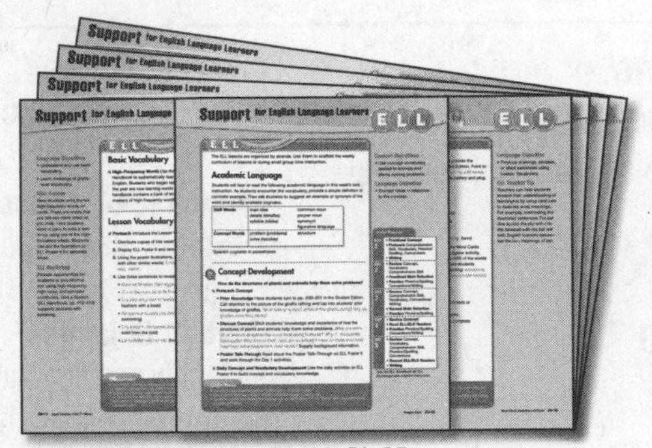
Teacher's Edition pages DI•16–DI•25

Differentiated Instruction for English language learners provides daily group activities that "frontload," or preteach, core instruction.

ELL Handbook pp. 59a–64

Find additional lesson materials that support the core lesson and the ELL instructional pages.

ELL Poster 6

ELL Reader 3.2.1

ELD Reader 3.2.1

Concept Literacy Reader

ELD, ELL Reader Teaching Guide

Concept Literacy Reader Teaching Guide

Technology

Online Teacher's Edition Use the digital version of the core Teacher's Edition for planning and instruction.

eReaders
This week's ELL and ELD Readers and Concept Literacy Reader are also available in digital format.

This Week's Content and Language Objectives by Strand

Concept Development/ Academic Language How do the structures of plants and animals help them solve problems?	**Content Objective** • Use concept vocabulary related to animals and plants solving problems. **Language Objective** • Express ideas in response to the concept.
Phonics and Spelling Syllables VC/V and V/CV	**Content Objective** • Identify spelling pattern VC/V and V/CV. **Language Objective** • Apply phonics and decoding skills to vocabulary used routinely in classroom materials.
Listening Comprehension Modified Read Aloud: "Desert Plants and Animals"	**Content Objectives** • Monitor and adjust oral comprehension. • Understand the general meaning and details of spoken language. **Language Objectives** • Discuss oral passages. • Use a graphic organizer to take notes.
Reading Comprehension Main Idea and Details	**Content Objectives** • Identify main idea and details. • Use main idea and details to aid comprehension. **Language Objectives** • Discuss main idea. • Retell details that support the main idea. • Draw and write the main idea and details. • Read grade-level text with accuracy.
Vocabulary Basic and Lesson Vocabulary	**Language Objectives** • Understand and use basic vocabulary. • Learn meanings of grade-level vocabulary. • Produce drawings, phrases, and short sentences to show understanding of Lesson Vocabulary.
Vocabulary Synonyms	**Content Objective** • Recognize synonyms. **Language Objective** • Discuss the meanings of synonyms.
Grammar and Conventions Common and Proper Nouns	**Content Objective** • Use common and proper nouns correctly. **Language Objective** • Write phrases and sentences with common and proper nouns.
Writing Writing Poems with Figurative Language	**Content Objective** • Identify figurative language. **Language Objectives** • Write a poem using figurative language. • Share feedback for editing and revising.

Word Cards for Vocabulary Activities

cuddles	**flippers**
frozen	**hatch**
pecks	**preen**
snuggles	

Teacher Note: Beginning Teach two to three words. **Intermediate** Teach three to four words. **Advanced** Teach four to five words. **Advanced High** Teach all words.

Name ___________________________

Picture It!

Main Idea and Details

Read the paragraph. **Look** at the pictures.

- Which sentence tells the main idea? **Write** that sentence in the *Main Idea* box.
- Which sentences tell the details? **Write** them in the *Detail* boxes.

Antarctic Animals

The animals that live in Antarctica are protected from the cold. Whales have a layer of fat to protect them. Fish have special blood that protects them from freezing in the water. Birds such as penguins have waterproof feathers. Some animals leave Antarctica during the coldest months, but many live there all year!

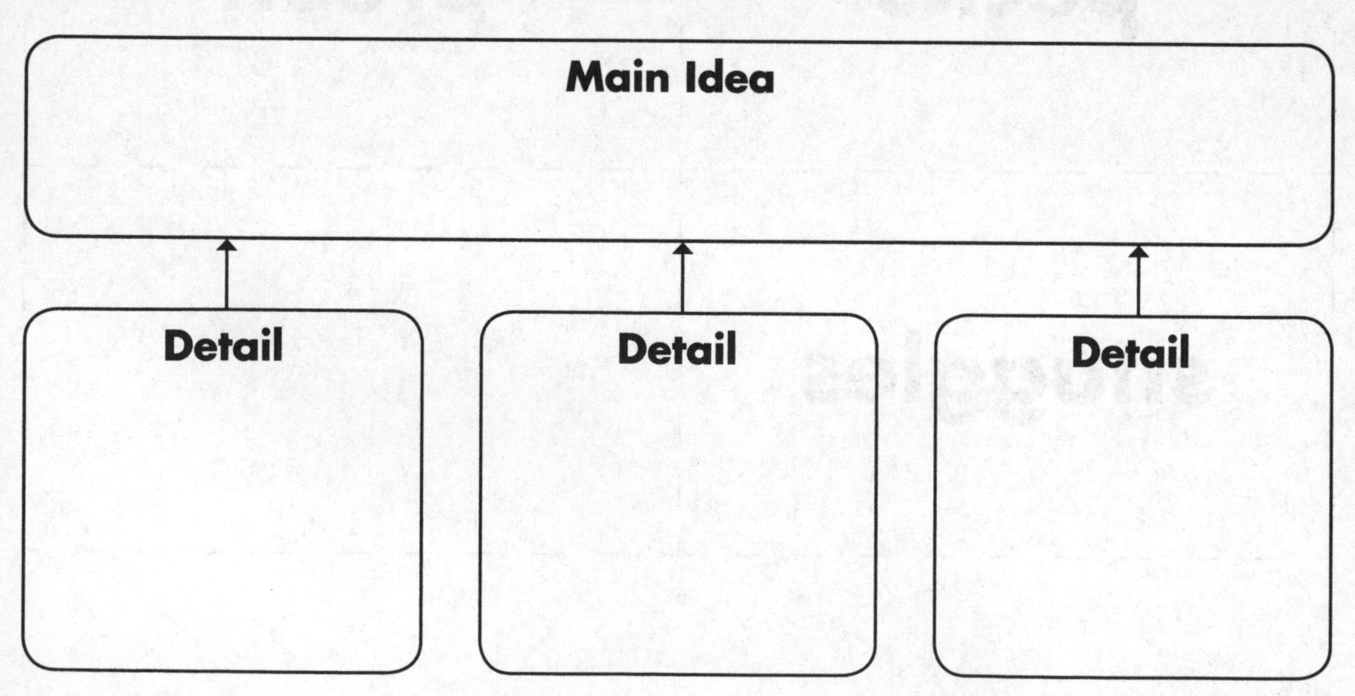

Main Idea and Details

Use this lesson to supplement or replace the skill lesson on page 204a of the Teacher's Edition. Display the Skill Points (at right) and share them with students.

Skill Points

- ✔ The most important idea in a paragraph is called the **main idea.**
- ✔ To find the main idea, ask: *What is this paragraph about?* Find out whether there is a sentence that tells the main idea.
- ✔ Other sentences in the paragraph tell about the main idea. They give **details** about the main idea.

Teach/Model

Beginning Display a photograph of the land in Antarctica. Ask: *What is this picture about? What is the main idea of this picture?* (Possible answer: This is a cold, snowy place.) *What details in the picture tell about the main idea?* (Possible answers: There is a lot of ice and snow. It looks cold.)

Intermediate Say: *Many kinds of penguins live in and near Antarctica. So do several kinds of seals. Some kinds of whales live in the ocean near Antarctica part of the year.* Work with students to decide what main idea the three details tell about. (Possible answer: Many kinds of penguins, seals, and whales live in or near Antarctica.)

Advanced Read aloud this paragraph: *Penguins are suited for swimming. They have flippers instead of wings. Their feathers help them float. Their shape helps them glide through the water.* Ask: *Which sentence tells the main idea?* (the first one) *Which sentences tell details?* (the second, third, and fourth sentences)

Advanced High Have students identify the main idea of a nonfiction selection they have read recently. Ask them to find details in the selection that support the main idea. Have them explain how these details support the main idea.

Then distribute copies of Picture It! page 60.

- Have students look at the pictures and describe what they see.
- Read the paragraph aloud. Ask: *What is this paragraph about?* (how Antarctic animals are protected from the cold)
- Review the Skill Points with students.
- Have students look at the pictures and words to identify the main idea and details.

Practice

Read aloud the directions on page 60. Reread the paragraph aloud, explaining the words *Antarctic/Antarctica* and *protect.* Have students refer to the pictures and the paragraph as they complete the graphic organizer.

Beginning Students can explain orally what they want to write and then dictate or write their answers for the graphic organizer. Provide help with English words and writing.

Intermediate Students can first orally identify the main idea and details and then write their answers in the boxes. Provide help with English words and writing.

Advanced Students can write their answers in the boxes and then check their sentences by quietly reading them aloud or comparing them with a partner's sentences.

Advanced High Students can write their answers in the boxes and then check their sentences by silently rereading the paragraph and making any necessary corrections.

Answers for page 60: *Main Idea:* Animals that live in Antarctica are protected from the cold. *Details:* Whales have a layer of fat. Fish have special blood that protects them from freezing. Birds such as penguins have waterproof feathers.

Multilingual Summaries

English

Penguin Chick

A female emperor penguin lays one egg each year. The male penguin holds the egg on his feet. The egg stays warm under his feathers. The cold temperature would freeze the egg if he left it.

The mother leaves to find food for the chick. She travels to the edge of the ice. She dives into the sea for fish and other food. She is gone for two months. The father stays with the egg.

When the mother returns, the egg has hatched. She stays and feeds the chick. The father goes in search of food. When the chick is bigger, it stays with other chicks. His mother or father still feeds him. After five months, the young penguin catches his own food. In about five years, he will have his own egg to take care of.

Spanish

El pingüino bebé

Un pingüino emperador hembra pone un huevo cada año. El pingüino macho incuba el huevo entre sus patas. El huevo se queda caliente debajo de sus plumas. Si él lo abandona, el huevo se puede congelar porque la temperatura es muy fría.

La madre se va a buscar comida para su pichón. Viaja hasta el borde de un bloque de hielo. Se sumerge en el mar para buscar pescado y otros tipos de comida. Se va por dos meses. El padre se queda con el huevo.

Cuando la madre regresa, el pichón ha salido del cascarón. La madre se queda y lo alimenta. El padre se va a buscar comida. Cuando el pichón crece, se queda con los demás pichones. Su madre o su padre lo siguen alimentando. Después de cinco meses, el joven pingüino caza su propia comida. Alrededor de cinco años después, tendrá e incubará su propio huevo.

Multilingual Summaries

Chinese

小企鵝

企鵝媽媽每年只生一隻蛋，企鵝爸爸把蛋小心翼翼地放在腳掌上，並用厚厚的皮毛為它保暖。如果爸爸離開，寒冷的天氣就會把蛋凍壞。

企鵝媽媽負責外出尋找食物。她要走到冰層邊上，跳進海裏找魚和其他吃的。這一走就是兩個月，企鵝爸爸都一刻不離地保護著蛋。

企鵝媽媽回來時，蛋已經孵化為小企鵝。這次她要留下來餵養，讓企鵝爸爸出去找食物。小企鵝一天天長大，長大後便和其他小企鵝待在一起，爸爸媽媽輪流餵養他。五個月過後，小企鵝就要自己去找食物啦！再過五年，他也將有自己的小寶寶，也會細心地照顧他。

Vietnamese

Chim Cánh Cụt Con

Một con chim mái loại cánh cụt hoàng đế mỗi năm đẻ một trứng. Chim trống giữ trứng trên chân của mình. Trứng được giữ ấm dưới lớp lông của chim trống. Nhiệt độ lạnh có thể làm đông trứng nếu chim trống bỏ mặc quả trứng.

Chim mẹ đi tìm thức ăn cho chim con. Chim mẹ đi đến bờ tảng băng. Chim mẹ lặn vào nước để tìm cá và các thức ăn khác. Chim mẹ bỏ đi hai tháng. Chim cha ở lại với quả trứng.

Khi chim mẹ trở về, quả trứng đã nở. Chim mẹ ở lại và cho chim con ăn. Chim cha đi tìm thức ăn. Khi chim con lớn ra, nó ở với những chim con khác. Mẹ và cha của chú chim này vẫn còn cho chú ăn. Sau năm tháng, chú chim cánh cụt non trẻ bắt được thức ăn cho riêng mình. Trong vòng năm năm, chú sẽ có trứng của riêng mình để chăm sóc.

Multilingual Summaries

Korean

새끼 펭귄

황제 펭귄 암컷은 해마다 알을 하나씩 낳고 수컷 펭귄은 그 알을 자신의 발 위에 품는다. 알은 수컷 깃털 아래에서 따뜻하게 유지된다. 만약 수컷이 알을 내버려둔다면 알은 차가운 기온 때문에 얼어버릴 것이다.

어미 펭귄은 새끼에게 줄 먹이를 찾아 나서는데 얼음 가장자리 끝까지 가서 물고기와 다른 먹을 것을 찾아 바닷속으로 잠수한다. 어미 펭귄이 두 달을 떠나있는 동안 아빠 펭귄은 알과 함께 남아있다.

어미가 돌아오면 알은 부화해있다. 이제 어미는 남아서 새끼를 먹여 키우고 아빠 펭귄이 먹이를 구하러 나선다. 새끼는 좀 더 자라면 다른 새끼 펭귄들과 함께 지내게 된다. 그러나 엄마 펭귄과 아빠 펭귄이 여전히 새끼 펭귄에게 먹이를 준다. 5개월이 지나면 어린 펭귄은 스스로 먹이를 잡을 수 있게 된다. 그리고 약 5년 내에 스스로 보살필 자신의 알을 갖게 될 것이다.

Hmong

Tus Os Dej Mos

Fab tim huabtais tus pojniam os dej nteg ib lub qe txhua txhua xyoo. Tus txiv os dej muab lub qe puag ntawm nws txhais ko taw. Lub qe no nyob sov so sab hauv nws cov plaub. Lub ciaj ntuj no yuav ua rau lub qe khov yog nws tsis ua li no.

Leejniam mus nrhiav khoom noj rau nws tus os dej mos. Nws mus nrhiav txog tom npoo naj kheem. Nws dhia mus rau hauv hiavtxwv mus muab ntses thiab lwm yam khoom noj. Nws mus ntev li ob lub hlis. Leejtxiv nyob zov lub qe.

Thaum leejniam rov los txog, lub qe twb daug lawm. Nws nyob thiab pub mov rau tus ob dej mos no. Leejtxiv ho mus nrhiav khoom los noj. Thaum tus ob dej mos no hlob los, nws nrog lwm cov menyuam ob dej nyob. Nws niam thiab nws txiv tseem pub rau nws noj nws haus. Tom qab tsib lub hlis, tus os dej no mam li mus nrhiav khoom rau nws noj. Li tsib xyoos tom ntej ces nws mam li muaj nws ib lub qe los tu thiab saib xyuas.

Name ____________________________

- **Read** *Different Beaks, Different Jobs* again.
- **Look** at the picture.
- **Write** the main idea of the reading on the lines below.

____

____

Family Link

Ask family members to think of birds that use their beaks to get food. Share their answers with your class

Weekly Resources Guide for English Language Learner Support

For this week's content and language objectives, see p. 65e.

Instructional Strand	Day 1	Day 2
Concept Development/Academic Language	TEACHER'S EDITION • Academic Language, p. DI•41 • Concept Development, p. DI•41 • Anchored Talk, pp. 232j—232–233 • Preteach Academic Vocabulary, p. 237a • Concept Talk Video ELL HANDBOOK • Hear It, See It, Say It, Use It, pp. xxxvi–xxxvii • ELL Poster Talk, Concept Talk, p. 65c ELL POSTER 7 • Day 1 Activities	TEACHER'S EDITION • Academic Language, p. DI•41 • Concept Development, p. DI•41 • Anchored Talk, p. 238a • Concept Talk Video ELL HANDBOOK • ELL Poster Talk, Concept Talk, p. 65c • Concept Talk Video Routine, p. 477 ELL POSTER 7 • Day 2 Activities
Phonics and Spelling	TEACHER'S EDITION • Phonics and Spelling, p. DI•45 • Decodable Practice Reader 7A, pp. 235a–235b	TEACHER'S EDITION • Phonics and Spelling, p. DI•45
Listening Comprehension	TEACHER'S EDITION • Modified Read Aloud, p. DI•44 • Read Aloud, p. 233b • Concept Talk Video ELL HANDBOOK • Concept Talk Video Routine, p. 477	TEACHER'S EDITION • Modified Read Aloud, p. DI•44 • AudioText of *I Wanna Iguana* • Concept Talk Video ELL HANDBOOK • AudioText CD Routine, p. 477 • Problem and Solution, p. 490
Reading Comprehension	TEACHER'S EDITION • Preteach Compare and Contrast, p. DI•46	TEACHER'S EDITION • Reteach Compare and Contrast, p. DI•46 • Frontloading Reading, p. DI•47 ELL HANDBOOK • Picture It! Skill Instruction, pp. 66–66a • Multilingual Summaries, pp. 67–69
Vocabulary **Basic and Lesson Vocabulary** **Vocabulary Skill: Unfamiliar Words**	TEACHER'S EDITION • Basic Vocabulary, p. DI•42 • Preteach Lesson Vocabulary, p. DI•42 • Unfamiliar Words, p. DI•45 ELL HANDBOOK • Word Cards, p. 65 • ELL Vocabulary Routine, p. 471 ELL POSTER 7 • Day 1 Activities	TEACHER'S EDITION • Basic Vocabulary, p. DI•42 • Reteach Lesson Vocabulary, p. DI•43 • Unfamiliar Words, p. DI•45 ELL HANDBOOK • Word Cards, p. 65 • Multilingual Vocabulary List, p. 433 ELL POSTER 7 • Day 2 Activities
Grammar and Conventions	TEACHER'S EDITION • Preteach Singular and Plural Nouns, p. DI•49	TEACHER'S EDITION • Reteach Singular and Plural Nouns, p. DI•49
Writing	TEACHER'S EDITION • Writing with Vivid Verbs, p. DI•50 • Writing for Tests: Fairy Tale, pp. 237e–237f	TEACHER'S EDITION • Writing for Tests: Fairy Tale, pp. 247d–247e

Unit 2 Week 2 I Wanna Iguana

This symbol indicates leveled instruction to address language proficiency levels.

Day 3	Day 4	Day 5
TEACHER'S EDITION • Academic Language, p. DI•41 • Concept Development, p. DI•41 • Anchored Talk, p. 248a • Concept Talk Video ELL HANDBOOK • ELL Poster Talk, Concept Talk, p. 65c ELL POSTER 7 • Day 3 Activities	TEACHER'S EDITION • Academic Language, p. DI•41 • Concept Development, p. DI•41 • Anchored Talk, p. 260a • Concept Talk Video ELL HANDBOOK • ELL Poster Talk, Concept Talk, p. 65c ELL POSTER 7 • Day 4 Activities	TEACHER'S EDITION • Academic Language, p. DI•41 • Concept Development, p. DI•41 • Concept Talk Video ELL HANDBOOK • ELL Poster Talk, Concept Talk, p. 65c ELL POSTER 7 • Day 5 Activities
ELL HANDBOOK • Phonics Transition Lesson, pp. 235, 239	ELL HANDBOOK • Phonics Transition Lesson, pp. 235, 239	TEACHER'S EDITION • Phonics and Spelling, p. DI•45
TEACHER'S EDITION • AudioText of *I Wanna Iguana* • Concept Talk Video ELL HANDBOOK • AudioText CD Routine, p. 477	TEACHER'S EDITION • Concept Talk Video	TEACHER'S EDITION • Concept Talk Video
TEACHER'S EDITION • Sheltered Reading, p. DI•47 ELL HANDBOOK • Multilingual Summaries, pp. 67–69	TEACHER'S EDITION • ELL/ELD Reader Guided Reading, p. DI•48 ELL HANDBOOK • ELL Study Guide, p. 70	TEACHER'S EDITION • ELL/ELD Reader Guided Reading, p. DI•48 ELL HANDBOOK • ELL Study Guide, p. 70
ELL HANDBOOK • High-Frequency Words Activity Bank, p. 446 ELL POSTER 7 • Day 3 Activities	ELL HANDBOOK • High-Frequency Words Activity Bank, p. 446	TEACHER'S EDITION • Unfamiliar Words, p. 265h ELL HANDBOOK • High-Frequency Words Activity Bank, p. 446
TEACHER'S EDITION • Grammar Jammer ELL HANDBOOK • Grammar Transition Lesson, pp. 316, 322 • Grammar Jammer Routine, p. 478	TEACHER'S EDITION • Grammar Jammer ELL HANDBOOK • Grammar Transition Lesson, pp. 316, 322	TEACHER'S EDITION • Grammar Jammer ELL HANDBOOK • Grammar Transition Lesson, pp. 316, 322
TEACHER'S EDITION • Let's Write It!, p. 258–259 • Writing for Tests: Evaluation, pp. 259a–259b	TEACHER'S EDITION • Writing for Tests: Fairy Tale, p. 265d	TEACHER'S EDITION • Writing for Tests: Conventions, pp. 265p–265q

Poster Talk, Concept Talk

Question of the Week

How do you know if a solution is a good solution?

Poster 7

Throughout the week, use the ELL Poster to help students produce and comprehend language, understand the concept, and build English vocabulary. Use the Question of the Week and other questions to help students share ideas in pairs, small groups, or the large group. Sample questions are shown, with examples of possible responses by students.

Weekly Concept and Language Goals

- Explain what makes a good solution
- Tell about problems that need solutions
- Identify some good solutions

By the end of the lesson, students should be able to talk about and write one or more sentences about good solutions.

Daily Team Talk

Day 1	Day 2	Day 3	Day 4	Day 5
After Day 1 activities on Poster, ask questions such as *In the poster picture, what is one problem the girl might have with her new pet iguana?*	After Day 2 activity on Poster, ask questions such as *The girl in the poster picture is worried that her iguana might escape from its tank. What do you think is a good solution for this problem?*	After Day 3 activity on Poster, ask questions such as *The girl buys a bigger tank that has a wire top on it. Why is this a good solution to the problem with the iguana's home?*	After Day 4 activity on Poster, ask questions such as *In the story* I Wanna Iguana, *Alex wants a pet iguana, but his mom does not. What is his solution to this problem?*	After Day 5 activity on Poster, ask questions such as *What is a problem you had, and how did you solve it?*
Beginning It can get out. **Intermediate** It might get out of the box. **Advanced** The iguana might climb out of its tank. **Advanced High** The iguana might climb out of its tank and escape into the house.	**Beginning** Get a big box. **Intermediate** She can get a box that has a lot of room. **Advanced** She can get a bigger tank. Then the iguana will not get out. **Advanced High** The girl can get a bigger tank that has higher sides. Then the iguana will have more room and it cannot climb out.	**Beginning** It won't get out. **Intermediate** The top will keep it from getting out. **Advanced** The iguana will not be able to get out of its tank. The girl will not lose her pet. **Advanced High** The iguana will be safe in a bigger tank with a top because it cannot escape. The girl will be happy because she will not lose her pet.	**Beginning** He writes letters. **Intermediate** He writes his mom letters that tell why he wants a pet. **Advanced** Alex writes letters to his mom explaining why he should get an iguana. **Advanced High** Alex writes letters to his mom explaining how much he wants a pet iguana. He also tells her that he will take good care of it.	**Beginning** My bike broke. My dad can fix it. **Intermediate** My bike broke. I can't fix it myself. I asked my dad. **Advanced** When my bike broke, I did not know how to fix it. I had to find help. **Advanced High** My bike broke while I was riding it. I did not know how to fix it myself, so I asked my dad for help.

This Week's Materials

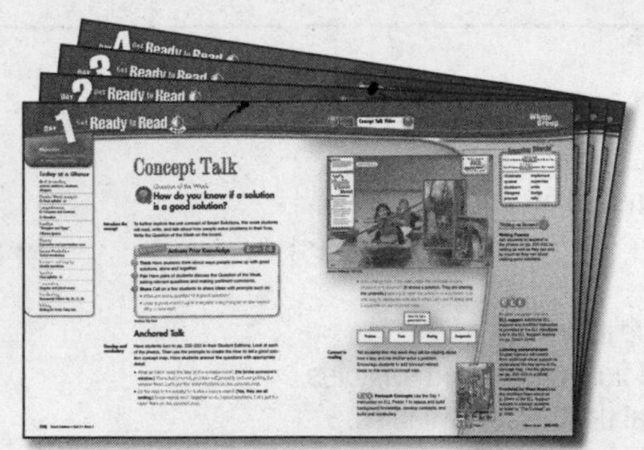

Teacher's Edition pages 232j–265q

See the support for English language learners throughout the lesson, including ELL strategies and scaffolded activities at points of use.

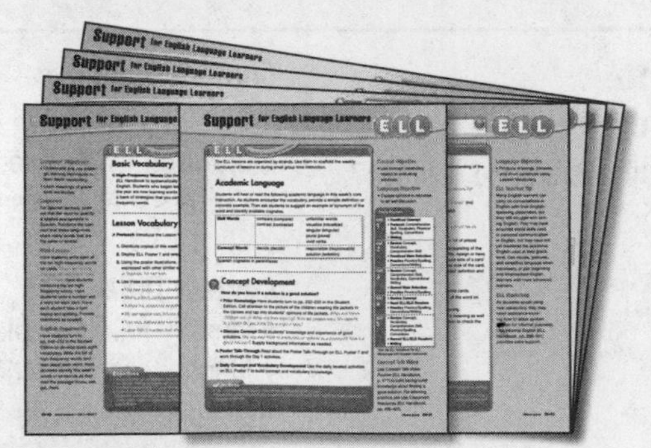

Teacher's Edition pages DI•41–DI•50

Differentiated Instruction for English language learners provides daily group activities that "frontload," or preteach, core instruction.

ELL Handbook pp. 65a–70

Find additional lesson materials that support the core lesson and the ELL instructional pages.

Do we have these?
Can we get them?

Concept Literacy Reader

ELD, ELL Reader Teaching Guide

Concept Literacy Reader Teaching Guide

Technology

Online Teacher's Edition Use the digital version of the core Teacher's Edition for planning and instruction.

eReaders
This week's ELL and ELD Readers and Concept Literacy Reader are also available in digital format.

This Week's Content and Language Objectives by Strand

Concept Development/ Academic Language How do you know if a solution is a good solution?	**Content Objective** • Use concept vocabulary related to evaluating solutions. **Language Objective** • Express ideas in response to art and discussion.
Phonics and Spelling Final Syllable *-le*	**Content Objectives** • Identify final syllable *–le* in words. • Identify and pronounce final unstressed syllables. • Decode words with final unstressed syllables. **Language Objective** • Correctly spell words with final syllable *-le.*
Listening Comprehension Modified Read Aloud: "The Best Name"	**Content Objective** • Monitor and adjust oral comprehension. **Language Objectives** • Discuss oral passages. • Use a graphic organizer to take notes.
Reading Comprehension Compare and Contrast	**Content Objectives** • Compare and contrast to aid comprehension. • Distinguish between formal and informal language. **Language Objectives** • Compare and contrast facts in a reading. • Adapt spoken language for formal purposes. • Use punctuation cues to read grade-level text with expression.
Vocabulary Basic and Lesson Vocabulary	**Language Objectives** • Understand and use basic vocabulary. • Learn meanings of grade-level vocabulary. • Produce drawings, phrases, and short sentences to show understanding of Lesson Vocabulary.
Vocabulary Unfamiliar Words	**Language Objective** • Apply phonics and decoding skills to vocabulary.
Grammar and Conventions Singular and Plural Nouns	**Content Objective** • Correctly form and use singular and plural nouns. **Language Objectives** • Speak using the pattern of singular and plural nouns. • Write phrases and sentences with singular and plural nouns.
Writing Writing with Vivid Verbs	**Content Objective** • Identify vivid verbs in a text. **Language Objectives** • Narrate and write a fairy tale using descriptive, vivid verbs. • Share feedback for editing and revising.

Word Cards for Vocabulary Activities

adorable	**compassionate**
exactly	**iguana**
mature	**mention**
trophies	

Teacher Note: Beginning Teach two to three words. **Intermediate** Teach three to four words. **Advanced** Teach four to five words. **Advanced High** Teach all words.

Name ______________________

Read Together

Picture It!
Compare and Contrast

Look at the picture. **Read** the paragraph.

- **Compare** Shelby to his mother. **Complete** the diagram.
- **Write** what is unique about Shelby on the left side.
- **Write** what is unique about his mother on the right side.
- **Write** what is the same about Shelby and his mother in the middle section.

Helping Mother

Shelby would like to help his mother with chores.

"You can help me cook dinner," says his mother.

They make macaroni and cheese. Shelby's mother teaches him to follow instructions. He also learns to be careful near the stove. Best of all, he helps his mother!

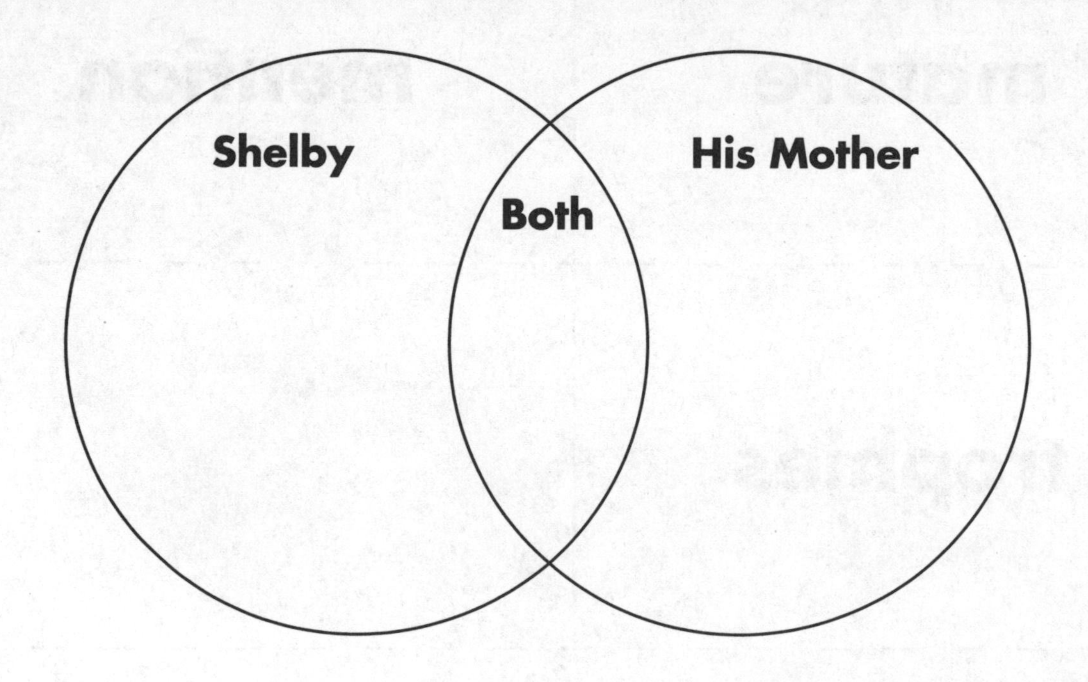

Picture It!

Compare and Contrast

Use this lesson to supplement or replace the skill lesson on page 236a of the Teacher's Edition. Display the Skill Points (at right) and share them with students.

> **Skill Points**
> ✔ When we **compare,** we look for the ways things are alike.
> ✔ When we **contrast,** we look for the ways things are different.

Teach/Model

Beginning Display an apple and a banana. Ask: *How are these alike?* (Possible answers: They are fruits. They are good for us.) *How are these different?* (Possible answers: One is red; one is yellow. One is round; one is long.) *When we tell how things are alike, we compare. When we tell how things are different, we contrast.*

Intermediate Draw a Venn diagram. Label the circles *Apple* and *Banana* and the intersection *Both.* Have students compare the apple and banana. Write their ideas under *Both.* Have students contrast them. Write their ideas under *Apple* or *Banana.* Show students how to use the diagram to state similarities and differences.

Advanced Have students name foods they eat for breakfast only, dinner only, or both meals. Write their responses. Draw a Venn diagram with appropriate labels. Have students tell where to write each food in the diagram. They can use it to orally compare and contrast the foods eaten at the two meals.

Advanced High Ask students to compare and contrast foods served at home with foods served at school. They can write and illustrate sentences or draw and fill in a Venn diagram to tell which foods are the same and which are different.

Then distribute copies of Picture It! page 66.

- Have students look at the picture and tell what is happening.
- Read the story aloud. Ask: *What happens in this story?* Have students tell how Shelby and his mother are alike and different.
- Review the Skill Points with students.
- Have students look at the pictures and words to compare and contrast the characters.

Practice

Read aloud the directions on page 66. Explain how to fill in the Venn diagram. Reread the story or have volunteers reread it aloud. Have students look at the picture and the story as they fill in the Venn diagram.

Beginning Students can point to each part of the diagram and say what they want to write there before filling in the diagram. Provide help with English words, filling in the diagram correctly, and writing.

Intermediate Students can first say what they want to write in the three parts of the diagram and then write their answers. Provide help with English words and writing.

Advanced Students can fill in the diagram and then check their answers by quietly rereading the story and marking the characters' similarities and differences.

Advanced High Students can fill in the diagram and then orally compare and contrast Shelby and his mother using information from the text and complete sentences.

Answers for page 66: *Both:* make macaroni and cheese, do chores, helpful; *Shelby:* child, boy, learns; *His Mother:* adult, woman, teaches

Multilingual Summaries

English

I Wanna Iguana

Alex's friend Mikey is moving. Alex wants Mikey's iguana when Mikey moves. Alex tries to tell his mom that the iguana will be a good pet. Alex says the iguana is quiet, cute, and a good friend. Alex's mom is not sure.

Alex's mom asks him how he will take care of the iguana. Alex says he would feed him every day. He also says he will clean his cage. Alex's mom says he can take care of the iguana for a week. Then she will decide if he can keep him.

Spanish

Quiero la iguana

Mikey, el amigo de Alex, se está cambiando de casa. Alex quiere la iguana de Mikey. Alex le dice a su mamá que la iguana será una buena mascota. Alex le dice que la iguana es tranquila, graciosa y una buena amiga. La mamá de Alex no está segura.

La mamá le pregunta cómo va a cuidar a la iguana. Alex dice que la alimentará todos los días. También dice que mantendrá limpia su jaula. La mamá dice que puede quedarse con la iguana por una semana. Después decidirá si puede conservarla.

Multilingual Summaries

Chinese

我想要一条鬣蜥

亚历克斯的朋友米奇快搬家了，当米奇搬家的时候，亚历克斯想要他的鬣蜥。亚历克斯跟妈妈说鬣蜥是一种很好的宠物，很内向、很可爱，是一个好朋友。妈妈不大相信他的话。

妈妈问亚历克斯怎么照顾鬣蜥，亚历克斯说他会每天喂养它，也会每天洗刷它的笼子。妈妈请他先照顾鬣蜥一个星期，然后她才决定他能不能有这个宠物。

Vietnamese

Tôi muốn con cự đà.

Mikey, bạn của Alex đang dọn nhà. Alex muốn con cự đà của Mikey khi Mikey dọn đi. Alex cố nói với mẹ rằng cự đà sẽ là con thú cưng tốt. Alex cho biết con cự đà yên lăng, xinh xắn và là một bạn tốt. Mẹ của Alex không tin.

Mẹ hỏi Alex sẽ chăm sóc con cự đà như thế nào. Alex nói nó sẽ cho cự đà ăn mỗi ngày. Nó cũng nói sẽ chùi rửa chuồng thú. Mẹ Alex nói nó có thể chăm sóc con cự đà trong một tuần. Sau đó mẹ sẽ quyết định xem nó có thể giữ lại con vật không.

Multilingual Summaries

Korean

이구아나 갖고 싶어요

알렉스의 친구 마이키는 이사를 갑니다. 알렉스는 마이키가 이사를 가면 마이키의 이구아나를 갖고 싶어합니다. 알렉스는 엄마에게 이구아나는 좋은 애완동물이 될 거라고 말합니다. 이구아나는 조용하고, 귀엽고, 좋은 친구라고 알렉스는 말합니다. 엄마는 확신이 서지 않습니다.

엄마는 알렉스가 어떻게 이구아나를 돌볼 건지 물어봅니다. 알렉스는 매일 먹이를 주겠다고 말합니다. 또 우리도 깨끗하게 치우겠다고 합니다. 엄마는 알렉스에에게 일주일동안 이구아나를 키워보라고 말합니다. 그리고 나서 알렉스가 계속 이구아나를 키울 수 있을 지 결정하겠다고 합니다.

Hmong

Kuv Xav Tau Tus Nab Qa Dev

Alex tus phoojywg Mikey yuav tsiv tsev. Alex xav tau Mickey tus nab qa dev thaus Mickey tsiv. Alex taij nwg niam tias tus nab qa dev yuav yog ib tus tsiaj zoo tu. Alex hais tias tus nab qa dev nyob ntsiag to, zoo nkauj, thiab yog ib tus phoojywg zoo. Alex niam ntseeg tsi tag.

Alex niam nus nwg tias nwg yuav tu tus nab qa dev li cas. Alex teb tias nwg mam muab mov rau nwg noj txhua txhia nub. Nwg hais ntxiv tias nwg mam ntxuav nwg lub nkuaj. Alex niam hais tsuas pub ib astihiv rau nwg tu tus nab qa dev. Tes nwg mam txiav txim siab saib puas cia Alex yuav.

Name ______________________

Mama's Birthday Garden

- **Read** *Mamá's Birthday Garden* again.
- **Find** details that support the main idea.
- **Write** them in the *Detail* boxes in the chart.

Main Idea:
Paula plants a garden for Mamá's birthday.

Detail (pages 2–3)	Detail (pages 4–5)	Detail (pages 6–8)
______	______	______

Family Link

Together with your family, draw your ideal flower garden. What flowers would it have? What shape would it be? How big would it be?

Weekly Resources Guide for English Language Learner Support

For this week's content and language objectives, see p. 71e.

Instructional Strand	Day 1	Day 2
Concept Development/Academic Language	TEACHER'S EDITION • Academic Language, p. DI•66 • Concept Development, p. DI•66 • Anchored Talk, pp. 266j—266–267 • Preteach Academic Vocabulary, p. 271a • Concept Talk Video ELL HANDBOOK • Hear It, See It, Say It, Use It, pp. xxxvi–xxxvii • ELL Poster Talk, Concept Talk, p. 71c ELL POSTER 8 • Day 1 Activities	TEACHER'S EDITION • Academic Language, p. DI•66 • Concept Development, p. DI•66 • Anchored Talk, p. 272a • Concept Talk Video ELL HANDBOOK • ELL Poster Talk, Concept Talk, p. 71c • Concept Talk Video Routine, p. 477 ELL POSTER 8 • Day 2 Activities
Phonics and Spelling	TEACHER'S EDITION • Phonics and Spelling, p. DI•70 • Decodable Practice Reader 8A, pp. 269a–269b	TEACHER'S EDITION • Phonics and Spelling, p. DI•70
Listening Comprehension	TEACHER'S EDITION • Modified Read Aloud, p. DI•69 • Read Aloud, p. 267b • Concept Talk Video ELL HANDBOOK • Concept Talk Video Routine, p. 477	TEACHER'S EDITION • Modified Read Aloud, p. DI•69 • AudioText of *Prudy's Problem and How She Solved It* • Concept Talk Video ELL HANDBOOK • AudioText CD Routine, p. 477 • Problem and Solution, p. 490
Reading Comprehension	TEACHER'S EDITION • Preteach Draw Conclusions, p. DI•71	TEACHER'S EDITION • Reteach Draw Conclusions, p. DI•71 • Frontloading Reading, p. DI•72 ELL HANDBOOK • Picture It! Skill Instruction, pp. 72–72a • Multilingual Summaries, pp. 73–75
Vocabulary **Basic and Lesson Vocabulary** **Vocabulary Skill: Compound Words**	TEACHER'S EDITION • Basic Vocabulary, p. DI•67 • Preteach Lesson Vocabulary, p. DI•67 • Compound Words, p. DI•70 ELL HANDBOOK • Word Cards, p. 71 • ELL Vocabulary Routine, p. 471 ELL POSTER 8 • Day 1 Activities	TEACHER'S EDITION • Basic Vocabulary, p. DI•67 • Reteach Lesson Vocabulary, p. DI•68 • Compound Words, p. DI•70 ELL HANDBOOK • Word Cards, p. 71 • Multilingual Vocabulary List, p. 434 ELL POSTER 8 • Day 2 Activities
Grammar and Conventions	TEACHER'S EDITION • Preteach Irregular Plural Nouns, p. DI•74	TEACHER'S EDITION • Teach Irregular Plural Nouns, p. DI•74
Writing	TEACHER'S EDITION • Writing with a Clear Purpose, p. DI•75 • Introduce Advertisement, pp. 271e–271f	TEACHER'S EDITION • Writing Trait: Focus/Ideas, pp. 281d–281e

Unit 2 Week 3 Prudy's Problem and How She Solved It

This symbol indicates leveled instruction to address language proficiency levels.

Day 3	Day 4	Day 5
TEACHER'S EDITION • Academic Language, p. DI•66 • Concept Development, p. DI•66 • Anchored Talk, p. 282a • Concept Talk Video ELL HANDBOOK • ELL Poster Talk, Concept Talk, p. 71c ELL POSTER 8 • Day 3 Activities	TEACHER'S EDITION • Academic Language, p. DI•66 • Concept Development, p. DI•66 • Anchored Talk, p. 294a • Concept Talk Video ELL HANDBOOK • ELL Poster Talk, Concept Talk, p. 71c ELL POSTER 8 • Day 4 Activities	TEACHER'S EDITION • Academic Language, p. DI•66 • Concept Development, p. DI•66 • Concept Talk Video ELL HANDBOOK • ELL Poster Talk, Concept Talk, p. 71c ELL POSTER 8 • Day 5 Activities
ELL HANDBOOK • Phonics Transition Lesson, pp. 278, 281	ELL HANDBOOK • Phonics Transition Lesson, pp. 278, 281	TEACHER'S EDITION • Phonics and Spelling, p. DI•70
TEACHER'S EDITION • AudioText of *Prudy's Problem and How She Solved It* • Concept Talk Video ELL HANDBOOK • AudioText CD Routine, p. 477	TEACHER'S EDITION • Concept Talk Video	TEACHER'S EDITION • Concept Talk Video
TEACHER'S EDITION • Sheltered Reading, p. DI•72 ELL HANDBOOK • Multilingual Summaries, pp. 73–75	TEACHER'S EDITION • ELL/ELD Reader Guided Reading, p. DI•73 ELL HANDBOOK • ELL Study Guide, p. 76	TEACHER'S EDITION • ELL/ELD Reader Guided Reading, p. DI•73 ELL HANDBOOK • ELL Study Guide, p. 76
ELL HANDBOOK • High-Frequency Words Activity Bank, p. 446 ELL POSTER 8 • Day 3 Activities	ELL HANDBOOK • High-Frequency Words Activity Bank, p. 446	TEACHER'S EDITION • Compound Words, p. 299h ELL HANDBOOK • High-Frequency Words Activity Bank, p. 446
TEACHER'S EDITION • Grammar Jammer ELL HANDBOOK • Grammar Transition Lesson, pp. 316, 322 • Grammar Jammer Routine, p. 478	TEACHER'S EDITION • Grammar Jammer ELL HANDBOOK • Grammar Transition Lesson, pp. 316, 322	TEACHER'S EDITION • Grammar Jammer ELL HANDBOOK • Grammar Transition Lesson, pp. 316, 322
TEACHER'S EDITION • Let's Write It!, p. 292–293 • Writer's Craft: Clear Purpose, pp. 293a–293b	TEACHER'S EDITION • Revising Strategy, pp. 299d–299e	TEACHER'S EDITION • Irregular Plural Nouns, pp. 299p–299q

Poster Talk, Concept Talk

Question of the Week

When is it time to find a solution?

Poster 8

Throughout the week, use the ELL Poster to help students produce and comprehend language, understand the concept, and build English vocabulary. Use the Question of the Week and other questions to help students share ideas in pairs, small groups, or the large group. Sample questions are shown, with examples of possible responses by students.

Weekly Concept and Language Goals

- Describe why finding solutions is important
- Tell about when to find solutions
- Explain ways to find solutions

By the end of the lesson, students should be able to talk about and write one or more sentences about finding solutions.

Daily Team Talk

Day 1	Day 2	Day 3	Day 4	Day 5
After Day 1 activities on Poster, ask questions such as *The librarian in the poster picture knows that some bookshelves are bending. When is a good time for her to find a solution to this problem?*	After Day 2 activity on Poster, ask questions such as *Why is it important to find a solution to the bending bookshelf problem?*	After Day 3 activity on Poster, ask questions such as *All the shelves in the library are filled. New books are coming. When is a good time for the librarian to find a solution to this problem?*	After Day 4 activity on Poster, ask questions such as *In the story* Prudy's Problem and How She Solved It, *what makes Prudy finally decide to find a solution to her problem?*	After Day 5 activity on Poster, ask questions such as *If you have a problem that needs to be solved, what is one way you can find a solution?*
Beginning Now. **Intermediate** Do something before they break. **Advanced** The librarian should find a solution before the shelves break. **Advanced High** The librarian should find a solution to the problem before the bookshelves break and the books fall.	**Beginning** It is a mess. **Intermediate** Books will fall on the floor. **Advanced** People might get hurt when the shelves break. **Advanced High** It is important to find a solution to the problem because people might get hurt when the bookshelves break and the books fall.	**Beginning** Before they get there. **Intermediate** Find a solution before the new books get there. **Advanced** She needs to find a solution before the new books arrive. **Advanced High** The librarian should find a solution to the problem before the new books arrive at the library.	**Beginning** It explodes. **Intermediate** She has so much stuff her room explodes. **Advanced** Prudy has so much stuff in her room that it explodes. **Advanced High** Prudy has collected so many things that her room cannot hold them all and it explodes.	**Beginning** See what others do. **Intermediate** I can see how others solve problems. **Advanced** I can see what solutions other people found for a problem like mine. **Advanced High** I can find out how other people have solved a problem like mine. Then I can decide whether one of those solutions will work for my problem.

This Week's Materials

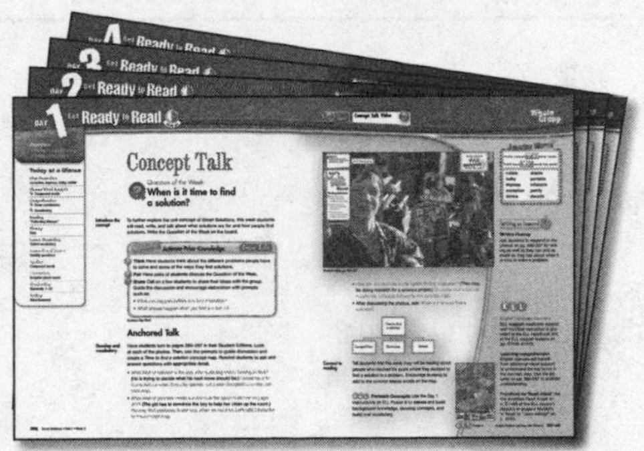
Teacher's Edition pages 266j–299q

See the support for English language learners throughout the lesson, including ELL strategies and scaffolded activities at points of use.

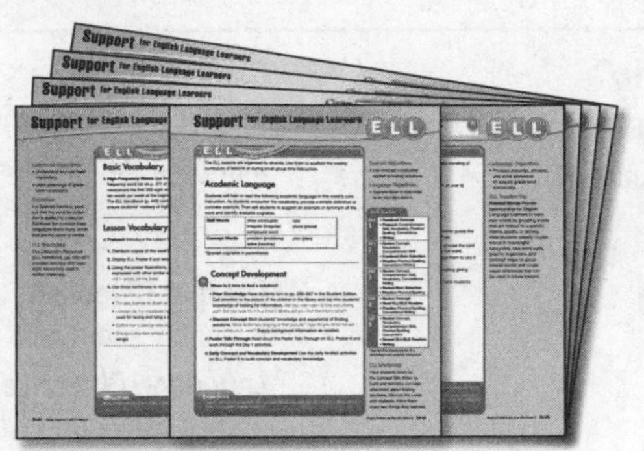
Teacher's Edition pages DI•66–DI•75

Differentiated Instruction for English language learners provides daily group activities that "frontload," or preteach, core instruction.

ELL Handbook pp. 71a–76

Find additional lesson materials that support the core lesson and the ELL instructional pages.

ELL Poster 8

ELL Reader 3.2.3

ELD Reader 3.2.3

Concept Literacy Reader

ELD, ELL Reader Teaching Guide

Concept Literacy Reader Teaching Guide

Technology

Online Teacher's Edition Use the digital version of the core Teacher's Edition for planning and instruction.

eReaders
This week's ELL and ELD Readers and Concept Literacy Reader are also available in digital format.

This Week's Content and Language Objectives by Strand

Concept Development/ Academic Language When is it time to find a solution?	**Content Objective** • Use concept vocabulary related to finding solutions. **Language Objective** • Express ideas in response to art and discussion.
Phonics and Spelling Compound Words	**Content Objective** • Identify and define words in compound words. **Language Objective** • Spell compound words.
Listening Comprehension Modified Read Aloud: "The First Blue Jeans"	**Content Objective** • Monitor and adjust oral comprehension. **Language Objectives** • Discuss oral passages. • Use a graphic organizer to take notes.
Reading Comprehension Draw Conclusions	**Content Objectives** • Use selection details and prior knowledge to draw conclusions. • Draw conclusions to aid comprehension. **Language Objectives** • Discuss evidence for drawing conclusions. • Retell facts that support a conclusion. • Draw conclusions and support answers. • Read grade-level text at the appropriate rate.
Vocabulary Basic and Lesson Vocabulary	**Language Objectives** • Understand and use basic vocabulary. • Learn meanings of grade-level vocabulary. • Produce drawings, phrases, and short sentences to show understanding of Lesson Vocabulary.
Vocabulary Compound Words	**Content Objective** • Learn new language structures heard during classroom instruction and interaction. **Language Objective** • Apply phonics and decoding skills to vocabulary.
Grammar and Conventions Irregular Plural Nouns	**Content Objectives** • Decode and use irregular plural nouns. • Correctly form irregular plural nouns. **Language Objectives** • Speak using irregular and regular plural nouns. • Write phrases and sentences with irregular plural nouns.
Writing Writing with a Clear Purpose	**Content Objective** • Identify a clear purpose in a text. **Language Objectives** • Write an advertisement with a clear purpose. • Share feedback for editing and revising.

Word Cards for Vocabulary Activities

butterflies	**collection**
enormous	**scattered**
shoelaces	**strain**

Teacher Note: Beginning Teach two to three words. **Intermediate** Teach three to four words. **Advanced** Teach four to five words. **Advanced High** Teach all words.

Name ______________________________

Look at the picture. **Read** the paragraph.

- **Notice** the details as you read the paragraph.

My Hobby

I am a stamp collector. I buy stamps at the post office. I also cut stamps off of letters. My grandmother sends me stamps too. Stamps help me learn about history. I learn about people and places. I also learn to be organized. Collecting stamps is fun!

Circle the letter of the correct answer for each question.

1. What do stamps help you do?
a. read **b.** shop **c.** learn

2. Where would you get a stamp?
a. post office **b.** library **c.** pet shop

3. What conclusion can you draw about stamps?
a. They cost a lot of money.
b. They come in many sizes.
c. They are used to mail letters.

Draw Conclusions

Use this lesson to supplement or replace the skill lesson on page 270a of the Teacher's Edition. Display the Skill Points (at right) and share them with students.

Teach/Model

Beginning Display an addressed, stamped envelope. Say: *This is a letter I wrote to my friend. What will I do with the letter? How do you know?* Guide students to draw the conclusion that you will put the letter in a mailbox or take it to a post office because a person mails a letter.

Intermediate Say and pantomime: *I put my letter into an envelope. I seal the envelope. I put a stamp on the envelope. What conclusion can you make about what I will do now?* (You will mail a letter.) *What helped you make that conclusion?* (To mail a letter, you must put a stamp on the envelope.)

Advanced Say: *I have many stamps from around the world. I have many pen pals around the world too. I write letters to them, and they write letters to me.* Ask students to tell a conclusion they can draw about your stamp collection. (You got your stamps from the letters your pen pals wrote to you.)

Advanced High Say: *I go to the post office. I mail a package. It is my aunt's birthday in one week. I hope the package is not late!* Ask: *What conclusion can you draw about the package?* (The package contains your aunt's birthday gift.) Have students write their conclusion.

Skill Points

- ✔ After you think about facts and details, you can figure something out, or **draw a conclusion.**
- ✔ Use facts and details, plus what you already know, to draw conclusions about why things happen or are done a certain way.

Then distribute copies of Picture It! page 72.

- Have students look at the picture and tell what they know about stamps.
- Read the paragraph aloud. Ask: *What can you figure out about where the narrator gets stamps?*
- Review the Skill Points with students.
- Have students look at the picture and words to identify facts and details. Help them draw a conclusion about stamp collecting (it is educational, stamps are used to mail letters).

Practice

Read aloud the directions on page 72. Reread the paragraph aloud, explaining any unfamiliar words or concepts. Have students look at the picture and the paragraph as they answer the questions.

Beginning Students can answer the questions orally and then mark their answers. Provide help with marking the correct choices.

Intermediate Students can first orally answer the questions and then mark their answers on the page.

Advanced Students can mark their answers and then check them by comparing them with a partner's answers.

Advanced High Students can mark their answers and then explain how they drew the conclusion in the last question.

Answers for page 72: 1. c; 2. a; 3. c

Multilingual Summaries

English

Prudy's Problem and How She Solved It

Prudy liked to collect things. She never threw anything away. She had many interesting collections. She had so many things that they covered the lawn, the living room, and her bedroom.

Prudy's parents told her that she had a problem. But Prudy always said there was no problem.

One day, Prudy wanted to add a gum wrapper to her collection. She tried to fit it into her room. But her room was so full that it exploded! Things flew everywhere.

Prudy saw that she did have a problem. She went to see collections in museums. Then she built a museum for all her collections.

Spanish

El problema de Prudy y cómo lo solucionó

A Prudy le gustaba coleccionar cosas. Nunca tiraba nada. Tenía muchas colecciones interesantes. Tenía tantas cosas que llenaban el césped, la sala y su habitación.

Los padres de Prudy le dijeron que ella tenía un problema. Pero Prudy decía que no había ningún problema.

Un día, Prudy quiso agregar una envoltura de chicle a su colección. Trató de acomodarla en la habitación. ¡Pero la habitación estaba tan llena que explotó! Las cosas volaron por todas partes.

Prudy comprendió que tenía un problema. Fue a ver colecciones a los museos. Luego, construyó un museo para todas sus colecciones.

Multilingual Summaries

Chinese

普魯迪的難題與解決辦法

普魯迪喜歡收藏東西，任何東西都不會扔掉。她有許多有趣的收藏品。可是東西越來越多，草坪、客廳和她的房間都堆滿了。

爸爸說這是一個大問題，可普魯迪說這一點也不成問題。

有一天，普魯迪要收藏一個漂亮的口香糖包裝盒。想放進房間裏，卻怎麼都塞不下了。用力一擠，擠破啦，裏面的東西撒得到處都是。

普魯迪終於知道遇到了大難題，於是特意去參觀博物館的收藏，回來後為她的收藏品建了一個博物館。

Vietnamese

Vấn Đề của Prudy và Cách Cô Bé Giải Quyết

Prudy thích thu thập đồ vật. Cô bé không bao giờ bỏ đi vật gì cả. Cô có nhiều bộ sưu tập thú vị. Cô có quá nhiều đồ vật đến mức chúng phủ đầy sân cỏ, phòng khách, và phòng ngủ của cô.

Ba mẹ của Prudy bảo rằng cô ấy có vấn đề. Nhưng Prudy luôn luôn nói rằng không có vấn đề gì.

Ngày nọ, Prudy muốn để thêm một miếng giấy bao kẹo cao su vào bộ sưu tập của cô. Cô cố nhét nó vào phòng của mình. Nhưng phòng của cô đầy đến nỗi nó nổ tung! Đồ vật bay đi khắp nơi.

Prudy thấy là mình thật sự có vấn đề. Cô đi xem các bộ sưu tập ở những viện bảo tàng. Rồi cô xây một bảo tàng cho tất cả các bộ sưu tập của mình.

Korean

프루디의 문제와 해결 방법

프루디는 수집하는 일을 좋아하여 무언가를 결코 버리는 법이 없었다. 그녀는 다수의 흥미로운 수집품들을 갖고 있었는데 그것이 너무도 많아서 잔디밭과 거실 그리고 그녀의 방을 뒤덮었다.

프루디의 부모님은 그녀에게 문제가 있다고 얘기했지만 프루디는 항상 아무 문제가 없다고 말했다.

어느 날 프루디는 자신의 수집품에 껌 종이를 포함시키고 싶었다. 그녀는 자신의 방에 그걸 끼워 넣으려고 했지만 방이 가득 차 있어서 터져버리고 말았다! 그리곤 물건들이 사방으로 날아갔다.

프루디는 자신에게 문제가 있음을 알고는 박물관들로 수집품들을 보러 갔다. 그리고 그녀는 자신의 모든 수집품들을 전시할 박물관을 세웠다.

Hmong

Prudy Cov Teebmeem thiab Nws Ho Kho Li Cas

Prudy nyiam sau ntau yam khoom los uake. Nws tsis kam muab ib yam dabtsi twg povtseg li. Cov khoom nws sau kuj muaj ntau yam ntxiv siab thiab. Cov khoom nws sau ntau yeej heev twb vov tag lub vaj, lub hoob nyob, thiab nws hoob txaj pw.

Prudy niam thiab txiv nkawd hais tias nws muaj teebmeem. Tiamsis Prudy yeej ib txwm hais tias nws yeej tsis muaj teebmeem.

Muaj ib hnub, Prudy xav sau ib tug ntawv qhwv khaub noom yaj. Tiamsis nws lub hoob twb pub nkaus lawm thiaj tsis yoj qhov khoom no. Ua rau nws hoob txaj tawg kiag. Txhua yam txhua tsav dhia thoob plaws txhua qhov txhia chaw.

Prudy mam li pom tias nws muaj teebmeem. Nws thiaj li mus xyuas lub tsev uas sau cov khoom no. Ces nws thiaj txua ib lub tsev rau cov khoom uas nws sau.

Name ______________________________

- **Read** *Jack's Library* again.
- **Find** details that support the main idea.
- **Write** them in the *Detail* boxes in the chart.

Main Idea:
Jack organizes his books into a library.

Detail (pages 2–4)	**Detail** (pages 5–6)	**Detail** (pages 7–8)

Family Link

Ask family members what kinds of books they would include in a library.

Weekly Resources Guide for English Language Learner Support

For this week's content and language objectives, see p. 77e.

Instructional Strand	Day 1	Day 2
Concept Development/Academic Language	TEACHER'S EDITION • Academic Language, p. DI•91 • Concept Development, p. DI•91 • Anchored Talk, pp. 300j—300–301 • Preteach Academic Vocabulary, p. 305a • Concept Talk Video ELL HANDBOOK • Hear It, See It, Say It, Use It, pp. xxxvi–xxxvii • ELL Poster Talk, Concept Talk, p. 77c ELL POSTER 9 • Day 1 Activities	TEACHER'S EDITION • Academic Language, p. DI•91 • Concept Development, p. DI•91 • Anchored Talk, p. 306a • Concept Talk Video ELL HANDBOOK • ELL Poster Talk, Concept Talk, p. 77c • Concept Talk Video Routine, p. 477 ELL POSTER 9 • Day 2 Activities
Phonics and Spelling	TEACHER'S EDITION • Phonics and Spelling, p. DI•95 • Decodable Practice Reader 9A, pp. 303a–303b	TEACHER'S EDITION • Phonics and Spelling, p. DI•95
Listening Comprehension	TEACHER'S EDITION • Modified Read Aloud, p. DI•94 • Read Aloud, p. 301b • Concept Talk Video ELL HANDBOOK • Concept Talk Video Routine, p. 477	TEACHER'S EDITION • Modified Read Aloud, p. DI•94 • AudioText of *Tops & Bottoms* • Concept Talk Video ELL HANDBOOK • AudioText CD Routine, p. 477 • Problem and Solution, p. 490
Reading Comprehension	TEACHER'S EDITION • Preteach Author's Purpose, p. DI•96	TEACHER'S EDITION • Reteach Author's Purpose, p. DI•96 • Frontloading Reading, p. DI•97 ELL HANDBOOK • Picture It! Skill Instruction, pp. 78–78a • Multilingual Summaries, pp. 79–81
Vocabulary **Basic and Lesson Vocabulary** **Vocabulary Skill: Antonyms**	TEACHER'S EDITION • Basic Vocabulary, p. DI•92 • Preteach Lesson Vocabulary, p. DI•92 • Antonyms, p. DI•95 ELL HANDBOOK • Word Cards, p. 77 • ELL Vocabulary Routine, p. 471 ELL POSTER 9 • Day 1 Activities	TEACHER'S EDITION • Basic Vocabulary, p. DI•92 • Reteach Lesson Vocabulary, p. DI•93 • Antonyms, p. DI•95 ELL HANDBOOK • Word Cards, p. 77 • Multilingual Vocabulary List, p. 434 ELL POSTER 9 • Day 2 Activities
Grammar and Conventions	TEACHER'S EDITION • Preteach Singular Possessive Nouns, p. DI•99	TEACHER'S EDITION • Reteach Singular Possessive Nouns, p. DI•99
Writing	TEACHER'S EDITION • Writing a Friendly Letter, p. DI•100 • Introduce Friendly Letter, pp. 305e–305f	TEACHER'S EDITION • Writing Trait: Focus/Ideas, pp. 317d–317e

This symbol indicates leveled instruction to address language proficiency levels.

Day 3	Day 4	Day 5
TEACHER'S EDITION • Academic Language, p. DI•91 • Concept Development, p. DI•91 • Anchored Talk, p. 318a • Concept Talk Video ELL HANDBOOK • ELL Poster Talk, Concept Talk, p. 77c ELL POSTER 9 • Day 3 Activities	TEACHER'S EDITION • Academic Language, p. DI•91 • Concept Development, p. DI•91 • Anchored Talk, p. 330a • Concept Talk Video ELL HANDBOOK • ELL Poster Talk, Concept Talk, p. 77c ELL POSTER 9 • Day 4 Activities	TEACHER'S EDITION • Academic Language, p. DI•91 • Concept Development, p. DI•91 • Concept Talk Video ELL HANDBOOK • ELL Poster Talk, Concept Talk, p. 77c ELL POSTER 9 • Day 5 Activities
ELL HANDBOOK • Phonics Transition Lesson, pp. 240, 242	ELL HANDBOOK • Phonics Transition Lesson, pp. 240, 242	TEACHER'S EDITION • Phonics and Spelling, p. DI•95
TEACHER'S EDITION • AudioText of *Tops & Bottoms* • Concept Talk Video ELL HANDBOOK • AudioText CD Routine, p. 477	TEACHER'S EDITION • Concept Talk Video	TEACHER'S EDITION • Concept Talk Video
TEACHER'S EDITION • Sheltered Reading, p. DI•97 ELL HANDBOOK • Multilingual Summaries, pp. 79–81	TEACHER'S EDITION • ELL/ELD Reader Guided Reading, p. DI•98 ELL HANDBOOK • ELL Study Guide, p. 82	TEACHER'S EDITION • ELL/ELD Reader Guided Reading, p. DI•98 ELL HANDBOOK • ELL Study Guide, p. 82
ELL HANDBOOK • High-Frequency Words Activity Bank, p. 446 ELL POSTER 9 • Day 3 Activities	ELL HANDBOOK • High-Frequency Words Activity Bank, p. 446	TEACHER'S EDITION • Antonyms, p. 333h ELL HANDBOOK • High-Frequency Words Activity Bank, p. 446
TEACHER'S EDITION • Grammar Jammer ELL HANDBOOK • Grammar Transition Lesson, pp. 317, 323 • Grammar Jammer Routine, p. 478	TEACHER'S EDITION • Grammar Jammer ELL HANDBOOK • Grammar Transition Lesson, pp. 317, 323	TEACHER'S EDITION • Grammar Jammer ELL HANDBOOK • Grammar Transition Lesson, pp. 317, 323
TEACHER'S EDITION • Let's Write It!, p. 328–329 • Writer's Craft: Set a Purpose, pp. 329a–329b	TEACHER'S EDITION • Revising Strategy, pp. 333d–333e	TEACHER'S EDITION • Possessive Nouns, pp. 333p–333q

Poster Talk, Concept Talk

Question of the Week

What can we do to make sure solutions are fair?

ELL Poster 9

Throughout the week, use the ELL Poster to help students produce and comprehend language, understand the concept, and build English vocabulary. Use the Question of the Week and other questions to help students share ideas in pairs, small groups, or the large group. Sample questions are shown, with examples of possible responses by students.

Weekly Concept and Language Goals

- Discuss the concept of fairness
- Explain why fair solutions are important
- Identify and describe unfair and fair solutions

By the end of the lesson, students should be able to talk about and write one or more sentences about fair solutions.

Daily Team Talk

Day 1	Day 2	Day 3	Day 4	Day 5
After Day 1 activities on Poster, ask questions such as *In the poster picture, if the boy in the yellow shirt stops picking tomatoes, will there be a problem? Why or why not?*	After Day 2 activity on Poster, ask questions such as *Is it fair for the boy in the yellow shirt to stop picking tomatoes? Why or why not?*	After Day 3 activity on Poster, ask questions such as *What if the boy in the yellow shirt stops picking tomatoes because he is tired? What is a fair solution to the problem now?*	After Day 4 activity on Poster, ask questions such as *In the story* Tops & Bottoms, *how is the bear unfair? How is the hare unfair?*	After Day 5 activity on Poster, ask questions such as *Why do you think it is important that we find fair solutions to our problems?*
Beginning Yes. He's not helping. **Intermediate** Yes. The girl will get mad. **Advanced** Yes. The girl working with him will get mad because he is not helping. **Advanced High** Yes. The girl who is picking tomatoes will be angry because the boy is not doing his share of the work.	**Beginning** No. He should help. **Intermediate** No. The girl will have to work more. **Advanced** No. The girl will have to pick all the tomatoes by herself. **Advanced High** It is not fair for the boy to stop picking tomatoes because the two children should share the work.	**Beginning** Stop for a while. **Intermediate** They can take turns picking and stopping. **Advanced** The two children can take turns picking the tomatoes and resting for a while. **Advanced High** A fair solution to the problem is taking turns. The boy rests while the girl picks. Then the girl rests while the boy picks. They both work and they both rest.	**Beginning** Bear doesn't help. Hare plays tricks. **Intermediate** The bear does not work. The hare tricks him. **Advanced** The bear does not help grow the plants. The hare tricks the bear. **Advanced High** The bear sleeps while the hare does all the work. The hare keeps tricking the bear so that he can get the best food.	**Beginning** We are happy. **Intermediate** When we are fair, people like it. **Advanced** When we find fair solutions, no one gets mad. **Advanced High** It is important because fair solutions are right and they make everyone happy.

This Week's Materials

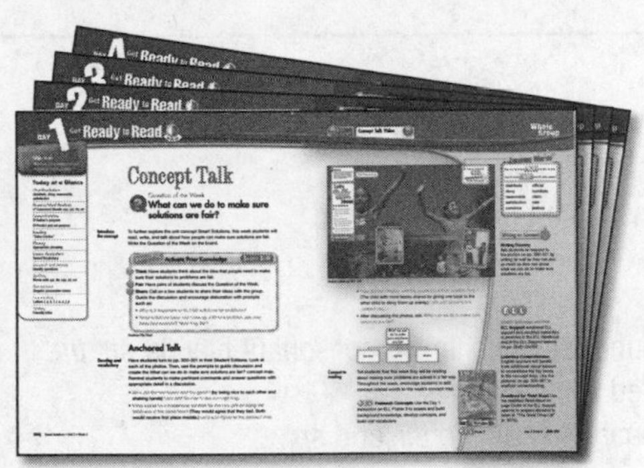

Teacher's Edition pages 300j–333q

See the support for English language learners throughout the lesson, including ELL strategies and scaffolded activities at points of use.

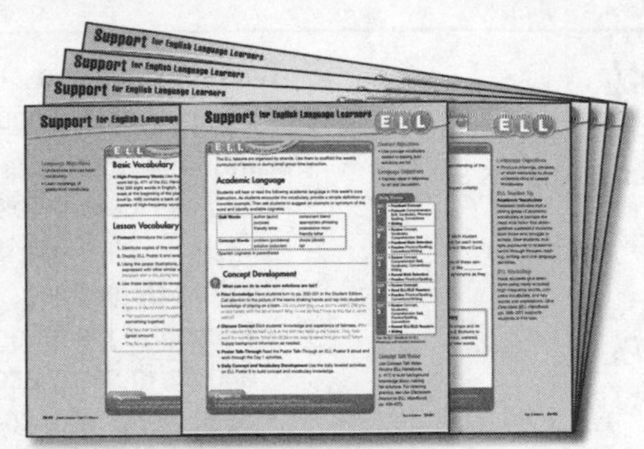

Teacher's Edition pages DI•91–DI•100

Differentiated Instruction for English language learners provides daily group activities that "frontload," or preteach, core instruction.

ELL Handbook pp. 77a–82

Find additional lesson materials that support the core lesson and the ELL instructional pages.

ELL Poster 9

ELL Reader 3.2.4

ELD Reader 3.2.4

Concept Literacy Reader

ELD, ELL Reader Teaching Guide

Concept Literacy Reader Teaching Guide

Technology

Online Teacher's Edition Use the digital version of the core Teacher's Edition for planning and instruction.

eReaders
This week's ELL and ELD Readers and Concept Literacy Reader are also available in digital format.

This Week's Content and Language Objectives by Strand

Concept Development/ Academic Language What can we do to make sure solutions are fair?	**Content Objective** • Use concept vocabulary related to making sure solutions are fair. **Language Objective** • Express ideas in response to art and discussion.
Phonics and Spelling Consonant Blends *str, thr, spl*	**Content Objectives** • Recognize the letter-sound relationships in consonant blends *str, thr,* and *spl* in newly acquired vocabulary. • Spell words with consonant blends *str, thr,* and *spl.* **Language Objective** • Read aloud words that contain consonant blends *str, thr,* and *spl* with accuracy.
Listening Comprehension Modified Read Aloud: "A Fair Divide"	**Content Objective** • Monitor and adjust oral comprehension. **Language Objectives** • Discuss oral passages. • Use a graphic organizer to take notes.
Reading Comprehension Author's Purpose	**Content Objectives** • Identify author's purpose. • Use author's purpose to aid comprehension. **Language Objectives** • Discuss evidence for and author's purpose. • Retell details that support an author's purpose. • Draw and write an author's purpose. • Read grade-level text with appropriate phrasing.
Vocabulary Basic and Lesson Vocabulary	**Language Objectives** • Understand and use basic vocabulary. • Learn meanings of grade-level vocabulary. • Produce drawings, phrases, and short sentences to show understanding of Lesson Vocabulary.
Vocabulary Antonyms	**Content Objective** • Identify antonyms to aid comprehension. **Language Objective** • Apply phonics and decoding skills to vocabulary.
Grammar and Conventions Singular Possessive Nouns	**Content Objectives** • Decode and use singular and possessive nouns. • Correctly form singular possessive nouns. **Language Objectives** • Speak using singular possessive nouns. • Write phrases and sentences with singular possessive nouns.
Writing Writing a Friendly Letter	**Content Objective** • Identify date, salutation, and closing in a letter. **Language Objectives** • Use newly acquired vocabulary to write a letter. • Write a letter with a date, salutation, and closing.

Word Cards for Vocabulary Activities

bottom	**cheated**
clever	**crops**
lazy	**partners**
wealth	

Teacher Note: Beginning Teach two to three words. **Intermediate** Teach three to four words. **Advanced** Teach four to five words. **Advanced High** Teach all words.

Name ____________________

Picture It!
Author's Purpose

Look at the pictures. **Read** the paragraph.

- **Answer** the questions below.

Tomato Plants and Marigolds

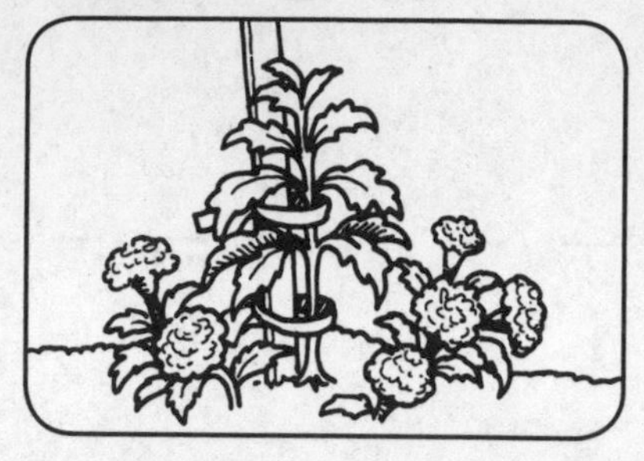

Delicious tomatoes are easy to grow with the help of marigolds. Plant the tomato plant in a sunny spot. Support the tall plant with a strong stick. Water the plant well. Plant some marigolds around your tomato plant. These small flowers will protect your tomato plant from insects. Soon you will have delicious tomatoes!

1. What are three ideas about tomato plants the author wants the reader to know?

____

____

____

2. What can you figure out about marigolds?

____

____

____

Author's Purpose

Use this lesson to supplement or replace the skill lesson on page 304a of the Teacher's Edition. Display the Skill Points (at right) and share them with students.

Teach/Model

Beginning Display a children's fiction book such as *Jack and the Beanstalk.* Ask: *Did the author write this book to entertain or to inform readers?* (to entertain) Repeat this process with a children's nonfiction book about plants. (to inform)

Intermediate Display a diagram of a plant and its parts in a science textbook. Ask: *What is the author's purpose for drawing this diagram? Is it to inform, to persuade, or to entertain?* (to inform)

Advanced Say: *I am reading a book called* Eat More Plants. *It tells why people need to eat more plants. What is the author's purpose?* (to persuade) Continue with these titles and purposes: *Maisie the Dancing Daisy*—to entertain; *The Life Cycle of a Plant*—to inform; *Planting a Vegetable Garden*—to explain how to do something.

Advanced High Ask students to select a fiction or nonfiction book about plants from the library. After they read the book, have them briefly describe it to the group. Ask them to identify the author's purpose and to explain how they know.

Skill Points

✔ The **author's purpose** is the reason an author writes something.

✔ An author may write to entertain, to inform, to express ideas, or to persuade.

✔ Sometimes the title helps you predict the author's purpose.

Then distribute copies of Picture It! page 78.

- Have students read the title and predict what the paragraph might be about.
- Review the Skill Points with students.
- Read the paragraph aloud. Ask: *What is the author's purpose? Why did the author write this paragraph?*
- Have students look at the pictures and words to identify the author's purpose.

Practice

Read aloud the directions on page 78. Reread the paragraph aloud, explaining any unfamiliar words or concepts. Have students look at the pictures and the paragraph as they answer the questions.

Beginning Students can answer the questions orally before writing words or phrases on the lines. Provide help with English words and writing.

Intermediate Students can first answer the questions orally and then write their answers on the lines. Provide help with writing.

Advanced Students can write their answers and then check them by comparing their answers with a partner's.

Advanced High Students can write their answers and then orally explain why they wrote what they wrote.

Answers for page 78: 1. Tomato plants are easy to grow. They need water and sun. Tomatoes are delicious. 2. Marigolds keep away insects. They grow with the same sun and water as tomatoes.

Multilingual Summaries

English

Tops & Bottoms

Lazy Bear did not farm his land. Hare had lost his land and his family was hungry. He made a deal with Bear. Hare would plant and harvest crops in Bear's field. Each would take half of the crops. Hare asked whether Bear wanted the top half or the bottom half. Bear chose the tops. When the harvest was done, Hare took the bottoms of the carrots, radishes, and beets. Bear was left with the leaves. Bear was angry. Hare agreed to plant more crops.

This time, Bear chose the bottoms. Hare took the tops of the lettuce and broccoli. Bear got the roots. Bear was angry again. Hare planted corn. Then Bear wanted tops and bottoms. Hare took the corn from the middle. Bear got roots and tassels. Bear decided to plant his own crops. Hare bought back his land. Hare and Bear stayed friends.

Spanish

Arriba y abajo

Oso Perezoso no cultivaba su tierra. Liebre había perdido su tierra y su familia estaba hambrienta. Hizo un trato con Oso. Liebre plantaría y cosecharía en el campo de Oso. Cada uno podría tener la mitad de la cosecha. Liebre le preguntó a Oso si él quería la parte de arriba o la parte de abajo. Oso eligió la parte de arriba. Cuando la cosecha terminó, Liebre tomó la parte de abajo de zanahorias, rábanos y remolachas. A Oso le tocaron las hojas. Oso estaba enojado. Liebre estuvo de acuerdo en plantar de nuevo para tener otra cosecha.

Esta vez Oso eligió la parte de abajo. Liebre tomó la parte de arriba de la lechuga y el bróculi. Oso quedó con las raíces. Oso estaba enojado. Liebre plantó maíz. Entonces Oso quería la parte de arriba y la parte de abajo. Liebre tomó el maíz del medio. Oso se quedó con las raíces y las borlas. Oso decidió plantar para tener sus propias cosechas. Liebre compró de nuevo su terreno. Liebre y Oso quedaron como amigos.

Multilingual Summaries

Chinese

上面與下面

懶熊從來不種地。兔子沒了土地，一家人餓得慌。于是兔子便和懶熊簽了一份合同，要借用他的地種莊稼，收成後每人各分一半。兔子問懶熊，你要上面還是下面，懶熊選上面。莊稼成熟後，兔子把胡蘿蔔、小蘿蔔與甜菜的下面部分拿走了，只給懶熊剩下葉子。懶熊非常生氣，兔子說下次多種點。

這回懶熊選下面。收成後兔子把萵苣與椰菜的上面部分拿走了，懶熊氣得大罵。第三次兔子種的是玉米，懶熊說上面下面他都要。兔子把玉米捧中間一段拿走了，只給懶熊留下根和穗。懶熊决定改掉毛病，以後自己種地。兔子也買回了土地，大家還是好朋友。

Vietnamese

Ngọn và Gốc

Gấu Lười không trồng trọt gì trên đất của mình. Thỏ bị mất đất và gia đình đang đói. Thỏ thương lượng với Gấu. Thỏ sẽ gieo trồng và thu hoạch mùa màng trên cánh đồng của Gấu. Mỗi người sẽ lấy phân nửa mùa màng. Thỏ hỏi Gấu muốn lấy phần ngọn hay phần gốc. Gấu chọn phần ngọn. Khi thu hoạch xong, Thỏ lấy phần gốc của cà-rốt, củ cải, và củ dền. Gấu bị để lại phần lá. Gấu tức giận. Thỏ đồng ý trồng thêm mùa màng.

Gấu chọn phần gốc. Thỏ lấy phần ngọn của rau diếp và bông cải xanh. Gấu lại tức giận lần nữa. Thỏ trồng bắp. Gấu muốn lấy phần ngọn và gốc. Thỏ lấy trái bắp ở chính giữa. Gấu lấy phần rễ và bông. Gấu quyết định tự mình trồng trọt mùa màng. Thỏ mua lại đất của mình. Thỏ và Gấu vẫn là bạn.

Multilingual Summaries

Korean

윗부분과 아랫부분

게으른 곰은 자신의 땅을 일구지 않았다. 산토끼는 자신의 땅을 잃었고 가족들은 굶주렸다. 산토끼는 곰과 계약을 맺었는데 산토끼가 곰의 들에서 작물을 심고 수확을 하면 각자 작물의 절반을 갖게 된다는 것이었다. 산토끼는 곰이 작물의 윗부분 반을 원하는지 아랫부분 반을 원하는지를 물었다. 곰은 윗부분을 택했다. 수확이 끝났을 때 산토끼는 당근과 무, 그리고 사탕무의 아랫부분을 차지했지만 곰에게 남겨진 것은 잎사귀들뿐이었다. 곰은 화가 났다. 그래서 산토끼는 작물을 좀더 심는 것에 동의했다.

이번에 곰은 아랫부분을 골랐다. 산토끼는 상추와 브로콜리의 윗부분을 차지했다. 곰은 다시 화가 났다. 산토끼는 옥수수를 심었고 곰은 윗부분과 아랫부분 모두를 원했다. 산토끼는 중간부분에서 옥수수를 따갔고 곰은 옥수수의 뿌리와 수염을 가지게 되었다. 이제 곰은 자신만의 작물을 심기로 결심했다. 산토끼는 그의 땅을 도로 샀다. 결국 산토끼와 곰은 친구로 남게 되었다.

Hmong

Saum Toj thiab Hauv Qab

Tus Dais tub nkeeg tsis ua liaj ua teb rau hauv nws daim teb. Hare daim teb tau poob ua rau nws tsevneeg tshaib plab. Nws thiaj sib koom tes nrog Dais. Hare mam li cog thiab nruam tej qoob tej loo uas nyob rau hauv Dais daim teb. Nws mam li faib cov qoob loo ib leeg ib nrab. Hare nug Dais seb nws yuav yuav cov qoob loo uas nyob saum toj losis hauv qab. Dais xaiv yav saum toj. Thaum nruam qoob loo tag, Hare yuav cov zaub uas nyob yav hauv qab. Qhov uas Dais tau ces tsuas yog nplooj xwb. Dais npau taws. Hare pom zoo cog dua qoob loo ntxiv.

Dais xaiv yav hauv qab. Hare xaiv yav saum toj uas muaj zaub paj thiab zaub ntsuab. Dais rov qab npau taws dua thiab. Hare thiaj li cog pobkws. Dais yuav hlo cov saum toj thiab cov hauv qab tibsi. Hare thiaj li yuav cov pobkws uas nyob nruab nrab. Dais tsuas tau cov cag nkaus xwb. Dais thiaj txiav txim mus cog nws li qoob loo. Hare thiaj yuav nws daim teb rov qab los. Hare thiab Dais nkawd thiaj li nyob ua phooj ua ywg txij ntawd los.

Name ____________________

A Garden for Everyone

- **Read** *A Garden for Everyone* again.
- **Draw** pictures to show what Jim's and Peter's gardens look like.
- **Write** words or sentences to describe each garden.

Jim's Garden	Peter's Garden
Words or Sentences	**Words or Sentences**
____________________	____________________
____________________	____________________
____________________	____________________

Family Link

Ask family members what their favorite vegetables are and how they use them.

Weekly Resources Guide for English Language Learner Support

For this week's content and language objectives, see p. 83e.

Instructional Strand	Day 1	Day 2
Concept Development/Academic Language	TEACHER'S EDITION • Academic Language, p. DI•116 • Concept Development, p. DI•116 • Anchored Talk, pp. 334j—334–335 • Preteach Academic Vocabulary, p. 339a • Concept Talk Video ELL HANDBOOK • Hear It, See It, Say It, Use It, pp. xxxvi–xxxvii • ELL Poster Talk, Concept Talk, p. 83c ELL POSTER 10 • Day 1 Activities	TEACHER'S EDITION • Academic Language, p. DI•116 • Concept Development, p. DI•116 • Anchored Talk, p. 340a • Concept Talk Video ELL HANDBOOK • ELL Poster Talk, Concept Talk, p. 83c • Concept Talk Video Routine, p. 477 ELL POSTER 10 • Day 2 Activities
Phonics and Spelling	TEACHER'S EDITION • Phonics and Spelling, p. DI•120 • Decodable Practice Reader 10A, pp. 337a–337b	TEACHER'S EDITION • Phonics and Spelling, p. DI•120
Listening Comprehension	TEACHER'S EDITION • Modified Read Aloud, p. DI•119 • Read Aloud, p. 335b • Concept Talk Video ELL HANDBOOK • Concept Talk Video Routine, p. 477	TEACHER'S EDITION • Modified Read Aloud, p. DI•119 • AudioText of *Amazing Bird Nests* • Concept Talk Video ELL HANDBOOK • AudioText CD Routine, p. 477 • Web, p. 486
Reading Comprehension	TEACHER'S EDITION • Preteach Main Idea and Details, p. DI•121	TEACHER'S EDITION • Reteach Main Idea and Details, p. DI•121 • Frontloading Reading, p. DI•122 ELL HANDBOOK • Picture It! Skill Instruction, pp. 84–84a • Multilingual Summaries, pp. 85–87
Vocabulary **Basic and Lesson Vocabulary** **Vocabulary Skill: Unfamiliar Words**	TEACHER'S EDITION • Basic Vocabulary, p. DI•117 • Preteach Lesson Vocabulary, p. DI•117 • Unfamiliar Words, p. DI•120 ELL HANDBOOK • Word Cards, p. 83 • ELL Vocabulary Routine, p. 471 ELL POSTER 10 • Day 1 Activities	TEACHER'S EDITION • Basic Vocabulary, p. DI•117 • Reteach Lesson Vocabulary, p. DI•118 • Unfamiliar Words, p. DI•120 ELL HANDBOOK • Word Cards, p. 83 • Multilingual Vocabulary List, p. 434 ELL POSTER 10 • Day 2 Activities
Grammar and Conventions	TEACHER'S EDITION • Preteach Plural Possessive Nouns, p. DI•124	TEACHER'S EDITION • Teach Plural Possessive Nouns, p. DI•124
Writing	TEACHER'S EDITION • Writing Introductory Statements, p. DI•125 • Introduce Directions, pp. 339e–339f	TEACHER'S EDITION • Writing Trait: Focus/Ideas, pp. 349d–349e

Unit 2 Week 5 Amazing Bird Nests

Leveled Support: This symbol indicates leveled instruction to address language proficiency levels.

Day 3	Day 4	Day 5
TEACHER'S EDITION • Academic Language, p. DI•116 • Concept Development, p. DI•116 • Anchored Talk, p. 350a • Concept Talk Video ELL HANDBOOK • ELL Poster Talk, Concept Talk, p. 83c ELL POSTER 10 • Day 3 Activities	TEACHER'S EDITION • Academic Language, p. DI•116 • Concept Development, p. DI•116 • Anchored Talk, p. 358a • Concept Talk Video ELL HANDBOOK • ELL Poster Talk, Concept Talk, p. 83c ELL POSTER 10 • Day 4 Activities	TEACHER'S EDITION • Academic Language, p. DI•116 • Concept Development, p. DI•116 • Concept Talk Video ELL HANDBOOK • ELL Poster Talk, Concept Talk, p. 83c ELL POSTER 10 • Day 5 Activities
ELL HANDBOOK • Phonics Transition Lesson, pp. 224, 227	ELL HANDBOOK • Phonics Transition Lesson, pp. 224, 227	TEACHER'S EDITION • Phonics and Spelling, p. DI•120
TEACHER'S EDITION • AudioText of *Amazing Bird Nests* • Concept Talk Video ELL HANDBOOK • AudioText CD Routine, p. 477	TEACHER'S EDITION • Concept Talk Video	TEACHER'S EDITION • Concept Talk Video
TEACHER'S EDITION • Sheltered Reading, p. DI•122 ELL HANDBOOK • Multilingual Summaries, pp. 85–87	TEACHER'S EDITION • ELL/ELD Reader Guided Reading, p. DI•123 ELL HANDBOOK • ELL Study Guide, p. 88	TEACHER'S EDITION • ELL/ELD Reader Guided Reading, p. DI•123 ELL HANDBOOK • ELL Study Guide, p. 88
ELL HANDBOOK • High-Frequency Words Activity Bank, p. 446 ELL POSTER 10 • Day 3 Activities	ELL HANDBOOK • High-Frequency Words Activity Bank, p. 446	TEACHER'S EDITION • Unfamiliar Words, p. 363h ELL HANDBOOK • High-Frequency Words Activity Bank, p. 446
TEACHER'S EDITION • Grammar Jammer ELL HANDBOOK • Grammar Transition Lesson, pp. 317, 323 • Grammar Jammer Routine, p. 478	TEACHER'S EDITION • Grammar Jammer ELL HANDBOOK • Grammar Transition Lesson, pp. 317, 323	TEACHER'S EDITION • Grammar Jammer ELL HANDBOOK • Grammar Transition Lesson, pp. 317, 323
TEACHER'S EDITION • Let's Write It!, p. 356–357 • Writing Trait: Organization, pp. 357a–357b	TEACHER'S EDITION • Revising Strategy, pp. 363d–363e	TEACHER'S EDITION • Plural Possessive Nouns, pp. 363p–363q

Poster Talk, Concept Talk

Question of the Week

How have plants and animals adapted to solve problems?

ELL Poster 10

Throughout the week, use the ELL Poster to help students produce and comprehend language, understand the concept, and build English vocabulary. Use the Question of the Week and other questions to help students share ideas in pairs, small groups, or the large group. Sample questions are shown, with examples of possible responses by students.

Weekly Concept and Language Goals

- Discuss why plants and animals adapt
- Identify and explain animal adaptations
- Explain plant adaptations

By the end of the lesson, students should be able to talk about and write one or more sentences about animal and plant adaptations.

Daily Team Talk

Day 1	Day 2	Day 3	Day 4	Day 5
After Day 1 activities on Poster, ask questions such as *In the poster picture, how is the bird's nest different from other birds' nests you have seen?*	After Day 2 activity on Poster, ask questions such as *Why do you think the bird is building its nest on the platform?*	After Day 3 activity on Poster, ask questions such as *In the poster picture, why do you think the plants are growing up the building and across the sidewalk?*	After Day 4 activity on Poster, ask questions such as *Think of the different ways birds make nests in* Amazing Bird Nests. *What is one way birds make nests?*	After Day 5 activity on Poster, ask questions such as *In what unusual place did you see a bird's nest? Why do you think the bird built it there?*
Beginning Not in a tree. **Intermediate** The bird's nest is not in a tree. **Advanced** The bird's nest is on a platform. Birds' nests are in trees and on buildings. **Advanced High** This bird is building its nest on a platform. Most birds build their nests in trees or on buildings.	**Beginning** No trees. **Intermediate** There are no trees to make a nest in. **Advanced** The bird builds its nest there because it cannot find any trees to build in. **Advanced High** The bird is building its nest on a platform because there are no trees; so it had to find another place.	**Beginning** No room. **Intermediate** There is no room for them to grow. **Advanced** There is not enough ground for them to grow, so they grow up and across. **Advanced High** The plants are growing up the building and across the sidewalk because there is no more ground. They had to find other places to grow.	**Beginning** With grass. **Intermediate** One bird makes a nest using pieces of grass. **Advanced** One kind of bird takes pieces of grass and sews them together. **Advanced High** The weaver bird takes strips of grass and weaves them together with its beak to make a nest.	**Beginning** Under the roof. **Intermediate** There is a nest under the edge of the house's roof. It is dry there. **Advanced** I saw a nest on top of a high wall. The bird would be safe there. **Advanced High** I saw a bird's nest in a crack in a wall. I think the bird built the nest there because it was warm and dry.

This Week's Materials

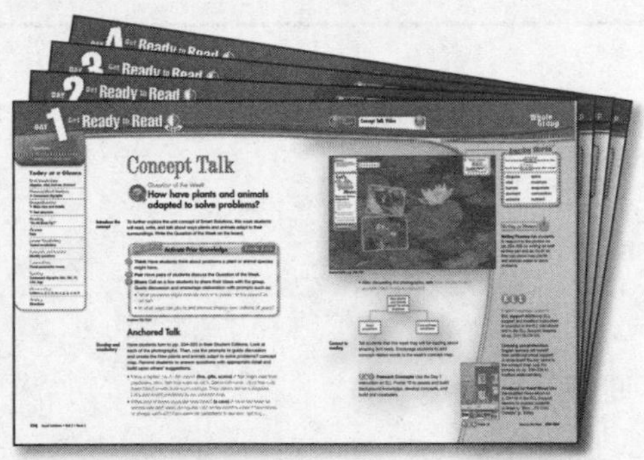

Teacher's Edition pages 334j–367a

See the support for English language learners throughout the lesson, including ELL strategies and scaffolded activities at points of use.

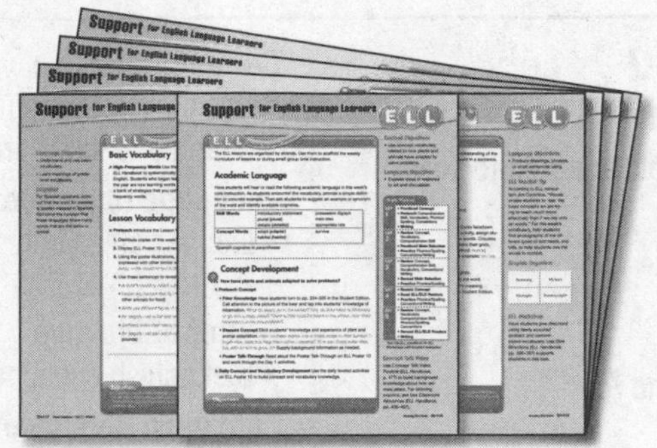

Teacher's Edition pages DI•116–DI•125

Differentiated Instruction for English language learners provides daily group activities that "frontload," or preteach, core instruction.

ELL Handbook pp. 83a–88

Find additional lesson materials that support the core lesson and the ELL instructional pages.

ELL Poster 10

ELL Reader 3.2.5

ELD Reader 3.2.5

Concept Literacy Reader

ELD, ELL Reader Teaching Guide

Concept Literacy Reader Teaching Guide

Technology

Online Teacher's Edition Use the digital version of the core Teacher's Edition for planning and instruction.

eReaders
This week's ELL and ELD Readers and Concept Literacy Reader are also available in digital format.

This Week's Content and Language Objectives by Strand

Concept Development/ Academic Language How have plants and animals adapted to solve problems?	**Content Objective** • Use concept vocabulary related to how plants and animals have adapted to solve problems. **Language Objective** • Express ideas in response to art and discussion.
Phonics and Spelling Consonant Digraphs /sh/ and /ch/	**Content Objective** • Distinguish consonant digraphs /sh/ and /ch/. **Language Objective** • Discuss consonant digraphs.
Listening Comprehension Modified Read Aloud: "Staying Warm in the Cold"	**Content Objective** • Monitor and adjust oral comprehension. **Language Objective** • Discuss oral passages.
Reading Comprehension Main Idea and Details	**Content Objectives** • Distinguish between main ideas and details. • Identify and understand main idea and details. **Language Objectives** • Retell main ideas and details from a reading. • Read grade-level text at an appropriate rate. • Summarize text using visual support.
Vocabulary Basic and Lesson Vocabulary	**Language Objectives** • Understand and use basic vocabulary. • Learn meanings of grade-level vocabulary. • Produce drawings, phrases, and short sentences to show understanding of Lesson Vocabulary.
Vocabulary Unfamiliar Words	**Content Objective** • Identify and understand unfamiliar words. **Language Objective** • Apply phonics and decoding skills to vocabulary.
Grammar and Conventions Plural Possessive Nouns	**Content Objectives** • Decode and use plural possessive nouns. • Correctly form plural possessive nouns. **Language Objectives** • Speak using the pattern of plural possessive nouns. • Write phrases and sentences with plural possessive nouns.
Writing Writing Introductory Statements	**Content Objective** • Identify introductory statements in text. **Language Objectives** • Write paragraphs using newly acquired vocabulary. • Share feedback for editing and revising.

Word Cards for Vocabulary Activities

bill	**goo**
hunters	**material**
platform	**tons**
twigs	

Teacher Note: Beginning Teach two to three words. **Intermediate** Teach three to four words. **Advanced** Teach four to five words. **Advanced High** Teach all words.

Name ______________________________

Picture It!
Main Idea and Details

Look at the pictures. **Read** the paragraph.

- Which sentences tell the details? **Write** them in the *Detail* circles.
- What is the main idea of the paragraph? **Write** it in the *Main Idea* circle.

Birds and Fish

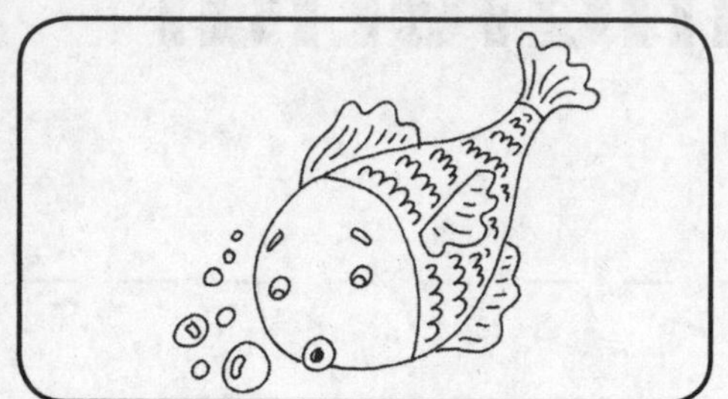

There are many kinds of birds and fish. Every bird has bones in its back, chest, and wings. All birds lay eggs. There are birds all over the world. All fish have bones in their backs and chests. Most have bones in their fins too. Some fish lay eggs. Fish live in waters all over Earth.

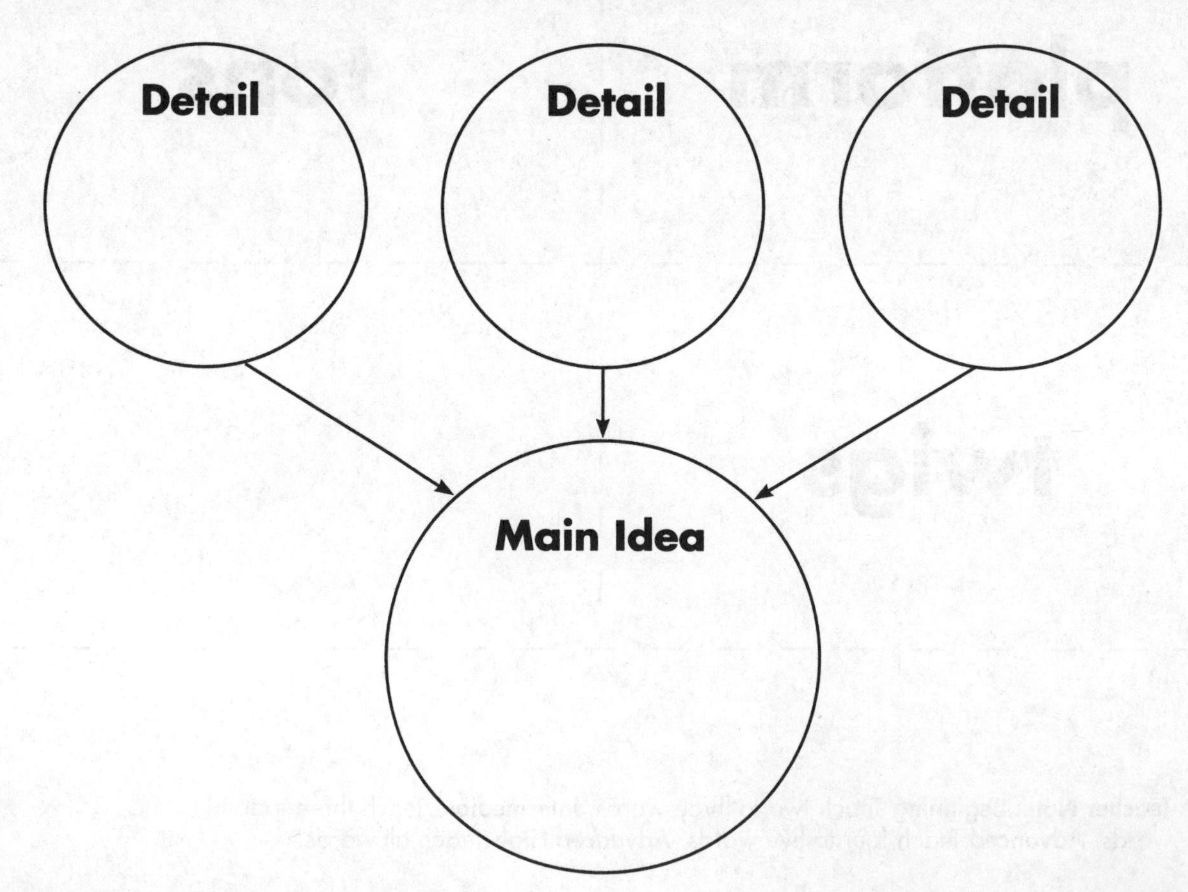

Main Idea and Details

Use this lesson to supplement or replace the skill lesson on page 338a of the Teacher's Edition. Display the Skill Points (at right) and share them with students.

Teach/Model

Beginning Write these sentences in a row and read them aloud: *Birds live in forests. Birds live in deserts. Birds live on mountains.* Say: *These are details. What main idea do all these details tell about?* Guide students to decide on a main idea such as Birds live in many places on Earth.

Intermediate Have students name as many kinds of birds as they can. Write the names in a list. Say: *Now let's write a main idea that all these details tell about.* Have students share main-idea sentences. (Possible answer: There are many kinds of birds.)

Advanced Write and read aloud these details: *Fish have fins. Fish can breathe underwater. Fish use their tails to steer.* Ask students to write a main idea that all the details tell about. (Possible answer: Fish are suited for swimming.)

Advanced High Have students read a section of the entry about fish in a children's encyclopedia. Ask them to share the details they learned. Then have them write the main idea that the details tell about. Suggest that they look at the title of the section.

Then distribute copies of Picture It! page 84.

- Have students look at the pictures and describe what they see.
- Read the paragraph aloud. Ask: *What is this paragraph about?* (how birds and fish are alike in some ways)
- Review the Skill Points with students.
- Have students look at the pictures and words to identify the main idea and details.

Practice

Read aloud the directions on page 84. Reread the paragraph aloud, encouraging students to tell what they know about birds and fish. Have students refer to the pictures and the paragraph as they complete the graphic organizer.

Beginning Students can explain orally what they want to write and then dictate or write their answers for the graphic organizer. Provide help with English words and writing.

Intermediate Students can first orally identify the main idea and details and then write their answers in the circles. Provide help with English words and writing.

Advanced Students can write their answers in the circles and then check their sentences by quietly reading them aloud or comparing them with a partner's sentences.

Advanced High Students can write their answers in the circles and then check their sentences by silently rereading the paragraph and making any necessary corrections.

Answers for page 84: *Main Idea:* Birds and fish are alike in some ways. *Details:* Birds and fish have bones in their backs and chests. Birds and fish lay eggs. Birds and fish live all over the world.

Skill Points

- ✔ The most important idea in a paragraph is called the **main idea.**
- ✔ To find the main idea, ask: *What is this paragraph about?* Find out whether there is a sentence that tells the main idea.
- ✔ Other sentences in the paragraph tell about the main idea. They give **details** about the main idea.

Multilingual Summaries

English

Amazing Bird Nests

Birds build nests and lay eggs in the spring. Nests are their safe spots. They protect the eggs and chicks from weather and predators.

Hummingbirds build very small nests. The American Bald Eagle builds very big nests. Each kind of bird builds a special type of nest.

Birds build their nests in many different places. City birds must build their nests in unusual places. Birds use strange things to build their nests. The swiftlet makes a goo and spits it out to build a nest.

No one teaches a bird to build a nest. Building a nest is a hard job. Birds do the job with their beaks with little help from their feet.

Spanish

Los sorprendentes nidos de las aves

Las aves hacen sus nidos y ponen sus huevos en la primavera. Los nidos son sus sitios seguros. Éstos protegen los huevos y a los polluelos del clima y de otros depredadores.

Los colibríes hacen unos nidos muy pequeños. El Águila Calva Americana hace unos nidos muy grandes. Cada tipo de ave hace un tipo diferente de nido.

Las aves hacen sus nidos en lugares diferentes. Las que se encuentran en las ciudades hacen sus nidos en sitios muy extraños. También usan cosas muy raras para construirlos. El vencejo hace una pelotita y la escupe para construir el nido.

Nadie le enseña a las aves a construir su nido. Hacer un nido es un trabajo arduo. Ellas los hacen sólo con la ayuda de su pico y casi no usan las patas.

Multilingual Summaries

Chinese

奇妙的鳥巢

小鳥在春天築巢下蛋。鳥巢是他們最安全的地方。這是因為，鳥巢不僅可以保護鳥蛋，而且可使雛鳥免受風吹雨打和掠食者的攻擊。

蜂鳥築的巢很小，而美國禿鷹築的巢卻很大。每一種鳥所築的巢樣子各不相同。

小鳥會在許多不同的地方築巢。城市裡的小鳥必須在不尋常的地方築巢。小鳥會使用奇怪的東西來築巢。小雨燕會吐出口水來築巢。

沒有人教小鳥如何築巢。築巢是份很辛苦的工作。小鳥主要用嘴來築巢，很少會用腳。

Vietnamese

Tổ Chim Ngộ Nghĩnh

Chim xây tổ và đẻ trứng vào mùa xuân. Tổ là nơi an toàn của chúng. Nó bảo vệ trứng và chim con tránh được thời tiết và các con vật săn mồi khác.

Chim vo vo xây tổ rất nhỏ. Chim ó trọc Mỹ xây tổ rất lớn. Mỗi loại chim xây một loại tổ đặc biệt.

Chim xây tổ ở nhiều nơi khác nhau. Chim ở thành phố phải xây tổ ở những nơi không bình thường. Chim dùng những vật kỳ lạ để xây tổ. Loại chim én cánh dài làm cụt nhớt và phun ra để xây tổ.

Không ai chỉ cho chim cách xây tổ. Xây tổ là một công việc khó nhọc. Chim xây tổ bằng mỏ của chúng với sự giúp đỡ chút ít của đôi chân.

Multilingual Summaries

Korean

굉장한 새 둥지

봄이 되면 새들은 둥지를 짓고 알을 낳는다. 둥지는 안전한 곳이다. 둥지는 날씨나 천적으로부터 알과 새끼를 보호한다.

벌새는 아주 작은 둥지를 짓는다. 흰머리수리는 아주 커다란 둥지를 짓는다. 새들은 종류에 따라 특정한 형태의 둥지를 짓는다.

새들은 매우 다양한 장소에 둥지를 짓는다. 도시의 새들은 별난 장소에 둥지를 지어야 하며 둥지를 짓는데 이상한 것들을 사용한다. 흰집칼새는 끈적이는 점액을 뱉어내어 둥지를 짓는다.

아무도 새에게 둥지 짓는 법을 가르치지 않았다. 둥지 짓기는 힘든 일이다. 새들은 발은 거의 쓰지 않으며 부리로 그 일을 한다.

Hmong

Zes Noog

Noog ua zes thiab nteg qe thaum lub caij ntuj tshiab. Zes noog yog qhov chaw puaj phais tshaj plaw. Nws tiv thaiv qe noog thiab me nyuam noog kom nag txhob ntub thiab txhob muaj tus dab noj.

Noog Kaus Zuag ua lub zes me me. Tus Noog Dav, American Bald Eagle, ua lub zes loj loj. Ib yam noog twg mas nyias ua nyias yam zes tshwj xeeb.

Noog ua zes nyob rau ntau qhov chaw txawv txawv kawg. Cov noog nyob hauv nroog mas lawv ua zes rau cov chaw txawv tshaj. Noob muab tau tej yam txawv txawv coj los ua lawv cov zes. Tus noog hus ua swiftlet nti aub ncaug thiab coj los ua zes.

Tsis muaj leeg twg qhia noog ua zes. Ua zes yogib txoj hauj lwm nyuaj. Noog muab lawv tus kaus ncauj los ua zes xwb ho lawv txais ko taw pab me me xwb.

Name ______________________________

- **Read** *Animals Adapt* again.
- **Draw** pictures to show where fish, beavers, turtles, and rabbits live.
- **Write** words or a sentence to go with your pictures.

Picture	Words or Sentence

Family Link

Ask family members if they have ever seen a fish, a beaver, a turtle, or a rabbit.

Weekly Resources Guide for English Language Learner Support

For this week's content and language objectives, see p. 89e.

Instructional Strand	Day 1	Day 2
Concept Development/Academic Language	TEACHER'S EDITION • Academic Language, p. DI•16 • Concept Development, p. DI•16 • Anchored Talk, pp. 370j—370–371 • Preteach Academic Vocabulary, p. 375a • Concept Talk Video ELL HANDBOOK • Hear It, See It, Say It, Use It, pp. xxxvi–xxxvii • ELL Poster Talk, Concept Talk, p. 89c ELL POSTER 11 • Day 1 Activities	TEACHER'S EDITION • Academic Language, p. DI•16 • Concept Development, p. DI•16 • Anchored Talk, p. 376a • Concept Talk Video ELL HANDBOOK • ELL Poster Talk, Concept Talk, p. 89c • Concept Talk Video Routine, p. 477 ELL POSTER 11 • Day 2 Activities
Phonics and Spelling	TEACHER'S EDITION • Phonics and Spelling, p. DI•20 • Decodable Practice Reader 11A, pp. 373a–373b	TEACHER'S EDITION • Phonics and Spelling, p. DI•20
Listening Comprehension	TEACHER'S EDITION • Modified Read Aloud, p. DI•19 • Read Aloud, p. 371b • Concept Talk Video ELL HANDBOOK • Concept Talk Video Routine, p. 477	TEACHER'S EDITION • Modified Read Aloud, p. DI•19 • AudioText of *How Do You Raise a Raisin?* • Concept Talk Video ELL HANDBOOK • AudioText CD Routine, p. 477 • Cause and Effect, p. 489
Reading Comprehension	TEACHER'S EDITION • Preteach Draw Conclusions, p. DI•21	TEACHER'S EDITION • Reteach Draw Conclusions, p. DI•21 • Frontloading Reading, p. DI•22 ELL HANDBOOK • Picture It! Skill Instruction, pp. 90–90a • Multilingual Summaries, pp. 91–93
Vocabulary **Basic and Lesson Vocabulary** **Vocabulary Skill: Homophones**	TEACHER'S EDITION • Basic Vocabulary, p. DI•17 • Preteach Lesson Vocabulary, p. DI•17 • Homophones, p. DI•20 ELL HANDBOOK • Word Cards, p. 89 • ELL Vocabulary Routine, p. 471 ELL POSTER 11 • Day 1 Activities	TEACHER'S EDITION • Basic Vocabulary, p. DI•17 • Reteach Lesson Vocabulary, p. DI•18 • Homophones, p. DI•20 ELL HANDBOOK • Word Cards, p. 89 • Multilingual Vocabulary List, p. 435 ELL POSTER 11 • Day 2 Activities
Grammar and Conventions	TEACHER'S EDITION • Preteach Action and Linking Verbs, p. DI•24	TEACHER'S EDITION • Teach Action and Linking Verbs, p. DI•24
Writing	TEACHER'S EDITION • Writing with an Engaging Tone, p. DI•25 • Introduce Fiction, pp. 375e–375f	TEACHER'S EDITION • Writing Trait: Voice, pp. 387d–387e

Unit 3 Week 1 How Do You Raise a Raisin?

This symbol indicates leveled instruction to address language proficiency levels.

Day 3	Day 4	Day 5
TEACHER'S EDITION • Academic Language, p. DI•16 • Concept Development, p. DI•16 • Anchored Talk, p. 388a • Concept Talk Video ELL HANDBOOK • ELL Poster Talk, Concept Talk, p. 89c ELL POSTER 11 • Day 3 Activities	TEACHER'S EDITION • Academic Language, p. DI•16 • Concept Development, p. DI•16 • Anchored Talk, p. 398a • Concept Talk Video ELL HANDBOOK • ELL Poster Talk, Concept Talk, p. 89c ELL POSTER 11 • Day 4 Activities	TEACHER'S EDITION • Academic Language, p. DI•16 • Concept Development, p. DI•16 • Concept Talk Video ELL HANDBOOK • ELL Poster Talk, Concept Talk, p. 89c ELL POSTER 11 • Day 5 Activities
ELL HANDBOOK • Phonics Transition Lesson, pp. 280, 283	ELL HANDBOOK • Phonics Transition Lesson, pp. 280, 283	TEACHER'S EDITION • Phonics and Spelling, p. DI•20
TEACHER'S EDITION • AudioText of *How Do You Raise a Raisin?* • Concept Talk Video ELL HANDBOOK • AudioText CD Routine, p. 477	TEACHER'S EDITION • Concept Talk Video	TEACHER'S EDITION • Concept Talk Video
TEACHER'S EDITION • Sheltered Reading, p. DI•22 ELL HANDBOOK • Multilingual Summaries, pp. 91–93	TEACHER'S EDITION • ELL/ELD Reader Guided Reading, p. DI•23 ELL HANDBOOK • ELL Study Guide, p. 94	TEACHER'S EDITION • ELL/ELD Reader Guided Reading, p. DI•23 ELL HANDBOOK • ELL Study Guide, p. 94
ELL HANDBOOK • High-Frequency Words Activity Bank, p. 446 ELL POSTER 11 • Day 3 Activities	ELL HANDBOOK • High-Frequency Words Activity Bank, p. 446	TEACHER'S EDITION • Homophones, p. 403h ELL HANDBOOK • High-Frequency Words Activity Bank, p. 446
TEACHER'S EDITION • Grammar Jammer ELL HANDBOOK • Grammar Transition Lesson, pp. 324, 327, 330, 336 • Grammar Jammer Routine, p. 478	TEACHER'S EDITION • Grammar Jammer ELL HANDBOOK • Grammar Transition Lesson, pp. 324, 327, 330, 336	TEACHER'S EDITION • Grammar Jammer ELL HANDBOOK • Grammar Transition Lesson, pp. 324, 327, 330, 336
TEACHER'S EDITION • Let's Write It!, p. 396–397 • Writer's Craft: Engaging Tone, pp. 397a–397b	TEACHER'S EDITION • Revising Strategy, pp. 403d–403e	TEACHER'S EDITION • Fiction, pp. 403p–403q

Poster Talk, Concept Talk

Question of the Week

How do people and nature interact?

Poster 11

Throughout the week, use the ELL Poster to help students produce and comprehend language, understand the concept, and build English vocabulary. Use the Question of the Week and other questions to help students share ideas in pairs, small groups, or the large group. Sample questions are shown, with examples of possible responses by students.

Weekly Concept and Language Goals

- Explain why people interact with nature
- Identify ways people interact with nature
- Tell favorite ways to interact with nature

By the end of the lesson, students should be able to talk about and write one or more sentences about people interacting with nature.

Daily Team Talk

Day 1	Day 2	Day 3	Day 4	Day 5
After Day 1 activities on Poster, ask questions such as *In the poster picture, how are people interacting with nature?*	After Day 2 activity on Poster, ask questions such as *In the poster picture, how have people had an effect on nature?*	After Day 3 activity on Poster, ask questions such as *Why do you think the people in the poster picture like to interact with nature?*	After Day 4 activity on Poster, ask questions such as *Why do you think the people in the poster picture planted a garden in the middle of the city?*	After Day 5 activity on Poster, ask questions such as *What is your favorite way to interact with nature?*
Beginning They are outside. **Intermediate** They are outside in a garden. **Advanced** The people are outside looking at and taking care of a garden. **Advanced High** The people are interacting with nature by enjoying and taking care of the plants in the garden and picking flowers and vegetables.	**Beginning** Made a garden. **Intermediate** They planted a garden. **Advanced** The people planted a garden in the city. **Advanced High** The people planted a garden in the middle of a city. They help take care of the trees, flowers, and vegetable plants in the garden.	**Beginning** It's nice. **Intermediate** Nature is pretty and fun. **Advanced** There are a lot of things to see and do in nature. **Advanced High** I think the people like to interact with nature because they like to look at pretty flowers and they like to grow vegetables to eat.	**Beginning** No plants there. **Intermediate** It's empty. **Advanced** The people planted a pretty garden to replace the empty lot. **Advanced High** The people planted a garden in an empty lot so they could enjoy nature in the city.	**Beginning** Go to the beach. **Intermediate** I like to go to the beach with my family. **Advanced** My family likes to go to the beach and swim in the ocean. **Advanced High** My family likes to go to the beach in the summer. We swim in the water and play in the sand.

This Week's Materials

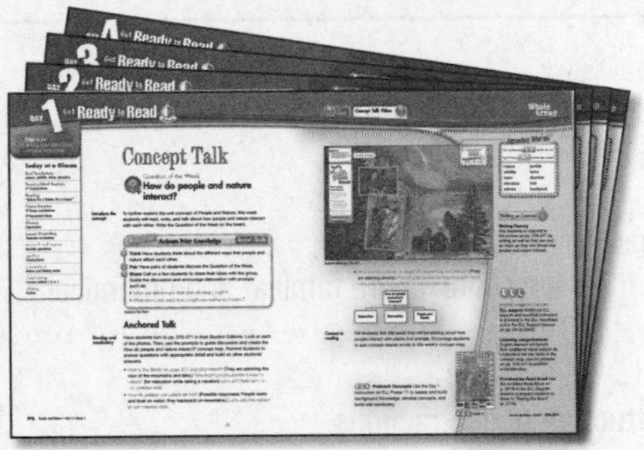
Teacher's Edition pages 370j–403q

See the support for English language learners throughout the lesson, including ELL strategies and scaffolded activities at points of use.

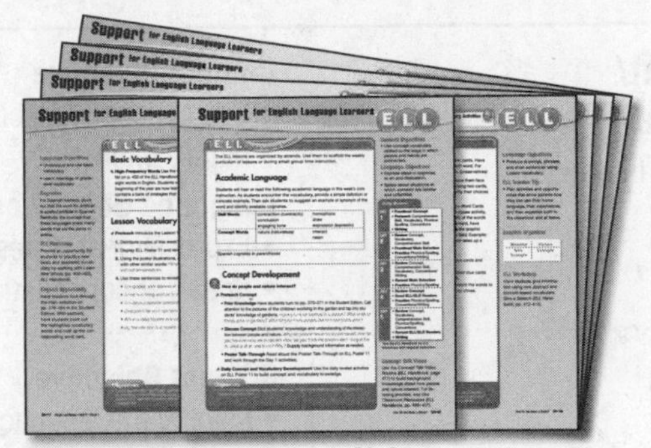
Teacher's Edition pages DI•16–DI•25

Differentiated Instruction for English language learners provides daily group activities that "frontload," or preteach, core instruction.

ELL Handbook pp. 89a–94

Find additional lesson materials that support the core lesson and the ELL instructional pages.

Poster 11

ELL Reader 3.3.1

ELD Reader 3.3.1

Concept Literacy Reader

ELD, ELL Reader Teaching Guide

Concept Literacy Reader Teaching Guide

Technology

Online Teacher's Edition Use the digital version of the core Teacher's Edition for planning and instruction.

eReaders
This week's ELL and ELD Readers and Concept Literacy Reader are also available in digital format.

This Week's Content and Language Objectives by Strand

Concept Development/ Academic Language How do people and nature interact?	**Content Objective** • Use concept vocabulary related to the ways in which people and nature interact. **Language Objectives** • Express ideas in response to discussion. • Speak about situations in which contexts are familiar and unfamiliar.
Phonics and Spelling Contractions	**Content Objective** • Identify the language structure of contractions. **Language Objectives** • Use spelling rules of contractions with increasing accuracy. • Monitor written language production and employ self-corrective techniques.
Listening Comprehension Modified Read Aloud: "The Bears of Big Bend"	**Content Objective** • Monitor and adjust oral comprehension **Language Objectives** • Discuss oral passages. • Use a graphic organizer to take notes.
Reading Comprehension Draw Conclusions	**Content Objectives** • Develop deductive reasoning strategies. • Use visual support to draw conclusions. **Language Objectives** • Write conclusions based on prior experiences. • Use academic language in speaking activities. • Expand vocabulary by retelling stories.
Vocabulary Basic and Lesson Vocabulary	**Language Objectives** • Understand and use basic and grade-level vocabulary. • Learn meanings of grade-level vocabulary. • Produce drawings, phrases, and short sentences to show understanding of Lesson Vocabulary.
Vocabulary Homophones	**Content Objective** • Identify homophones. **Language Objective** • Write using newly acquired basic vocabulary.
Grammar and Conventions Action and Linking Verbs	**Content Objective** • Decode and use action and linking verbs. **Language Objectives** • Speak using action and linking verbs correctly. • Write phrases and sentences with action and linking verbs.
Writing Writing with an Engaging Tone	**Content Objective** • Recognize engaging tone in a text. **Language Objective** • Write paragraphs using an engaging tone and complex grammatical structures.

Word Cards for Vocabulary Activities

area	**artificial**
grapevine	**preservative**
proof	**raise**
raisin	

Teacher Note: Beginning Teach two to three words. **Intermediate** Teach three to four words. **Advanced** Teach four to five words. **Advanced High** Teach all words.

Name ______________________________

Read the paragraph. Then fill in the four boxes that follow to show what the story is about.

- **Write** details from the text in the first two boxes.
- **Write** something from your own knowledge in the third box.
- **Write** a conclusion telling what the story is about in the fourth box.

A Gardener's Best Friend?

Some ladybugs eat insects that can hurt plants. Many people call them a gardener's best friend. Some gardeners even buy ladybugs for their gardens. Other kinds of ladybugs eat plants that gardeners grow. These ladybugs are enemies to a vegetable garden. They are called squash beetles.

Detail	→	Detail	→	What I Know	→	Conclusion

Picture It!

Draw Conclusions

Use this lesson to supplement or replace the skill lesson on page 374a of the Teacher's Edition. Display the Skill Points (at right) and share them with students.

Teach/Model

Beginning Say: *I buy a jade plant. I forget to give it water. The jade plant does not grow.* Discuss these details and what students know about plants. Help students draw a conclusion about why the jade plant does not grow. (It needs water to grow.)

Intermediate Tell these details about your garden: *My plants look sick. They have holes in their leaves. I see bugs on them.* Ask: *What do you know about plants and bugs?* (Some bugs eat plants.) Ask: *What conclusion can you draw about my garden?* (The bugs are eating your plants.)

Advanced Show a magazine photograph of a healthy, thriving garden. Ask: *What information can help you draw a conclusion about this garden?* (visual details; my own knowledge of plants) Have students draw and record conclusions about the garden.

Advanced High Ask students to think of simple gardening situations and share them with the group. Have the group identify and record details and any prior knowledge for each situation. Then have students compare notes to draw and record conclusions.

Then distribute copies of Picture It! page 90.

- Have students look at the picture and tell what they know about ladybugs and gardens.
- Read the paragraph aloud. Ask: *Did you learn anything new about ladybugs or gardens?*
- Review the Skill Points with students.
- Have students look at the picture and words to identify details. Help them draw a conclusion about ladybugs and gardens. (Some ladybugs help gardens, but other ladybugs hurt them.)

Skill Points

✔ After you think about facts and details, you can figure something out, or **draw a conclusion.**

✔ Use facts and details, plus what you already know, to draw conclusions about why things happen or are done a certain way.

Practice

Read aloud the directions on page 90. Have students reread the paragraph aloud. Then have them look at the picture and the paragraph as they complete the graphic organizer.

Beginning Students can first draw pictures and write words to complete the graphic organizer and then orally describe their pictures. Provide help with English words and writing.

Intermediate Students can first orally answer and then write words and phrases to complete the graphic organizer. Provide help with English words and writing.

Advanced Students can write sentences to complete the graphic organizer and then check their sentences by exchanging them with a partner.

Advanced High Students can write sentences to complete the graphic organizer and then orally explain how they drew their conclusions.

Answers for page 90: *Detail:* Some ladybugs eat harmful insects. *Detail:* Other kinds of ladybugs eat plants instead of insects. *What I Know:* Some bugs kill plants. *Conclusion:* Some ladybugs are good for gardens. Not all ladybugs are good for gardens.

Multilingual Summaries

English

How Do You Raise a Raisin?

Raisins are dried grapes. They are grown in many countries. Raisins grow best in places where there is hot weather and plenty of water. Most raisins in the U.S. are grown in California.

Grapevines grow on wires tied to branches. Grape pickers cut the grapes from the vines. They lay the grapes on trays to dry in the sun. As they bake, the raisins get wrinkles. After many weeks, they are put in packages.

It is hard to remove the seeds from raisins. William Thompson brought a seedless grape to California. Most California raisins come from Thompson Seedless grapes. Raisins are healthy to eat. They can be used to make many foods.

Spanish

¿Qué pasa con las pasas?

Las pasas son uvas secas. Crecen en un muchos países. Se dan mejor en climas cálidos y con agua. La mayoría de las pasas de Estados Unidos son de California.

La vid crece sobre alambres que amarrados a ramas. Los trabajadores cortan las uvas de la vid. Ellos las ponen en bandejas, bajo el sol. Conforme se secan, les salen arrugas. Luego se colocan en paquetes.

Es difícil quitarles las semillas. William Thompson llevó la uva sin semilla a California. La mayoría de las pasas de California vienen de las uvas Thompson. Las pasas son saludables. Se usan en usar para hacer muchos alimentos.

Multilingual Summaries

Chinese

怎样种葡萄干？

葡萄干是干了的葡萄。很多国家都种葡萄，葡萄最好生长在炎热、水源充足的地方。在美国，很多葡萄来自加州。

葡萄绕着支撑它的茎秆的棚架生长，收割的人把葡萄从茎秆剪下，然后把葡萄放在一个盘子上，利用太阳把葡萄晒干。葡萄在阳光下逐渐露出皱纹，变成葡萄干，几个星期以后，葡萄干就被包装出售。

葡萄干里面的核是很难被去掉的。威廉汤普森把一粒无核葡萄带到加州，从此，很多加州的葡萄干都来自汤普森的无核葡萄。葡萄干对身体很好，也可以用来做很多不同的食物。

Vietnamese

Làm Sao Để Trồng Nho?

Nho khô là trái nho phơi khô. Nho được trồng tại nhiều nước. Nho khô trồng tốt nhất là ở những nơi khí hậu nóng và có nhiều nước. Phần lớn nho khô ở Hoa Kỳ được trồng tại California.

Cây nho sinh trưởng trên dây cột vào các cành cây. Người hái nho cắt những chùm nho khỏi cây nho. Họ đặt trái nho trên khay để phơi nắng. Khi trái nho rám nắng, vỏ nó nhăn lại. Sau nhiều tuần lễ, nho được đóng gói.

Khó mà lấy hột ra khỏi trái nho khô. William Thompson đem nho không hột đến California. Phần lớn nho khô là từ nho không hột của Thompson. Ăn nho tốt cho sức khỏe. Nho có thể dùng để làm ra nhiều loại thực phẩm.

Multilingual Summaries

Korean

어떻게 건포도를 키우나요?

건포도는 말린 포도입니다. 건포도는 많은 나라에서 재배됩니다. 건포도는 날이 덥고 물이 충분한 곳에서 가장 잘 자랍니다. 미국 대부분의 건포도는 캘리포니아에서 재배됩니다.

포도덩굴은 가지에 연결된 철사줄에서 자랍니다. 포도 재배자는 포도를 덩굴에서 잘라냅니다. 그리고 포도를 쟁반에 펼쳐서 햇볕에서 말립니다. 마르면서 포도는 쭈글쭈글해집니다. 몇 주 후에, 건포도는 포장이 됩니다.

건포도에서 씨를 제거하기 어렵습니다. 윌리엄 톰슨은 씨없는 포도를 캘리포니아로 들여왔습니다. 대부분의 캘리포니아 건포도는 톰슨씨의 씨없는 포도로 만듭니다. 건포도는 건강에 좋습니다. 건포도는 또 여러가지 음식에 쓰이기도 합니다.

Hmong

Koj Yuav Tu Txiv Quav Ntswg Qhuav Loj Hlob Li Cas?

Txiv quav ntswg qhuav yog cov txiv quav ntswg uas qhaa qhuav. Cov txiv no cog loj hlob nyob ntau lub tebchaws. Txiv quav ntswg qhuav loj hlob zoo tshaj rau thaj chaw uas kub kub heev thiab muaj dej. Feem ntau cov txiv quav ntswg hauv U.S. yog cog loj hlob rau California.

Txiv quav ntswg loj hlob ntawm ib txoj mab uas ncau los ntawm cov ceg ntoo. Cov tub de txiv quav ntswg txiav cov txiv ntawm txoj mab. Lawv muab cov txiv quav ntswg coj mus tso rau ib lub phaj tes cia lub nub ziab. Thaus ziab lawm, cov txiv quav ntswg qhuav pib ntsws tuaj. Tom qab ob peb asthiv lawm, lawv muab coj los ntim cia hauv nab.

Trho cov noob tawm ntawm cov txiv quav ntswg qhuav mas nyuab heev. William Thompson coj tau cov txiv quav ntswg uas tsi muaj noob tuaj rau California. Feem ntau California cov txiv quav ntswg qhuav yog los ntawm Thompson Seedless cov txiv quav ntswg. Txiv quav ntswg qhuav noj zoo rau lub cev. Cov txiv no siv ua tau ntau yam zaub mov.

Name ____________________ **Nana's Herb Garden**

- **Read** *Nana's Herb Garden* again.
- **Draw** pictures to show what happens in the beginning, middle, and end.
- **Write** words or sentences that tell why each thing happens.

Beginning (pages 2–5)

Middle (pages 6–7)

End (page 8)

Family Link

Ask family members what they would plant in an herb garden.

Weekly Resources Guide for English Language Learner Support

For this week's content and language objectives, see p. 95e.

Instructional Strand	Day 1	Day 2
Concept Development/Academic Language	TEACHER'S EDITION • Academic Language, p. DI•41 • Concept Development, p. DI•41 • Anchored Talk, pp. 404j—404–405 • Preteach Academic Vocabulary, p. 409a • Concept Talk Video ELL HANDBOOK • Hear It, See It, Say It, Use It, pp. xxxvi–xxxvii • ELL Poster Talk, Concept Talk, p. 95c ELL POSTER 12 • Day 1 Activities	TEACHER'S EDITION • Academic Language, p. DI•41 • Concept Development, p. DI•41 • Anchored Talk, p. 410a • Concept Talk Video ELL HANDBOOK • ELL Poster Talk, Concept Talk, p. 95c • Concept Talk Video Routine, p. 477 ELL POSTER 12 • Day 2 Activities
Phonics and Spelling	TEACHER'S EDITION • Phonics and Spelling, p. DI•45 • Decodable Practice Reader 12A, pp. 407a–407b	TEACHER'S EDITION • Phonics and Spelling, p. DI•45
Listening Comprehension	TEACHER'S EDITION • Modified Read Aloud, p. DI•44 • Read Aloud, p. 405b • Concept Talk Video ELL HANDBOOK • Concept Talk Video Routine, p. 477	TEACHER'S EDITION • Modified Read Aloud, p. DI•44 • AudioText of *Pushing Up the Sky* • Concept Talk Video ELL HANDBOOK • AudioText CD Routine, p. 477 • Cause and Effect, p. 489
Reading Comprehension	TEACHER'S EDITION • Preteach Literary Elements: Character, Setting, Plot, p. DI•46	TEACHER'S EDITION • Reteach Literary Elements: Character, Setting, Plot, p. DI•46 • Frontloading Reading, p. DI•47 ELL HANDBOOK • Picture It! Skill Instruction, pp. 96–96a • Multilingual Summaries, pp. 97–99
Vocabulary **Basic and Lesson Vocabulary** **Vocabulary Skill: Unknown Words**	TEACHER'S EDITION • Basic Vocabulary, p. DI•42 • Preteach Lesson Vocabulary, p. DI•42 • Unknown Words, p. DI•45 ELL HANDBOOK • Word Cards, p. 95 • ELL Vocabulary Routine, p. 471 ELL POSTER 12 • Day 1 Activities	TEACHER'S EDITION • Basic Vocabulary, p. DI•42 • Reteach Lesson Vocabulary, p. DI•43 • Unknown Words, p. DI•45 ELL HANDBOOK • Word Cards, p. 95 • Multilingual Vocabulary List, p. 435 ELL POSTER 12 • Day 2 Activities
Grammar and Conventions	TEACHER'S EDITION • Preteach Main and Helping Verbs, p. DI•49	TEACHER'S EDITION • Teach Main and Helping Verbs, p. DI•49
Writing	TEACHER'S EDITION • Writing with Dialogue, p. DI•50 • Introduce Drama: Play, pp. 409e–409f	TEACHER'S EDITION • Writing Trait: Organization, pp. 417d–417e

Unit 3 Week 2 Pushing Up the Sky

This symbol indicates leveled instruction to address language proficiency levels.

Day 3	Day 4	Day 5
TEACHER'S EDITION • Academic Language, p. DI•41 • Concept Development, p. DI•41 • Anchored Talk, p. 418a • Concept Talk Video **ELL HANDBOOK** • ELL Poster Talk, Concept Talk, p. 95c **ELL POSTER 12** • Day 3 Activities	**TEACHER'S EDITION** • Academic Language, p. DI•41 • Concept Development, p. DI•41 • Anchored Talk, p. 428a • Concept Talk Video **ELL HANDBOOK** • ELL Poster Talk, Concept Talk, p. 95c **ELL POSTER 12** • Day 4 Activities	**TEACHER'S EDITION** • Academic Language, p. DI•41 • Concept Development, p. DI•41 • Concept Talk Video **ELL HANDBOOK** • ELL Poster Talk, Concept Talk, p. 95c **ELL POSTER 12** • Day 5 Activities
ELL HANDBOOK • Phonics Transition Lesson, pp. 284, 291	**ELL HANDBOOK** • Phonics Transition Lesson, pp. 284, 291	**TEACHER'S EDITION** • Phonics and Spelling, p. DI•45
TEACHER'S EDITION • AudioText of *Pushing Up the Sky* • Concept Talk Video **ELL HANDBOOK** • AudioText CD Routine, p. 477	**TEACHER'S EDITION** • Concept Talk Video	**TEACHER'S EDITION** • Concept Talk Video
TEACHER'S EDITION • Sheltered Reading, p. DI•47 **ELL HANDBOOK** • Multilingual Summaries, pp. 97–99	**TEACHER'S EDITION** • ELL/ELD Reader Guided Reading, p. DI•48 **ELL HANDBOOK** • ELL Study Guide, p. 100	**TEACHER'S EDITION** • ELL/ELD Reader Guided Reading, p. DI•48 **ELL HANDBOOK** • ELL Study Guide, p. 100
ELL HANDBOOK • High-Frequency Words Activity Bank, p. 446 **ELL POSTER 12** • Day 3 Activities	**ELL HANDBOOK** • High-Frequency Words Activity Bank, p. 446	**TEACHER'S EDITION** • Unknown Words, p. 437h **ELL HANDBOOK** • High-Frequency Words Activity Bank, p. 446
TEACHER'S EDITION • Grammar Jammer **ELL HANDBOOK** • Grammar Transition Lesson, pp. 324, 327, 330, 335 • Grammar Jammer Routine, p. 478	**TEACHER'S EDITION** • Grammar Jammer **ELL HANDBOOK** • Grammar Transition Lesson, pp. 324, 327, 330, 335	**TEACHER'S EDITION** • Grammar Jammer **ELL HANDBOOK** • Grammar Transition Lesson, pp. 324, 327, 330, 335
TEACHER'S EDITION • Let's Write It!, p. 426–427 • Writing Subtrait: Dialogue, pp. 427a–427b	**TEACHER'S EDITION** • Revising Strategy, pp. 437d–437e	**TEACHER'S EDITION** • Drama, pp. 437p–437q

Poster Talk, Concept Talk

Question of the Week

How do people explain things in nature?

Poster 12

Throughout the week, use the ELL Poster to help students produce and comprehend language, understand the concept, and build English vocabulary. Use the Question of the Week and other questions to help students share ideas in pairs, small groups, or the large group. Sample questions are shown, with examples of possible responses by students.

Weekly Concept and Language Goals

- Tell why people want to explain nature
- Discuss how myths explained nature for people in the past
- Share ways that people explain things in nature today

By the end of the lesson, students should be able to talk about and write one or more sentences about explaining things in nature.

Daily Team Talk

Day 1	Day 2	Day 3	Day 4	Day 5
After Day 1 activities on Poster, ask questions such as *In the poster picture, why do the students think a moose drops its antlers?*	After Day 2 activity on Poster, ask questions such as *The students write a play to explain something in nature. How is this similar to the way people explained things in nature in the past?*	After Day 3 activity on Poster, ask questions such as *How do people explain things in nature today?*	After Day 4 activity on Poster, ask questions such as *Why did the Snohomish people tell the story of* Pushing Up the Sky?	After Day 5 activity on Poster, ask questions such as *Think about what you have learned in your science class. What is one thing science explains about nature?*
Beginning Too heavy. **Intermediate** They get too big and heavy. They bump into things. **Advanced** They get so big they bump into things. They are too heavy to carry. Now they drop off. **Advanced High** The big antlers bumped into things and were too heavy to carry, so all the moose decided to have their antlers drop off each year.	**Beginning** They tell stories. **Intermediate** People told stories to explain nature. **Advanced** People told stories to explain things in nature they did not know. **Advanced High** In the past, people told stories to explain things in nature they did not understand. The students told a story about nature in their play.	**Beginning** With science. **Intermediate** We use science to explain things in nature. **Advanced** Scientists figure out things in nature and explain them to people. **Advanced High** Scientists study things in nature to figure out how they work. People use what scientists learn to explain things in nature.	**Beginning** To tell about the sky. **Intermediate** To explain why the sky is so high. **Advanced** They told this story to explain why the sky is so high up. **Advanced High** The Snohomish told this story to explain why the sky is so high above us and why we can see stars in the sky.	**Beginning** How plants grow. **Intermediate** Science explains how plants grow. **Advanced** Science explains how plants start as seeds and then grow into big plants. **Advanced High** In science class I learned how plants grow. My science book explains that a plant starts as a seed and then grows roots, a stem, leaves, flowers, and seeds.

This Week's Materials

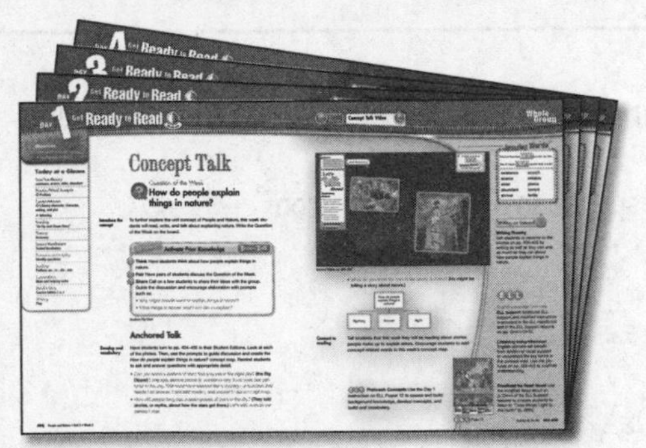

Teacher's Edition pages 404j–437q

See the support for English language learners throughout the lesson, including ELL strategies and scaffolded activities at points of use.

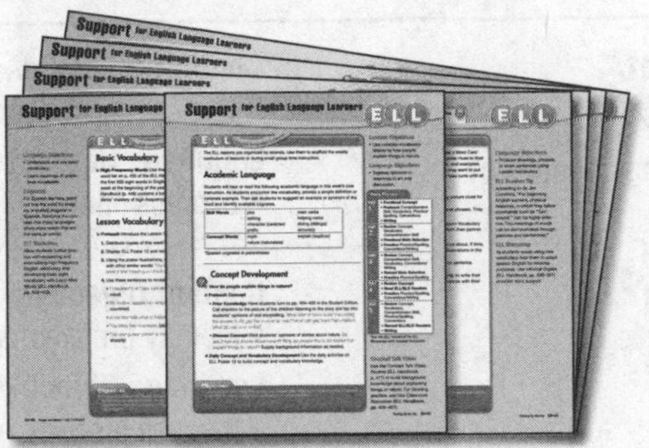

Teacher's Edition pages DI•41–DI•50

Differentiated Instruction for English language learners provides daily group activities that "frontload," or preteach, core instruction.

ELL Handbook pp. 95a–100

Find additional lesson materials that support the core lesson and the ELL instructional pages.

ELL Poster 12

ELL Reader 3.3.2

ELD Reader 3.3.2

Concept Literacy Reader

ELD, ELL Reader Teaching Guide

Concept Literacy Reader Teaching Guide

Technology

Online Teacher's Edition Use the digital version of the core Teacher's Edition for planning and instruction.

eReaders
This week's ELL and ELD Readers and Concept Literacy Reader are also available in digital format.

This Week's Content and Language Objectives by Strand

Concept Development/ Academic Language How do people explain things in nature?	**Content Objective** • Use concept vocabulary related to how people explain things in nature. **Language Objective** • Express opinions in response to art and discussion.
Phonics and Spelling Prefixes	**Content Objective** • Identify prefixes *un-*, *re-*. **Language Objective** • Discuss prefixes *un-*, *re-*.
Listening Comprehension Modified Read Aloud: "How the North Got its Light"	**Content Objective** • Monitor and adjust oral comprehension. **Language Objectives** • Discuss oral passages. • Use a graphic organizer to take notes.
Reading Comprehension Literary Elements: Character, Setting, Plot	**Content Objectives** • Identify literary elements based on evidence found in a text. • Provide evidence for your identification of literary elements based on familiar and unfamiliar contexts. **Language Objectives** • Discuss evidence for your identification of literary elements. • Write literary elements as you identify them. • Summarize text using visual support.
Vocabulary Basic and Lesson Vocabulary	**Language Objectives** • Understand and use basic and grade-level vocabulary. • Learn meanings of grade-level vocabulary. • Produce drawings, phrases, and short sentences to show understanding of Lesson Vocabulary.
Vocabulary Unknown Words	**Content Objective** • Identify unknown words. **Language Objective** • Apply phonics and decoding skills to vocabulary.
Grammar and Conventions Main and Helping Verbs	**Content Objective** • Decode and use main and helping verbs. **Language Objectives** • Speak using main and helping verbs correctly. • Write phrases and sentences with main and helping verbs.
Writing Writing with Dialogue	**Content Objective** • Recognize the use of dialogue in a text. **Language Objectives** • Write short dialogues using newly acquired vocabulary. • Share feedback for editing and revising.

Word Cards for Vocabulary Activities

antlers	**imagined**
languages	**narrator**
overhead	**poked**

Leveled Support

Teacher Note: Beginning Teach two to three words. **Intermediate** Teach three to four words. **Advanced** Teach four to five words. **Advanced High** Teach all words.

Name ___________________________

Look at the picture. **Read** the paragraph.

- **Notice** the details as you read the paragraph.

Grandmother's Molas

My grandmother grew up in Central America. She was a Kuno Indian. Grandmother made molas as a child. Molas are a kind of fabric art. When I visited her home, Grandmother wanted to teach me to make molas. I like to play with her farm animals, though. I do not like to sew, and Grandmother was very disappointed. Finally, she found an animal design I could make. Together we made a mola of a beautiful bird.

Circle the letter of the correct answer for each question.

1. Who is telling the story?
a. the grandmother **b.** the granddaughter **c.** the mother

2. Where does the story take place?
a. the grandmother's house **b.** Central America **c.** the girl's home

3. What is the problem in the story?
a. The grandmother forgot how to make molas.
b. The girl thought making molas was too hard.
c. The girl thought she would not like making molas.

Character, Setting, and Plot

Use this lesson to supplement or replace the skill lesson on page 408a of the Teacher's Edition. Display the Skill Points (at right) and share them with students.

Teach/Model

Beginning Say: *Dad and I were going camping. It rained. I had an idea. I put the tent inside. We camped in the house!* Ask students to draw pictures to show the events in the plot of the story. Have them label the characters and the setting in their pictures.

Intermediate Tell students a short story about your family. Ask them to identify the characters, setting, and plot of the story. List their responses. Have students use these notes to write simple sentences about the story elements.

Advanced Display a magazine photograph of a family. Say: *Let's write a story about this family.* Have students choose names for the characters and a setting and brainstorm events for the plot. Write their plan on the board. Have each student write and illustrate a sentence telling about one event in the plot.

Advanced High Pair students. Have one partner tell a story about his or her family. Have the other partner identify the characters and setting of the story and write a few sentences about the plot. Then the partners trade roles.

Then distribute copies of Picture It! page 96.

- Have students look at the picture and title and tell what they think the story is about.
- Read the story aloud. Ask: *What happens in this story?*
- Review the Skill Points with students.
- Have students identify the characters, setting, and plot of the story.

Skill Points

✔ A **character** is a person or animal who appears in a story.

✔ The **setting** is the time and place of a story.

✔ The **plot** is the series of important events that happen in the beginning, middle, and end of a story.

Practice

Read aloud the directions on page 96. Have students reread the story with partners. Have them look at the picture and the story as they answer the questions.

Beginning Students can answer the questions orally and then mark their answers. Provide help with circling the correct answers.

Intermediate Students can first orally answer and then circle the letters of their answers.

Advanced Students can circle the letters of their answers and then check their answers by comparing them with a partner's.

Advanced High Students can circle the letters of their answers and then check them by rereading the story and underlining the details that answer the questions.

Answers for page 96: 1. b; 2. a; 3. c

Multilingual Summaries

English

Pushing Up the Sky

The Snohomish people are not happy. The sky is too close. They bump their heads on it. They lose their balls in the sky. Children get lost when they climb tall trees. The people must do something.

The seven wisest chiefs have a meeting. They decide to push up the sky. The people all find long poles and start pushing. At first, it does not work. Then, when they all push together, the sky moves. People will not bump their heads on the sky anymore. Stars shine through the holes that their poles poked into the sky.

Spanish

Levantar el cielo

La gente del pueblo de Snohomish no está feliz. El cielo está demasiado cerca. Se pegan en la cabeza con él. Pierden sus pelotas si las lanzan hacia el cielo. Los niños se pierden cuando trepan en los árboles altos. La gente tiene que hacer algo.

Los siete jefes sabios tienen una reunión. Deciden empujar y levantar el cielo. Todos buscan palos y comienzan a empujar. Al principio no pasa nada. Luego, cuando todos empujan a la vez, el cielo se mueve. La gente ya nunca volverá a pegarse con el cielo en la cabeza. Las estrellas brillan a través de los agujeros que hicieron con los palos cuando levantaron el cielo.

Multilingual Summaries

Chinese

把天空推高一點

斯諾霍米什這個地方的人不快樂，因為天空離他們太近了，害他們的頭時常撞到天空，球抛到天空上也會不見了，小朋友爬高樹的時候也會迷路。他們都想解決這個問題。

地方上七個最聰明的首領召開會議，決定要把天空推高一點。大家找來長竿子開始推。剛開始的時候，一點用也沒有，後來，他們合力一起推的時候，天空竟然動了。人們的頭不會再撞到天空了。他們用竿子在天空上戳破的洞裡，也會有星星發出光芒來。

Vietnamese

Đẩy Trời Lên Cao

Người của bộ lạc Snohomish không được vui. Bầu trời gần họ quá. Họ va đầu vào đó. Họ bị mất mấy quả bóng trong bầu trời. Trẻ em thất lạc khi chúng leo lên các cây cao. Dân chúng cần phải hành động.

Bảy vị thủ lĩnh thông thái mở cuộc họp. Họ quyết định đẩy trời lên cao. Dân chúng tìm những cây gậy dài và bắt đầu đẩy. Thoạt đầu, việc này không có kết quả. Sau đó, khi mọi người cùng đẩy, bầu trời chuyển động. Người ta sẽ không còn va đầu vào bầu trời nữa. Các vì sao chiếu qua những lỗ tròn mà những cây gậy của họ đã đâm vào bầu trời.

Multilingual Summaries

Korean

하늘 밀어 올리기

스노호미쉬 사람들은 행복하지 않다. 하늘이 너무 가까워서 하늘에 머리를 부딪히고 하늘에다 공을 잃어버리며 아이들은 높은 나무에 올라갈 때마다 길을 잃는다. 사람들은 뭔가 조치를 해야만 한다.

일곱 명의 가장 현명한 우두머리들이 회의를 열고 하늘을 밀어 올리기로 결정한다. 사람들은 모두 기다란 막대기를 찾아 하늘을 밀어 올리기 시작하는데 처음에는 잘 되지 않는다. 이후 사람들 모두가 함께 밀어 올리자 하늘이 움직인다. 사람들은 더 이상 하늘에 머리를 부딪히지 않는다. 그리고 막대기로 찔렀던 구멍으로 별들이 빛난다.

Hmong

Thawb Lub Ntuj Rov Sauv

Cov neeg Snohomish tsis zoo siab. Lub ntuj nyob ris dhau lawm. Lawv tsoo lawv tau hau sauv. Lawv ua lawv tej pob xiam sauv. Menyuam poob zoo thaum lawv nce ntoo siab siab. Cov neeg yuav tsum ua li cas.

Xya leej thawj coj uas txawj tse tsaj plaws muaj ib lub roob sib tham. Lawv txhiav txim siab thawb lub ntuj rov sauv. Neeg sawvdaws nrhiav tau ib cov nreg siab siab thiab pib thawb. Thaum xub thawj, nws tsis ua hauj lwm. Ces, thaum lawv sawvdaws thawb ua ke, lub ntuj. Tib neeg tsis tsoo taub hauv saum ntuj lawm. Hnub qub ci tuaj tawm ntawm cov qhov uas lawv cov nreg tau tshum sauv ntuj.

Name ______________________________

- **Read** *The Legend of the North Star* again.
- What is the problem in the story? **Write** it in the box.
- What is the solution? **Write** it in the box.

Problem

____

____

____

Solution

____

____

____

Family Link

Ask family members to share legends they have heard about how things came to be. Compare and contrast the problems and solutions from these legends with those from *The Legend of the North Star.*

Weekly Resources Guide for English Language Learner Support

For this week's content and language objectives, see p. 101e.

Instructional Strand	Day 1	Day 2
Concept Development/Academic Language	TEACHER'S EDITION • Academic Language, p. DI•66 • Concept Development, p. DI•66 • Anchored Talk, pp. 438j—438–439 • Preteach Academic Vocabulary, p. 443a • Concept Talk Video ELL HANDBOOK • Hear It, See It,Say It, Use It, pp. xxxvi–xxxvii • ELL Poster Talk, Concept Talk, p. 101c ELL POSTER 13 • Day 1 Activities	TEACHER'S EDITION • Academic Language, p. DI•66 • Concept Development, p. DI•66 • Anchored Talk, p. 444a • Concept Talk Video ELL HANDBOOK • ELL Poster Talk, Concept Talk, p. 101c • Concept Talk Video Routine, p. 477 ELL POSTER 13 • Day 2 Activities
Phonics and Spelling	TEACHER'S EDITION • Phonics and Spelling, p. DI•70 • Decodable Practice Reader 13A, pp. 441a–441b	TEACHER'S EDITION • Phonics and Spelling, p. DI•70
Listening Comprehension	TEACHER'S EDITION • Modified Read Aloud, p. DI•69 • Read Aloud, p. 439b • Concept Talk Video ELL HANDBOOK • Concept Talk Video Routine, p. 477	TEACHER'S EDITION • Modified Read Aloud, p. DI•69 • AudioText of *Seeing Stars* • Concept Talk Video ELL HANDBOOK • AudioText CD Routine, p. 477 • K-W-L Chart, p. 480
Reading Comprehension	TEACHER'S EDITION • Preteach Graphic Sources, p. DI•71	TEACHER'S EDITION • Reteach Graphic Sources, p. DI•71 • Frontloading Reading, p. DI•72 ELL HANDBOOK • Picture It! Skill Instruction, pp. 102–102a • Multilingual Summaries, pp. 103–105
Vocabulary **Basic and Lesson Vocabulary** **Vocabulary Skill: Unknown Words**	TEACHER'S EDITION • Basic Vocabulary, p. DI•67 • Preteach Lesson Vocabulary, p. DI•67 • Unknown Words, p. DI•70 ELL HANDBOOK • Word Cards, p. 101 • ELL Vocabulary Routine, p. 471 ELL POSTER 13 • Day 1 Activities	TEACHER'S EDITION • Basic Vocabulary, p. DI•67 • Reteach Lesson Vocabulary, p. DI•68 • Unknown Words, p. DI•70 ELL HANDBOOK • Word Cards, p. 101 • Multilingual Vocabulary List, pp. 435–436 ELL POSTER 13 • Day 2 Activities
Grammar and Conventions	TEACHER'S EDITION • Preteach Subject-Verb Agreement, p. DI•74	TEACHER'S EDITION • Reteach Subject-Verb Agreement, p. DI•74
Writing	TEACHER'S EDITION • Writing with Correct Commas and Capitalization in a Formal Letter, p. DI•75 • Introduce Formal Letter, pp. 443e–443f	TEACHER'S EDITION • Writer's Craft: Narrow Your Topic, pp. 451d–451e

This symbol indicates leveled instruction to address language proficiency levels.

Day 3	Day 4	Day 5
TEACHER'S EDITION • Academic Language, p. DI•66 • Concept Development, p. DI•66 • Anchored Talk, p. 452a • Concept Talk Video ELL HANDBOOK • ELL Poster Talk, Concept Talk, p. 101c ELL POSTER 13 • Day 3 Activities	TEACHER'S EDITION • Academic Language, p. DI•66 • Concept Development, p. DI•66 • Anchored Talk, p. 462a • Concept Talk Video ELL HANDBOOK • ELL Poster Talk, Concept Talk, p. 101c ELL POSTER 13 • Day 4 Activities	TEACHER'S EDITION • Academic Language, p. DI•66 • Concept Development, p. DI•66 • Concept Talk Video ELL HANDBOOK • ELL Poster Talk, Concept Talk, p. 101c ELL POSTER 13 • Day 5 Activities
ELL HANDBOOK • Phonics Transition Lesson, pp. 272, 275	ELL HANDBOOK • Phonics Transition Lesson, pp. 272, 275	TEACHER'S EDITION • Phonics and Spelling, p. DI•70
TEACHER'S EDITION • AudioText of *Seeing Stars* • Concept Talk Video ELL HANDBOOK • AudioText CD Routine, p. 477	TEACHER'S EDITION • Concept Talk Video	TEACHER'S EDITION • Concept Talk Video
TEACHER'S EDITION • Sheltered Reading, p. DI•72 ELL HANDBOOK • Multilingual Summaries, pp. 103–105	TEACHER'S EDITION • ELL/ELD Reader Guided Reading, p. DI•73 ELL HANDBOOK • ELL Study Guide, p. 106	TEACHER'S EDITION • ELL/ELD Reader Guided Reading, p. DI•73 ELL HANDBOOK • ELL Study Guide, p. 106
ELL HANDBOOK • High-Frequency Words Activity Bank, p. 446 ELL POSTER 13 • Day 3 Activities	ELL HANDBOOK • High-Frequency Words Activity Bank, p. 446	TEACHER'S EDITION • Unknown Words, p. 467h ELL HANDBOOK • High-Frequency Words Activity Bank, p. 446
TEACHER'S EDITION • Grammar Jammer ELL HANDBOOK • Grammar Transition Lesson, pp. 340, 349 • Grammar Jammer Routine, p. 478	TEACHER'S EDITION • Grammar Jammer ELL HANDBOOK • Grammar Transition Lesson, pp. 340, 349	TEACHER'S EDITION • Grammar Jammer ELL HANDBOOK • Grammar Transition Lesson, pp. 340, 349
TEACHER'S EDITION • Let's Write It!, p. 460–461 • Writing Trait: Conventions, pp. 461a–461b	TEACHER'S EDITION • Revising Strategy, pp. 467d–467e	TEACHER'S EDITION • Formal Letter, pp. 467p–467q

Poster Talk, Concept Talk

Question of the Week

What can we learn about nature by investigating?

ELL Poster 13

Throughout the week, use the ELL Poster to help students produce and comprehend language, understand the concept, and build English vocabulary. Use the Question of the Week and other questions to help students share ideas in pairs, small groups, or the large group. Sample questions are shown, with examples of possible responses by students.

Weekly Concept and Language Goals

- Explain why people investigate to learn about nature
- Identify a tool people use to investigate space
- Discuss what people can learn about stars by investigating them

By the end of the lesson, students should be able to talk about and write one or more sentences about what they can learn by investigating nature.

Daily Team Talk

Day 1	Day 2	Day 3	Day 4	Day 5
After Day 1 activities on Poster, ask questions such as *In the poster picture, what are the girl and her father doing?*	After Day 2 activity on Poster, ask questions such as *Think of all you know about stars. How do people know things about stars?*	After Day 3 activity on Poster, ask questions such as *How are the girl and her father like the scientists who investigate stars?*	After Day 4 activity on Poster, ask questions such as *In the selection* Seeing Stars, *what is one tool people use to investigate space?*	After Day 5 activity on Poster, ask questions such as *What can you learn by looking at the stars?*
Beginning Looking at stars. **Intermediate** They are looking at the stars in the sky. **Advanced** The girl and her father are looking for patterns in the stars. **Advanced High** The girl and her father are looking for patterns made by the stars in the night sky. Her father is pointing at one of the star patterns.	**Beginning** From science. **Intermediate** Science tells people things about stars. **Advanced** Scientists learn things about the stars and then tell people what they learn. **Advanced High** Scientists investigate the stars by asking questions, using tools, and finding answers. Then they tell people what they find out.	**Beginning** They look at stars. **Intermediate** They both look at the stars. **Advanced** Scientists look at stars to learn about them, like the girl and her father do. **Advanced High** The girl and her father look at the stars. Scientists investigate stars by looking at them too.	**Beginning** A telescope. **Intermediate** People use a telescope. **Advanced** People use a telescope to see things that are far away in space. **Advanced High** Scientists use a telescope to see things in space. A telescope makes things that are far away look like they are close.	**Beginning** There are patterns. **Intermediate** The stars can make patterns in the sky. **Advanced** There are many patterns in the sky. Some stars are brighter than others. **Advanced High** There are millions of stars in the sky. Some are bright, and others are dim. Some stars form patterns called constellations.

This Week's Materials

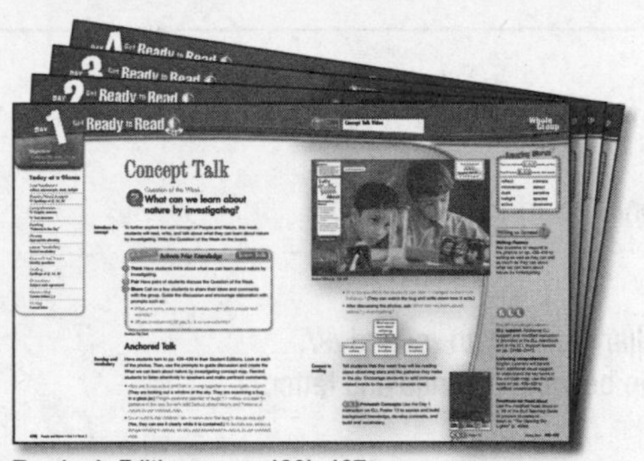
Teacher's Edition pages 438j–467q

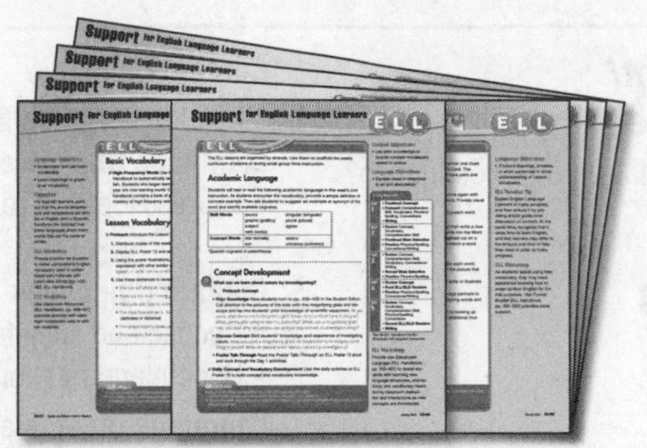
Teacher's Edition pages DI•66–DI•75

ELL Handbook pp. 101a–106

See the support for English language learners throughout the lesson, including ELL strategies and scaffolded activities at points of use.

Differentiated Instruction for English language learners provides daily group activities that "frontload," or preteach, core instruction.

Find additional lesson materials that support the core lesson and the ELL instructional pages.

Poster 13

ELL Reader 3.3.3

ELD Reader 3.3.3

Concept Literacy Reader

ELD, ELL Reader Teaching Guide

Concept Literacy Reader Teaching Guide

Technology

Online Teacher's Edition Use the digital version of the core Teacher's Edition for planning and instruction.

eReaders
This week's ELL and ELD Readers and Concept Literacy Reader are also available in digital format.

This Week's Content and Language Objectives by Strand

Concept Development/ Academic Language What can we learn about nature by investigating?	**Content Objective** • Use prior knowledge to acquire concept vocabulary related to space. **Language Objective** • Express ideas in response to art and discussion.
Phonics and Spelling Spellings of /s/ and /k/	**Content Objectives** • Decode and spell familiar words with /s/ and /k/. • Understand relationship between sounds and letters. **Language Objective** • Use phonics and spelling skills to write familiar vocabulary accurately.
Listening Comprehension Modified Read Aloud: "Northern Lights"	**Content Objective** • Monitor and adjust oral comprehension. **Language Objectives** • Discuss oral passages using accessible language. • Use visual support of a graphic organizer to understand spoken language.
Reading Comprehension Graphic Sources	**Content Objectives** • Identify graphic sources. • Use graphic sources to aid comprehension. **Language Objectives** • Discuss graphic sources. • Demonstrate comprehension by retelling a text. • Summarize text by collaborating with peers.
Vocabulary Basic and Lesson Vocabulary	**Language Objectives** • Understand and use basic and grade-level vocabulary. • Learn meanings of grade-level vocabulary. • Produce drawings, phrases, and short sentences to show understanding of Lesson Vocabulary.
Vocabulary Unknown Words	**Content Objective** • Use a dictionary to find the meaning of unknown words. **Language Objective** • Discuss how to find the meaning of unknown words.
Grammar and Conventions Subject-Verb Agreement	**Content Objectives** • Identify correct subject-verb agreement. • Form sentences with correct subject-verb agreement. **Language Objectives** • Speak using correct subject-verb agreement. • Write phrases and sentences with correct subject-verb agreement.
Writing Writing with Correct Commas and Capitalization in a Formal Letter	**Content Objective** • Identify the main features of a formal letter. **Language Objective** • Write a formal letter using a variety of sentence lengths and specificity and detail.

Word Cards for Vocabulary Activities

dim	**gas**
gigantic	**ladle**
patterns	**shine**
temperature	

Teacher Note: Beginning Teach two to three words. **Intermediate** Teach three to four words. **Advanced** Teach four to five words. **Advanced High** Teach all words.

Name ____________________

Picture It!
Graphic Sources

Look at the picture. **Read** the story.

- Use the information in the paragraph to **label** the picture.

Parts of a Plant

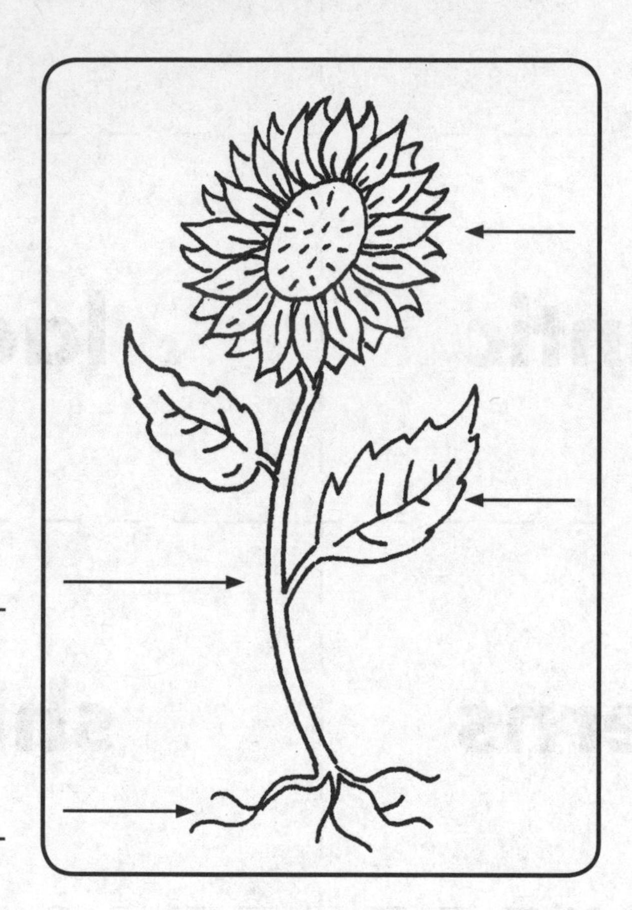

Plants have many parts. The parts have jobs. The *flower* is the part that blossoms. It has the parts that make seeds for new flowers. The *roots* are under the ground. Roots help the plant get nutrients from the soil. The *stem* is the part above the ground that holds the flower and leaves up. The *leaves* of the plant may be green and flat. The leaves take in sunlight. They also take in important gases from the air around the plant.

Graphic Sources

Use this lesson to supplement or replace the skill lesson on page 442a of the Teacher's Edition. Display the Skill Points (at right) and share them with students.

Skill Points

✔ **Graphic sources** are charts, photos, graphs, and diagrams that help you understand information in the text.

Teach/Model

Beginning Display a map, a photograph, a graph, and a chart in textbooks. Point to the map. Say: *This is a map. What does a map tell us?* (where things are located) Repeat this process with the other graphic sources.

Intermediate Display a magazine photograph of a plant and a textbook diagram of a plant. Ask: *What do both graphic sources tell about?* (a plant) Point to each example in turn and ask: *What can we learn about the plant from this graphic source?* (where it grows; what it looks like; what parts it has)

Advanced Display a diagram of a tree, with the roots, trunk, branches, and leaves labeled. Ask: *How does this diagram make the information easier to understand?* (It clearly identifies the parts of a tree.) Have students respond by writing a sentence about the diagram.

Advanced High Ask students to look in the classroom for examples of maps, illustrations, charts, graphs, and diagrams. Have students identify their graphic sources and explain how each helps readers understand information.

Then distribute copies of Picture It! page 102.

- Have students look at the diagram and tell what they know about plants.
- Read the paragraph aloud. Ask: *What parts does a plant have?*
- Review the Skill Points with students.
- Have students look at the picture and words. Ask: *What words can you use to label the picture? How can you tell?*

Practice

Read aloud the directions on page 102. Reread or have volunteers take turns rereading the paragraph aloud. Have students look at the picture and the paragraph as they complete the diagram.

Beginning Students can first orally answer as they point to the parts of the picture and then write the words on the lines to complete the diagram. Provide help with English words.

Intermediate Students can first orally answer and then write their answers to label the parts of the diagram.

Advanced Students can write their answers to complete the diagram and then check their work by rereading the paragraph and making any necessary corrections.

Advanced High Students can write their answers to complete the diagram and then explain the function and location of each plant part.

Answers for page 102: *Left-hand labels:* stem, roots; *Right-hand labels:* flower, leaves

Multilingual Summaries

Read Together

English

Seeing Stars

Stars are always in the sky, but you can't see them during the day. Stars are giant spheres of gas. Light pollution and smog make it hard to see stars in cities. In the country, you can see thousands of stars with just your eyes. You can use a telescope to see millions of stars that are far away.

Some stars are bright and some are dim. They all look white, but they are actually different colors. Stars also have different temperatures. It looks like the stars move, but it is the Earth moving.

Constellations are named after animals, shapes, and characters from mythology. Some constellations are Orion, Sirius, Canis Major, and Ursa Major.

Spanish

School + Home

Viendo estrellas

Las estrellas están siempre en el cielo, pero no podemos verlas durante el día. Las estrellas son gigantescas esferas de gas. La contaminación hace que las estrellas sean difíciles de ver en las ciudades. En el campo puedes ver miles de estrellas tan sólo con tus ojos. Puedes usar un telescopio para observar millones de estrellas que se encuentran muy lejos.

Algunas estrellas son muy brillantes y otras son opacas. Todas ellas se ven blancas, pero realmente son de diferentes colores. Las estrellas también tienen diferentes temperaturas. Parece que las estrellas se mueven, pero es el planeta Tierra el que se mueve.

A las constelaciones les dieron nombres de animales, de formas geométricas y personajes mitológicos. Algunas de las constelaciones son Orión, Sirio, Can Mayor y La Osa Mayor.

Multilingual Summaries

Chinese

看星星

星星一直高掛在天上，但是白天卻看不到它們。 星星是由氣體構成的巨大球體。 由於城市裡有光害和煙塵，所以很難看到星星。 在鄉下，僅用肉眼就可以看到成千上萬的星星。 你用望遠鏡可以看到數百萬顆距離地球很遠的星星。

有些星星很亮，而有些星星則很暗。 儘管他們看起來都是白色的，但實際上他們的顏色各不相同。 星星的溫度也不一樣。 我們會覺得是星星在移動，但實際上是地球在轉動。

星座是依據動物、形狀和神話中的人物命名的， 例如獵戶座、天狼座、大犬座和大熊座。

Vietnamese

Xem Các Ngôi Sao

Các ngôi sao lúc nào cũng có trên bầu trời, nhưng bạn không thể nhìn thấy nó vào ban ngày. Ngôi sao là những hình cầu bằng hơi vĩ đại. Sự ô nhiễm không khí và khói ở thành phố làm cho chúng ta khó thấy được các ngôi sao. Ở đồng quê, bạn có thể thấy được cả vạn ngôi sao ngay trước mắt. Bạn có thể dùng kính thiên văn để nhìn cả triệu ngôi sao ở nơi xa thẳm.

Có một số ngôi sao sáng và còn một số thì mờ. Chúng đều nhìn màu trắng, nhưng thật ra chúng có nhiều màu khác nhau. Các ngôi sao cũng có nhiệt độ khác nhau. Nhìn các ngôi sao thấy giống như di động, nhưng thật ra là do quả Đất đi chuyển.

Các chòm sao được đặt tên từ thú vật, hình dáng, và đặc điểm từ các câu chuyện thần thoại. Một số chòm sao là Orion, Sirius, Canis Major, và Ursa Major.

Multilingual Summaries

Korean

별 보기

별들은 하늘에 항상 있지만 낮에는 볼 수 없다. 별은 기체로 된 거대한 구이다. 도시의 불빛과 스모그가 별 보기를 어렵게 한다. 시골에서는 맨눈으로도 수천 개의 별을 볼 수 있다. 망원경을 사용하면 멀리 있는 수백만 개의 별을 볼 수 있다.

어떤 별은 밝고 어떤 별은 희미하다. 별은 모두 흰색으로 보이지만 실제로는 색이 다양하다. 별의 온도도 다양하다. 우리에겐 별이 움직이는 것처럼 보이지만 움직이는 것은 지구다.

별자리는 신화 속의 동물이나 모양이나 등장인물을 따라 이름이 붙었다. 별자리에는 오리온, 시리우스, 큰개자리, 큰곰자리가 있다.

Hmong

Pom Hnub Qub

Hnub qub mas yeej ib txwm nyob saum ntuj, tabsis yus tsis pom nws thaum nruab hnub xwb. Hnub qub ib pa roj loj loj kawg. Duab tshaj ntuj ua rau thiab pa ua rau tsis pom hnub qub nyob hauv tej zos. Nyob rau hauv teb chaw, koj yeej pom txog phav lub hnub qub nrog koj ob lub qhov muag. Koj yeej siv lub telescope los tsom mus pom txog pua pua phav lub hnub qub deb deb kawg.

Muaj ib co hnub qub ci ci thiab muaj ib co qauj quaj. Lawv tas nro mas yog xim dawb, tabsis qhov tseeb tiag lawm nyias muaj nyias xim. Hnub qublos kuj tseem muaj lub kub lub txia sib txawv. Nws zoo li cov hnub qub txav, tabsis yog lub ntiaj teb txav xwb.

Tej kab lig ntuj mas raug tis npe rau li tej tsiaj, nws zoo licas, thiab nws muaj nyob licas tas los lawm xwb. Muaj ib co kab lig ntuj yog Orion, Sirius, Canis Major, thiab Ursa Major.

Name ______________________________

Exploring the Rocky Mountains

- **Read** *Exploring the Rocky Mountains* again. Look at the pictures of the plants and animals and where they live.
- **Draw** pictures to show one animal or plant that lives at the top, middle, and bottom of a mountain.
- **Write** the names of the living things on the lines.

	Top of the Mountain
	______________________
	______________________
	______________________

	Middle of the Mountain
	______________________
	______________________
	______________________

	Bottom of the Mountain
	______________________
	______________________
	______________________

Family Link

Ask your family members if they have ever seen any of the animals you read about. Share their stories with your class.

Weekly Resources Guide for English Language Learner Support

For this week's content and language objectives, see p. 107e.

Instructional Strand	Day 1	Day 2
Concept Development/Academic Language	TEACHER'S EDITION • Academic Language, p. DI•91 • Concept Development, p. DI•91 • Anchored Talk, pp. 468j—468–469 • Preteach Academic Vocabulary, p. 473a • Concept Talk Video ELL HANDBOOK • Hear It, See It, Say It, Use It, pp. xxxvi–xxxvii • ELL Poster Talk, Concept Talk, p. 107c ELL POSTER 14 • Day 1 Activities	TEACHER'S EDITION • Academic Language, p. DI•91 • Concept Development, p. DI•91 • Anchored Talk, p. 474a • Concept Talk Video ELL HANDBOOK • ELL Poster Talk, Concept Talk, p. 107c • Concept Talk Video Routine, p. 477 ELL POSTER 14 • Day 2 Activities
Phonics and Spelling	TEACHER'S EDITION • Phonics and Spelling, p. DI•95 • Decodable Practice Reader 14A, pp. 471a–471b	TEACHER'S EDITION • Phonics and Spelling, p. DI•95
Listening Comprehension	TEACHER'S EDITION • Modified Read Aloud, p. DI•94 • Read Aloud, p. 469b • Concept Talk Video ELL HANDBOOK • Concept Talk Video Routine, p. 477	TEACHER'S EDITION • Modified Read Aloud, p. DI•94 • AudioText of *A Symphony of Whales* • Concept Talk Video ELL HANDBOOK • AudioText CD Routine, p. 477
Reading Comprehension	TEACHER'S EDITION • Preteach Generalize, p. DI•96	TEACHER'S EDITION • Reteach Generalize, p. DI•96 • Frontloading Reading, p. DI•97 ELL HANDBOOK • Picture It! Skill Instruction, pp. 108–108a • Multilingual Summaries, pp. 109–111
Vocabulary **Basic and Lesson Vocabulary** **Vocabulary Skill: Unfamiliar Words**	TEACHER'S EDITION • Basic Vocabulary, p. DI•92 • Preteach Lesson Vocabulary, p. DI•92 • Unfamiliar Words, p. DI•95 ELL HANDBOOK • Word Cards, p. 107 • ELL Vocabulary Routine, p. 471 ELL POSTER 14 • Day 1 Activities	TEACHER'S EDITION • Basic Vocabulary, p. DI•92 • Reteach Lesson Vocabulary, p. DI•93 • Unfamiliar Words, p. DI•95 ELL HANDBOOK • Word Cards, p. 107 • Multilingual Vocabulary List, p. 436 ELL POSTER 14 • Day 2 Activities
Grammar and Conventions	TEACHER'S EDITION • Preteach Past, Present, and Future Tense, p. DI•99	TEACHER'S EDITION • Reteach Past, Present, and Future Tense, p. DI•99
Writing	TEACHER'S EDITION • 5Ws and How, p. DI•100 • Introduce News Article, pp. 473e–473f	TEACHER'S EDITION • Writer's Craft: The 5Ws and How, pp. 485d–485e

Unit 3 Week 4 A Symphony of Whales

This symbol indicates leveled instruction to address language proficiency levels.

Day 3	Day 4	Day 5
TEACHER'S EDITION • Academic Language, p. DI•91 • Concept Development, p. DI•91 • Anchored Talk, p. 486a • Concept Talk Video **ELL HANDBOOK** • ELL Poster Talk, Concept Talk, p. 107c **ELL POSTER 14** • Day 3 Activities	**TEACHER'S EDITION** • Academic Language, p. DI•91 • Concept Development, p. DI•91 • Anchored Talk, p. 496a • Concept Talk Video **ELL HANDBOOK** • ELL Poster Talk, Concept Talk, p. 107c **ELL POSTER 14** • Day 4 Activities	**TEACHER'S EDITION** • Academic Language, p. DI•91 • Concept Development, p. DI•91 • Concept Talk Video **ELL HANDBOOK** • ELL Poster Talk, Concept Talk, p. 107c **ELL POSTER 14** • Day 5 Activities
ELL HANDBOOK • Phonics Transition Lesson, pp. 287, 294	**ELL HANDBOOK** • Phonics Transition Lesson, pp. 287, 294	**TEACHER'S EDITION** • Phonics and Spelling, p. DI•95
TEACHER'S EDITION • AudioText of *A Symphony of Whales* • Concept Talk Video **ELL HANDBOOK** • AudioText CD Routine, p. 477	**TEACHER'S EDITION** • Concept Talk Video	**TEACHER'S EDITION** • Concept Talk Video
TEACHER'S EDITION • Sheltered Reading, p. DI•97 **ELL HANDBOOK** • Multilingual Summaries, pp. 109–111	**TEACHER'S EDITION** • ELL/ELD Reader Guided Reading, p. DI•98 **ELL HANDBOOK** • ELL Study Guide, p. 112	**TEACHER'S EDITION** • ELL/ELD Reader Guided Reading, p. DI•98 **ELL HANDBOOK** • ELL Study Guide, p. 112
ELL HANDBOOK • High-Frequency Words Activity Bank, p. 446 **ELL POSTER 14** • Day 3 Activities	**ELL HANDBOOK** • High-Frequency Words Activity Bank, p. 446	**TEACHER'S EDITION** • Unfamiliar Words, p. 501h **ELL HANDBOOK** • High-Frequency Words Activity Bank, p. 446
TEACHER'S EDITION • Grammar Jammer **ELL HANDBOOK** • Grammar Transition Lesson, pp. 324–325, 330–332 • Grammar Jammer Routine, p. 478	**TEACHER'S EDITION** • Grammar Jammer **ELL HANDBOOK** • Grammar Transition Lesson, pp. 324–325, 330–332	**TEACHER'S EDITION** • Grammar Jammer **ELL HANDBOOK** • Grammar Transition Lesson, pp. 324–325, 330–332
TEACHER'S EDITION • Let's Write It!, p. 494–495 • Writer's Craft: Headlines and Subheads, pp. 495a–495b	**TEACHER'S EDITION** • Revising Strategy, pp. 501d–501e	**TEACHER'S EDITION** • News Article, pp. 501p–501q

Poster Talk, Concept Talk

Question of the Week

How can people help animals in danger?

Poster 14

Throughout the week, use the ELL Poster to help students produce and comprehend language, understand the concept, and build English vocabulary. Use the Question of the Week and other questions to help students share ideas in pairs, small groups, or the large group. Sample questions are shown, with examples of possible responses by students.

Weekly Concept and Language Goals

- Describe how animals can be in danger
- Name ways people can put animals in danger
- Explain how people can help animals in danger

By the end of the lesson, students should be able to talk about and write one or more sentences about helping animals.

Daily Team Talk

Day 1	Day 2	Day 3	Day 4	Day 5
After Day 1 activities on Poster, ask questions such as *In the poster picture, how are the whales in danger?*	After Day 2 activity on Poster, ask questions such as *In the poster picture, why are the people outside using picks?*	After Day 3 activity on Poster, ask questions such as *How can a ship be able to help the whales get free?*	After Day 4 activity on Poster, ask questions such as *In the story* A Symphony of Whales, *the whales are too scared to follow the ship to the ocean. What does the captain do to get the whales to follow?*	After Day 5 activity on Poster, ask questions such as *What is something people do that puts animals in danger?*
Beginning They're stuck. **Intermediate** The whales have ice all around them. **Advanced** The whales are trapped by ice. They need to get to the ocean. **Advanced High** The whales need to get to open water in the ocean, but the ice is surrounding them and they are trapped.	**Beginning** They are helping. **Intermediate** They want to help get the whales free. **Advanced** The people use the picks to break the ice. They want to help the whales. **Advanced High** The people are using the picks to break the ice and make a channel so the whales can swim out into the ocean.	**Beginning** Cut the ice. **Intermediate** A ship can cut through the ice. **Advanced** A ship can break a path in the ice for the whales to swim through. **Advanced High** A ship can cut a channel through the ice. The whales can swim through the channel to get to the ocean.	**Beginning** Plays music. **Intermediate** The captain plays music so they will follow him. **Advanced** The captain plays different kinds of music until the whales start to follow the ship. **Advanced High** At first the captain plays whale sounds, but the whales do not follow the ship. Then he plays different kinds of music until they finally start to follow him to the ocean.	**Beginning** Throw garbage. **Intermediate** People throw garbage everywhere. **Advanced** People leave trash. Trash can hurt animals that try to pick it up or eat it. **Advanced High** People leave garbage where animals can get to it. Animals can get stuck in jars, cans, or plastic rings. They can eat things that are bad for them.

This Week's Materials

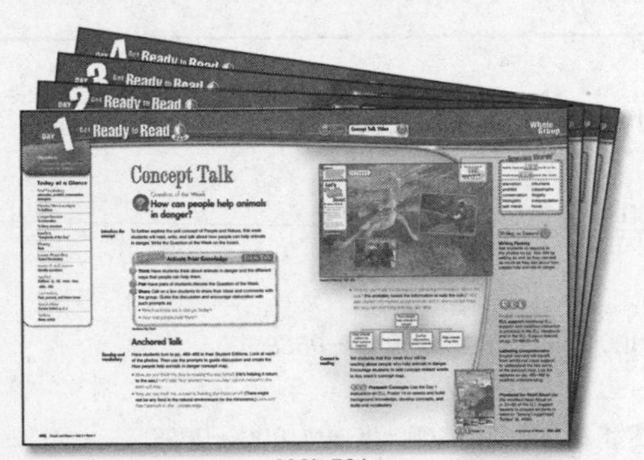

Teacher's Edition pages 468j–501q

See the support for English language learners throughout the lesson, including ELL strategies and scaffolded activities at points of use.

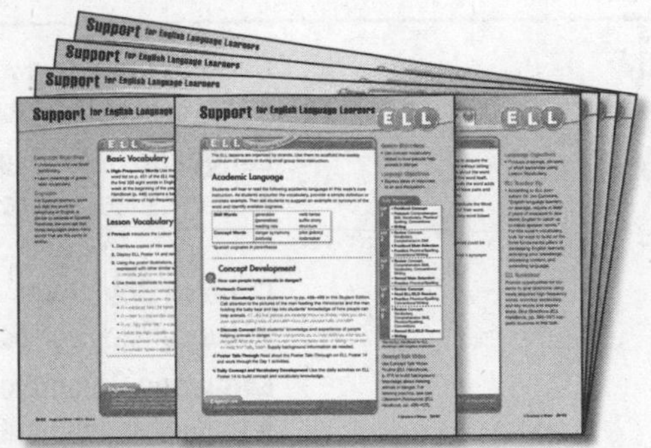

Teacher's Edition pages DI•91–DI•100

Differentiated Instruction for English language learners provides daily group activities that "frontload," or preteach, core instruction.

ELL Handbook pp. 107a–112

Find additional lesson materials that support the core lesson and the ELL instructional pages.

Poster 14

ELL Reader 3.3.4

Concept Literacy Reader

ELD, ELL Reader Teaching Guide

Concept Literacy Reader Teaching Guide

ELD Reader 3.3.4

Technology

Online Teacher's Edition Use the digital version of the core Teacher's Edition for planning and instruction.

eReaders
This week's ELL and ELD Readers and Concept Literacy Reader are also available in digital format.

This Week's Content and Language Objectives by Strand

Concept Development/ Academic Language How can people help animals in danger?	**Content Objective** • Use concept vocabulary related to how people help animals in danger. **Language Objective** • Express ideas in response to art and discussion.
Phonics and Spelling Suffixes *–ly, -ful* and *-ness*	**Content Objective** • Use suffixes correctly, including *–ly, -ful,* and *–ness.* **Language Objective** • Understand the meanings of the suffixes *–ly, -ful,* and *–ness.*
Listening Comprehension Modified Read Aloud: "Humans Help the Turtles"	**Content Objective** • Monitor and adjust oral comprehension. **Language Objectives** • Discuss oral passages. • Use a graphic organizer to take notes.
Reading Comprehension Generalize	**Content Objective** • Use story structure to generalize about the story's content. **Language Objectives** • Discuss ways to make a generalization. • Recognize generalizations in a reading. • Make generalizations from personal experience. • Summarize the action of the text by filling out a story map.
Vocabulary Basic and Lesson Vocabulary	**Language Objectives** • Understand and use basic and grade-level vocabulary. • Learn meanings of grade-level vocabulary. • Produce drawings, phrases, and short sentences to show understanding of Lesson Vocabulary.
Vocabulary Unfamiliar Words	**Content Objective** • Identify unfamiliar words. **Language Objective** • Use context clues to determine meaning of unfamiliar words.
Grammar and Conventions Past, Present, and Future Tense	**Content Objectives** • Use past, present, and future tense. • Correctly form past, present and future tense. **Language Objectives** • Speak using past, present, and future tense correctly. • Write and edit sentences that contain past, present, and future tense verbs.
Writing 5Ws and How	**Content Objective** • Understand how to write using *5Ws* and *How.* **Language Objective** • Write paragraphs using *5Ws* and *How* technique and content based vocabulary.

Word Cards for Vocabulary Activities

anxiously	**bay**
blizzards	**channel**
chipped	**melody**
supplies	**surrounded**
symphony	

Teacher Note: Beginning Teach three to four words. **Intermediate** Teach four to six words. **Advanced** Teach six to seven words. **Advanced High** Teach all words.

Name ______________________

Look at the picture. **Read** the paragraph.

- **List** three ideas that are similar. **Write** a generalization about the ideas.

Mammals of the Sea

A mammal is a type of animal. All mammals breathe air, have warm blood, and feed milk to their babies. Dogs, cats, and cows are mammals. Did you know that whales and dolphins are mammals too? They live in the water, but they come up to the surface to breathe air. They also have warm blood and feed their babies milk.

Similar Ideas:

1. ______________________________
____

2. ______________________________
____

3. ______________________________
____

Generalization:

____

____

Generalize

Use this lesson to supplement or replace the skill lesson on page 472a of the Teacher's Edition. Display the Skill Points (at right) and share them with students.

> **Skill Points**
> ✔ After reading about similar ideas, you can make a **generalization** about all of the ideas together.
> ✔ Clue words such as *all, many,* and *most* signal generalizations.

Teach/Model

Beginning Display a picture of a whale. Say: *Whales live in water. Is this true for all whales?* (yes) *Since this is true for all whales, we can make a generalization.* Write and read aloud this sentence: *All whales live in water.* Guide students in recognizing *all* as a clue word for the generalization.

Intermediate Write and read aloud this sentence: *Most dolphins live in the sea. How are most dolphins alike?* (They live in the sea.) *When I tell you a way that most dolphins are alike, I am making a generalization about dolphins.* Have students identify the clue word that tells them the sentence is a generalization. (most)

Advanced Write these sentences: *Many people love dolphins. They are smart creatures. Most of them are friendly.* Read the sentences aloud and have students listen for words that indicate generalizations. (many, most) Have them identify the generalizations and explain how the clue words helped them.

Advanced High Ask each student to write two sentences about mammals, including one generalization. Ask: *What clue words can you use to show you are making a generalization?* (most, all, many) Pair students and have them take turns identifying each other's generalization.

Then distribute copies of Picture It! page 108.

- Have students look at the picture and describe what they see.
- Read the paragraph aloud. Ask: *What animals are mammals?*
- Review the Skill Points with students.
- Ask: *Which ideas are similar? What generalization can you make?*

Practice

Read aloud the directions on page 108. Have students reread the paragraph silently. Have them look at the picture and the paragraph as they fill in the graphic organizer.

Beginning Students can first say what they want to write and then write words and phrases in the boxes. Provide help with English words and writing.

Intermediate Students can first say their answers and then write sentences in the boxes. Provide help with English words and writing.

Advanced Students can write their answers in the boxes and then check them by discussing them with a partner.

Advanced High Students can write their answers in the boxes and then orally explain how they used the similar ideas to make a generalization.

Answers for page 108: Possible answers: *Similar Ideas:* Mammals are animals. Dogs, cats, and cows are mammals. Whales and dolphins are mammals. *Generalization:* Many animals are mammals.

Multilingual Summaries

English

Read Together

A Symphony of Whales

Glashka lives in a village near the Arctic Ocean. The village is very cold, dark, and snowy in the winter. One winter, Glashka hears music. The old people in her village say that she hears the voice of Narna the whale.

After a blizzard, Glashka and her family go to the next village for supplies. When they return, they find many whales in the bay. The ice has frozen over the channel, the whales' pathway to the ocean. The whales are surrounded by ice. They are trapped. They could die. Glashka and her family use the emergency radio to call an icebreaker ship. The ship can break the ice.

The icebreaker comes and breaks the ice. But the whales will not follow the ship to the ocean. Glashka knows that they need Narna's songs. The ship plays music to the whales. The whales follow the music to the ocean.

Spanish

School + Home

Una sinfonía para las ballenas

Glashka vive en una aldea cercana al océano Ártico. La aldea es fría, oscura y está cubierta de nieve en el invierno. Una vez, durante el invierno, Glashka escucha música. Los ancianos del pueblo dicen que ella escucha la voz de Narna, la ballena.

Después de una ventisca, Glashka y su familia salen para buscar provisiones a una aldea cercana. De regreso, encuentran muchas ballenas en la bahía. El hielo se ha congelado en el canal, que es el camino de las ballenas hacia el océano. Las ballenas están rodeadas de hielo. Están atrapadas y en peligro de morir. Glashka y su familia usan el radio de emergencia para llamar a un barco rompehielos. El barco puede romper el hielo.

El rompehielos viene y separa el hielo. Pero las ballenas no siguen al barco hacia el océano. Glashka sabe que necesitan la melodías de Narna. El barco pone melodías para las ballenas. Las ballenas siguen la música hacia el océano.

Multilingual Summaries

Chinese

鯨魚交響曲

可萊西卡住在北極洋附近的村莊裡，那裡又冷又暗，冬天會下很多雪。有一年冬天，可萊西卡聽到遠處飄來美妙的聲音，村莊裡的老人說，她聽到的是鯨魚納那的歌聲。

暴風雪過後，可萊西卡和家人去隔壁村莊買東西。在回家的路上，他們發現海灣裡有很多鯨魚。原來是水道結冰了，鯨魚無法游過去。鯨魚四周都是冰，牠們被困住了，可能會死掉。可萊西卡和家人趕快用緊急聯絡無線電叫來一艘破冰船，這種船可以打碎冰塊。

破冰船來了，順利地打碎困住鯨魚的冰塊。但是，鯨魚不會跟著破冰船游回海洋。可萊西卡知道牠們需要納那的歌聲指引。破冰船於是開始放鯨魚交響曲給鯨魚聽，這群鯨魚果然就乖乖地跟著樂聲游回海洋了。

Vietnamese

Bản Nhạc Giao Hưởng của Cá Voi

Glashka sống trong một làng gần Đại Dương Bắc Cực. Vào mùa đông ngôi làng rất lạnh, tối tăm, và đầy tuyết. Một mùa đông nọ, Glashka nghe tiếng nhạc. Những người già trong làng nói rằng cô bé nghe giọng hát của cá voi tên Narna.

Sau một trận bão tuyết lớn, Glashka và gia đình đi đến làng bên cạnh để tìm thêm đồ dự trữ. Khi trở về, họ thấy có nhiều cá voi trong vùng vịnh. Băng đóng kín eo biển, là con đường để cá voi trở ra đại dương. Các con cá voi bị băng bao quanh. Chúng bị kẹt. Chúng có thể chết. Glashka và gia đình dùng máy rađiô cấp cứu để gọi một chiếc tàu phá băng. Chiếc tàu này có thể phá băng.

Tàu đến phá băng. Nhưng những con cá voi không chịu bơi theo tàu ra đại dương. Glashka biết là họ cần có những bài hát của Narna. Tàu phát những bài hát cá voi cho các con cá voi nghe. Những con cá voi bơi theo nhạc ra đại dương.

Multilingual Summaries

Korean

고래들의 교향곡

글래쉬카는 북극해 근처의 한 마을에 사는데 그 마을은 겨울에 매우 춥고 어두우며 눈이 많이 내린다. 어느 겨울 글래쉬카는 음악소리를 듣는다. 마을 어른들은 그녀가 고래인 나르나의 목소리를 듣는 것이라고 말한다.

한 차례의 눈보라가 지나간 후 글래쉬카의 가족은 양식을 구하러 옆 동네로 간다. 집으로 돌아올 때 그들은 만에서 많은 고래들을 발견한다. 고래들이 바다로 나가는 통로인 해협 위로 얼음이 얼어 있었던 것이다. 고래들은 얼음에 둘러싸여 갇혀있었고 죽을 수도 있었다. 글래쉬카의 가족들은 얼음을 부술 수 있는 쇄빙선을 부르기 위해 긴급 무전을 이용한다.

쇄빙선이 와서 얼음을 부수지만 고래들은 배를 따라 바다로 나가지 않는다. 글래쉬카는 고래에게 나르나의 노래가 필요하다는 것을 안다. 배가 고래들에게 고래 노래를 연주해주자 고래들은 음악을 따라 바다로 나간다.

Hmong

Ib Pab Ntses Loj (Whales)

Glashka nyob ib lub zos me me nyob ze hiav txwv Arctic Ocean. Lub zos no no kawg nkaus, tsaus ntuj nti, thiab los teb (xas naus) lub caij ntuaj no. Muab ib lub caij ntuj no, Glashka hnov hnov phee. Cov neeg laus hauv nws lub zos hais tias nws hnov Narna tus ntses loj lub suab.

Tom qab nag xob nag cua nro daus, Glashka thiab nws tsev neeg mus rau lub zos tom ub mus yuav khoom. Thaum lawv rov qab los, lawv pom ib cov ntses loj coob coob nyob tom dug dej. Hav dej khov tag lawm, uas yog cov ntses loj txoj kev rov mus rau pem hiav txwv. Nas kuab ncig cov ntses loj ib vuag. Lawv raug cuab tag lawm. Lawv kuj tuag tauv. Glashka thiab nws tsev neeg siv lub xov tooj cua emergency hu ib lub nkoj tsoos nas kuab. Lub nkoj ntawd tsoos tau nas kuab.

Lub nkoj tsoos nas kuab tuaj txog thiab tsoos nas kuab. Tiam si cov ntses loj tsis kam tsaws lub nkoj mus pem hiav txwv. Glashka paub tias lawv yuav tsum tau Narna cov nkauj. Lub nkoj tso nkauj rau cov ntses. Cov ntses tsaws txoj phee rau pem hiav txwv.

Name ______________________________

Whale Rescue at Cape Cod Bay

- **Read** *Whale Rescue at Cape Cod Bay* again.
- **Write** the general idea of each section.
- **Use** complete sentences. The first one is done for you.

Pages	Heading	General Idea
2	Whales in Danger	56 whales were stuck on a beach.
3	Why Were the Whales Stuck?	
4–7	The Rescue	
8	What's Next?	

Family Link

Ask family members if they have ever seen a whale, and how they felt when they saw it.

Weekly Resources Guide for English Language Learner Support

For this week's content and language objectives, see p. 113e.

Instructional Strand	Day 1	Day 2
Concept Development/Academic Language	TEACHER'S EDITION • Academic Language, p. DI•116 • Concept Development, p. DI•116 • Anchored Talk, pp. 502j—502–503 • Preteach Academic Vocabulary, p. 507a • Concept Talk Video ELL HANDBOOK • Hear It, See It, Say It, Use It, pp. xxxvi–xxxvii • ELL Poster Talk, Concept Talk, p. 113c ELL POSTER 15 • Day 1 Activities	TEACHER'S EDITION • Academic Language, p. DI•116 • Concept Development, p. DI•116 • Anchored Talk, p. 508a • Concept Talk Video ELL HANDBOOK • ELL Poster Talk, Concept Talk, p. 113c • Concept Talk Video Routine, p. 477 ELL POSTER 15 • Day 2 Activities
Phonics and Spelling	TEACHER'S EDITION • Phonics and Spelling, p. DI•120 • Decodable Practice Reader 15A, pp. 505a–505b	TEACHER'S EDITION • Phonics and Spelling, p. DI•120
Listening Comprehension	TEACHER'S EDITION • Modified Read Aloud, p. DI•119 • Read Aloud, p. 503b • Concept Talk Video ELL HANDBOOK • Concept Talk Video Routine, p. 477	TEACHER'S EDITION • Modified Read Aloud, p. DI•119 • AudioText of *Around One Cactus* • Concept Talk Video ELL HANDBOOK • AudioText CD Routine, p. 477 • T-Chart, p. 493
Reading Comprehension	TEACHER'S EDITION • Preteach Cause and Effect, p. DI•121	TEACHER'S EDITION • Reteach Cause and Effect, p. DI•121 • Frontloading Reading, p. DI•122 ELL HANDBOOK • Picture It! Skill Instruction, pp. 114–114a • Multilingual Summaries, pp. 115–117
Vocabulary **Basic and Lesson Vocabulary** **Vocabulary Skill: Prefixes and Suffixes**	TEACHER'S EDITION • Basic Vocabulary, p. DI•117 • Preteach Lesson Vocabulary, p. DI•117 • Prefixes and Suffixes, p. DI•120 ELL HANDBOOK • Word Cards, p. 113 • ELL Vocabulary Routine, p. 471 ELL POSTER 15 • Day 1 Activities	TEACHER'S EDITION • Basic Vocabulary, p. DI•117 • Reteach Lesson Vocabulary, p. DI•118 • Prefixes and Suffixes, p. DI•120 ELL HANDBOOK • Word Cards, p. 113 • Multilingual Vocabulary List, p. 436 ELL POSTER 15 • Day 2 Activities
Grammar and Conventions	TEACHER'S EDITION • Preteach Irregular Verbs, p. DI•124	TEACHER'S EDITION • Reteach Irregular Verbs, p. DI•124
Writing	TEACHER'S EDITION • Writing to Compare and Contrast, p. DI•125 • Writing for Tests: Compare-and-Contrast Composition, pp. 507e–507f	TEACHER'S EDITION • Writing for Tests: Compare-and-Contrast Composition, pp. 517d–517e

Unit 3 Week 5 Around One Cactus

This symbol indicates leveled instruction to address language proficiency levels.

Day 3	Day 4	Day 5
TEACHER'S EDITION • Academic Language, p. DI•116 • Concept Development, p. DI•116 • Anchored Talk, p. 518a • Concept Talk Video **ELL HANDBOOK** • ELL Poster Talk, Concept Talk, p. 113c **ELL POSTER 15** • Day 3 Activities	**TEACHER'S EDITION** • Academic Language, p. DI•116 • Concept Development, p. DI•116 • Anchored Talk, p. 532a • Concept Talk Video **ELL HANDBOOK** • ELL Poster Talk, Concept Talk, p. 113c **ELL POSTER 15** • Day 4 Activities	**TEACHER'S EDITION** • Academic Language, p. DI•116 • Concept Development, p. DI•116 • Concept Talk Video **ELL HANDBOOK** • ELL Poster Talk, Concept Talk, p. 113c **ELL POSTER 15** • Day 5 Activities
ELL HANDBOOK • Phonics Transition Lesson, pp. 244–245	**ELL HANDBOOK** • Phonics Transition Lesson, pp. 244–245	**TEACHER'S EDITION** • Phonics and Spelling, p. DI•120
TEACHER'S EDITION • AudioText of *Around One Cactus* • Concept Talk Video **ELL HANDBOOK** • AudioText CD Routine, p. 477	**TEACHER'S EDITION** • Concept Talk Video	**TEACHER'S EDITION** • Concept Talk Video
TEACHER'S EDITION • Sheltered Reading, p. DI•122 **ELL HANDBOOK** • Multilingual Summaries, pp. 115–117	**TEACHER'S EDITION** • ELL/ELD Reader Guided Reading, p. DI•123 **ELL HANDBOOK** • ELL Study Guide, p. 118	**TEACHER'S EDITION** • ELL/ELD Reader Guided Reading, p. DI•123 **ELL HANDBOOK** • ELL Study Guide, p. 118
ELL HANDBOOK • High-Frequency Words Activity Bank, p. 446 **ELL POSTER 15** • Day 3 Activities	**ELL HANDBOOK** • High-Frequency Words Activity Bank, p. 446	**TEACHER'S EDITION** • Prefixes and Suffixes, p. 537h **ELL HANDBOOK** • High-Frequency Words Activity Bank, p. 446
TEACHER'S EDITION • Grammar Jammer **ELL HANDBOOK** • Grammar Transition Lesson, pp. 325, 334 • Grammar Jammer Routine, p. 478	**TEACHER'S EDITION** • Grammar Jammer **ELL HANDBOOK** • Grammar Transition Lesson, pp. 325, 334	**TEACHER'S EDITION** • Grammar Jammer **ELL HANDBOOK** • Grammar Transition Lesson, pp. 325, 334
TEACHER'S EDITION • Let's Write It!, p. 530–531 • Writing for Tests: Evaluation, pp. 531a–531b	**TEACHER'S EDITION** • Writing for Tests: Writing Trait: Word Choice, p. 537d	**TEACHER'S EDITION** • Writing for Tests: Writing Trait: Sentences, pp. 537p–537q

Poster Talk, Concept Talk

Question of the Week

What can we observe in different environments?

Poster 15

Throughout the week, use the ELL Poster to help students produce and comprehend language, understand the concept, and build English vocabulary. Use the Question of the Week and other questions to help students share ideas in pairs, small groups, or the large group. Sample questions are shown, with examples of possible responses by students.

Weekly Concept and Language Goals

- Know that there are special things about every environment
- Identify things in a desert environment
- Explain how environments are different

By the end of the lesson, students should be able to talk about and write one or more sentences about what they can observe in different environments.

Daily Team Talk

Day 1	Day 2	Day 3	Day 4	Day 5
After Day 1 activities on Poster, ask questions such as *In the poster picture, what are some special things you see in a desert environment?*	After Day 2 activity on Poster, ask questions such as *In the poster picture, why is the rattlesnake the same color as the sand?*	After Day 3 activity on Poster, ask questions such as *In the poster picture, why do you think the owl makes its home in the cactus?*	After Day 4 activity on Poster, ask questions such as *Why do you think the animals come out at night in the story* Around One Cactus*?*	After Day 5 activity on Poster, ask questions such as *What is one way that the desert is different from or similar to where we live?*
Beginning Animals and cactuses. **Intermediate** There are cactuses, sand, snakes, and lizards. **Advanced** The desert has some plants such as cactuses and grass. It has some animals such as coyotes, snakes, lizards, and owls. **Advanced High** Cactuses, coyotes, rattlesnakes, scorpions, lizards, and owls live in the desert. These plants and animals can survive in this dry environment.	**Beginning** So it can hide. **Intermediate** It helps the snake hide. **Advanced** The snake is the same color as the sand so it can hide from other animals. **Advanced High** The rattlesnake is the same color as the sand so it can blend in with its environment and stay hidden from the other animals.	**Beginning** No trees. **Intermediate** A cactus is like a tree. **Advanced** Its home is in a cactus because the desert has no trees. **Advanced High** Most birds make their homes in trees. There are no trees in the desert, so the owl makes its home in a cactus, which is like a tree.	**Beginning** It is not hot. **Intermediate** The night is not hot like the day. **Advanced** The animals come out at night because it is not hot then. **Advanced High** The animals wait to come out at night because it is cooler at night. The animals will be more comfortable.	**Beginning** We have grass and trees. **Intermediate** The desert is dry. We get lots of rain. **Advanced** Not much grows in the desert. Many kinds of plants grow where we live. **Advanced High** Scorpions and lizards are common animals in the desert. Squirrels and rabbits are common animals in our environment.

This Week's Materials

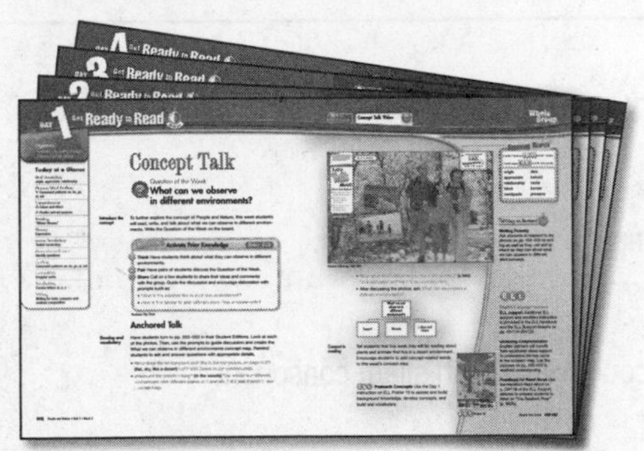
Teacher's Edition pages 502j–541a

See the support for English language learners throughout the lesson, including ELL strategies and scaffolded activities at points of use.

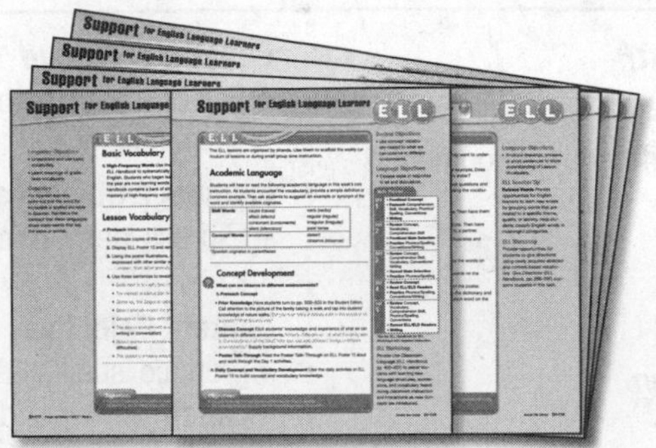
Teacher's Edition pages DI•116–DI•125

Differentiated Instruction for English language learners provides daily group activities that "frontload," or preteach, core instruction.

ELL Handbook pp. 113a–118

Find additional lesson materials that support the core lesson and the ELL instructional pages.

ELL Poster 15

ELL Reader 3.3.5

ELD Reader 3.3.5

Concept Literacy Reader

ELD, ELL Reader Teaching Guide

Concept Literacy Reader Teaching Guide

Technology

Online Teacher's Edition Use the digital version of the core Teacher's Edition for planning and instruction.

eReaders
This week's ELL and ELD Readers and Concept Literacy Reader are also available in digital format.

This Week's Content and Language Objectives by Strand

Concept Development/ Academic Language What can we observe in different environments?	**Content Objective** • Use concept vocabulary related to what we can observe in different environments. **Language Objective** • Express ideas in response to art and discussion.
Phonics and Spelling Silent Consonants *wr, kn, gn*	**Content Objective** • Produce, spell, and decode words with silent consonant pattern *wr, kn,* and *gn.* **Language Objective** • Accurately write words with silent consonant patterns.
Listening Comprehension Modified Read Aloud: "The Chicago River Changes Course"	**Content Objective** • Monitor and adjust oral comprehension. **Language Objectives** • Discuss oral passages. • Use a graphic organizer to take notes.
Reading Comprehension Cause and Effect	**Content Objectives** • Identify causes and effects. • Use causes and effects to aid comprehension. **Language Objectives** • Discuss causes and effects. • Retell causes and effects in a text. • Write using causes and effects. • Summarize using visual support.
Vocabulary Basic and Lesson Vocabulary	**Language Objectives** • Understand and use basic and grade-level vocabulary. • Learn meanings of grade-level vocabulary. • Produce drawings, phrases, and short sentences to show understanding of Lesson Vocabulary.
Vocabulary Prefixes and Suffixes	**Content Objective** • Use prefixes and suffixes to understand the meanings of new words. **Language Objective** • Discuss meanings of prefixes and suffixes.
Grammar and Conventions Irregular Verbs	**Content Objectives** • Identify irregular verbs. • Form sentences with irregular verbs. **Language Objectives** • Speak using irregular verbs. • Write and edit sentences with irregular verbs.
Writing Writing to Compare and Contrast	**Content Objective** • Identify words used to compare and contrast in a text. **Language Objectives** • Write an expository paragraph using words to compare and contrast. • Share feedback for editing and revising.

Word Cards for Vocabulary Activities

incredible	**lofty**
noble	**search**
stinging	**survivors**
topic	**unseen**
waterless	

Teacher Note: Beginning Teach three to four words. **Intermediate** Teach four to six words. **Advanced** Teach six to seven words. **Advanced High** Teach all words.

Name ______________________________

Picture It!
Cause and Effect

Look at the picture. **Read** the paragraph.

- Which sentence describes why something happens? **Write** it in the *Cause* circle.
- Which sentences describe what happens? **Write** them in the *Effect* circles.

Space Camp!

Kiki cannot wait to go to Space Camp today! This is why she quickly washes her face. She almost forgets to change out of her pajamas!

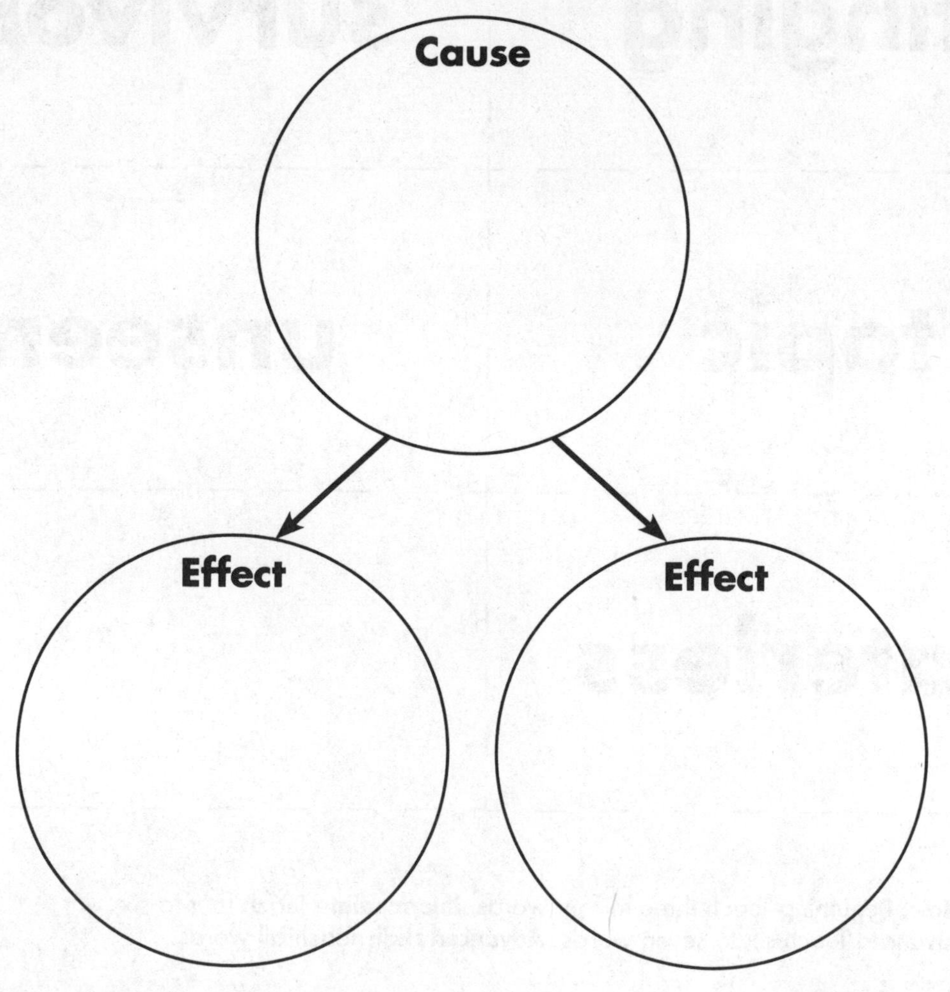

Cause and Effect

Use this lesson to supplement or replace the skill lesson on page 506a of the Teacher's Edition. Display the Skill Points (at right) and share them with students.

> **Skill Points**
> ✔ A **cause** tells why something happens.
> ✔ An **effect** tells what happens.
> ✔ Words such as *because, so,* and *why* are clues. They tell you that you are reading about a cause-and-effect relationship.

Teach/Model

Beginning Say: *My hands are dirty. I wash my hands.* Guide students in identifying the cause (My hands are dirty) and the effect (I wash my hands). Tell students you can use clue words to show the cause and the effect: *My hands are dirty, so I wash them. I wash my hands because they are dirty.*

Intermediate Write and read aloud this sentence: *My hair is all tangled, so I brush it.* Have students copy the sentence and label the cause and the effect. Ask them to circle the clue word that helped them identify the cause and the effect. (so)

Advanced Say: *I put on a sweater. Why would I put on a sweater?* (Possible answer: I feel cold.) Ask students to write the two sentences in a way that shows the cause-and-effect relationship. (Because I feel cold, I put on a sweater. I feel cold, so I put on a sweater.)

Advanced High Pair students. One partner writes a cause-and-effect sentence, and the other partner reads the sentence and identifies the cause and the effect. Then the partners trade roles.

Then distribute copies of Picture It! page 114.

- Have students look at the picture and tell what is happening.
- Read the paragraph aloud. Ask: *Where is Kiki going?*
- Review the Skill Points with students.
- Ask: *What does Kiki do because she cannot wait to go to Space Camp?* Guide students to name the two effects.

Practice

Read aloud the directions on page 114. Ask a volunteer to reread the story aloud. Have students look at the picture and the story as they fill in the graphic organizer.

Beginning Students can first say what they want to write and then write words and phrases in the circles. Provide help with English words and writing.

Intermediate Students can first orally state the cause and effects and then write sentences in the circles. Provide help with English words and writing.

Advanced Students can write their answers in the circles and then check them by comparing them with a partner's answers.

Advanced High Students can write their answers in the circles and then check them by constructing cause-and-effect sentences using the word *because*.

Answers for page 114: *Cause:* Kiki cannot wait to go to Space Camp. *Effects:* She quickly washes her face. She almost forgets to change out of her pajamas.

Multilingual Summaries

English

Read Together

Around One Cactus

A desert is a hot, dry, rocky place. The desert is full of life, though. A saguaro cactus is a safe place for many animals that live in the desert. Many kinds of animals live in and around this cactus.

A kangaroo rat builds a nest in the ground by the cactus. The long-nose bat spreads pollen from flower to flower. The elf owl builds a nest up high in the cactus. A rattlesnake slides along the ground. Scorpions move along trails near the cactus. Kit foxes clean their fur in a den. A gila monster crawls from a hole, in search of food.

The area in and around the saguaro cactus is home for all these animals.

Spanish

School + Home

Alrededor de un cacto

El desierto es cálido, seco y rocoso, pero está lleno de vida. El cacto saguaro es un lugar seguro para muchos animales. Varios viven cerca del cacto o en él.

La rata canguro hace un nido cerca del cacto. El murciélago lleva polen de una flor a otra. El búho hace un nido a lo alto serpiente de cascabel se desliza. Los escorpiones pasan cerca. Los zorros limpian su pelaje en la madriguera. Un monstruo gila se arrastra se busca comida.

El área que rodea al cacto es el hogar de estos animales.

Multilingual Summaries

Chinese

仙人掌的旁边

沙漠很热、很干，也有很多岩石，但沙漠充满生机。巨柱仙人掌是很多沙漠动物的避难所，很多不同种类的动物都住在这种仙人掌的里面和旁边。

袋鼠鼠在仙人掌旁边的土建窝巢；长鼻蝙蝠在花丛中飞舞，传播花粉；姬鸮在高高的仙人掌的上面建窝巢；响尾蛇在地上滑行；蝎子在仙人掌的旁边追踪嗅迹；沙狐在洞穴里清洁自己的毛皮；希拉怪物在洞里爬出来，寻找食物。

巨柱仙人掌的里面和旁边都是这些动物的家。

Vietnamese

Quanh Một Cây Xương Rồng

Sa mac là nơi nóng, khô và có nhiều đá. Tuy nhiên sa mac có đầy sức sống. Cây xương rồng lớn là nơi an toàn cho nhiều loài động vật sống trên sa mạc. Nhiều loài thú sống bên trong và quanh cây xương rồng.

Con đại thử có túi xây ổ dưới đất gần bên cây xương rồng. Con dơi mũi dài rải phấn hoa từ đóa hoa này sang đóa hoa khác. Con cú tinh ranh xây tổ cao trên cây xương rồng. Con rắn hổ mang bò trên mặt đất. Con bọ cạp bò theo vệt dài gần cây xương rồng. Con cáo con liếm sạch lông trong hang. Con thằn lằn độc bò ra khỏi hang đi tìm mồi.

Khu vực bên trong và chung quanh cây xương rồng lớn là nơi ở của tất cả các động vật đó.

Multilingual Summaries

Korean

한 그루의 선인장 주변에는

사막은 덥고, 건조하고, 바위가 많은 곳이다. 그러나 사막은 생명체로 가득하다. 사과로 선인장은 사막에서 많은 동물들이 안전하게 살아가는 곳이다. 많은 종류의 동물들이 이 선인장 주변에 산다.

캥거루 쥐는 선인장 옆 땅 속에 보금자리를 짓는다. 긴 코 박쥐는 꽃에서 꽃으로 꽃가루를 퍼뜨린다. 난장이 올빼미는 선인장 꼭대기에 집을 짓는다. 방울뱀은 땅을 기어다닌다. 전갈은 선인장 주변을 돌아다닌다. 키트 여우는 굴 안에서 자기 털을 깨끗하게 한다. 독도마뱀은 먹이를 찾으로 구멍 안에서 기어나온다.

사과로 선인장 안과 주변 지역은 이 모든 동물들의 집이다.

Hmong

Ib Ncig Ib Tsob Ntoo Pos

Thaj chaw moj siab qhua mas kub heev, qhuav, thiab ua pobzeb kawg. Thaj chaw moj siab qhua tseem muaj sia nyob thiab. Tsob ntoo pos saguaro yog ib lub chaw uas muaj ntau tus tsiaj ua tsev nyob. Muaj tsiaj ntau yam nyob ib ncig tsob ntoo pos.

Niag nastsuag loj ua lub zes rau hauv av ntawm tsob ntoo pos. Niag puav uas qhov ntswg ntev ywg hmoov paj dhau ib tsob paj mus rau ib tsob. Niag nplas taublaub ua lub zes nyob siab siab sau tsob ntoo pos. Niag nab uas tw nchus nrov nrov nkag hauv peg teb ib ncig. Niag raubris teb khiav ib ncig tsob ntoo pos. Niag ma me me ntxuav nws cov plaub hauv nws lub chaw nkaum. Niag nab qa dev nkag tawm ntawm nws lub qhov mus nrhiav mov noj.

Thaj chaw no thiab ib ncig tsob ntoo pos saguaro yog tsev rau ntau tus tsiaj nyob.

Name ______________________________

Rainforests Around the World

- **Read** *Rainforests Around the World* again.
- Look for **causes** or reasons why things happen.
- Look for **effects** or things that happen for a reason.
- Use information from your reading. **Write** the cause or effect that is missing. The first example is done for you.

Cause	Effect
Areas close to the equator are hot and wet.	Tropical rainforests exist there.
The green mamba snake has scales.	______________________
______________________	The grey parrot can repeat almost any sound.
Mangrove trees have tall roots.	______________________
Tree kangaroos have short legs and strong arms.	______________________
______________________	We depend on rainforests.

Family Link

Tell a family member about your favorite animal that you learned about in this book. Work with them to draw a picture of it. Bring your drawing to school and share it with the class.

Weekly Resources Guide for English Language Learner Support

For this week's content and language objectives, see p. 119e.

Instructional Strand	Day 1	Day 2
Concept Development/Academic Language	TEACHER'S EDITION • Academic Language, p. DI•16 • Concept Development, p. DI•16 • Anchored Talk, pp. 20j—20–21 • Preteach Academic Vocabulary, p. 25a • Concept Talk Video ELL HANDBOOK • Hear It, See It, Say It, Use It, pp. xxxvi–xxxvii • ELL Poster Talk, Concept Talk, p. 119c ELL POSTER 16 • Day 1 Activities	TEACHER'S EDITION • Academic Language, p. DI•16 • Concept Development, p. DI•16 • Anchored Talk, p. 26a • Concept Talk Video ELL HANDBOOK • ELL Poster Talk, Concept Talk, p. 119c • Concept Talk Video Routine, p. 477 ELL POSTER 16 • Day 2 Activities
Phonics and Spelling	TEACHER'S EDITION • Phonics and Spelling, p. DI•20 • Decodable Practice Reader 16A, pp. 23a–23b	TEACHER'S EDITION • Phonics and Spelling, p. DI•20
Listening Comprehension	TEACHER'S EDITION • Modified Read Aloud, p. DI•19 • Read Aloud, p. 21b • Concept Talk Video ELL HANDBOOK • Concept Talk Video Routine, p. 477	TEACHER'S EDITION • Modified Read Aloud, p. DI•19 • AudioText of *The Man Who Invented Basketball* • Concept Talk Video ELL HANDBOOK • AudioText CD Routine, p. 477 • Story Map A, p. 483
Reading Comprehension	TEACHER'S EDITION • Preteach Generalize, p. DI•21	TEACHER'S EDITION • Reteach Generalize, p. DI•21 • Frontloading Reading, p. DI•22 ELL HANDBOOK • Picture It! Skill Instruction, pp. 120–120a • Multilingual Summaries, pp. 121–123
Vocabulary **Basic and Lesson Vocabulary** **Vocabulary Skill: Unfamiliar Words**	TEACHER'S EDITION • Basic Vocabulary, p. DI•17 • Preteach Lesson Vocabulary, p. DI•17 • Unfamiliar Words, p. DI•20 ELL HANDBOOK • Word Cards, p. 119 • ELL Vocabulary Routine, p. 471 ELL POSTER 16 • Day 1 Activities	TEACHER'S EDITION • Basic Vocabulary, p. DI•17 • Reteach Lesson Vocabulary, p. DI•18 • Unfamiliar Words, p. DI•20 ELL HANDBOOK • Word Cards, p. 119 • Multilingual Vocabulary List, p. 437 ELL POSTER 16 • Day 2 Activities
Grammar and Conventions	TEACHER'S EDITION • Preteach Singular and Plural Pronouns, p. DI•24	TEACHER'S EDITION • Reteach Singular and Plural Pronouns, p. DI•24
Writing	TEACHER'S EDITION • Conjunctions, p. DI•25 • Introduce Persuasive Text, pp. 25e–25f	TEACHER'S EDITION • Writing Trait: Focus/Ideas, pp. 35d–35e

Unit 4 Week 1 The Man Who Invented Basketball

This symbol indicates leveled instruction to address language proficiency levels.

Day 3	Day 4	Day 5
TEACHER'S EDITION • Academic Language, p. DI•16 • Concept Development, p. DI•16 • Anchored Talk, p. 36a • Concept Talk Video **ELL HANDBOOK** • ELL Poster Talk, Concept Talk, p. 119c **ELL POSTER 16** • Day 3 Activities	**TEACHER'S EDITION** • Academic Language, p. DI•16 • Concept Development, p. DI•16 • Anchored Talk, p. 46a • Concept Talk Video **ELL HANDBOOK** • ELL Poster Talk, Concept Talk, p. 119c **ELL POSTER 16** • Day 4 Activities	**TEACHER'S EDITION** • Academic Language, p. DI•16 • Concept Development, p. DI•16 • Concept Talk Video **ELL HANDBOOK** • ELL Poster Talk, Concept Talk, p. 119c **ELL POSTER 16** • Day 5 Activities
ELL HANDBOOK • Phonics Transition Lesson, pp. 268, 270	**ELL HANDBOOK** • Phonics Transition Lesson, pp. 268, 270	**TEACHER'S EDITION** • Phonics and Spelling, p. DI•20
TEACHER'S EDITION • AudioText of *The Man Who Invented Basketball* • Concept Talk Video **ELL HANDBOOK** • AudioText CD Routine, p. 477	**TEACHER'S EDITION** • Concept Talk Video	**TEACHER'S EDITION** • Concept Talk Video
TEACHER'S EDITION • Sheltered Reading, p. DI•22 **ELL HANDBOOK** • Multilingual Summaries, pp. 121–123	**TEACHER'S EDITION** • ELL/ELD Reader Guided Reading, p. DI•23 **ELL HANDBOOK** • ELL Study Guide, p. 124	**TEACHER'S EDITION** • ELL/ELD Reader Guided Reading, p. DI•23 **ELL HANDBOOK** • ELL Study Guide, p. 124
ELL HANDBOOK • High-Frequency Words Activity Bank, p. 446 **ELL POSTER 16** • Day 3 Activities	**ELL HANDBOOK** • High-Frequency Words Activity Bank, p. 446	**TEACHER'S EDITION** • Unfamiliar Words, p. 53h **ELL HANDBOOK** • High-Frequency Words Activity Bank, p. 446
TEACHER'S EDITION • Grammar Jammer **ELL HANDBOOK** • Grammar Transition Lesson, pp. 362–369 • Grammar Jammer Routine, p. 478	**TEACHER'S EDITION** • Grammar Jammer **ELL HANDBOOK** • Grammar Transition Lesson, pp. 362–369	**TEACHER'S EDITION** • Grammar Jammer **ELL HANDBOOK** • Grammar Transition Lesson, pp. 362–369
TEACHER'S EDITION • Let's Write It!, p. 44–45 • Writer's Craft: Persuasive Elements, pp. 45a–45c	**TEACHER'S EDITION** • Revising Strategy, pp. 53d–53e	**TEACHER'S EDITION** • Singular and Plural Nouns, pp. 53p–53q

Poster Talk, Concept Talk

Question of the Week

How do talents make someone unique?

ELL Poster 16

Throughout the week, use the ELL Poster to help students produce and comprehend language, understand the concept, and build English vocabulary. Use the Question of the Week and other questions to help students share ideas in pairs, small groups, or the large group. Sample questions are shown, with examples of possible responses by students.

Weekly Concept and Language Goals

- Explain how talents can make someone unique
- Tell why talents make people unique
- Name and describe unique talents

By the end of the lesson, students should be able to talk about and write one or more sentences about how talents make someone unique.

Daily Team Talk

Day 1	Day 2	Day 3	Day 4	Day 5
After Day 1 activities on Poster, ask questions such as *In the poster picture, what talents do the basketball players have?*	After Day 2 activity on Poster, ask questions such as *In the poster picture, what talents does the basketball coach have?*	After Day 3 activity on Poster, ask questions such as *What talent do the children in the other room in the poster picture have that makes them unique?*	After Day 4 activity on Poster, ask questions such as *One person has a talent for running. Another person has a talent for playing the piano. How do their talents make these people unique?*	After Day 5 activity on Poster, ask questions such as *What special talent do you have that makes you unique?*
Beginning They run. **Intermediate** They know what to do. **Advanced** The players can run and throw the ball in the hoop. **Advanced High** The basketball players know how to play the game. They can pass the ball to one another and score points.	**Beginning** She leads. **Intermediate** She leads the team. **Advanced** The coach tells the players what to do. She cheers for them. **Advanced High** The coach teaches the players how to play basketball. She gives them instructions and helps them play well.	**Beginning** They read. **Intermediate** They want to read books. **Advanced** The children read books instead of watching the basketball game. **Advanced High** Those children can read and study while a basketball game is going on next to the room.	**Beginning** They are not the same. **Intermediate** They have different talents. **Advanced** The people are unique because they have different talents. **Advanced High** Every person has different talents. These different talents make each person unique.	**Beginning** I sing. **Intermediate** I can paint pictures. **Advanced** I know how to play chess. **Advanced High** My special talent is writing stories. My stories make people laugh.

This Week's Materials

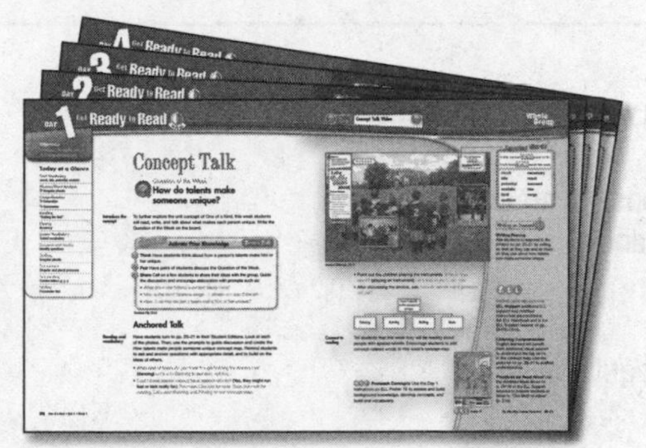

Teacher's Edition pages 20j–53q

See the support for English language learners throughout the lesson, including ELL strategies and scaffolded activities at points of use.

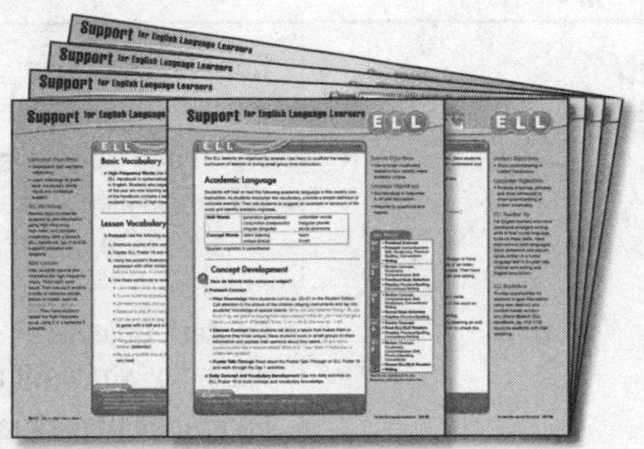

Teacher's Edition pages DI•16–DI•25

Differentiated Instruction for English language learners provides daily group activities that "frontload," or preteach, core instruction.

ELL Handbook pp. 119a–124

Find additional lesson materials that support the core lesson and the ELL instructional pages.

ELL Poster 16

ELL Reader 3.4.1

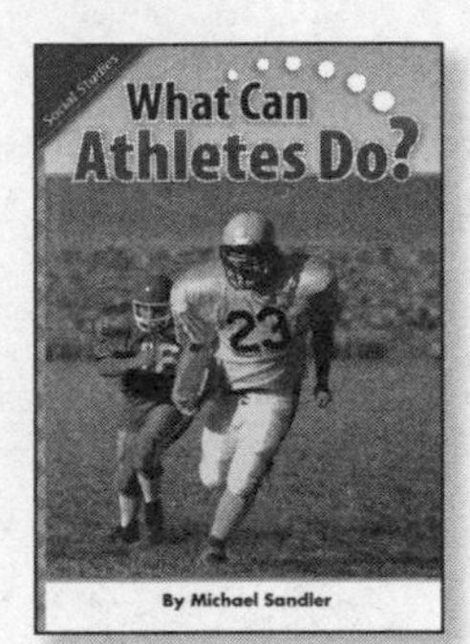

ELD Reader 3.4.1

Concept Literacy Reader

ELD, ELL Reader Teaching Guide

Concept Literacy Reader Teaching Guide

Technology

Online Teacher's Edition Use the digital version of the core Teacher's Edition for planning and instruction.

eReaders
This week's ELL and ELD Readers and Concept Literacy Reader are also available in digital format.

This Week's Content and Language Objectives by Strand

Concept Development/ Academic Language How do talents make someone unique?	**Content Objective** • Use concept vocabulary related to how talents make someone unique. **Language Objectives** • Express ideas in response to art and discussion. • Respond to questions and requests.
Phonics and Spelling Irregular Plurals	**Content Objective** • Identify words with irregular plurals. **Language Objectives** • Apply spelling rules to irregular plurals. • Discuss how to create irregular plurals.
Listening Comprehension Modified Read Aloud: "Do Not Fly Too Close to the Sun"	**Content Objective** • Monitor and adjust oral comprehension. **Language Objectives** • Discuss oral passages. • Use a graphic organizer to take notes.
Reading Comprehension Generalize	**Content Objectives** • Use summary statements to generalize about a story. • Recognize generalizations in a reading. **Language Objectives** • Use deductive reasoning to make generalizations. • Write a summary that is a generalization. • Understand main points of spoken language. • Summarize text using visual support.
Vocabulary Basic and Lesson Vocabulary	**Language Objectives** • Understand and use basic and grade-level vocabulary. • Learn meanings of grade-level vocabulary. • Produce drawings, phrases, and short sentences to show understanding of Lesson Vocabulary.
Vocabulary Unfamiliar Words	**Content Objective** • Identify unfamiliar words using contextual support. **Language Objective** • Use context clues to determine the meanings of Unfamiliar Words.
Grammar and Conventions Singular and Plural Pronouns	**Content Objectives** • Decode and use singular and plural pronouns. • Correctly write sentences with singular and plural pronouns. **Language Objectives** • Speak using singular and plural pronouns. • Write sentences with singular and plural pronouns.
Writing Conjunctions	**Content Objective** • Identify conjunctions in a text. **Language Objectives** • Write sentences using conjunctions. • Share feedback for editing and revising.

Word Cards for Vocabulary Activities

disease	**guard**
freeze	**terrible**
study	**popular**
sports	**basketball**

Teacher Note: Beginning Teach three to four words. **Intermediate** Teach four to six words. **Advanced** Teach six to seven words. **Advanced High** Teach all words.

Name ______________________

Picture It!
Generalize

Look at the pictures. **Read** the story.

- Use what you read to **answer** the questions below.

Living with Dragons

All dragons can breathe fire. Most dragons are nice. They can hold their breath. Many years ago, the people in Dragonland made homes of wood. A few dragons breathed and burned some homes! Today, people in Dragonland build homes from stone. Living with dragons is easier.

1. What are two sentences that tell what the story is about?

____

____

2. After reading the story, what can you generalize about dragons and people?

____

____

Generalize

Use this lesson to supplement or replace the skill lesson on page 24a of the Teacher's Edition. Display the Skill Points (at right) and share them with students.

> **Skill Points**
> ✔ After reading about similar ideas, you can make a **generalization** about all of the ideas together.
> ✔ Clue words such as *all, many,* and *most* signal generalizations.

Teach/Model

Beginning Read aloud these sentences: *Bees are insects. They have wings. Many insects have wings.* Ask: *Which sentence is a generalization?* (Many insects have wings.) *What is the word that helps you know this is a generalization?* (many)

Intermediate Write and read aloud these sentences: *People like different pets. Most people like furry pets. A few people like slimy pets.* Ask students to identify the generalization. (Most people like furry pets.) Have a volunteer circle the word that helped students know which sentence was the generalization. (most)

Advanced Ask students to think of ways that all or most fish are alike. List their responses. Have students use the list to help them as they write and illustrate one or more generalizations about fish.

Advanced High Ask each student to write a generalization about reptiles. Ask: *How can you let your readers know you are making a generalization?* (I can use clue words such as *most, all,* and *many.*) Have students present their generalizations to the group.

Then distribute copies of Picture It! page 120.

- Have students look at the pictures and describe what they see.
- Read the story aloud. Ask: *How did the people of Dragonland solve the problem of living with dragons?*
- Review the Skill Points with students.
- Ask: *Which sentences tell how dragons are all or mostly alike? What words let you know these sentences are generalizations?*

Practice

Read aloud the directions on page 120. Have students reread the story with partners. Have them look at the pictures and the story as they answer the questions.

Beginning Students can orally answer the questions before writing words or phrases on the lines. Provide help with English words and writing.

Intermediate Students can first orally answer the questions and then write their answers on the lines. Provide help with English words and writing.

Advanced Students can write their answers to the questions and then check them by rereading the story and making any necessary corrections.

Advanced High Students can write their answers to the questions and then orally explain how they made their generalizations.

Answers for page 102: Possible answers: 1. Many years ago, the people in Dragonland made homes of wood. Today, people in Dragonland build homes from stone. 2. Most dragons try not to breathe fire. Most people in Dragonland have learned how to live with dragons.

Multilingual Summaries

Read Together

English

The Man Who Invented Basketball

James Naismith was born in Canada in 1861. His parents died when he was a boy. He was very poor growing up. He decided to go to college and become a minister.

James took a job teaching sports at a YMCA. At this job, he invented a game that could be played in the winter. In the game, players used two peach baskets as goals. The game became very popular. Over time, the game changed and improved.

Later, James studied to become a doctor. He spent his life working as a teacher, a minister, and a doctor. But he is best known for inventing basketball.

Spanish

School + Home

El hombre que inventó el basquetbol

James Naismith nació en Canadá en 1861. Sus padres murieron cuando era niño. James fue muy pobre. Fue a la universidad y se convirtió en ministro religioso.

James consiguió trabajo de profesor de deportes en YMCA. Ahí inventó un deporte que se podía jugar durante el invierno. Los jugadores lanzaban pelotas a canastas de duraznos. El juego se volvió muy popular. Con el tiempo, cambió y mejoró.

Tiempo después, James estudió para ser médico. Pasó su vida trabajando como maestro, ministro religioso y médico, pero es conocido por haber inventado el basquetbol.

Multilingual Summaries

Chinese

发明篮球的人

詹姆斯•奈史密斯生于一八六一年的加拿大，小时候已经父母双亡。他长大的时候很穷，所以决定上大学并成为一位牧师。

他在基督教青年会找到一份体育教师的工作，工作期间，他发明了一种可以在冬天玩的游戏，参与的人以两个桃篮为目标。这种游戏逐渐流行起来，而且在多年间不断改变和改良。

后来，詹姆斯学习成为一个医生，并在余生当教师、牧师和医生，但令他最出名的始终是发明了篮球。

Vietnamese

Người Phát Minh Ra Môn Bóng Rổ.

James Naismith ra đời tại Canada năm 1861. Cha mẹ ông mất lúc ông còn bé. Ông lớn lên trong nghèo khó. Ông quyết định vào trường Đại học để trở nên mục sư.

James nhận một công việc dạy thể thao tại YMCA. Tại đó ông phát minh một môn thể thao có thể chơi trong mùa Đông. Trong môn chơi này, đấu thủ dùng hai rổ trái đào làm mục tiêu. Môn chơi trở nên rất thịnh hành. Lâu dần, môn chơi được thay đổi và cải tiến.

Về sau, James học thành bác sĩ. Suốt cuộc đời, ông làm việc như một giáo viên, một mục sư và một bác sĩ. Nhưng ông được biết nhiều nhất vì đã phát minh ra môn bóng rổ.

Multilingual Summaries

Korean

농구를 고안한 사람

제임스 나이스미스는 1861년 캐나다에서 태어났다. 그의 부모님은 그가 어렸을 때 돌아가셨다. 제임스는 자라면서 무척 가난했다. 그는 대학에 가서 성직자가 되기로 결심했다.

제임스는 YMCA에서 체육을 가르쳤다. 여기서 그는 겨울에도 할 수 있는 경기를 고안해냈다.선수들은 두 개의 복숭아 바구니를 골로 사용했다. 이 경기는 매우 인기가 많아졌다. 시간이 흐르면서 경기는 바뀌고 향상되었다.

후에, 제임스는 의사가 되기 위해 공부하였다. 그는 일생을 선생으로, 성직자로, 의사로 보냈다. 그러나 그는 농구를 고안한 사람으로 가장 유명하다.

Hmong

School
+ Home

Tus Txivneej Uas Tsim Basketball

James Naismith yug hauv Canada rau 1861. Nwg niam thiab txiv tuag thaus nwg yog ib tus menyuam tub. Nwg txomnyem heev thaus nwg loj hlob. Nwg txiav txim siab mus kawm ntawv qeb siab mus ua ib tus Xibhwb cev Vajtswv txoj lus.

James txais ib txog haujlwm qhia sis tw uasi tom YMCA. Ntawm nwg txoj haujlwm, nwg tsim tau ib txoj kev sis tw uasi uas pov npas thaus lub caij ntuj no. Hauv txoj kev sis tw uasi, cov tub pov npas yuav siv ob lub tawb txiv duaj los cim ntaus yeej. Txoj kev sis tw uasi no pib nto npe. Dhau ib ntus rau yav tom ntej, txoj kev sis tw uasi no hloov thiab kho lomzem ntxiv.

Tom qab, James mus kawm ua ib tus kws kho mob. Nwg siv tag nwg lub neej ua ib tus xibhwb, ib tus xibhwb qhia Vajtswv txoj lus, thiab ib tus kws kho mob. Tiamsis lawv paub txog nwg zoo tsaj yog ua tus tsim basketball.

Name ______________________________

My Good Friend

- **Read** *My Good Friend* again.
- **Write** words to describe Luz. **Write** words to describe your best friend.
- **Write** a sentence to compare Luz with your best friend.

Luz	My Best Friend

____

____

Family Link

Ask family members to say what they look for in a good friend.

Weekly Resources Guide for English Language Learner Support

For this week's content and language objectives, see p. 125e.

Instructional Strand	Day 1	Day 2
Concept Development/Academic Language	TEACHER'S EDITION • Academic Language, p. DI•41 • Concept Development, p. DI•41 • Anchored Talk, pp. 54j—54–55 • Preteach Academic Vocabulary, p. 59a • Concept Talk Video ELL HANDBOOK • Hear It, See It, Say It, Use It, pp. xxxvi–xxxvii • ELL Poster Talk, Concept Talk, p. 125c ELL POSTER 17 • Day 1 Activities	TEACHER'S EDITION • Academic Language, p. DI•41 • Concept Development, p. DI•41 • Anchored Talk, p. 60a • Concept Talk Video ELL HANDBOOK • ELL Poster Talk, Concept Talk, p. 125c • Concept Talk Video Routine, p. 477 ELL POSTER 17 • Day 2 Activities
Phonics and Spelling	TEACHER'S EDITION • Phonics and Spelling, p. DI•45 • Decodable Practice Reader 17A, pp. 57a–57b	TEACHER'S EDITION • Phonics and Spelling, p. DI•45
Listening Comprehension	TEACHER'S EDITION • Modified Read Aloud, p. DI•44 • Read Aloud, p. 55b • Concept Talk Video ELL HANDBOOK • Concept Talk Video Routine, p. 477	TEACHER'S EDITION • Modified Read Aloud, p. DI•44 • AudioText of *Hottest, Coldest, Highest, Deepest* • Concept Talk Video ELL HANDBOOK • AudioText CD Routine, p. 477 • K-W-L Chart, p. 480
Reading Comprehension	TEACHER'S EDITION • Preteach Graphic Sources, p. DI•46	TEACHER'S EDITION • Reteach Graphic Sources, p. DI•46 • Frontloading Reading, p. DI•47 ELL HANDBOOK • Picture It! Skill Instruction, pp. 126–126a • Multilingual Summaries, pp. 127–129
Vocabulary **Basic and Lesson Vocabulary** **Vocabulary Skill: Unknown Words**	TEACHER'S EDITION • Basic Vocabulary, p. DI•42 • Preteach Lesson Vocabulary, p. DI•42 • Unknown Words, p. DI•45 ELL HANDBOOK • Word Cards, p. 125 • ELL Vocabulary Routine, p. 471 ELL POSTER 17 • Day 1 Activities	TEACHER'S EDITION • Basic Vocabulary, p. DI•42 • Reteach Lesson Vocabulary, p. DI•43 • Unknown Words, p. DI•45 ELL HANDBOOK • Word Cards, p. 125 • Multilingual Vocabulary List, p. 437 ELL POSTER 17 • Day 2 Activities
Grammar and Conventions	TEACHER'S EDITION • Preteach Subject and Object Pronouns, p. DI•49	TEACHER'S EDITION • Reteach Subject and Object Pronouns, p. DI•49
Writing	TEACHER'S EDITION • Complex Sentences, p. DI•50 • Introduce Imaginative Story, pp. 59e–59f	TEACHER'S EDITION • Writer's Craft: Generating Ideas, pp. 69d–69e

Unit 4 Week 2 Hottest, Coldest, Highest, Deepest

This symbol indicates leveled instruction to address language proficiency levels.

Day 3	Day 4	Day 5
TEACHER'S EDITION • Academic Language, p. DI•41 • Concept Development, p. DI•41 • Anchored Talk, p. 70a • Concept Talk Video ELL HANDBOOK • ELL Poster Talk, Concept Talk, p. 125c ELL POSTER 17 • Day 3 Activities	TEACHER'S EDITION • Academic Language, p. DI•41 • Concept Development, p. DI•41 • Anchored Talk, p. 80a • Concept Talk Video ELL HANDBOOK • ELL Poster Talk, Concept Talk, p. 125c ELL POSTER 17 • Day 4 Activities	TEACHER'S EDITION • Academic Language, p. DI•41 • Concept Development, p. DI•41 • Concept Talk Video ELL HANDBOOK • ELL Poster Talk, Concept Talk, p. 125c ELL POSTER 17 • Day 5 Activities
ELL HANDBOOK • Phonics Transition Lesson, pp. 262–265	ELL HANDBOOK • Phonics Transition Lesson, pp. 262–265	TEACHER'S EDITION • Phonics and Spelling, p. DI•45
TEACHER'S EDITION • AudioText of *Hottest, Coldest, Highest, Deepest* • Concept Talk Video ELL HANDBOOK • AudioText CD Routine, p. 477	TEACHER'S EDITION • Concept Talk Video	TEACHER'S EDITION • Concept Talk Video
TEACHER'S EDITION • Sheltered Reading, p. DI•47 ELL HANDBOOK • Multilingual Summaries, pp. 127–129	TEACHER'S EDITION • ELL/ELD Reader Guided Reading, p. DI•48 ELL HANDBOOK • ELL Study Guide, p. 130	TEACHER'S EDITION • ELL/ELD Reader Guided Reading, p. DI•48 ELL HANDBOOK • ELL Study Guide, p. 130
ELL HANDBOOK • High-Frequency Words Activity Bank, p. 446 ELL POSTER 17 • Day 3 Activities	ELL HANDBOOK • High-Frequency Words Activity Bank, p. 446	TEACHER'S EDITION • Unknown Words, p. 85h ELL HANDBOOK • High-Frequency Words Activity Bank, p. 446
TEACHER'S EDITION • Grammar Jammer ELL HANDBOOK • Grammar Transition Lesson, pp. 362, 365–366 • Grammar Jammer Routine, p. 478	TEACHER'S EDITION • Grammar Jammer ELL HANDBOOK • Grammar Transition Lesson, pp. 362, 365–366	TEACHER'S EDITION • Grammar Jammer ELL HANDBOOK • Grammar Transition Lesson, pp. 362, 365–366
TEACHER'S EDITION • Let's Write It!, p. 78–79 • Writer's Craft: Dialogue, pp. 79a–79b	TEACHER'S EDITION • Revising Strategy, pp. 85d–85e	TEACHER'S EDITION • Subject and Object Pronouns, pp. 85p–85q

Poster Talk, Concept Talk

Question of the Week

What makes nature's record holders unique?

ELL Poster 17

Throughout the week, use the ELL Poster to help students produce and comprehend language, understand the concept, and build English vocabulary. Use the Question of the Week and other questions to help students share ideas in pairs, small groups, or the large group. Sample questions are shown, with examples of possible responses by students.

Weekly Concept and Language Goals

- Give an example of a record holder in nature
- Name unique features of nature's record holders
- Describe natural features in nature

By the end of the lesson, students should be able to talk about and write one or more sentences about nature's unique record holders.

Daily Team Talk

Day 1	Day 2	Day 3	Day 4	Day 5
After Day 1 activities on Poster, ask questions such as *What natural features do you see in the top picture?*	After Day 2 activity on Poster, ask questions such as *How could the mountains in the top picture be record holders?*	After Day 3 activity on Poster, ask questions such as *How could the desert in the bottom picture be a record holder?*	After Day 4 activity on Poster, ask questions such as *In the poster picture, what natural feature do both the beach and the desert have? How are they different?*	After Day 5 activity on Poster, ask questions such as *What is a record holder in nature that you have seen?*
Beginning Water and trees. **Intermediate** There are mountains, trees, and water. **Advanced** There are mountains with trees on them. I also see waterfalls and a lake. **Advanced High** The high, rocky mountains have trees on them. Tall waterfalls flow down the mountains into a lake.	**Beginning** They're big. **Intermediate** The mountains are tall. **Advanced** The mountains are very tall. They could be the tallest mountains. **Advanced High** These mountains could be record holders if they are the tallest mountains in the world.	**Beginning** It's big. **Intermediate** The desert is big and dry. **Advanced** The desert looks very dry and hot. It could be the driest desert or the hottest desert. **Advanced High** This desert could be a record holder if it is the driest place or the hottest place in the world. It could also be the biggest desert in the world.	**Beginning** They have sand. **Intermediate** Both have sand, but the desert does not have water. **Advanced** They both have a lot of sand. The beach has water, but the desert does not. **Advanced High** The beach and the desert are both covered with sand. The desert does not get much water, but the beach has a lot of water because it is by the ocean.	**Beginning** A big lake. **Intermediate** We saw a big lake. **Advanced** We saw one of the Great Lakes. **Advanced High** We walked on the shore of one of the Great Lakes.

This Week's Materials

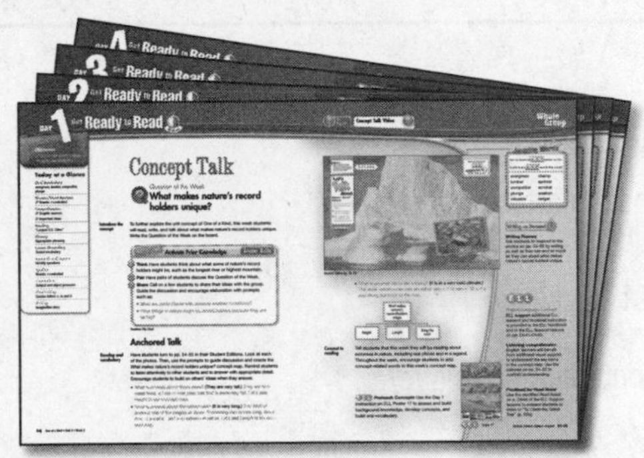
Teacher's Edition pages 54j–85q

See the support for English language learners throughout the lesson, including ELL strategies and scaffolded activities at points of use.

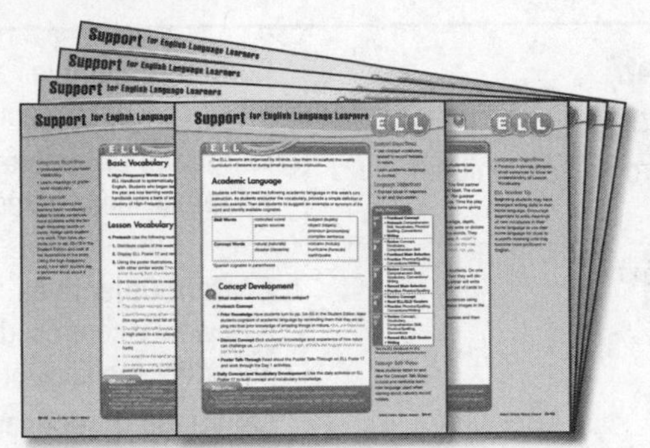
Teacher's Edition pages DI•41–DI•50

Differentiated Instruction for English language learners provides daily group activities that "frontload," or preteach, core instruction.

ELL Handbook pp. 125a–130

Find additional lesson materials that support the core lesson and the ELL instructional pages.

Poster 17

ELL Reader 3.4.2

ELD Reader 3.4.2

Extremes
By Myka-Lynne Sokoloff

Concept Literacy Reader

ELD, ELL Reader Teaching Guide

Concept Literacy Reader Teaching Guide

Technology

Online Teacher's Edition Use the digital version of the core Teacher's Edition for planning and instruction.

eReaders
This week's ELL and ELD Readers and Concept Literacy Reader are also available in digital format.

This Week's Content and Language Objectives by Strand

Concept Development/ Academic Language What makes nature's record holders unique?	**Content Objective** • Use concept vocabulary related to record holders in nature. **Language Objective** • Express ideas in response to art and discussion.
Phonics and Spelling *r*-Controlled Vowels:/ė/	**Content Objectives** • Review *r*-controlled vowels. • Identify spellings of *r*-controlled vowels /ė/. **Language Objectives** • Apply spelling rules to irregular plurals. • Discuss how to create irregular plurals.
Listening Comprehension Modified Read Aloud: "He Climbed the Tallest Tree"	**Content Objectives** • Monitor and adjust oral comprehension. • Learn essential language. **Language Objective** • Discuss oral passages.
Reading Comprehension Graphic Sources	**Content Objectives** • Identify graphic sources. • Understand how graphics enhance information in text. **Language Objectives** • Discuss information in graphic sources. • Use punctuation cues to phrase appropriately when reading aloud.
Vocabulary Basic and Lesson Vocabulary	**Language Objectives** • Understand and use basic and grade-level vocabulary. • Learn meanings of grade-level vocabulary. • Produce drawings, phrases, and short sentences to show understanding of Lesson Vocabulary.
Vocabulary Unknown Words	**Content Objective** • Identify unknown words in a sentence. **Language Objective** • Use a dictionary to determine the meanings of unknown words.
Grammar and Conventions Subject and Object Pronouns	**Content Objectives** • Identify subject and object pronouns. • Understand the difference between subject and object pronouns. **Language Objectives** • Speak using a variety of grammatical structures. • Write sentences using subject and object pronouns.
Writing Complex Sentences	**Content Objectives** • Identify complex sentence patterns. • Identify clauses and connecting words in complex sentence patterns. **Language Objective** • Write complex sentence using content-based grade-level vocabulary.

average	**depth**
deserts	**erupted**
outrun	**peak**
tides	**waterfalls**

Teacher Note: Beginning Teach three to four words. **Intermediate** Teach four to six words. **Advanced** Teach six to seven words. **Advanced High** Teach all words.

Name ______________________________

Picture It!
Graphic Sources

Look at the picture. What do you think the paragraph is going to be about?

1. Write your guess.

____

Read the paragraph. **Answer** the questions that follow.

Two American Cities

Chicago and San Diego are large cities with different climates. Chicago has cold winters and warm summers. San Diego is warm all year long. In both cities, people enjoy spending time at the beach. Chicago's beaches are on Lake Michigan, but San Diego's are on the Pacific Ocean.

2. What is the paragraph about?

____

____

3. What things and places shown in the picture are also mentioned in the paragraph?

____

____

Graphic Sources

Use this lesson to supplement or replace the skill lesson on page 58a of the Teacher's Edition. Display the Skill Points (at right) and share them with students.

Skill Points

✔ **Graphic sources** are charts, photos, graphs, and diagrams that help you understand information in the text.

Teach/Model

Beginning Say: *I am writing a report about our town. How can I use a map in my report?* (to show where our town is located) Repeat the question for other graphic sources, such as a photograph and a chart.

Intermediate Display a diagram and a graph in a science textbook. Ask students to identify the graphic sources. Discuss what information each graphic source shows and why this is a good way to show the information.

Advanced Write and read aloud the following: *In my hometown, the average temperatures are 45°F in winter, 70°F in spring, 82°F in summer, and 68°F in fall.* Pair students and have partners make a chart that shows this information.

Advanced High Write these sentence frames on the board: *This graphic source is a ___. It tells me about ___. It helps me ___.* Ask students to find graphic sources in classroom books. Have them copy and complete the sentence frames about each graphic source.

Then distribute copies of Picture It! page 126.

- Have students look at the picture and predict what the paragraph will be about. Then have them tell what they know about the cities of Chicago and San Diego.
- Read the paragraph aloud.
- Review the Skill Points with students.
- Have students look at the picture and words to identify the graphic source and tell how it supports the text.

Practice

Read aloud the directions on page 126. Reread the paragraph aloud. Have students look at the picture and the paragraph as they answer the questions.

Beginning Students can say what they want to write for each answer before writing words and phrases on the lines. Provide help with English words and writing.

Intermediate Students can first orally answer the questions and then write their answers on the lines. Provide help as necessary.

Advanced Students can write their answers to the questions and then check them by silently rereading the paragraph and revising their predictions.

Advanced High Students can write their answers to the questions and then orally explain how the graphic source helped them better understand the information in the paragraph.

Answers for page 126: 1. Possible answer: I think it will be about two American cities that are near water. 2. It is about two large American cities, Chicago and San Diego. 3. The cities' climates and beaches are shown in the picture and mentioned in the paragraph.

Multilingual Summaries

English

Hottest, Coldest, Highest, Deepest

There are many different climates and landforms on Earth. The longest river is the Nile, in Africa. The oldest and deepest lake is Lake Baikal in Russia. Mount Everest is the highest mountain. Mauna Kea in Hawaii is really the tallest mountain, but most of it is underwater.

The hottest place is Al Aziziyah, Libya, in the Sahara Desert. The coldest place is Vostok, Antarctica. The wettest place is Tutunendo, Colombia. The driest place is the Atacama Desert in Chile.

Mount Washington in New Hampshire is the windiest place on Earth. The highest waterfall is in Venezuela. The deepest part of the ocean is the Marianas Trench in the Philippines. Ecuador has the most active volcano. The world's biggest tides occur in the Bay of Fundy in Nova Scotia, Canada. Mount Rainier in Washington gets the most snow.

Spanish

Caluroso, frío, alto y profundo

En la Tierra hay una gran variedad de climas y accidentes geográficos. El río más largo es el Nilo, en África. El lago más antiguo y profundo es el Baikal, en Rusia. El monte Everest es la montaña más alta. El Mauna Kea, en Hawai, es realmente la montaña más alta, pero la mayoría está bajo el agua.

El lugar más caluroso de la Tierra es Al Aziziyah, en el desierto del Sahara, Libia. El lugar más frío es Vostock, en la Antártida. El lugar más húmedo es el pueblo Tutunendo, en Colombia. El lugar más seco es el desierto de Atacama, en Chile.

El monte Washington, que está en New Hampshire, es el lugar con más vientos de la Tierra. La catarata más alta está en Venezuela. La parte más profunda del océano está en la fosa de las Marianas en Filipinas. Ecuador tiene el volcán más activo. Las mareas más altas se dan en la bahía de Fundy en Nueva Escocia en Canadá. El monte Rainer, en el estado de Washington, es donde cae más nieve.

Multilingual Summaries

Chinese

地球上最熱、最冷、最高和最深的地方

地球上有許多不同的氣候和地形。最長的河是非洲的尼羅河。最古老和最深的湖是俄羅斯的貝加爾湖。聖母峰是世界上最高的山。其實夏威夷的茂納基亞山才是最高的,不過它大部分都在水面下。

最熱的地方是利比亞的埃爾阿爾奇亞,在撒哈拉沙漠裡。最冷的地方是南極的沃斯托克。最潮濕的地方是哥倫比亞的圖特納多。最乾燥的地方是智利的阿他加馬沙漠。

新罕布夏州的華盛頓山是世界上風最大的地方。最高的瀑布在委內瑞拉。最深的海底在菲律賓的馬里亞納海溝。厄瓜多爾有地球上最多的活火山。世界最大的潮汐出現在新斯科細亞省的芬地灣。華盛頓州的祖父山雪下得最多。

Vietnamese

Nóng Nhất Lạnh Nhất Cao Nhất Sâu Nhất

Có nhiều địa hình và khí hậu khác nhau trên Trái Đất. Con sông dài nhất là sông Nile, ở Phi Châu. Hồ xưa nhất và sâu nhất là hồ Baikal ở Nga. Đỉnh Everest là ngọn núi cao nhất. Đỉnh Mauna Kea ở Hawaii thật sự là ngọn núi cao nhất, nhưng phần lớn của núi này nằm dưới biển.

Nơi nóng nhất là Al Aziziyah, Libya, trong Sa Mạc Sahara. Nơi lạnh nhất là Vostok, Nam Cực. Nơi nhiều mưa nhất là Tutunendo, Columbia. Nơi khô nhất là Sa Mạc Atacama ở Chile.

Ngọn núi Washington ở New Hampshire là nơi nhiều gió nhất trên Trái Đất. Thác nước cao nhất ở Venezuela. Phần sâu nhất của đại dương là Marianas Trench ở Philippines. Ecuador có ngọn núi lửa phun thường xuyên nhất. Thủy triều lớn nhất thế giới xảy ra ở Vịnh Fundy ở Nova Scotia, Canada. Ngọn núi Rainier ở Washington có nhiều tuyết nhất.

Multilingual Summaries

Korean

가장 덥고 가장 춥고 가장 높고 가장 깊은 곳

지구에는 매우 다른 기후와 지형이 있다. 가장 긴 강은 아프리카에 있는 나일강이고 가장 오래되고 깊은 호수는 러시아의 바이칼호이며 가장 높은 산은 에베레스트산이다. 하와이의 마우나 케아가 사실은 가장 높은 산이지만 거의 대부분이 물 속에 잠겨있다.

가장 더운 곳은 사하라 사막에 있는 리비아의 알 아지지아이고 가장 추운 곳은 남극대륙의 보스토크이며 가장 습한 지역은 콜롬비아의 투테넨도, 그리고 가장 건조한 곳은 칠레의 아타카마 사막이다.

뉴햄프셔의 워싱턴산은 지구에서 바람이 가장 많은 지역이고 가장 높은 폭포는 베네수엘라에 있다. 해양의 가장 깊은 곳은 필리핀의 마리아나 화구이며 에콰도르에는 가장 활동적인 화산이 있다. 세계에서 가장 큰 파도는 캐나다 노바스코샤 주의 펀디만에서 발생한다. 워싱턴의 레이니어산은 눈이 가장 많이 내린다.

Hmong

Sov Tshaj No Tshaj Siab Tshaj Tob Tshaj

Muaj ntau tsav ntau yam huab cua thiab dej av nyob rau ntiaj teb Earth no. Tub dej ntev tshaj plaws yog tub Nile, nyob rau Africa. Lub pas dej qub thiab tob tshaj plaws yog Lake Baikal nyob rau Russia. Mount Everest yog lub roob siab tshaj plaws. Mauna Kea nyob rau Hawaii thiag thiag yog lub roob siab tshaj plaws tiam si feem ntau nyob hauv qab dej.

Qhov chaw sov tshaj plaws yog Al Aziziyah, nyob rau Libya, nyob rau Sahara Desert. Qhov chaw no tshaj plaws yog Vostok, nyob rau Antartica. Qhov chaw ntuv tshaj plaws yog Tutunendo, nyob rau Columbia. Qhov chaws qhuas tshaj plaws yog Atacama Desert nyob rau Chile.

Mount Washington nyob rau New Hampshire yog qhov uas cua hlob tshaj plaws nyob rau ntiaj teb Earth no. Tus dej tsaws tsag siab tshaj plaws nyob rau Venezuela. Qhov chaws tob tshaj plaws nyob hauv hiav txwv yog Marianas Trench nyob rau Philippines. Ecuador muaj lub roob hluav taws ciaj tshaj plaws. Ntiaj teb qhov chaws uas dej hiav txwv siab thiab ris tshaj plaws nyob rau Bay of Fundy nyob Nova Scotia. Mount Rainier nyob rau Washington tau te ntau tshaj plaws.

Name ______________________________

How Big? How Strong?

- **Read** *How Big? How Strong?* again.
- **Write** answers to the questions.

pages 2–3

1. Which type of hurricane is stronger, a Category 5 or a Category 2?

____

pages 4–5

2. Why was Florida a disaster area in September of 2004?

____

____

page 6

3. What kind of damage does an earthquake measuring 7.0 on the Richter scale do?

____

pages 7–8

4. Look at the pictures of earthquake damage. What kinds of things do earthquakes destroy?

____

____

Family Link

Ask family members if they have ever experienced a hurricane or an earthquake. Ask them to share what happened.

Weekly Resources Guide for English Language Learner Support

For this week's content and language objectives, see p. 131e.

Instructional Strand	Day 1	Day 2
Concept Development/Academic Language	TEACHER'S EDITION • Academic Language, p. DI•66 • Concept Development, p. DI•66 • Anchored Talk, pp. 86j—86–87 • Preteach Academic Vocabulary, p. 91a • Concept Talk Video ELL HANDBOOK • Hear It, See It, Say It, Use It, pp. xxxvi–xxxvii • ELL Poster Talk, Concept Talk, p. 131c ELL POSTER 18 • Day 1 Activities	TEACHER'S EDITION • Academic Language, p. DI•66 • Concept Development, p. DI•66 • Anchored Talk, p. 92a • Concept Talk Video ELL HANDBOOK • ELL Poster Talk, Concept Talk, p. 131c • Concept Talk Video Routine, p. 477 ELL POSTER 18 • Day 2 Activities
Phonics and Spelling	TEACHER'S EDITION • Phonics and Spelling, p. DI•70 • Decodable Practice Reader 18A, pp. 89a–89b	TEACHER'S EDITION • Phonics and Spelling, p. DI•70
Listening Comprehension	TEACHER'S EDITION • Modified Read Aloud, p. DI•69 • Read Aloud, p. 87b • Concept Talk Video ELL HANDBOOK • Concept Talk Video Routine, p. 477	TEACHER'S EDITION • Modified Read Aloud, p. DI•69 • AudioText of *Rocks in His Head* • Concept Talk Video ELL HANDBOOK • AudioText CD Routine, p. 477 • Story Map A, p. 483
Reading Comprehension	TEACHER'S EDITION • Preteach Fact and Opinion, p. DI•71	TEACHER'S EDITION • Reteach Fact and Opinion, p. DI•71 • Frontloading Reading, p. DI•72 ELL HANDBOOK • Picture It! Skill Instruction, pp. 132–132a • Multilingual Summaries, pp. 133–135
Vocabulary **Basic and Lesson Vocabulary** **Vocabulary Skill: Multiple-Meaning Words**	TEACHER'S EDITION • Basic Vocabulary, p. DI•67 • Preteach Lesson Vocabulary, p. DI•67 • Multiple-Meaning Words, p. DI•70 ELL HANDBOOK • Word Cards, p. 131 • ELL Vocabulary Routine, p. 471 ELL POSTER 18 • Day 1 Activities	TEACHER'S EDITION • Basic Vocabulary, p. DI•67 • Reteach Lesson Vocabulary, p. DI•68 • Multiple-Meaning Words, p. DI•70 ELL HANDBOOK • Word Cards, p. 131 • Multilingual Vocabulary List, pp. 437–438 ELL POSTER 18 • Day 2 Activities
Grammar and Conventions	TEACHER'S EDITION • Preteach Possessive Pronouns, p. DI•74	TEACHER'S EDITION • Reteach Possessive Pronouns, p. DI•74
Writing	TEACHER'S EDITION • Combining Short, Choppy Sentences, p. DI•75 • Introduce Biography, pp. 91e–91f	TEACHER'S EDITION • Writer's Craft: Sequence, pp. 99d–99e

Leveled Support: This symbol indicates leveled instruction to address language proficiency levels.

Day 3	Day 4	Day 5
TEACHER'S EDITION • Academic Language, p. DI•66 • Concept Development, p. DI•66 • Anchored Talk, p. 100a • Concept Talk Video ELL HANDBOOK • ELL Poster Talk, Concept Talk, p. 131c ELL POSTER 18 • Day 3 Activities	TEACHER'S EDITION • Academic Language, p. DI•66 • Concept Development, p. DI•66 • Anchored Talk, p. 110a • Concept Talk Video ELL HANDBOOK • ELL Poster Talk, Concept Talk, p. 131c ELL POSTER 18 • Day 4 Activities	TEACHER'S EDITION • Academic Language, p. DI•66 • Concept Development, p. DI•66 • Concept Talk Video ELL HANDBOOK • ELL Poster Talk, Concept Talk, p. 131c ELL POSTER 18 • Day 5 Activities
ELL HANDBOOK • Phonics Transition Lesson, pp. 285–286, 292–293	ELL HANDBOOK • Phonics Transition Lesson, pp. 285–286, 292–293	TEACHER'S EDITION • Phonics and Spelling, p. DI•70
TEACHER'S EDITION • AudioText of *Rocks in His Head* • Concept Talk Video ELL HANDBOOK • AudioText CD Routine, p. 477	TEACHER'S EDITION • Concept Talk Video	TEACHER'S EDITION • Concept Talk Video
TEACHER'S EDITION • Sheltered Reading, p. DI•72 ELL HANDBOOK • Multilingual Summaries, pp. 133–135	TEACHER'S EDITION • ELL/ELD Reader Guided Reading, p. DI•73 ELL HANDBOOK • ELL Study Guide, p. 136	TEACHER'S EDITION • ELL/ELD Reader Guided Reading, p. DI•73 ELL HANDBOOK • ELL Study Guide, p. 136
ELL HANDBOOK • High-Frequency Words Activity Bank, p. 446 ELL POSTER 18 • Day 3 Activities	ELL HANDBOOK • High-Frequency Words Activity Bank, p. 446	TEACHER'S EDITION • Multiple-Meaning Words, p. 115h ELL HANDBOOK • High-Frequency Words Activity Bank, p. 446
TEACHER'S EDITION • Grammar Jammer ELL HANDBOOK • Grammar Transition Lesson, pp. 363, 367 • Grammar Jammer Routine, p. 478	TEACHER'S EDITION • Grammar Jammer ELL HANDBOOK • Grammar Transition Lesson, pp. 363, 367	TEACHER'S EDITION • Grammar Jammer ELL HANDBOOK • Grammar Transition Lesson, pp. 363, 367
TEACHER'S EDITION • Let's Write It!, p. 108–109 • Writing Trait: Sentences, pp. 109a–109b	TEACHER'S EDITION • Revising Strategy, pp. 115d–115e	TEACHER'S EDITION • Possessive Pronouns, pp. 115p–115q

Poster Talk, Concept Talk

Question of the Week

Why is it valuable to have unique interests?

ELL Poster 18

Throughout the week, use the ELL Poster to help students produce and comprehend language, understand the concept, and build English vocabulary. Use the Question of the Week and other questions to help students share ideas in pairs, small groups, or the large group. Sample questions are shown, with examples of possible responses by students.

Weekly Concept and Language Goals

- Discuss unique interests
- Identify some unique interests of others
- Explain how unique interests lead to new discoveries

By the end of the lesson, students should be able to talk about and write one or more sentences about unique interests.

Daily Team Talk

Day 1	Day 2	Day 3	Day 4	Day 5
After Day 1 activities on Poster, ask questions such as *In the poster picture, what unique interest does the girl have?*	After Day 2 activity on Poster, ask questions such as *How can collecting stamps help the girl in the poster picture discover new things?*	After Day 3 activity on Poster, ask questions such as *In the poster picture, what unique interest does the girl's mother have?*	After Day 4 activity on Poster, ask questions such as *In the story* Rocks in His Head, *what unique interest does the writer's father have? How does that interest help him?*	After Day 5 activity on Poster, ask questions such as *What is a unique interest you have? What can you learn from your unique interest?*
Beginning She likes stamps. **Intermediate** She likes to collect stamps. **Advanced** The girl likes to collect stamps with people on them. **Advanced High** The girl is interested in stamp collecting. She likes stamps with famous people on them.	**Beginning** Learn about people. **Intermediate** She can learn new things about the people. **Advanced** The girl can discover things about the people on the stamps. **Advanced High** The girl can discover things she did not know before about the people on the stamps.	**Beginning** She likes schools. **Intermediate** She likes to help make new schools. **Advanced** Her mother helps make new schools. She thinks schools are important. **Advanced High** The girl's mother is interested in planning new schools. She thinks education is important.	**Beginning** He likes rocks. **Intermediate** He likes rocks. It gets him a job. **Advanced** The writer's father likes collecting rocks. He gets a job at the museum. **Advanced High** The writer's father enjoys collecting and learning about rocks. He is offered a job at the museum because he knows so much about rocks.	**Beginning** I like kites. **Intermediate** I can learn what makes the best kite. **Advanced** I like flying kites. I can learn what kind of kite flies best. **Advanced High** By trying out different kinds of kites, I can learn what materials and design make the best kite.

This Week's Materials

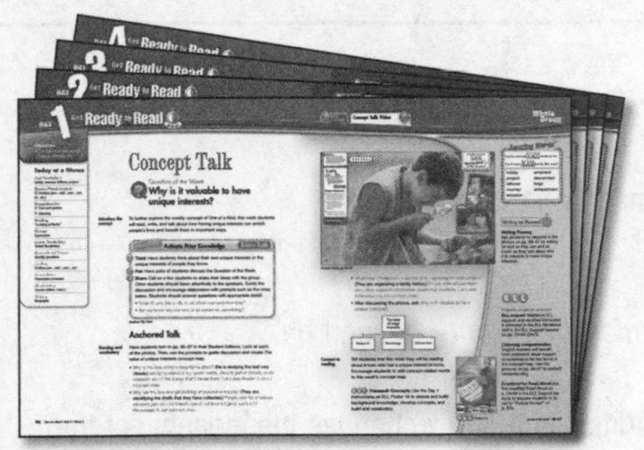
Teacher's Edition pages 86j–115q

See the support for English language learners throughout the lesson, including ELL strategies and scaffolded activities at points of use.

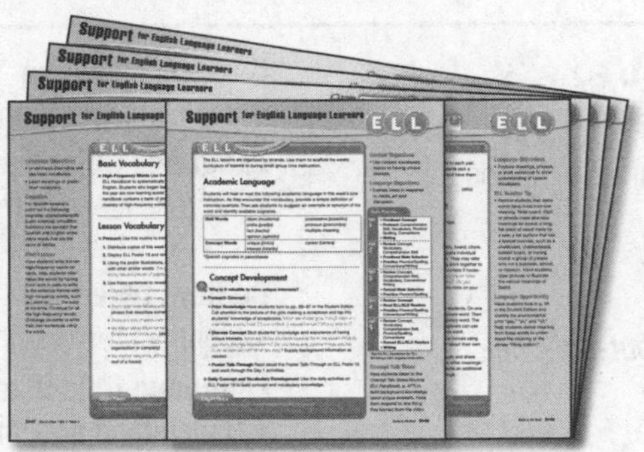
Teacher's Edition pages DI•66–DI•75

Differentiated Instruction for English language learners provides daily group activities that "frontload," or preteach, core instruction.

ELL Handbook pp. 131a–136

Find additional lesson materials that support the core lesson and the ELL instructional pages.

ELL Poster 18

ELL Reader 3.4.3

What Careers Interest You?

ELD Reader 3.4.3

Concept Literacy Reader

ELD, ELL Reader Teaching Guide

Concept Literacy Reader Teaching Guide

Technology

Online Teacher's Edition Use the digital version of the core Teacher's Edition for planning and instruction.

eReaders
This week's ELL and ELD Readers and Concept Literacy Reader are also available in digital format.

This Week's Content and Language Objectives by Strand

Concept Development/ Academic Language Why is it valuable to have unique interests?	**Content Objective** • Use concept vocabulary related to having unique interests. **Language Objective** • Express ideas in response to art and discussion.
Phonics and Spelling Prefixes *pre-*, *mid-*, *over-*, *out-*, *bi-*, *de-*	**Content Objective** • Identify prefixes *pre-*, *mid-*, *over-*, *out-*, *bi-*, and *de*. **Language Objective** • Understand how the addition of a prefix changes the meaning of the base or root of the word.
Listening Comprehension Modified Read Aloud: "Pictures In His Hand"	**Content Objective** • Monitor and adjust oral comprehension. **Language Objectives** • Discuss oral passages. • Use a graphic organizer to demonstrate listening comprehension.
Reading Comprehension Fact and Opinion	**Content Objectives** • Distinguish between fact and opinion. • Recognize clue words that signal opinions. **Language Objectives** • Distinguish between formal and informal English. • Learn when to use formal and informal English. • Read aloud with appropriate expression.
Vocabulary Basic and Lesson Vocabulary	**Language Objectives** • Understand and use basic and grade-level vocabulary. • Learn meanings of grade-level vocabulary. • Produce drawings, phrases, and short sentences to show understanding of Lesson Vocabulary.
Vocabulary Multiple-Meaning Words	**Content Objective** • Identify and understand multiple-meaning words. **Language Objective** • Apply phonics and decoding skills to spelling.
Grammar and Conventions Possessive Pronouns	**Content Objectives** • Identify possessive pronouns. • Use possessive pronouns correctly. **Language Objectives** • Practice using possessive pronouns in speaking. • Write sentences using possessive pronouns.
Writing Combining Short, Choppy Sentences	**Content Objectives** • Identify choppy sentences. • Identify connecting words to combine sentences. **Language Objectives** • Write and speak by using connecting words. • Share feedback for editing and revising.

Word Cards for Vocabulary Activities

attic	**board**
chores	**customer**
labeled	**spare**
stamps	

Teacher Note: Beginning Teach two to three words. **Intermediate** Teach three to four words. **Advanced** Teach four to five words. **Advanced High** Teach all words.

Name ____________________

Picture It!
Fact and Opinion

Look at the pictures. **Read** the paragraph.

- **Write** a fact from the story. **Write** how you can prove it.
- **Write** an opinion from the story. **Write** the clue word.

Chile

Many people visit Chile for fun. You can ski on the mountains. They are covered with snow. I think the mountains are too cold! I like to visit the beaches in Chile better. They are warmer than the mountains. You can swim in the warm sea. The sea is prettier than the mountains too.

Fact: ____________________

____

____

____

Opinion: ____________________

____

____

Picture It!

Fact and Opinion

Use this lesson to supplement or replace the skill lesson on page 90a of the Teacher's Edition. Display the Skill Points (at right) and share them with students.

> **Skill Points**
>
> ✔ A statement of **fact** tells something that can be proven. It is either true or false. You can prove it by reading about it or asking an expert.
>
> ✔ An **opinion** tells someone's ideas or feelings. Clue words such as *fun, best,* and *like* tell you that a statement is an opinion.

Teach/Model

Beginning Display a map of North America. Say: *Mexico is in North America. Is this a fact or an opinion?* (fact) *How can you prove it is true?* (Look at the map.) Say: *I like Mexican food best. Is this a fact or an opinion?* (opinion) *How do you know?* (It tells your feelings. It cannot be proven true or false.)

Intermediate Write and read aloud these sentences: *Chile is a country in South America. It would be fun to visit Chile.* Ask students to copy the opinion. Have them circle the words that tell them this is an opinion. (would, fun)

Advanced Read aloud these sentences: *Brazil has rain forests. Brazil's rain forests are beautiful.* Have students explain how they can tell which statement is a fact and which statement is an opinion.

Advanced High Ask students to write one fact and one opinion. Pair students. One partner reads aloud his or her statements, and the other partner identifies the fact and the opinion. Then the partners trade roles.

Then distribute copies of Picture It! page 132.

- Have students look at the pictures. Read the paragraph aloud.
- Review the Skill Points with students.
- Ask: *What is one fact?* (Answers will vary.) *Where can you check to see if it is true?* (Possible answer: in an encyclopedia or on the Internet)

Practice

Read aloud the directions on page 132. Have students reread the paragraph silently. Have them look at the pictures and the paragraph as they fill in the boxes.

Beginning Students can say what facts and opinions they want to write before writing their answers on the lines. Provide help with English words and writing.

Intermediate Students can first orally answer and then write sentences on the lines. Provide help with writing.

Advanced Students can write their answers and then check them by rereading the paragraph and making any necessary corrections.

Advanced High Students can write their answers and then orally explain how they decided which are facts and which are opinions.

Answers for page 132: Possible answers: *Fact:* The beaches are warmer than the mountains. You can prove it by looking at a weather web site. *Opinion:* I like to visit the beaches in Chile better. The clue words are *like* and *better.*

Multilingual Summaries

English

Read Together

Rocks in His Head

A boy collected rocks. He wanted to work with rocks when he grew up. He opened a gas station instead. He sold gas and fixed cars. He still collected rocks.

Bad times came. People stopped buying gas. The man had to close the gas station. He and his family moved to an old house. He kept his rocks in the attic. He read books about rocks. He looked for a job.

Sometimes the man visited the science museum to see the rocks there. The director of the museum noticed he often visited. She talked to him about his rock collection. He took her to his house to show her his rocks. She gave him a job as a janitor. But soon she hired him to be in charge of the museum's rocks.

Spanish

School + Home

Rocas en su cabeza

Un niño coleccionaba rocas. Quería trabajar con rocas cuando fuera grande. En vez de hacer esto, cuando creció, abrió una estación de gasolina. Vendía gasolina y arreglaba autos. Pero aún seguía coleccionando rocas.

Llegaron tiempos difíciles. La gente dejó de comprar gasolina. El hombre tuvo que cerrar la estación de gasolina. Él y su familia se mudaron para una casa vieja. En el ático de la casa, el hombre guardó sus rocas. Él seguía leyendo libros sobre las rocas. Fue a buscar trabajo.

A veces el hombre visitaba el museo de ciencias para ver las rocas que había allí. La directora del museo notó sus frecuentes visitas. Ella habló con él sobre su colección de rocas. Él la llevó a su casa para mostrarle su colección de rocas. Ella le dio un trabajo como portero, pero muy pronto lo dejó a cargo de las rocas del museo.

Multilingual Summaries

Chinese

滿腦子都是石頭

有個小男孩很喜歡收集石頭，他希望長大以後可以做跟石頭有關的工作。不過他後來卻開了一家加油站，專門賣汽油和修理汽車，但他還是在收集石頭。

經濟不景氣，大家都不買汽油，這個男人不得已只好把加油站關了。他和家人改住舊房子，但是他還是沒有把石頭丟掉。他一邊讀跟石頭有關的書，一邊忙著找工作。

這個男人有時候會去參觀博物館，看看裡面收藏的石頭。博物館館長注意到他經常來，於是和男人聊起他收集的石頭，男人很熱心地帶她到家裡看石頭。館長給男人一份博物館工友的工作，不久之後，她又正式雇用男人，要他負責照料博物館裡的石頭。

Vietnamese

Đá Sỏi Trong Đầu

Một cậu bé thu thập đá sỏi. Cậu muốn làm việc với đá sỏi khi khôn lớn. Nhưng khi lớn lên ông này lại mở một trạm xăng. Ông bán xăng và sửa chữa xe hơi. Ông vẫn còn thu thập đá.

Thời kỳ khốn khó đến. Người ta thôi không mua xăng. Ông phải đóng cửa trạm xăng. Ông và gia đình dọn đến một ngôi nhà cũ kỹ. Ông giữ những viên đá của mình trên gác xép. Ông đọc sách về đá. Ông tìm việc làm.

Thỉnh thoảng ông này đến việc bảo tàng khoa học để xem những viên đá ở đó. Vị giám đốc viện bảo tàng để ý thấy ông thường đến xem. Bà ta nói chuyện với ông về bộ đá ông thu thập. Ông đưa bà về nhà để cho bà xem những viên đá của ông. Bà cho ông vào làm người quét dọn. Nhưng chẳng bao lâu bà mướn ông cai quản đá của viện bảo tàng.

Multilingual Summaries

Korean

바위 생각으로 가득 찬 남자

한 소년이 바위를 수집한다. 그는 커서 바위를 갖고 일하길 원하지만 대신 주유소를 열어 기름을 팔고 차를 수리한다. 그래도 그는 여전히 바위를 모은다.

어려운 시기가 닥쳐온다. 사람들이 기름을 사지 않게 되자 남자는 주유소를 닫고 가족들은 낡은 집으로 이사한다. 그는 다락방에 바위들을 보관하고 바위에 관한 책을 읽으며 일자리를 찾는다.

가끔 남자는 바위를 보기 위해 과학 박물관에 갔고 박물관장 여자는 이 남자가 박물관에 종종 들린다는 걸 알게 된다. 그녀는 그의 바위 수집품에 관해 이야기를 하고 그는 자기의 바위들을 보여주려고 여자를 집으로 데리고 간다. 박물관장은 그에게 건물 수위 자리를 주지만 그녀는 곧 박물관의 바위를 책임지는 자리에 남자를 고용한다.

Hmong

Pobzeb nyob hauv Nws Taub Hau

Muaj ib tug me tub ua khaws pobzeb. Nws xa ua hauj lwm nrog pobzeb thaum nws loj. Nws qhib ib lub lab muag roj theej qhov ntawd. Nws muag roj thiab kho tsheb. Nws tseem khaws pobzeb.

Sib hawm phem tuaj lawm. Neeg tsis yuav roj lawm. Tus txiv neej ntawd tau kaw lus lab muag roj. Nws thiab nws tsev neeg lawv tsiv mus nyob ib lub tsev qub qub. Nws khaws nws cov pobzeb sauv nthab. Nws nyeem ntawv txog pobzeb. Nws nrhiav hauj lwm.

Muaj tej zaum tus txiv neej ntawd mus tom science museum mus xyuas pobzeb tov. Tus coj ntawm lub museum pom tias nws tuaj heev. Nws nrog nws tham txog nws txoj kev khaws pobzeb. Nws coj nws mus tom nws tsev mus xyuas nws cov pobzeb. Nws muab ib txoj hauj lwm rau nws ua ib tug neeg tu vaj tu tsev cheb vaj cheb tsev. Tiam si tsis ntev nws txais nws los ua tus saib xyuas cov pobzeb hauv lub museum.

Name ______________________

What Careers Interest You?

- **Read** *What Careers Interest You?* again.
- **Use** the information in the book. **Write** on the first line who uses these tools in his or her job.
- **Write** on the next two lines some things you think a person with this job likes to do.

Tools	Who uses them? What does this person like to do?
	1. ______________________ ______________________ ______________________
	2. ______________________ ______________________ ______________________
	3. ______________________ ______________________ ______________________
	4. ______________________ ______________________ ______________________

Family Link

Ask family members about careers they have or would like to have.

Weekly Resources Guide for English Language Learner Support

For this week's content and language objectives, see p. 137e.

Instructional Strand	Day 1	Day 2
Concept Development/Academic Language	TEACHER'S EDITION • Academic Language, p. DI•91 • Concept Development, p. DI•91 • Anchored Talk, pp. 116j—116–117 • Preteach Academic Vocabulary, p. 121a • Concept Talk Video ELL HANDBOOK • Hear It, See It, Say It, Use It, pp. xxxvi–xxxvii • ELL Poster Talk, Concept Talk, p. 137c ELL POSTER 19 • Day 1 Activities	TEACHER'S EDITION • Academic Language, p. DI•91 • Concept Development, p. DI•91 • Anchored Talk, p. 122a • Concept Talk Video ELL HANDBOOK • ELL Poster Talk, Concept Talk, p. 137c • Concept Talk Video Routine, p. 477 ELL POSTER 19 • Day 2 Activities
Phonics and Spelling	TEACHER'S EDITION • Phonics and Spelling, p. DI•95 • Decodable Practice Reader 19A, pp. 119a–119b	TEACHER'S EDITION • Phonics and Spelling, p. DI•95
Listening Comprehension	TEACHER'S EDITION • Modified Read Aloud, p. DI•94 • Read Aloud, p. 117b • Concept Talk Video ELL HANDBOOK • Concept Talk Video Routine, p. 477	TEACHER'S EDITION • Modified Read Aloud, p. DI•94 • AudioText of *America's Champion Swimmer: Gertrude Ederle* • Concept Talk Video ELL HANDBOOK • AudioText CD Routine, p. 477 • Cause and Effect, p. 489
Reading Comprehension	TEACHER'S EDITION • Preteach Fact and Opinion, p. DI•96	TEACHER'S EDITION • Reteach Fact and Opinion, p. DI•96 • Frontloading Reading, p. DI•97 ELL HANDBOOK • Picture It! Skill Instruction, pp. 138–138a • Multilingual Summaries, pp. 139–141
Vocabulary **Basic and Lesson Vocabulary** **Vocabulary Skill: Multiple-Meaning Words**	TEACHER'S EDITION • Basic Vocabulary, p. DI•92 • Preteach Lesson Vocabulary, p. DI•92 • Multiple-Meaning Words, p. DI•95 ELL HANDBOOK • Word Cards, p. 137 • ELL Vocabulary Routine, p. 471 ELL POSTER 19 • Day 1 Activities	TEACHER'S EDITION • Basic Vocabulary, p. DI•92 • Reteach Lesson Vocabulary, p. DI•93 • Multiple-Meaning Words, p. DI•95 ELL HANDBOOK • Word Cards, p. 137 • Multilingual Vocabulary List, p. 438 ELL POSTER 19 • Day 2 Activities
Grammar and Conventions	TEACHER'S EDITION • Preteach Contractions, p. DI•99	TEACHER'S EDITION • Reteach Contractions, p. DI•99
Writing	TEACHER'S EDITION • Writing Headings and Subheads, p. DI•100 • Introduce Autobiography, pp. 121e–121f	TEACHER'S EDITION • Writing Trait: Organization, pp. 131d–131e

Unit 4 Week 4 *Gertrude Ederle*

This symbol indicates leveled instruction to address language proficiency levels.

Day 3	Day 4	Day 5
TEACHER'S EDITION • Academic Language, p. DI•91 • Concept Development, p. DI•91 • Anchored Talk, p. 132a • Concept Talk Video **ELL HANDBOOK** • ELL Poster Talk, Concept Talk, p. 137c **ELL POSTER 19** • Day 3 Activities	**TEACHER'S EDITION** • Academic Language, p. DI•91 • Concept Development, p. DI•91 • Anchored Talk, p. 144a • Concept Talk Video **ELL HANDBOOK** • ELL Poster Talk, Concept Talk, p. 137c **ELL POSTER 19** • Day 4 Activities	**TEACHER'S EDITION** • Academic Language, p. DI•91 • Concept Development, p. DI•91 • Concept Talk Video **ELL HANDBOOK** • ELL Poster Talk, Concept Talk, p. 137c **ELL POSTER 19** • Day 5 Activities
ELL HANDBOOK • Phonics Transition Lesson, pp. 289, 296	**ELL HANDBOOK** • Phonics Transition Lesson, pp. 289, 296	**TEACHER'S EDITION** • Phonics and Spelling, p. DI•95
TEACHER'S EDITION • AudioText of *America's Champion Swimmer: Gertrude Ederle* • Concept Talk Video **ELL HANDBOOK** • AudioText CD Routine, p. 477	**TEACHER'S EDITION** • Concept Talk Video	**TEACHER'S EDITION** • Concept Talk Video
TEACHER'S EDITION • Sheltered Reading, p. DI•97 **ELL HANDBOOK** • Multilingual Summaries, pp. 139–141	**TEACHER'S EDITION** • ELL/ELD Reader Guided Reading, p. DI•98 **ELL HANDBOOK** • ELL Study Guide, p. 142	**TEACHER'S EDITION** • ELL/ELD Reader Guided Reading, p. DI•98 **ELL HANDBOOK** • ELL Study Guide, p. 142
ELL HANDBOOK • High-Frequency Words Activity Bank, p. 446 **ELL POSTER 19** • Day 3 Activities	**ELL HANDBOOK** • High-Frequency Words Activity Bank, p. 446	**TEACHER'S EDITION** • Multiple-Meaning Words, p. 149h **ELL HANDBOOK** • High-Frequency Words Activity Bank, p. 446
TEACHER'S EDITION • Grammar Jammer **ELL HANDBOOK** • Grammar Transition Lesson, pp. 328, 337 • Grammar Jammer Routine, p. 478	**TEACHER'S EDITION** • Grammar Jammer **ELL HANDBOOK** • Grammar Transition Lesson, pp. 328, 337	**TEACHER'S EDITION** • Grammar Jammer **ELL HANDBOOK** • Grammar Transition Lesson, pp. 328, 337
TEACHER'S EDITION • Let's Write It!, p. 142–143 • Writing Trait: Organization, pp. 143a–143b	**TEACHER'S EDITION** • Revising Strategy, pp. 149d–149e	**TEACHER'S EDITION** • Autobiography, pp. 149p–149q

Poster Talk, Concept Talk

Question of the Week

What unique traits does it take to be the first to do something?

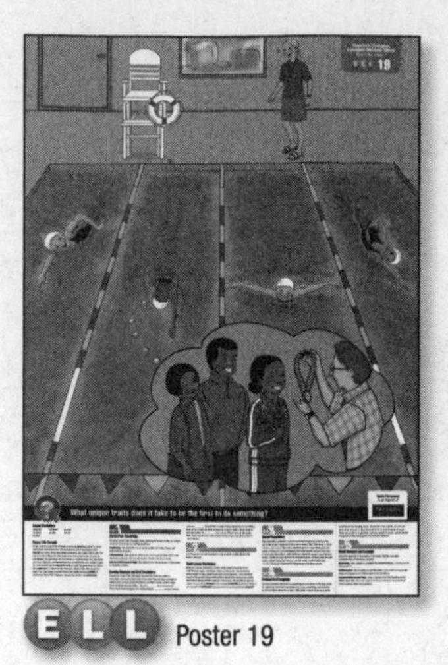

Poster 19

Throughout the week, use the ELL Poster to help students produce and comprehend language, understand the concept, and build English vocabulary. Use the Question of the Week and other questions to help students share ideas in pairs, small groups, or the large group. Sample questions are shown, with examples of possible responses by students.

Weekly Concept and Language Goals

- Participate in a discussion about unique traits
- Name and explain some unique traits
- Share ways that unique traits can help a person do new things

By the end of the lesson, students should be able to talk about and write one or more sentences about unique traits and being the first to do something.

Daily Team Talk

Day 1	Day 2	Day 3	Day 4	Day 5
After Day 1 activities on Poster, ask questions such as *In the poster picture, what are the girls in the pool doing?*	After Day 2 activity on Poster, ask questions such as *In the poster picture, what does the girl in the second lane dream of doing?*	After Day 3 activity on Poster, ask questions such as *In the poster picture, what unique trait do you think the girl in the second lane has that can help her win a medal?*	After Day 4 activity on Poster, ask questions such as *Other than practicing every day, what is another unique trait that can help the girl in the poster picture win a medal for swimming?*	After Day 5 activity on Poster, ask questions such as *In the story* America's Champion Swimmer, *how did her unique trait of courage help Gertrude swim the English Channel?*
Beginning Swimming. **Intermediate** They are swimming in the pool. **Advanced** The girls in the pool are practicing different ways to swim. **Advanced High** The girls in the pool are practicing different swimming strokes.	**Beginning** Winning. **Intermediate** She wants to win a medal. **Advanced** The girl dreams of winning a medal for swimming. **Advanced High** The girl dreams of being the first person in her family to win a medal for swimming.	**Beginning** Swims a lot. **Intermediate** She swims every day. **Advanced** The girl likes to swim. She practices every day. **Advanced High** The girl loves swimming and practices every day. When you practice doing something, you get better at doing it.	**Beginning** She wants it. **Intermediate** She knows what she wants. **Advanced** The girl can plan how to get to her goal. **Advanced High** The girl knows what her final goal is. She can plan the steps she must take to reach that goal.	**Beginning** She keeps going. **Intermediate** She does not stop when it is hard. **Advanced** Gertrude's courage helped her keep swimming, even when it got tough. **Advanced High** Gertrude's courage kept her from giving up, even when people told her she should. She was scared and tired, but she kept going.

This Week's Materials

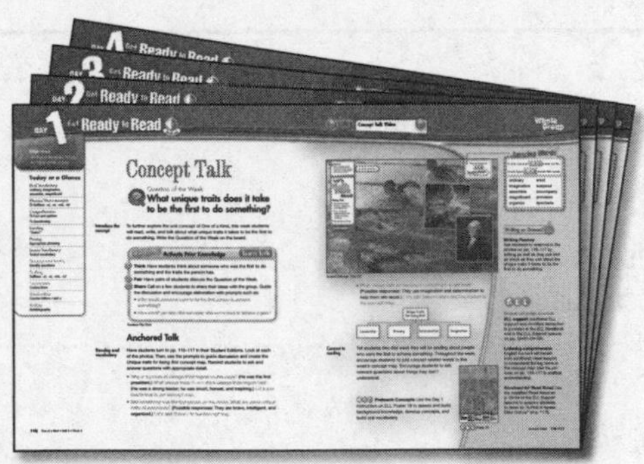

Teacher's Edition pages 116j–149q

See the support for English language learners throughout the lesson, including ELL strategies and scaffolded activities at points of use.

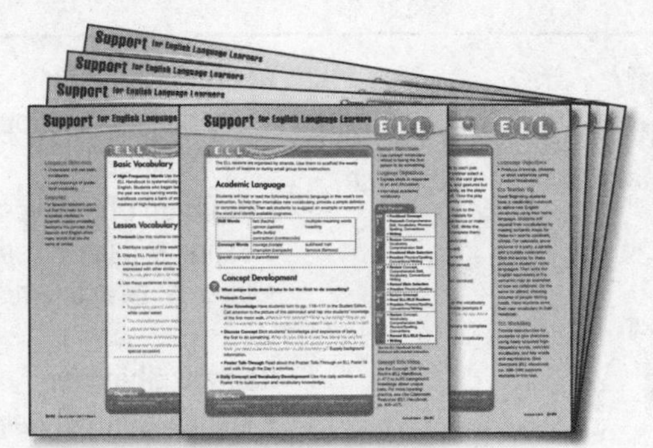

Teacher's Edition pages DI•91–DI•100

Differentiated Instruction for English language learners provides daily group activities that "frontload," or preteach, core instruction.

ELL Handbook pp. 137a–142

Find additional lesson materials that support the core lesson and the ELL instructional pages.

ELL Poster 19

ELL Reader 3.4.4

ELD Reader 3.4.4

Concept Literacy Reader

ELD, ELL Reader Teaching Guide

Concept Literacy Reader Teaching Guide

Technology

Online Teacher's Edition Use the digital version of the core Teacher's Edition for planning and instruction.

eReaders
This week's ELL and ELD Readers and Concept Literacy Reader are also available in digital format.

This Week's Content and Language Objectives by Strand

Concept Development/ Academic Language What unique traits does it take to be the first to do something?	**Content Objective** • Use concept vocabulary related to being the first person to do something. **Language Objectives** • Express ideas in response to art and discussion. • Internalize academic vocabulary.
Phonics and Spelling Suffixes *–er, -or, -ist*	**Content Objective** • Identify suffixes *–er, -or, -ist*. **Language Objective** • Understand how the addition of a suffix changes the meaning of the base or root of the word.
Listening Comprehension Modified Read Aloud: "First to Reach a Goal"	**Content Objective** • Monitor and adjust oral comprehension. **Language Objectives** • Discuss oral passages. • Use a graphic organizer to demonstrate listening comprehension.
Reading Comprehension Fact and Opinion	**Content Objectives** • Distinguish between fact and opinion. • Recognize clue words that signal opinions. **Language Objectives** • Formulate questions to distinguish between facts and opinions. • Speak using academic vocabulary. • Read aloud with appropriate phrasing.
Vocabulary Basic and Lesson Vocabulary	**Language Objectives** • Understand and use basic and grade-level vocabulary. • Learn meanings of grade-level vocabulary. • Produce drawings, phrases, and short sentences to show understanding of Lesson Vocabulary.
Vocabulary Multiple-Meaning Words	**Content Objective** • Identify and use context to understand multiple-meaning words. **Language Objective** • Apply phonics and decoding skills to spelling.
Grammar and Conventions Contractions	**Content Objectives** • Identify contractions. • Understand function of apostrophe in contractions. **Language Objectives** • Practice using contractions in speaking. • Write sentences using contractions.
Writing Writing Headings and Subheads	**Content Objectives** • Identify vivid details. • Use vivid details to describe character traits. **Language Objectives** • Use vivid language in writing. • Organize writing using heads and subheads.

Word Cards for Vocabulary Activities

celebrate	**continued**
current	**drowned**
medals	**stirred**
strokes	

Teacher Note: Beginning Teach two to three words. **Intermediate** Teach three to four words. **Advanced** Teach four to five words. **Advanced High** Teach all words.

Name ______________________________

Picture It!
Fact and Opinion

Look at the picture. **Read** the paragraph.

- **Write** a fact from the story. **Write** how you can prove it.
- **Write** an opinion from the story. **Write** the clue word.

Different Strokes

I am on the swim team at school. It is fun to swim on a team. We swim different strokes, such as butterfly, crawl, and backstroke. I do not like the backstroke. I cannot see where I am going!

Fact: ______________________________

____

How to prove: ______________________________

____

Opinion: ______________________________

____

Clue word: ______________________________

____

Fact and Opinion

Use this lesson to supplement or replace the skill lesson on page 120a of the Teacher's Edition. Display the Skill Points (at right) and share them with students.

Skill Points

✔ A statement of **fact** tells something that can be proven. It is either true or false. You can prove it by reading about it or asking an expert.

✔ An **opinion** tells someone's ideas or feelings. Clue words such as *fun, best,* and *like* tell you that a statement is an opinion.

Teach/Model

Beginning Say: *Swimming can make people strong. Is this a fact or an opinion?* (fact) *How can you prove it is a fact?* (Look in a reference book. Ask an expert.) *Swimming is fun. Is this a fact or an opinion?* (opinion) *How do you know?* (It tells how you feel.)

Intermediate Say: *Summer is the best time for swimming lessons. What clue word tells you that this is an opinion?* (best) *I take swimming lessons in the summer. How can you prove this is a fact?* (Ask your swimming teacher.)

Advanced Say: *The pool is open from 8:00 A.M. to 7:00 P.M. The pool should stay open until 8:00 P.M.* Have students explain how they can tell which statement is a fact and which statement is an opinion.

Advanced High Ask each student to find one fact and one opinion in a classroom text. Have them copy the statements, circle clue words that indicate the opinion, and tell what they could do to prove the fact.

Then distribute copies of Picture It! page 138.

- Have students look at the picture and tell what is happening.
- Read the paragraph aloud. Ask: *What strokes does the girl like to swim?*
- Review the Skill Points with students.
- Ask: *What is one fact?* (Possible answer: The narrator is on the school's swim team.) *Where can you check to find out if it is true?* (Possible answer: Ask the swim coach.)

Practice

Read aloud the directions on page 138. Have students reread the paragraph aloud. Have them look at the picture and the paragraph as they fill in the boxes.

Beginning Students can say what they want to write in the boxes before writing words or phrases on the lines. Provide help with English words and writing.

Intermediate Students can first orally answer and then write sentences in the boxes. Provide help with English words and writing.

Advanced Students can write their answers in the boxes and then check their answers by discussing them with a partner.

Advanced High Students can write their answers in the boxes and then orally explain how they decided which are facts and which are opinions.

Answers for page 138: Possible answers: *Facts:* I am on the swim team at school. We swim different strokes. I cannot see where I am going! *How to prove:* Ask the swim coach. Watch the swimmers. Look at the picture. *Opinions:* It is fun to swim on a team. I do not like the backstroke. Clue words: *fun, like*

Multilingual Summaries

English

America's Champion Swimmer: Gertrude Ederle

Gertrude Ederle was called Trudy. When she was seven years old, she almost drowned. So her father taught her to swim. She swam better than the other children. She joined a swimming club when she was thirteen. She won her first race when she was fifteen. The next year she swam from Manhattan to New Jersey and set a new record.

In 1924, Trudy won three Olympic medals. Then she trained to swim the English Channel. No woman had ever done that. The first time she tried, she did not finish. She got a new trainer and tried again a year later. On August 6, 1926, she crossed the channel. She beat the men's record.

When Trudy returned to New York, there was a parade for her. She had proven that women could be as strong as men.

Spanish

La campeona norteamericana de natación: Gertrude Ederle

A Gertrude Ederle la llamaban Trudy. Cuando tenía siete años, casi se ahoga. Entonces, su padre le enseñó a nadar. Nadaba mejor que los demás niños. Cuando cumplió trece años, entró a un club de natación. A los quince años, ganó su primera competencia. Al año siguiente, nadó desde Manhattan hasta New Jersey y estableció un nuevo récord.

En 1924, Trudy ganó tres medallas olímpicas. Después, se entrenó para nadar en el Canal de la Mancha. Nunca una mujer había hecho esto. La primera vez no pudo terminar. Buscó a un nuevo entrenador y volvió a intentarlo un año después. El 6 de agosto de 1926, cruzó el canal. Superó también el récord de los hombres.

Cuando Trudy regresó a Nueva York, la recibieron con un desfile en las calles. Ella había probado que las mujeres pueden ser tan fuertes como los hombres.

Multilingual Summaries

Chinese

美國游泳冠軍：葛魯德·艾德莉

大家都叫葛魯德・艾德莉「魯蒂」。魯蒂七歲時，差一點淹死，所以她父親就教她游泳，她游得比其他小朋友好。十三歲時，她參加了游泳隊，十五歲，魯蒂贏得她人生中的第一個冠軍。第二年，她從曼哈頓游到新澤西，創了新紀錄。

1924 年，魯蒂贏了三面奧運獎牌。接著，她接受訓練，準備游泳橫越英吉利海峽，之前從來沒有女泳手這樣做。第一次橫越沒有成功，於是她請了一個新教練，繼續努力練習，一年後又再次挑戰英吉利海峽。1926 年 8 月 6 日，魯蒂成功游泳橫越英吉利海峽，還破了男人創下的紀錄。

當魯蒂回到紐約時，群眾遊行慶祝她載譽歸國。魯蒂證明，女人也能像男人一樣優秀。

Vietnamese

Nhà Bơi Vô Địch của Hoa Kỳ: Gertrude Ederle

Gertrude Ederle được gọi là Trudy. Khi cô lên bảy, cô suýt bị chết đuối. Vì vậy ba của cô dạy cô bơi. Cô bơi giỏi hơn những đứa trẻ khác. Cô tham gia câu lạc bộ bơi lội khi cô mười ba tuổi. Cô thắng kỳ bơi đua đầu tiên của mình vào năm mười lăm tuổi. Năm sau đó cô bơi từ Manhattan đến New Jersey và lập một kỷ lục mới.

Vào năm 1924, Trudy thắng ba huy chương Thế Vận Hội. Rồi cô tập luyện để bơi qua eo biển Anh. Không một người phụ nữ nào từng làm điều này. Lần đầu tiên, cô không bơi hết. Cô có một huấn luyện viên mới và cố gắng lần nữa vào năm sau. Vào ngày 6 Tháng Tám, 1926, cô băng qua eo biển Anh. Cô phá cả kỷ lục của nam giới.

Khi Trudy trở lại New York, có diễn hành tiếp đón. Cô đã chứng minh rằng phụ nữ cũng mạnh được như nam.

Multilingual Summaries

Korean

미국의 수영 챔피언: 게르투르드 에덜리

트루디라 불리는 게르투르드 에덜리는 일곱 살이었을 때 물에 빠져 거의 죽을 뻔했다. 그래서 에덜리 아버지는 그녀에게 수영을 가르쳤고 그녀는 다른 아이들보다 수영을 잘 했다. 열 세 살이 되었을 때 그녀는 수영 클럽에 들어갔고 열 다섯 살 때 처음 경주에서 우승을 했다. 다음 해 그녀는 맨하튼에서 뉴저지까지 수영을 했고 새로운 기록을 달성했다.

1924년 트루디는 세 개의 올림픽 메달을 땄다. 이후 그녀는 영국 해협을 헤엄쳐 건너기 위해 훈련을 했고 여자로서 그 일을 해낸 사람은 아직 아무도 없었다. 첫 번째 시도에서 그녀는 성공하지 못했지만 새 트레이너를 구하고 1년 후에 다시 도전해서 1926년 8월 6일 해협을 건넜다. 그녀가 남자 기록을 깨뜨린 것이다.

트루디가 뉴욕으로 돌아왔을 때 그녀를 위한 퍼레이드가 벌어졌다. 그녀는 여자도 남자만큼 강할 수 있다는 것을 증명해 보인 것이다.

Hmong

Miskas Teb Tus Neeg Ua Luam Dej Keej Tshaj Plaws: Gertrude Ederle

Lawv muab Gertrude Ederle hu ua Trudy. Thaum nws muaj xya xyoo, nws yuav hluag poob dej. Ces nws txiv thiaj li qhia nws ua luam dej. Nws ua luam dej keej tshaj lwm cov menyuam. Nws tau koom ib lub koos haum ua luam dej thaum nws muaj kaum peb xyoo. Nws yeej nws thawj thawj txoj kev sib tw thaum nws muaj kaum tsib xyoo. Xyoo tom qab ntawd, nws ua luam dej pib pem Manhattan mus rau New Jersey thiab tau tsim ib qhov xeev xwm txheej tsiab.

Thaum xyoo 1924, Trudy yeej peb lub kib Olympic. Ces nws txawm txhij nws tus kheej kom luam tau dej hauv tus English Channel. Tsis muaj ib tug poj niam twg uas tau ua li ntawd duab li. Thawj thawj zaug, nws luam tsis tiav. Nws tau ib tug neeg qhia nws tshiab thiab xyaum ntxiv ib xyoo tom qab. Hnub vas thij rau lub yim hli ntuj xyoo 1926, nws luam dej hla tau tus channel. Nws ua tau zoo tshaj cov txiv neej cov xeev xwm txheej.

Thaum Trudy rov qab mus rau New York, lawv ua ib qhov kev zoo siab parade rau nws. Nws tau ua yam txwv tias poj niam kuj muaj zog npaum li txiv neej thiag.

Name ______________________________ **Helen Wills Moody**

- **Read** *Helen Wills Moody* again.
- **Look** at the dates in the book. **Look** at the time line below.
- **Write** one fact about Helen Wills Moody for each date on the time line.

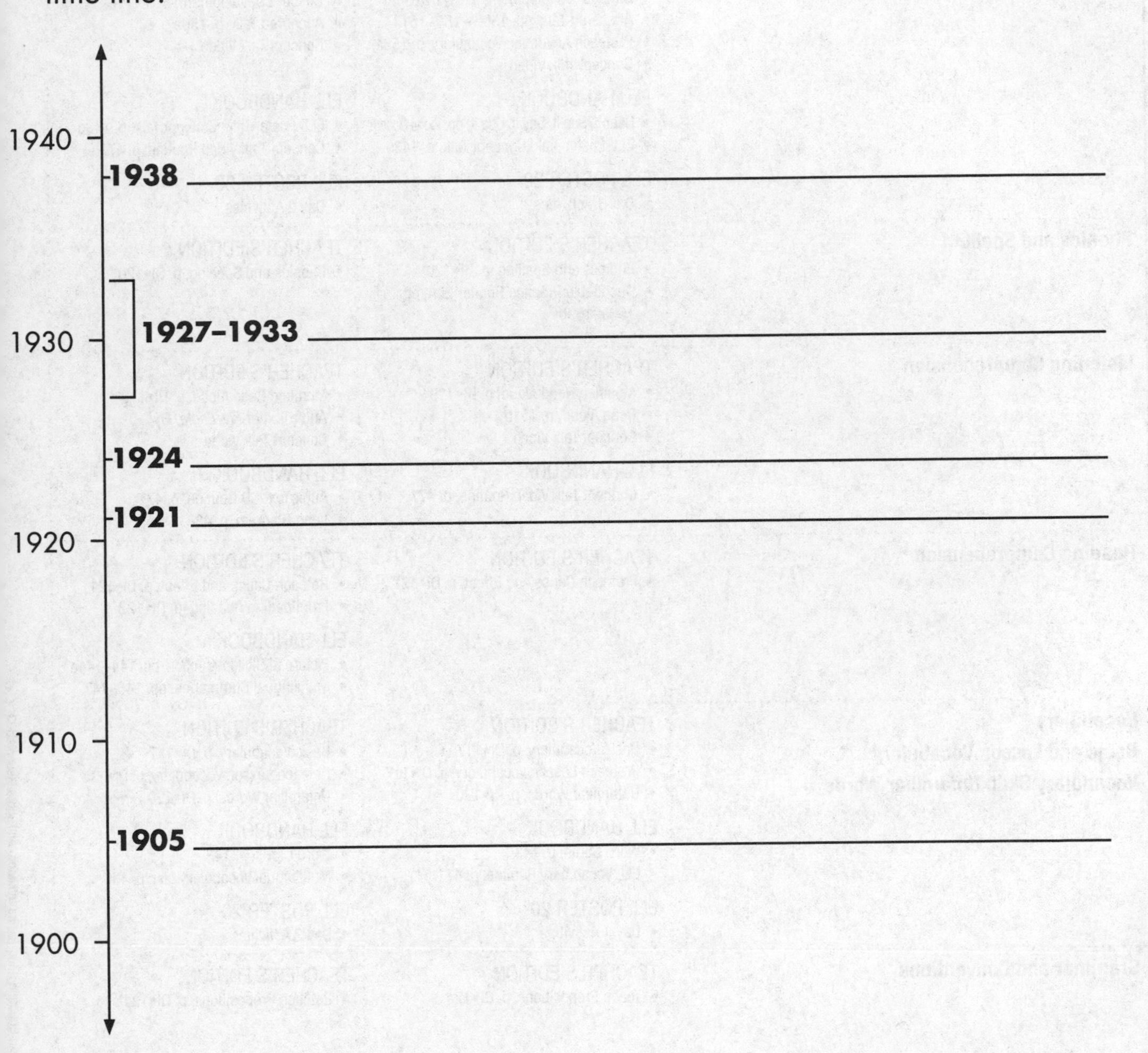

Family Link

Ask family members what they know about tennis and tennis players.

Weekly Resources Guide for English Language Learner Support

For this week's content and language objectives, see p. 143e.

Instructional Strand	Day 1	Day 2
Concept Development/Academic Language	TEACHER'S EDITION • Academic Language, p. DI•116 • Concept Development, p. DI•116 • Anchored Talk, pp. 150j—150–151 • Preteach Academic Vocabulary, p. 155a • Concept Talk Video ELL HANDBOOK • Hear It, See It, Say It, Use It, pp. xxxvi–xxxvii • ELL Poster Talk, Concept Talk, p. 143c ELL POSTER 20 • Day 1 Activities	TEACHER'S EDITION • Academic Language, p. DI•116 • Concept Development, p. DI•116 • Anchored Talk, p. 156a • Concept Talk Video ELL HANDBOOK • ELL Poster Talk, Concept Talk, p. 143c • Concept Talk Video Routine, p. 477 ELL POSTER 20 • Day 2 Activities
Phonics and Spelling	TEACHER'S EDITION • Phonics and Spelling, p. DI•120 • Decodable Practice Reader 20A, pp. 153a–153b	TEACHER'S EDITION • Phonics and Spelling, p. DI•120
Listening Comprehension	TEACHER'S EDITION • Modified Read Aloud, p. DI•119 • Read Aloud, p. 151b • Concept Talk Video ELL HANDBOOK • Concept Talk Video Routine, p. 477	TEACHER'S EDITION • Modified Read Aloud, p. DI•119 • AudioText of *Fly, Eagle, Fly!* • Concept Talk Video ELL HANDBOOK • AudioText CD Routine, p. 477 • Venn Diagram, p. 488
Reading Comprehension	TEACHER'S EDITION • Preteach Cause and Effect, p. DI•121	TEACHER'S EDITION • Reteach Cause and Effect, p. DI•121 • Frontloading Reading, p. DI•122 ELL HANDBOOK • Picture It! Skill Instruction, pp. 144–144a • Multilingual Summaries, pp. 145–147
Vocabulary **Basic and Lesson Vocabulary** **Vocabulary Skill: Unfamiliar Words**	TEACHER'S EDITION • Basic Vocabulary, p. DI•117 • Preteach Lesson Vocabulary, p. DI•117 • Unfamiliar Words, p. DI•120 ELL HANDBOOK • Word Cards, p. 143 • ELL Vocabulary Routine, p. 471 ELL POSTER 20 • Day 1 Activities	TEACHER'S EDITION • Basic Vocabulary, p. DI•117 • Reteach Lesson Vocabulary, p. DI•118 • Unfamiliar Words, p. DI•120 ELL HANDBOOK • Word Cards, p. 143 • Multilingual Vocabulary List, p. 438 ELL POSTER 20 • Day 2 Activities
Grammar and Conventions	TEACHER'S EDITION • Teach Prepositions, p. DI•124	TEACHER'S EDITION • Reteach Prepositions, p. DI•124
Writing	TEACHER'S EDITION • Writing Time-Order Transition Words, p. DI•125 • Writing for Tests: Summary, pp. 155e–155f	TEACHER'S EDITION • Writing for Tests: Summary, pp. 167d–167e

Unit 4 Week 5 Fly, Eagle, Fly!

This symbol indicates leveled instruction to address language proficiency levels.

Day 3	Day 4	Day 5
TEACHER'S EDITION • Academic Language, p. DI•116 • Concept Development, p. DI•116 • Anchored Talk, p. 168a • Concept Talk Video ELL HANDBOOK • ELL Poster Talk, Concept Talk, p. 143c ELL POSTER 20 • Day 3 Activities	TEACHER'S EDITION • Academic Language, p. DI•116 • Concept Development, p. DI•116 • Anchored Talk, p. 176a • Concept Talk Video ELL HANDBOOK • ELL Poster Talk, Concept Talk, p. 143c ELL POSTER 20 • Day 4 Activities	TEACHER'S EDITION • Academic Language, p. DI•116 • Concept Development, p. DI•116 • Concept Talk Video ELL HANDBOOK • ELL Poster Talk, Concept Talk, p. 143c ELL POSTER 20 • Day 5 Activities
ELL HANDBOOK • Phonics Transition Lesson, pp. 234, 238	ELL HANDBOOK • Phonics Transition Lesson, pp. 234, 238	TEACHER'S EDITION • Phonics and Spelling, p. DI•120
TEACHER'S EDITION • AudioText of *Fly, Eagle, Fly!* • Concept Talk Video ELL HANDBOOK • AudioText CD Routine, p. 477	TEACHER'S EDITION • Concept Talk Video	TEACHER'S EDITION • Concept Talk Video
TEACHER'S EDITION • Sheltered Reading, p. DI•122 ELL HANDBOOK • Multilingual Summaries, pp. 145–147	TEACHER'S EDITION • ELL/ELD Reader Guided Reading, p. DI•123 ELL HANDBOOK • ELL Study Guide, p. 148	TEACHER'S EDITION • ELL/ELD Reader Guided Reading, p. DI•123 ELL HANDBOOK • ELL Study Guide, p. 148
ELL HANDBOOK • High-Frequency Words Activity Bank, p. 446 ELL POSTER 20 • Day 3 Activities	ELL HANDBOOK • High-Frequency Words Activity Bank, p. 446	TEACHER'S EDITION • Unknown Words, p. 183h ELL HANDBOOK • High-Frequency Words Activity Bank, p. 446
TEACHER'S EDITION • Grammar Jammer ELL HANDBOOK • Grammar Transition Lesson, pp. 379–380 • Grammar Jammer Routine, p. 478	TEACHER'S EDITION • Grammar Jammer ELL HANDBOOK • Grammar Transition Lesson, pp. 379–380	TEACHER'S EDITION • Grammar Jammer ELL HANDBOOK • Grammar Transition Lesson, pp. 379–380
TEACHER'S EDITION • Let's Write It!, p. 174–175 • Writing for Tests: Evaluation, pp. 175a–175b	TEACHER'S EDITION • Writing for Tests, p. 183d	TEACHER'S EDITION • Writing for Tests, pp. 183p–183q

Poster Talk, Concept Talk

Question of the Week

What behaviors are unique to different animals?

Poster 20

Throughout the week, use the ELL Poster to help students produce and comprehend language, understand the concept, and build English vocabulary. Use the Question of the Week and other questions to help students share ideas in pairs, small groups, or the large group. Sample questions are shown, with examples of possible responses by students.

Weekly Concept and Language Goals

- Explain unique behaviors of animals
- Give examples of animals with protective behaviors
- Tell how unique animal behaviors help animals survive

By the end of the lesson, students should be able to talk about and write one or more sentences about unique animal behaviors.

Daily Team Talk

Day 1	Day 2	Day 3	Day 4	Day 5
After Day 1 activities on Poster, ask questions such as *In the poster picture, what is unique about how an anteater finds its food?*	After Day 2 activity on Poster, ask questions such as *What unique behavior do gazelles have that helps protect them?*	After Day 3 activity on Poster, ask questions such as *In the poster picture, how do you think the elephant protects itself from the heat?*	After Day 4 activity on Poster, ask questions such as *In the poster picture, how can the baboons' unique behavior help them survive?*	After Day 5 activity on Poster, ask questions such as *What unique behavior helps an animal that lives in our area survive?*
Beginning Uses its nose. **Intermediate** It uses its long nose. **Advanced** An anteater has a very long nose that it uses to look for food. **Advanced High** An anteater uses its long, skinny nose to poke around and search for food.	**Beginning** They're fast. **Intermediate** Gazelles can run fast. **Advanced** Gazelles can run away from things quickly. **Advanced High** Gazelles protect themselves by running quickly away from danger.	**Beginning** With water. **Intermediate** It uses water. **Advanced** It sprays water from its trunk. **Advanced High** The elephant uses its trunk to spray water on itself. The water helps keep it cool.	**Beginning** They go up trees. **Intermediate** They climb trees to get food. **Advanced** Baboons can climb trees. They eat the leaves of the trees. **Advanced High** Because baboons can climb trees, they can get to the leaves they want to eat. They are also safe from animals on the ground.	**Beginning** Squirrels get nuts. **Intermediate** Squirrels look for nuts and hide them. **Advanced** Squirrels store nuts for the winter. **Advanced High** Squirrels gather and store nuts and other food so they have something to eat during the winter.

This Week's Materials

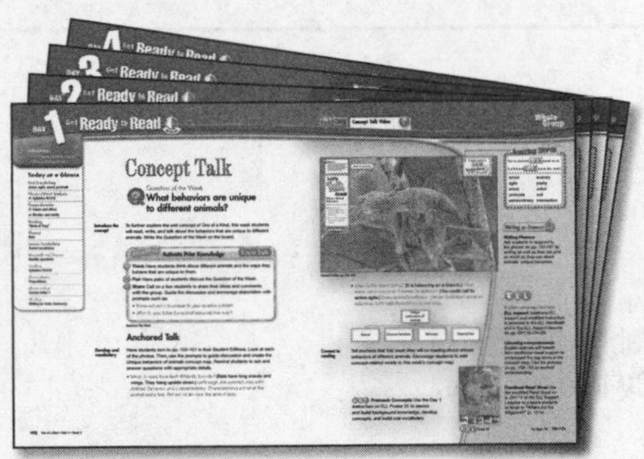

Teacher's Edition pages 150j–187a

See the support for English language learners throughout the lesson, including ELL strategies and scaffolded activities at points of use.

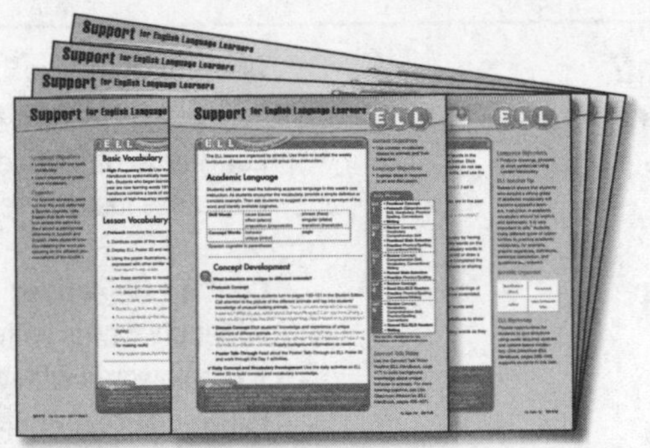

Teacher's Edition pages DI•116–DI•125

Differentiated Instruction for English language learners provides daily group activities that "frontload," or preteach, core instruction.

ELL Handbook pp. 143a–148

Find additional lesson materials that support the core lesson and the ELL instructional pages.

Poster 20

ELL Reader 3.4.5

ELD Reader 3.4.5

Concept Literacy Reader

ELD, ELL Reader Teaching Guide

Concept Literacy Reader Teaching Guide

Technology

Online Teacher's Edition Use the digital version of the core Teacher's Edition for planning and instruction.

eReaders
This week's ELL and ELD Readers and Concept Literacy Reader are also available in digital format.

This Week's Content and Language Objectives by Strand

Concept Development/ Academic Language What behaviors are unique to different animals?	**Content Objective** • Use concept vocabulary related to animals and their behaviors. **Language Objective** • Express ideas in response to art and discussion.
Phonics and Spelling Syllables VCCCV	**Content Objectives** • Identify words with syllables VCCCV. • Break words with VCCCV into syllables. **Language Objective** • Apply phonics and decoding skills to vocabulary.
Listening Comprehension Modified Read Aloud: "The American Alligator"	**Content Objective** • Monitor and adjust oral comprehension **Language Objectives** • Discuss oral passages. • Use a graphic organizer to understand the main points of spoken language.
Reading Comprehension Cause and Effect	**Content Objectives** • Identify an effect as something that happens. • Determine the cause or why a thing happens. **Language Objectives** • Use *if... then* clauses to talk about cause and effect. • Use sentences with *if... then* to talk about things that happen in the classroom. • Read grade-level text at the appropriate rate.
Vocabulary Basic and Lesson Vocabulary	**Language Objectives** • Understand and use basic vocabulary. • Learn meanings of grade-level vocabulary. • Produce drawings, phrases, and short sentences to show understanding of Lesson Vocabulary.
Vocabulary Unfamiliar Words	**Content Objective** • Identify unknown words. **Language Objective** • Use dictionary to find the meanings of unknown words.
Grammar and Conventions Prepositions	**Content Objectives** • Identify prepositions in a sentence. • Understand that prepositions tell where things are. **Language Objectives** • Use prepositions to tell where something is. • Write sentences with prepositions.
Writing Writing Time-Order Transition Words	**Content Objective** • Identify time-order transition words in a text. **Language Objectives** • Write paragraphs using time-order transition words. • Share feedback for editing and revising.

Word Cards for Vocabulary Activities

clutched	**echoed**
gully	**reeds**
scrambled	**thatch**
valley	

Teacher Note: Beginning Teach two to three words. **Intermediate** Teach three to four words. **Advanced** Teach four to five words. **Advanced High** Teach all words.

Name ____________________

Look at the picture. **Read** the paragraph.

- What causes Lulu to be a good hunter? **Underline** the clue words. Then **write** the two causes and the effect in the first set of boxes below.
- What causes Lulu to be able to go fishing? **Underline** the clue words. Then **write** the two causes and the effect in the second set of boxes below.

Lulu Goes Fishing

Lulu can see better than most animals. She flies quickly. She has giant claws, so she can hold prey. These reasons make Lulu a good hunter. Because she can see underwater, Lulu can even catch fish. Thanks to her strong legs, Lulu can carry a fish while she flies!

Cause

Cause

Effect

Cause

Cause

Effect

Cause and Effect

Use this lesson to supplement or replace the skill lesson on page 154a of the Teacher's Edition. Display the Skill Points (at right) and share them with students.

Teach/Model

Beginning Say: *The robin is hungry, so it looks for worms. What does the robin do?* (It looks for worms.) *Why does it do this?* (It is hungry.) *What the robin does is the effect. Why it does that is the cause.* Ask students to repeat the cause and the effect.

Intermediate Write and read aloud this sentence: *The ducks fly south because winter is coming.* Ask: *What clue word tells us there is a cause-and-effect relationship in this sentence?* (because) Have students copy the sentence. Ask them to circle the cause (winter is coming) and underline the effect (the ducks fly south).

Advanced Write and read aloud this sentence: *The baby birds cannot fly because they are too young.* Ask students to identify the cause (they are too young) and the effect (the baby birds cannot fly). Write and read aloud this sentence: *The babies are too young, so they cannot fly.* Ask students whether it tells the same cause and effect. (yes)

Advanced High Have each student write a cause-and-effect sentence. Pair students. One partner reads his or her sentence aloud and the other partner identifies the cause and the effect. Then the partners trade roles.

Then distribute copies of Picture It! page 144.

- Have students look at the picture and tell what is happening.
- Read the paragraph aloud. Ask: *What kind of bird is Lulu?*
- Review the Skill Points with students.
- Ask: *What causes Lulu to be a good hunter?* Guide students to recognize that because Lulu sees well, flies quickly, and has giant claws, she is a good hunter.

Skill Points

- ✔ A **cause** tells why something happens.
- ✔ An **effect** tells what happens.
- ✔ Words such as *because, so,* and *why* are clues. They tell you that you are reading about a cause-and-effect relationship.

Practice

Read aloud the directions on page 144. Reread the paragraph aloud, explaining the word *prey.* Have students look at the picture and the paragraph as they fill in the graphic organizer.

Beginning Students can say the causes and effects they want to write before writing their answers in the graphic organizer. Provide help with filling in the cause and effect boxes correctly.

Intermediate Students can first orally answer, pointing to the information in the paragraph, and then write their answers in the graphic organizer. Provide help with English words and writing.

Advanced Students can write sentences to fill in the boxes in the graphic organizer. They can check their answers by circling causes and underlining effects in the paragraph.

Advanced High Students can write their answers to complete the graphic organizer. They can check their answers by using their causes and effects to construct sentences with the word *because.*

Answers for page 144: Underline the words *These reasons* and *Because. Cause:* Lulu can see better than most animals. She has giant claws for holding prey. *Effect:* Lulu is a good hunter. *Cause:* Lulu can see underwater. Lulu can carry a fish with her strong legs. *Effect:* Lulu can go fishing.

Multilingual Summaries

English

Read Together

Fly, Eagle, Fly!

A farmer found a baby eagle that had fallen from its nest. He took it home and put it with his chickens. The eagle grew up with the chickens. It acted like a chicken.

The farmer's friend saw the eagle. He thought the eagle should fly, not live on the ground. Twice, the friend tried to make the eagle fly. Both times the eagle went back to the ground with the chickens.

On the third day, the farmer and his friend climbed into the mountains. They carried the eagle with them. They waited for the sun to rise. The friend knew the eagle would fly when it saw the sun rise. They waited. The sun rose. The eagle spread its wings and flew.

Spanish

School + Home

¡Vuela águila, vuela!

Un granjero encontró un águila bebé que se había caído del nido. La llevó para su casa y la dejó con sus gallinas. El águila creció con las gallinas. Actuaba de la misma forma que las gallinas.

Un amigo del granjero vio el águila. Pensó que el águila tendría que volar en vez de vivir en el suelo. Dos veces, el amigo trató de hacer volar al águila. Las dos veces el águila regresó con las gallinas.

Al tercer día, el granjero y su amigo subieron a las montañas. Llevaban el águila con ellos. Esperaron a que amaneciera. El amigo sabía que el águila iba a poder volar cuando viera el amanecer. Esperaron. Amaneció. El águila abrió sus alas y voló.

Multilingual Summaries

Chinese

勇敢地飛吧，老鷹！

有個農夫偶然發現有隻小鷹寶寶從鳥巢裡掉下來，於是農夫把牠帶回家，跟雞養在一起。小鷹和雞群一起長大，牠的一舉一動簡直就跟雞沒有兩樣。

農夫的朋友看到了這隻老鷹，他覺得老鷹應該是在天空中飛翔的，而不是在地上生活。這個朋友試了兩次，想辦法要讓老鷹飛起來，可是兩次老鷹都嚇得趕緊回地面找牠的雞兄弟。

第三天，農夫和他的朋友帶著老鷹一起上山。他們在等日出，因為這個朋友知道，老鷹看到日出就會飛。他們等著等著太陽終於升起了。老鷹終於展開翅膀，飛出去了！

Vietnamese

Bay Đi, Đại Bàng, Bay Đi!

Một bác nông phu tìm được một con chim đại bàng bé bị rơi khỏi tổ. Bác đem chim về và để chung với những con gà của mình. Chim đại bàng khôn lớn với những chú gà. Nó cư xử giống như gà.

Bạn của bác nông phu thấy chim đại bàng này. Ông nghĩ là chim đại bàng nên bay chứ không chỉ sống ở dưới đất. Người bạn thử làm cho đại bàng bay hai lần. Cả hai lần chim đại bàng đều trở về đất với những chú gà.

Đến ngày thứ ba, bác nông phu và người bạn đi leo núi. Họ mang chim đại bàng theo. Họ chờ mặt trời mọc. Người bạn biết đại bàng sẽ bay khi nó thấy mặt trời mọc. Họ chờ. Mặt trời mọc lên. Đại bàng giang đôi cánh bay.

Multilingual Summaries

Korean

날아라 독수리야, 날아라

한 농부가 둥지에서 떨어진 아기 독수리를 발견한다. 그는 독수리를 집으로 데려가 병아리들과 함께 둔다. 독수리는 병아리들과 같이 자라고 병아리처럼 행동한다.

농부의 친구가 그 독수리를 보고 독수리는 땅에서 사는 게 아니라 날아 다녀야 한다고 생각한다. 그 친구는 독수리를 날게 만들어보려고 두 번이나 시도했지만 두 번 다 독수리는 병아리가 있는 땅으로 돌아온다.

셋째 날 농부와 친구는 독수리를 데리고 산으로 올라간다. 그들은 태양이 떠오르기를 기다린다. 친구는 독수리가 태양이 떠오르는 걸 보면 날아오른다는 것을 알고 있다. 그들은 기다린다. 그리고 태양이 뜨자 독수리는 날개를 펴고 날아오른다.

Hmong

Ya, Dav, Ya!

Muaj ib tug tswv teb uas nrhiav tau ib lub qe dav uas poob saum nws lub zes los. Nws nqa lub qe ntawd mus tsev thiab muab tso nrog cov qaib. Tus dav ntawd loj hlob nrog cov qaib. Nws coj li ib tug qaib.

Tus tswv teb tus phooj ywg pom tus dav. Nws xav tias tus dav yuav tsum ya, es tsis txhob nyob hauv av. Muaj ob zaug, uas tus phooj ywg ntawd tau ua kom tus dav ya. Txhua zaus tus dav rov qab mus hauv av mus nyob nrog cov qaib.

Hnub thib peb, tus tswv teb thiab nws tus phooj ywg nce mus pem roob. Nkawd nqa tus dav nrog nkawd mus. Nkawd tos kom lub hnub tawm tuaj. Tus phooj ywg twb paub lawm tias tus dav yeej yuav ya thaum nws pom lub hnub tuaj. Nkawd tos. Lub hnub tuaj. Tus dav dhuav or could be nto tis thiab ya mus lawm.

Name ______________________________

Mealtime in Madagascar

- **Read** *Mealtime in Madagascar* again.
- **Draw** pictures to show what happens in the beginning, in the middle, and at the end of the story.
- **Write** words or a sentence to go with your pictures.

Beginning (pages 2–3)

Middle (pages 4–9)

End (pages 10–12)

Family Link

Ask family members if they have ever watched wild animals eat.

Weekly Resources Guide for English Language Learner Support

For this week's content and language objectives, see p. 149e.

Instructional Strand	Day 1	Day 2
Concept Development/Academic Language	TEACHER'S EDITION • Academic Language, p. DI•16 • Concept Development, p. DI•16 • Anchored Talk, pp. 190j—190–191 • Preteach Academic Vocabulary, p. 195a • Concept Talk Video ELL HANDBOOK • Hear It, See It, Say It, Use It, pp. xxxvi–xxxvii • ELL Poster Talk, Concept Talk, p. 149c ELL POSTER 21 • Day 1 Activities	TEACHER'S EDITION • Academic Language, p. DI•16 • Concept Development, p. DI•16 • Anchored Talk, p. 196a • Concept Talk Video ELL HANDBOOK • ELL Poster Talk, Concept Talk, p. 149c • Concept Talk Video Routine, p. 477 ELL POSTER 21 • Day 2 Activities
Phonics and Spelling	TEACHER'S EDITION • Phonics and Spelling, p. DI•20 • Decodable Practice Reader 21A, pp. 193a–193b	TEACHER'S EDITION • Phonics and Spelling, p. DI•20
Listening Comprehension	TEACHER'S EDITION • Modified Read Aloud, p. DI•19 • Read Aloud, p. 191b • Concept Talk Video ELL HANDBOOK • Concept Talk Video Routine, p. 477	TEACHER'S EDITION • Modified Read Aloud, p. DI•19 • AudioText of *Suki's Kimono* • Concept Talk Video ELL HANDBOOK • AudioText CD Routine, p. 477 • Story Map A, p. 483
Reading Comprehension	TEACHER'S EDITION • Preteach Compare and Contrast, p. DI•21	TEACHER'S EDITION • Reteach Compare and Contrast, p. DI•21 • Frontloading Reading, p. DI•22 ELL HANDBOOK • Picture It! Skill Instruction, pp. 150–150a • Multilingual Summaries, pp. 151–153
Vocabulary **Basic and Lesson Vocabulary** **Vocabulary Skill: Synonyms**	TEACHER'S EDITION • Basic Vocabulary, p. DI•17 • Preteach Lesson Vocabulary, p. DI•17 • Synonyms, p. DI•20 ELL HANDBOOK • Word Cards, p. 149 • ELL Vocabulary Routine, p. 471 ELL POSTER 21 • Day 1 Activities	TEACHER'S EDITION • Basic Vocabulary, p. DI•17 • Reteach Lesson Vocabulary, p. DI•18 • Synonyms, p. DI•20 ELL HANDBOOK • Word Cards, p. 149 • Multilingual Vocabulary List, p. 439 ELL POSTER 21 • Day 2 Activities
Grammar and Conventions	TEACHER'S EDITION • Preteach Adjectives and Articles, p. DI•24	TEACHER'S EDITION • Reteach Adjectives and Articles, p. DI•24
Writing	TEACHER'S EDITION • Supporting Details, p. DI•25 • Introduce Letter to the Editor, pp. 195e–195f	TEACHER'S EDITION • Writing Trait: Organization, pp. 205d–205e

This symbol indicates leveled instruction to address language proficiency levels.

Day 3	Day 4	Day 5
TEACHER'S EDITION • Academic Language, p. DI•16 • Concept Development, p. DI•16 • Anchored Talk, p. 206a • Concept Talk Video ELL HANDBOOK • ELL Poster Talk, Concept Talk, p. 149c ELL POSTER 21 • Day 3 Activities	TEACHER'S EDITION • Academic Language, p. DI•16 • Concept Development, p. DI•16 • Anchored Talk, p. 216a • Concept Talk Video ELL HANDBOOK • ELL Poster Talk, Concept Talk, p. 149c ELL POSTER 21 • Day 4 Activities	TEACHER'S EDITION • Academic Language, p. DI•16 • Concept Development, p. DI•16 • Concept Talk Video ELL HANDBOOK • ELL Poster Talk, Concept Talk, p. 149c ELL POSTER 21 • Day 5 Activities
ELL HANDBOOK • Phonics Transition Lesson, pp. 233, 237	ELL HANDBOOK • Phonics Transition Lesson, pp. 233, 237	TEACHER'S EDITION • Phonics and Spelling, p. DI•20
TEACHER'S EDITION • AudioText of *Suki's Kimono* • Concept Talk Video ELL HANDBOOK • AudioText CD Routine, p. 477	TEACHER'S EDITION • Concept Talk Video	TEACHER'S EDITION • Concept Talk Video
TEACHER'S EDITION • Sheltered Reading, p. DI•22 ELL HANDBOOK • Multilingual Summaries, pp. 151–153	TEACHER'S EDITION • ELL/ELD Reader Guided Reading, p. DI•23 ELL HANDBOOK • ELL Study Guide, p. 154	TEACHER'S EDITION • ELL/ELD Reader Guided Reading, p. DI•23 ELL HANDBOOK • ELL Study Guide, p. 154
ELL HANDBOOK • High-Frequency Words Activity Bank, p. 446 ELL POSTER 21 • Day 3 Activities	ELL HANDBOOK • High-Frequency Words Activity Bank, p. 446	TEACHER'S EDITION • Synonyms, p. 221h ELL HANDBOOK • High-Frequency Words Activity Bank, p. 446
TEACHER'S EDITION • Grammar Jammer ELL HANDBOOK • Grammar Transition Lesson, pp. 370, 373–374 • Grammar Jammer Routine, p. 478	TEACHER'S EDITION • Grammar Jammer ELL HANDBOOK • Grammar Transition Lesson, pp. 370, 373–374	TEACHER'S EDITION • Grammar Jammer ELL HANDBOOK • Grammar Transition Lesson, pp. 370, 373–374
TEACHER'S EDITION • Let's Write It!, p. 214–215 • Writing Trait: Focus/Ideas, pp. 215a–215b	TEACHER'S EDITION • Revising Strategy, pp. 221d–221e	TEACHER'S EDITION • Adjectives and Articles, pp. 221p–221q

Poster Talk, Concept Talk

Question of the Week

How does culture influence the clothes we wear?

Poster 21

Throughout the week, use the ELL Poster to help students produce and comprehend language, understand the concept, and build English vocabulary. Use the Question of the Week and other questions to help students share ideas in pairs, small groups, or the large group. Sample questions are shown, with examples of possible responses by students.

Weekly Concept and Language Goals

- Discuss clothing from different cultures
- Identify different kinds of clothes
- Tell about favorite articles of clothing

By the end of the lesson, students should be able to talk about and write one or more sentences about clothing and cultures.

Daily Team Talk

Day 1	Day 2	Day 3	Day 4	Day 5
After Day 1 activities on Poster, ask questions such as *In the poster picture, what is the woman in the bottom left corner wearing?*	After Day 2 activity on Poster, ask questions such as *Who is wearing a uniform in the poster picture?*	After Day 3 activity on Poster, ask questions such as *In the poster picture, what is special about the clothes the two people in the top right corner are wearing?*	After Day 4 activity on Poster, ask questions such as *In the story* Suki's Kimono, *why is Suki's kimono her favorite clothing to wear?*	After Day 5 activity on Poster, ask questions such as *What is your favorite piece of clothing? Why is it your favorite?*
Beginning A dress and a hat. **Intermediate** She is wearing a green dress and a hat. **Advanced** The woman is wearing a green dress with flowers and a pink hat. **Advanced High** The woman is wearing a green dress with yellow flowers and a pink hat with a flower on it.	**Beginning** The woman on the horse. **Intermediate** The woman on the horse has a uniform. **Advanced** The police officer and the people in the band are wearing uniforms. **Advanced High** The police officer is wearing a police uniform. The members of the marching band are wearing band uniforms.	**Beginning** They are different. **Intermediate** The clothes are from their country. **Advanced** The people are wearing clothes that people from their country wear. **Advanced High** The people are from Nigeria. The clothes they are wearing are part of the culture in Nigeria.	**Beginning** From her grandma. **Intermediate** Her grandma gave it to Suki. **Advanced** Her grandma gave Suki the kimono and showed her a traditional dance. **Advanced High** Her grandmother gave the kimono to Suki. She took Suki to a festival and showed her a traditional dance. The kimono is part of Suki's culture.	**Beginning** My blue sweater. **Intermediate** I like the blue sweater my mom made for me. **Advanced** My favorite is the blue sweater my mom made for my birthday. **Advanced High** My favorite piece of clothing is the sweater my mom gave me for my birthday. She knitted it with many shades of blue yarn.

This Week's Materials

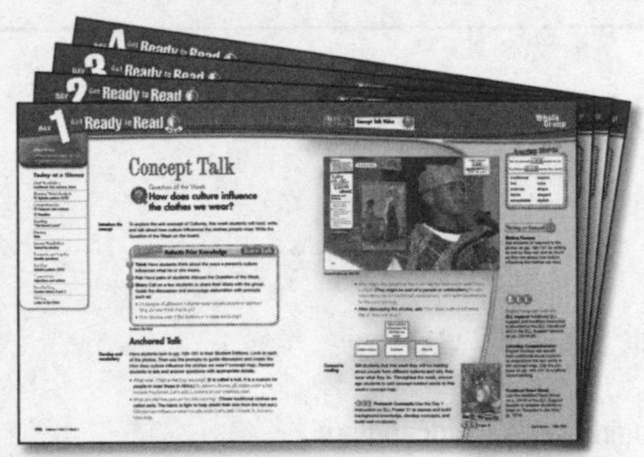

Teacher's Edition pages 190j–221q

See the support for English language learners throughout the lesson, including ELL strategies and scaffolded activities at points of use.

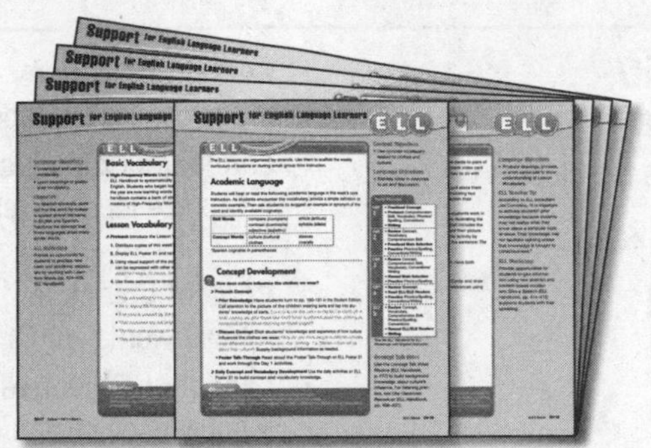

Teacher's Edition pages DI•16–DI•25

Differentiated Instruction for English language learners provides daily group activities that "frontload," or preteach, core instruction.

ELL Handbook pp. 149a–154

Find additional lesson materials that support the core lesson and the ELL instructional pages.

ELL Poster 21

ELL Reader 3.5.1

ELD Reader 3.5.1

Concept Literacy Reader

ELD, ELL Reader Teaching Guide

Concept Literacy Reader Teaching Guide

Technology

Online Teacher's Edition Use the digital version of the core Teacher's Edition for planning and instruction.

eReaders
This week's ELL and ELD Readers and Concept Literacy Reader are also available in digital format.

This Week's Content and Language Objectives by Strand

Concept Development/ Academic Language How does culture influence the clothes we wear?	**Content Objective** • Use concept vocabulary related to clothes and culture. **Language Objective** • Express ideas in response to art and discussion.
Phonics and Spelling Syllable Pattern CV/VC	**Content Objective** • Read words with syllable pattern CV/VC. **Language Objective** • Apply phonics and decoding skills to vocabulary.
Listening Comprehension Modified Read Aloud: "Clothes for the Cultural Fair"	**Content Objective** • Monitor and adjust oral comprehension. **Language Objectives** • Discuss oral passages. • Use a graphic organizer to understand the main points of spoken language.
Reading Comprehension Compare and Contrast	**Content Objectives** • Identify the difference between compare and contrast. **Language Objectives** • Compare and contrast a character in a reading. • Write comparisons and contrasts about a character in a reading. • Understand meaning in familiar context by comparing and contrasting.
Vocabulary Basic and Lesson Vocabulary	**Language Objectives** • Understand and use basic and grade-level vocabulary. • Learn meanings of grade-level vocabulary. • Produce drawings, phrases, and short sentences to show understanding of Lesson Vocabulary.
Vocabulary Synonyms	**Content Objective** • Identify synonyms of words. **Language Objective** • Discuss meanings of synonyms.
Grammar and Conventions Adjectives and Articles	**Content Objective** • Decode and use adjectives and articles. **Language Objectives** • Speak using adjectives and articles. • Write sentences with adjectives and articles.
Writing Supporting Details	**Content Objective** • Identify details in a text. **Language Objectives** • Write paragraphs using descriptive details. • Share feedback for editing and revising by summarizing the important details.

Word Cards for Vocabulary Activities

cotton	**festival**
graceful	**handkerchief**
paces	**pale**
rhythm	**snug**

Teacher Note: Beginning Teach three to four words. **Intermediate** Teach four to six words. **Advanced** Teach six to seven words. **Advanced High** Teach all words.

Name ______________________________

Picture It!
Compare and Contrast

Look at the pictures. **Read** the story.

- How are Ky and Ben similar? **Write** your ideas in the middle section of the Venn diagram.
- How are they different? **Describe** Ky in the left-hand side of the diagram. **Describe** Ben in the right-hand side of the diagram.

Breakfast Time

Ky and Ben are friends. They both eat breakfast before they go to school.

Ky's Breakfast

Ky is from Japan. He eats white rice and miso soup for breakfast. He uses chopsticks to eat the rice and a spoon to eat the soup.

Ben's Breakfast

Ben is from the United States. Ben has cereal with strawberries and milk for breakfast. He uses a spoon to eat his cereal. He also has a glass of orange juice.

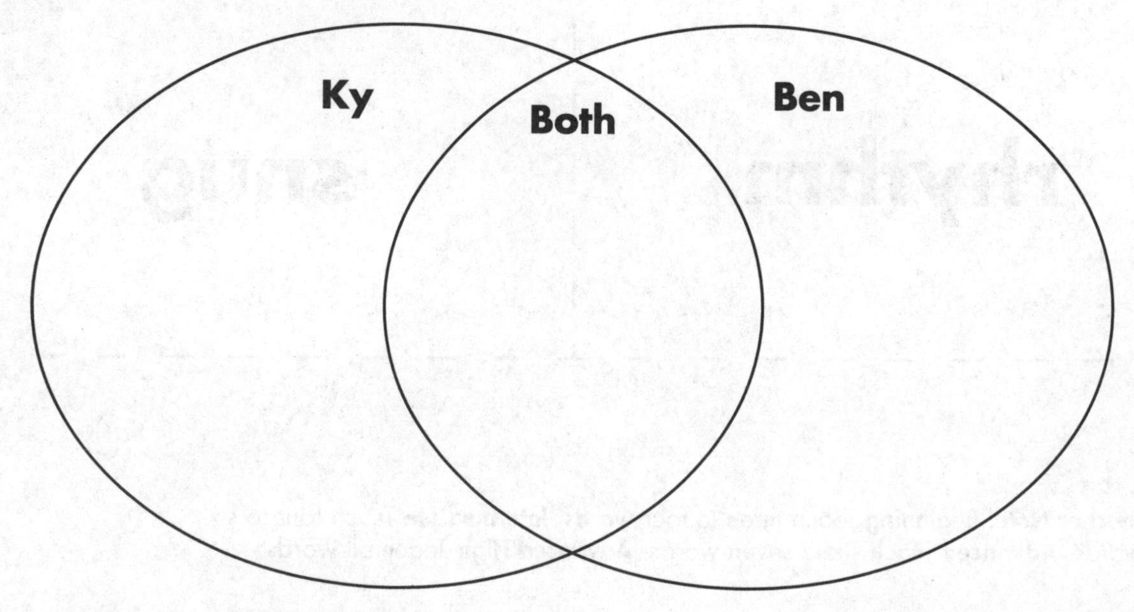

Picture It!

Compare and Contrast

Use this lesson to supplement or replace the skill lesson on page 194a of the Teacher's Edition. Display the Skill Points (at right) and share them with students.

Skill Points

✔ When we **compare,** we look for the ways things are alike.

✔ When we **contrast,** we look for the ways things are different.

Teach/Model

Beginning Display pictures of a salad and a bowl of soup. Ask: *How are soup and salad the same? How are they different?* Draw a Venn diagram. Label one circle *Salad*, the other circle *Soup*, and the intersection *Both*. Record students' responses in the appropriate sections.

Intermediate Write and read aloud: *Jan and I both like rice. I like rice mixed with beans, but Jan does not like beans.* Have students copy the sentences, circle the sentence that compares, underline the sentence that contrasts, and point out the clue words (both, but).

Advanced Say: *In Japan, people eat rice with breakfast, lunch, and dinner. In the United States, most people eat rice only with lunch or dinner.* Ask students to use the sentences to compare and contrast when people eat rice. Ask: *What words helped you compare and contrast?* (In Japan, In the United States, most, only)

Advanced High Have students write about their favorite food, including its color, its taste, how it is made, and when it is eaten. Ask pairs of students to compare and contrast their favorite foods. Suggest that they use clue words as they write sentences telling how their favorite foods are alike and different.

Then distribute copies of Picture It! page 150.

- Have students look at the pictures and describe what they see.
- Read the story aloud. Ask: *Who are Ky and Ben? Where are they from?*
- Review the Skill Points with students.
- Say: *Look at Ky's breakfast and Ben's breakfast. How are they the same and different?*

Practice

Read aloud the directions on page 150. Ask three volunteers to reread each part aloud. Then have students use the pictures and the story as they complete the Venn diagram.

Beginning Students can say what they want to write in each section of the Venn diagram before writing words in the appropriate sections. Provide help with filling in the diagram and writing.

Intermediate Students can first orally tell how Ky and Ben are alike and different and then write words and phrases in the appropriate sections of the Venn diagram. Provide help with writing.

Advanced Students can write their ideas and descriptions to fill in the diagram and then check their answers by silently rereading the story and making any necessary corrections.

Advanced High Students can write their answers in the diagram and then use it to orally compare and contrast Ky's and Ben's breakfasts.

Answers for page 150: *Ky:* white rice, miso soup, eats with chopsticks; *Ben:* cereal with strawberries and milk, orange juice; *Both:* eat before going to school, eat from bowls, use spoons

Multilingual Summaries

English

Suki's Kimono

On the first day of school, Suki wants to wear her kimono. Her sisters say that people will laugh. Suki's sisters will wear their new clothes. Suki does not care. Suki wants to wear her favorite thing. Her favorite thing is her kimono. Suki's grandmother, her *obāchan*, gave the kimono to Suki.

In the schoolyard, some children laugh at Suki's kimono. She does not care. In class, two boys tease Suki about her kimono. She does not pay attention to them.

The teacher asks the children to tell what they did during the summer. Suki tells the class about her grandma's visit. Suki tells the class that she and her *obāchan* went to a festival. Suki tells about the dancing at the festival. Then, Suki dances. Everyone is quiet. Then everyone claps for her.

No one notices Suki's sisters' new clothes. But Suki smiles and dances all the way home.

Spanish

El kimono de Suki

El primer día de clase Suki quiere vestirse con su kimono. Sus hermanas le dicen que la gente se va a reír. Las hermanas de Suki se van a poner su ropa nueva. A Suki no le importa. Ella quiere vestirse con su ropa favorita, su kimono. La abuela de Suki, su *obāchan*, le dio el kimono a Suki.

En el patio de recreo algunos niños se ríen del kimono de Suki. A ella no le importa. En la clase, dos niños se burlan de ella por su kimono. Ella no les presta atención.

La maestra le pregunta a los niños qué hicieron durante el verano. Suki le cuenta a la clase sobre la visita de su abuela. Suki le dice a la clase que ella y su *obāchan* fueron a un festival. Suki les cuenta de la danza en el festival. Después, Suki baila. Todos están en silencio. Luego todos aplauden.

Nadie se da cuenta de la ropa nueva de las hermanas de Suki. Pero Suki sonríe y baila todo el tiempo en camino a su casa.

Multilingual Summaries

Chinese

淑惠的和服

第一天上學，淑惠想穿和服，可是姐姐說別人肯定會笑話。淑惠的姐姐們都穿新衣裳上學，淑惠可不在意，她只想穿最喜歡的衣服，就是奶奶送給她的那件和服。

淑惠在學校操場上遭到同學的取笑，可是她不在乎。在教室裏，兩個男同學嘲笑她，淑惠一點兒也不理睬。

老師問同學們在暑假做了些什麼。淑惠告訴大家她的奶奶來了，她和奶奶一起過節，看了跳舞表演，接著就給大家跳起了舞，同學們都被吸引住了，一點吵鬧的聲音都沒有，最後都為淑惠鼓掌。

沒有人注意到淑惠的姐姐們穿了新衣裳。這天淑惠笑得很開心，回家的路上還一直跳著舞呢！

Vietnamese

Áo Kimônô của Suki

Vào ngày đầu nhập học, Suki muốn mặc chiếc áo kimônô của mình. Các chị của cô bé nói là người ta sẽ cười. Các chị của Suki sẽ mặc đồ mới của họ. Suki chẳng quan tâm. Suki muốn mặc đồ mà mình ưa thích. Đồ mà cô ưa thích là áo kimônô của mình. Bà của Suki, "obachan," đã cho Suki chiếc áo kimônô này.

Ở sân trường, vài đứa trẻ cười nhạo áo kimônô của Suki. Cô bé chẳng quan tâm. Trong lớp học, có hai đứa con trai trêu chọc Suki vì chiếc áo kimônô của cô. Cô bé chẳng để ý đến chúng.

Cô giáo kêu các học sinh kể lại những gì chúng đã làm vào mùa hè. Suki kể cho lớp nghe về chuyến viếng thăm của bà mình. Suki kể cho lớp nghe là cô và bà của cô đã đi đến một lễ hội. Suki kể về việc nhảy múa ở lễ hội. Kế đến, Suki múa. Mọi người yên lặng. Rồi mọi người vỗ tay khen ngợi cô bé.

Không ai để ý đến quần áo mới của các chị của Suki. Nhưng Suki cười và nhảy múa suốt chặng đường về nhà.

Multilingual Summaries

Korean

수키의 기모노

학교 첫 날 기모노를 입고 싶어하는 수키에게 언니들은 사람들이 비웃을 거라고 말한다. 언니들은 새 옷을 입겠다고 하지만 수키는 상관하지 않고 자기가 가장 좋아하는 옷인 기모노를 입고 싶어한다. 수키의 할머니 '오바아짱' 은 수키에게 기모노를 준다.

학교 운동장에서 몇몇 아이들이 기모노를 입은 수키를 보고 놀려대지만 수키는 신경 쓰지 않는다. 수업 시간에 남자 아이 두 명이 수키의 기모노를 갖고 수키를 놀려대지만 수키는 상관하지 않는다.

선생님은 아이들에게 방학 동안 한 일들에 대해 묻는다. 수키는 반 친구들에게 할머니가 놀러오신 일을 이야기하며 '오바아짱' 과 함께 축제에 가 춤을 췄다고 얘기해준다. 그리고 나서 수키가 춤을 추자 모두들 조용히 있다가 박수를 친다.

아무도 수키의 언니들이 새 옷을 입고 온 줄 모른다. 수키는 집에 가는 내내 웃으며 춤을 춘다.

Hmong

Suki Lub Tsho Tshaj Sab

Hnub kawm ntawv thib ib, Suki xav hnav nws lub tsho tshaj sab. Nws cov viv ncaus hais tias cov neeg yuav luag nws. Suki cov viv ncaus yuav hnav zam khaub ncaws tshiab. Suki tsis quav ntsej txog. Suki xav hnav qhov uas nws nyiam tshaj. Qhov uas nws nyiam tshaj yog nws lub tsho tshaj sab. Suki tus pog, los hu ua obachan, tau pub tsho tshaj sab no rau Suki.

Nyob tsev kawm ntawv ntawm tshav ua si, ib co menyuam luag vim yog Suki lub tsho tshaj sab. Suki tsis quav nstej txog. Nyob hauv hoob kawm, ob tug hluas nraug thuam zes Suki vim nws hnav tsho tshaj sab. Nws tsis quav nstej lawv hlo li.

Tus Nai Khu thov kom cov menyuam qhia tej yam lawv ua thaum caij sov sov. Suki hais txog nws tus pog kev tuaj xyuas. Suki qhia cov menyuam tias nws thiab nws obachan tau mus txog chaw ua koob tsheej. Suki qhia txog kev ua las voos ntawm chaw ua koob tsheej ntawd. Ces, Suki txawm ua las voos. Puav leej ntsiag twb to. Ces txhua leej txhua tus npuaj tes rau nws.

Tsis muaj leejtwg quav ntsej txog Suki cov viv ncaus khaub ncaws tshiab. Tab sis Suki luag ntxhwb ntxhi thiab ua las voos tas kev txog tsev.

Name ______________________ **School Days in Japan**

- **Read** *School Days in Japan* again.
- Use the information in the book to **answer** the questions. Try to **write** complete sentences if you can.

pages 2–3

1. How long is a school year for Japanese students?

____

____

2. What do Japanese students wear to school?

____

____

____

pages 4–8

3. What subjects do Japanese students study?

____

____

____

4. What is one way Japanese students are different from students in your school?

____

____

Family Link

Ask family members to describe schools they have attended.

Weekly Resources Guide for English Language Learner Support

For this week's content and language objectives, see p. 155e.

Instructional Strand	Day 1	Day 2
Concept Development/Academic Language	TEACHER'S EDITION • Academic Language, p. DI•41 • Concept Development, p. DI•41 • Anchored Talk, pp. 222j—222–223 • Preteach Academic Vocabulary, p. 227a • Concept Talk Video ELL HANDBOOK • Hear It, See It, Say It, Use It, pp. xxxvi–xxxvii • ELL Poster Talk, Concept Talk, p. 155c ELL POSTER 22 • Day 1 Activities	TEACHER'S EDITION • Academic Language, p. DI•41 • Concept Development, p. DI•41 • Anchored Talk, p. 228a • Concept Talk Video ELL HANDBOOK • ELL Poster Talk, Concept Talk, p. 155c • Concept Talk Video Routine, p. 477 ELL POSTER 22 • Day 2 Activities
Phonics and Spelling	TEACHER'S EDITION • Phonics and Spelling, p. DI•45 • Decodable Practice Reader 22A, pp. 225a–225b	TEACHER'S EDITION • Phonics and Spelling, p. DI•45
Listening Comprehension	TEACHER'S EDITION • Modified Read Aloud, p. DI•44 • Read Aloud, p. 223b • Concept Talk Video ELL HANDBOOK • Concept Talk Video Routine, p. 477	TEACHER'S EDITION • Modified Read Aloud, p. DI•44 • AudioText of *I Love Saturdays y domingos* • Concept Talk Video ELL HANDBOOK • AudioText CD Routine, p. 477 • Venn Diagram, p. 488
Reading Comprehension	TEACHER'S EDITION • Preteach Main Idea and Details, p. DI•46	TEACHER'S EDITION • Reteach Main Idea and Details, p. DI•46 • Frontloading Reading, p. DI•47 ELL HANDBOOK • Picture It! Skill Instruction, pp. 156–156a • Multilingual Summaries, pp. 157–159
Vocabulary **Basic and Lesson Vocabulary** **Vocabulary Skill: Homophones**	TEACHER'S EDITION • Basic Vocabulary, p. DI•42 • Preteach Lesson Vocabulary, p. DI•42 • Homophones, p. DI•45 ELL HANDBOOK • Word Cards, p. 155 • ELL Vocabulary Routine, p. 471 ELL POSTER 22 • Day 1 Activities	TEACHER'S EDITION • Basic Vocabulary, p. DI•42 • Reteach Lesson Vocabulary, p. DI•43 • Homophones, p. DI•45 ELL HANDBOOK • Word Cards, p. 155 • Multilingual Vocabulary List, p. 439 ELL POSTER 22 • Day 2 Activities
Grammar and Conventions	TEACHER'S EDITION • Preteach Comparative and Superlative Adjectives, p. DI•49	TEACHER'S EDITION • Reteach Comparative and Superlative Adjectives, p. DI•49
Writing	TEACHER'S EDITION • Consistent Verb Tense, p. DI•50 • Writing for Tests: Personal Narrative, pp. 227e–227f	TEACHER'S EDITION • Writing for Tests: Personal Narrative, pp. 237d–237e

Unit 5 Week 2 I Love Saturdays y domingos

This symbol indicates leveled instruction to address language proficiency levels.

Day 3	Day 4	Day 5
TEACHER'S EDITION • Academic Language, p. DI•41 • Concept Development, p. DI•41 • Anchored Talk, p. 238a • Concept Talk Video ELL HANDBOOK • ELL Poster Talk, Concept Talk, p. 155c ELL POSTER 22 • Day 3 Activities	TEACHER'S EDITION • Academic Language, p. DI•41 • Concept Development, p. DI•41 • Anchored Talk, p. 250a • Concept Talk Video ELL HANDBOOK • ELL Poster Talk, Concept Talk, p. 155c ELL POSTER 22 • Day 4 Activities	TEACHER'S EDITION • Academic Language, p. DI•41 • Concept Development, p. DI•41 • Concept Talk Video ELL HANDBOOK • ELL Poster Talk, Concept Talk, p. 155c ELL POSTER 22 • Day 5 Activities
ELL HANDBOOK • Phonics Transition Lesson, pp. 279, 282	ELL HANDBOOK • Phonics Transition Lesson, pp. 279, 282	TEACHER'S EDITION • Phonics and Spelling, p. DI•45
TEACHER'S EDITION • AudioText of *I Love Saturdays y domingos* • Concept Talk Video ELL HANDBOOK • AudioText CD Routine, p. 477	TEACHER'S EDITION • Concept Talk Video	TEACHER'S EDITION • Concept Talk Video
TEACHER'S EDITION • Sheltered Reading, p. DI•47 ELL HANDBOOK • Multilingual Summaries, pp. 157–159	TEACHER'S EDITION • ELL/ELD Reader Guided Reading, p. DI•48 ELL HANDBOOK • ELL Study Guide, p. 160	TEACHER'S EDITION • ELL/ELD Reader Guided Reading, p. DI•48 ELL HANDBOOK • ELL Study Guide, p. 160
ELL HANDBOOK • High-Frequency Words Activity Bank, p. 446 ELL POSTER 22 • Day 3 Activities	ELL HANDBOOK • High-Frequency Words Activity Bank, p. 446	TEACHER'S EDITION • Homophones, p. 253h ELL HANDBOOK • High-Frequency Words Activity Bank, p. 446
TEACHER'S EDITION • Grammar Jammer ELL HANDBOOK • Grammar Transition Lesson, pp. 371, 375 • Grammar Jammer Routine, p. 478	TEACHER'S EDITION • Grammar Jammer ELL HANDBOOK • Grammar Transition Lesson, pp. 371, 375	TEACHER'S EDITION • Grammar Jammer ELL HANDBOOK • Grammar Transition Lesson, pp. 371, 375
TEACHER'S EDITION • Let's Write It!, p. 248–249 • Writing for Tests: Evaluation, pp. 249a–249b	TEACHER'S EDITION • Writing for Tests: Personal Narrative, p. 253d	TEACHER'S EDITION • Writing for Tests: Editing Skill: Conventions, pp. 253p–253q

Poster Talk, Concept Talk

Question of the Week

How are cultures alike and different?

ELL Poster 22

Throughout the week, use the ELL Poster to help students produce and comprehend language, understand the concept, and build English vocabulary. Use the Question of the Week and other questions to help students share ideas in pairs, small groups, or the large group. Sample questions are shown, with examples of possible responses by students.

Weekly Concept and Language Goals

- Be aware of differences and similarities among cultures
- Compare and contrast cultures
- Tell about aspects of different cultures, such as language

By the end of the lesson, students should be able to talk about and write one or more sentences about the similarities and differences among cultures.

Daily Team Talk

Day 1	Day 2	Day 3	Day 4	Day 5
After Day 1 activities on Poster, ask questions such as *In the poster picture, what is one thing the two families do that is the same?*	After Day 2 activity on Poster, ask questions such as *In the poster picture, what is one thing the two families do that is different?*	After Day 3 activity on Poster, ask questions such as *In the poster picture, how are the foods the two families eat different? How are the foods the same?*	After Day 4 activity on Poster, ask questions such as *In the story* I Love Saturdays y domingos, *why do you think the narrator uses different languages when she tells about her Saturdays and Sundays?*	After Day 5 activity on Poster, ask questions such as *How is your family different from the two families in the poster picture?*
Beginning No shoes in the house. **Intermediate** They do not wear shoes in the house. **Advanced** The families do not wear their shoes in the house. They wear slippers. **Advanced High** Both families take off their outside shoes and put on slippers when they are inside their houses.	**Beginning** How they eat. **Intermediate** One family eats with their hands. **Advanced** One family eats with chopsticks. The other family eats with their hands. **Advanced High** The two families eat in different ways. The Japanese family eats with chopsticks, while the Moroccan family eats with their hands.	**Beginning** One eats fish. One eats bread. **Intermediate** One family eats fish. One family eats bread. They both drink tea. **Advanced** One family eats fish and rice. The other family eats bread. Both families drink tea. **Advanced High** The Japanese family is eating fish and rice. The Moroccan family is dipping bread in a bowl. Both families drink tea with their meal.	**Beginning** Because of her grandparents. **Intermediate** She visits her grandparents on Saturdays and Sundays. **Advanced** She visits her grandparents. They are from different cultures. **Advanced High** She visits her grandparents on Saturdays and Sundays. Her grandparents come from different cultures and speak different languages.	**Beginning** We use forks. **Intermediate** We eat with forks and knives. **Advanced** We use forks and knives when we eat. They do not. **Advanced High** My family eats food with forks and knives. The two families in the poster pictures eat their food with chopsticks or their hands.

This Week's Materials

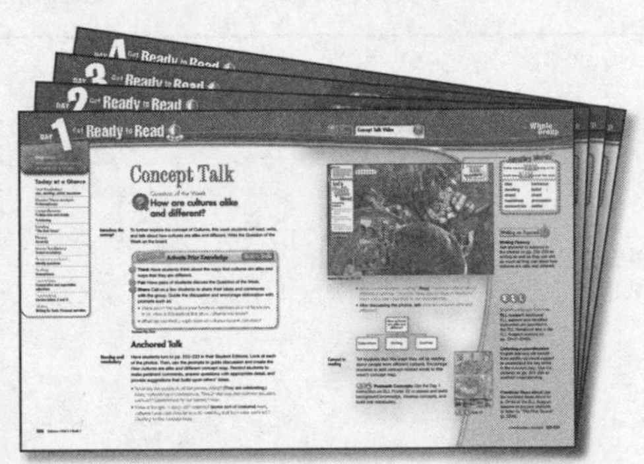

Teacher's Edition pages 222j–253q

See the support for English language learners throughout the lesson, including ELL strategies and scaffolded activities at points of use.

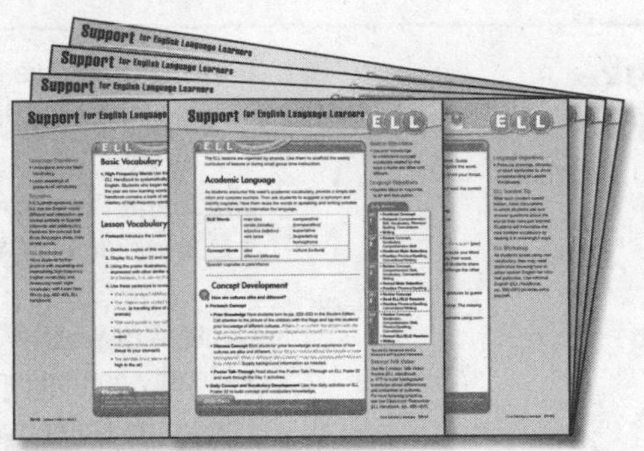

Teacher's Edition pages DI•41–DI•50

Differentiated Instruction for English language learners provides daily group activities that "frontload," or preteach, core instruction.

ELL Handbook pp. 155a–160

Find additional lesson materials that support the core lesson and the ELL instructional pages.

Poster 22

ELL Reader 3.5.2

ELD Reader 3.5.2

Concept Literacy Reader

ELD, ELL Reader Teaching Guide

Concept Literacy Reader Teaching Guide

Technology

Online Teacher's Edition Use the digital version of the core Teacher's Edition for planning and instruction.

eReaders
This week's ELL and ELD Readers and Concept Literacy Reader are also available in digital format.

This Week's Content and Language Objectives by Strand

Concept Development/ Academic Language How are cultures alike and different?	**Content Objective** • Use concept vocabulary related to the ways cultures are alike and different. **Language Objective** • Express ideas in response to art and discussion.
Phonics and Spelling Homophones	**Content Objective** • Identify homophones. **Language Objective** • Read and write homophones.
Listening Comprehension Modified Read Aloud: "The Caddo and the Comanche"	**Content Objective** • Monitor and adjust oral comprehension **Language Objectives** • Discuss oral passages. • Use a graphic organizer to scaffold understanding of details in spoken language.
Reading Comprehension Main Idea and Details	**Content Objectives** • Distinguish between main idea and details. • Identify the main idea and details to aid comprehension. **Language Objectives** • Retell the main idea and details from a reading. • Write main idea and details from personal experience. • Demonstrate listening comprehension by taking notes.
Vocabulary Basic and Lesson Vocabulary	**Language Objectives** • Understand and use basic and grade-level vocabulary. • Learn meanings of grade-level vocabulary. • Produce drawings, phrases, and short sentences to show understanding of Lesson Vocabulary.
Vocabulary Homophones	**Content Objective** • Read and write homophones. **Language Objective** • Apply phonics and decoding skills to vocabulary.
Grammar and Conventions Comparative and Superlative Adjectives	**Content Objective** • Use comparative and superlative adjectives orally and in writing. **Language Objectives** • Speak using comparative and superlative adjectives. • Write sentences using comparative and superlative adjectives.
Writing Consistent Verb Tense	**Content Objective** • Identify verb tense. **Language Objectives** • Write narrative paragraphs with consistent verb tense. • Share feedback for editing and revising for consistent verb tense.

Word Cards for Vocabulary Activities

bouquet	**circus**
difficult	**nibbling**
pier	**soars**
swallow	

Teacher Note: Beginning Teach two to three words. **Intermediate** Teach three to four words. **Advanced** Teach four to five words. **Advanced High** Teach all words.

Name ______________________________

Picture It!
Main Idea and Details

Look at the picture. **Read** the story.

Birthdays

People celebrate birthdays differently. In the United States, birthdays are celebrated on the day a person was born. The birthday child often gets presents. The child blows out the candles on a special cake. In Vietnam, everyone's birthday is celebrated on New Year's Day. The birthday child gets money. The family eats long noodles for lunch. No matter how you celebrate, birthdays are a special day.

Circle the letter of the correct answer.

1. What is the main idea of the story?
  a. Birthdays are the same around the world.
  b. Not everyone celebrates birthdays.
  c. Birthdays are celebrated differently in different countries.

2. Write two details that support this main idea.

____

____

____

____

Main Idea and Details

Use this lesson to supplement or replace the skill lesson on page 226a of the Teacher's Edition. Display the Skill Points (at right) and share them with students.

Skill Points

- ✔ The most important idea in a paragraph is called the **main idea.**
- ✔ To find the main idea, ask: *What is this paragraph about?* Find out whether there is a sentence that tells the main idea.
- ✔ Other sentences in the paragraph tell about the main idea. They give **details** about the main idea.

Teach/Model

Beginning Say: *My birthday party was fun! I had a special cake. I played games with my friends. They gave me nice gifts.* Ask students to identify the main idea (first sentence) and the details that support the main idea (other sentences).

Intermediate Write and read aloud: *It is fun to celebrate birthdays.* Ask students to think of a detail that supports this main idea. Have each student write his or her detail in a complete sentence and share it with the group.

Advanced Write and read aloud this paragraph: *We play fun games on my birthday. We make a special meal on Dad's birthday. We go to the park on Mom's birthday.* Have students write possible main idea sentences for the paragraph. (We celebrate our birthdays in different ways.)

Advanced High Discuss celebrations with students. Together think of a main idea, such as *We celebrate when good things happen.* Write it on the board and circle it. Have students write supporting details in circles around the main idea.

Then distribute copies of Picture It! page 156.

- Have students look at the pictures and tell what is happening.
- Read the paragraph aloud. Ask: *What is this paragraph about?* (birthdays in the United States and Vietnam)
- Review the Skill Points with students.
- Have students look at the pictures and words to identify the main idea and details.

Practice

Read aloud the directions on page 156. Have students reread the paragraph with a partner. Then have them use the pictures and the paragraph as they answer the questions.

Beginning Students can orally answer the questions before circling and writing their answers. Provide help with circling the correct answer and with English words and writing.

Intermediate Students can point out the answers in the paragraph and then circle and write their answers on the page. Provide help with English words and writing.

Advanced Students can circle and write their answers and then check them by comparing them with a partner's answers.

Advanced High Students can circle and write their answers and then explain how the two details support the main idea of the paragraph.

Answers for page 156: 1. c; 2. In the United States, children eat cake. In Vietnam, they eat noodles. In the United States, children celebrate on the day they were born. In Vietnam, they celebrate on New Year's Day.

Multilingual Summaries

English

I Love Saturdays y domingos

The little girl loves Saturdays and Sundays. She visits Grandma and Grandpa on Saturday. She visits *Abuelito* and *Abuelita* on Sundays.

Grandma makes pancakes for breakfast. *Abuelita* makes *huevos rancheros*. Grandma has a cat. *Abuelita* has a dog.

Grandma and Grandpa play a movie about the circus. *Abuelito* and *Abuelita* take the little girl to the circus. Both Grandpa and *Abuelito* have surprises for her and tell her stories. Grandma and *Abuelita* tell her about their families.

Grandma and Grandpa come to the little girl's birthday party. They brought her a new doll and dress for the doll. *Abuelito* and *Abuelita* come to the birthday party too. They bring her a dollhouse and dress to match her doll's dress.

Spanish

Me gustan los *Saturdays* y los domingos

A la pequeña niña le gustan los *Saturdays* y los domingos. Los *Saturdays* ella visita a la *Grandma* y a *Grandpa*. Los domingos ella va de visita a casa de Abuelita y Abuelito.

Grandma hace panqueques para el desayuno. Abuelita hace huevos rancheros. *Grandma* tiene un gato. Abuelita tiene un perro.

Grandma y *Grandpa* ponen una película sobre el circo. Abuelito y Abuelita llevan a la pequeña niña al circo. Ambos, *Grandpa* y Abuelito le cuentan historias y le traen sorpresas. *Grandma* y Abuelita le hablan sobre sus familias.

Grandma y *Grandpa* visitan a la pequeña niña el día de su cumpleaños. Le llevan una muñeca nueva y los trajes para vestirla. Abuelito y Abuelita también llegan a la fiesta de cumpleaños. Le llevan una casita de muñecas y más vestidos para vestir su muñeca.

Multilingual Summaries

Chinese

我喜歡過星期六和星期日

小女孩喜歡過星期六和星期日。 因為星期六她可以去爺爺奶奶家玩。 而星期日她又可以去外公外婆家玩。

早餐時奶奶會做薄餅給她吃， 而外婆會做墨西哥煎蛋給她吃。 奶奶家養了一隻貓， 而外婆家卻養了一隻狗。

爺爺奶奶會放馬戲團的電影給小女孩看， 而外公外婆會帶小女孩去看馬戲團的表演。 爺爺和外公都為小女孩準備了驚喜，並講故事給她聽。 奶奶和外婆則會給她講她們家族的事情。

奶奶和爺爺來參加小女孩的慶生會。 他們送給她一個新娃娃和一件給娃娃穿的衣服。 外公和外婆也來參加她的慶生會。 他們送給她一間娃娃屋，以及另一件可搭配娃娃衣服穿的衣服。

Vietnamese

Tôi Thích Ngày Thứ Bảy và Chủ Nhật

Cô bé gái thích ngày thứ Bảy và Chủ Nhật. Cô đi thăm Ông Bà vào thứ Bảy. Cô thăm Abuelito và Abuelita vào Chủ Nhật.

Bà làm bánh kẹp cho bữa điểm tâm. Abuelita làm huevos rancheros. Bà có con mèo. Abuelita có con chó.

Ông Bà cho cô xem phim về gánh xiệc. Abuelito và Abuelita dẫn cô đi xem xiệc. Cả hai Ông và Abuelito lúc nào cũng dành sự kinh ngạc cho cô và kể chuyện cho cô nghe. Bà và Abuelita thì kể cho cô nghe về gia đình.

Ông Bà đến dự tiệc sinh nhật của cô bé. Họ cho cô búp bê mới và quần áo cho nó mặc. Abuelito và Abuelita cũng đến dự tiệc nữa. Họ cho cô nhà cho búp bê ở và áo đầm cho cô mặc giống như áo của búp bê.

Multilingual Summaries

Korean

나는 토요일과 도밍고가 좋다

한 꼬마 여자아이는 토요일과 일요일을 좋아한다. 그 아이는 토요일에 할머니와 할아버지에게 간다. 일요일에는 아부엘리토와 아부엘리타에게 간다.

할머니는 아침으로 팬케이크를 만든다. 아부엘리타는 휴보스 란체로스를 만든다. 할머니에겐 고양이가 있고, 아부엘리타에겐 개가 있다.

할머니와 할아버지는 서커스에 관한 영화를 보여준다. 아부엘리토와 아부엘리타는 꼬마 여자아이를 서커스에 데려간다. 할아버지와 아부엘리토는 모두 놀랄 만한 선물을 준비하며 아이에게 이야기를 들려준다. 할머니와 아부엘리토는 가족에 관해 얘기해준다.

할머니와 할아버지가 꼬마 여자아이의 생일 잔치에 온다. 그들은 새 인형과 인형의 드레스를 선물한다. 아부엘리토와 아부엘리타도 생일 잔치에 온다. 그들은 인형 집과 인형 옷에 어울리는 아이의 드레스를 선물한다.

Hmong

Kuv Nyiam Hnub Vasxaum thiab Vasthiv

Tus me nyuam ntxhais nyiam hnub Vasxaum thiab Vasthiv. Nws mus saib nws Pog thiab Yawg rau hnub Vasxaum. Nws mus saib niam tais Abuelito thiab yawm txiv Abuelita hnub Vasthiv.

Pog ua khob noom khev rau nws noj ua tshais. Abuelita ua cov huevos rancheros. Pog muaj miv. Niam tais Abuelita muaj dev.

Pog thiab Yawg tso xisnesmas txog kev cob tsiaj ua si saib. Niam tais Abuelito thiab yawm txiv Abuelita coj tus me nyuam ntxhais mus saib tsiaj ua si. Pog thiab niam tais Abuelito puav leej mus yam ua rau nws ceeb thiab qhia nws tej zaj dab neeg. Pog thiab niam tais Abuelita tham lawv tej tsev neeg qhia rau nws.

Pog thiab Yawg kuj tuaj thaum txog tus me nyuam ntxhais lub hnub yug. Lawv coj me nyuam roj hmab thiab poj tiab tuaj pub nws. Niam tais Abuelito thiab yawm txiv Abuelita los kuj tuaj ib yam. Nkawd nqa ib lub me nyuam tsev rau tus me nyuam roj hmab thiab poj tiab rau nws.

Name ______________________

Cultures Around the World

- **Read** *Cultures Around the World* again.
- Fill in the chart. **Write** two facts from the story and two opinions you have about different cultures.

Facts from the Story
1. ______________________
2. ______________________

Your Opinions
1. ______________________
2. ______________________

Family Link

Ask family members what they know about different cultures.

Weekly Resources Guide for English Language Learner Support

For this week's content and language objectives, see p. 161e.

Instructional Strand	Day 1	Day 2
Concept Development/Academic Language	TEACHER'S EDITION • Academic Language, p. DI•66 • Concept Development, p. DI•66 • Anchored Talk, pp. 254j—254–255 • Preteach Academic Vocabulary, p. 259a • Concept Talk Video ELL HANDBOOK • Hear It, See It, Say It, Use It, pp. xxxvi–xxxvii • ELL Poster Talk, Concept Talk, p. 161c ELL POSTER 23 • Day 1 Activities	TEACHER'S EDITION • Academic Language, p. DI•66 • Concept Development, p. DI•66 • Anchored Talk, p. 260a • Concept Talk Video ELL HANDBOOK • ELL Poster Talk, Concept Talk, p. 161c • Concept Talk Video Routine, p. 477 ELL POSTER 23 • Day 2 Activities
Phonics and Spelling	TEACHER'S EDITION • Phonics and Spelling, p. DI•70 • Decodable Practice Reader 23A, pp. 257a–257b	TEACHER'S EDITION • Phonics and Spelling, p. DI•70
Listening Comprehension	TEACHER'S EDITION • Modified Read Aloud, p. DI•69 • Read Aloud, p. 255b • Concept Talk Video ELL HANDBOOK • Concept Talk Video Routine, p. 477	TEACHER'S EDITION • Modified Read Aloud, p. DI•69 • AudioText of *Good-Bye, 382 Shin Dang Dong* • Concept Talk Video ELL HANDBOOK • AudioText CD Routine, p. 477 • Story Map A, p. 483
Reading Comprehension	TEACHER'S EDITION • Preteach Sequence of Events, p. DI•71	TEACHER'S EDITION • Reteach Sequence of Events, p. DI•71 • Frontloading Reading, p. DI•72 ELL HANDBOOK • Picture It! Skill Instruction, pp. 162–162a • Multilingual Summaries, pp. 163–165
Vocabulary **Basic and Lesson Vocabulary** **Vocabulary Skill: Compound Words**	TEACHER'S EDITION • Basic Vocabulary, p. DI•67 • Preteach Lesson Vocabulary, p. DI•67 • Compound Words, p. DI•70 ELL HANDBOOK • Word Cards, p. 161 • ELL Vocabulary Routine, p. 471 ELL POSTER 23 • Day 1 Activities	TEACHER'S EDITION • Basic Vocabulary, p. DI•67 • Reteach Lesson Vocabulary, p. DI•68 • Compound Words, p. DI•70 ELL HANDBOOK • Word Cards, p. 161 • Multilingual Vocabulary List, pp. 439–440 ELL POSTER 23 • Day 2 Activities
Grammar and Conventions	TEACHER'S EDITION • Preteach Adverbs, p. DI•74	TEACHER'S EDITION • Reteach Adverbs, p. DI•74
Writing	TEACHER'S EDITION • Figurative Language, p. DI•75 • Introduce Poetry: Free Verse, pp. 259e–259f	TEACHER'S EDITION • Organization, pp. 271d–271e

Unit 5 Week 3 *Good-Bye, 382 Shin Dang Dong*

This symbol indicates leveled instruction to address language proficiency levels.

Day 3	Day 4	Day 5
TEACHER'S EDITION • Academic Language, p. DI•66 • Concept Development, p. DI•66 • Anchored Talk, p. 272a • Concept Talk Video ELL HANDBOOK • ELL Poster Talk, Concept Talk, p. 161c ELL POSTER 23 • Day 3 Activities	TEACHER'S EDITION • Academic Language, p. DI•66 • Concept Development, p. DI•66 • Anchored Talk, p. 284a • Concept Talk Video ELL HANDBOOK • ELL Poster Talk, Concept Talk, p. 161c ELL POSTER 23 • Day 4 Activities	TEACHER'S EDITION • Academic Language, p. DI•66 • Concept Development, p. DI•66 • Concept Talk Video ELL HANDBOOK • ELL Poster Talk, Concept Talk, p. 161c ELL POSTER 23 • Day 5 Activities
ELL HANDBOOK • Phonics Transition Lesson, pp. 273, 276	ELL HANDBOOK • Phonics Transition Lesson, pp. 273, 276	TEACHER'S EDITION • Phonics and Spelling, p. DI•70
TEACHER'S EDITION • AudioText of *Good-Bye, 382 Shin Dang Dong* • Concept Talk Video ELL HANDBOOK • AudioText CD Routine, p. 477	TEACHER'S EDITION • Concept Talk Video	TEACHER'S EDITION • Concept Talk Video
TEACHER'S EDITION • Sheltered Reading, p. DI•72 ELL HANDBOOK • Multilingual Summaries, pp. 163–165	TEACHER'S EDITION • ELL/ELD Reader Guided Reading, p. DI•73 ELL HANDBOOK • ELL Study Guide, p. 166	TEACHER'S EDITION • ELL/ELD Reader Guided Reading, p. DI•73 ELL HANDBOOK • ELL Study Guide, p. 166
ELL HANDBOOK • High-Frequency Words Activity Bank, p. 446 ELL POSTER 23 • Day 3 Activities	ELL HANDBOOK • High-Frequency Words Activity Bank, p. 446	TEACHER'S EDITION • Compound Words, p. 287h ELL HANDBOOK • High-Frequency Words Activity Bank, p. 446
TEACHER'S EDITION • Grammar Jammer ELL HANDBOOK • Grammar Transition Lesson, pp. 372, 377 • Grammar Jammer Routine, p. 478	TEACHER'S EDITION • Grammar Jammer ELL HANDBOOK • Grammar Transition Lesson, pp. 372, 377	TEACHER'S EDITION • Grammar Jammer ELL HANDBOOK • Grammar Transition Lesson, pp. 372, 377
TEACHER'S EDITION • Let's Write It!, p. 282–283 • Writer's Craft: Figurative Language, pp. 283a–283b	TEACHER'S EDITION • Revising Strategy, pp. 287d–287e	TEACHER'S EDITION • Proofread for Adverbs, pp. 287p–287q

Poster Talk, Concept Talk

Question of the Week

Why is it hard to adapt to a new culture?

ELL Poster 23

Throughout the week, use the ELL Poster to help students produce and comprehend language, understand the concept, and build English vocabulary. Use the Question of the Week and other questions to help students share ideas in pairs, small groups, or the large group. Sample questions are shown, with examples of possible responses by students.

Weekly Concept and Language Goals

- Compare and contrast cultures
- Tell reasons why it can be hard to adapt to a new culture
- Describe ways to adapt to a new culture

By the end of the lesson, students should be able to talk about and write one or more sentences about adapting to a new culture.

Daily Team Talk

Day 1	Day 2	Day 3	Day 4	Day 5
After Day 1 activities on Poster, ask questions such as *In the poster picture, how is the boy's new home different from his old home?*	After Day 2 activity on Poster, ask questions such as *Why is it hard for the boy in the poster picture to adapt to his new home?*	After Day 3 activity on Poster, ask questions such as *How will having a new friend help the boy in the poster picture adapt to his new home?*	After Day 4 activity on Poster, ask questions such as *The desert is a very dry place. How has the boy in the poster picture adapted to the rain?*	After Day 5 activity on Poster, ask questions such as *In the story* Good-Bye, 382 Shin Dang Dong, *what makes Jangmi start to feel better about her new home?*
Beginning It's a city. **Intermediate** He lived in the desert. Now he lives in the city. **Advanced** The boy moved from the desert to the city. It is raining. **Advanced High** The boy used to live in the desert where it is very dry. Then he moved across the country. Now he lives in the city, and it is raining outside.	**Beginning** He is sad. **Intermediate** He misses his friend from his old home. **Advanced** The boy misses his friend and playing in the desert. He is not used to the city and the rain. **Advanced High** The boy is sad because he misses his neighbor and the desert. The city is very different from the desert.	**Beginning** He won't be sad. **Intermediate** If he has a new friend, he will not feel sad. **Advanced** A new friend will help him feel less sad about leaving his old friend. **Advanced High** Having a new friend will help the boy feel better about moving away from his old friend. He will have someone to talk to and to play with in the city.	**Beginning** Uses an umbrella. **Intermediate** He uses an umbrella to stay dry. **Advanced** The boy has learned to use an umbrella to keep dry in the rain. **Advanced High** The boy has adapted to the rain by learning to use an umbrella to keep dry.	**Beginning** A new friend. **Intermediate** She meets a girl named Mary. They become friends. **Advanced** She becomes friends with a girl named Mary. She eats honeydew. **Advanced High** Jangmi becomes friends with a girl named Mary, who reminds her of her best friend in Korea. She also eats honeydew, which reminds her of home.

This Week's Materials

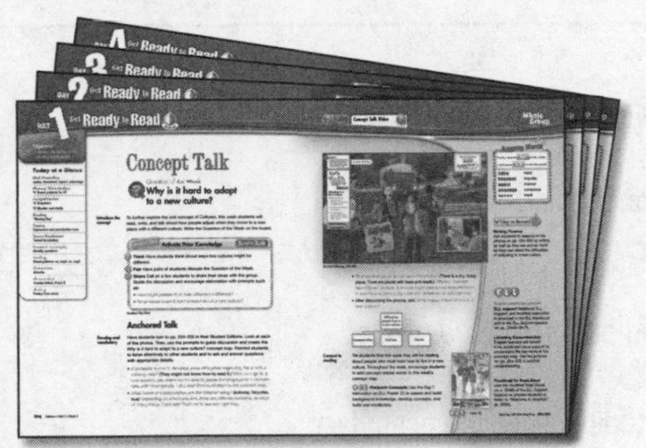

Teacher's Edition pages 254j–287q

See the support for English language learners throughout the lesson, including ELL strategies and scaffolded activities at points of use.

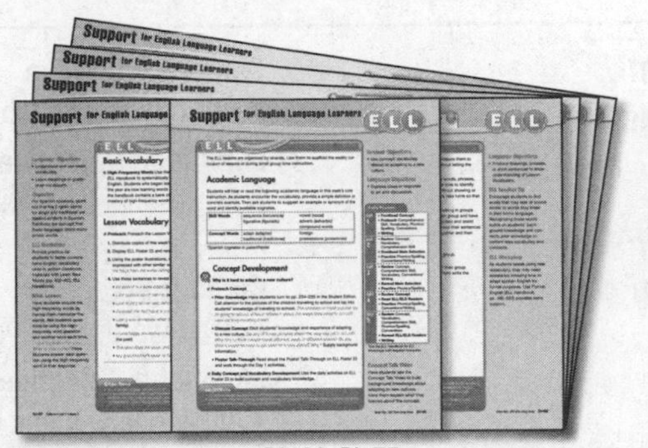

Teacher's Edition pages DI•66–DI•75

Differentiated Instruction for English language learners provides daily group activities that "frontload," or preteach, core instruction.

ELL Handbook pp. 161a–166

Find additional lesson materials that support the core lesson and the ELL instructional pages.

ELL Poster 23

ELL Reader 3.5.3

ELD Reader 3.5.3

Concept Literacy Reader

ELD, ELL Reader Teaching Guide

Concept Literacy Reader Teaching Guide

Technology

Online Teacher's Edition Use the digital version of the core Teacher's Edition for planning and instruction.

eReaders
This week's ELL and ELD Readers and Concept Literacy Reader are also available in digital format.

This Week's Content and Language Objectives by Strand

Concept Development/ Academic Language Why is it hard to adapt to a new culture?	**Content Objective** • Use concept vocabulary related to adapting to a new culture. **Language Objective** • Express ideas in response to art and discussion.
Phonics and Spelling Vowel Patterns	**Content Objective** • Read words with vowel patterns *a, au, aw, al.* **Language Objective** • Apply phonics and decoding skills to vocabulary.
Listening Comprehension Modified Read Aloud: "Coming to America"	**Content Objective** • Monitor and adjust oral comprehension **Language Objectives** • Discuss oral passages. • Use a graphic organizer to take notes.
Reading Comprehension Sequence	**Content Objective** • Identify the sequence of events in a story. **Language Objectives** • Retell the sequence of events in a reading. • Write and give information using a sequence of events. • Read grade-level text with varied intonation patterns.
Vocabulary Basic and Lesson Vocabulary	**Language Objectives** • Understand and use basic and grade-level vocabulary. • Learn meanings of grade-level vocabulary. • Produce drawings, phrases, and short sentences to show understanding of Lesson Vocabulary.
Vocabulary Compound Words	**Content Objective** • Identify and define words in compound words. **Language Objective** • Read and write compound words.
Grammar and Conventions Adverbs	**Content Objective** • Identify and use adverbs. **Language Objectives** • Speak using adverbs. • Write phrases and sentences with adverbs.
Writing Figurative Language	**Content Objective** • Identify figurative language in a text. **Language Objectives** • Write paragraphs using figurative language. • Share feedback for editing and revising.

Word Cards for Vocabulary Activities

airport	**cellar**
curious	**delicious**
described	**farewell**
homesick	**memories**
raindrops	

Teacher Note: Beginning Teach three to four words. **Intermediate** Teach four to six words. **Advanced** Teach six to seven words. **Advanced High** Teach all words.

Name ______________________________

Look at the pictures. **Read** the story.

- What does Anita do? **Write** the events in the correct sequence.

Moving Day

Anita's family is moving. They need to pack many things. Anita helps Dad pack the tools.

Next, Mom asks for help. Anita helps her pack the dishes.

Now, it is time for Anita to work on her room. She packs all of her books.

It has been a long day. Anita falls asleep in her chair.

First ______________________________

Next ______________________________

Then ______________________________

Last ______________________________

Sequence

Use this lesson to supplement or replace the skill lesson on page 258a of the Teacher's Edition. Display the Skill Points (at right) and share them with students.

Teach/Model

Beginning Say: *First, I pack my things in boxes. Next, I put the boxes in a truck. Then I drive the truck to my new home. Last, I unpack everything.* Have students pantomime and tell the events in the story in the correct sequence using the clue words *first, next, then,* and *last.*

Intermediate Display an empty box, a book, a roll of tape, and a marker. Show how to pack, seal, and label the box without narrating the steps. Have students tell the steps in sequence. Remind them to use the clue words *first, next, then,* and *last.*

Advanced Tell students how to get to the school's library without using clue words that indicate sequence. Ask: *How can we use clue words to make the sequence easier to understand and follow?* List suggested clue words. Have volunteers use them to retell the directions.

Advanced High Pair students. Have partners make up a story that has a sequence of at least four events. They can write sentences about the events using the words *first, next, then,* and *last.* Have pairs take turns reading their stories to the group.

Skill Points

- ✔ **Sequence** is the order in which things happen.
- ✔ Look for clue words such as *first, next, then,* and *last.*
- ✔ Sometimes a story will not have clue words.

Then distribute copies of Picture It! page 162.

- Have students look at the pictures and tell what is happening.
- Read the story aloud. Ask: *What does Anita pack first? Then what does she pack?*
- Review the Skill Points with students.
- Ask students to find clue words in the story that help them identify the sequence.

Practice

Read aloud the directions on page 162. Have volunteers take turns rereading the parts of the story aloud. Then have students use the pictures and the story as they list the sequence.

Beginning Students can point to each picture and orally explain the event before writing their answers on the lines. Provide help with English words and writing.

Intermediate Students can first orally answer, beginning their sentences with the words shown, and then write their answers on the lines. Provide help with writing.

Advanced Students can write their answers and then check them by comparing them with a partner's.

Advanced High Students can write their answers and then check them by retelling the events in the story in the same order but in their own words.

Answers for page 162: *First:* Anita helps Dad pack the tools. *Next:* She helps Mom pack the dishes. *Then:* She packs all of her books. *Last:* Anita falls asleep in her chair.

Multilingual Summaries

English

Good-Bye, 382 Shin Dang Dong

When she is eight years old, Jangmi moves from Korea to America. The family's Korean address is 382 Shin Dang Dong. When they move, Jangmi's family has a good-bye lunch. She says good-bye to her best friend Kisuni. For the last time, the girls eat melon called *chummy* together.

The family flies to America in an airplane. Jangmi is sad. America is very different from Korea. Her new house feels strange.

The movers come with the family's things. People from the neighborhood come too. They bring food for Jangmi's family. A girl named Mary gives Jangmi some melon balls. Jangmi thinks that the honeydew melon balls taste like *chummy*. Mary asks what fruit Jangmi ate in Korea. Jangmi has a new friend.

Spanish

Adiós, 382 Shin Dang Dong

A los ocho años, Jangmi se muda de Corea para América del Norte. La dirección de su familia en Corea es 382 Shin Dang Dong. Cuando se mudan, la familia de Jangmi preparan un almuerzo de despedida. Ella se despide de su mejor amiga Kisuni. Las niñas comen melón, llamado *chummy,* juntas por última vez.

La familia vuela a América del Norte en avión. Jangmi está triste. América del Norte es muy diferente a Corea. Su nueva casa le parece extraña.

Los de la mudanza llegan con las cosas de la familia. La gente del barrio viene también. Le ofrecen comida a la familia de Jangmi. Una niña llamada Mary le da a Jangmi algunas bolas de melón. Jangmi piensa que las bolas de melón le saben a *chummy.* Mary le pregunta a Jangmi qué fruta comía en Corea. Jangmi tiene una nueva amiga.

Multilingual Summaries

Chinese

再見，史丹東路382號

吉米八歲時，她家從韓國搬到美國。一家人原本韓國的家在史丹東路382號。搬家那天，家裏特意請朋友來吃午餐。吉米要和最好的朋友杰蘇妮告別，兩人最後一起吃甜瓜。

一家人乘飛機來到美國。吉米非常傷心，她發現美國與韓國完全不一樣，新家讓她感到很陌生。

搬運公司運來了家具。隔壁鄰居也來拜訪，送來吃的東西。有個小女孩叫瑪麗，送給吉米一些蜜瓜球。吉米想甜甜的蜜瓜球就是真摯的友情，瑪麗還問吉米韓國有什麼水果。吉米有了新朋友。

Vietnamese

School
+ Home

Từ Biệt, Nhà Số 382 Shin Dang Dong

Khi được tám tuổi, Jangmi dọn đến Hoa Kỳ từ Hàn Quốc. Địa chỉ của gia đình ở Hàn Quốc là 382 Shin Dang Dong. Khi họ dọn đi, gia đình của Jangmi có tổ chức một buổi ăn trưa từ giã. Cô bé chào từ biệt người bạn thân nhất của mình là Kisuni. Hai cô bé cùng ăn dưa với nhau lần cuối cùng.

Gia đình đi máy bay đến Hoa Kỳ. Jangmi buồn. Hoa Kỳ rất khác lạ so với Hàn Quốc. Ngôi nhà mới của cô cảm thấy lạ.

Những người khuân dọn nhà mang đồ đạc của gia đình đến. Những người từ khu xóm cũng đến. Họ mang thức ăn đến cho gia đình của Jangmi. Một cô gái tên Mary cho Jangmi ít viên dưa. Jangmi nghĩ là những viên dưa xanh có hương vị giống như “chummy”. Mary hỏi Jangmi đã ăn loại trái cây gì ở Hàn Quốc. Jangmi có một người bạn mới.

Multilingual Summaries

Korean

잘 있어, 신당동 382번지

장미는 여덟 살 때 한국에서 미국으로 이주한다. 장미 가족의 한국 주소는 신당동 382번지이다. 장미 가족은 이사하면서 작별 점심을 먹는다. 장미는 가장 친한 친구인 기순이에게 작별 인사를 하고 마지막으로 참외를 같이 먹는다.

장미의 가족은 비행기를 타고 미국에 온다. 미국은 한국과 아주 많이 달라서 장미는 슬프다. 새집은 낯설게 느껴진다.

이삿짐 업체에서 가족의 물건들을 가지고 오자 이웃 사람들도 찾아 온다. 이웃 사람들은 장미의 가족에게 음식을 가져오는데 메리라는 한 소녀는 장미에게 메론 몇 개를 준다. 장미는 그 단물이 나는 메론 덩어리들에게서 친근한 맛이 난다고 생각한다. 메리는 장미에게 한국에서 어떤 과일을 먹었느냐고 묻고 장미와 곧 새로운 친구가 된다.

Hmong

School
+ Home

Sib Ntsib Dua, 382 Shin Dang Dong

Thaum Jangmi muaj yim xyoos, nws tsiv tsev ntawm Korea tuaj txog tebchaws Amelikas. Nws tsev neeg chaws nyob Korea yog 382 Shin Dang Dong. Ua ntej lawv tsiv, Jangmi tsev neeg noj su hais sib ntsib dua. Nws hais sib ntsib dua rau nws tus phoojywg zoo tshaj hu ua Kisuni. Ob tug hluas nkauj no noj dib liab ua ke zaum kawg.

Nws tsev neeg ya tuaj txog Amelikas rau hauv dav hlau. Jangmi tu siab heev. Amelikas thiab Korea nyias txawv nyias. Nws lub tsev tshiab los txawv zog thiab.

Lab luam pab tsiv tsev thauj nws tsev neeg tej khoom tuaj. Neeg zej zog los pab zog thiab. Lawv nqa mov tuaj rau Jangmi tsev neeg noj. Ib tug hluas nkauj npe hu ua Mary pub cov pob dib rau nws noj. Jangmi muaj xav hais tias cov pob dib pag qab luaj chummy. Mary noog seb Jangmi noj txiv dabtsi ntawm Korea. Jangmi muaj ib tug phoojywg tshiab.

Name ______________________________

A New Country

- **Read** *A New Country* again.
- Find details that support the conclusion shown below. **Write** one detail in each *Supporting Detail* box.

Conclusion: There are differences between life in the United States and other countries.

Supporting Detail (pages 2–4)

____
____
____
____
____

Supporting Detail (pages 5–6)

____
____
____
____
____

Supporting Detail (pages 7–8)

____
____
____
____
____

Family Link

Ask family members if they have lived in a different place. How does life differ from one place to the other?

Weekly Resources Guide for English Language Learner Support

For this week's content and language objectives, see p. 167e.

Instructional Strand	Day 1	Day 2
Concept Development/Academic Language	TEACHER'S EDITION • Academic Language, p. DI•91 • Concept Development, p. DI•91 • Anchored Talk, pp. 288j—288–289 • Preteach Academic Vocabulary, p. 293a • Concept Talk Video ELL HANDBOOK • Hear It, See It, Say It, Use It, pp. xxxvi–xxxvii • ELL Poster Talk, Concept Talk, p. 167c ELL POSTER 24 • Day 1 Activities	TEACHER'S EDITION • Academic Language, p. DI•91 • Concept Development, p. DI•91 • Anchored Talk, p. 294a • Concept Talk Video ELL HANDBOOK • ELL Poster Talk, Concept Talk, p. 167c • Concept Talk Video Routine, p. 477 ELL POSTER 24 • Day 2 Activities
Phonics and Spelling	TEACHER'S EDITION • Phonics and Spelling, p. DI•95 • Decodable Practice Reader 24A, pp. 291a–291b	TEACHER'S EDITION • Phonics and Spelling, p. DI•95
Listening Comprehension	TEACHER'S EDITION • Modified Read Aloud, p. DI•94 • Read Aloud, p. 289b • Concept Talk Video ELL HANDBOOK • Concept Talk Video Routine, p. 477	TEACHER'S EDITION • Modified Read Aloud, p. DI•94 • AudioText of *Jalapeño Bagels* • Concept Talk Video ELL HANDBOOK • AudioText CD Routine, p. 477 • T-Chart, p. 493
Reading Comprehension	TEACHER'S EDITION • Preteach Draw Conclusions, p. DI•96	TEACHER'S EDITION • Reteach Draw Conclusions, p. DI•96 • Frontloading Reading, p. DI•97 ELL HANDBOOK • Picture It! Skill Instruction, pp. 168–168a • Multilingual Summaries, pp. 169–171
Vocabulary **Basic and Lesson Vocabulary** **Vocabulary Skill: Unfamiliar Words**	TEACHER'S EDITION • Basic Vocabulary, p. DI•92 • Preteach Lesson Vocabulary, p. DI•92 • Unfamiliar Words, p. DI•95 ELL HANDBOOK • Word Cards, p. 167 • ELL Vocabulary Routine, p. 471 ELL POSTER 24 • Day 1 Activities	TEACHER'S EDITION • Basic Vocabulary, p. DI•92 • Reteach Lesson Vocabulary, p. DI•93 • Unfamiliar Words, p. DI•95 ELL HANDBOOK • Word Cards, p. 167 • Multilingual Vocabulary List, p. 440 ELL POSTER 24 • Day 2 Activities
Grammar and Conventions	TEACHER'S EDITION • Preteach Comparative and Superlative Adverbs, p. DI•99	TEACHER'S EDITION • Reteach Comparative and Superlative Adverbs, p. DI•99
Writing	TEACHER'S EDITION • Purpose, p. DI•100 • Introduce Invitation, pp. 293e–293f	TEACHER'S EDITION • Writing Trait: Focus/Ideas, pp. 303d–303e

Unit 5 Week 4 Jalapeño Bagels

This symbol indicates leveled instruction to address language proficiency levels.

Day 3	Day 4	Day 5
TEACHER'S EDITION • Academic Language, p. DI•91 • Concept Development, p. DI•91 • Anchored Talk, p. 304a • Concept Talk Video **ELL HANDBOOK** • ELL Poster Talk, Concept Talk, p. 167c **ELL POSTER 24** • Day 3 Activities	**TEACHER'S EDITION** • Academic Language, p. DI•91 • Concept Development, p. DI•91 • Anchored Talk, p. 314a • Concept Talk Video **ELL HANDBOOK** • ELL Poster Talk, Concept Talk, p. 167c **ELL POSTER 24** • Day 4 Activities	**TEACHER'S EDITION** • Academic Language, p. DI•91 • Concept Development, p. DI•91 • Concept Talk Video **ELL HANDBOOK** • ELL Poster Talk, Concept Talk, p. 167c **ELL POSTER 24** • Day 5 Activities
ELL HANDBOOK • Phonics Transition Lesson, pp. 254, 256	**ELL HANDBOOK** • Phonics Transition Lesson, pp. 254, 256	**TEACHER'S EDITION** • Phonics and Spelling, p. DI•95
TEACHER'S EDITION • AudioText of *Jalapeño Bagels* • Concept Talk Video **ELL HANDBOOK** • AudioText CD Routine, p. 477	**TEACHER'S EDITION** • Concept Talk Video	**TEACHER'S EDITION** • Concept Talk Video
TEACHER'S EDITION • Sheltered Reading, p. DI•97 **ELL HANDBOOK** • Multilingual Summaries, pp. 169–171	**TEACHER'S EDITION** • ELL/ELD Reader Guided Reading, p. DI•98 **ELL HANDBOOK** • ELL Study Guide, p. 172	**TEACHER'S EDITION** • ELL/ELD Reader Guided Reading, p. DI•98 **ELL HANDBOOK** • ELL Study Guide, p. 172
ELL HANDBOOK • High-Frequency Words Activity Bank, p. 446 **ELL POSTER 24** • Day 3 Activities	**ELL HANDBOOK** • High-Frequency Words Activity Bank, p. 446	**TEACHER'S EDITION** • Unfamiliar Words, p. 319h **ELL HANDBOOK** • High-Frequency Words Activity Bank, p. 446
TEACHER'S EDITION • Grammar Jammer **ELL HANDBOOK** • Grammar Transition Lesson, pp. 372, 378 • Grammar Jammer Routine, p. 478	**TEACHER'S EDITION** • Grammar Jammer **ELL HANDBOOK** • Grammar Transition Lesson, pp. 372, 378	**TEACHER'S EDITION** • Grammar Jammer **ELL HANDBOOK** • Grammar Transition Lesson, pp. 372, 378
TEACHER'S EDITION • Let's Write It!, p. 312–313 • Writing Trait: Purpose, pp. 313a–313b	**TEACHER'S EDITION** • Revising Strategy, pp. 319d–319e	**TEACHER'S EDITION** • Adverbs, pp. 319p–319q

Poster Talk, Concept Talk

Question of the Week

How can different cultures contribute to the foods we eat?

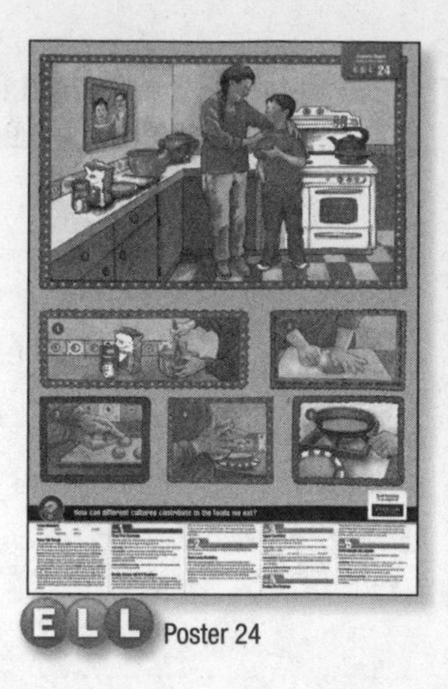

Poster 24

Throughout the week, use the ELL Poster to help students produce and comprehend language, understand the concept, and build English vocabulary. Use the Question of the Week and other questions to help students share ideas in pairs, small groups, or the large group. Sample questions are shown, with examples of possible responses by students.

Weekly Concept and Language Goals

- Discuss food from different cultures
- Name some favorite foods from other cultures
- Tell about the ingredients used to make different foods

By the end of the lesson, students should be able to talk about and write one or more sentences about food from different cultures.

Daily Team Talk

Day 1	Day 2	Day 3	Day 4	Day 5
After Day 1 activities on Poster, ask questions such as *Why do you think tortillas are important to the grandmother in the poster picture?*	After Day 2 activity on Poster, ask questions such as *How does the grandmother make tortillas? What ingredients does she use?*	After Day 3 activity on Poster, ask questions such as *In* Jalapeño Bagels, *why does Pablo decide to bring jalapeño bagels to school?*	After Day 4 activity on Poster, ask questions such as *What other foods do you know that come from different cultures?*	After Day 5 activity on Poster, ask questions such as *What is your favorite food from another culture?*
Beginning They are from her home. **Intermediate** They are part of her Mexican culture. **Advanced** Tortillas are an important part of Mexican culture. They remind her of home. **Advanced High** The grandmother remembers her Mexican culture when she eats Mexican foods such as tortillas.	**Beginning** Flour, salt, and water. **Intermediate** She uses flour, salt, and water to make dough. **Advanced** She makes dough out of flour, salt, and water. Then she cooks it in a hot pan. **Advanced High** The grandmother mixes flour, salt, and water to make dough. She rolls it into small balls and flattens it. She cooks the flat dough in a hot frying pan.	**Beginning** They are like his mom and dad. **Intermediate** They are both Mexican and Jewish, like him. **Advanced** Pablo brings them because they are like him, both Mexican and Jewish. **Advanced High** Pablo decides to bring jalapeño bagels to school because they represent him. Bagels show his Jewish culture, and jalapeños show his Mexican culture.	**Beginning** Pasta from Italy. **Intermediate** People in Italy eat pasta. **Advanced** Pasta is from Italy, and curry is from India. **Advanced High** Italy is known for pasta, India is known for curry, and Japan is known for sushi.	**Beginning** Spaghetti. **Intermediate** I like enchiladas. They are Mexican. **Advanced** My favorite food is ravioli. It is an Italian food. **Advanced High** My favorite food from another culture is moo shu chicken. It is a Chinese food.

This Week's Materials

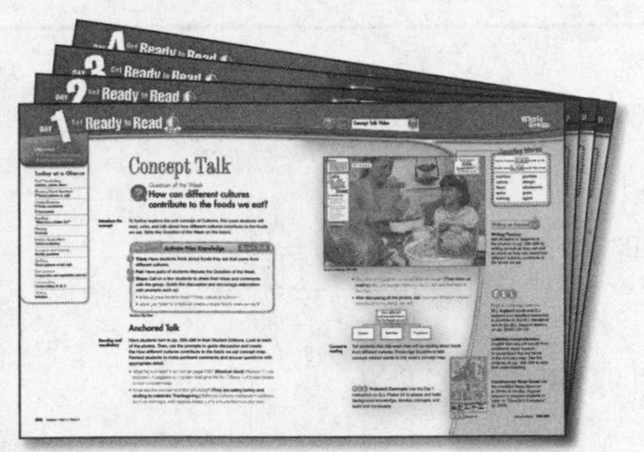

Teacher's Edition pages 288j–319q

See the support for English language learners throughout the lesson, including ELL strategies and scaffolded activities at points of use.

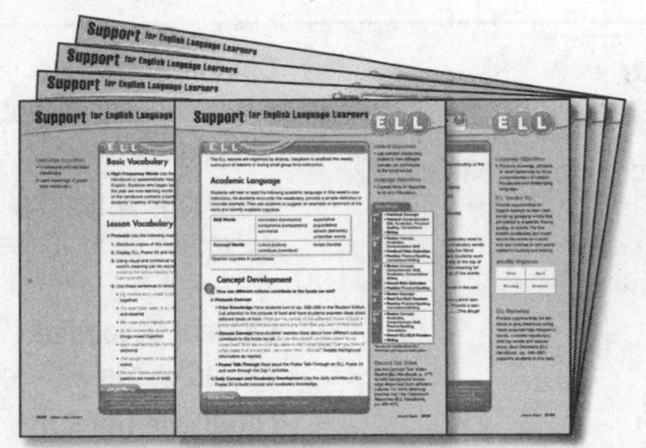

Teacher's Edition pages DI•91–DI•100

Differentiated Instruction for English language learners provides daily group activities that "frontload," or preteach, core instruction.

ELL Handbook pp. 167a–172

Find additional lesson materials that support the core lesson and the ELL instructional pages.

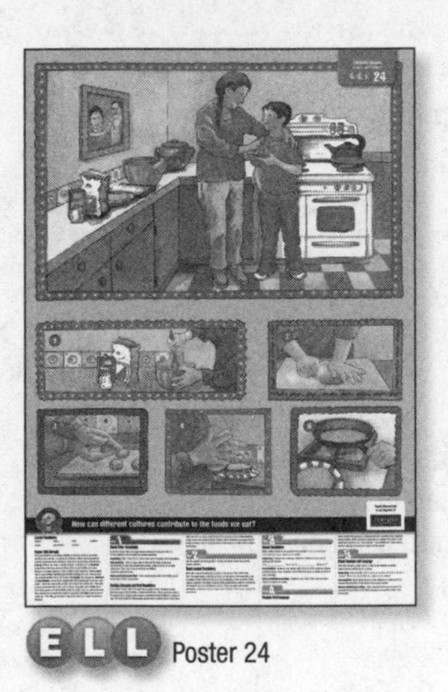

ELL Poster 24

ELL Reader 3.5.4

ELD Reader 3.5.4

Concept Literacy Reader

ELD, ELL Reader Teaching Guide

Concept Literacy Reader Teaching Guide

Technology

Online Teacher's Edition Use the digital version of the core Teacher's Edition for planning and instruction.

eReaders
This week's ELL and ELD Readers and Concept Literacy Reader are also available in digital format.

This Week's Content and Language Objectives by Strand

Concept Development/ Academic Language How can different cultures contribute to the foods we eat?	**Content Objective** • Use concept vocabulary related to how different cultures contribute to the foods we eat. **Language Objective** • Express ideas in response to art and discussion.
Phonics and Spelling Vowel Patterns	**Content Objective** • Read words with vowel digraphs *ei* and *eigh*. **Language Objective** • Apply phonics and decoding skills to vocabulary.
Listening Comprehension Modified Read Aloud: "What is American Food?"	**Content Objective** • Monitor and adjust oral comprehension **Language Objectives** • Discuss oral passages with accessible language. • Use a graphic organizer to take notes.
Reading Comprehension Draw Conclusions	**Content Objective** • Identify how to draw conclusions from a text. **Language Objectives** • Draw conclusions from a reading. • Write by drawing conclusions. • Read grade-level text with accuracy. • Summarize text using visual support.
Vocabulary Basic and Lesson Vocabulary	**Language Objectives** • Understand and use basic and grade-level vocabulary. • Learn meanings of grade-level vocabulary. • Produce drawings, phrases, and short sentences to show understanding of Lesson Vocabulary.
Vocabulary Unfamiliar Words	**Content Objective** • Use contextual support to understand unfamiliar words. **Language Objective** • Write sentences with unfamiliar words.
Grammar and Conventions Comparative and Superlative Adverbs	**Content Objectives** • Decode and use comparative and superlative adverbs. • Correctly form comparative and superlative adverbs. **Language Objectives** • Speak using comparative and superlative adverbs. • Write phrases and sentences with comparative and superlative adverbs.
Writing Purpose	**Content Objective** • Identify the purpose of a text. **Language Objectives** • Write and narrate paragraphs with a specific purpose. • Share feedback for editing and revising.

Word Cards for Vocabulary Activities

bakery	**batch**
boils	**braided**
dough	**ingredients**
mixture	

Teacher Note: Beginning Teach two to three words. **Intermediate** Teach three to four words. **Advanced** Teach four to five words. **Advanced High** Teach all words.

Name ______________________________

Picture It!
Draw Conclusions

Look at the pictures. **Read** the story.
Answer the questions that follow.

Bakery Scents

Bob and his wife, Rita, wake up at 3:00 A.M. They go downstairs to their bakery. They start working.

In a few hours, people start waking up. Mmm! They smell bread, cake, and cookies.

At 7:00 A.M., Bob opens the door. People come in and buy warm bread.

Circle the letter of the correct answer.

1. What do Bob and Rita do?
a. work late **b.** wake people
c. work in a school **d.** bake bread

2. What do people say when they smell the bread?
a. Oh, no! **b.** Yuck!
c. Mmm! **d.** What is that smell?

3. What **conclusion** can you draw about the bakery?
a. People love it. **b.** It is closed.
c. It opens late. **d.** People do not like it.

Draw Conclusions

Use this lesson to supplement or replace the skill lesson on page 292a of the Teacher's Edition. Display the Skill Points (at right) and share them with students.

Skill Points

- ✔ After you think about facts and details, you can figure something out, or **draw a conclusion.**
- ✔ Use facts and details, plus what you already know, to draw conclusions about why things happen or are done a certain way.

Teach/Model

Beginning Say: *My favorite foods are raisin bread, raisin granola, and raisin bars. What conclusion can you make about my favorite foods?* (You like raisins.) Have students explain how they made that conclusion. (All the foods have raisins in them.)

Intermediate Say: *I go in the kitchen. The oven is warm. I smell something sweet.* Ask students to draw a conclusion from the details. (Something is baking.) Ask them to identify clue words that helped them draw that conclusion. (kitchen, oven, warm, sweet)

Advanced Say: *I go to the bakery to buy rolls. There are no rolls left. The bakery is sold out! What conclusion can you draw about the bakery's rolls?* (They must be really good.) Have students explain how they drew that conclusion. (People bought all of them.)

Advanced High Write the following: *Whole grain bread is full of fiber. Our bodies need fiber to stay healthy.* Ask students to read the facts and think about what they already know about healthy foods. Have them write and share conclusions they can draw about the topic. (Whole grain bread is good for our bodies. Whole grain bread is healthy.)

Then distribute copies of Picture It! page 168.

- Have students look at the pictures and tell what they know about bakeries.
- Read the story aloud. Ask: *Have you ever smelled bread baking? Why do the people go to the bakery?* (The bread smells delicious, and they want to eat some.)
- Review the Skill Points with students.
- Have students look at the pictures and words to draw conclusions.

Practice

Read aloud the directions on page 168. Have volunteers reread the story aloud. Then have students use the pictures and the story as they answer the questions.

Beginning Students can first orally answer the questions and then circle their answers. Provide help with circling the correct choices.

Intermediate Students can read the questions, look for the answers in the story, and then circle their answers on the page.

Advanced Students can circle their answers and then check them by silently rereading the story and making any necessary corrections.

Advanced High Students can circle their answers and then orally explain how what they read in the story and what they already knew helped them draw the conclusions.

Answers for page 168: 1. d; 2. c; 3. a

Multilingual Summaries

English

Jalapeño Bagels

Pablo is bringing food to school for International Day. He cannot decide which food to bring. His mother will let him bring something from the family bakery. In exchange, Pablo must help in the bakery. Pablo agrees to help.

At the bakery, Pablo helps his mother make Mexican sweet bread, pumpkin turnovers, and chocolate chip bars. Then Pablo helps his father. They make bagels. They also make *challah*, Jewish braided bread. Then, the whole family makes jalapeño bagels together.

Finally, Pablo decides to bring jalapeño bagels. He chooses them because they represent both sides of his family.

Spanish

Bagels de jalapeño

Pablo va a llevar comida a la escuela para el Día Internacional. No se puede decidir sobre qué comida llevar. Su mamá le dejará llevar algo de la panadería familiar. A cambio, Pablo tiene que ayudar en la panadería. Pablo está de acuerdo en ayudar.

En la panadería, Pablo ayuda a su mamá a hacer pan dulce mexicano, tartas de calabaza y barras con pedacitos de chocolate. Luego Pablo ayuda a su papá. Hacen *bagels*. También hacen *challah*, el pan trenzado que comen los judíos. Después, la familia entera hace *bagels* de jalapeño.

Finalmente, Pablo decide llevar *bagels* de jalapeño a la escuela. Los elige porque representan los dos lados de su familia.

Multilingual Summaries

Chinese

賈拉皮那貝果

國際節那天，帕布魯要帶些吃的回學校。他不知道帶什麼東西最好，媽媽說他可以從家裏的麵包店拿些東西，不過必須幫忙在店裏幹活，帕布魯高興地答應了。

在店裏，帕布魯先是幫媽媽做墨西哥甜麵包、南瓜餅和巧克力條。然後幫爸爸做百吉圈餅，還做了麻花辮一樣的猶太人哈拉麵包。最後全家人一起做賈拉皮那貝果。

帕布魯決定帶賈拉皮那貝果回學校，因為它是全家人一起勞動的成果。

Vietnamese

Bánh Mì Vòng Tròn Có Vị Ớt Jalapeđo

Pablo sắp mang thức ăn đến trường vào Ngày Quốc Tế. Cậu không quyết định được là sẽ mang thức ăn gì. Mẹ của cậu sẽ cho cậu mang một món gì đó từ tiệm bánh của gia đình. Bù lại, Pablo phải giúp việc trong tiệm bánh. Pablo đồng ý phụ giúp.

Ở tiệm bánh, Pablo giúp mẹ của cậu làm bánh mì ngọt của Mễ Tây Cơ, bánh bí nướng, và các thẻ bánh sô-cô-la. Rồi Pablo giúp ba của cậu. Họ làm những cái bánh mì vòng tròn. Họ cũng làm bánh "challah", bánh mì thắt bím của người Do Thái. Kế đến, cả gia đình cùng nhau làm những cái bánh mì vòng tròn có vị ớt jalapeđo.

Cuối cùng, Pablo quyết định mang những cái bánh mì vòng tròn có vị ớt jalapeđo. Cậu chọn chúng vì những chiếc bánh này tiêu biểu cho cả hai bên gia đình của cậu.

Multilingual Summaries

Korean

할라뻬뇨 베이글

파블로는 '국제의 날'에 학교로 음식을 가지고 가려고 하는데 어떤 음식을 가져가야 할 지 정하지 못했다. 파블로의 어머니가 가족이 운영하는 빵집에서 뭔가를 가져가게 해 주겠지만 대신 파블로는 빵집 일을 도와드려야 한다. 파블로는 도와드리기로 한다.

빵집에서 파블로는 어머니를 도와 멕시코식 달콤한 빵과 호박 파이, 그리고 초콜릿 칩 바를 만든다. 그 다음에는 아버지를 도와 베이글과 꼬인 모양의 유대인 빵인 '할라'를 만든다. 그리고 나서 온 가족이 함께 할라뻬뇨 베이글을 만든다.

마침내 파블로는 학교에 자기 가족의 모든 모습을 모두 보여주는 할라뻬뇨 베이글을 가져가기로 한다.

Hmong

School
+ Home

Mov Ci Kheej Xyaw Kua Txob Mev

Pablo yuav nqa mov noj mus txog tsev kawm ntawv rau Hnub Xav txog Pej Kum Teb. Nws txiav txim siab tsis tau nqa mov twg mus. Nws leej niam kheev nws nqa dabtsi ntawm lawv tsev neeg lab ua mov ci noj mus. Tab si Pablo yuav tsum pab ua mov ci hauv lab kom pauj txiaj ntsig. Pablo yib los pab.

Nyob ntawm lab ua mov ci noj, Pablo pab nws leej niam ua mov ci mev qab zib, mov ci xyaw dib daj, thiab ncuav qhob noom. Ces Pablo pab nws txiv. Nkawd ua mov ci kheej. Nkawd ua challah, los yog mov ci sib ntswj Jewish. Ces, nws tsev neeg sawvdaws ua mov ci kheej xyaw kua txob mev ua ke.

Pablo txawm txiav txim siab nqa mov ci xyaw kua txob mev mus. Nws xaiv lawv rau qhov lawv muaj keebkwm ntawm nws tsevneeg ob tog.

Name ______________________________ **The Story of Pizza**

- **Read** *The Story of Pizza* again.
- **Draw** what you like on your pizza.
- **Finish** the sentence.

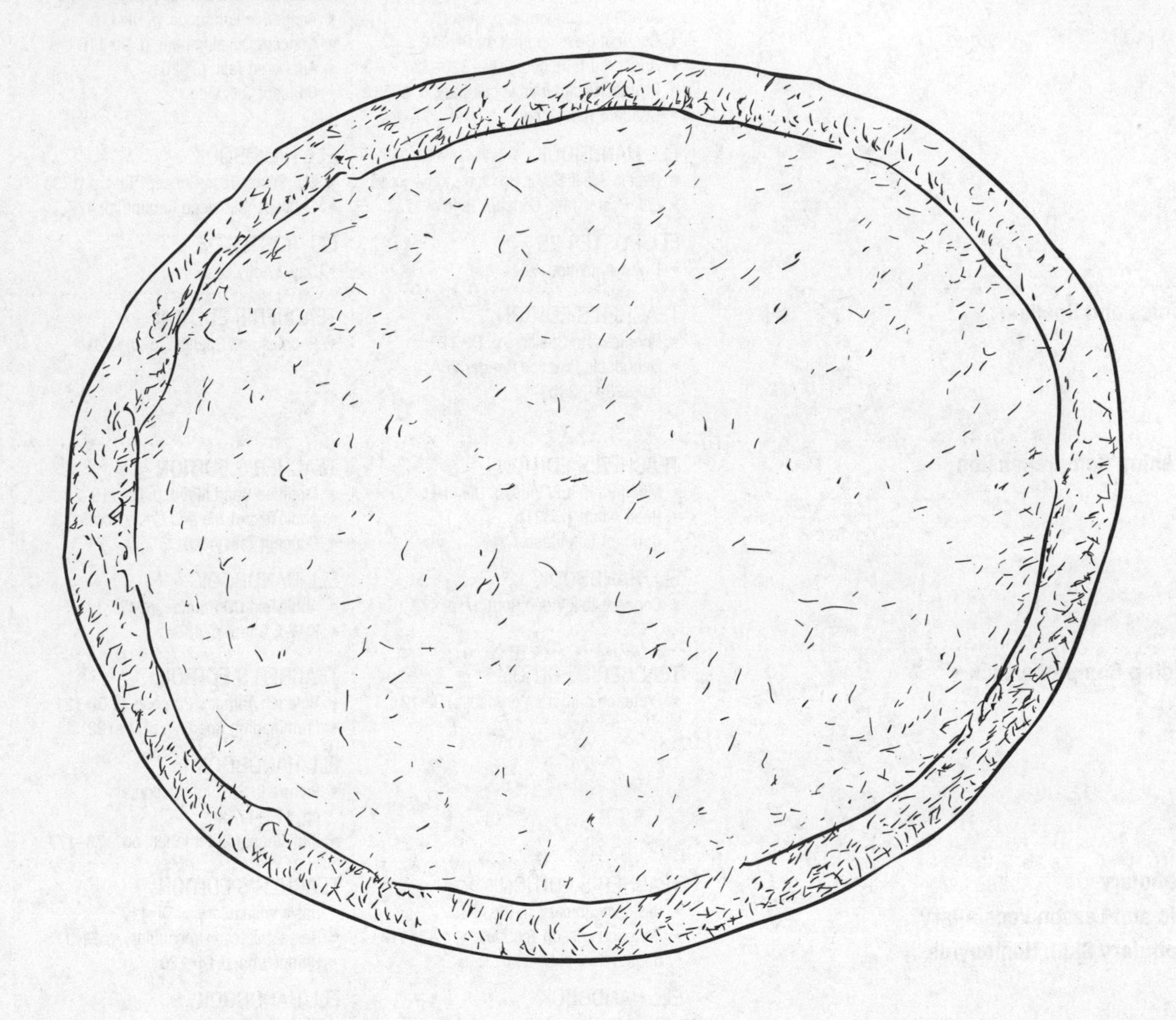

I like pizza with ______________________________

______________________________.

Family Link

Ask family members what they like on their pizza. What kind of pizza is most popular in your family?

Weekly Resources Guide for English Language Learner Support

For this week's content and language objectives, see p. 173e.

Instructional Strand	Day 1	Day 2
Concept Development/Academic Language	TEACHER'S EDITION • Academic Language, p. DI•116 • Concept Development, p. DI•116 • Anchored Talk, pp. 320j—320–321 • Preteach Academic Vocabulary, p. 325a • Concept Talk Video ELL HANDBOOK • Hear It, See It, Say It, Use It, pp. xxxvi–xxxvii • ELL Poster Talk, Concept Talk, p. 173c ELL POSTER 25 • Day 1 Activities	TEACHER'S EDITION • Academic Language, p. DI•116 • Concept Development, p. DI•116 • Anchored Talk, p. 326a • Concept Talk Video ELL HANDBOOK • ELL Poster Talk, Concept Talk, p. 173c • Concept Talk Video Routine, p. 477 ELL POSTER 25 • Day 2 Activities
Phonics and Spelling	TEACHER'S EDITION • Phonics and Spelling, p. DI•120 • Decodable Practice Reader 25A, pp. 323a–323b	TEACHER'S EDITION • Phonics and Spelling, p. DI•120
Listening Comprehension	TEACHER'S EDITION • Modified Read Aloud, p. DI•119 • Read Aloud, p. 321b • Concept Talk Video ELL HANDBOOK • Concept Talk Video Routine, p. 477	TEACHER'S EDITION • Modified Read Aloud, p. DI•119 • AudioText of *Me and Uncle Romie* • Concept Talk Video ELL HANDBOOK • AudioText CD Routine, p. 477 • K-W-L Chart, p. 480
Reading Comprehension	TEACHER'S EDITION • Preteach Author's Purpose, p. DI•121	TEACHER'S EDITION • Reteach Author's Purpose, p. DI•121 • Frontloading Reading, p. DI•122 ELL HANDBOOK • Picture It! Skill Instruction, pp. 174–174a • Multilingual Summaries, pp. 175–177
Vocabulary **Basic and Lesson Vocabulary** **Vocabulary Skill: Homonyms**	TEACHER'S EDITION • Basic Vocabulary, p. DI•117 • Preteach Lesson Vocabulary, p. DI•117 • Homonyms, p. DI•120 ELL HANDBOOK • Word Cards, p. 173 • ELL Vocabulary Routine, p. 471 ELL POSTER 25 • Day 1 Activities	TEACHER'S EDITION • Basic Vocabulary, p. DI•117 • Reteach Lesson Vocabulary, p. DI•118 • Homonyms, p. DI•120 ELL HANDBOOK • Word Cards, p. 173 • Multilingual Vocabulary List, p. 440 ELL POSTER 25 • Day 2 Activities
Grammar and Conventions	TEACHER'S EDITION • Preteach Conjunctions, p. DI•124	TEACHER'S EDITION • Reteach Conjunctions, p. DI•124
Writing	TEACHER'S EDITION • Check Your Work, p. DI•125 • Introduce Book Review, pp. 325e–325f	TEACHER'S EDITION • Book Review, pp. 339d–339e

Unit 5 Week 5 Me and Uncle Romie

This symbol indicates leveled instruction to address language proficiency levels.

Day 3	Day 4	Day 5
TEACHER'S EDITION • Academic Language, p. DI•116 • Concept Development, p. DI•116 • Anchored Talk, p. 340a • Concept Talk Video **ELL HANDBOOK** • ELL Poster Talk, Concept Talk, p. 173c **ELL POSTER 25** • Day 3 Activities	**TEACHER'S EDITION** • Academic Language, p. DI•116 • Concept Development, p. DI•116 • Anchored Talk, p. 354a • Concept Talk Video **ELL HANDBOOK** • ELL Poster Talk, Concept Talk, p. 173c **ELL POSTER 25** • Day 4 Activities	**TEACHER'S EDITION** • Academic Language, p. DI•116 • Concept Development, p. DI•116 • Concept Talk Video **ELL HANDBOOK** • ELL Poster Talk, Concept Talk, p. 173c **ELL POSTER 25** • Day 5 Activities
ELL HANDBOOK • Phonics Transition Lesson, pp. 290, 297	**ELL HANDBOOK** • Phonics Transition Lesson, pp. 290, 297	**TEACHER'S EDITION** • Phonics and Spelling, p. DI•120
TEACHER'S EDITION • AudioText of *Me and Uncle Romie* • Concept Talk Video **ELL HANDBOOK** • AudioText CD Routine, p. 477	**TEACHER'S EDITION** • Concept Talk Video	**TEACHER'S EDITION** • Concept Talk Video
TEACHER'S EDITION • Sheltered Reading, p. DI•122 **ELL HANDBOOK** • Multilingual Summaries, pp. 175–177	**TEACHER'S EDITION** • ELL/ELD Reader Guided Reading, p. DI•123 **ELL HANDBOOK** • ELL Study Guide, p. 178	**TEACHER'S EDITION** • ELL/ELD Reader Guided Reading, p. DI•123 **ELL HANDBOOK** • ELL Study Guide, p. 178
ELL HANDBOOK • High-Frequency Words Activity Bank, p. 446 **ELL POSTER 25** • Day 3 Activities	**ELL HANDBOOK** • High-Frequency Words Activity Bank, p. 446	**TEACHER'S EDITION** • Homonyms, p. 359h **ELL HANDBOOK** • High-Frequency Words Activity Bank, p. 446
TEACHER'S EDITION • Grammar Jammer **ELL HANDBOOK** • Grammar Transition Lesson, pp. 379, 381 • Grammar Jammer Routine, p. 478	**TEACHER'S EDITION** • Grammar Jammer **ELL HANDBOOK** • Grammar Transition Lesson, pp. 379, 381	**TEACHER'S EDITION** • Grammar Jammer **ELL HANDBOOK** • Grammar Transition Lesson, pp. 379, 381
TEACHER'S EDITION • Let's Write It!, p. 352–353 • Writing: Book Review, p. 353a • Writer's Craft: Check Your Work, p. 353b	**TEACHER'S EDITION** • Revising Strategy, pp. 359d–359e	**TEACHER'S EDITION** • Writing Trait: Conventions, pp. 359p–359q

Poster Talk, Concept Talk

Question of the Week

How does city life compare to life in the country?

Poster 25

Throughout the week, use the ELL Poster to help students produce and comprehend language, understand the concept, and build English vocabulary. Use the Question of the Week and other questions to help students share ideas in pairs, small groups, or the large group. Sample questions are shown, with examples of possible responses by students.

Weekly Concept and Language Goals

- Describe urban and rural areas
- Compare and contrast aspects of urban and rural life
- Explain preferences for urban life or rural life

By the end of the lesson, students should be able to talk about and write one or more sentences comparing city life and country life.

Daily Team Talk

Day 1	Day 2	Day 3	Day 4	Day 5
After Day 1 activities on Poster, ask questions such as *Look at the boys playing baseball in the poster picture. Where do you think they live?*	After Day 2 activity on Poster, ask questions such as *Look at the park in the poster picture. Why is a park important in an urban area?*	After Day 3 activity on Poster, ask questions such as *How is a rural area different from an urban area?*	After Day 4 activity on Poster, ask questions such as *How are the ways people get around different in an urban area and a rural area?*	After Day 5 activity on Poster, ask questions such as *Would you rather live in a rural area or an urban area? Why?*
Beginning In the building. **Intermediate** In a tall building near the park. **Advanced** They live in an apartment building near the park. **Advanced High** I think the boys live in an apartment in a tall building near the park and the library.	**Beginning** It's a place to play. **Intermediate** People need places to play. **Advanced** Many people living in apartments don't have yards to play in. They need a park. **Advanced High** In an urban area, many people live in apartment buildings that don't have backyards. A park gives people a place to play and be outside.	**Beginning** Not many people. **Intermediate** A rural area does not have many people. **Advanced** A rural area has houses and more open space. An urban area has many buildings and many people. **Advanced High** A rural area has fewer buildings and people than an urban area. There is more entertainment in the city.	**Beginning** They walk and drive. **Intermediate** They can walk to places in an urban area. **Advanced** In an urban area, they can walk from place to place. In a rural area, they have to drive from place to place. **Advanced High** Places are closer together in an urban area, so people can walk from place to place. Places are farther apart in a rural area, so people drive from place to place.	**Beginning** A rural area. More space. **Intermediate** An urban area, so my friends are close. **Advanced** I would like to live in an urban area because my friends would live nearby. **Advanced High** I think it would be fun to live in a rural area because I would have lots of room to run and play.

This Week's Materials

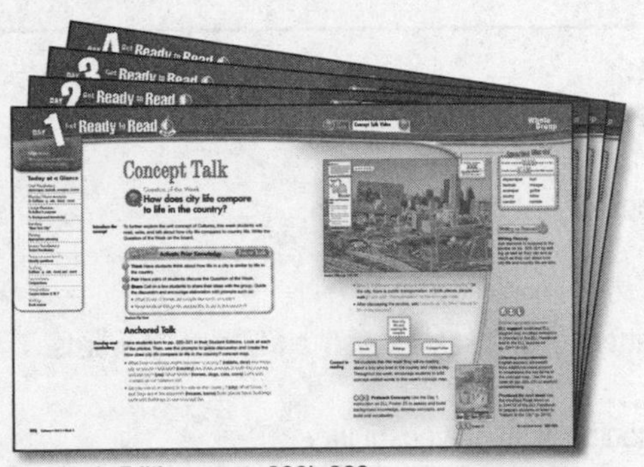
Teacher's Edition pages 320j–363a

See the support for English language learners throughout the lesson, including ELL strategies and scaffolded activities at points of use.

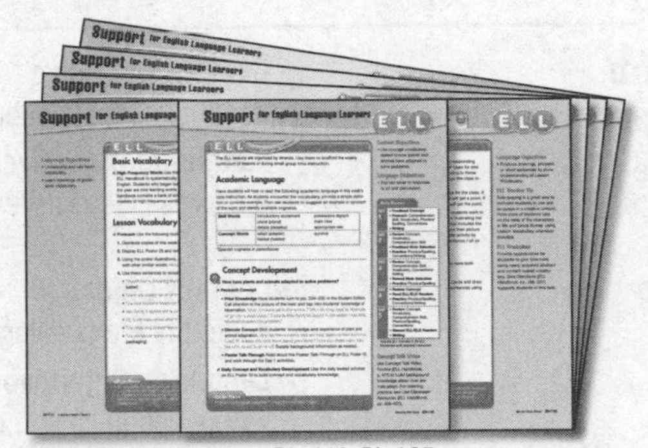
Teacher's Edition pages DI•116–DI•125

Differentiated Instruction for English language learners provides daily group activities that "frontload," or preteach, core instruction.

ELL Handbook pp. 173a–178

Find additional lesson materials that support the core lesson and the ELL instructional pages.

Poster 25

ELL Reader 3.5.5

ELD Reader 3.5.5

Concept Literacy Reader

ELD, ELL Reader Teaching Guide

Concept Literacy Reader Teaching Guide

Technology

Online Teacher's Edition Use the digital version of the core Teacher's Edition for planning and instruction.

eReaders
This week's ELL and ELD Readers and Concept Literacy Reader are also available in digital format.

This Week's Content and Language Objectives by Strand

Concept Development/ Academic Language How does city life compare to life in the country?	**Content Objective** • Use concept vocabulary related to city life and country life. **Language Objective** • Express ideas in response to art and discussion.
Phonics and Spelling Suffixes	**Content Objective** • Identify the spelling pattern in suffixes *–y*, *-ish*, and *-ment* in words. **Language Objective** • Apply phonics and decoding skills to vocabulary.
Listening Comprehension Modified Read Aloud: "Keeping Nature in the City"	**Content Objective** • Monitor and adjust oral comprehension **Language Objectives** • Discuss oral passages. • Use a graphic organizer to take notes.
Reading Comprehension Author's Purpose	**Content Objective** • Identify the various purposes an author may have for writing. **Language Objectives** • Discuss the various different kinds of purposes authors have for writing. • Express feelings and seek clarification about the author's purpose.
Vocabulary Basic and Lesson Vocabulary	**Language Objectives** • Understand and use basic and grade-level vocabulary. • Learn meanings of grade-level vocabulary. • Produce drawings, phrases, and short sentences to show understanding of Lesson Vocabulary.
Vocabulary Homonyms	**Content Objective** • Identify homonyms. **Language Objective** • Read, comprehend, and write homonyms.
Grammar and Conventions Conjunctions	**Content Objectives** • Decode and use conjunctions. • Correctly write sentences with conjunctions. **Language Objectives** • Speak using conjunctions. • Write sentences with conjunctions with accuracy and ease.
Writing Check Your Work	**Content Objective** • Identify how to check your work. **Language Objectives** • Write paragraphs with correct spelling, grammar, and punctuation. • Share feedback for editing and revising.

Word Cards for Vocabulary Activities

cardboard	**feast**
fierce	**flights**
pitcher	**ruined**
stoops	**treasure**

Teacher Note: Beginning Teach three to four words. **Intermediate** Teach four to five words. **Advanced** Teach six to seven words. **Advanced High** Teach all words.

Name ____________________

Picture It!
Author's Purpose

Look at the pictures. **Read** the paragraph.

- Why did the author write this story? **Write** your answer in the *Author's Purpose* box.
- What details give clues to the author's purpose? **Write** them in the *Detail* boxes.

Visit New York City

There are so many things to see in New York City! You can explore the Statue of Liberty. It is magnificent. You can see the famous Empire State Building. No other city is quite so exciting. You should visit New York City one day.

Author's Purpose

Detail	**Detail**	**Detail**

Picture It!

Author's Purpose

Use this lesson to supplement or replace the skill lesson on page 324a of the Teacher's Edition. Display the Skill Points (at right) and share them with students.

Teach/Model

Beginning Write and read aloud these sentences: *I love New York City. About eight million people live in New York City.* Ask students which sentence was written to inform (the second) and which sentence was written to express the author's feelings (the first).

Intermediate Read aloud part of the entry for New York City in a children's encyclopedia. Ask: *What is the author's purpose?* (to give information about the city) Have students tell details that helped them identify the author's purpose.

Advanced Say: *An author wrote a book about funny things that happen to a character on her first trip to New York City. What is the author's purpose?* (to entertain) *Why do you think that?* Repeat this process with other books written for different purposes.

Advanced High Write *to inform, to entertain, to persuade,* and *to express feelings* on strips of paper. Have students select a strip and write a three-sentence paragraph for that purpose. Read each paragraph aloud and ask the group to determine the author's purpose.

Then distribute copies of Picture It! page 174.

- Have students look at the pictures, read the title, and tell what they already know about New York City.
- Review the Skill Points with students.
- Read the paragraph aloud. Ask: *What is the author's purpose? Does the author want you to visit New York City? How do you know?*

Skill Points

- ✔ The **author's purpose** is the reason an author writes something.
- ✔ An author may write to entertain, to inform, to express ideas, or to persuade.
- ✔ Sometimes the title helps you predict the author's purpose.

Practice

Read aloud the directions on page 174. Reread the paragraph aloud, explaining the words *magnificent* and *famous.* Then have students use the pictures and the paragraph as they complete the graphic organizer.

Beginning Students can say what they want to write for the author's purpose and details before writing words or phrases in the boxes. Provide help with English words and writing.

Intermediate Students can first orally answer and then write their answers in the boxes. Provide help with English words and writing.

Advanced Students can write sentences to complete the organizer and then check them by comparing them with a partner's answers.

Advanced High Students can write sentences to complete the organizer and then explain how clue words helped them identify the author's purpose.

Answers for page 174: *Author's Purpose:* to persuade people to visit New York City; *Possible detail answers:* so many things to see; no city quite as exciting; you should visit New York City

Multilingual Summaries

English

Me and Uncle Romie

James will spend the summer in New York City with his Uncle Romie and Aunt Nanette. James is sad because he will not be home on his birthday. On his birthday, James always has lemon cake and goes to a baseball game.

James rides on a train from North Carolina to New York City. Uncle Romie is busy in his art studio. Aunt Nanette takes James to Harlem. He plays stickball. He eats ice cream. James likes the sounds and sights of the city.

Aunt Nanette goes on a visit. Uncle Romie makes a special birthday breakfast. He takes James to a baseball game. Aunt Nanette makes a lemon and mango birthday cake.

James learns that he and Uncle Romie are alike in many ways. When James gets on the train to go home, Uncle Romie gives James a painting. When he returns home, James makes a painting for Uncle Romie.

Spanish

Tío Romie y yo

James pasará el verano con el tío Romie y la tía Nanette en la ciudad de Nueva York. James está triste porque no estará en casa el día de su cumpleaños. El día de su cumpleaños, James siempre come pastel de limón y va a ver un juego de béisbol.

James viaja en tren desde Carolina del Norte hasta Nueva York. El tío Romie está ocupado en su estudio de arte. La tía Nanette lleva a James a Harlem. Allí se une a un juego de béisbol callejero. También va a comer helado. A James le gustan los sonidos y los lugares interesantes de la ciudad.

La tía Nanette se va a hacer una visita. El tío Romie prepara un desayuno especial de cumpleaños. Lleva a James a un juego de béisbol. La tía Nanette hace un pastel de cumpleaños de limón y mango.

James aprende que su tío Romie y él se parecen en muchas cosas. Cuando James sube al tren para regresar a casa, el tío Romie le da una de sus pinturas. Cuando regresa a casa, James hace una pintura para el tío Romie.

Multilingual Summaries

Chinese

羅密叔叔和詹姆斯

今年的暑假，詹姆斯將要到紐約，跟羅密叔叔和納內特嬸嬸一起住。由於生日不能回家，詹姆斯很不開心。以前每逢生日，他都可以吃檸檬蛋糕和玩棒球。

詹姆斯從北卡羅來納坐火車到紐約。羅密叔叔忙著畫畫，於是納內特嬸嬸帶詹姆斯去哈萊姆玩曲棍球和吃霜淇淋，詹姆斯開始喜歡紐約了。

有一天，納內特嬸嬸有事外出，羅密叔叔為詹姆斯特別做了生日早餐，還帶他一起玩棒球。嬸嬸回來後做了檸檬芒果生日蛋糕。

詹姆斯察覺到他和羅密叔叔有很多相似的地方。乘火車回家時，羅密叔叔送給他一幅畫。回家後，詹姆斯也要畫畫送給羅密叔叔。

Vietnamese

Chú Romie và Tôi

James sẽ trải qua mùa hè ở Thành Phố New York với Chú Romie và Cô Nanette. James buồn vì sẽ không được ở nhà vào dịp sinh nhật của mình. Vào lễ sinh nhật của cậu, James luôn luôn được có bánh chanh và đi xem bóng chày.

James đi xe lửa từ North Carolina đến Thành Phố New York. Chú Romie bận rộn trong phòng họa của mình. Cô Nanette đưa James đến Harlem. Cậu chơi đánh bóng gậy. Cậu ăn kem. James thích âm thanh và cảnh vật của thành phố.

Cô Nanette đi vắng. Chú Romie làm một bữa ăn sáng cho ngày sinh nhật đặc biệt. Chú dẫn James đi xem bóng chày. Cô Nanette làm một bánh sinh nhật chanh và xoài.

James học hỏi được rằng cậu và Chú Romie giống nhau về nhiều mặt. Khi James lên xe lửa trở về nhà, Chú Romie đưa cho James một bức tranh vẽ. Khi cậu về đến nhà, James vẽ một bức tranh cho Chú Romie.

Multilingual Summaries

Korean

나와 로미 삼촌

제임스는 로미 삼촌과 나네트 숙모와 함께 뉴욕에서 여름을 보낼 것이다. 제임스는 자신의 생일날 집을 떠나온 것 때문에 서운하다. 생일이면 제임스는 항상 레몬 케이크를 먹고 야구경기를 하러 갔기 때문이다.

제임스는 노스캐롤라이나에서 뉴욕까지 기차를 타고 간다. 로미 삼촌은 예술 스튜디오에서 일하느라 바빠서 나네트 숙모가 제임스를 할렘에 데려다 준다. 제임스는 약식야구 경기를 하고 아이스크림을 먹는다. 제임스는 도시의 소리와 경치를 좋아한다.

나네트 숙모가 집에 들른다. 로미 삼촌은 특별한 생일 아침 식사를 준비하고 제임스를 야구 경기에 데리고 간다. 나네트 숙모는 레몬과 망고 생일 케이크를 만든다.

제임스는 자기와 로미 삼촌이 많은 면에서 비슷하다는 것을 알게 된다. 제임스가 집에 가는 기차에 올라탔을 때 로미 삼촌은 제임스에게 그림을 하나 준다. 제임스는 집에 돌아와서 로미 삼촌을 위해 그림을 그린다.

Hmong

Kuv thiab Txiv Ntxawm Romie

Mus txog lub caij sov sov tas James yuav nrog nws tus Txiv Ntxawm Romie thiab Niam Ntxawm Nanette nyob Nroog New York. James tu siab rau qhov nws yuav tsis nyob tsev thaum txog nws hnub yug. Thaum txog nws hnub yug, James ib txwm noj mov ci qab zib xyaw txiv qaub thiab mus ua si xuas qws ntau pob.

James caij tsheb nqajhlau txij xeev North Carolina mus txog Nroog New York. Txiv Ntxawm Romie khwv khwv hauv chav pleev duab. Niam Ntxawm Nanette thauj James mus txog Harlem. Nws xuas qws ntau pob. Nws noj kua mis nyuj nkoog. James nyiam yam uas nws pom thiab hnov hauv lub nroog.

Niam Ntxawm Nanette mus cuav zos. Txiv Ntxawm Romie ua pluag tshais nco hnub yug. Nws coj James mus saib cov kws xuas qws ntau pob. Niam Ntxawm ua mov ci qab zib xyaw txiv qaub thiab txiv nkhaus taw.

James kawm paub tias nws thiab Txiv Ntxawm Romie coj cwjpwm zoo sib xws. Thaum James nkag tsheb nqajhlau mus tsev, Txiv Ntxawm Romie pub ib daim duab pleev rau James. Thaum nws mus txog tsev lawm, James pleev duab rau Txiv Ntxawm Romie thiab.

Name ______________________________

From a Small Town to a Big City

- **Read** *From a Small Town to a Big City* again.
- Do you think the author would rather live in a small town or a big city? **Draw** a picture of where you would like to live.
- **Write** a sentence that tells why.

____

____

____

Family Link

Ask family members to share their opinions about life in a small town and life in a big city.

Weekly Resources Guide for English Language Learner Support

For this week's content and language objectives, see p. 179e.

Instructional Strand	Day 1	Day 2
Concept Development/Academic Language	TEACHER'S EDITION • Academic Language, p. DI•16 • Concept Development, p. DI•16 • Anchored Talk, pp. 366j—366–367 • Preteach Academic Vocabulary, p. 371a • Concept Talk Video ELL HANDBOOK • Hear It, Say It, See It, Use It, pp. xxxvi–xxxvii • ELL Poster Talk, Concept Talk, p. 179c ELL POSTER 26 • Day 1 Activities	TEACHER'S EDITION • Academic Language, p. DI•16 • Concept Development, p. DI•16 • Anchored Talk, p. 372a • Concept Talk Video ELL HANDBOOK • ELL Poster Talk, Concept Talk, p. 179c • Concept Talk Video Routine, p. 477 ELL POSTER 26 • Day 2 Activities
Phonics and Spelling	TEACHER'S EDITION • Phonics and Spelling, p. DI•20 • Decodable Practice Reader 26A, pp. 369a–369b	TEACHER'S EDITION • Phonics and Spelling, p. DI•20
Listening Comprehension	TEACHER'S EDITION • Modified Read Aloud, p. DI•19 • Read Aloud, p. 367b • Concept Talk Video ELL HANDBOOK • Concept Talk Video Routine, p. 477	TEACHER'S EDITION • Modified Read Aloud, p. DI•19 • AudioText of *The Story of the Statue of Liberty* • Concept Talk Video ELL HANDBOOK • AudioText CD Routine, p. 477 • Main Idea, p. 487
Reading Comprehension	TEACHER'S EDITION • Preteach Fact and Opinion, p. DI•21	TEACHER'S EDITION • Reteach Fact and Opinion, p. DI•21 • Frontloading Reading, p. DI•22 ELL HANDBOOK • Picture It! Skill Instruction, pp. 180–180a • Multilingual Summaries, pp. 181–183
Vocabulary **Basic and Lesson Vocabulary** **Vocabulary Skill: Prefix *un-***	TEACHER'S EDITION • Basic Vocabulary, p. DI•17 • Preteach Lesson Vocabulary, p. DI•17 • Prefix *un-*, p. DI•20 ELL HANDBOOK • Word Cards, p. 179 • ELL Vocabulary Routine, p. 471 ELL POSTER 26 • Day 1 Activities	TEACHER'S EDITION • Basic Vocabulary, p. DI•17 • Reteach Lesson Vocabulary, p. DI•18 • Prefix *un-*, p. DI•20 ELL HANDBOOK • Word Cards, p. 179 • Multilingual Vocabulary List, p. 431 ELL POSTER 26 • Day 2 Activities
Grammar and Conventions	TEACHER'S EDITION • Preteach Capital Letters, p. DI•24	TEACHER'S EDITION • Reteach Capital Letters, p. DI•24
Writing	TEACHER'S EDITION • Paraphrasing, p. DI•25 • Introduce Notes, pp. 371e–371f	TEACHER'S EDITION • Writing Trait: Focus/Ideas, pp. 381d–381e

Unit 6 Week 1 The Story of the Statue of Liberty

This symbol indicates leveled instruction to address language proficiency levels.

Day 3	Day 4	Day 5
TEACHER'S EDITION • Academic Language, p. DI•16 • Concept Development, p. DI•16 • Anchored Talk, p. 382a • Concept Talk Video ELL HANDBOOK • ELL Poster Talk, Concept Talk, p. 179c ELL POSTER 26 • Day 3 Activities	TEACHER'S EDITION • Academic Language, p. DI•16 • Concept Development, p. DI•16 • Anchored Talk, p. 390a • Concept Talk Video ELL HANDBOOK • ELL Poster Talk, Concept Talk, p. 179c ELL POSTER 26 • Day 4 Activities	TEACHER'S EDITION • Academic Language, p. DI•16 • Concept Development, p. DI•16 • Concept Talk Video ELL HANDBOOK • ELL Poster Talk, Concept Talk, p. 179c ELL POSTER 26 • Day 5 Activities
ELL HANDBOOK • Phonics Transition Lesson, pp. 254, 259	ELL HANDBOOK • Phonics Transition Lesson, pp. 254, 259	TEACHER'S EDITION • Phonics and Spelling, p. DI•20
TEACHER'S EDITION • AudioText of *The Story of the Statue of Liberty* • Concept Talk Video ELL HANDBOOK • AudioText CD Routine, p. 477	TEACHER'S EDITION • Concept Talk Video	TEACHER'S EDITION • Concept Talk Video
TEACHER'S EDITION • Sheltered Reading, p. DI•22 ELL HANDBOOK • Multilingual Summaries, pp. 181–183	TEACHER'S EDITION • ELL/ELD Reader Guided Reading, p. DI•23 ELL HANDBOOK • ELL Study Guide, p. 184	TEACHER'S EDITION • ELL/ELD Reader Guided Reading, p. DI•23 ELL HANDBOOK • ELL Study Guide, p. 184
ELL HANDBOOK • High-Frequency Words Activity Bank, p. 446 ELL POSTER 26 • Day 3 Activities	ELL HANDBOOK • High-Frequency Words Activity Bank, p. 446	TEACHER'S EDITION • Prefix *un-*, p. 393h ELL HANDBOOK • High-Frequency Words Activity Bank, p. 446
TEACHER'S EDITION • Grammar Jammer ELL HANDBOOK • Grammar Transition Lesson, pp. 314–315, 319–321 • Grammar Jammer Routine, p. 478	TEACHER'S EDITION • Grammar Jammer ELL HANDBOOK • Grammar Transition Lesson, pp. 314–315, 319–321	TEACHER'S EDITION • Grammar Jammer ELL HANDBOOK • Grammar Transition Lesson, pp. 314–315, 319–321
TEACHER'S EDITION • Let's Write It!, p. 388–389 • Writer's Craft: Paraphrase, pp. 389a–389b	TEACHER'S EDITION • Revising Strategy, pp. 393d–393e	TEACHER'S EDITION • Notes, pp. 393p–393q

Poster Talk, Concept Talk

Question of the Week

Why do we have symbols that represent freedom?

ELL Poster 26

Throughout the week, use the ELL Poster to help students produce and comprehend language, understand the concept, and build English vocabulary. Use the Question of the Week and other questions to help students share ideas in pairs, small groups, or the large group. Sample questions are shown, with examples of possible responses by students.

Weekly Concept and Language Goals

- Understand the concept of symbols of freedom
- Identify symbols of freedom
- Explain how the U.S. flag is a symbol of freedom

By the end of the lesson, students should be able to talk about and write one or more sentences about symbols of freedom.

Daily Team Talk

Day 1	Day 2	Day 3	Day 4	Day 5
After Day 1 activities on Poster, ask questions such as *How can you describe the Statue of Liberty to a friend?*	After Day 2 activity on Poster, ask questions such as *What does the tablet the statue is holding represent?*	After Day 3 activity on Poster, ask questions such as *How do you think going to see the Statue of Liberty would make you feel?*	After Day 4 activity on Poster, ask questions such as *Besides the Statue of Liberty, what other symbol of freedom is in the poster picture?*	After Day 5 activity on Poster, ask questions such as *Why is the United States flag a symbol of freedom?*
Beginning It is tall. **Intermediate** The statue is a tall woman in a robe and a crown. **Advanced** The Statue of Liberty is a tall woman wearing a robe and a crown. She is holding up a torch. **Advanced High** The Statue of Liberty is a statue of a woman. She is wearing a robe and a crown. She holds a torch in her right hand and a tablet in her left hand.	**Beginning** The Fourth of July. **Intermediate** The tablet has the date July 4, 1776. **Advanced** The statue is holding a tablet that has the date July 4, 1776. That is our country's birthday. **Advanced High** The tablet the statue is holding has the date July 4, 1776, on it. That is the date that our country declared its freedom.	**Beginning** Excited. **Intermediate** I would feel excited and proud. **Advanced** I would feel proud because the statue is a symbol of our country. **Advanced High** I think I would feel amazed because the statue is so big. I would also feel proud because it represents the freedom we have in our country.	**Beginning** Our flag. **Intermediate** I see the United States flag. **Advanced** The United States flag is another symbol of freedom. **Advanced High** The United States flag is flying next to the statue. Our flag is also a symbol of freedom.	**Beginning** It stands for our country. **Intermediate** The flag stands for our country and freedom. **Advanced** The United States flag represents our country and the freedom that people have in our country. **Advanced High** Our country protects people's freedom, and the flag represents our country, so the flag is a symbol of freedom.

This Week's Materials

Teacher's Edition pages 366j–393q

See the support for English language learners throughout the lesson, including ELL strategies and scaffolded activities at points of use.

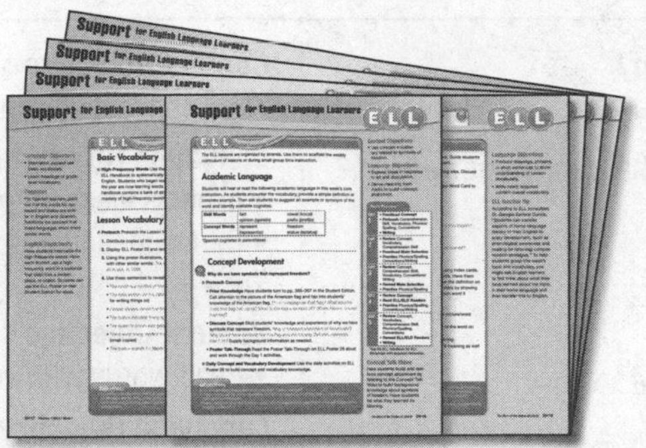

Teacher's Edition pages DI•16–DI•25

Differentiated Instruction for English language learners provides daily group activities that "frontload," or preteach, core instruction.

ELL Handbook pp. 179a–184

Find additional lesson materials that support the core lesson and the ELL instructional pages.

ELL Poster 26

ELL Reader 3.6.1

ELD Reader 3.6.1

Concept Literacy Reader

ELD, ELL Reader Teaching Guide

Concept Literacy Reader Teaching Guide

Technology

Online Teacher's Edition Use the digital version of the core Teacher's Edition for planning and instruction.

eReaders
This week's ELL and ELD Readers and Concept Literacy Reader are also available in digital format.

This Week's Content and Language Objectives by Strand

Concept Development/ Academic Language Why do we have symbols that represent freedom?	**Content Objective** •Use concept vocabulary related to symbols of freedom. **Language Objectives** • Express ideas in response to art and discussion. • Derive meaning from media to build concept attainment.
Phonics and Spelling Vowel Sounds *oo, ew, ue, ui*	**Content Objective** • Read words with vowel sounds *oo, ew, ue,* and *ui.* **Language Objective** • Apply phonics and decoding skills to words with *oo, ew, ue,* and *ui.*
Listening Comprehension Modified Read Aloud: "The Liberty Bell"	**Content Objective** • Monitor and adjust oral comprehension. **Language Objectives** • Discuss oral passages. • Use a graphic organizer to take notes.
Reading Comprehension Fact and Opinion	**Content Objectives** • Distinguish between facts and opinions. • Identify facts and opinions to aid comprehension. **Language Objectives** • Discuss evidence for facts and opinions. • Retell facts and opinions from a reading. • Understand that opinions often express feelings.
Vocabulary Basic and Lesson Vocabulary	**Language Objectives** • Internalize, expand use basic vocabulary. • Learn meanings of grade-level vocabulary. • Produce drawings, phrases, and short sentences to show understanding of Lesson Vocabulary.
Vocabulary Prefix *un-*	**Content Objective** • Identify words with prefix *un-*. **Language Objectives** • Discuss meaning of words with prefix *un-*. • Write words with prefix *un-*.
Grammar and Conventions Capital Letters	**Content Objectives** • Use capital letters. • Correctly write phrases and sentences with capital letters. **Language Objective** • Write phrases and sentences with capital letters.
Writing Paraphrasing	**Content Objective** • Learn how to paraphrase a text. **Language Objectives** • Paraphrase a portion of text. • Share feedback for editing and revising.

Word Cards for Vocabulary Activities

crown	**liberty**
models	**symbol**
tablet	**torch**
unforgettable	**unveiled**

Teacher Note: Beginning Teach three to four words. **Intermediate** Teach four to six words. **Advanced** Teach six to seven words. **Advanced High** Teach all words.

Name ______________________________

Picture It!
Fact and Opinion

Look at the picture. **Read** the story.

- Which sentences are facts? Which sentences are opinions? **Write** your answers in the boxes below.

The Chinese American Story

Life was hard for some early Chinese immigrants to the United States. Most Chinese immigrants were men. Many left their families in China. They were alone for a long time. Some of the men made money by building railroads. That's a hard job! Other people did not want the job. Today, the Chinese American community has grown. The people have had great success.

Fact: ______________________________

____

____

____

Opinion: ______________________________

____

____

Fact and Opinion

Use this lesson to supplement or replace the skill lesson on page 370a of the Teacher's Edition. Display the Skill Points (at right) and share them with students.

Skill Points

- ✔ A statement of **fact** tells something that can be proven. It is either true or false. You can prove it by reading about it or asking an expert.
- ✔ An **opinion** tells someone's ideas or feelings. Clue words such as *fun, best,* and *like* tell you that a statement is an opinion.

Teach/Model

Beginning Display a globe. Point to China and Japan. Say: *China is a bigger country than Japan. I think a plane ride to China is too long. Which sentence tells an opinion? Which sentence tells a fact? How can the globe prove that the fact is true?*

Intermediate Say: *Everyone should visit a different country. How do you know this is an opinion?* (*Should* is a clue word that indicates opinion.) *I have visited Mexico and England. How do you know this is a fact?* (It can be proven.)

Advanced Ask students to make a two-column chart labeled *Facts* and *Opinions.* Write facts and opinions on the board. For example: *The best way to travel is by train. Mexico is south of the United States.* Ask students to write the sentences in the appropriate columns. Discuss how they decided which sentences belong in each column.

Advanced High Pair students. One partner tells a fact and an opinion about traveling. The other partner identifies which is the fact and which is the opinion and explains how he or she knows. Then the partners trade roles.

Then distribute copies of Picture It! page 180.

- Have students look at the picture. Read the paragraph aloud.
- Review the Skill Points with students.
- Ask: *What is one fact? Where can you check to find out if it is true?* (Possible answer: check a book or a reliable website)

Practice

Read aloud the directions on page 180. Reread the paragraph aloud, explaining the words *immigrants, community,* and *success.* Then have students use the picture and the paragraph as they fill in the boxes.

Beginning Students can say what facts and opinions they want to write before writing their answers in the boxes. Provide help with English words and writing.

Intermediate Students can first orally answer and then write their answers in the boxes. Provide help with English words and writing.

Advanced Students can write facts and opinions in the boxes and then check their answers by comparing them with a partner's answers.

Advanced High Students can write their answers in the boxes and then orally explain how they decided which are facts and which are opinions.

Answers for page 180: *Possible facts:* Most Chinese immigrants were men. Some of the men made money by building railroads. Other people did not want the job. *Possible opinions:* Life was hard for some early Chinese immigrants to the United States. That's a hard job!

Multilingual Summaries

English

The Story of the Statue of Liberty

Frédéric Auguste Bartholdi was a French sculptor. He wanted to make a statue for the United States. The statue would stand on an island in New York Harbor. He started making the statue in 1871. The statue was of a woman he called Liberty. He wanted the statue to be a symbol of freedom.

The statue was very big. Before it was finished, parts of the statue were shown. The arm that held the torch was shown in Philadelphia and New York. The head was shown in Paris.

The statue was finished in 1884. It was sent to America in pieces, on a ship. The base for the statue was finished, and the statue was put together in 1886. There was a big celebration. Since that time, the Statue of Liberty has welcomed people who come to New York.

Spanish

La historia de la Estatua de la Libertad

Frédéric Auguste Bartholdi era un escultor francés. Él quería hacer una estatua para Estados Unidos. La estatua podría colocarse en una isla en la bahía de Nueva York. Él comenzó a hacer la estatua en 1871. La estatua era una mujer que él llamó Libertad. Él quería que la estatua fuera un símbolo de libertad.

La estatua era muy grande. Antes de terminarla, algunas de sus partes fueron presentadas en exhibiciones. El brazo que sostenía la antorcha fue exhibido en Filadelfia y en Nueva York. La cabeza fue exhibida en París.

La estatua fue terminada en 1884. Fue enviada a Estados Unidos en piezas, en un barco. La base para la estatua se terminó y se unieron todas sus piezas en 1886. Hubo una gran celebración. Desde aquel momento, la Estatua de la Libertad le ha dado la bienvenida a las personas que llegan a Nueva York.

Multilingual Summaries

Chinese

自由女神像

腓德列克・奥古斯特・巴托迪是法國雕塑家。他想創作一座雕像獻給美國，佇立在紐約港口的小島上。這項工作由1871年開始。巴托迪把雕像叫做自由女神，希望她成為自由的象徵。

整座雕像很大，在完成之前，部份雕像就做過展覽。在費城與紐約展出了舉著火炬的手臂，在巴黎展出了頭像。

1884年終於全部完成，分拆後用船運到美國。雕像基座建好後，1886年正式組合。人們舉行了盛大的慶祝活動。從那以後，自由女神像就一直在紐約港口歡迎來自各地的人們。

Vietnamese

Câu Chuyện về Tượng Nữ Thần Tự Do

Frédéric Auguste Bartholdi là một nhà điêu khắc người Pháp. Ông muốn làm một bức tượng cho Hoa Kỳ. Bức tượng này sẽ được dựng lên trên một hòn đảo ở Cảng New York. Ông bắt đầu làm bức tượng vào năm 1871. Bức tượng là một người phụ nữ mà ông gọi là Tự Do. Ông muốn bức tượng này là biểu tượng của sự tự do.

Tượng này rất lớn. Trước khi được hoàn thành, những phần của bức tượng được mang đi trưng bày. Cánh tay cầm cây đuốc được trưng bày ở Philadelphia và New York. Đầu tượng được trưng bày ở Paris.

Bức tượng này được hoàn thành vào năm 1884. Tượng được gởi đến Hoa Kỳ bằng nhiều miếng, trên một chiếc tàu. Trụ của bức tượng được hoàn tất, và bức tượng được lắp ráp lại với nhau vào năm 1886. Có một lễ ăn mừng lớn. Kể từ lúc đó, Tượng Nữ Thần Tự Do đã chào đón mọi người đến New York.

Multilingual Summaries

Korean

자유의 여신상 이야기

프레데리크 오귀스트 바르톨디는 프랑스의 조각가였다. 그는 미국을 위해 조각상을 하나 만들고 싶었다. 그 조각상은 뉴욕항의 어느 섬에 세워질 것이었다. 그는 1871년부터 조각상을 만들기 시작했는데 그가 '자유' 라고 이름 붙인 한 여인의 동상이었다. 그는 그 조각상이 자유의 상징이 되기를 바랐다.

그 동상은 상당히 컸다. 작품이 완성되기 전 그 동상의 일부가 공개되었다. 횃불을 든 팔은 필라델피아와 뉴욕에서, 두상은 파리에서 공개되었다.

조각상은 1884년에 완성되었으며 조각으로 나뉘어져 배편으로 미국에 보내졌다. 조각상은 토대가 완성된 후 1886년에 조립되었고 성대한 축하행사가 열렸다. 그때 이후로 뉴욕에 오는 많은 사람들이 자유의 여신상을 관람하고 있다.

Hmong

Zaj Dab Neeg txog Mlom Nco Kev YwjPheej.

Frederic Auguste Bartholdi yog tus kws puab mlom Fagkis. Nws xav puab mlom pub rau tebchaws Amelikas. Tus mlom ntawd yuav sawv ntsug saum koog pov txwv ntawm chaws nres nkos New York. Nws pib puab mlom xyoos 1871. Tus mlom yog ib tug pojniam hu ua Kev YwjPheej. Nws xav kom tus mlom ua ib lub cim nco txog kev YwjPheej.

Tus mlom ntawd loj ua luaj. Ua ntej nws muab txuas tas, tej feem mlom raug muab saib. Txhais caj npab uas tuav tsau raug muab saib hauv Philadelphia thiab New York ob xeev. Lub taubhau raug muab saib ntawm nroog Paris.

Tus mlom raug puab tas xyoos 1884. Nws raug xa rau tebchaws Amelikas ua tej dwb daim. Lub hauvpaus mlom raug txhim tsa tas, thiab tus mlom raug muab txuas tas xyoos 1886. Txawm muaj qhov kev zoo siab loj. Txij hnub ntawd los txog tav no Tus Mlom Nco Kev YwjPheej txais tos txhua tus uas tuaj xyuas xeev New York.

Name ___________________________

The Eagle: A Symbol of Freedom

- **Read** *The Eagle, A Symbol of Freedom* again.
- Use the information in the book. **Write** facts and opinions in the chart. The first fact has been done for you.
- In the *Fact* column, **write** facts from the book. In the *Opinion* column, **write** opinions of your own about the facts you chose.

Fact	Opinion
1. *The Bald Eagle is an American symbol for freedom.*	1. ___________________
2.	2. ___________________
3.	3. ___________________
4.	4. ___________________

Family Link

What animal would you choose for your symbol? Why? Ask family members the same questions. Share your ideas with them.

Weekly Resources Guide for English Language Learner Support

For this week's content and language objectives, see p. 185e.

Instructional Strand	Day 1	Day 2
Concept Development/Academic Language	TEACHER'S EDITION • Academic Language, p. DI•41 • Concept Development, p. DI•41 • Anchored Talk, pp. 394j—394–395 • Preteach Academic Vocabulary, p. 399a • Concept Talk Video ELL HANDBOOK • Hear It, See It, Say It, Use It, pp. xxxvi–xxxvii • ELL Poster Talk, Concept Talk, p. 185c ELL POSTER 27 • Day 1 Activities	TEACHER'S EDITION • Academic Language, p. DI•41 • Concept Development, p. DI•41 • Anchored Talk, p. 400a • Concept Talk Video ELL HANDBOOK • ELL Poster Talk, Concept Talk, p. 185c • Concept Talk Video Routine, p. 477 ELL POSTER 27 • Day 2 Activities
Phonics and Spelling	TEACHER'S EDITION • Phonics and Spelling, p. DI•45 • Decodable Practice Reader 27A, pp. 397a–397b	TEACHER'S EDITION • Phonics and Spelling, p. DI•45
Listening Comprehension	TEACHER'S EDITION • Modified Read Aloud, p. DI•44 • Read Aloud, p. 395b • Concept Talk Video ELL HANDBOOK • Concept Talk Video Routine, p. 477	TEACHER'S EDITION • Modified Read Aloud, p. DI•44 • AudioText of *Happy Birthday Mr. Kang* • Concept Talk Video ELL HANDBOOK • AudioText CD Routine, p. 477 • Story Map B, p. 484
Reading Comprehension	TEACHER'S EDITION • Preteach Cause and Effect, p. DI•46	TEACHER'S EDITION • Reteach Cause and Effect, p. DI•46 • Frontloading Reading, p. DI•47 ELL HANDBOOK • Picture It! Skill Instruction, pp. 186–186a • Multilingual Summaries, pp. 187–189
Vocabulary **Basic and Lesson Vocabulary** **Vocabulary Skill: Antonyms**	TEACHER'S EDITION • Basic Vocabulary, p. DI•42 • Preteach Lesson Vocabulary, p. DI•42 • Antonyms, p. DI•45 ELL HANDBOOK • Word Cards, p. 185 • ELL Vocabulary Routine, p. 471 ELL POSTER 27 • Day 1 Activities	TEACHER'S EDITION • Basic Vocabulary, p. DI•42 • Reteach Lesson Vocabulary, p. DI•43 • Antonyms, p. DI•45 ELL HANDBOOK • Word Cards, p. 185 • Multilingual Vocabulary List, p. 441 ELL POSTER 27 • Day 2 Activities
Grammar and Conventions	TEACHER'S EDITION • Preteach Abbreviations, p. DI•49	TEACHER'S EDITION • Reteach Abbreviations, p. DI•49
Writing	TEACHER'S EDITION • Structure of a Limerick, p. DI•50 • Introduce Poetry: Limerick, pp. 399e–399f	TEACHER'S EDITION • Writer's Craft: Structure of a Limerick, pp. 411d–411e

Unit 6 Week 2 Happy Birthday Mr. Kang

This symbol indicates leveled instruction to address language proficiency levels.

Day 3	Day 4	Day 5
TEACHER'S EDITION • Academic Language, p. DI•41 • Concept Development, p. DI•41 • Anchored Talk, p. 412a • Concept Talk Video ELL HANDBOOK • ELL Poster Talk, Concept Talk, p. 185c ELL POSTER 27 • Day 3 Activities	TEACHER'S EDITION • Academic Language, p. DI•41 • Concept Development, p. DI•41 • Anchored Talk, p. 424a • Concept Talk Video ELL HANDBOOK • ELL Poster Talk, Concept Talk, p. 185c ELL POSTER 27 • Day 4 Activities	TEACHER'S EDITION • Academic Language, p. DI•41 • Concept Development, p. DI•41 • Concept Talk Video ELL HANDBOOK • ELL Poster Talk, Concept Talk, p. 185c ELL POSTER 27 • Day 5 Activities
ELL HANDBOOK • Phonics Transition Lesson, pp. 266–267	ELL HANDBOOK • Phonics Transition Lesson, pp. 266–267	TEACHER'S EDITION • Phonics and Spelling, p. DI•45
TEACHER'S EDITION • AudioText of *Happy Birthday Mr. Kang* • Concept Talk Video ELL HANDBOOK • AudioText CD Routine, p. 477	TEACHER'S EDITION • Concept Talk Video	TEACHER'S EDITION • Concept Talk Video
TEACHER'S EDITION • Sheltered Reading, p. DI•47 ELL HANDBOOK • Multilingual Summaries, pp. 187–189	TEACHER'S EDITION • ELL/ELD Reader Guided Reading, p. DI•48 ELL HANDBOOK • ELL Study Guide, p. 190	TEACHER'S EDITION • ELL/ELD Reader Guided Reading, p. DI•48 ELL HANDBOOK • ELL Study Guide, p. 190
ELL HANDBOOK • High-Frequency Words Activity Bank, p. 446 ELL POSTER 27 • Day 3 Activities	ELL HANDBOOK • High-Frequency Words Activity Bank, p. 446	TEACHER'S EDITION • Antonyms, p. 429h ELL HANDBOOK • High-Frequency Words Activity Bank, p. 446
TEACHER'S EDITION • Grammar Jammer ELL HANDBOOK • Grammar Transition Lesson, pp. 315, 320 • Grammar Jammer Routine, p. 478	TEACHER'S EDITION • Grammar Jammer ELL HANDBOOK • Grammar Transition Lesson, pp. 315, 320	TEACHER'S EDITION • Grammar Jammer ELL HANDBOOK • Grammar Transition Lesson, pp. 315, 320
TEACHER'S EDITION • Let's Write It!, p. 422–423 • Writer's Craft: Structure, pp. 423a–423b	TEACHER'S EDITION • Revising Strategy, pp. 429d–429e	TEACHER'S EDITION • Poetry: Limerick, pp. 429p–429q

Poster Talk, Concept Talk

Question of the Week

What does it mean to grant freedom?

Poster 27

Throughout the week, use the ELL Poster to help students produce and comprehend language, understand the concept, and build English vocabulary. Use the Question of the Week and other questions to help students share ideas in pairs, small groups, or the large group. Sample questions are shown, with examples of possible responses by students.

Weekly Concept and Language Goals

- Tell what granting freedom means
- Give examples of granting freedom
- Explain the importance of freedom

By the end of the lesson, students should be able to talk about and write one or more sentences about granting freedom.

Daily Team Talk

Day 1	Day 2	Day 3	Day 4	Day 5
After Day 1 activity on Poster, ask questions such as *What does it mean to grant freedom to someone or something?*	After Day 2 activities on Poster, ask questions such as *Do you think the boy in the poster picture granted Jack, the dog, his freedom? Why or why not?*	After Day 3 activity on Poster, ask questions such as *What kind of freedom do you think Jack wants to have?*	After Day 4 activity on Poster, ask questions such as *When the boy in the poster picture finds Jack, what do you think he will do?*	After Day 5 activity on Poster, ask questions such as *Why is freedom important?*
Beginning To let them go. **Intermediate** To let them be free and go where they want. **Advanced** When you grant freedom to people, you let them go free so they can go wherever they want. **Advanced High** To grant freedom to people or animals means to set them free. They can go any place that they want to go.	**Beginning** No. **Intermediate** No, Jack is lost. **Advanced** No, Jack got lost. The boy did not let him go. **Advanced High** No, the boy did not grant Jack his freedom. That would mean he let Jack go free. But Jack ran away on his own.	**Beginning** To run and play. **Intermediate** He wants to run and play everywhere. **Advanced** Jack might want to run and play, but I think he would miss the boy. **Advanced High** Jack might want the freedom to run and play anywhere he wants, but I think he would miss his friend.	**Beginning** Hug him. **Intermediate** He will hug him and play with him. **Advanced** I think Jack and the boy will run and play together. **Advanced High** I think the boy will be happy to get Jack back. I also think he will be more careful not to lose his dog again.	**Beginning** We want it. **Intermediate** We want to be able to do and say what we want. **Advanced** We don't want someone else to tell us what to say and do. We want to be free to choose. **Advanced High** Everyone has the right to live as he or she chooses. No one wants to be told how to live.

This Week's Materials

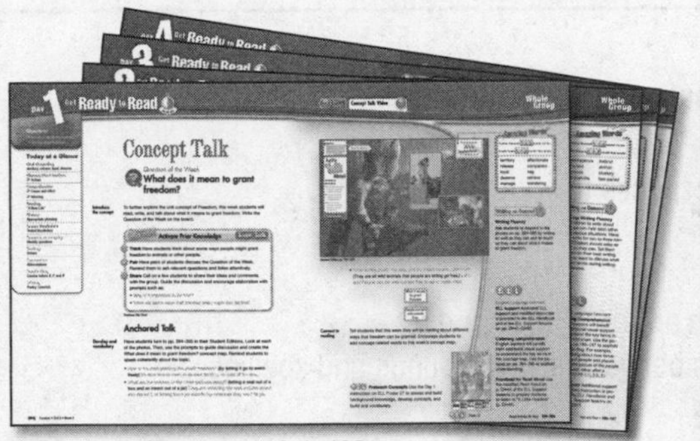

Teacher's Edition pages 394j–429q

See the support for English language learners throughout the lesson, including ELL strategies and scaffolded activities at points of use.

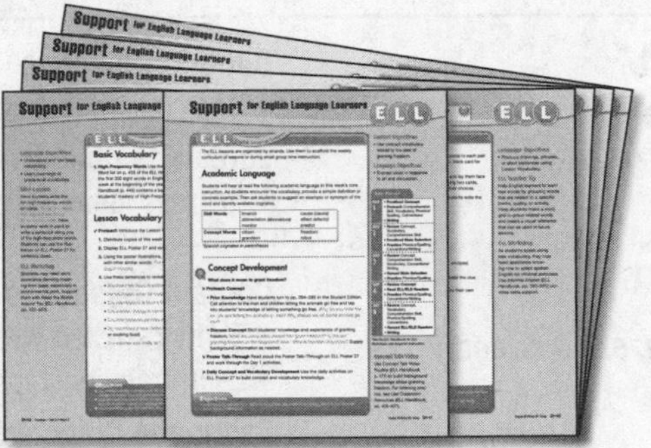

Teacher's Edition pages DI•41–DI•50

Differentiated Instruction for English language learners provides daily group activities that "frontload," or preteach, core instruction.

ELL Handbook pp. 185a–190

Find additional lesson materials that support the core lesson and the ELL instructional pages.

ELL Poster 27

ELL Reader 3.6.2

ELD Reader 3.6.2

Concept Literacy Reader

ELD, ELL Reader Teaching Guide

Concept Literacy Reader Teaching Guide

Technology

Online Teacher's Edition Use the digital version of the core Teacher's Edition for planning and instruction.

eReaders
This week's ELL and ELD Readers and Concept Literacy Reader are also available in digital format.

This Week's Content and Language Objectives by Strand

Concept Development/ Academic Language What does it mean to grant freedom?	**Content Objective** • Use concept vocabulary related to freedom. **Language Objective** • Express ideas in response to art and discussion.
Phonics and Spelling Schwa (ə) spelled with an *a, e, i, o, u,* and *y*	**Content Objectives** • Schwa spelled with an *a, e, i, o, u,* and *y.* • Learn relationships between schwa sounds and spellings. **Language Objective** • Identify and pronounce words that contain the schwa sound.
Listening Comprehension Modified Read Aloud: "JAK and JIL Ask for Freedom"	**Content Objective** • Monitor and adjust oral comprehension. **Language Objectives** • Discuss oral passages. • Use a graphic organizer to take notes.
Reading Comprehension Cause and Effect	**Content Objectives** • Distinguish cause and effect. • Identify cause and effect to aid comprehension. **Language Objectives** • Discuss the connections between causes and effects. • Pronounce transition words that suggest cause and effect relationships. • Write about causes and effects from personal experience.
Vocabulary Basic and Lesson Vocabulary	**Language Objectives** • Internalize, expand use basic vocabulary. • Learn meanings of grade-level vocabulary. • Produce drawings, phrases, and short sentences to show understanding of Lesson Vocabulary.
Vocabulary Antonyms	**Content Objective** • Identify antonyms. **Language Objective** • Apply phonics and decoding skills to vocabulary.
Grammar and Conventions Abbreviations	**Content Objectives** • Identify abbreviations in reading. • Decode abbreviations in reading. **Language Objectives** • Read aloud passages that contain abbreviations. • Write abbreviations accurately.
Writing Structure of a Limerick	**Content Objective** • Identify the structure of a limerick. **Language Objectives** • Write about the structure of limericks. • Share feedback for editing and revising.

Word Cards for Vocabulary Activities

bows	**chilly**
foolish	**foreign**
narrow	**perches**
recipe	

Teacher Note: Beginning Teach two to three words. **Intermediate** Teach three to four words. **Advanced** Teach four to five words. **Advanced High** Teach all words.

Name ________________________________

Picture It!
Cause and Effect

Look at the pictures. **Read** the captions. **Choose** one cause and effect.

- Why does something happen? **Write** it in the *Cause* circle.
- What happens? **Write** it in the *Effect* circle.

First Day of School

The teacher asks Benito a question.

Benito cannot answer because he does not speak English yet.

Since Carmen is bilingual, she tells Benito what the teacher said.

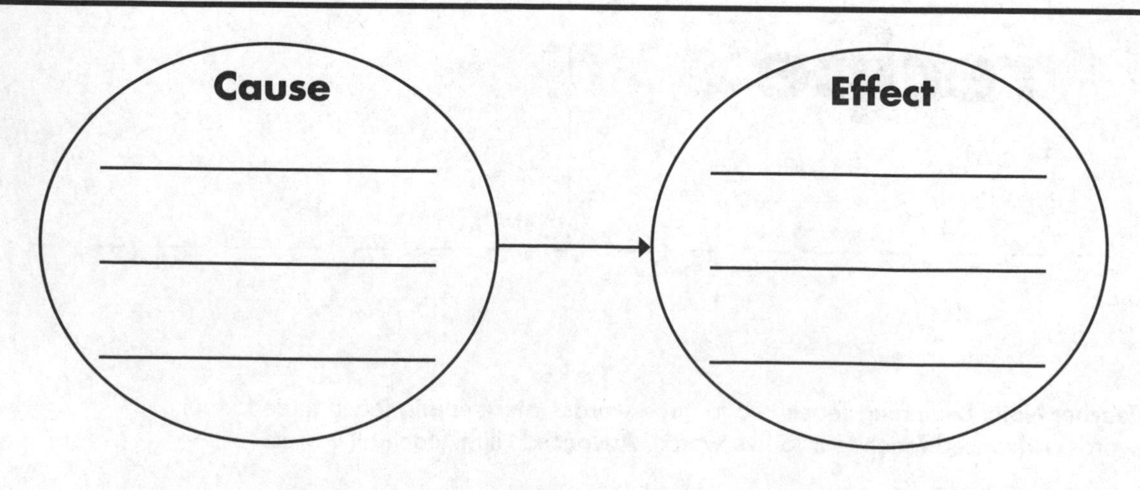

Picture It!

Cause and Effect

Use this lesson to supplement or replace the skill lesson on page 398a of the Teacher's Edition. Display the Skill Points (at right) and share them with students.

Teach/Model

Beginning Put a pencil on a table and push it so that it rolls. Say: *I push the pencil. The pencil rolls. What happens?* (The pencil rolls.) *That is the effect. Why does this happen?* (You push it.) *That is the cause. The pencil rolls because I push it.*

Intermediate Write and read aloud this sentence: *Because I want to learn to cook, I am taking cooking classes.* Have students copy the sentence. Ask: *What clue word helps you know this sentence tells about a cause and an effect?* (because) Ask students to write cause and effect above the appropriate parts of the sentence.

Advanced Write and read aloud these sentences: *We listen to our teacher because we want to learn. Since we want to learn, we listen to our teacher.* Point to the first sentence and have students identify the cause and the effect. Repeat the process with the second sentence.

Advanced High Pair students. Have each partner write a cause-and-effect sentence with a clue word and then exchange papers. Ask students to identify the cause and the effect in their partners' sentences.

Then distribute copies of Picture It! page 186.

- Have students look at the pictures and tell what is happening.
- Read the story aloud. Ask: *What happens because Benito cannot speak English?* (He cannot answer the teacher.)
- Review the Skill Points with students.
- Have students look at the pictures and words to find causes and effects.

Skill Points

- ✔ A **cause** tells why something happens.
- ✔ An **effect** tells what happens.
- ✔ Words such as *because* and *since* are clues. They tell you that you are reading about a cause-and-effect relationship.

Practice

Read aloud the directions on page 186. Have a volunteer reread the story aloud. Then have students use the pictures and the story as they fill in the cause-and-effect diagram. Remind them to look for clue words that indicate cause-and-effect relationships.

Beginning Students can say what cause and what effect they want to write before writing words or phrases in the circles. Provide help with English words and writing.

Intermediate Students can first orally respond and then write their answers on the lines in the circles. Provide help with English words and writing.

Advanced Students can write sentences to fill in the diagram and then check their answers by discussing the story with a partner.

Advanced High Students can write sentences to fill in the diagram and then orally explain how they recognized causes and effects in the story.

Answers for page 186: *Cause:* Benito does not speak English yet. *Effect:* He cannot answer the teacher's question; or *Cause:* Carmen is bilingual. *Effect:* Carmen can tell Benito what the teacher said.

Multilingual Summaries

English

Happy Birthday Mr. Kang

For many years, Mr. Kang has worked in a restaurant. When he is seventy years old, he stops working. He wants to read the newspaper, write poems, and have a hua mei bird.

Every Sunday, Mr. Kang takes his bird to the park. One Sunday his grandson, Sam, goes with him. Mr. Kang meets his friends. His friends have also taken their birds to the park. Mr. Kang recites poems as he talks with his friends. Sam thinks the birds want to fly away. He thinks that they want to be free. Mr. Kang thinks about that. Finally, he agrees. His friends tell him no. Mrs. Kang tells him no. Sam gets frightened and tells his grandpa to wait. But Mr. Kang opens the cage door. The bird flies away.

When Mr. Kang and Sam get home, the bird is waiting for them. Mr. Kang writes a new poem about the bird and Sam.

Spanish

Feliz cumpleaños Sr. Kang

El Sr. Kang ha trabajado en un restaurante durante muchos años. Cuando cumple setenta años, deja de trabajar. Él quiere leer el periódico, escribir poemas y tener un pájaro hua mei.

Todos los domingos, el Sr. Kang va al parque con su pájaro. Un domingo su nieto Sam va con él. El Sr. Kang se encuentra con sus amigos. Sus amigos también han venido con sus pájaros al parque. El Sr. Kang recita poemas mientras habla con sus amigos. Sam piensa que los pájaros quieren volar lejos. Piensa que los pájaros quieren ser libres. El Sr. Kang piensa sobre eso. Finalmente, está de acuerdo. Sus amigos le dicen que no. La Sra. Kang le dice que no. Sam se asusta y le dice a su abuelo que espere. Pero el Sr. Kang abre la jaula. El pájaro se va volando.

Cuando el Sr. Kang y Sam regresan a casa, el pájaro los está esperando. El Sr. Kang escribe un nuevo poema sobre Sam y el pájaro.

Multilingual Summaries

Chinese

康爺爺生日快樂

康爺爺在餐館裏工作了很多年，七十歲的時候終于退休了。他希望以後可以讀讀報紙、寫寫詩歌、再養一隻畫眉鳥。

每個星期天，康爺爺都帶著畫眉鳥去公園。有一次，他的小孫子薩姆也跟他一起去。在公園，康爺爺遇到許多老朋友，他們也帶來了自己養的鳥。康爺爺一邊和朋友聊天一邊朗讀詩歌。這時薩姆想，這些鳥兒一定很想在天空自由飛翔，不願意被關在籠子裏。康爺爺想了想同意放了畫眉鳥，但他的朋友們都說不行，康奶奶也說不好。一想到畫眉鳥要獨自生活了，薩姆很擔心，叫爺爺等一會。但康爺爺還是打開鳥籠，讓畫眉鳥飛走了。

康爺爺和薩姆回到家，發現畫眉鳥早已飛回家等著他們了！康爺爺說，要將小鳥與薩姆的故事寫進他的詩歌裏。

Vietnamese

Mừng Ông Kang được Sinh Nhật Vui Vẻ

Ông Kang đã làm việc cho một nhà hàng qua nhiều năm. Khi ông bảy mươi tuổi, ông ngưng làm việc. Ông muốn được đọc báo, viết văn thơ, và có một con chim họa mi.

Mỗi chủ nhật, Ông Kang mang chim của mình đến khu công viên. Có một ngày chủ nhật cháu trai của ông là Sam đi với ông. Ông Kang gặp gỡ bạn bè của mình. Bạn của ông cũng mang những con chim của họ đến khu công viên. Ông Kang đọc lại những bài thơ khi ông trò chuyện với bạn ông. Sam nghĩ là những chú chim muốn được bay đi. Cậu nghĩ là chúng muốn được tự do. Ông Kang nghĩ ngợi về chuyện này. Cuối cùng, ông đồng ý. Các bạn bảo ông đừng. Bà Kang bảo ông đừng. Sam thấy sợ và kêu ông của mình hãy chờ. Nhưng Ông Kang mở cửa lồng. Chim bay đi.

Khi Ông Kang và Sam trở về nhà, chú chim đang chờ họ. Ông Kang viết một bài thơ mới về Sam và chú chim.

Multilingual Summaries

Korean

생일 축하합니다 강씨 할아버지

강씨 할아버지는 수년간 어느 음식점에서 일해왔다. 70세가 되던 해 일을 그만둔 할아버지는 화메이 새 한 마리를 기르면서 신문을 읽고 시를 쓰는 삶을 소망한다.

매주 일요일마다 강씨 할아버지는 새를 데리고 공원에 간다. 어느 일요일 손자인 샘이 할아버지와 함께 공원에 간다. 강씨 할아버지는 그곳에서 친구들을 만나는데 친구들도 공원에 새를 데리고 왔다. 강씨 할아버지는 친구들과 이야기하면서 시를 낭송한다. 샘은 새들이 멀리 날아가고 싶고 자유로워지고 싶어할 거라고 생각한다. 강씨 할아버지는 그 점에 대해 생각해 보고 마침내 새를 날려보내려고 하지만 할아버지의 친구들과 강씨 할머니는 안 된다고 말한다. 샘은 겁이 나 할아버지에게 기다리라고 말하지만 강씨 할아버지는 새장 문을 연다. 그리고 새는 멀리 날아간다.

강씨 할아버지와 샘이 집에 돌아왔을 때 새가 이들을 기다리고 있다. 강씨 할아버지는 새와 샘에 대한 새로운 시를 짓는다.

Hmong

Zoo Siab Hnub Yug Mr. Kang

Tau ntau ntau xyoo, Mr. Kang ua num rau hauv tsev ua mov noj. Txog hnub nyoog xya caum, nws yuav lawb haujlwm tas li. Nws xav twm ntawv xov xwm, sau zaj paj huam, thiab tau ib tug noog hua mei.

Txhua hnub vas nthiv, Mr. Kang nqa nws tus noog mus txog tshav ua si. Muaj ib hnub vas nthiv nws tus xeeb ntxwv nrog nws mus. Mr. Kang ntsib nws cov phoojywg. Nws cov phoojywg yeej nqa lawv cov noog mus txog tshav ua si. Mr. Kang hais qog tawm cov paj huam thaum nws nrog nws cov phoojywg sib tham. Sam muaj xav tias cov noog xav ya mus. Nws muaj xav tias lawv xav nyob yam ywjpheej. Mr. Kang xav txog qhov ntawd. Nws txawm yib lawm. Nws cov phoojywg hais kom nws tsis txhob ua. Sam ntxhov siab thiab nws thov kom nws tus yawg tos. Tab sis mas Mr. Kang muab tawb noog lub qhov rooj qhib plho. Tus noog ya tawm.

Thaum Mr. Kang thiab Sam mus txog tsev, tus noog nyob tos lawv. Mr. Kang txawm sau ib zaj paj huam tshiab txog tus noog thiab Sam.

Name ______________________

Gina Becomes a Citizen

- **Read** *Gina Becomes a Citizen* again.
- **Write** information from the story to fill in the chart.

What happens?	Why does it happen?
1. Gina wants to learn English.	1. ______________________ ______________________
2. ______________________ ______________________	2. Gina studied hard.
3. Gina said that she would follow the laws in the United States.	3. ______________________ ______________________
4. ______________________ ______________________	4. Gina can vote now.

Family Link

Ask family members to talk about what it means to be a citizen of the United States.

Weekly Resources Guide for English Language Learner Support

For this week's content and language objectives, see p. 191e.

Instructional Strand	Day 1	Day 2
Concept Development/Academic Language	TEACHER'S EDITION • Academic Language, p. DI•66 • Concept Development, p. DI•66 • Anchored Talk, pp. 430j—430–431 • Preteach Academic Vocabulary, p. 435a • Concept Talk Video ELL HANDBOOK • Hear It, See It, Say It, Use It, pp. xxxvi–xxxvii • ELL Poster Talk, Concept Talk, p. 191c ELL POSTER 28 • Day 1 Activities	TEACHER'S EDITION • Academic Language, p. DI•66 • Concept Development, p. DI•66 • Anchored Talk, p. 436a • Concept Talk Video ELL HANDBOOK • ELL Poster Talk, Concept Talk, p. 191c • Concept Talk Video Routine, p. 477 ELL POSTER 28 • Day 2 Activities
Phonics and Spelling	TEACHER'S EDITION • Phonics and Spelling, p. DI•70 • Decodable Practice Reader 28A, pp. 433a–433b	TEACHER'S EDITION • Phonics and Spelling, p. DI•70
Listening Comprehension	TEACHER'S EDITION • Modified Read Aloud, p. DI•69 • Read Aloud, p. 431b • Concept Talk Video ELL HANDBOOK • Concept Talk Video Routine, p. 477	TEACHER'S EDITION • Modified Read Aloud, p. DI•69 • AudioText of *Talking Walls* • Concept Talk Video ELL HANDBOOK • AudioText CD Routine, p. 477 • Main Idea, p. 487
Reading Comprehension	TEACHER'S EDITION • Preteach Graphic Sources, p. DI•71	TEACHER'S EDITION • Reteach Graphic Sources, p. DI•71 • Frontloading Reading, p. DI•72 ELL HANDBOOK • Picture It! Skill Instruction, pp. 192–192a • Multilingual Summaries, pp. 193–195
Vocabulary **Basic and Lesson Vocabulary** **Vocabulary Skill: Unknown Words**	TEACHER'S EDITION • Basic Vocabulary, p. DI•67 • Preteach Lesson Vocabulary, p. DI•67 • Unknown Words, p. DI•70 ELL HANDBOOK • Word Cards, p. 191 • ELL Vocabulary Routine, p. 471 ELL POSTER 28 • Day 1 Activities	TEACHER'S EDITION • Basic Vocabulary, p. DI•67 • Reteach Lesson Vocabulary, p. DI•68 • Unknown Words, p. DI•70 ELL HANDBOOK • Word Cards, p. 191 • Multilingual Vocabulary List, pp. 441–442 ELL POSTER 28 • Day 2 Activities
Grammar and Conventions	TEACHER'S EDITION • Preteach Combining Sentences, p. DI•74	TEACHER'S EDITION • Teach Combining Sentences, p. DI•74
Writing	TEACHER'S EDITION • Sensory Details, p. DI•75 • Introduce Description, pp. 435e–435f	TEACHER'S EDITION • Writer's Craft: Sensory Details, pp. 445d–445e

Unit 6 Week 3 Talking Walls: Art for the People

This symbol indicates leveled instruction to address language proficiency levels.

Day 3	Day 4	Day 5
TEACHER'S EDITION • Academic Language, p. DI•66 • Concept Development, p. DI•66 • Anchored Talk, p. 446a • Concept Talk Video ELL HANDBOOK • ELL Poster Talk, Concept Talk, p. 191c ELL POSTER 28 • Day 3 Activities	TEACHER'S EDITION • Academic Language, p. DI•66 • Concept Development, p. DI•66 • Anchored Talk, p. 456a • Concept Talk Video ELL HANDBOOK • ELL Poster Talk, Concept Talk, p. 191c ELL POSTER 28 • Day 4 Activities	TEACHER'S EDITION • Academic Language, p. DI•66 • Concept Development, p. DI•66 • Concept Talk Video ELL HANDBOOK • ELL Poster Talk, Concept Talk, p. 191c ELL POSTER 28 • Day 5 Activities
ELL HANDBOOK • Phonics Transition Lesson, pp. 288, 295	ELL HANDBOOK • Phonics Transition Lesson, pp. 288, 295	TEACHER'S EDITION • Phonics and Spelling, p. DI•70
TEACHER'S EDITION • AudioText of *Talking Walls* • Concept Talk Video ELL HANDBOOK • AudioText CD Routine, p. 477	TEACHER'S EDITION • Concept Talk Video	TEACHER'S EDITION • Concept Talk Video
TEACHER'S EDITION • Sheltered Reading, p. DI•72 ELL HANDBOOK • Multilingual Summaries, pp. 193–195	TEACHER'S EDITION • ELL/ELD Reader Guided Reading, p. DI•73 ELL HANDBOOK • ELL Study Guide, p. 196	TEACHER'S EDITION • ELL/ELD Reader Guided Reading, p. DI•73 ELL HANDBOOK • ELL Study Guide, p. 196
ELL HANDBOOK • High-Frequency Words Activity Bank, p. 446 ELL POSTER 28 • Day 3 Activities	ELL HANDBOOK • High-Frequency Words Activity Bank, p. 446	TEACHER'S EDITION • Unknown Words, p. 459h ELL HANDBOOK • High-Frequency Words Activity Bank, p. 446
TEACHER'S EDITION • Grammar Jammer ELL HANDBOOK • Grammar Transition Lesson, pp. 344, 356 • Grammar Jammer Routine, p. 478	TEACHER'S EDITION • Grammar Jammer ELL HANDBOOK • Grammar Transition Lesson, pp. 344, 356	TEACHER'S EDITION • Grammar Jammer ELL HANDBOOK • Grammar Transition Lesson, pp. 344, 356
TEACHER'S EDITION • Let's Write It!, p. 454–455 • Writing Trait: Word Choice, pp. 455a–455b	TEACHER'S EDITION • Revising Strategy, pp. 459d–459e	TEACHER'S EDITION • Description, pp. 459p–459q

Poster Talk, Concept Talk

Question of the Week

Why is freedom of expression important?

Poster 28

Throughout the week, use the ELL Poster to help students produce and comprehend language, understand the concept, and build English vocabulary. Use the Question of the Week and other questions to help students share ideas in pairs, small groups, or the large group. Sample questions are shown, with examples of possible responses by students.

Weekly Concept and Language Goals

- Understand the concept of freedom of expression
- Give an example of free expression
- Discuss why freedom to express ideas is important

By the end of the lesson, students should be able to talk about and write one or more sentences about freedom of expression.

Daily Team Talk

Day 1	Day 2	Day 3	Day 4	Day 5
After Day 1 activities on Poster, ask questions such as *What is the artist in the poster picture making?*	After Day 2 activity on Poster, ask questions such as *Why does the artist in the poster picture make sculptures?*	After Day 3 activity on Poster, ask questions such as *What is the artist in the poster picture making her sculptures for?*	After Day 4 activity on Poster, ask questions such as *What idea do you think the artist is expressing with her sculptures?*	After Day 5 activity on Poster, ask questions such as *Think of a time when you used art to express your ideas or feelings. What did you make?*
Beginning Dolls. **Intermediate** She is making dolls. **Advanced** The artist is making sculptures of children. **Advanced High** The artist is making sculptures of children from different cultures.	**Beginning** She likes them. **Intermediate** She has ideas for them. **Advanced** The artist shares her ideas by making sculptures. **Advanced High** The artist makes sculptures because that is how she expresses and shares her ideas.	**Beginning** The library. **Intermediate** She is making them for the library. **Advanced** The artist is making the sculptures to put in her city's library. **Advanced High** The artist is making the sculptures for her community. She will put them in the local library.	**Beginning** People can live together. **Intermediate** Different people can live together in one place. **Advanced** The children are all different from one another. People from different places live together in the city. **Advanced High** The sculptures show children from different cultures standing together. The artist wants people from different countries to feel welcome in her community.	**Beginning** I made a picture. **Intermediate** I made a drawing of my family. **Advanced** I drew a picture of my family at my grandma's. **Advanced High** I drew a picture of all my relatives at my grandma's house. I wanted to remember that special time.

This Week's Materials

Teacher's Edition pages 430j–459q

See the support for English language learners throughout the lesson, including ELL strategies and scaffolded activities at points of use.

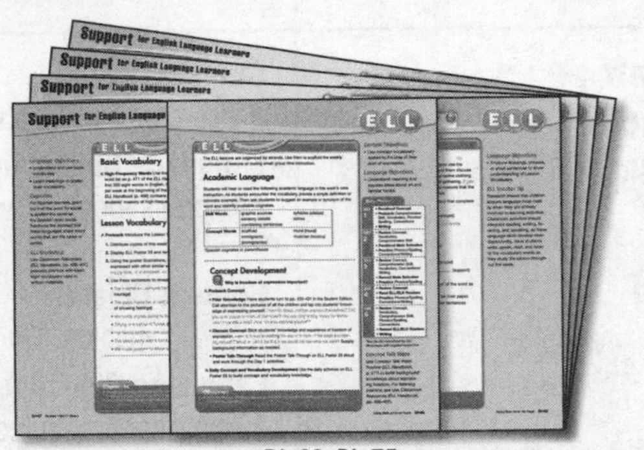

Teacher's Edition pages DI•66–DI•75

Differentiated Instruction for English language learners provides daily group activities that "frontload," or preteach, core instruction.

ELL Handbook pp. 191a–196

Find additional lesson materials that support the core lesson and the ELL instructional pages.

Poster 28

ELL Reader 3.6.3

ELD Reader 3.6.3

Concept Literacy Reader

ELD, ELL Reader Teaching Guide

Concept Literacy Reader Teaching Guide

Technology

Online Teacher's Edition Use the digital version of the core Teacher's Edition for planning and instruction.

eReaders
This week's ELL and ELD Readers and Concept Literacy Reader are also available in digital format.

This Week's Content and Language Objectives by Strand

Concept Development/ Academic Language Why is freedom of expression important?	**Content Objective** • Use concept vocabulary related to the idea of freedom of expression. **Language Objective** • Express ideas in response to art and discussion.
Phonics and Spelling Final Syllables *–tion, -ture, -ive, -ize*	**Content Objective** • Final syllables *-tion, -ion, -ture, -ive,* and *-ize.* **Language Objective** • Apply spelling rules with final syllables *–tion, -ture, -ive,* and *-ize.*
Listening Comprehension Modified Read Aloud: "Not All Artists Are the Same"	**Content Objective** • Monitor and adjust oral comprehension. **Language Objectives** • Discuss oral passages. • Use a graphic organizer to take notes.
Reading Comprehension Graphic Sources	**Content Objectives** • Distinguish information presented in graphic sources. • Gather information from graphic sources. **Language Objectives** • Discuss information in a graphic source. • Explain the content of a graphic source.
Vocabulary Basic and Lesson Vocabulary	**Language Objectives** • Internalize, expand use basic vocabulary. • Learn meanings of grade-level vocabulary. • Produce drawings, phrases, and short sentences to show understanding of Lesson Vocabulary.
Vocabulary Unknown Words	**Content Objective** • Determine the meanings of unknown words. **Language Objective** • Use a dictionary to determine the meanings of unknown words.
Grammar and Conventions Combining Sentences	**Content Objective** • Combine sentences accurately. **Language Objectives** • Speak in complete sentences. • Write sentences with a plural subject or predicate.
Writing Sensory Details	**Content Objective** • Identify sensory details in reading materials. **Language Objectives** • Write paragraphs using sensory details. • Share feedback for editing and revising.

Word Cards for Vocabulary Activities

encourages	**expression**
local	**native**
settled	**social**
support	

Teacher Note: Beginning Teach two to three words. **Intermediate** Teach three to four words. **Advanced** Teach four to five words. **Advanced High** Teach all words.

Name ______________________________

Picture It!
Graphic Sources

Read the paragraph. **Look** at the map.

- Use the information in the paragraph to **label** the map.

Mexican Muralists

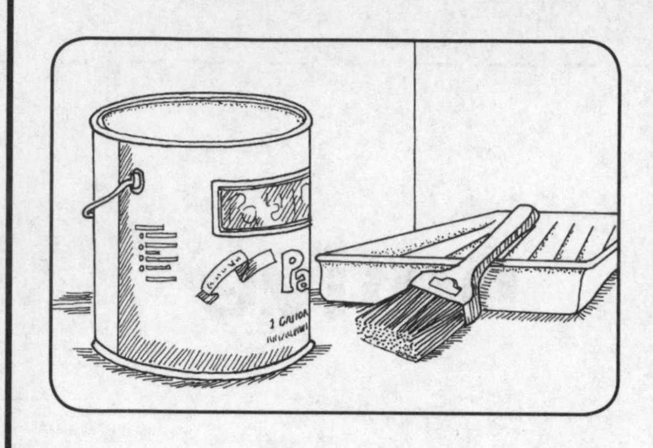

Many Mexican artists painted murals in the United States. José Clemente Orozco painted murals at Dartmouth College in New Hampshire. It took him two years to paint them. Diego Rivera created murals all over the United States. He painted a famous mural in Detroit, Michigan. David Alfara Siqueiros traveled all over the world. He painted murals and other works of art. Siqueiros spent just six months in Los Angeles, California. In that time he painted three murals.

Write the name of the artist by the city where his mural is located.

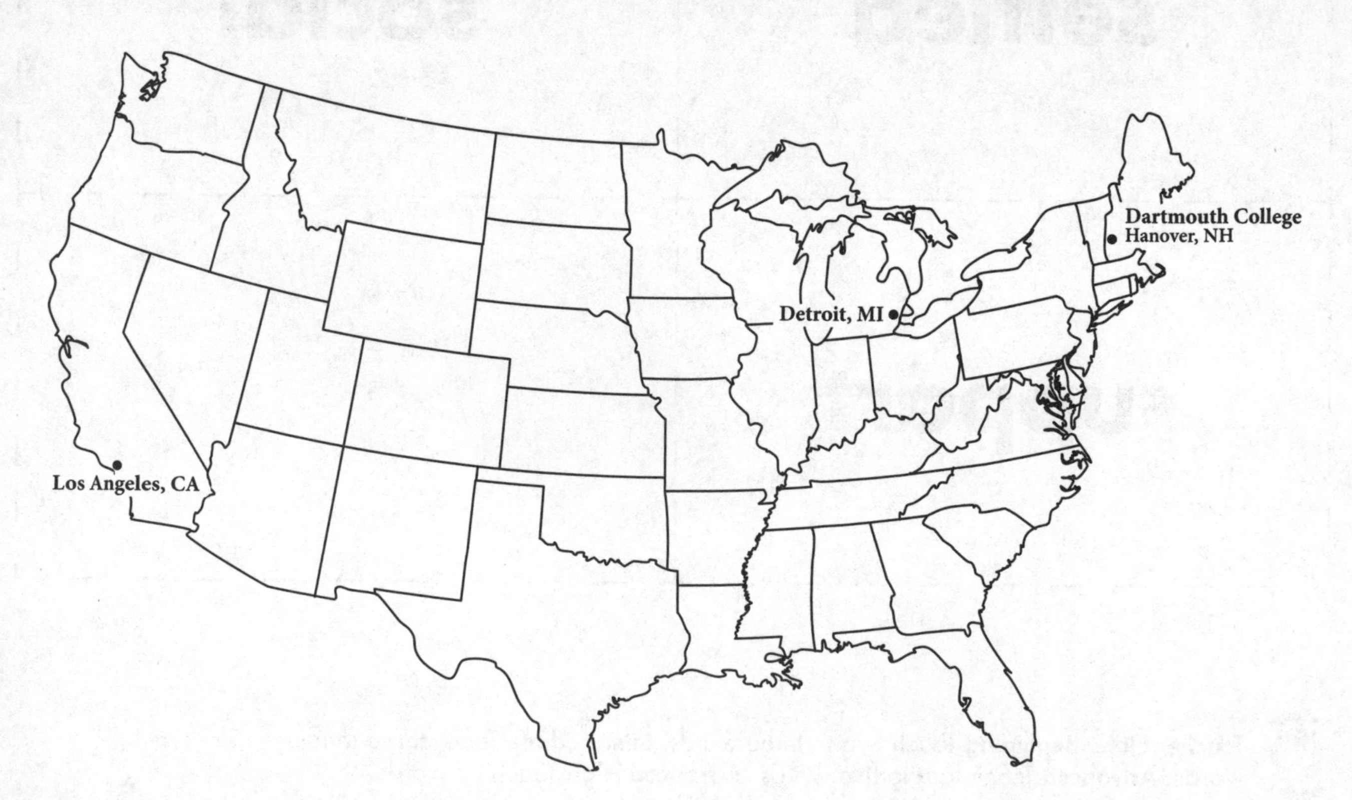

Graphic Sources

Use this lesson to supplement or replace the skill lesson on page 434a of the Teacher's Edition. Display the Skill Points (at right) and share them with students.

Teach/Model

Beginning Display a map of the United States. Ask: *What information does this graphic source tell us?* (the locations of cities, states, mountains, lakes, rivers, etc.) Ask students to tell about a time they or someone they know used a map.

Intermediate Display an illustration of hieroglyphics in a children's encyclopedia. Read the description of the hieroglyphics. Ask: *How does this illustration help you understand the text?* Discuss how the illustration makes the information easier to see and understand.

Advanced Display a graph or chart from a newspaper. Discuss with students what kind of information the graphic source tells them. Ask: *How does the title help you to know what information is in this graph (chart)?* Have students write a sentence that tells something they learned from the graphic source.

Advanced High Read aloud several states' populations from a current almanac. Ask students how a graphic source could help them better understand the information. Write the information on the board. Pair students and have partners show the information in an appropriate graphic source.

Then distribute copies of Picture It! page 192.

- Have students look at the picture and tell what they know about painting murals.
- Read the paragraph aloud. Ask: *What graphic sources go with the paragraph?* (picture, map)
- Review the Skill Points with students.
- Ask: *What other graphic sources could go with the paragraph?* (photos of the murals, photos of the artists)

Skill Points

✔ **Graphic sources** are charts, photos, illustrations, diagrams, and graphs that help you understand information in the text.

✔ A **caption** is text that explains a graphic source. A caption appears near the graphic source it explains.

Practice

Read aloud the directions on page 192. Reread the paragraph aloud. Then have students use the paragraph as they label the map. Remind them they can use the names in the paragraph as models for their writing.

Beginning Students can point to each city on the map and say what they want to write for each label before writing the artists' names. Provide help with labeling and writing.

Intermediate Students can first orally say the names of the cities and the artists and then write the artists' names by the cities' names.

Advanced Students can write their labels and then check them by comparing them with a partner's labels.

Advanced High Students can write their labels and then orally explain how adding labels to the map makes the paragraph easier to understand.

Answers for page 192: Students should correctly label the map: Orozco/Hanover, New Hampshire; Rivera/Detroit, Michigan; Siqueiros/Los Angeles, California

Multilingual Summaries

English

Talking Walls: Art for the People

Muralists are artists who paint on walls. Muralists can create works of art on buildings. Hector Ponce is a muralist. His mural is entitled *Immigrant*. The mural celebrates the hard work of American immigrants.

Joshua Sarantitis is also a muralist. He has painted a mural called *Reach High and You Will Go Far*. The mural shows a girl reaching toward the sky. Sarantitis wants the mural to inspire children.

Another mural that is meant to inspire school children is Paul Botello's *A Shared Hope*. It shows students, teachers, and parents working together to help children learn.

David Botello and Wayne Healy have their own mural company. They made their first mural together in third grade! David has a mural called *Dreams of Flight*. David hopes that the mural will encourage children to dream.

These and other murals inspire, teach, and tell stories.

Spanish

Paredes que hablan

Los muralistas son artistas que pintan en las paredes. Los muralistas pueden crear obras de arte en los edificios. Héctor Ponce es un muralista. Su mural se llama *Inmigrante*. El mural celebra el duro trabajo de los inmigrantes norteamericanos.

Joshua Sarantitis también es muralista. Pintó un mural llamado *Aspira alto y llegarás lejos*. El mural muestra a una niña alcanzando el cielo. Sarantitis quiere que el mural inspire a los niños.

Otro mural que desea inspirar a los niños es el de Paul Botello, *Una esperanza compartida*. Muestra a estudiantes, maestros y padres trabajando juntos para que los niños aprendan.

David Botello y Wayne Healy tienen su propia compañía de murales. ¡Ellos hicieron su primer mural juntos en tercer grado! David tiene un mural llamado *Sueños voladores*. David tiene la esperanza de que el mural anime a los niños a soñar.

Estos y otros murales inspiran, enseñan y cuentan historias.

Multilingual Summaries

Chinese

有意義的壁畫藝術

壁畫家是指在牆上畫畫的藝術家，他們創作的藝術讓房子變得非常漂亮。赫克托。龐塞就是一個壁畫家，他畫了一幅名叫“移民”的壁畫，歌頌辛勤工作的美國移民。

約書亞。薩拉提提斯也是一位壁畫家，他的壁畫名叫“站得高看得遠”，說的是一個小女孩夢想著碰到天空，薩拉提提斯希望用他的畫激發孩子們的大膽想像力。

保羅。博特略也用壁畫來鼓勵學生，他創作的“分享希望”講的是孩子們在老師和家長的幫助下不斷成長的故事。

大衛。博特略與韋恩。希利有自己的壁畫公司，三年級時他們就一起創作了兩人的第一幅壁畫！大衛有一幅畫名叫“飛行之夢”，鼓勵孩子們要擁有自己的夢想。

在全國各地有許多壁畫，它們不僅講述故事，還能給我們各種啟迪。

Vietnamese

Các Bức Tường Biết Nói Nghệ Thuật Cho Công Chúng

Những nhà họa sĩ tranh tường là những họa sĩ vẽ tranh trên các bức tường. Các họa sĩ tranh tường có thể sáng tạo những tác phẩm nghệ thuật trên các tòa nhà. Hector Ponce là một họa sĩ tranh tường. Bức tranh tường của ông với nhan đề “Người Di Dân”. Bức tranh này ca ngợi sự cần cù của những người di dân đến Hoa Kỳ.

Joshua Sarantitis cũng là một họa sĩ tranh tường. Ông đã vẽ một bức tranh tường gọi là “Hãy Vươn Cao và Bạn Sẽ Tiến Xa.” Bức tranh tường này có hình một em gái vươn đến bầu trời. Sarantitis muốn bức tranh tường này thôi thúc trẻ em.

Một bức tranh tường khác có ý thôi thúc các em học sinh là của Paul Botello “San Sẻ Hy Vọng.” Tranh này cho thấy học sinh, giáo viên và phụ huynh cùng hợp tác để giúp các em học tập.

David Botello và Wayne Healy có công ty vẽ tranh tường của riêng họ. Họ đã cùng nhau làm ra một bức tranh tường khi còn học lớp ba! David có một bức tranh tường được gọi là “Giấc Mơ Bay.” David hy vọng rằng bức tranh này sẽ khuyến khích các em nhỏ biết ước mơ.

Những bức tranh này và những bức tranh tường khác trên toàn quốc đều để thôi thúc, dạy dỗ, và kể chuyện.

Multilingual Summaries

Korean

말하는 벽
사람들을 위한 예술

벽화가란 벽에 그림을 그리는 예술가를 말한다. 벽화가는 건물 벽에 예술 작품을 창조할 수 있다. 헥터 폰스는 벽화가다. 그의 벽화에는 '이민자' 라는 제목이 붙어 있는데 이것은 미국에 온 이민자들의 고된 노동을 기념하고 있다.

조슈아 사란티티스 또한 벽화가다. 그는 '높은 곳에 다다르면 더 멀리 갈 수 있다' 라는 벽화를 그렸는데 거기엔 하늘에 가까이 닿으려는 한 소녀가 그려져 있다. 사란티티스는 그 벽화가 어린이들에게 영감을 주기를 바란다.

폴 보텔로의 '희망 나누기' 라는 벽화 또한 학교에 다니는 어린이들에게 영감을 심어주려는 목적을 가지고 있다. 이 벽화에는 학생들과 교사들, 그리고 부모들이 함께 어린이들의 공부를 돕는 모습이 그려져 있다.

데이비드 보텔로와 웨인 힐리는 자신들만의 벽화 회사를 세웠다. 그들은 3학년 때 처음으로 함께 벽화를 그렸다. 데이비드에게는 '비행의 꿈' 이라는 벽화가 있는데 그는 이 벽화가 어린이들이 꿈을 가질 수 있도록 격려해주기를 바란다.

전국 곳곳에 있는 이러한 벽화들은 영감과 가르침을 주며 우리에게 많은 이야기를 해준다.

Hmong

School + Home

Phab Ntsa Hais Lus
Pleev Duab rau Pejxeem

Muralist yog tus kws pleev duab uas pleev duab loj ntawm phab ntsa. Muralist pleev taus duab ntawm tej tsev lab luam siab siab. Hector Ponce yog ib tug muralist. Nws li duab pleev loj hu ua "Neeg Thoj Nam." Duab pleev loj no ua kom nco txog neeg thoj nam Amelikas kev ua haujlwm hnyav.

Joshua Sarantitis kuj yog ib tug muralist. Nws pleev duab loj hu ua "Tsa Tes Siab thiab Yus Mus Tau Deb Kiag." Duab pleev loj no muaj ib tus hluas nkauj tsa tes rau saum ntuj. Sarantis xav kom Duab pleev loj no yuav ua rau cov menyuam muaj siab loj.

Ib lwm duab pleev loj uas raug pleev kom cov menyuam kawm ntawv muaj siab loj yog Paul Botello duab pleev hu ua "Sib Faib Kev Cia Siab." Nws muaj cov kawm ntawv, cov nai khu, thiab cov niamtxiv ua haujlwm ua ke pab cov menyuam kawm tau ntawv.

David Botello thiab Wayne Healy muaj ib lab luam pleev duab loj. Nkawd pleev duab loj ua ke xub thawj thaum nyob hoob kawm peb. David muaj duab pleev hu ua "Zaj NpauSuav txog Kev Ya." David cia siab hais tias duab pleev no yuav yaum kom cov menyuam muaj ib zaj npausuav tso siab rau.

Cov no thiab lwm cov duab pleev loj nyob thoob tebchaws no deev siab deev ntsws, pab kawm, thiab qhia dab neeg.

The Wall of Names

Name ______________________________

- **Read** *The Wall of Names* again.
- **Add** information about the Vietnam Veterans Memorial.

Who?	Maya Lin
What?	
When?	
Where?	
Why?	

Family Link

Ask family members what they know about the Vietnam Veterans Memorial.

Weekly Resources Guide for English Language Learner Support

For this week's content and language objectives, see p. 197e.

Instructional Strand	Day 1	Day 2
Concept Development/Academic Language	TEACHER'S EDITION • Academic Language, p. DI•91 • Concept Development, p. DI•91 • Anchored Talk, pp. 460j—460–461 • Preteach Academic Vocabulary, p. 465a • Concept Talk Video ELL HANDBOOK • Hear It, See It, Say It, Use It, pp. xxxvi–xxxvii • ELL Poster Talk, Concept Talk, p. 197c ELL POSTER 29 • Day 1 Activities	TEACHER'S EDITION • Academic Language, p. DI•91 • Concept Development, p. DI•91 • Anchored Talk, p. 466a • Concept Talk Video ELL HANDBOOK • ELL Poster Talk, Concept Talk, p. 197c • Concept Talk Video Routine, p. 477 ELL POSTER 29 • Day 2 Activities
Phonics and Spelling	TEACHER'S EDITION • Phonics and Spelling, p. DI•95 • Decodable Practice Reader 29A, pp. 463a–463b	TEACHER'S EDITION • Phonics and Spelling, p. DI•95
Listening Comprehension	TEACHER'S EDITION • Modified Read Aloud, p. DI•94 • Read Aloud, p. 461b • Concept Talk Video ELL HANDBOOK • Concept Talk Video Routine, p. 477	TEACHER'S EDITION • Modified Read Aloud, p. DI•94 • AudioText of *Two Bad Ants* • Concept Talk Video ELL HANDBOOK • AudioText CD Routine, p. 477 • Story Map A, p. 483
Reading Comprehension	TEACHER'S EDITION • Preteach Plot and Theme, p. DI•96	TEACHER'S EDITION • Reteach Plot and Theme, p. DI•96 • Frontloading Reading, p. DI•97 ELL HANDBOOK • Picture It! Skill Instruction, pp. 198–198a • Multilingual Summaries, pp. 199–201
Vocabulary **Basic and Lesson Vocabulary** **Vocabulary Skill: Prefixes and Suffixes**	TEACHER'S EDITION • Basic Vocabulary, p. DI•92 • Preteach Lesson Vocabulary, p. DI•92 • Prefixes and Suffixes, p. DI•95 ELL HANDBOOK • Word Cards, p. 197 • ELL Vocabulary Routine, p. 471 ELL POSTER 29 • Day 1 Activities	TEACHER'S EDITION • Basic Vocabulary, p. DI•92 • Reteach Lesson Vocabulary, p. DI•93 • Prefixes and Suffixes, p. DI•95 ELL HANDBOOK • Word Cards, p. 197 • Multilingual Vocabulary List, p. 442 ELL POSTER 29 • Day 2 Activities
Grammar and Conventions	TEACHER'S EDITION • Preteach Commas, p. DI•99	TEACHER'S EDITION • Reteach Commas, p. DI•99
Writing	TEACHER'S EDITION • Writing Dialogue, p. DI•100 • Introduce Comic Book, pp. 465e–465f	TEACHER'S EDITION • Comic Book, pp. 477d–477e

Leveled Support: This symbol indicates leveled instruction to address language proficiency levels.

Day 3	Day 4	Day 5
TEACHER'S EDITION • Academic Language, p. DI•91 • Concept Development, p. DI•91 • Anchored Talk, p. 478a • Concept Talk Video ELL HANDBOOK • ELL Poster Talk, Concept Talk, p. 197c ELL POSTER 29 • Day 3 Activities	TEACHER'S EDITION • Academic Language, p. DI•91 • Concept Development, p. DI•91 • Anchored Talk, p. 490a • Concept Talk Video ELL HANDBOOK • ELL Poster Talk, Concept Talk, p. 197c ELL POSTER 29 • Day 4 Activities	TEACHER'S EDITION • Academic Language, p. DI•91 • Concept Development, p. DI•91 • Concept Talk Video ELL HANDBOOK • ELL Poster Talk, Concept Talk, p. 197c ELL POSTER 29 • Day 5 Activities
ELL HANDBOOK • Phonics Transition Lesson, pp. 285, 292	ELL HANDBOOK • Phonics Transition Lesson, pp. 285, 292	TEACHER'S EDITION • Phonics and Spelling, p. DI•95
TEACHER'S EDITION • AudioText of *Two Bad Ants* • Concept Talk Video ELL HANDBOOK • AudioText CD Routine, p. 477	TEACHER'S EDITION • Concept Talk Video	TEACHER'S EDITION • Concept Talk Video
TEACHER'S EDITION • Sheltered Reading, p. DI•97 ELL HANDBOOK • Multilingual Summaries, pp. 199–201	TEACHER'S EDITION • ELL/ELD Reader Guided Reading, p. DI•98 ELL HANDBOOK • ELL Study Guide, p. 202	TEACHER'S EDITION • ELL/ELD Reader Guided Reading, p. DI•98 ELL HANDBOOK • ELL Study Guide, p. 202
ELL HANDBOOK • High-Frequency Words Activity Bank, p. 446 ELL POSTER 29 • Day 3 Activities	ELL HANDBOOK • High-Frequency Words Activity Bank, p. 446	TEACHER'S EDITION • Prefixes and Suffixes, p. 493h ELL HANDBOOK • High-Frequency Words Activity Bank, p. 446
TEACHER'S EDITION • Grammar Jammer ELL HANDBOOK • Grammar Transition Lesson, pp. 346, 359 • Grammar Jammer Routine, p. 478	TEACHER'S EDITION • Grammar Jammer ELL HANDBOOK • Grammar Transition Lesson, pp. 346, 359	TEACHER'S EDITION • Grammar Jammer ELL HANDBOOK • Grammar Transition Lesson, pp. 346, 359
TEACHER'S EDITION • Let's Write It!, p. 488–489 • Writer's Craft: Dialogue, pp. 489a–489b	TEACHER'S EDITION • Revising Strategy, pp. 493d–493e	TEACHER'S EDITION • Comic Book, pp. 493p–493q

Poster Talk, Concept Talk

Question of the Week

Why are rules and laws important to freedom?

Poster 29

Throughout the week, use the ELL Poster to help students produce and comprehend language, understand the concept, and build English vocabulary. Use the Question of the Week and other questions to help students share ideas in pairs, small groups, or the large group. Sample questions are shown, with examples of possible responses by students.

Weekly Concept and Language Goals

- Explain why we have rules and laws
- Name some rules and laws
- Share reasons why rules and laws are important

By the end of the lesson, students should be able to talk about and write one or more sentences about rules and laws.

Daily Team Talk

Day 1	Day 2	Day 3	Day 4	Day 5
After Day 1 activities on Poster, ask questions such as *What rules and laws do you think the park in the poster picture has?*	After Day 2 activity on Poster, ask questions such as *Do you think the girl and her father are following the park's rules and laws? How can you tell?*	After Day 3 activity on Poster, ask questions such as *Why is it important for the girl and her father to follow the park's rules and laws?*	After Day 4 activity on Poster, ask questions such as *What could happen if the girl and her father do not follow the park's rules and laws?*	After Day 5 activity on Poster, ask questions such as *What rules and laws does our school have for the playground?*
Beginning Do not litter. **Intermediate** Do not litter and keep on the path. **Advanced** People cannot litter. They should stay on the trails. **Advanced High** People should not leave litter on the ground. They should stay on the trails and leave the park before it closes.	**Beginning** Yes. **Intermediate** Yes. They are staying on the path. **Advanced** Yes. They are staying on the trails, and they do not leave the mitten. **Advanced High** Yes, they are following the park's rules and laws. They do not leave the trails, and they go back to find the mitten so they do not leave it on the ground.	**Beginning** To be safe. **Intermediate** They will keep them safe. **Advanced** The rules and laws will keep them safe and keep the park clean. **Advanced High** The rules and laws help keep people safe and make sure the park stays clean so everyone can enjoy it.	**Beginning** They get lost. **Intermediate** They can get lost if they leave the path. **Advanced** If the girl and her father do not stay on the path, they could get lost. **Advanced High** If the girl and her father wander off the trails or if they stay after the park closes and it gets dark, they could get lost.	**Beginning** Be nice. **Intermediate** Stay on the playground, and take turns. **Advanced** We are supposed to play with others and go in when the bell rings. **Advanced High** The rules say stay on the playground, be safe, and give everyone a turn.

This Week's Materials

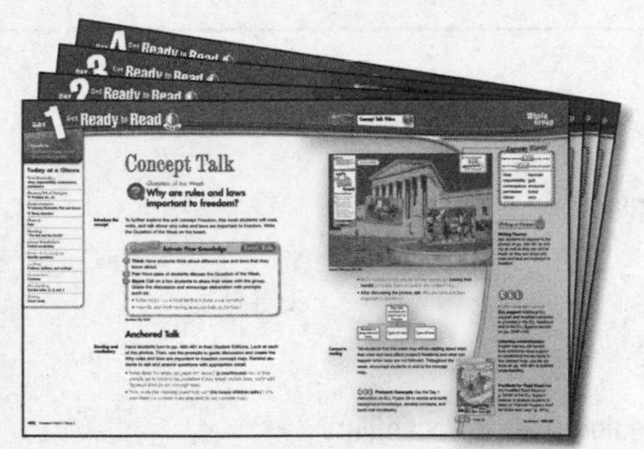
Teacher's Edition pages 460j–493q

See the support for English language learners throughout the lesson, including ELL strategies and scaffolded activities at points of use.

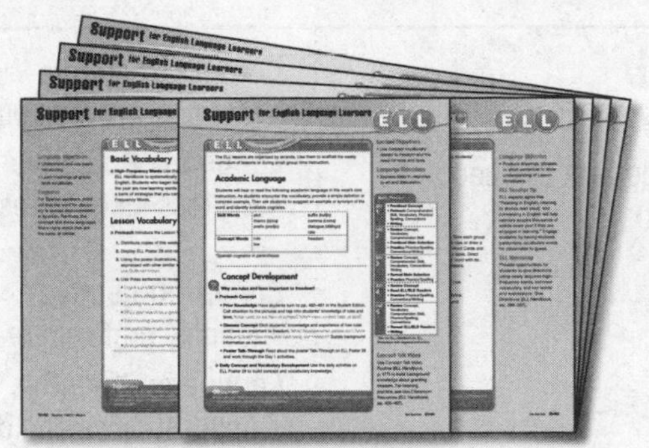
Teacher's Edition pages DI•91–DI•100

Differentiated Instruction for English language learners provides daily group activities that "frontload," or preteach, core instruction.

ELL Handbook pp. 197a–202

Find additional lesson materials that support the core lesson and the ELL instructional pages.

ELL Poster 29

ELL Reader 3.6.4

ELD Reader 3.6.4

Concept Literacy Reader

ELD, ELL Reader Teaching Guide

Concept Literacy Reader Teaching Guide

Technology

Online Teacher's Edition Use the digital version of the core Teacher's Edition for planning and instruction.

eReaders
This week's ELL and ELD Readers and Concept Literacy Reader are also available in digital format.

This Week's Content and Language Objectives by Strand

Concept Development/ Academic Language Why are rules and laws important to freedom?	**Content Objective** • Use concept vocabulary related to freedom, rules, and laws. **Language Objective** • Express ideas in response to art and discussion.
Phonics and Spelling Prefixes *im-* and *in-*	**Content Objective** • Identify prefixes *im-* and *in-*. **Language Objective** • Apply phonics and decoding skills to vocabulary.
Listening Comprehension Modified Read Aloud: "Hannah's List of Rules and Laws"	**Content Objective** • Monitor and adjust oral comprehension. **Language Objectives** • Discuss oral passages. • Use a graphic organizer to take notes.
Reading Comprehension Plot and Theme	**Content Objectives** • Define the terms plot and theme. • Identify the plot and theme of the story. **Language Objectives** • Learn and use academic language to summarize the plot of the story. • Read grade-level text at a smooth conversational rate.
Vocabulary Basic and Lesson Vocabulary	**Language Objectives** • Understand and use basic and grade-level vocabulary. • Learn meanings of grade-level vocabulary. • Produce drawings, phrases, and short sentences to show understanding of Lesson Vocabulary.
Vocabulary Prefixes and Suffixes	**Content Objective** • Identify prefixes and suffixes in word structure. **Language Objective** • Discuss prefixes and suffixes in word structure.
Grammar and Conventions Commas	**Content Objectives** • Identify commas. • Correctly use commas in dates and in a series. **Language Objective** • Write sentences with commas in a series and in dates.
Writing Writing Dialogue	**Content Objective** • Identify dialogue in written selections. **Language Objectives** • Write dialogue using quotation marks and speaker tags. • Share feedback for editing and revising.

Word Cards for Vocabulary Activities

crystal	**disappeared**
discovery	**goal**
journey	**joyful**
scoop	**unaware**

Teacher Note: Beginning Teach three to four words. **Intermediate** Teach four to six words. **Advanced** Teach six to seven words. **Advanced High** Teach all words.

Name ______________________________

Look at the pictures. **Read** the story. **Write** the important things that happen in the beginning, in the middle, and at the end of the story.

Ant Adventure

Two ants came to a river. "It's too deep to cross here," said Artie.

"I will climb the grass and look for a shallow place," said Andy.

"Oh, no!" Andy cried. Then he saw where he was falling.

"Sometimes the solution to a problem comes in an unexpected way," said Artie.

Beginning

Middle

End

Plot and Theme

Use this lesson to supplement or replace the skill lesson on page 464a of the Teacher's Edition. Display the Skill Points (at right) and share them with students.

Skill Points

✔ The **plot** is the series of important events that happen in the beginning, middle, and end of a story.

✔ The big idea of a story is called the **theme.** Ask yourself: *What does the author want me to learn from this story?* Sometimes the theme is a lesson or moral.

Teach/Model

Review the fable "The Ant and the Grasshopper."

Beginning Ask: *What happens in the beginning, middle, and end of "The Ant and the Grasshopper"?* When students are finished, say: *This is the plot of the story. What lesson does the story teach readers?* (Possible answer: Don't put off until tomorrow what you should do today.) *This is the lesson or moral of the story. It is also the story's theme.*

Intermediate Ask students to draw three pictures that show the beginning, middle, and end of the plot of "The Ant and the Grasshopper" and write a sentence about each picture. Together decide what the big idea, or theme, of the story is.

Advanced Have students write sentences that tell the plot of "The Ant and the Grasshopper." Ask: *What is the theme of the story?* (Possible answer: Prepare today for things you will need tomorrow.) *How can we apply this lesson to our lives?*

Advanced High Together think of a theme. For example: If at first you don't succeed, try again. Make up a story based on the big idea. Have students write sentences that tell what happens in the beginning, middle, and end of the story's plot.

Then distribute copies of Picture It! page 198.

- Have students look at the pictures and tell what is happening.
- Read the story aloud. Ask: *Who are the characters in this story?*
- Review the Skill Points with students.
- Ask: *What happens in the story? What lesson do the ants learn?* (The solution to a problem can come in an unexpected way.) *This is the moral, or theme, of the story.*

Practice

Read aloud the directions on page 198. Have students take turns rereading the story with a partner. Then have them use the pictures and the story as they fill in the graphic organizer.

Beginning Students can say what they want to write for the beginning, middle, and end of the story before writing their ideas in the boxes. Provide help with English words and writing.

Intermediate Students can first orally respond and then write sentences about the plot in the boxes. Provide help with writing.

Advanced Students can write their answers in the boxes and then check them by discussing the story's plot and theme with a partner.

Advanced High Students can write their answers in the boxes and then orally tell about the story's theme and explain how the story shows that theme.

Answers for page 198: *Beginning:* The ants cannot cross the river. *Middle:* Andy Ant climbs a blade of grass, and it bends over the river. *End:* The ants can both cross the river safely.

Multilingual Summaries

English

Two Bad Ants

An ant brought a sugar crystal to the queen. She ate it all. She wanted more. The first ant led the ants on a long march. They reached what seemed to be a mountain. It was the side of a house. They climbed the wall and went through a kitchen window. They found the sugar bowl. Each ant took a crystal and began to march home.

Two ants stayed behind. These two bad ants wanted more sugar. A big spoon scooped them into a cup of hot coffee. The spoon stirred them around and around. Then they crawled onto a piece of bread. The bread was in a hot toaster. Then they crawled down the sink drain. They were almost washed down the drain.

The other ants came back for more sugar crystals. The two bad ants joined the line of ants. They each picked up a crystal and marched home.

Spanish

Dos hormigas traviesas

Una hormiga le llevó a la reina un cristal de azúcar. La reina se lo comió todo y quería más. La primera hormiga condujo a las otras en una larga caminata. Llegaron a lo que parecía ser una montaña. En realidad era la pared de una casa. Subieron por la pared y entraron por la ventana de la cocina. Allí encontraron la azucarera. Cada hormiga agarró un cristal de azúcar y se fue de regreso a casa.

Dos hormigas se quedaron atrás. Estas dos hormigas traviesas querían más azúcar. De repente, una cuchara las metió en una taza de café caliente. La cuchara les dio vueltas y vueltas. Luego las hormigas se arrastraron hasta un pedazo de pan. El pan estaba en la tostadora caliente. Después, se arrastraron hasta el desagüe del fregadero. Casi se fueron para abajo por él.

Las otras hormigas regresaron por más cristales de azúcar. Las dos hormigas traviesas se unieron a la fila de hormigas. Cada una agarró un cristal y regresaron a casa.

Multilingual Summaries

Chinese

兩隻壞螞蟻

有一隻螞蟻偷了一粒糖給蟻后。蟻后一下子就吃光了，而且還想吃。于是蟻后就命令偷糖的螞蟻領著大家再去找。他們走過很長的路，來到山一樣高的地方，那是一堵墻。他們悄悄爬上去，溜進厨房的窗戶，找到了放糖的碗。每只螞蟻都偷一粒糖背回家。

兩隻壞螞蟻走在最後，這兩個傢夥還想要多拿。忽然一把大調羹伸過來，把他們舀進熱咖啡，攪得他們天旋地轉。好不容易爬上一塊麵包，却被放進了烤箱。他們爬進排水管，又差點讓水沖進臭水溝。

螞蟻們第二次來偷糖了。那兩隻壞螞蟻趕緊混入隊伍，每只螞蟻背一粒，溜回家了。

Vietnamese

Hai Con Kiến Hư

Một con kiến mang một hạt đường đến kiến chúa. Kiến chúa ăn hết. Kiến chúa muốn ăn thêm. Con kiến đầu tiên dẫn đầu đàn kiến đi thành một hàng dài. Chúng đến một nơi trông giống như một ngọn núi. Đó là vách bên hông của một ngôi nhà. Chúng leo lên tường và đi qua cửa sổ nhà bếp. Chúng tìm gặp hủ đường. Mỗi con kiến lấy một hạt đường và bắt đầu đi về ổ.

Có hai con kiến ở lại. Hai con kiến hư này muốn có thêm đường. Một chiếc thìa to múc đổ chúng vào một tách cà phê nóng. Chiếc thìa quậy chúng quanh tròn. Rồi chúng bò ra lên trên miếng bánh mì. Miếng bánh mì đang ở trong lò nướng bánh nóng. Rồi chúng bò xuống lỗ thoát nước của bồn rửa chén. Chúng suýt bị dội xuống rãnh.

Các con kiến khác trở lại để lấy thêm đường. Hai con kiến hư này gia nhập vào hàng kiến. Mỗi con nhặt một hạt đường và đi về ổ.

Multilingual Summaries

Korean

나쁜 개미 두 마리

한 개미가 여왕개미에게 설탕 한 덩이를 가져다 준다. 여왕개미는 설탕을 다 먹은 후 더 먹고 싶어한다. 첫 번째 개미가 다른 개미들을 이끌고 긴 행렬에 나선다. 그들은 산처럼 보이는 곳에 도착했는데 그곳은 어느 집의 측면이었다. 그들은 벽을 기어 올라 부엌 창문을 통해 들어간다. 그리고 그곳에서 설탕 그릇을 발견하고는 설탕 한 덩이씩을 들고 집으로 행진해 간다.

두 개미가 뒤에 남아있었다. 이 두 나쁜 개미는 좀 더 많은 설탕을 갖고 싶어한다. 그 때 커다란 숟가락 하나가 그들을 떠내어 뜨거운 커피 잔 안에 넣는다. 숟가락은 개미들을 계속 휘저었다. 그리고 나서 그들은 빵 조각 위로 기어갔는데 그 빵은 뜨거운 토스터기 안에 있었다. 이번에는 싱크대 배수구로 기어 내려가는데 그들은 거기서 거의 배수구 아래로 쓸려 내려갈 뻔 한다.

다른 개미들이 설탕 덩어리를 더 가져가려고 돌아온다. 그 두 나쁜 개미들은 개미들의 행렬에 합류했고 그들 각각은 설탕 덩어리를 하나씩 들고 집으로 행진해간다.

Hmong

Ob Tug Ntsaum Phem

Ib tug ntsaum nqa tau ib lub piam thaj los rau tus ntsaum poj noj. Nws muab noj tag lawm. Nws xav noj ntxiv. Thawj tug ntsaum coj cov ntsaum kev mus deb deb kawg. Lawm mus txog ib qhov chaw uas ntxim li ib lub ntsoob. Nws yog ib sab tsev. Lawv nce lub phab ntsa rau saum lub qhov tsai ces nqag qhov ntsai rau hauv lawm. Lawv nrhiav pom lub tais piam thaj. Lawv ib leeg nqa ib lub piam thaj ces rov thaum kev mus tsev.

Ob tug ntsaum nyob tau qab. Ob tug ntawd xav tau piam thaj ntau tshaj. Ib tsab diav loj loj cia li los daus tau nkawv coj mus do hauv ib lub khob kasfes (coffee). Tsab diav muab nkawv nto nto nto. Ces nkawd ho nkag mus rau saum ib daim khob qij. Luag muab daim khob qij ntawd ci hauv qhov cub. Ces nkawd nkag mus rau hauv lub qhov dej ntawm lub dab ntxuav tais. Nkawd yuav luag tsaug ntxuav mus rau puag hauv lub qhov dej.

Lwm cov ntsaum tsov qab los nqa piam thaj ntxiv. Ob tug ntsaum phem ntawd thiaj li rov qab mus koom nrog lawv. Lawv ib leeg nqa ib lub piam thaj thiab rov mus tsev lawm.

Study Guide

Name ______________________________

The Story of Our Freedom

- **Read** *The Story of Our Freedom* again.
- Use the information in the book to **answer** the questions below.

pages 2–3

1. What are two freedoms that we have?

____

____

pages 4–5

2. Who protects our rights?

____

pages 6–7

3. When was the Declaration of Independence signed?

____

pages 8–9

4. What is a constitution?

____

pages 10–12

5. Why did our leaders want to protect our rights?

____

Family Link

Have family members talk about why we celebrate the Fourth of July.

Weekly Resources Guide for English Language Learner Support

For this week's content and language objectives, see p. 203e.

Instructional Strand	Day 1	Day 2
Concept Development/Academic Language	TEACHER'S EDITION • Academic Language, p. DI•116 • Concept Development, p. DI•116 • Anchored Talk, pp. 494j—494–495 • Preteach Academic Vocabulary, p. 499a • Concept Talk Video ELL HANDBOOK • Hear It, See It, Say It, Use It, pp. xxxvi–xxxvii • ELL Poster Talk, Concept Talk, p. 203c ELL POSTER 30 • Day 1 Activities	TEACHER'S EDITION • Academic Language, p. DI•116 • Concept Development, p. DI•116 • Anchored Talk, p. 500a • Concept Talk Video ELL HANDBOOK • ELL Poster Talk, Concept Talk, p. 203c • Concept Talk Video Routine, p. 477 ELL POSTER 30 • Day 2 Activities
Phonics and Spelling	TEACHER'S EDITION • Phonics and Spelling, p. DI•120 • Decodable Practice Reader 30A, pp. 497a–497b	TEACHER'S EDITION • Phonics and Spelling, p. DI•120
Listening Comprehension	TEACHER'S EDITION • Modified Read Aloud, p. DI•119 • Read Aloud, p. 495b • Concept Talk Video ELL HANDBOOK • Concept Talk Video Routine, p. 477	TEACHER'S EDITION • Modified Read Aloud, p. DI•119 • AudioText of *Atlantis* • Concept Talk Video ELL HANDBOOK • AudioText CD Routine, p. 477
Reading Comprehension	TEACHER'S EDITION • Preteach Generalize, p. DI•121	TEACHER'S EDITION • Reteach Generalize, p. DI•121 • Frontloading Reading, p. DI•122 ELL HANDBOOK • Picture It! Skill Instruction, pp. 204–204a • Multilingual Summaries, pp. 205–207
Vocabulary **Basic and Lesson Vocabulary** **Vocabulary Skill: Homographs**	TEACHER'S EDITION • Basic Vocabulary, p. DI•117 • Preteach Lesson Vocabulary, p. DI•117 • Homographs, p. DI•120 ELL HANDBOOK • Word Cards, p. 203 • ELL Vocabulary Routine, p. 471 ELL POSTER 30 • Day 1 Activities	TEACHER'S EDITION • Basic Vocabulary, p. DI•117 • Reteach Lesson Vocabulary, p. DI•118 • Homographs, p. DI•120 ELL HANDBOOK • Word Cards, p. 203 • Multilingual Vocabulary List, p. 442 ELL POSTER 30 • Day 2 Activities
Grammar and Conventions	TEACHER'S EDITION • Preteach Quotations and Parentheses, p. DI•124	TEACHER'S EDITION • Reteach Quotations and Parentheses, p. DI•124
Writing	TEACHER'S EDITION • Writing Specific Adjectives, p. DI•125 • Writing for Tests: Historical Fiction, pp. 499e–499f	TEACHER'S EDITION • Writing for Tests: Historical Fiction, pp. 511d–511e

Leveled Support: This symbol indicates leveled instruction to address language proficiency levels.

Day 3	Day 4	Day 5
TEACHER'S EDITION • Academic Language, p. DI•116 • Concept Development, p. DI•116 • Anchored Talk, p. 512a • Concept Talk Video ELL HANDBOOK • ELL Poster Talk, Concept Talk, p. 203c ELL POSTER 30 • Day 3 Activities	TEACHER'S EDITION • Academic Language, p. DI•116 • Concept Development, p. DI•116 • Anchored Talk, p. 524a • Concept Talk Video ELL HANDBOOK • ELL Poster Talk, Concept Talk, p. 203c ELL POSTER 30 • Day 4 Activities	TEACHER'S EDITION • Academic Language, p. DI•116 • Concept Development, p. DI•116 • Concept Talk Video ELL HANDBOOK • ELL Poster Talk, Concept Talk, p. 203c ELL POSTER 30 • Day 5 Activities
ELL HANDBOOK • Phonics Transition Lesson, pp. 284–297	ELL HANDBOOK • Phonics Transition Lesson, pp. 284–297	TEACHER'S EDITION • Phonics and Spelling, p. DI•120
TEACHER'S EDITION • AudioText of *Atlantis* • Concept Talk Video ELL HANDBOOK • AudioText CD Routine, p. 477	TEACHER'S EDITION • Concept Talk Video	TEACHER'S EDITION • Concept Talk Video
TEACHER'S EDITION • Sheltered Reading, p. DI•122 ELL HANDBOOK • Multilingual Summaries, pp. 205–207	TEACHER'S EDITION • ELL/ELD Reader Guided Reading, p. DI•123 ELL HANDBOOK • ELL Study Guide, p. 208	TEACHER'S EDITION • ELL/ELD Reader Guided Reading, p. DI•123 ELL HANDBOOK • ELL Study Guide, p. 208
ELL HANDBOOK • High-Frequency Words Activity Bank, p. 446 ELL POSTER 30 • Day 3 Activities	ELL HANDBOOK • High-Frequency Words Activity Bank, p. 446	TEACHER'S EDITION • Homographs, p. 531h ELL HANDBOOK • High-Frequency Words Activity Bank, p. 446
TEACHER'S EDITION • Grammar Jammer ELL HANDBOOK • Grammar Transition Lesson, pp. 347, 360–361 • Grammar Jammer Routine, p. 478	TEACHER'S EDITION • Grammar Jammer ELL HANDBOOK • Grammar Transition Lesson, pp. 347, 360–361	TEACHER'S EDITION • Grammar Jammer ELL HANDBOOK • Grammar Transition Lesson, pp. 347, 360–361
TEACHER'S EDITION • Let's Write It!, p. 522–523 • Writing for Tests: Evaluation, pp. 523a–523b	TEACHER'S EDITION • Writing for Tests: Historical Fiction, p. 531d	TEACHER'S EDITION • Writing for Tests: Editing Skill: Concluding Statements, pp. 531p–531q

Poster Talk, Concept Talk

Question of the Week

What is the best way to keep your freedom?

Poster 30

Throughout the week, use the ELL Poster to help students produce and comprehend language, understand the concept, and build English vocabulary. Use the Question of the Week and other questions to help students share ideas in pairs, small groups, or the large group. Sample questions are shown, with examples of possible responses by students.

Weekly Concept and Language Goals

- Discuss how people in the past kept their freedom
- Share ways that people today keep their freedom
- Identify ways people lost freedom in the past

By the end of the lesson, students should be able to talk about and write one or more sentences about maintaining freedom.

Daily Team Talk

Day 1	Day 2	Day 3	Day 4	Day 5
After Day 1 activities on Poster, ask questions such as *Look at the people in the poster picture. How did people in the past keep their freedom?*	After Day 2 activity on Poster, ask questions such as *In the poster picture, what do you think the king would do if the people did not work together?*	After Day 3 activity on Poster, ask questions such as *In the story* Atlantis, *what do the people of Atlantis do that makes them lose their freedom?*	After Day 4 activity on Poster, ask questions such as *How do people today keep their freedom?*	After Day 5 activity on Poster, ask questions such as *What do you do to keep your freedom at school?*
Beginning Work for the king. **Intermediate** They worked for the king and listened to him. **Advanced** People worked hard and listened to what the king told them. **Advanced High** People in the past kept their freedom by working together to build their community and by listening to what their king told them.	**Beginning** He will get mad. **Intermediate** The king will get mad and they will lose freedom. **Advanced** The king would be angry with them and they could lose their freedom. **Advanced High** If the people did not work together, the king would get angry. He might take away their freedom until they learned to work together.	**Beginning** Fight. **Intermediate** They fight with each other. **Advanced** The people get greedy and they start to fight with each other. **Advanced High** The people of Atlantis become greedy and start fighting with each other. Atlantis is not a safe place anymore.	**Beginning** They vote. **Intermediate** They vote for their leaders and write them letters. **Advanced** People can vote for leaders and write letters to leaders telling how they feel. **Advanced High** People today keep their freedom by voting for the president and other leaders. People also tell leaders how they feel by writing letters or signing petitions.	**Beginning** Follow the rules. **Intermediate** I follow the rules and listen to my teacher. **Advanced** I obey the school rules and do what my teacher tells me. **Advanced High** To keep my freedom at school, I learn the school's rules and my teacher's rules and I obey them.

This Week's Materials

Teacher's Edition pages 494j–535a

See the support for English language learners throughout the lesson, including ELL strategies and scaffolded activities at points of use.

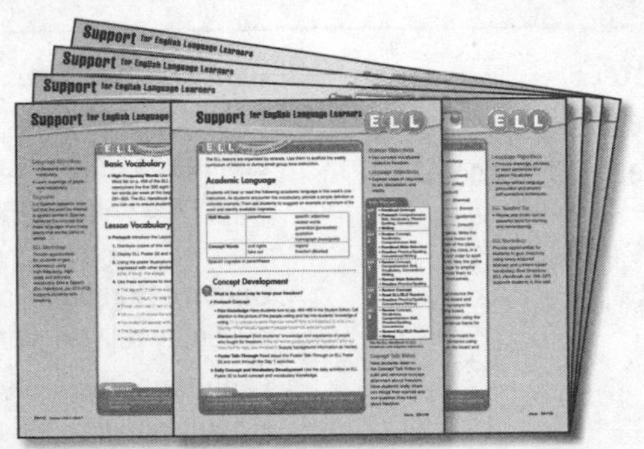
Teacher's Edition pages DI•116–DI•125

Differentiated Instruction for English language learners provides daily group activities that "frontload," or preteach, core instruction.

ELL Handbook pp. 203a–208

Find additional lesson materials that support the core lesson and the ELL instructional pages.

ELL Poster 30

ELL Reader 3.6.5

ELD Reader 3.6.5

Concept Literacy Reader

ELD, ELL Reader Teaching Guide

Concept Literacy Reader Teaching Guide

Technology

Online Teacher's Edition Use the digital version of the core Teacher's Edition for planning and instruction.

eReaders
This week's ELL and ELD Readers and Concept Literacy Reader are also available in digital format.

This Week's Content and Language Objectives by Strand

Concept Development/ Academic Language What is the best way to keep your freedom?	**Content Objective** • Use concept vocabulary related to freedom. **Language Objective** • Express ideas in response to art, discussion, and media.
Phonics and Spelling Related Words	**Content Objective** • Identify related words. **Language Objective** • Apply phonics and decoding skills to vocabulary.
Listening Comprehension Modified Read Aloud: "I Have a Dream"	**Content Objective** • Monitor and adjust oral comprehension. **Language Objectives** • Discuss oral passages. • Use a graphic organizer to take notes.
Reading Comprehension Generalize	**Content Objectives** • Identify generalizations. • Distinguish between generalizations and specific facts. **Language Objectives** • Write generalizations. • Read grade-level text with expression.
Vocabulary Basic and Lesson Vocabulary	**Language Objectives** • Understand and use basic vocabulary. • Learn meanings of grade-level vocabulary. • Produce drawings, phrases, and short sentences to show understanding of Lesson Vocabulary.
Vocabulary Homographs	**Content Objective** • Use context clues for homograph meaning. **Language Objective** • Discuss the different meanings of homographs.
Grammar and Conventions Quotations and Parentheses	**Content Objectives** • Identify quotation marks and parentheses. • Correctly use quotation marks in dialogue and parentheses to set off additional information. **Language Objective** • Write sentences with quotation marks.
Writing Writing Specific Adjectives	**Content Objective** • Identify specific adjectives in a text. **Language Objective** • Write a narrative paragraph, describing specific adjectives.

Word Cards for Vocabulary Activities

aqueducts	**crouched**
guidance	**honor**
pillar	**thermal**
content	

Teacher Note: Beginning Teach two to three words. **Intermediate** Teach three to four words. **Advanced** Teach four to five words. **Advanced High** Teach all words.

Name ______________________________

Read the paragraph. Then **complete** the graphic organizer.

- **Write** a generalization about lead crystal.
- **Write** the information from the text that supports that generalization.

Lead Crystal

Lead crystal, also called lead glass, is a special type of glass. Artists have been making lead crystal items since the 1600s. People still use lead crystal to make items such as vases, bowls, and sculptures. It sparkles more than normal glass. It is also easier to cut. Artists cut the glass to make the glass reflect more light.

Generalization:

____

____

Supporting Information:

____

____

____

Picture It!

Generalize

Use this lesson to supplement or replace the skill lesson on page 498a of the Teacher's Edition. Display the Skill Points (at right) and share them with students.

Skill Points

✔ After reading about similar ideas, you can make a **generalization** about all of the ideas together.

✔ Clue words such as *all, many,* and *most* signal generalizations.

Teach/Model

Beginning Display a glass. Say: *I should be careful with this glass. Many glass objects can break easily. Which sentence tells a way that many glass objects are alike?* (the second sentence) *Which sentence is a generalization?* (the second one) Point out that the word *many* is a clue word for recognizing a generalization.

Intermediate Write and read aloud this sentence: *Most people do not drink enough water each day.* Ask: *What makes this sentence a generalization?* (It tells a way most people are alike. It uses the word *most.*)

Advanced Write a generalization on the board. For example: *All birds have feathers.* Ask students why this is a generalization. Have them write sentences that support the generalization. If necessary, point out that naming different kinds of birds supports the generalization and write the first support sentence: *Robins and gulls have feathers.*

Advanced High Pair students. Provide a topic, such as animals, and have partners write a generalization about it. Say: *Remember to use a clue word such as* all, many, *or* most *in your generalization.* Have partners write a fact that supports their generalization.

Then distribute copies of Picture It! page 204.

- Have students look at the picture and title. Read the paragraph aloud.
- Review the Skill Points with students.
- Ask: *Which ideas about lead crystal are similar? What can you generalize about these ideas?*

Practice

Read aloud the directions on page 204. Reread the paragraph aloud. Then have students use the picture and the paragraph to complete the graphic organizer.

Beginning Students can say what they want to write before writing words or phrases in the graphic organizer. Provide help with English words and writing.

Intermediate Students can first orally respond and then write sentences to complete the graphic organizer. Provide help with English words and writing.

Advanced Students can write sentences to complete the graphic organizer and then check their answers by silently rereading the paragraph.

Advanced High Students can write sentences to complete the graphic organizer and then orally explain how they made their generalization.

Answers for page 204: *Generalization:* Many artists like using lead crystal to make items. *Support:* Artists have been making lead crystal items since the 1600s. Artists are still using lead crystal to make items today. Artists can cut lead crystal to make it reflect more light.

Multilingual Summaries

English

Atlantis: The Legend of a Lost City

A family lived on a small rocky island on the sea. Poseidon, the god of the sea, saw their daughter, Cleito. He fell in love with her, and they married.

Poseidon changed the island into a paradise. The people of the island built a great city. They named the island Atlantis. The people of Atlantis obeyed Poseidon's laws. The people of Atlantis were wise and peaceful. Then Poseidon left Atlantis. The people of Atlantis disobeyed Poseidon's laws. Poseidon saw them and sent the island to the bottom of the sea.

Some people think Atlantis was a real place. Other people think it is just a legend.

Spanish

La Atlántida: La leyenda de una ciudad perdida

Una familia vivía en una pequeña isla rocosa. Poseidón, el dios del mar, vio a su hija, Cleito. Él se enamoró de ella y se casaron.

Poseidón convirtió la isla en un paraíso. Los habitantes de la isla construyeron una gran ciudad. La llamaron la Atlántida. Los habitantes de la Atlántida obedecieron las leyes de Poseidón. Los habitantes de la Atlántida eran sabios y pacíficos. Entonces, Poseidón abandonó la Atlántida. Los habitantes de la Atlántida desobedecieron las leyes de Poseidón. Poseidón se dio cuenta y mandó la isla al fondo del mar.

Algunas personas creen que la Atlántida era un lugar real. Otras personas creen que es sólo una leyenda.

Chinese

阿特兰蒂斯：传说中的失落古城

有一个家庭住在一个海中并布满岩石的小岛上面。海神波塞冬看见了他们的女儿克利托以后，就爱上她，并与她结婚。

波塞冬把小岛变成了天堂。岛上的人建造了一个伟大的城市，并把这个城市叫做阿特兰蒂斯。阿特兰蒂斯的居民遵守波塞冬的法律；他们都很有智慧，生活得很和平。波塞冬离开了阿特兰蒂斯以后，人们就开始不遵守他的法律，波塞冬知道了以后，就把整个岛送到海底里去。

有些人认为世上真有阿特兰蒂斯这地方，但有些人却认为这是传说。

Vietnamese

Atlantis: Huyền Thoại Về Một Thành Phố Đã Mất

Có một gia đình đã sống trên một hòn đảo đá ngoài biển. Thần Biển Poseidon trông thấy Cleito, con gái của họ và đem lòng yêu cô ta, rồi hai người kết hôn.

Thần Poseidon biến hòn đảo thành thiên đàng. Dân trên đảo xây dựng một thành phố lớn. Họ đặt tên đảo là Atlantis. Dân chúng Atlantis tuân theo luật lệ của thần Poseidon. Dân chúng Atlantis khôn ngoan và sống hoà bình. Rồi thần Poseidon rời Atlantis. Dân chúng Atlantis không tuân thủ luật lệ của thần Poseidon nữa. Thần Poseidon thấy vậy bèn nhận hòn đảo chìm sâu xuống đáy biển.

Có người nghỉ rằng Atlantis có thât. Có những người khác nghĩ rằng đó chỉ là huyền thoại.

Multilingual Summaries

Korean

아틀란티스: 잃어버린 도시의 전설

한 가족이 바닷가 돌섬에서 살고 있었습니다. 바다의 신 포세이돈은 그 가족의 딸인 클레이토를 보고 사랑에 빠져, 둘은 결혼하게 되었습니다.

포세이돈은 돌섬을 천국으로 바꾸었습니다. 그 섬에 살던 사람들은 훌륭한 도시를 만들었고 그 이름을 아틀란티스라고 지었습니다. 아틀란티스 사람들은 포세이돈의 법에 복종했습니다. 아틀란티스 사람들은 현명하고 평화로운 사람들이었습니다. 그리고 포세이돈은 아틀란티스를 떠났습니다. 아틀란티스 사람들은 포세이돈의 법을 무시했습니다. 포세이돈은 그 사람들을 보고 섬을 바다 밑으로 보내 버렸습니다.

어떤 사람은 아틀란티스를 실재 존재했던 곳으로 생각합니다. 다른 사람들은 그것을 전설이라고 생각합니다.

Hmong

Atlantis: Zaj Dabneeg Txog Lub Zog Uas Ploj

Muaj ib tsev tibneeg nyob ntawm ib thaj av uas muaj pobzeb ntau ntau thiab dej hiavtxwv nyob ib ncig. Poseidon, tus dab tswj dej hiavtxwv, pom lawv tus ntxhais, Cleito. Nwg ciali nyiam lawv tus ntxhais, thiab nkawv sis yuav.

Poseidon hloov lawv thaj av ib ncig dej hiavtxwv uas ib thaj av zoo nkauj cuag ceebtsheej. Cov tibneeg nyob ntawm thaj av ib ncig dej hiavtxwv tsim tau ib lub zog zoo heev. Lawv tis npe hu ua Atlantis. Cov tibneeg hauv Atlantis coj Poseidon txoj cai. Cov tibneeg hauv Atlantis ntse thiab coj tug. Ces Poseidon muab Atlantis tseg cia. Cov tibneeg huav Atlantis ciali tsi coj Poseidon txoj cai. Poseidon pom lawv ua li ntawd thiab muab thaj av ib ncig dej hiavtxwv ntawv xa mus rau qabthu.

Ib txhia tibneeg xav tias Atlantis yog ib lub chaw tiag tiag. Lwv cov tibneeg xav tias nwg tsuas yog ib zaj dabneeg xwb.

Name ______________________________

Freedom for All

- **Read** *Freedom for All* again.
- Use the information in the book to **answer** the questions below.

pages 2–3

1. What was Nelson Mandela's name as a child? What does it mean?

____

____

pages 4–6

2. How do you know that Nelson was a good student?

____

pages 7–9

3. How did Nelson help the people of South Africa?

____

____

4. What happened to Nelson?

____

pages 10–12

5. What was the author's purpose in writing this book?

____

Family Link

Ask family members to tell you what they know about Nelson Mandela.

Answer Key

page 30, Picture It!
He goes to the market with his mom.
He is at the farmers' market.
He learns that sometimes different foods taste good.

page 34, ELL Reader Study Guide
Answers should include the following information:
Beginning: Elena learns about the Spanish club.
Middle: Elena tells her mother about the Spanish club. She feels excited and nervous about joining.
End: Elena goes to the Spanish club. She learns a new song in Spanish. She makes a new friend, Diego.

page 36, Picture It!
Sequence words: *first, next, then;* Story events: Albert feels lonely, reads, draws, plays outside, and meets a new friend.

page 40, ELL Reader Study Guide
Answers should include:
Page 3: He fixed a sign; Pages 4–5: hammer merchant; Pages 6–7: He made a new shelf.

page 42, Picture It!
Sequence words: *Monday, Tuesday, Wednesday, Thursday; walk the dog, mow the lawn, sell lemonade, buy mom a gift.*

page 46, ELL Reader Study Guide
Answers should include the following information:
First: She made a schedule of her activities.
Next: She practices with her friends or her father.
Then: She practices by herself.
Last: She feels ready for the tryouts.

page 48, Picture It!
1. Both like apples. They buy them every week.
2. Anna lives in the country, and Henry lives in the city. Anna walks to a farm, and Henry takes the bus to a store. Anna pays less for her apples than Henry pays.

page 52, ELL Reader Study Guide
Answers should include:
Next, they bought tomatoes.
Then, they bought a fish.
Last, their neighbor gave them parsley.

page 54, Picture It!
1. a
2. c

page 58, ELL Reader Study Guide
Students should draw and write about what they would buy with $5.

page 60, Picture It!
Main Idea: Animals that live in Antarctica are protected from the cold.
Details: Whales have layers of fat; Fish have special blood; Birds have waterproof feathers.

page 64, ELL Reader Study Guide
Main Idea: Birds use different kinds of beaks to get food.

page 66, Picture It!
Both: make macaroni and cheese, do chores; Shelby: child, boy, learns; His Mother: adult, woman, teaches

page 70, ELL Reader Study Guide
Students should include details from the story that support the idea of planting a garden.

page 72, Picture It!
1. c
2. a
3. c

page 76, ELL Reader Study Guide
Sample Answers
Details: Jack had lots of books in his room.
His mother asked him to clean up his scattered books.
Jack decided to put the books into alphabetical order by title.

page 78, Picture It!
1. Tomato plants are easy to grow. They need water and sun. Tomatoes are delicious.
2. Marigolds repel insects. They grow with the same sun and water as tomatoes.

page 82, ELL Reader Study Guide
Jim's garden contains three rows of lettuce and four tomato plants.
Peter's garden contains two rows of peppers and four rows of corn.

page 84, Picture It!
Main Idea: Birds and fish are alike in many ways.
Details: Birds and fish have bones in their backs and chests; Birds and fish lay eggs; Birds and fish live all over the world.

page 88, ELL Reader Study Guide
Responses include: fish live in any body of water; beavers live near water in a beaver lodge; turtles live on land and near water; rabbits live on land in holes

page 90, Picture It!
Details: Some ladybugs eat harmful insects; Other kinds of ladybugs eat plants instead of insects.
What I Know: Some bugs kill plants.
Conclusion: Some ladybugs are good for gardens. Not all ladybugs are good for gardens.

page 94, ELL Reader Study Guide
Students should draw the three main events from the story and describe them with labels or sentences.

page 96, Picture It!
1. b
2. a
3. c

page 100, ELL Reader Study Guide
Problem: Na-gah climbed to the top of the tallest mountain and can't get down.
Solution: His father turns him into the North Star so he will shine forever.

page 102, Picture It!
Children should correctly label the plant parts.

page 106, ELL Reader Study Guide
Students should draw an animal or plant they can see on each part of the mountain and write words or sentences about each.

page 108, Picture It!
Similar Ideas: Mammals are animals; Dogs, cats, and cows are mammals; Whales and dolphins are mammals.
Generalization: Many animals are mammals.

page 112, ELL Reader Study Guide
Page 3 Nobody can explain why.
Pages 4–7 Volunteers helped to rescue the whales.
Page 8 Whales will get stuck again, and people will help them again.

page 114, Picture It!
Cause: Kiki cannot wait to go to Space Camp today.
Effects: She quickly washes her face; She almost forgets to change out of her pajamas!

page 118, ELL Reader Study Guide
Causes: The grey parrot is very smart; We eat food that grows there and use rain forest plants for medicine.
Effects: It can hold the branches; They keep straight; They can climb and hop through trees.

page 120, Picture It!
1. Many years ago, the people in Dragonland made homes of wood. Today, people in Dragonland build homes from stone.
2. Most dragons try not to breathe fire. Most people in Dragonland have learned how to live with dragons.

page 124, ELL Reader Study Guide
Children should list facts about both Luz and their best friends. In a phrase or sentence, they should tell how Luz and their friends are alike and different.

page 126, Picture It!
1. Answers will vary.
2. Two large cities (Chicago and San Diego) with different climates.
3. Climates and beaches

page 130, ELL Reader Study Guide
1. Category 5
2. Four hurricanes hit the state in six weeks.
3. major damage
4. buildings, homes, cars, roads

page 132, Picture It!
Facts: Many people visit Chile for fun; You can ski on the mountains; The beaches are warmer than the mountains. Prove it: Look up weather

page 132, Picture It!
Facts: Many people visit Chile for fun; You can ski on the mountains; The beaches are warmer than the mountains. Prove it: Look up tourist or weather information.
Opinions: I think the mountains are too cold. I like to visit the beaches in Chile better. The sea is prettier than the mountains too. Clue words: *think, like, prettier*

page 136, ELL Reader Study Guide
1. astronaut: work in computers and spacecraft
2. gardener: help plants and trees grow
3. teacher: help students learn
4. baker: bake cakes and/or baked goods

page 138, Picture It!
Facts: I am on the swim team at school. We swim different strokes. I cannot see where I am going! *How to prove:* by asking the coach, by trying the backstroke by watching swimmers, by looking at the picture; *Opinions:* It is fun to swim on a team. I do not like the backstroke. *Clue words:* fun, like.

page 142, ELL Reader Study Guide
1938: Helen retired. *1927–1933:* Helen won 180 matches in a row. *1924:* Helen won the gold medal for tennis at the Olympics. *1921:* Helen won the California State Women's Championship. *1905:* Helen was born.

page 144, Picture It!
Causes: Lulu can see better than most animals. She flies quickly.
Effect: She is a good hunter.
Causes: Lulu can see underwater. Lulu has strong legs.
Effect: Lulu can catch fish.

page 148, ELL Reader Study Guide
Beginning: Tina the chameleon and Ringo the lemur meet each other.
Middle: Tina and Ringo talk about how different they are. They meet Fred the fossa who scares them. He wants to eat them.
End: Both Tina and Ringo hide from Fred. Fred goes away.

page 150, Picture It!
Both: eat breakfast; eat before school
Ky: eats white rice and soup; uses chopsticks
Ben: eats cereal with strawberries and milk; drinks a glass of orange juice

page 154, ELL Reader Study Guide
1. The school year lasts 11 months *or* The school year lasts 240 days.
2. Some students wear uniforms. Other students wear everyday clothes. Many wear yellow hats.
3. They study math, reading, science, social studies, computers, and English.
4. Answers will vary. Possible responses: They help clean the school. They study Japanese. They belong to clubs.

page 156, Picture It!
1. c
2. In the U.S., kids eat cake, and in Vietnam they eat noodles. In the U.S., kids celebrate on the day on which they were born. In Vietnam, they celebrate on New Year's Day.

page 160, ELL Reader Study Guide
Possible answers:
Facts: Culture is how people live their lives. People's foods, language, and music are their culture. The United States has people and cultures from all over the world. Pizza comes from Italy. The word *hamburger* means "from Hamburg, Germany." (Accept other responses that can be proven to be true or false.) *Opinions:* Pizza is my favorite food. I think hamburgers taste the best.

page 162, Picture It!
Anita helps Dad pack the tools.
She helps Mom pack the dishes.
She packs her books.
She falls asleep.

page 166, ELL Reader Study Guide
Possible answers: People in the United States speak English fast. People in the U.S. don't visit their families a lot. In Mexico, people greet each other with a kiss on the cheek. In the U.S., people smile and say, "Hi." In Colombia, it's polite to leave some food on your plate. In the U.S., it's polite to eat everything on your plate.

page 168, Picture It!

1. d
2. c
3. a

page 172, ELL Reader Study Guide

Possible answer: I like pizza with pepperoni, sausage, and cheese.

page 174, Picture It!

Author's Purpose: to persuade people to visit New York City; *Possible detail answers:* so many things to see; It is magnificent; It is the most exciting city; You should visit New York City.

page 178, ELL Reader Study Guide

Answers will vary. Possible response: *I would rather live in the country where it's quiet and peaceful and the air is clean.*

page 180, Picture It!

Facts: Most Chinese immigrants were men. Many left their families in China. Some of the men made money by building railroads. Other people did not want the job. Today, the Chinese American community has grown.
Opinions: Life was hard for some early Chinese immigrants to the United States. That's a hard job! The people have had great success.

page 184, ELL Reader Study Guide

Facts should be information that can be proven true or false. Opinions are ideas or beliefs.

page 186, Picture It!

Possible response:
Cause: Benito does not speak English yet.
Effect: He cannot answer the teacher's question.

page 190, ELL Reader Study Guide

She wants to pass a citizenship test; Gina passed the test; Gina wants to become a citizen; Gina becomes a citizen.

page 192, Picture It!

Students should correctly label the map: Orozco/New Hampshire; Rivera/Detroit; Siqueiros/Los Angeles

page 196, ELL Reader Study Guide

What: a V-shaped design; *When:* 1980; *Where:* Washington, D.C.; *Why:* to honor Vietnam veterans

page 198, Picture It!

Beginning: Two ants come to a deep river.
Middle: Andy climbs a piece of grass to find a place to cross.
End: The ants use the grass to cross the river.

page 202, ELL Reader Study Guide

1. We are free to say or write what we think. We are free to gather. We are free to vote for our leaders.
2. Our government protects our rights.
3. It was signed on July 4, 1776.
4. A constitution is a written statement of laws.
5. They did not want the people to be ruled by a king again.

page 204, Picture It!

Generalization: Many artists like using lead crystal to make items.
Support: Artists have been making lead crystal items since the 1600s. Artists can cut lead crystal to make it reflect more light. Artists are still using lead crystal to make items today.

page 208, ELL Reader Study Guide

1. His name was Rolihlahla. It means *troublemaker.*
2. Possible answer: His teacher gave him the name Nelson, which means "son of a champion."
3. Possible answers: He started the first office for black lawyers. He wanted to make the laws fair to everyone. He wanted people to have more freedom.
4. He went to jail for thirty years.
5. Possible answers: Nelson is no longer a troublemaker. He fought for equality and freedom.

Part 3
Phonics Instruction for English Language Learners

Contents

Introduction to the Phonics Transition Lessons

Phonological and phonemic awareness, phonics, and word study are critical components of literacy instruction for English learners. The core lessons in *Reading Street* provide the explicit, systematic instruction that all children need to become fluent readers and writers. The following Phonics Transition Lessons and Practice Pages will supplement the core instruction with customized lessons that meet the particular needs of English learners. Lessons and Practice Pages are divided into three sections:

- **Phonological Awareness and Concepts of Print** English learners may not have learned to distinguish word boundaries, syllables, rhymes, or phonemes within words in English, or even in their home languages. Some children also may be unfamiliar with English print conventions, such as the alphabet and left-to-right directionality. This section provides activities that can be used at any time to develop phonological awareness and concepts of print.
- **Problem Sounds in English** These lessons cover the phonemes that are typically the most challenging for English learners, such as easily confused consonants and short vowel sounds. In some cases, a Model Lesson is provided along with notes for using the same lesson format with related phonics skills. Lessons in this section include Pronunciation Tips that teachers can use to help children produce the target phonemes. A Practice Page for every lesson provides strong visual support for instruction and offers additional practice.
- **Word Study** An understanding of word parts and word origins is a powerful tool for English learners. The Word Study Lessons reinforce the core instruction and include suggestions for making connections with the home language. The Practice Pages provide visual support and context for the target skills.

Throughout the Phonics Transition Lessons, a **Transfer Skills** feature identifies specific challenges faced by English language learners as they acquire the target skills.

In addition to the Phonics Transition Lessons and Practice Pages, you can supplement core phonics instruction with routines such as the following:

- **Strengthen oral language skills.** Allow beginning speakers to work with partners when completing phonics activities. Encourage children to talk about their work with English, and provide other oral language opportunities with the target words.
- **Teach word meanings.** Before teaching the phonics skills, introduce the target words orally to children by using them in activities such as riddle games, songs, chants, or asking and answering questions that use the words.
- **Provide alternate instruction.** If children have limited literacy skills, use resources such as the *Reading Street Intervention Kit* or *Early Reading Intervention (ERI)* to provide literacy instruction at the level where children can participate and learn.
- **Relate to the home language.** Whenever possible, help children build on what they already know by making connections between each target phonics skill and the home language. Use available resources such as bilingual staff members, bilingual dictionaries, and language Web sites to gather information about the home language.
- **Engage children as active learners.** Children who are acquiring English may have a stronger awareness of language than monolingual speakers. Build their knowledge with engaging activities that explicitly show the patterns and structures of language. Consider using games such as **Four by Four** and **Word Hunt** on the next page.

Four by Four

Use with page 217.

Make and distribute copies of page 217. Work with students to generate a class list of twenty or more words that reflect the target phonics or word study skills that students have recently studied—for example, words that begin with the prefixes *im-* and *in-*. Write each word on a card. Have students choose sixteen words from the list and write them in random order in the squares on page 217. Have students cut out the star markers at the bottom of the page. Shuffle the cards, and read aloud one card at a time. Students should look for each word on their paper and cover it with a star marker. The first one to have four marked words in a row (horizontally, vertically, or diagonally) calls out "Four by Four!" Note: For students in early stages of literacy, write consonants in the squares, and have students listen for words that begin with the consonants.

Word Hunt

Use with page 218.

Choose a target phonics or word study skill, such as "Words with long *a*" or "Words with the suffix *-ly*," and list it at the top of page 218. Make and distribute copies to individuals, partners, or small groups. Have students look around the classroom and school, in books and magazines, and perhaps at home, for words that have the particular phonics feature. They can list the words in the chart on page 218, and either draw or attach (with glue or tape) pictures that illustrate the words. Conclude by having students share the words they find.

Name ___________________________

Four by Four

- **Write** the words that your teacher gives you. Write one word in each square.
- **Listen** to the words. When you hear a word that is in a square, **cover** it with a star marker.
- When you have four covered words in a row, **say** "Four by Four!"

- **Cut out** the star markers. **Use** them in the game.

Name ________________________________

Word Hunt: Words with ____________

- **Find** words that share a sound or a spelling pattern.
- **Write** the words. **Add** pictures or definitions for the words.
- **Tell** your words to a friend.

Word	Picture or Definition

Transfer Skills

Many factors can influence students' understanding of print conventions. The students may be emergent readers of non-alphabetic languages or languages with alphabets similar to or different from the English alphabet. Some English learners may be familiar with reading left to right and top to bottom, as in English. Others may be accustomed to reading text from right to left, or from the bottom to the top of the page. Some have little experience with printed text. For students who are unfamiliar with English print conventions, activities such as these will help develop print awareness and strengthen literacy skills.

Print Awareness Activities

Parts of a Book Show students how to hold a book. Point out and explain the title, author byline, and illustrator's name. Turn to the selection pages and read a sentence or two. Discuss how the illustrations go with the text. Page through the book, and show how the narrative continues. Point to the text on each page. Then have students practice holding the book correctly, finding the title and author's name, turning the pages, and pointing to the text on each page.

Words, Sentences, Paragraphs Display a few paragraphs of printed text in a large format or on an overhead transparency. Frame one word with your fingers, and read it aloud. Explain that it is a word, and point out the spacing before and after the word. Then read aloud a sentence, running your finger under each word as you read. Point out the sentence boundaries: a capital letter at the beginning of the sentence and the end punctuation. Then circle a paragraph with your finger, and explain that a paragraph is a group of related sentences. Point out the indent at the beginning of the paragraph. Have students practice finding words, sentences, and paragraphs in other texts.

Directionality As you read a book aloud, put your finger on the starting point in the text on each page. Show that you read from left to right and from top to bottom by moving your finger along lines of text. Use your finger to show how to sweep back from the end of a line to the beginning of another, and how to move to the next page. Then have students use their fingers to show the correct movement as you read the text aloud again.

Writing the Alphabet Students should be introduced systematically to all the letters of the English alphabet, in manuscript and cursive writing. Students can practice writing letters, punctuation marks, and numbers, using pages 220, 221, and 222 as handwriting guides.

Name ______________________

The Alphabet

- **Practice** writing the letters of the alphabet.
- **Write** more of the letters on other paper.

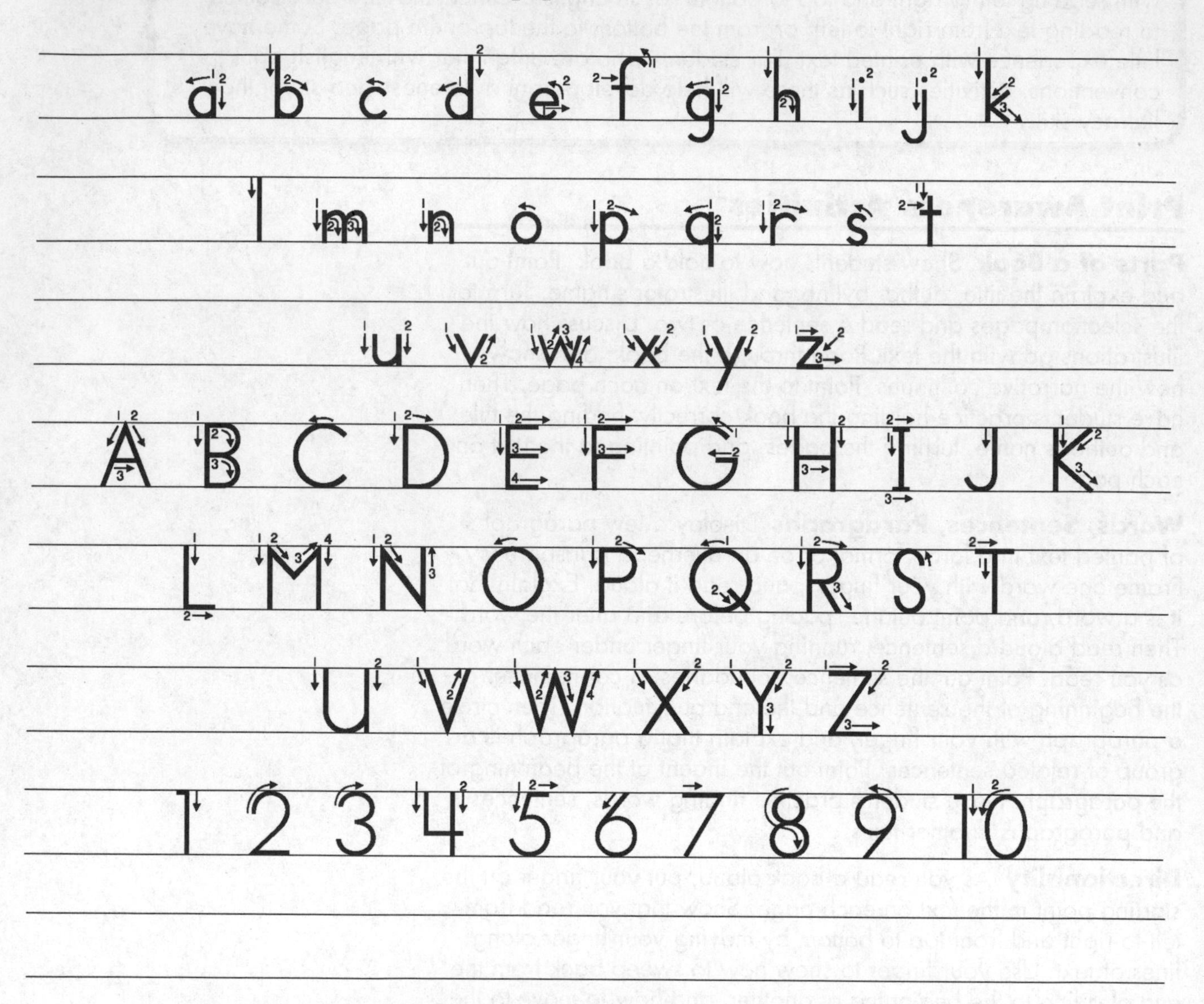

Name ___________________________________

The D'Nealian™ Alphabet

- **Practice** writing the letters of the alphabet.
- **Write** more of the letters on other paper.

a b c d e f g h i j k

l m n o p q r s t

u v w x y z

A B C D E F G H I J K

L M N O P Q R S T

U V W X Y Z

1 2 3 4 5 6 7 8 9 10

Name ______________________________

The D'Nealian™ Cursive Alphabet

- **Practice** writing the letters of the alphabet in cursive.
- **Write** more of the letters on other paper.

a b c d e f g h i j k

l m n o p q r s t

u v w x y z

A B C D E F G H I J K

L M N O P Q R S T

U V W X Y Z

1 2 3 4 5 6 7 8 9 10

The phonemes of certain English consonants may be unfamiliar to English language learners or easily confused with other phonemes. For example, consonant digraphs such as /th/, /sh/, and /ch/ may sound alike to some English language learners. Spanish speakers may hear and write /n/ at the end of words ending with /m/. The following lessons provide practice with certain consonant pairs that English language learners may find troublesome. You can develop similar lessons for other consonant sounds that are difficult for your students. This model lesson gives you a pattern for teaching.

☆ Model Lesson: Words with *b* and *v*

Use with page 226.

Preteach Copy and distribute page 226. Have students point to the picture of the box at the top of the page. Say: *This is a box. The word* box *begins with /b/. Say it with me: /b/, /b/, /b/, box.* Repeat the procedure with the word *van,* using the other picture at the top of the page.

Teach/Model Guide students to distinguish between /b/ and /v/, using the Pronunciation Tip. Then, direct students' attention to Row 1. Name each of the items shown, one by one: *boat, vest, bat, vase.* Continue: *I'll say each word one more time. If the word starts with the letter* b, *circle* b *under the picture. If the word starts with the letter* v, *circle* v. Read the words aloud once more, giving students enough time to circle the corresponding letter.

Repeat the process for Row 2, omitting the directions: *violin, vine, basketball, bike.*

Practice Have students look at the pictures in Row 3. Ask them to tell what the pictures show *(box, van)* and then write those words on the appropriate blank line.

Read the practice sentence aloud and have students find the words with *b* and *v (Val, Billy, dove, wave).* After they've had a chance to repeat the sentence several times, challenge students to say it as quickly as they can.

Assess Make letter cards for *b* and *v,* and give one of each to each student. Tell students: *I will say some words. Hold up the card that matches the sound you hear at the beginning of each word:* boat, vote, bolt, volt, vanilla, basket, very, berry, bent, vent, best, vest, vane. Then have students repeat the contrasting word pairs after you, striving for the correct pronunciation of /b/ and /v/. Keep in mind that students who have difficulty distinguishing /b/ and /v/ may still be able to comprehend words they hear or read that start with these consonants.

Pronunciation Tip
b* and *v *When you say /b/, your lips start out together. Then they open and a tiny puff of air comes out of your mouth. If you touch your throat, you can feel it move because your voice box is on. Can you hold a /b/ sound? Try it: /b/, /b/. No, you can't hold it. When you say /v/, you can hold it: /vvvv/. Your voice box is still on. Your top teeth touch your bottom lip. Say /v/ and feel your teeth touch your bottom lip. Hold the sound. Try it: /vvvv/, /vvvv/. Try both sounds: /b/, /vvvv/.*

Adapting the ☆ Model Lesson

Use the same lesson format above to teach the following consonants and digraphs: /ch/, /sh/, /d/, /th/, /l/, /r/, /m/, /n/, and /s/. The following information will help you to customize each lesson.

Notes for Additional Lessons

Words with *ch* and *sh*

Use with page 227.

Teach/Model Use these words: *child, shop.* Row 1 of page 227: *shoe, cherry, chair, sheep.*

Practice Row 2: *shark, shell, chicken, chalk.* Row 3: *child, shop.* Practice sentence: *Sherry the Shark chewed and chewed on a shiny shoe.*

Assess Use these words: *chew, shoe, chin, shin, chomp, cherry, Sherry, shell, chain, chair, share.*

Pronunciation Tip
ch* and *sh *When you say /ch/, your lips are open and your teeth are close together. Your tongue moves as you make the sound. Can you hold a /ch/ sound? Try it: /ch/, /ch/. No, you can't hold it. When you say /sh/, your lips are also open and your teeth are close together. But your tongue doesn't move, and you can hold the sound: /shhhhh/. Try it: /shhhhh/, /shhhhh/. Try both sounds: /ch/, /shhhhh/.*

Words with *d* and *th*

Use with page 228.

Teach/Model Use these words: *desk, third.* Row 1 of page 228: *door, thorn, thirty, dinosaur.*

Practice Row 2: *thermos, thumb, dish, dog.* Row 3: *third, desk.* Practice sentence: *Think a thought about a daring dog walking through thick grass.*

Assess Use these words: *thigh, dye, think, thirty, dirty, duck, though, dough, there, dare.*

Pronunciation Tip
d* and *th *When you say /d/, the tip of your tongue touches above your top teeth. Say /d/ and feel the tip of your tongue touch above your top teeth: /d/. Is your voice box on? Yes, you can feel your throat move when you say /d/. Can you hold a /d/ sound? Try it: /d/, /d/. No, you can't hold it. When you say /ŦH/ in a word like this, your voice box is also on: /ŦH/. But your tongue is between your teeth, and you can hold the sound. Try it: /ŦHHHHH/, /ŦHHHHH/. Try both sounds: /d/, /ŦHHHHH/. When you say /th/ in a word like thin, your voice box is off, and you can hold the sound: /thhhhh/. The tip of your tongue comes out between your teeth and air comes out, but no sound. Try it: /thhhhh/, /thhhhh/. Try both th sounds: /ŦHHHHH/, /thhhhh/.*

Notes for Additional Lessons

Words with *l* and *r*

Use with page 229.

Teach/Model Use these words: *leg, ring.* Row 1 of page 229: *radio, lake, light, ruler.*

Practice Row 2: *rose, lizard, leaf, river.* Row 3: *leg, ring.* Practice sentence: *The red river runs into a little lake.*

Assess Use these words: *rake, lake, rip, lip, red, rice, late, rate, load, road, loud, lean.*

Pronunciation Tip
l* and *r *When you say /l/, the tip of your tongue touches above your top teeth and stays there. Say /l/ and feel your throat move. Your voice box is on when you say /l/. Try it: /l/, /l/. When you say /r/, your voice box is on again. The tip of your tongue goes toward the roof of your mouth, but doesn't touch it. Try it: /r/, /r/. Try both sounds: /l/, /r/.*

Words with *m* and *n*

Use with page 230.

Teach/Model Use these words: *mask, nest.* Row 1 of page 230: *nose, net, mouse, match.*

Practice Focus on ending sounds for Row 2: *jam, pen, stem, fan.* Row 3: *mask, nest.* Practice sentence: *The man in the moon eats ice cream with a spoon.*

Assess Use these words: *meat, neat, mole, next, moat, note, Pam, pan, tone, time, some, sun.*

Pronunciation Tip
m* and *n *When you say /m/, your lips come together and a little air comes out of your nose. Can you hold the sound /m/? Try it: /mmmm/, /mmmm/. Yes, you can hold the sound. You can also hold the /n/ sound. Try it: /nnnn/. But when you say /n/, your lips are open. Your tongue is behind your top teeth. Say it again: /n/, /n/. Try both sounds: /m/, /n/.*

Words with *s* and *th*

Use with page 231.

Teach/Model Use these words: *sun, thorn.* Row 1 of page 231: *saw, thumb, thermos, soap.*

Practice Row 2: *sandwich, soup, thigh, thirteen.* Row 3: *sun, thorn.* Practice sentence: *Sara sipped thick soup.*

Assess Use these words: *some, thumb, so, think, sink, sock, thin, thing, sing, thank.*

Pronunciation Tip
s* and *th *When you say /s/, the tip of your tongue touches above your top teeth. It makes a snake sound, and you can hold the sound. Try it: /ssss/, /ssss/. When you say /th/ in a word like thick, the tip of your tongue comes out between your teeth. You can feel air come out of your mouth. Try it: /thhhh/, /thhhh/. Try both sounds: /ssss/, /thhhh/.*

Name ___________________________

Words with *b* and *v*

- If the word begins with the sound of *b* in *box*, **circle** the *b*.
- If the word begins with the sound of *v* in *van*, **circle** the *v*.

ROW 1

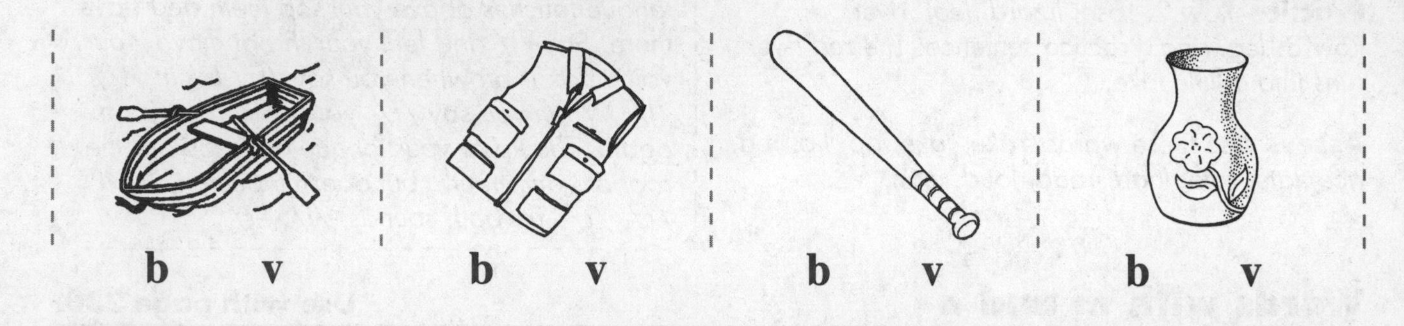

b **v** **b** **v** **b** **v** **b** **v**

ROW 2

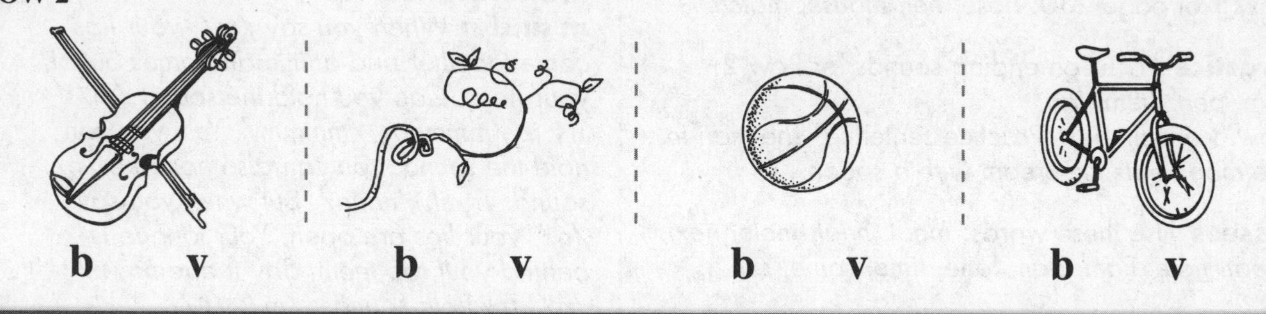

b **v** **b** **v** **b** **v** **b** **v**

- **Look** at each picture. **Say** its name. **Write** the word.

ROW 3

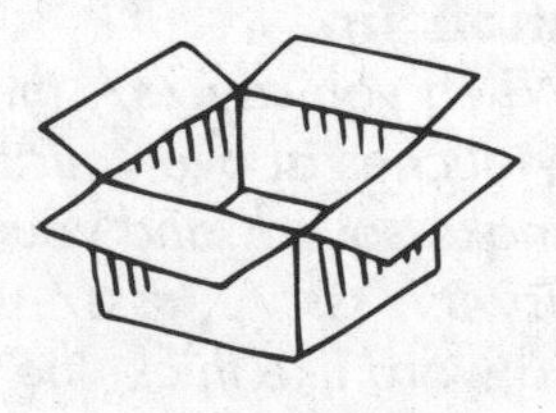

___________________ ___________________

Find *b* and *v* in this sentence. Then **practice** chanting or singing the sentence.

Val and Billy dove into the wave.

Name ______________________________

Words with *ch* and *sh*

- If the word begins with the sound of *ch* in *child*, **circle** the *ch*.
- If the word begins with the sound of *sh* in *shop*, **circle** the *sh*.

ROW 1

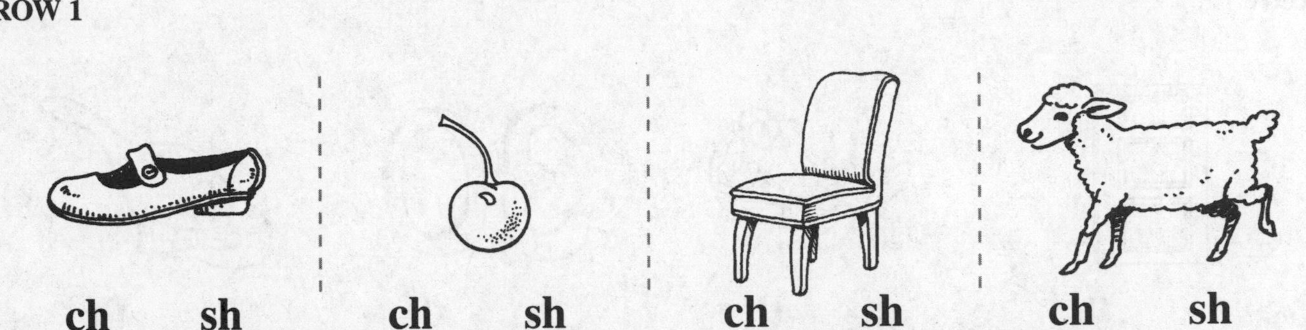

ch sh | ch sh | ch sh | ch sh

ROW 2

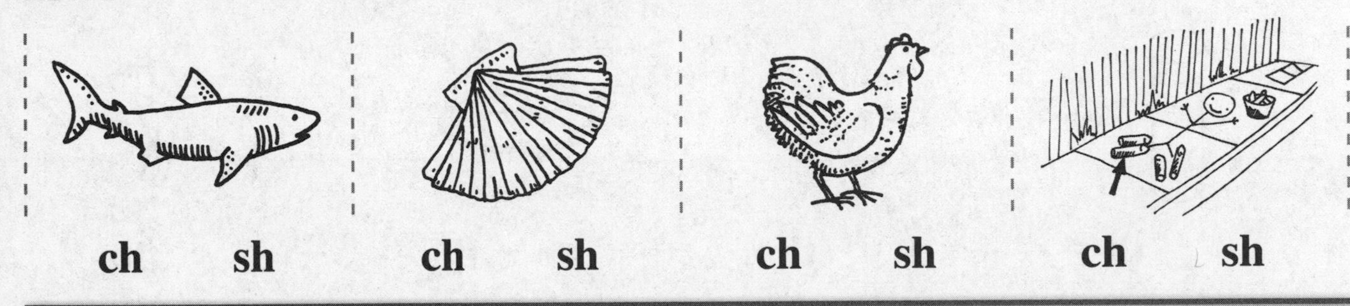

ch sh | ch sh | ch sh | ch sh

- **Look** at each picture. **Say** its name. **Write** the word.

ROW 3

______________________ ______________________

Find *ch* and *sh* in this sentence. Then **practice** chanting or singing the sentence.

Sherry the Shark chewed and chewed on a shiny shoe.

Name ______________________________

Words with *d* and *th*

- If the word begins with the sound of *d* in *desk*, **circle** the *d*.
- If the word begins with the sound of *th* in *third*, **circle** the *th*.

ROW 1

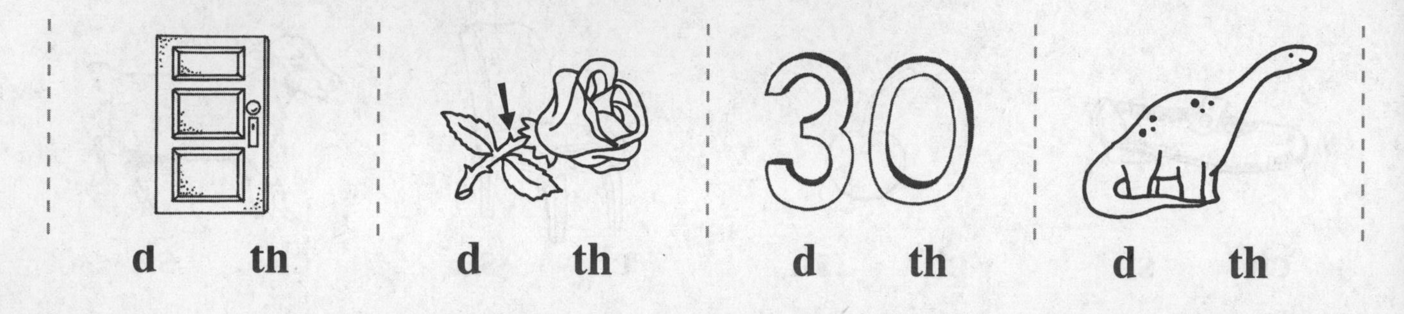

d **th** | **d** **th** | **d** **th** | **d** **th**

ROW 2

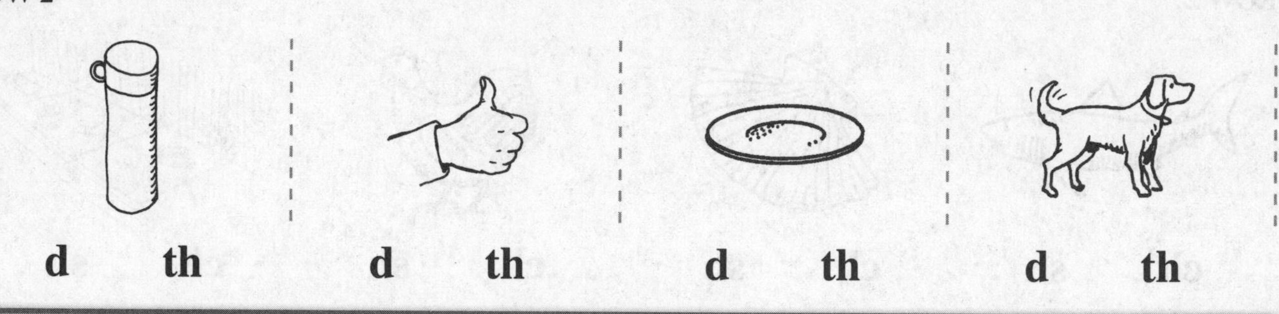

d **th** | **d** **th** | **d** **th** | **d** **th**

- **Look** at each picture. **Say** its name. **Write** the word.

ROW 3

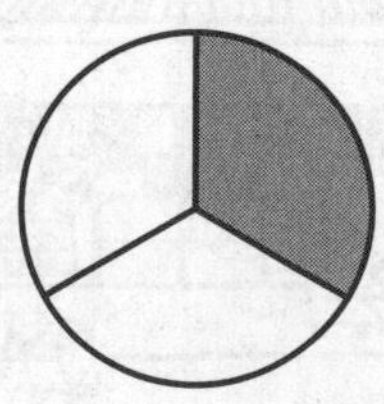

______________________ ______________________

Find *th* and *d* in this sentence. Then **practice** chanting or singing the sentence.

Think a thought about a daring dog walking through thick grass.

Name ___________________________

Words with *l* and *r*

- If the word begins with the sound of *l* in *leg*, **circle** the *l*.
- If the word begins with the sound of *r* in *ring*, **circle** the *r*.

ROW 1

l r

l r

l r

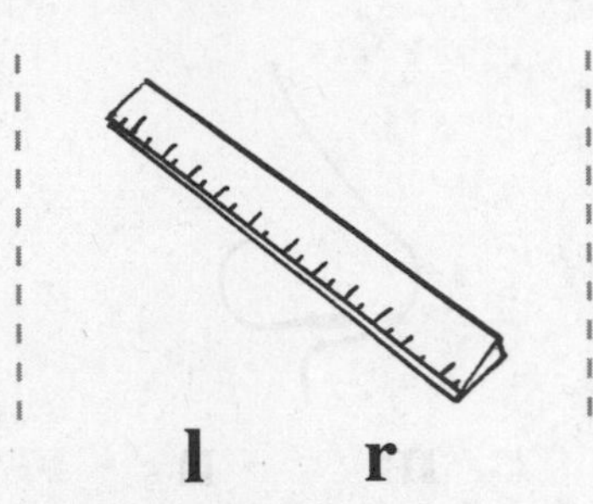

l r

ROW 2

l r

l r

l r

l r

- **Look** at each picture. **Say** its name. **Write** the word.

ROW 3

____

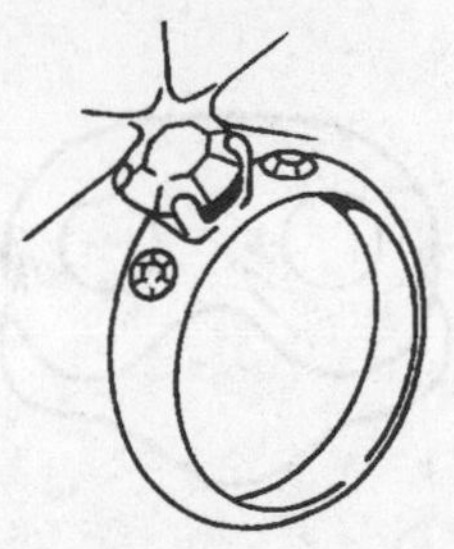

____

Find *l* and *r* in this sentence. Then **practice** chanting or singing the sentence.

The red river runs into a little lake.

Name ___________________________

Words with *m* and *n*

- If the word has the sound of *m* in *mask*, **circle** the *m*.
- If the word has the sound of *n* in *nest*, **circle** the *n*.

ROW 1

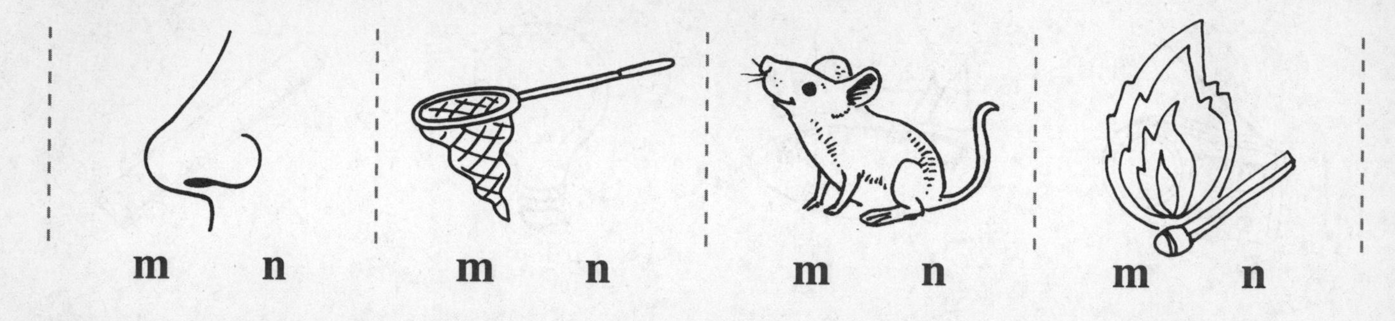

m n **m n** **m n** **m n**

ROW 2

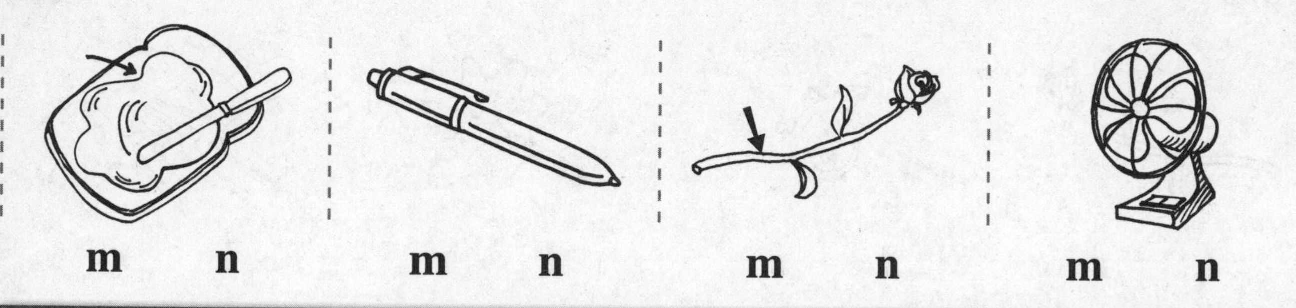

m n **m n** **m n** **m n**

- **Look** at each picture. **Say** its name. **Write** the word.

ROW 3

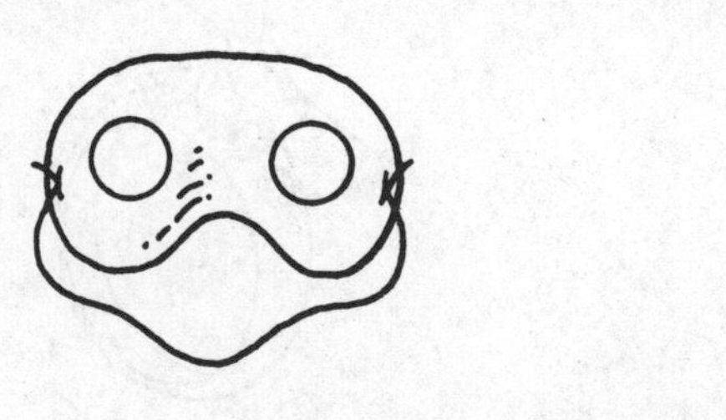

___________________ ___________________

Find *m* and *n* in this sentence. Then **practice** chanting or singing the sentence.

The man in the moon eats ice cream with a spoon.

Name ________________________________

Words with *s* and *th*

- If the word begins with the sound of *s* in *sun*, **circle** the *s*.
- If the word begins with the sound of *th* in *thorn*, **circle** the *th*.

ROW 1

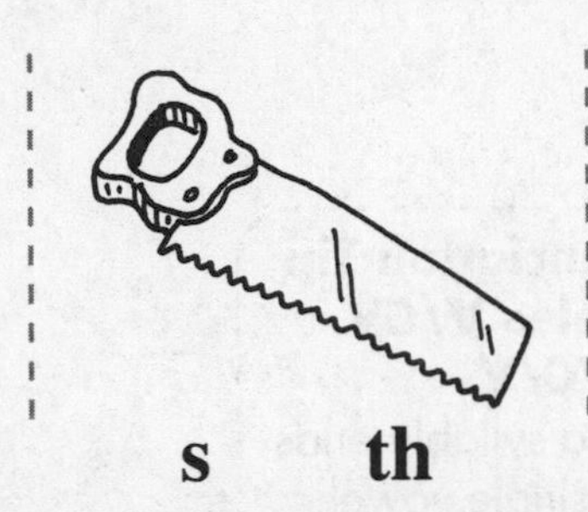

s **th**

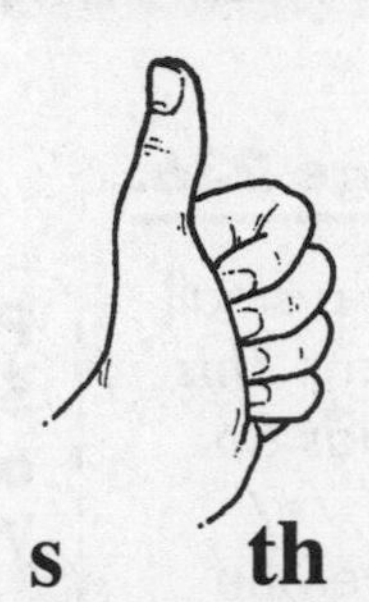

s **th**

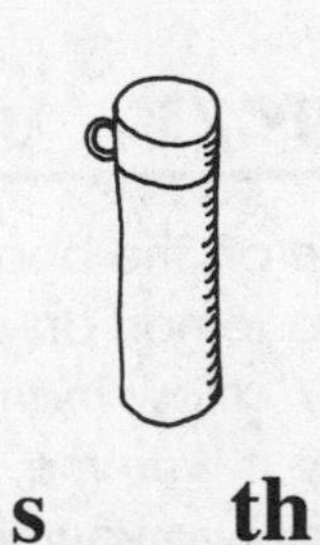

s **th**

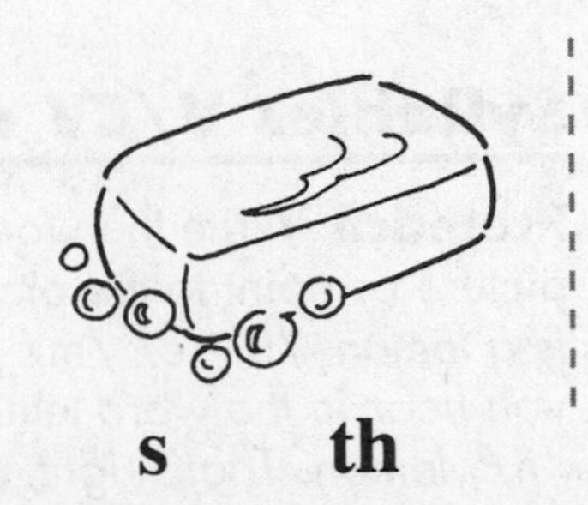

s **th**

ROW 2

s **th**

s **th**

s **th**

s **th**

- **Look** at each picture. **Say** its name. **Write** the word.

ROW 3

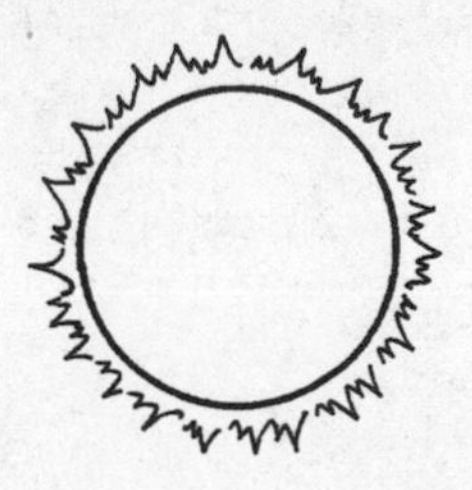

____

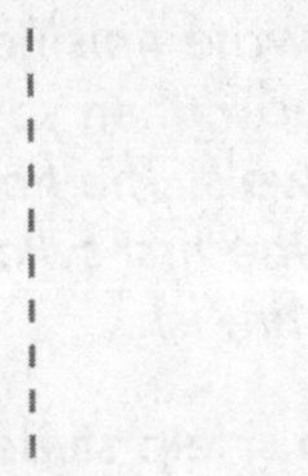

____

Find *s* and *th* in this sentence. Then **practice** chanting or singing the sentence.

Sara sipped thick soup.

Transfer Skills

The writing systems of languages such as Arabic and Hebrew focus on consonant sounds and long vowels. Short vowels are indicated with separate marks that are often optional. Speakers of these languages may need extra help in spelling words with short vowels or multiple vowel sounds.

Syllables V/CV and VC/V **Use with page 236.**

Preteach Write the word *lemon* on the board and draw a small picture or point to the picture of a lemon on page 236. Say: *This is a lemon, /l/ /e/ /m/ /ə/ /n/. How many vowel sounds do you hear in the word* lemon? *Say it with me, /l/ /e/ /m/ /ə/ /n/, lemon. That's right, there are two vowel sounds.* Cover the *mon*. Say: *If the syllable ended after the* e, *I would pronounce the word with a long* e: *lē mon. This does not make a word that I know.* Cover the *on*, then say: *I will try it with a short* e, */l/ /e/ /m/ /ə/ /n/. Now I pronounce the word* lemon, *and I recognize it. The short vowel sound is correct.* Repeat with the words *broken* and *finish*, emphasizing the short or long vowel sound in the first syllable.

Pronunciation Tip Syllables V/CV and VC/V
When a syllable ends with a single vowel, the vowel sound is usually long. When a syllable ends with a consonant, the vowel sound is usually short.

Teach/Model Write the word *pupil* on the board. Draw a line between the two syllables and tell students: *When you hear a word with more than one vowel sound, divide it into parts.* Explain that when there is one consonant between two vowels, it is important to figure out if the first vowel has a short or long sound in order to know where to divide the syllable.

Point out that because the first syllable in *pupil* has a long vowel sound, it ends after the first vowel. Then write *finish* on the board. Draw a line between the *n* and the second *i*, then say: *This word also has one consonant between two vowels. The first vowel sound in* finish *is short, so we know that the first syllable ends with a consonant. Say it with me: finish, fin/ish.*

Practice Copy and distribute page 236. Help students read the words in the box on page 236. Clap as you read each word to emphasize the syllable break in the word. Say: *I am going to read the words again. This time, circle each word with a long vowel sound in the first syllable. Underline each word with a short vowel sound in the first syllable.* Review the answers as a class *(Circle: broken, frozen, music, tulip; Underline: salad, lemon)*.

Assess Make word cards with these word parts: *bro, ken, si, lent, sev, en, fe, male, rap, id*. In pairs, give students the pile of word cards. Have students put the various word parts together to create complete words. If necessary, list the words *broken, silent, seven, female,* and *rapid* on the board.

Speakers of monosyllabic languages such as Cantonese, Hmong, Khmer, Korean, and Vietnamese may pronounce a two-syllable word as two separate words. Have students practice saying multisyllabic words.

Syllables CV/VC

Use with page 237.

Pronunciation Tip Syllables CV/VC Remind students that a word has as many syllables as it has vowel sounds.

Preteach Write the word *violin* on the board and draw a small picture or point to the picture of a violin on page 237. Say: *This is a violin, /v/ /ī/ /ə/ /l/ /i/ /n/. How many vowel sounds do you hear in the word* violin? *Say it with me, /v/ /ī/ /ə/ /l/ /i/ /n/, violin. That's right, there are three vowel sounds.* Explain that if a word in English has three vowel sounds, it must also have three syllables. Repeat with the words *computer* and *calendar,* emphasizing vowel sounds and reviewing what students have learned about breaking words into syllables.

Teach/Model Write the word *create* on the board. Draw a line between the first *e* and *a* and tell students: *When you hear a word with more than one vowel sound, divide it into parts.* Explain that when there are two vowels side-by-side, you must put a syllable break between the two vowels.

Practice breaking multisyllabic words with the CV/VC syllable pattern into meaningful parts. Write the word *reorganize.* Point out the prefix *re-* and say: *We know that the prefix* re- *is its own syllable and means "again."* Then cover up the prefix so that only *organize* is visible. Say: Organize *means "to put in order." We know that* organize *has three vowel sounds, so it has three syllables.* Uncover the prefix, draw lines between the syllables, and blend the word. Have students repeat the word after you. Have them explain the meaning of *reorganize.* Repeat this exercise with the words *reunite, deactivate,* and *scientists.*

Practice Copy and distribute page 237. Read the directions aloud, and help students read the words if necessary. After students complete the activities, practice saying the multisyllabic words aloud. (See answers on page 308.)

Assess Make word cards with the word parts in Part 2 of page 237. Put students in pairs. Give one student the word parts from column 1. Give the second student the word parts from column 2. Once students have pieced the words together, have them write out the words and draw lines between each syllable.

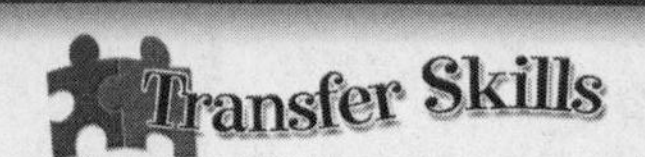

Speakers of monosyllabic languages such as Cantonese, Hmong, Khmer, Korean, and Vietnamese may pronounce a two-syllable word as two separate words. Have students practice saying multisyllabic words.

Syllables VCCCV

Use with page 238.

Preteach Write *dolphin* on the board and draw a small picture. Say: *This is a dolphin,* /d/ /o/ /l/ /f/ /i/ /n/. Point out that there are two vowel sounds in *dolphin,* and therefore two syllables. Say: *How many consonants do you see between the vowels* o *and* i *in the word* dolphin*?* Point to the l, p, and h as you say: *That's right, there are three consonants between the vowels.* Remind students that when two consonants, such as the *ph* in *dolphin* make one sound, those letters stay together when you divide the word into syllables. Say: *Now let's break the word* dolphin *into syllables: dol/phin, dolphin.* Repeat with the words *huddle* and *contract,* emphasizing vowel sounds and reviewing what students have learned about breaking words into syllables.

Pronunciation Tip
Syllables VCCCV
Remind students that a word has as many syllables as it has vowel sounds.

Teach/Model Write *surprise* on the board. Underline the three consonants between the vowels *u* and *i* and tell students: *There are three consonants between two vowels in this word. Each vowel means that there is a syllable, so we know that there are two syllables in this pattern.* Since it is hard to generalize where the syllable break comes in a word with the VCCCV syllable pattern, help students understand that they must look at each word separately to find its syllable breaks.

Practice breaking words with the VCCCV syllable pattern. Distribute several copies of a dictionary and point out how each word is divided into syllables. Write the word *complain* on the board. Ask: *How many syllables does this word have?* (2) *What is the first syllable?* (com) *What's the second syllable?* (plain) Repeat this exercise with the words *explore, sample, enclose,* and *hundred.*

Practice Copy and distribute page 238. Read the directions aloud, and have students look at the sample answer to help them get started. After students complete the activity, have them break each of the words into syllables. (See answers on page 308.)

Assess Write the following words on the board: *address, district, substance, complete,* and *control.* Have students write the words on a piece of paper, showing the syllable divisions. Students should use what they know about dividing words into syllables. If they have difficulty with a word, they may use a dictionary to see how a word is divided into syllables.

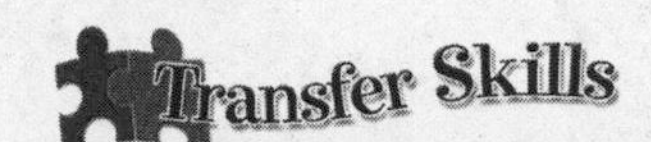

Many languages do not have the schwa /ə/ sound, so English learners may have difficulty pronouncing and spelling the unstressed syllable in words such as *table* and *apple*. Provide additional practice pronouncing these words.

C + *-le*

Use with page 239.

Preteach Say the word *candle* and draw a small picture or point to the picture of a candle on page 239. Say: *This is a candle, /k/ /a/ /n/ /d/ /əl/. How many syllables do you hear in the word* candle? *That's right, there are two syllables.* Sound out and blend the following words with *-le: bubble, puddle, table.* Point out that the first syllable in each word carries more stress than the second syllable.

Teach/Model Write *candle* on the board. Draw a line between the two syllables and tell students: *When you hear a word with more than one vowel sound, divide it into parts.* Cover *can.* Say: *If a word ends with* -le, *then the consonant before the* -le *is part of the last syllable.* Show that in the word *candle,* the letter *d* comes right before the *-le* and is part of the second syllable. Now write *double* on the board. Draw a line between the *u* and the *b* and say: *In the word* double, *the letter* b *comes before the* -le *and is part of the second syllable. Say it with me: double, dou/ble.*

Practice Copy and distribute page 239. Help students name the words that are pictured on the top half of page 239. Then read the words in the box. Clap as you read each word to emphasize the syllable break in the word. Say: *I am going to read the words again. This time write the word below the correct picture.* Review the answers as a class (*bubble, puddle, eagle, candle*), then tell students to break the words into syllables.

Assess Tell students: *I will say some words. Put your thumb up if you hear a consonant with* -le *at the end of the word. Put your thumb down if you do not:* purple, bubble, puppy, people, softball, broken, noodle. Then have students repeat the C + *-le* words back to you.

Pronunciation Tip C + *-le*
When a word ends in *-le,* the consonant that comes before the *-le* must be part of the last syllable.

Name ___________________________

Syllables V/CV and VC/V

- **Read** the words in the box. **Circle** each word with a **long vowel sound** in the first syllable. **Underline** each word with a **short vowel sound** in the first syllable.
- **Write** a word on the line by each picture.

music	tulip
lemon	broken
frozen	salad

____

____

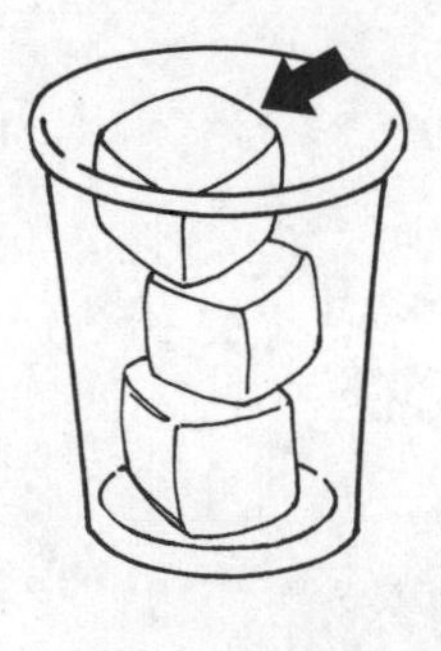

____

____

____

____

Name ______________________________

Syllables CV/VC

PART 1

- **Read** the words.
- **Find** the syllables in each word. **Draw** a line between each syllable.

scientist

piano

violin

video

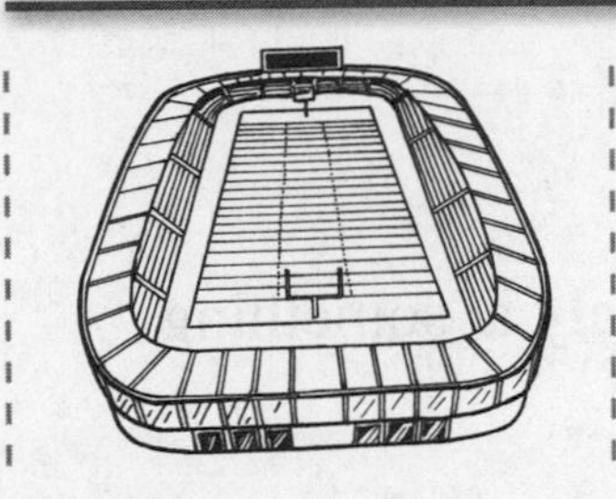

stadium

radio

rodeo

meteor

PART 2

- **Read** the two lists of words.
- **Connect** word parts from each list to make words.

studi-	-neer
cre-	-onic
ide-	-o
me-	-ate
pio-	-dium
immedi-	-ance
bi-	-a
reli-	-ate

Name ______________________________

Syllables *VCCCV*

- **Read** the words in the box.
- **Look** at the pictures. **Read** the meanings.
- **Write** the correct word on each blank line.

inspect
children
purchase
surprise
explode
address

1.  **purchase** = to buy something

2. 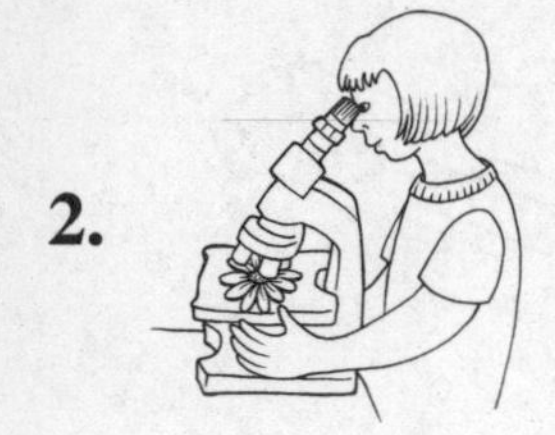 ________________ = to look closely at something

3. 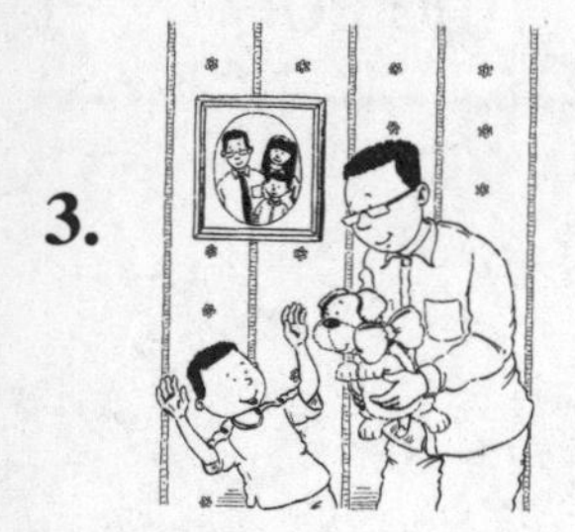 ________________ = something unexpected

4.  ________________ = more than one child

5.  ________________ = blow apart with a loud noise

6. 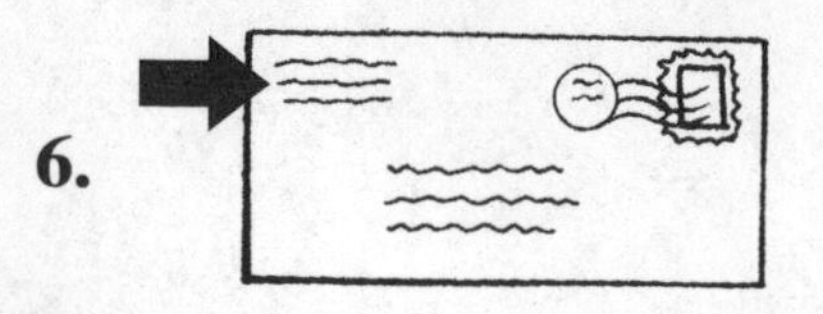 ________________ = the street where someone lives

Name ______________________________

C + -le

PART 1

- **Look** at the pictures.
- **Read** the words in the box.
- **Write** the word on the line.

_______________ _______________ _______________ _______________

puddle	bubble	candle	eagle

PART 2

- **Read** the word.
- **Write** the two syllable parts that make up the word.

_______________ + _______________ = marble

_______________ + _______________ = middle

_______________ + _______________ = double

_______________ + _______________ = little

_______________ + _______________ = title

_______________ + _______________ = handle

Consonant Blends

Transfer Skills

Consonant blends in English words often are challenging for English language learners because their home languages may not combine consonant phonemes in similar ways at the beginnings and ends of words. For example, consonant blends with *l* and *r* can be particularly difficult for speakers of Asian languages such as Chinese, Korean, and Vietnamese. Speakers of Arabic may insert vowel sounds between the consonants within a blend. The following lessons provide practice with consonant blends. If your students are struggling with particular blends, you can develop similar lessons targeted to those blends.

Initial Consonant Blends

Use with page 242.

Preteach Copy and distribute page 242. Have students point to the picture of the crib at the top of the page. Say: *This is a crib. The word* crib *begins with /kr/.* Write *crib* on the board. Say: *Usually, when two letters come before a vowel* (underline the *cr*), *we blend the sounds of the letters: /k/ /r/... /kr/ /i/ /b/. Say it with me: /kr/ /i/ /b/,* crib. Repeat for *clap.*

Teach/Model Direct students' attention to Row 1. Name each of the items shown, one by one: *crab, crown, clock, cloth.* Continue: *I'll say each word one more time. If the word starts with the letters* cr, *circle* cr *under the picture. If the word starts with the letters* cl, *circle* cl. Read the words aloud once more, giving students enough time to circle the corresponding letter.

Tell students that there are many beginning blends in English. Write a 10-column chart on the board with the headings: *br, cr, cl, fl, gr, pr, pl, sn, sp, st.* List the words *crib* and *clap* in the columns where they belong. Add the words from Row 1 to the chart. Give several more examples. Invite children to suggest other words that begin with these blends that can be added to the chart.

Practice Have students look at the pictures in Row 2. Name the items shown *(princess, plant, price, plug),* and pause to let students circle their answer choices. Repeat the procedure for Row 3 (*straw, string, steak, starfish).*

Read the practice sentence aloud, and have students find the words with beginning blends *(clock, struck, students, snapped).* After they've had a chance to repeat the sentence several times, challenge students to say it as quickly as they can.

Assess Prepare sets of cards with a blend written on each one: *cr, cl, pr, pl, tr, dr, st, str.* Give each student a set of cards. Say a list of words, and have students display the correct initial blends: *crawl, please, claw, preen, tree, street, draw, stall.* Then have students repeat the words after you, striving for the correct pronunciation of the initial blends. Keep in mind that students who have difficulty pronouncing the initial blends may still be able to comprehend words they hear or read that start with these consonants.

Pronunciation Tip Initial Consonant Blends *When a word begins with two consonants like* c *and* r, *you blend the sounds of the two consonants together. In the word* crib, *take the /k/ sound and /r/ sound and put them together: /kr/. Try it: /kr/, /kr/, /kr/ /i/ /b/,* crib.

Final Consonant Blends — Use with page 243.

Preteach Copy and distribute page 243. Have students point to the picture of the pond at the top of the page. Say: *This is a pond. The word* pond *ends with /nd/. Usually, when two letters come after a vowel* (underline the *nd*), *we blend the sounds of the letters: /n/ /d/.../p/ /o/ /n/ /d/. Say it with me:* pond, /p/ /o/ /n/ /d/. Repeat for *sink*.

Teach/Model Direct students' attention to Row 1. Name each of the items shown, one by one: *(band, trunk, hand, bank)*. Continue: *I'll say each word one more time. If the word ends with the letters* nd, *circle* nd *under the picture. If the word ends with the letters* nk, *circle* nk. Read the words aloud once more, giving students enough time to circle the corresponding letter.

Tell students that there are many ending blends in English. Write a 9-column chart on the board with the headings *lt, mp, nch, nd, nk, nt, sk, sp, st.* List the words *pond* and *sink* in the columns where they belong. Add the words from Row 1 to the chart. Give several more examples. Invite children to suggest other words that end with these blends that can be added to the chart.

Practice Have students look at the pictures in Row 2. Name the items shown *(ant, paint, branch, inch)*, and pause to let students circle their answer choices. Repeat the procedure for Row 3 *(desk, vest, cast, mask)*.

Read the practice sentence aloud, and have students find the words with ending blends *(must, ask, band, paint, bench)*. After they've had a chance to read the sentence several times, challenge students to say it from memory.

Assess Prepare sets of cards with a blend written on each one: *nd, nk, nt, nch, sk, st.* Give each student a set of cards. Say a list of words, and have students display the correct final blends: *sink, cinch, bank, band, inch, ink, dusk, dust, ant, and, paint, pond.* Then have students repeat the words after you, striving for the correct pronunciation of the final blends. Keep in mind that students who have difficulty pronouncing the final blends may still be able to comprehend words they hear or read that end with these consonants.

Pronunciation Tip
Final Consonant Blends *When a word ends with two consonants like* s *and* k, *you blend the sounds of the two consonants together. In the word* desk, *take the /s/ sound and /k/ sound and put them together: /sk/. Try it: /sk/, /sk/, desk.*

Name ______________________________

Initial Consonant Blends

- If the word begins with the sound of *cr* in *crib*, **circle** the *cr.*
- If the word begins with the sound of *cl* in *clap*, **circle** the *cl.*

ROW 1

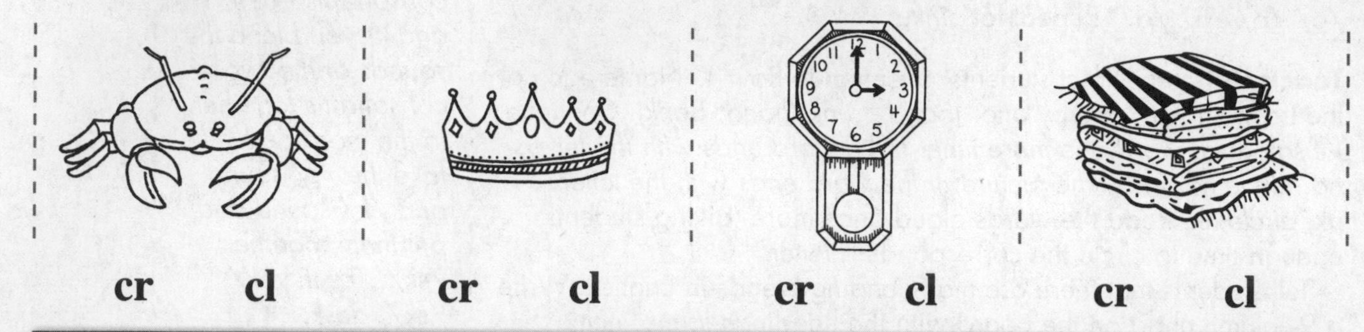

cr **cl** **cr** **cl** **cr** **cl** **cr** **cl**

- If the word begins with the sound of *pl* in *plum*, **circle** the *pl.*
- If the word begins with the sound of *pr* in *prize*, **circle** the *pr.*

ROW 2

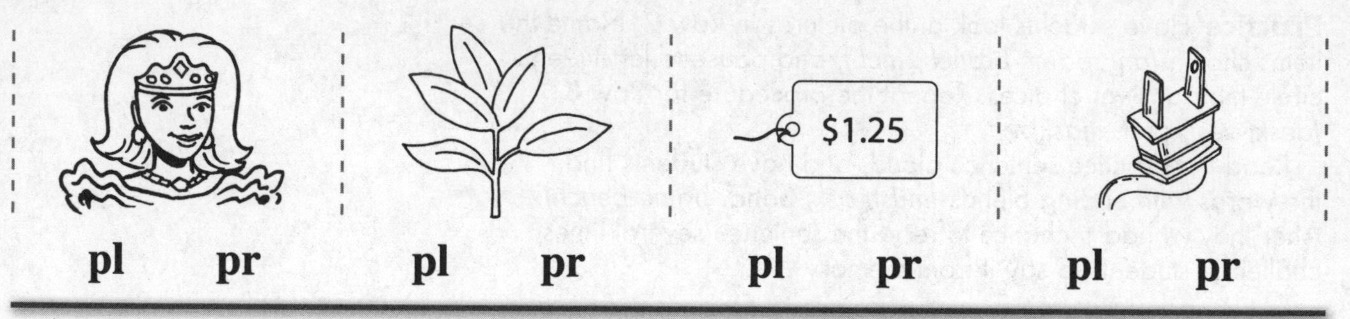

pl **pr** **pl** **pr** **pl** **pr** **pl** **pr**

- If the word begins with the sound of *str* in *stripe*, **circle** the *str.*
- If the word begins with the sound of *st* in *stick*, **circle** the *st.*

ROW 3

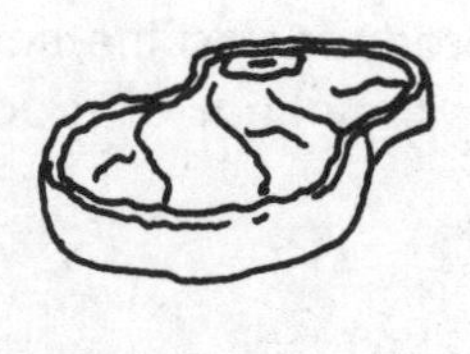

str **st** **str** **st** **str** **st** **str** **st**

Find the beginning blends in this sentence. Then **practice** chanting or singing the sentence.

When the clock struck one, the students snapped their fingers.

Name ______________________________

Final Consonant Blends

- If the word ends with the sound of *nd* in *pond*, **circle** the *nd*.
- If the word ends with the sound of *nk* in *sink*, **circle** the *nk*.

ROW 1

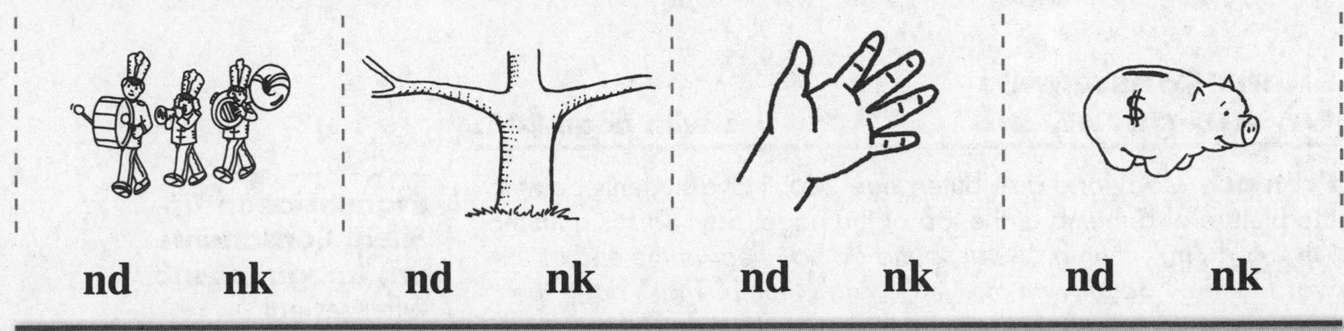

- If the word ends with the sound of *nt* in *cent*, **circle** the *nt*.
- If the word ends with the sound of *nch* in *bench*, **circle** the *nch*.

ROW 2

- If the word ends with the sound of *st* in *nest*, **circle** the *st*.
- If the word ends with the sound of *sk* in *tusk*, **circle** the *sk*.

ROW 3

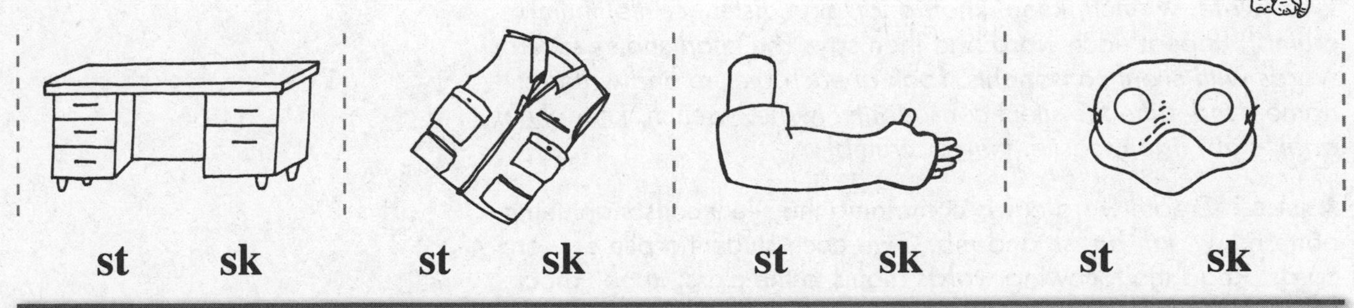

Find the ending blends in this sentence. Then **practice** chanting or singing the sentence.

You must ask the band to paint the bench.

Silent Consonants

Transfer Skills

Students who are literate in their home language(s) may be familiar with the concept of silent letters. In Spanish, the letter *h* is always silent, and the letter *u* is silent when it follows a *q*. In French, the letter *s* at the end of a word is often silent. Discuss students' awareness of silent letters in their home languages before introducing *wr, kn, gn, st,* and *mb.*

Silent Consonants *wr, kn, gn, st, mb*

Use with page 245.

Preteach Copy and distribute page 245. Have students point to the picture of a thumb at the top of the page. Say: *This is a thumb, /th/ /u/ /m/, thumb. What sound do you hear at the end of the word* thumb? *Say it with me: /m/, /m/, thumb. That's right, the ending sound is /m/.* Now point to the *castle.* Ask: *What sound do you hear in the middle of the word? Listen: /k/ /a/ /s/ /əl/. Yes, the middle sound is /s/.*

Teach/Model Write the word *thumb* on the board. Underline the *mb* in the word and tell students: *The sound /m/ in* thumb *is spelled* mb. *Say it with me: thumb, /th/ /u/ /m/. The letters* mb *make the sound /m/ in* thumb. *The letter* b *is not pronounced.* Now write *castle* on the board. Underline the *st* in the word and say: *The sound /s/ is in the middle of the word* castle. *Say it with me:* castle. *The letters* st *make the sound /s/ in* castle. *The letter* t *is not pronounced.*

Help students name the items in Row 1 on page 245 *(climb, wrist, gnat, knot, knit).* Repeat each word, stretching out the sounds. Say: *I am going to read the words again. This time, circle the silent consonants in each word.* Review the answers as a class *(mb, wr, gn, kn, kn).*

Practice Have students name the items in the chart on page 245 *(write, wrench, knee, knot, gnat, sign, listen, castle, thumb, crumb).* Repeat each word and then say: *The chart shows several words with silent consonants. Look at each picture and write its name. Underline the silent consonants. (<u>wr</u>ite, <u>wr</u>ench, <u>kn</u>ee, <u>kn</u>ot, <u>g</u>nat, si<u>g</u>n, li<u>st</u>en, ca<u>st</u>le, thu<u>mb</u>, cru<u>mb</u>).*

Assess Create word cards containing the silent consonant letter patterns *wr, kn, gn, st,* and *mb.* Give each student a pile of word cards. Read the following words aloud to the class: *knob, knock, knit, write, wrist, wreath, sign, gnat, design, listen, hustle, bustle, lamb, comb,* and *numb.* Pause after each word so students can find and hold up the card that contains the silent consonant letter pattern that corresponds to each word.

Pronunciation Tip Silent Consonants *wr, kn, gn, st, mb*
Offer several examples of words containing letter patterns with silent consonants *(knee, knob, wrist, sign, castle, lamb).* See if students can point out the silent letter as they look at and listen to each word.

Name ______________________________

Silent Consonants *wr, kn, gn, st, mb*

- **Listen** for the beginning and ending sounds.
- **Circle** the correct letters.

ROW 1

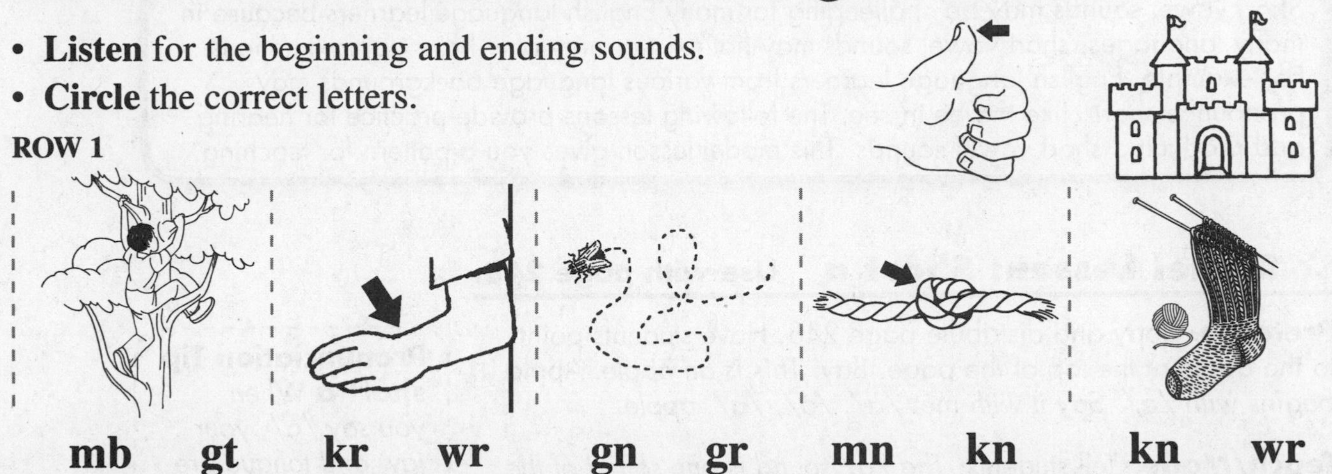

mb **gt** | **kr** **wr** | **gn** **gr** | **mn** **kn** | **kn** **wr**

- **Look** at the pictures in each column. **Write** the word for each picture.

Silent Consonants				
wr	kn	gn	st	mb
______	______	______	______	______
______	______	______	______	______

Short Vowels

Transfer Skills

Short vowel sounds may be challenging for many English language learners because in many languages, short vowel sounds may not exist or may only have approximations. For example, English language learners from various language backgrounds may pronounce short *i* like the *ee* in *see*. The following lessons provide practice for hearing and producing short vowel sounds. This model lesson gives you a pattern for teaching.

☆ Model Lesson: Short *a* Use with page 248.

Preteach Copy and distribute page 248. Have students point to the apple at the top of the page. Say: *This is an apple.* Apple *begins with /a/. Say it with me: /a/, /a/, /a/, apple.*

Teach/Model Tell students: *The /a/ sound is one sound of the letter* a. *We call this sound the short* a. *Repeat these /a/ words after me:* cap, am, mat, pan.

Ask students to name the items in Row 1 on page 248 *(acrobat, mop, bat, ant)*. Repeat each word, clearly pronouncing the vowel each time. Then say: *I'll say these words again. If you hear the /a/ sound, circle the picture:* acrobat, mop, bat, ant. Students should circle the *acrobat, bat,* and *ant* pictures—but not the *mop*.

Practice Have students look at the pictures in Row 2 on page 248. Have them read the words below each picture and circle the word that names it *(cap, man, map, can)*. Then have them look at the pictures in Row 3, say the name of each picture, and write the names *(man, bat, ant, hat)*.

Read the practice sentence aloud, and have students find the short *a* words *(acrobat, an, apple, bat, act)*. Invite students to chant the sentence together, clapping each time they hear short *a*.

Assess Tell students: *I will say some word pairs. Raise your hand when you hear the /a/ sound:* pat, pet; hot, hat; bad, bed; man, main; tug, tag. Then have students repeat the word pairs after you, striving for the correct pronunciation of /a/. Keep in mind that students who have difficulty pronouncing /a/ may still be able to comprehend short *a* words that they hear or read.

Pronunciation Tip
short *a* *When you say /a/, your jaw and tongue are down. Say /a/ and feel your jaw and tongue go down.*

Adapting the ☆ Model Lesson

Use the same lesson format above to teach the short vowels /e/, /i/, /o/, and /u/. The following information will help you to customize each lesson.

Notes for Additional Lessons

Short *e*

Use with page 249.

Teach/Model Use these /e/ words: *enter, exit, elephant, elk.* Row 1 of page 249: *vest, elephant, tiger, tent.*

Practice Row 2: *pen, web, bell, bed;* Row 3: *ten, bell, nest, web.* Practice sentence: *The elephant entered the tent with an elegant step.*

Assess Use these word pairs: *set, sat; ten, tan; net, not; sell, sale.*

Pronunciation Tip
short e *When you say /e/, your mouth is open. Your tongue is behind your bottom teeth. Say /e/. Did your mouth open? Say /e/ again.*

Short *i*

Use with page 250.

Teach/Model Use these /i/ words: *it, sit, if, thin, with.* Row 1 of page 250: *dinner, gift, ice, inch.*

Practice Row 2: *pin, zip, dig, sit;* Row 3: *zip, gift, pig, six.* Practice sentence: *Six pigs with bibs grinned and did a jig in a minute.*

Assess Use these word pairs: *tin, ten; six, socks; pig, pine; trip, trap.*

Pronunciation Tip
short *i* *When you say /i/, your mouth is open and your tongue is slightly lowered. Say /i/. Is your mouth open, and is your tongue slightly lowered? Practice: /i/.* In Spanish, the letter *i* is pronounced /ē/. Point out that this letter has different sounds in English.

Short *o*

Use with page 251.

Teach/Model Use these /o/ words: *on, olive, Oscar, opposite.* Row 1 of page 251: *elephant, dog, octopus, box.*

Practice Row 2: *lock, rock, fox, hop;* Row 3: *box, dog, lock, mop.* Practice sentence: *I opened the lock and a fox jumped out of the box.*

Assess Use these word pairs: *hop, hope; top, tape; dog, dig; lock, lake.*

Pronunciation Tip
short o *When you say /o/, your mouth is open and your jaw drops. Put your hand under your chin and say /o/. See, your mouth opened and your jaw dropped.* In Spanish, the sound of letter *a* is similar to /o/ in English. Examples: *mami/mom; mapa/mop.*

Short *u*

Use with page 252.

Teach/Model Use these /u/ words: *up, bump, slump, plug.* Row 1 of page 252: *truck, plane, puppy, train.*

Practice Row 2: *bus, duck, tub, rug;* Row 3: *bus, truck, duck, sun.* Practice sentence: *A bug on a rug jumped up and landed on a pup.*

Assess Use these word pairs: *bug, bag; tub, tube; cup, cap; cub, cube.*

Pronunciation Tip
short u *When you say /u/, your mouth is open and your tongue is down. Say /u/ again. Is your mouth open? Is your tongue down?*

Name ______________________________

Words with Short *a*

- **Listen** for the sound of *a* in *apple.*
- **Circle** the pictures of words that have this sound.

ROW 1

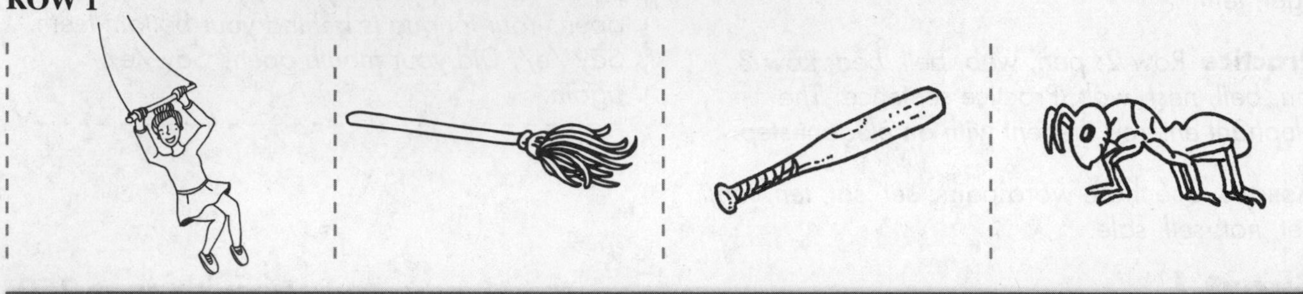

- **Look** at each picture. **Say** its name.
- **Circle** the word that names each picture.

ROW 2

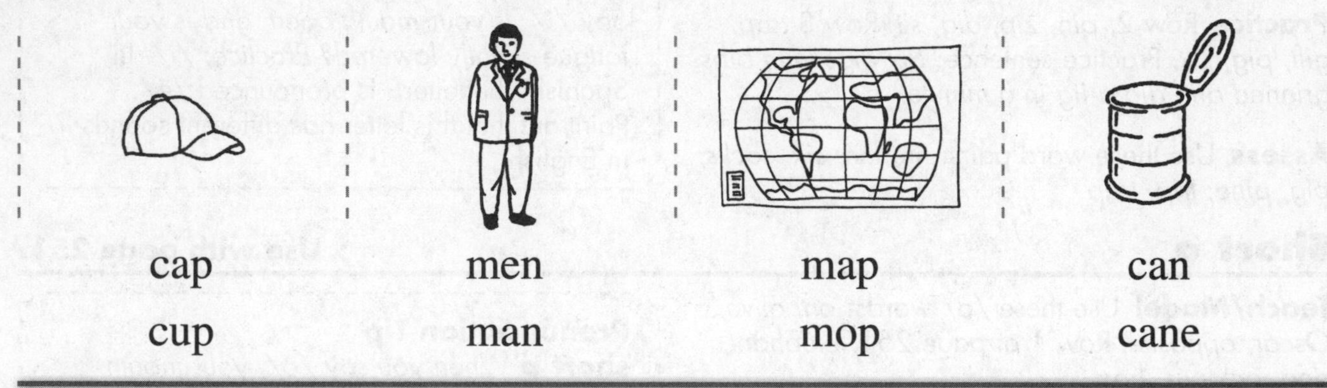

cap	men	map	can
cup	man	mop	cane

- **Look** at each picture. **Say** its name.
- **Write** the name of the picture.

ROW 3

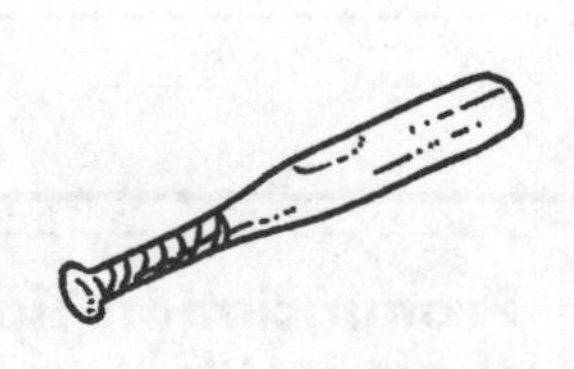

______________ ______________ ______________ ______________

Find short *a* in this sentence. Then **practice** chanting or singing the sentence.

The acrobat hit an apple with a bat in the middle of her act.

Name ______________________________

Words with Short e

- **Listen** for the sound of *e* in *elbow.*
- **Circle** the pictures of words that have this sound.

ROW 1

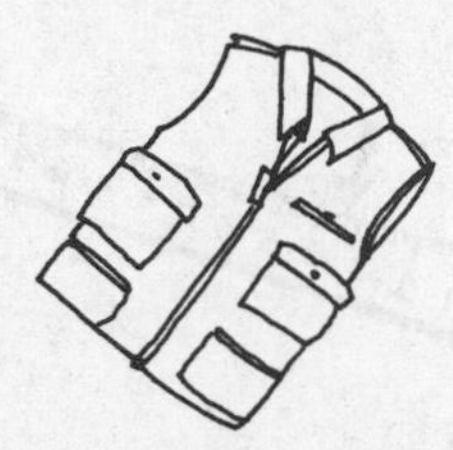   

- **Look** at each picture. **Say** its name.
- **Circle** the word that names each picture.

ROW 2

   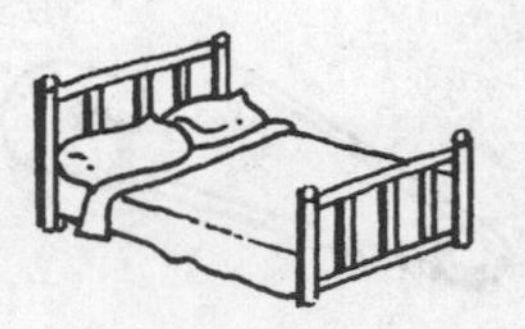

pine	web	ball	bed
pen	weed	bell	bead

- **Look** at each picture. **Say** its name.
- **Write** the name of the picture.

ROW 3

______________ ______________ ______________ ______________

Find short *e* in this sentence. Then **practice** chanting or singing the sentence.

The elephant entered the tent with an elegant step.

Name ______________________________

Words with Short *i*

- **Listen** for the sound of *i* in *pig*.
- **Circle** the pictures of words that have this sound.

ROW 1

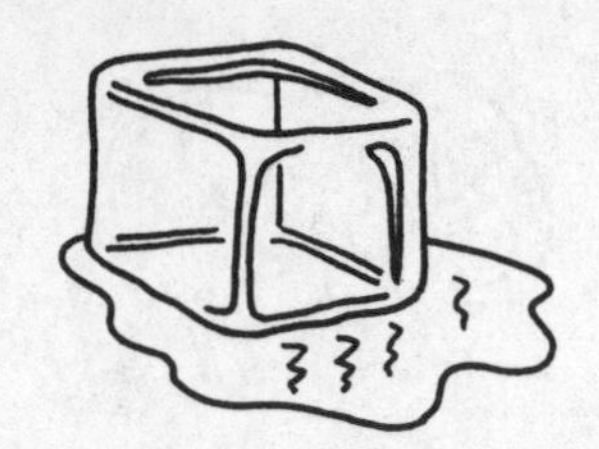

- **Look** at each picture. **Say** its name.
- **Circle** the word that names each picture.

ROW 2

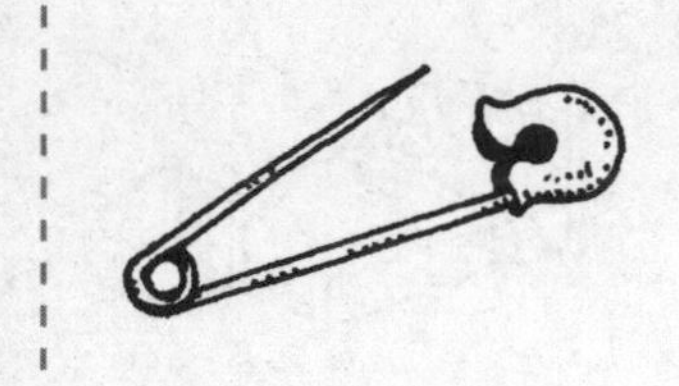

pin
pine

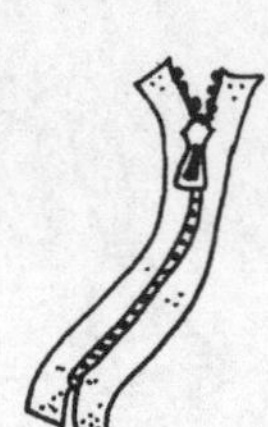

zip
zap

dog
dig

set
sit

- **Look** at each picture. **Say** its name.
- **Write** the name of the picture.

ROW 3

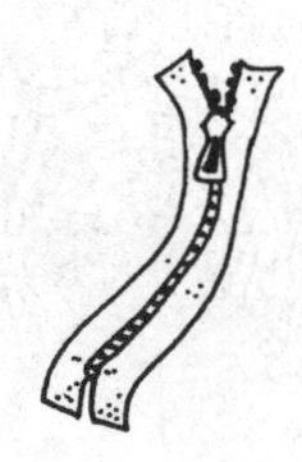

______________ ______________ ______________ ______________

Find short *i* in this sentence. Then **practice** chanting or singing the sentence.

Six pigs with bibs grinned and did a jig in a minute.

Name ______________________________

Words with Short o

- **Listen** for the sound of *o* in *ox.*
- **Circle** the pictures of words that have this sound.

ROW 1

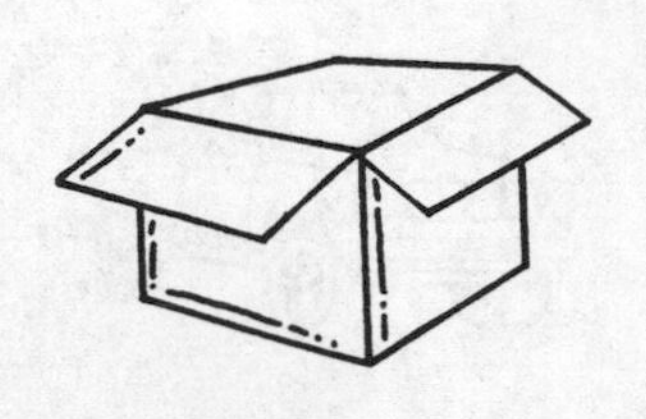

- **Look** at each picture. **Say** its name.
- **Circle** the word that names each picture.

ROW 2

lick	rock	fox	hop
lock	rack	fix	hope

- **Look** at each picture. **Say** its name.
- **Write** the name of the picture.

ROW 3

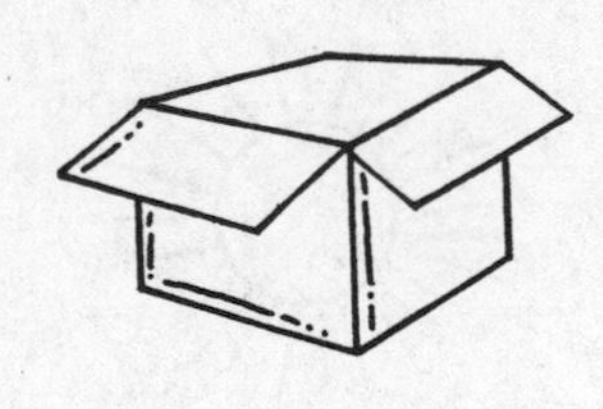

______________ ______________ ______________ ______________

Find short *o* in this sentence. Then **practice** chanting or singing the sentence.

I opened the lock and a fox jumped out of the box.

Name ___________________________

Words with Short *u*

- **Listen** for the sound of *u* in *sun.*
- **Circle** the pictures of words that have this sound.

ROW 1

 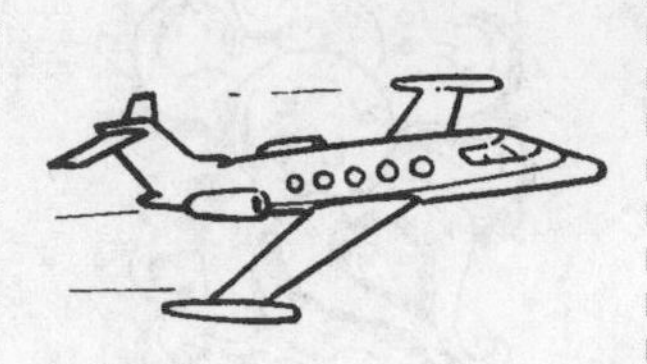  

- **Look** at each picture. **Say** its name.
- **Circle** the word that names each picture.

ROW 2

   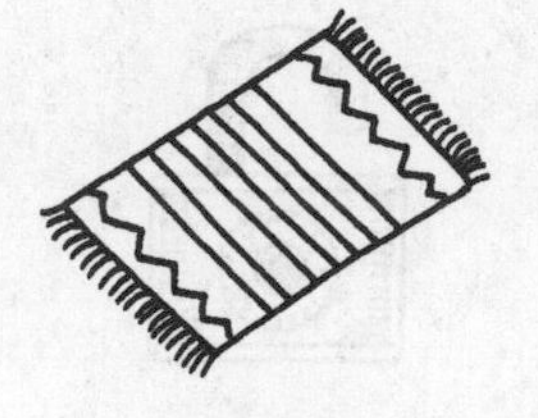

bus	dock	tub	rug
boss	duck	tube	rag

- **Look** at each picture. **Say** its name.
- **Write** the name of the picture.

ROW 3

_______________ _______________ _______________ _______________

Find short *u* in this sentence. Then **practice** chanting or singing the sentence.

A bug on a rug jumped up and landed on a pup.

Long vowels and the vowel digraphs that produce long vowel sounds can be confusing for English language learners. For example, some long vowel sounds in English are similar to the sounds made by different vowels or vowel combinations in Spanish. As a result, Spanish speakers may spell long *a* words with an *e*, or long *i* words with *ai*. The following lessons provide practice for hearing, producing, and spelling long vowel sounds. This model lesson gives you a pattern for teaching.

☆ Model Lesson: Long *a*   Use with page 255.

Preteach Copy and distribute page 255. Have students point to the bunch of grapes at the top of the page. Say: *These are grapes.* Grapes *has the sound of /ā/. Say it with me: /ā/, /ā/, grapes.* Repeat for *rain* and *tray.*

Teach/Model Tell students: *The /ā/ sound is one sound of the letter* a. *We call this sound the long* a. *Repeat these /ā/ words after me:* age, name, make, place, state.

Ask students to name the items in Row 1 on page 255 *(rake, cat, train, plate)*. Repeat each word, clearly pronouncing the vowel each time. Then say: *I'll say these words again. If you hear the /ā/ sound, circle the picture:* rake, cat, train, plate. Students should circle the *rake, train,* and *plate* pictures—but not the *cat.*

Point out that there are different ways of spelling long *a* words. Write a 3-column chart on the board with the headings *a_e, ai,* and *ay.* List the words *grapes, rain,* and *tray* in the columns where they belong. Add the long *a* words from Row 1 to the chart. Invite students to suggest other long *a* words they know that can be added to the chart.

Practice Have students look at the pictures in Row 2 on page 255. Have them read the words below each picture and circle the word that names it *(snake, chain, plane, hay)*. Then have them look at the pictures in Row 3, say the name of each picture, and write the names *(grapes, tray, rake, rain)*.

Read the practice sentence aloud, and have students find the long *a* words *(came, gate, cave, waited, Dave)*. Invite students to chant the sentence together, clapping each time they hear long *a.*

Assess Tell students: *I will say some word pairs. Raise your hand if both words have the /ā/ sound:* sell, sale; cage, rage; ate, late; gate, get; rack, rake. Then have students repeat the word pairs after you, striving for the correct pronunciation of /ā/. Keep in mind that students who have difficulty pronouncing /ā/ may still be able to comprehend long *a* words that they hear or read.

Pronunciation Tip
long *a* *When you start to say /ā/, your mouth is open. Your tongue is in the middle of your mouth. To finish the sound /ā/, your tongue and your jaw move up a little. Try it: /ā/, /ā/, ape.* The long *a* sound is similar to the Spanish digraph *ei*. Example: *rain/reina* (queen).

Adapting the ☆ Model Lesson

Use the same lesson format above to teach the long vowels /ē/, /ī/, /ō/, and /ū/. The following information will help you to customize each lesson.

Notes for Additional Lessons

Long *e*

Use with page 256.

Teach/Model Use these /ē/ words: *bee, beaver, me, team*. Row 1 of page 256: *eagle, teeth, eye, feet*. Make a 4-column chart for long e words.

Practice Row 2: *he, wheel, thirty, leaf*. Row 3: *tree, leaf, me, bee*. Practice sentence: See the leaves on the trees on our street.

Assess Use these word pairs: *team, Tim; meat, met; leaf, lean; seen, seat; wheat, wet*.

Pronunciation Tip
long e *When you say /ē/, your lips are stretched wide. Your mouth has a little smile when you say /ē/. Try it: /ē/, /ē/, /ē/*. The long e sound is similar to the sound of *i* in Spanish. Examples: *need/nido* (nest); *see/sí* (yes).

Long *i*

Use with page 257.

Teach/Model Use these /ī/ words: *kite, five, sky, why*. Row 1 of page 257: *bike, night, mice, fish*. Make a 5-column chart for long *i* words.

Practice Row 2: *ice, child, tie, light*. Row 3: *five, kite, light, sky*. Practice sentence: Five kites in the sky are flying high.

Assess Use these word pairs: *fight, fit; sky, sly; mice, miss; rice, price; light, lit*.

Pronunciation Tip
long *i* *When you say /ī/, your mouth is open and your jaw drops. Your tongue is down. To finish the sound /ī/, your tongue and your jaw move up. Try it: /ī/, /ī/, /ī/*. The long *i* sound is similar to the Spanish digraphs *ai* and *ay*. Examples: *I/hay* (there is/are); *bike/baile* (dance).

Long *o*

Use with page 258.

Teach/Model Use these /ō/ words: *rose, goat, pillow, smoke*. Row 1 of page 258: *rope, lock, nose, bone*. Make a 4-column chart for long *o* words.

Practice Row 2: *robe, gold, bow, boat*. Row 3: *goat, rose, snow(man), gold*. Practice sentence: Joan wrote a note and rode on a boat.

Assess Use these word pairs: *boat, bought; globe, lobe; low, blow; hose, toes; coat, cot*.

Pronunciation Tip
long o *When you say /ō/, your mouth is round. Try it: /ō/, /ō/, /ō/*. The long *o* sound is similar to the sound of *o* in Spanish. Example: *no/no*.

Long *u*

Use with page 259.

Teach/Model Use these /ū/ words: *flute, balloon, cube, use, news, true, blue*. Row 1 of page 259: *boat, boot, suitcase, foot*. Make a 5-column chart for long *u* words.

Practice Row 2: *glue, stool, fruit, mule*. Row 3: *fruit, flute, moon, cube*. Practice sentence: Sue used blue when she drew the moon.

Assess Use these word pairs: *tune, ton; rule, tool; soon, son; glue, blue; too, toe*.

Pronunciation Tip
long u *When you say /ū/ in a word like* rule, *your mouth is round and the opening is small. Try it: /ū/, /ū/. When you say /ū/ in a word like* use, *your lips start out in a line. Then they move into a circle. Try it: /ū/, /ū/*. The long *u* sound in *tube* is similar to the sound of *u* in Spanish: *tube/tubo*. The long *u* sound in *unit* is similar to the sound of *iu* or *yu* in Spanish: *unit/yugo*.

Name ______________________________

Words with Long *a*

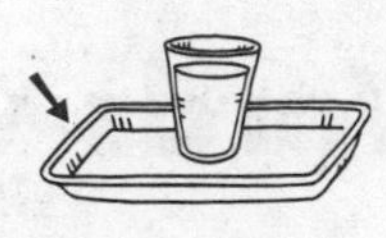

- **Listen** for the sound of *a* in *grapes*.
- **Circle** the pictures of words that have this sound.

ROW 1

- **Look** at each picture. **Say** its name.
- **Circle** the word that names each picture.

ROW 2

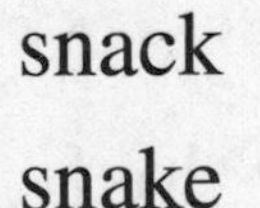

snack	chin	plan	hay
snake	chain	plane	hat

- **Look** at each picture. **Say** its name.
- **Write** the name of the picture.

ROW 3

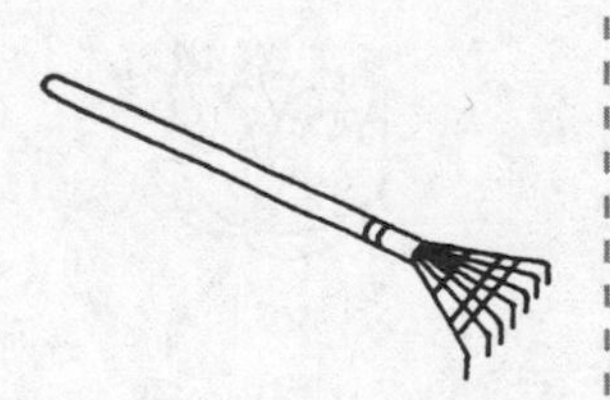

______________ ______________ ______________ ______________

Find long *a* in this sentence. Then **practice** chanting or singing the sentence.

We came to a gate by the cave and waited for Dave.

Name ______________________________

Words with Long e

- **Listen** for the sound of *e* in *bee.*
- **Circle** the pictures of words that have this sound.

ROW 1

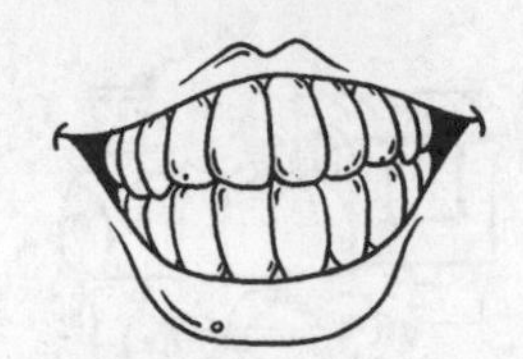

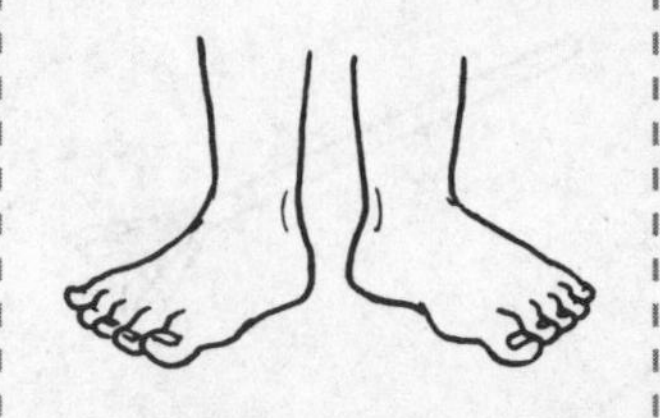

- **Look** at each picture. **Say** its name.
- **Circle** the word that names each picture.

ROW 2

he	well	thirst	leaf
hi	wheel	thirty	loaf

- **Look** at each picture. **Say** its name.
- **Write** the name of the picture.

ROW 3

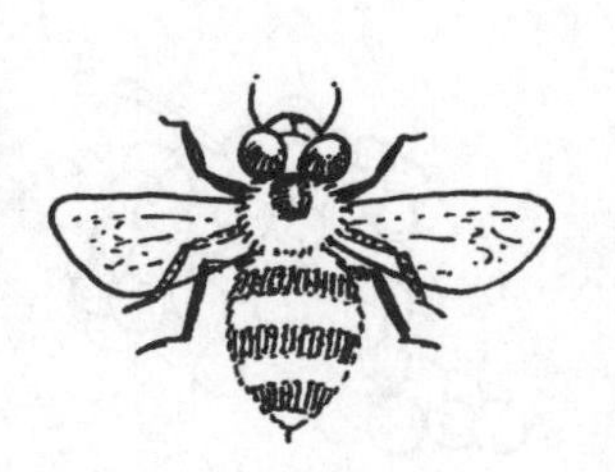

______________ ______________ ______________ ______________

Find long *e* in this sentence. Then **practice** chanting or singing the sentence.

See the leaves on the trees on our street.

Name ________________________________

Words with Long *i*

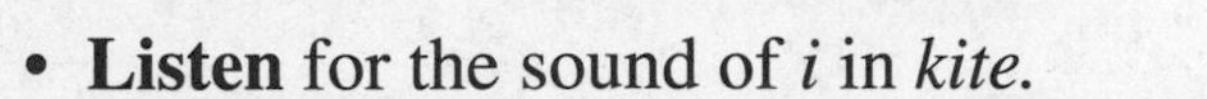

- **Listen** for the sound of *i* in *kite.*
- **Circle** the pictures of words that have this sound.

ROW 1

- **Look** at each picture. **Say** its name.
- **Circle** the word that names each picture.

ROW 2

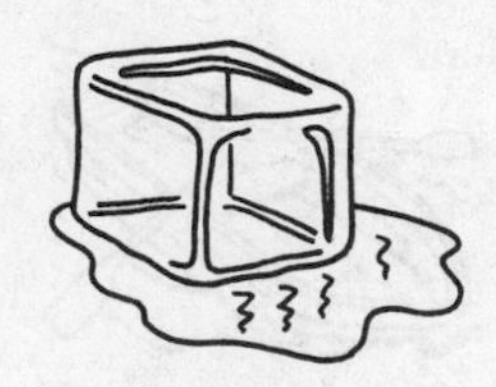			
ice	child	tie	lit
ace	chill	tea	light

- **Look** at each picture. **Say** its name.
- **Write** the name of the picture.

ROW 3

________________ ________________ ________________ ________________

Find long *i* in this sentence. Then **practice** chanting or singing the sentence.

Five kites in the sky are flying high.

Name ___________________________

Words with Long o

- **Listen** for the sound of *o* in *goat.*
- **Circle** the pictures of words that have this sound.

ROW 1

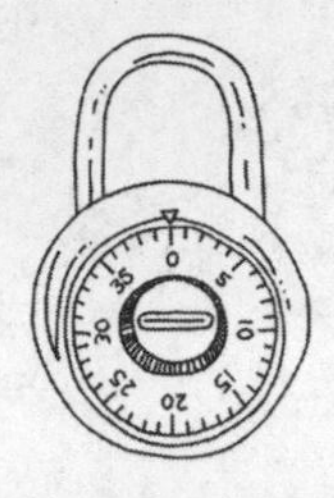

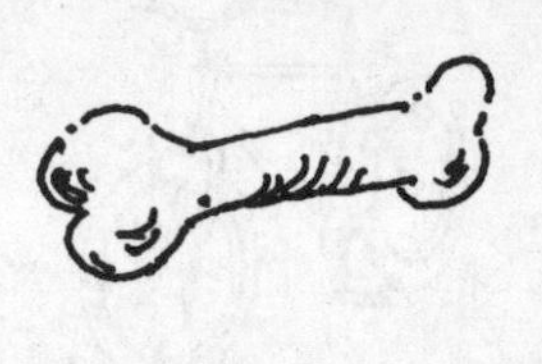

- **Look** at each picture. **Say** its name.
- **Circle** the word that names each picture.

ROW 2

rob	gold	bow	bat
robe	good	box	boat

- **Look** at each picture. **Say** its name.
- **Write** the name of the picture.

ROW 3

_______________ _______________ _______________ _______________

Find long *o* in this sentence. Then **practice** chanting or singing the sentence.

Joan wrote a note and rode on a boat.

Name ______________________________

Words with Long *u*

- **Listen** for the sound of *u* in *flute*.
- **Circle** the pictures of words that have this sound.

ROW 1

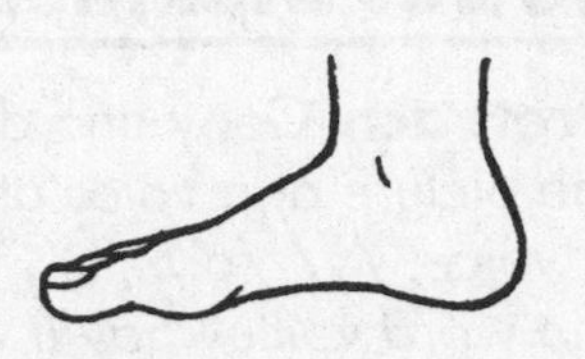

- **Look** at each picture. **Say** its name.
- **Circle** the word that names each picture.

ROW 2

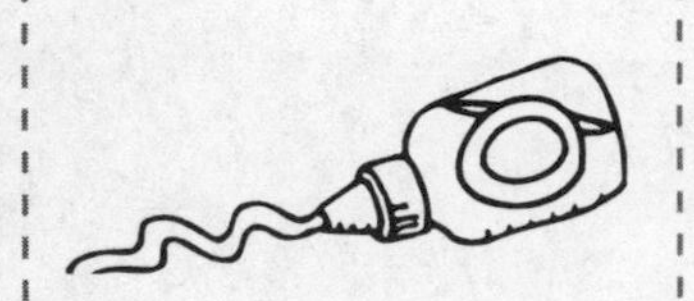

glue	stole	fright	mole
glow	stool	fruit	mule

- **Look** at each picture. **Say** its name.
- **Write** the name of the picture.

ROW 3

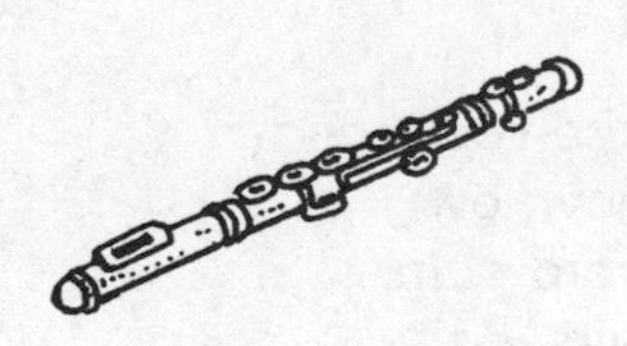

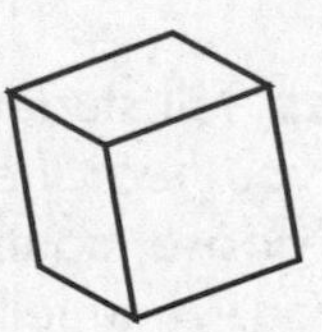

__________ __________ __________ __________

Find long *u* in this sentence. Then **practice** chanting or singing the sentence.

Sue used blue when she drew the moon.

Vowel Diphthongs

Transfer Skills

Explain to Spanish speakers that the Spanish vowel sounds *au* and *oy* are similar in pronunciation to /ou/ *ow* and /oi/ *oy* in English. Display and discuss the examples *jaula (birdcage), flauta (flute), hoy (today),* and *soy (I am).*

Vowel Diphthongs

Use with page 261.

Pronunciation Tip
Vowel Diphthongs
In a diphthong, each vowel contributes to the sound that is produced or heard.

Preteach Copy and distribute page 261. Have students point to the picture of a *voice* at the top of the page. Say: *This child has a voice, /v/ /oi/ /s/, voice. What vowel sound do you hear in the word voice? Say it with me: voice, /oi/, /oi/, voice. That's right, the sound is* /oi/. Now point to the *cloud*. Ask: *What vowel sound do you hear in the word* cloud? *Listen: /c/ /l/ /ou/ /d/. Yes, the sound is* /ou/. Repeat this drill for the words *royal* and *plow.*

Teach/Model Write the word *voice* on the board. Underline the *oi* and tell students: *The sound /oi/ in* voice *is spelled* oi. Now write *royal* on the board. Underline the *oy* in the word and say: *The sound /oi/ in* royal *is spelled* oy. Then write *cloud* on the board. Underline the *ou* and say: *The sound /ou/ in* cloud *is spelled* ou. Repeat for the word *plow.*

Help students name the items in Row 1 on page 261 *(soil, boy, coin, box).* Repeat each name, clearly pronouncing the vowel sound in each word. Say: *I am going to say these words again:* soil, boy, coin, box. *Circle the pictures of words that have the /oi/ sound as in* voice. (Students should circle *soil, boy,* and *coin,* but not *box.*)

Practice Have students look at the pictures in Row 2 on page 261. Help students name each picture *(crowd, count, towel, plow).* Have them choose and circle the word that correctly names each picture. Have students look at the pictures in Row 3, say the name of each picture, and write the names *(cow, toy, voice, cloud).*

Assess Tell students: *I will say some word pairs. Raise your hand when you hear the /ou/ sound:* plow, blow; grow, how; owl, snow; goose, south. Then have students repeat the word pairs after you. Then tell the class: *Here are more word pairs. Raise your hand when you hear the /oi/ sound:* soy, soon; enjoy, rock; choice, short; toil, coat; join, born. Have the class repeat the word pairs after you, striving for the correct pronunciation of /oi/.

Name ________________________________

Vowel Diphthongs

- **Listen** to the sound of *oi* in *voice* and *oy* in *royal.*
- **Circle** the pictures of words that have this sound.

ROW 1

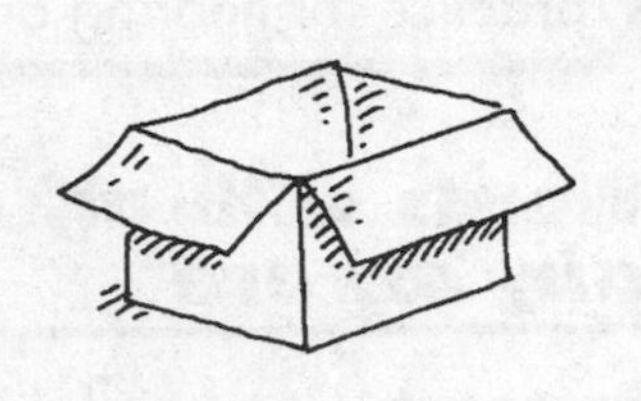

- **Look** at each picture. **Say** its name.
- **Circle** the word that names the picture.

ROW 2

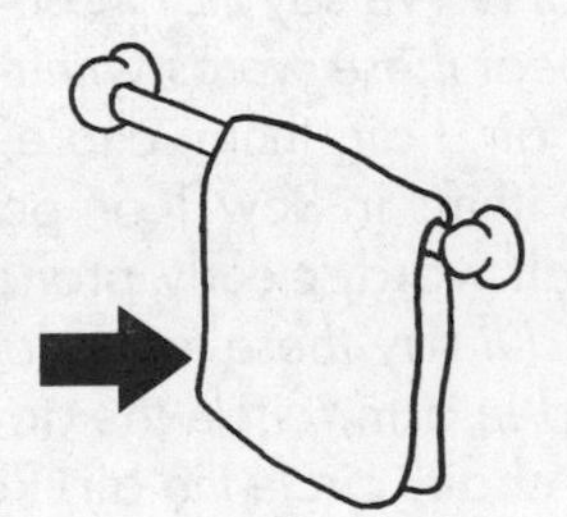

crowd	cob	towel	plow
crop	count	toil	pot

- **Look** at each picture. **Say** its name.
- **Write** the name of the picture.

ROW 3

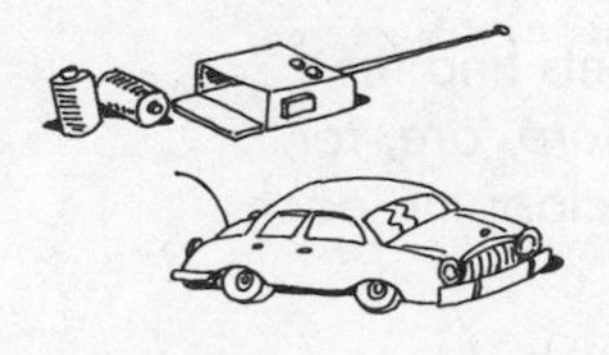

____________ ____________ ____________ ____________

Find the vowel diphthongs in this sentence. Then **practice** chanting or singing the sentence.

The boy will count his toy cows.

r-Controlled Vowels

Transfer Skills

The /r/ sound is flapped or rolled in languages such as Spanish, Polish, Farsi, and Arabic, so speakers of these languages may have difficulty pronouncing words with *r*-controlled vowels, especially in words such as *part* and *turn,* when *r* is followed by a consonant. Also, Spanish does not have a sound that is equivalent to /er/, so Spanish speakers may pronounce *bird* as *beerd* or *later* as *la-tair.* The following lessons provide practice for hearing and pronouncing words with *r*-controlled vowels.

Words with *ar, are, air, or, ore*

Use with page 264.

Preteach Copy and distribute page 264. Have students point to the picture of the arm at the top of the page. Say: *This is an arm.* Arm *has the sound of /är/. Say it with me: /är/, /är/, arm.* Repeat the procedure for the sound of /âr/ in the word *chair,* and the sound of /ôr/ in the word *horn.*

Teach/Model Tell students: *The sound of a vowel changes when it is followed by the sound of* r. *We say that these kinds of vowels are* r-*controlled vowels. Repeat these words with* r-*controlled vowels:* barn, harp, jar, care, stare, air, hair, thorn, chore, more, core.

Ask students to name the items in Row 1 on page 264 *(stair, shark, car, fair).* Repeat each word, clearly pronouncing the vowel each time. Then say: *I'll say these words again. If you hear the* r-*controlled vowel sound in* arm, *circle the* ar. *If you hear the* r-*controlled vowel sound in* chair, *circle the* air. Repeat the words one more time, pausing as you go to give students time to circle their choice. Then ask students to name the items in Row 2 *(corn, horse, car, fork).* Repeat each word, clearly pronouncing the vowel each time. Then say: *I'll say these words again. If you hear the* r-*controlled vowel sound in* horn, *circle the picture.* Students should circle the pictures of the *corn, horse,* and *fork.*

Practice Have students look at the pictures in Row 3 on page 264. Have them name the pictures *(star, hair, store, porch).* Then ask them to circle the correct word below each picture. Finally, have them write the words.

Read the practice sentence aloud, and have students find the words with *r*-controlled vowels *(chairs, forks, corn, more, are, for, store).* Invite students to chant the sentence together, clapping each time they hear the *r*-controlled vowels.

Assess Tell students: *I will say some words. Put your thumb up if you hear an* r-*controlled vowel. Put your thumb down if you do not:* chair, chew, chore, far, feet, stare, stand, store, car, more. Then have students repeat the *r*-controlled words after you, striving for the correct pronunciation of the *r*-controlled vowels. Keep in mind that students who have difficulty pronouncing the *r*-controlled vowels may still be able to comprehend words with *r*-controlled vowels that they hear or read.

Pronunciation Tip Words with *ar, are, air, or, ore* *When you say words like* far, dare, *and* more, *you make the vowel sound first. Then you bring your lips together for the /r/ sound. Try:* far, dare, more.

Words with *er, ir, or, ur, eer, ear*

Use with page 265.

Preteach Copy and distribute page 265. Have students point to the picture of the purse at the top of the page. Say: *This is a purse. Purse has the sound /ėr/. Say it with me: /ėr/, /ėr/, purse.* Repeat the procedure for the sound of /ir/ in the word *tear.*

Teach/Model Tell students: *The sound of a vowel changes when it is followed by the sound of* r. *We say that these kinds of vowels are* r-*controlled vowels. Repeat these words with* r-*controlled vowels:* fern, third, curve, dear, cheer, clear.

Ask students to name the items in Row 1 on page 265 *(nurse, ear, surf, spear)*. Repeat each word, clearly pronouncing the vowel each time. Then say: *I'll say these words again. If you hear the* r-*controlled vowel sound in* purse, *circle the* ur. *If you hear the* r-*controlled vowel sound in* tear, *circle the* ear. Repeat the words one more time, pausing as you go to give students time to circle their choice.

Practice Have students look at the pictures in Row 2 on page 265 *(bird, deer, butter, skirt)* and circle the pictures of words that have the sound of *-ir* in *shirt.* Students should circle the pictures of the bird, butter, and skirt. Then have them look at the pictures in Row 3. Have them read the words below each picture, circle the correct words *(worm, deer, purse, shirt)*, and write the words.

Read the practice sentence aloud, and have students find the words with *r*-controlled vowels (dear, girl, tear, purse, near, here). Invite students to chant the sentence together, clapping each time they hear the *r*-controlled vowels.

Assess Tell students: *I will say some word pairs. Raise your hand when you hear a sound with er, eer, or ear:* cheer, chair; steer, stare; her, hair; deer, door; fear, for. Then have students repeat the word pairs after you, striving for the correct pronunciation of the *r*-controlled vowels. Keep in mind that students who have difficulty pronouncing the *r*-controlled vowels may still be able to comprehend words with *r*-controlled vowels that they hear or read.

Pronunciation Tip Words with *er, ir, or, ur, eer, ear* *When you say words like* sir *and* word, *you put your lips close together and hold them: /ėr/, /ėr/. When you say a word like* fear, *your lips start out in a line. Then you bring your lips together for the /ir/ sound. Try it: /ir/, /ir/,* fear.

Name ______________________________

Words with *ar, are, air, or, ore*

- If the word has the sound of *ar* in *arm*, **circle** the *ar.*
- If the word has the sound of *air* in *chair*, **circle** the *air.*

ROW 1

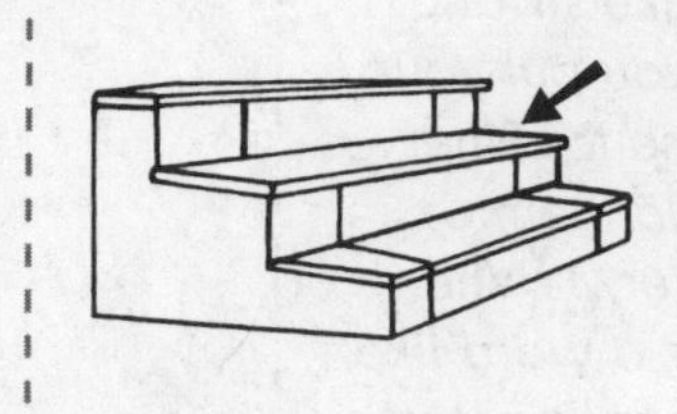

ar **air** | **ar** **air** | **ar** **air** | **ar** **air**

- If the picture has the sound of *or* in *horn*, **circle** it.

ROW 2

- **Look** at each picture. **Say** its name.
- **Circle** the correct word. **Write** the name of the picture.

ROW 3

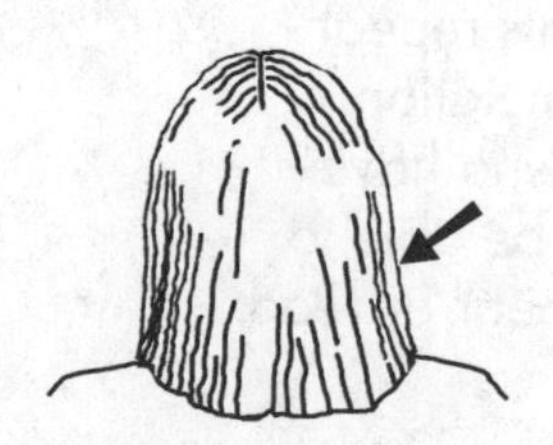

stair	hair	stare	porch
star	here	store	perch

____________ ____________ ____________ ____________

Find words with r in this sentence. Then **practice** chanting or singing the sentence.

Chairs, forks, corn, and so much more are all for sale in the store.

Name ____________________

Words with *er, ir, or, ur, eer, ear*

- If the word has the sound of *ur* in *purse*, **circle** the *ur.*
- If the word has the sound of *ear* in *tear*, **circle** the *ear.*

ROW 1

ear **ur**

ear **ur**

ear **ur**

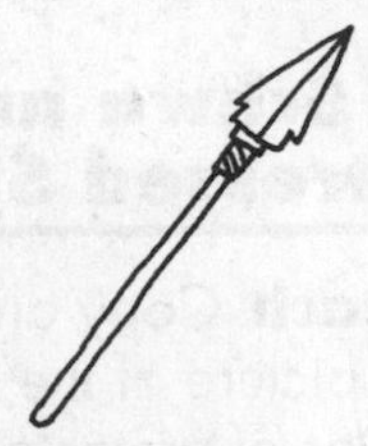

ear **ur**

- If the picture has the sound of *ir* in *shirt*, **circle** it.

ROW 2

- **Look** at each picture. **Say** its name.
- **Circle** the correct word. **Write** the name of the picture.

ROW 3

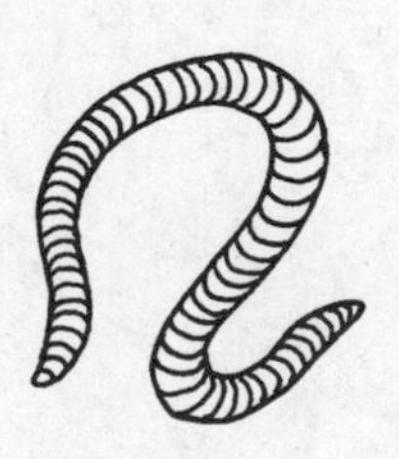

warm
worm

deer
door

purse
pass

short
shirt

________________ ________________ ________________ ________________

Find words with *r* in this sentence. Then **practice** chanting or singing the sentence.

"Oh, dear," said the girl with a tear. "My purse is not near here."

The Schwa and Unstressed Syllables

Transfer Skills

Some languages are "syllable-timed" languages: the syllables within words are each pronounced in the same amount of time. In English, by contrast, vowels in stressed syllables are pronounced more distinctly. Vowels in unstressed syllables often take a more neutral schwa sound. This lesson provides practice with the schwa sound, which English learners may have difficulty pronouncing and spelling.

The Schwa and Unstressed Syllables

Use with page 267.

Preteach Copy and distribute page 267. Have students point to the picture of the pretzel. Say: *This is a pretzel. Say the two syllables of* pretzel *with me: PRET-zel. Which syllable sounds louder? Yes, the first syllable. It is called the stressed syllable. The second syllable is the unstressed syllable, and it sounds quieter. Look at Row 1. Listen to the vowel sound in the unstressed syllables of these words: a-LARM, a-FRAID, BOT-tle, DRAG-on. The vowel sound in the unstressed syllables sounds like this: /ə/. We call this the schwa sound. Say the schwa sound in these words: PRET-zel, a-FRAID.*

Teach/Model Tell students: *In English, unstressed syllables often have a schwa sound. The schwa sound can be at the beginning, middle, or end of a word:* about, alone, animal, avenue, ribbon, table.

Have students look at Row 1on page 267. Repeat each word. Say: *Circle the words that have the /ə/ sound in the first syllable. Underline the words that have the /ə/ sound in the last syllable.* Read the words aloud one more time. Students should circle *alarm* and *afraid*. They should underline *bottle* and *dragon*.

Tell students: *It can be hard to know how to spell syllables that have a schwa sound, because this sound can be spelled with any vowel. It can also be spelled with a consonant +* -le, *as in* table.

Practice Ask students to name the items in the chart on page 267 *(medal, sandal, nickel, shovel, table, apple, wagon, button)*. Repeat each word and then say: *The chart shows some of the ways that the schwa sound can be spelled at the end of words. Look at each picture and write its name.*

Read the practice sentence aloud, and have students find the words with the schwa sound *(apples, bagels, alarm, a, pretzel, table)*. Invite students to chant the sentence together, raising a finger each time they hear the schwa sound.

Assess Tell students: *I will say a list of words. Put your hand up when you hear a word with the /ə/ sound:* asleep, asking, final, panel, pancake, cradle, crazy, lesson, ribbon, backbone. Then have students repeat the words with a schwa sound: *asleep, final, panel, cradle, lesson,* and *ribbon*. Keep in mind that students who have difficulty pronouncing the schwa may still be able to comprehend words with /ə/.

Pronunciation Tip
schwa *When you say the schwa sound, it sounds a little like the /u/ sound in up. But you say it quickly and without any stress on the syllable: /ə/, /ə/, /ə/. Try these words with a schwa sound:* about, around, final, little, taken, pencil, jungle, able.

Name ______________________________

The Schwa and Unstressed Syllables

- **Say** each word. If you hear the schwa sound in the first syllable, **circle** the word.
- If you hear the schwa sound in the last syllable, **underline** the word.

ROW 1

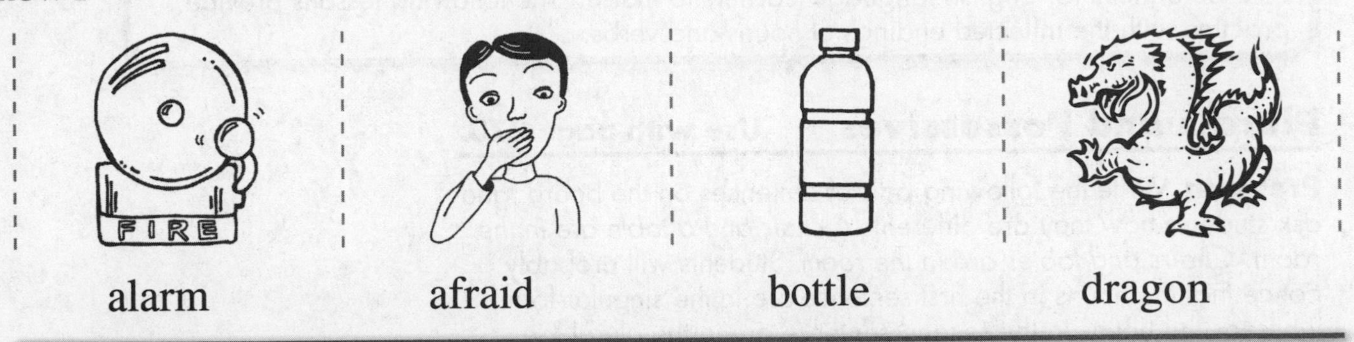

- **Look** at the pictures in each column. **Write** the word for each picture.

Final Syllables with Schwa			
-al	-el	-le	-on
____________	____________	____________	____________
____________	____________	____________	____________

Find words with a schwa sound in this sentence. Then **practice** chanting or singing the sentence.

There are three apples, two bagels, one alarm clock, and a pretzel on the table.

Inflected endings may be challenging for English language learners. For example, languages such as Chinese, Hmong, and Vietnamese do not use inflected endings to form verb tenses. Students may need help understanding that adding *-ed* to a verb indicates that the action happened in the past. Spelling changes in inflected verbs may also be difficult for English language learners to master. The following lessons provide practice with the inflected endings of nouns and verbs.

Plurals and Possessives Use with page 270.

Preteach Write the following pair of sentences on the board, and ask students how they are different: *A chair and a table are in the room. Chairs and tables are in the room.* Students will probably notice that the nouns in the first sentence are in the singular form, whereas the nouns in the second sentence are in the plural form.

Next, write these two sentences on the board, again asking students what they notice about them: *The pen of the teacher is red. The teacher's pen is red.* Both sentences mean the same, but they use different ways to show possession, or ownership.

Teach/Model Copy the following chart on the board, and use it to teach students how to form plurals and possessives in English.

	Rules	Examples
Plurals	• Add *-s* to the singular form of most nouns. • Add *-es* to words that end with *sh, ch, x, s,* and *z.* • For words that end with a consonant and *y,* change the *y* to *i* before adding *-es.*	• *boys, girls, pens, balls, teachers* • *boxes, classes, brushes, dishes* • *cities, stories, candies*
Possessives with an apostrophe	• Add an apostrophe and *s* to most singular nouns. • Add an apostrophe to plural nouns that end in *s.*	• Juana's idea, Kin's report, Carlos's dog • the girls' uniforms, the boys' team

Practice Copy and distribute page 270. Read the directions aloud, and direct students' attention to the pictures of the children and their pets. Have students complete the sentences by writing each word in parentheses in the plural or possessive form, as appropriate. (See answers on page 310.)

Assess Tell students to write pairs of sentences about a friend and a family member. The first sentence should introduce the person, and the second sentence tells about something that person has or owns. Write this example on the board: *My friend's name is Samuel. Samuel's wheelchair can go fast.*

Verb Endings *-s, -ed, -ing* Use with page 271.

Preteach Write these verbs on the board and read them aloud for the class, asking students to pay close attention to the sound at the end of each word: *washes, cleans, writes, sleeps, fixes, plays, swims, talks.* Ask students if they noticed a difference in the way the final -s was pronounced in certain words. Confirm for them that *writes, sleeps,* and *talks* are pronounced with the sound of /s/ at the end, and that *washes, cleans, fixes, plays,* and *swims* are pronounced with the sound of /z/.

In a similar way, ask students to determine if the following words end with the sound of /d/ or /t/: *walked, enjoyed, liked, talked, played, measured.*

Finally, have students practice saying the following gerunds aloud, modeling correct pronunciation as necessary: *playing, cleaning, jogging, talking, washing, swimming.*

Teach/Model The following rules may help students know which pronunciation to use with words that end in *-s* and *-ed.* Remind students that these are general guidelines, and that they should listen carefully to native speakers for further guidance.

For words that end in *-s,*
- use the sound of /s/ if the letter before it is *k, p,* or *t.*
- use the sound of /z/ if the letter before it is *b, f, g, m, n,* or a vowel.

Note: If a word ends in silent *e,* the sound of *-s* depends on the letter before the *e.*

For words that end in *-ed,*
- use the sound of /d/ if the letter before it is *b, l, m, n,* or a vowel.
- use the sound of /t/ if the letter before it is *ch, k, p, s, sh,* or x.

To make the *-ing* form of a verb,
- add *-ing* to the simple verb.
- double final *b, g, m, n,* or *p* before adding *-ing.*
- drop silent *e* before adding *-ing.*

Practice Copy and distribute page 271. Read the directions aloud, and have students look at the sample answers to help them get started. After students complete the activities, practice saying the verbs in each chart aloud. (See answers on page 310.)

Assess Ask students to write three sentences using a verb from each of the three charts on page 271, keeping the verb in the same form as in the chart.

Name ______________________________

Plurals and Possessives

- **Look** at the pictures. **Read** the children's names.
- **Complete** each sentence. Use the word in parentheses. Make the word possessive or plural.

1. The children's (pet) ________________ are nice and friendly.

2. (Martin) ________________ lizard is very tame.

3. The (birds) ________________ cage is open.

4. (Mia) ________________ cat likes to sit on her lap.

5. (Carlos) ________________ dog is still a puppy.

6. When dogs are (puppy) ________________, they like to play.

Name ________________________________

Verb Endings *-s, -ed, -ing*

Part 1

- **Read** the verbs in the box.
- **Write** the *-s* form of the verb in the correct column of the chart.

ask	call	help	write
play	run	walk	see

/s/	/z/
asks	

Part 2

- **Read** the verbs in the box.
- **Write** the *-ed* form of the verb in the correct column of the chart.

call	fix	help	open
play	rub	walk	wash

/d/	/t/
called	

Part 3

- **Read** the words in the chart.
- **Write** the correct *-ing* form of the verb in the second column.

Verb	*-ing* Form
call	
hope	
play	
run	

Transfer Skills

English learners may benefit from extra practice distinguishing between /j/ and /ch/ sounds. Have students pronounce the sounds while placing their hands on their throats. Have them feel how the /j/ is voiced from their throats and the /ch/ sound is unvoiced and originates in their mouth.

Spellings of /j/, /s/, /k/ Use with page 275.

Preteach Copy and distribute page 275. Have students point to the picture of a bridge at the top of the page. Say: *This is a bridge, /b/ /r/ /i/ /j/. Where do you hear the /j/ sound in the word? Say it with me: /j/, /j/, bridge. That's right, the sound /j/ comes at the end of the word.* Now point to the *sailboat.* Ask: *Do you hear the /s/ sound in this word? Where? Listen: /s/ /ā/ /l/ /b/ /ō/ /t/. Yes, the /s/ sound is at the beginning of the word.* Repeat this drill for the word *kick.*

Teach/Model Write *bridge, jump,* and *judge* on the board. Say the words aloud, and point to the letters that make the /j/ sound in each. Write *bus* and *mice* on the board. Say the words aloud, and point to the letters that make the /s/ sound in each. Then write *care, back, kite,* and *chrome.* Say the words aloud, and point to the letters that make the /k/ sound. Review each set of words. Have students repeat the words after you.

Practice Help students name the items in Row 1 on page 275 *(jet, cage, tree, jam).* Say: *I will say the words again. This time, circle the picture if the word has the sound of* j, *as in* bridge. Repeat each name, stretching out the sound of each letter so students can hear the /j/ sound in each word. Students should circle *jet, cage, jam,* but not *tree.* Repeat the process for Rows 2 and 3.

Read the practice sentence aloud and have students find the words with /j/, /s/, and /k/ sounds *(Jessica, checks, crossing, bridge).* After they have repeated the sentence several times, challenge students to say it as quickly as they can.

Assess Make another copy of page 275 and cut out all of the pictures. Prepare a sheet of paper with three columns that are labeled with the letters *j, k,* and *s.* Give each student the pile of pictures. Have students say the names of the pictures and place each one under the sound that the word contains.

Pronunciation Tip Spellings of /j/, /s/, /k/ The sound /j/ can be spelled *g, j,* or *dge.* The sound /s/ can be spelled *s* or *c.* The sound /k/ can be spelled *c, k, ck,* or *ch.*

In Spanish, each vowel has only one sound. Spanish speakers may benefit from extra practice pronouncing and spelling words with variant vowel sounds in English. Let students practice saying and writing groups of words that have the sound /ȯ/ in *ball* and *walk: all, fault, awe, scald.*

Spellings of /ȯ/ (Vowel Sound in ball): *a, au, aw, al*

Use with page 276.

Preteach Copy and distribute page 276. Have students point to the picture of a ball at the top of the page. Say: *This is a ball, /b/ /ȯ/ /l/. What vowel sound do you hear in the word* ball*? Say it with me: /ȯ/, /ȯ/,* ball.

Teach/Model Write *call, sauce, yawn,* and *talk* on the board. Underline the *a, au, aw,* and *al* sound spellings in the words. Tell students: *The sound /ȯ/ can be spelled* a, au, aw, *and* al. *When* a *is followed by* u, l, *or* w, *it usually stands for the sound you hear in* ball. Point out the sound spellings for /ȯ/ in the words *call, sauce, yawn,* and *talk*. Segment and blend each of the words as a class.

Help students name the items in Row 1 on page 276 *(saw, sausage, fence, straw)*. Repeat each name, stretching out the sound of each letter so students can hear the vowel sound in each word. Read the words again. This time, tell students to circle the pictures for words that contain the sound /ȯ/. Review the answers as a class *(saw, sausage, straw)*.

Practice Have students look at the pictures in Row 2 on page 276. Help them read the words in the box. Have them write the word that names each picture *(applause, lawn, walnut, salt)*. Then students can work with a partner to fill in the chart at the bottom of the page. When they are finished, share answers, and teach any new words students do not know.

Assess Have students write the /ȯ/ sound spellings *a, au, aw,* and *al* on index cards. Then read the following words aloud to the class: *all, fault, raw, bald, talk, sauce, yawn, saw, crawl, call.* Pause after each word so students can find and hold up the card that contains the sound-spelling pattern that corresponds to the word.

Pronunciation Tip
Spellings of /ȯ/ in *a, au, aw, al*
When words end in the sound /ȯ/, the sound /ȯ/ is usually spelled *aw*.

Transfer Skills

Students may need assistance with words spelled *augh* and *ough* as in *caught* and *fought,* in which the *gh* is silent. Practice the words along with words containing the vowel patterns *aw, au,* and *al* as in *claw, jaunt,* and *call*. Display the words on the board as you practice.

Spellings of /ȯ/ as in *thought:* in *augh, ough*

Use with page 277.

Preteach Display and say the word *thought*. Ask: *What vowel sound do you hear in the word* thought? *Say it with me: /ȯ/, /ȯ/, thought.* Display and say the word *caught*. Ask: *What vowel sound do you hear in the word* caught? *Say it with me: /ȯ/, /ȯ/, caught. In the words* thought *and* caught, *the vowel sound is /ȯ/.*

Teach/Model Write *thought* and *caught* on the board. Underline the *ough* and *augh* sound spellings in the words. Tell students: *The sound /ȯ/ can be spelled* ough *and* augh. *When you see the spellings* ough *and* augh, *you know the word will have the /ȯ/ vowel sound.* Point out the sound spellings for /ȯ/ in the words *thought* and *caught*. Segment and blend each of the words as a class.

Write two columns on the board, labeled *ough* and *augh*. As a class, brainstorm a list of words with *ough* and *augh* sound spellings such as *sought, ought, brought, taught, daughter,* and *fraught.* Have students repeat the words after you, and then have them practice saying the words with a partner.

Practice Copy and distribute page 277. Read the directions aloud, and discuss the meanings of the words in the box. Then do the first example together. Have students choose and write a logical word in the blank. Then have students read the sentences aloud with a partner. (See answers on page 310.)

Assess Have students write the /ȯ/ sound spellings *ough* and *augh* on index cards. Then read the following words aloud to the class: *brought, caught, daughter, fraught, taught, thought, fought.* Pause after each word so students can hold up the card that contains the sound-spelling pattern that corresponds to the word.

Name ______________________________

Sounds of j, s, k

- If the word has the sound of *j* as in *bridge*, **circle** it.

ROW 1

- If the word has the sound of *s* as in *sail*, **circle** it.

ROW 2

- If the word has the sound of *k* as in *kick*, **circle** it.

ROW 3

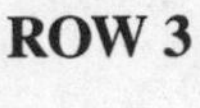

   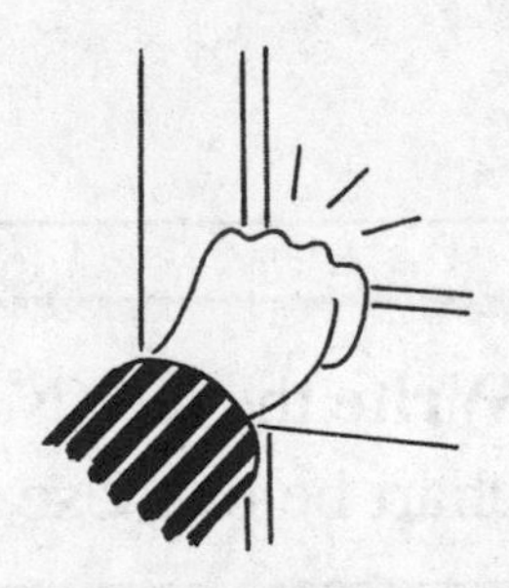

Find the sounds of *j, s,* and *k* in this sentence. Then **practice** chanting it.

Jessica checks both ways before crossing the bridge.

Name ___________________________

Vowel Sound in *ball*

- **Listen** for the vowel sound in *ball.* This sound can be spelled *a, au, aw,* or *al.*
- **Circle** the pictures of words that have this sound.

ROW 1

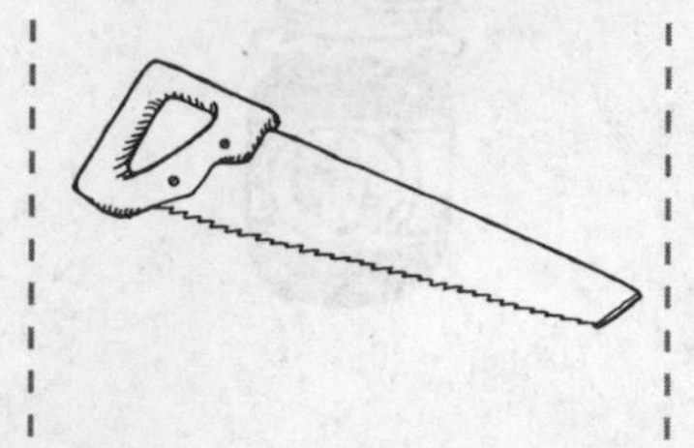
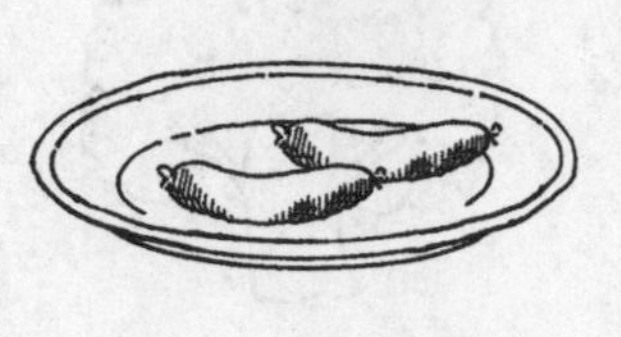
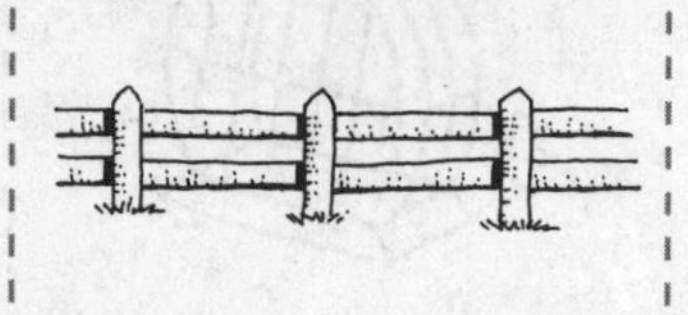

- **Look** at each picture. **Read** the words in the box.
- **Write** the word that names each picture.

lawn	walnut	salt	applause

ROW 2

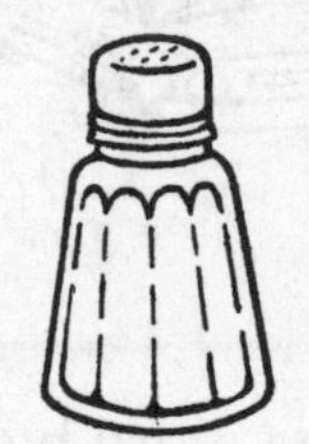

______________ ______________ ______________ ______________

- **Write** the words with the same vowel sound as in *ball* spelled *a, au, aw,* and *al* in the chart below. **Use** adictionary to **find** more words.

a	au	aw	al

Name ______________________________

Vowel Sound in *thought*: *augh, ough*

- **Read** the sentences.
- **Choose** the correct word from the box to complete each sentence.
- **Write** the word on the blank line.

thought
brought
fought
taught
daughter
caught

1. We ________________ sandwiches for lunch today.

2. My neighbor has a new baby ________________.

3. The boy ________________ he locked the door.

4. The two puppies ________________ over a ball.

5. I ________________ the ball at the baseball game.

6. My mom ________________ me how to plant a tree.

Compound Words, Homophones, and Contractions

Compound words exist in many languages, including Spanish, Vietnamese, Haitian Creole, German, and Russian. Children may readily understand the concept of compound words, but may need additional help with decoding to break English compound words into their parts. **Homophones** are also common in other languages, but English learners may not recognize that English homophone pairs have the same pronunciation despite their different spellings. They may need to learn to use their knowledge of word meaning to choose the correct spelling of homophones. Some languages, such as the Romance languages, include **contractions**, but English learners may need help recognizing them in English and using apostrophes correctly. The following lessons provide practice with compound words, homophones, and contractions.

Compound Words Use with page 281.

Preteach On two separate index cards, write the words *story* and *teller*. Ask students to define each word. If necessary, define *teller* as "a person who talks or tells something" (as opposed to a teller at a bank). Then hold the cards side by side, ask students what *storyteller* means, and confirm that it means "a person who tells stories." Explain that the new word is a compound word. It is made up of two smaller words.

Teach/Model Tell students: *When you make a compound word, you put two words together to make a new word. Usually, there isn't any change to the spellings of the two smaller words.*

Write the following pairs of words on separate index cards: *butter, fly; milk, shake; hand, writing; sun, flower.* Discuss the meaning of each separate word, and then show how the words can be combined to create a new word. Point out that neither of the smaller words has a spelling change. The words are simply put together to create a new word. Ask students to share any other compounds that they know. Spanish examples include *abrelatas* (can opener), *rascacielos* (skyscraper), and *parasol* (parasol).

Practice Copy and distribute page 281. Read the directions aloud, and help students read the words if necessary. After students complete the activities, practice saying the compound words aloud. (See answers on page 310.)

Assess Form pairs of students, and provide partners with a set of word cards with words from page 281. Challenge students to match the cards to create a complete set of compound words. To check comprehension, ask each pair to make an oral sentence with three words from their set.

Homophones

Use with page 282.

Preteach Tell students this joke in the form of a question and answer: *What is black and white and read all over? A newspaper!* Explain to students that the question seems to be asking about colors (black, white, and red), but there is a play on the word *red*. The color red sounds the same as *read*, a past tense form of the verb *read*. Explain that this joke is based on a pair of homophones *(red* and *read)*, two words that sound the same but are spelled differently and mean completely different things.

Teach/Model Write the following homophone pairs on the board: *pair, pear; flour, flower; ceiling, sealing; week, weak.* Explain the meaning of each word and point out the two different spellings. Model the pronunciation, emphasizing that the two words in each pair are pronounced in exactly the same way. Invite students to share any other homophones that they know. Spanish examples include *casa/caza* (house/hunt), *hola/ola* (hello/wave), and *ciento/siento* (one hundred/I feel).

Practice Copy and distribute page 282. Read the directions aloud, and help students answer the first item in each exercise. Help students read the words if necessary. When they are finished, invite volunteers to write their answers on the board. Review the meanings of the words. Make corrections as necessary, and tell students to correct their own work as well. (See answers on page 310.)

Assess Ask students to write three sentences that include a pair of homophones, such as: *Our English class is an hour long.* Encourage students to make simple jokes with the homophones; they can also write sentences that are fanciful or silly, as in: *On Monday, I was too weak to make it through the whole week.* Alternatively, you can dictate pairs of sentences using homophones from page 282; for example: *Mo threw the ball. The ball went through the window.* Check students' work to make sure that they used the correct homophone in each sentence.

Contractions

Use with page 283.

Preteach Write the following sentences on the board, and ask students to tell you how they are different:

I am sorry for being late to class. → I'm sorry for being late to class.

Confirm that *I am* has been shortened to *I'm* in the second sentence. Tell students that this is a contraction. Summarize: *The pronoun* I *and the verb* am *are put together with an apostrophe to form one word,* I'm. *The letter a is dropped from the word* am, *and the apostrophe takes its place.*

Teach/Model Write the following chart on the board, asking students to tell you how to write each contraction as you go:

The Verb "be"	The Verb "have"	Negatives
I am → I'm	I have → I've	has not → hasn't
You are → You're	You have → You've	have not → haven't
He is → He's	He has → He's	are not → aren't
She is → She's	She has → She's	is not → isn't
It is → It's	It has → It's	should not → shouldn't
We are → We're	We have → We've	can not → can't
They are → They're	They have → They've	will not → won't
		do not → don't
		did not → didn't

Conclude by showing how the future tense marker *will* can be shortened and connected to a pronoun using *'ll: I'll, you'll, she'll,* etc.

Practice Copy and distribute page 283. Read the directions aloud, and complete the first line together. Help students read the dialogue if necessary. After students complete the activities, have them practice the dialogue. (See answers on page 310.)

Assess Form pairs of students, and have partners create their own dialogue between a parent and child. Tell them to include a contraction in each line of dialogue. Circulate as they work to provide assistance. When they are finished, invite students to read their dialogues aloud for the class.

Name ________________________________

Compound Words

PART 1

- **Read** the compound words.
- **Draw** a line between the two words in each compound.

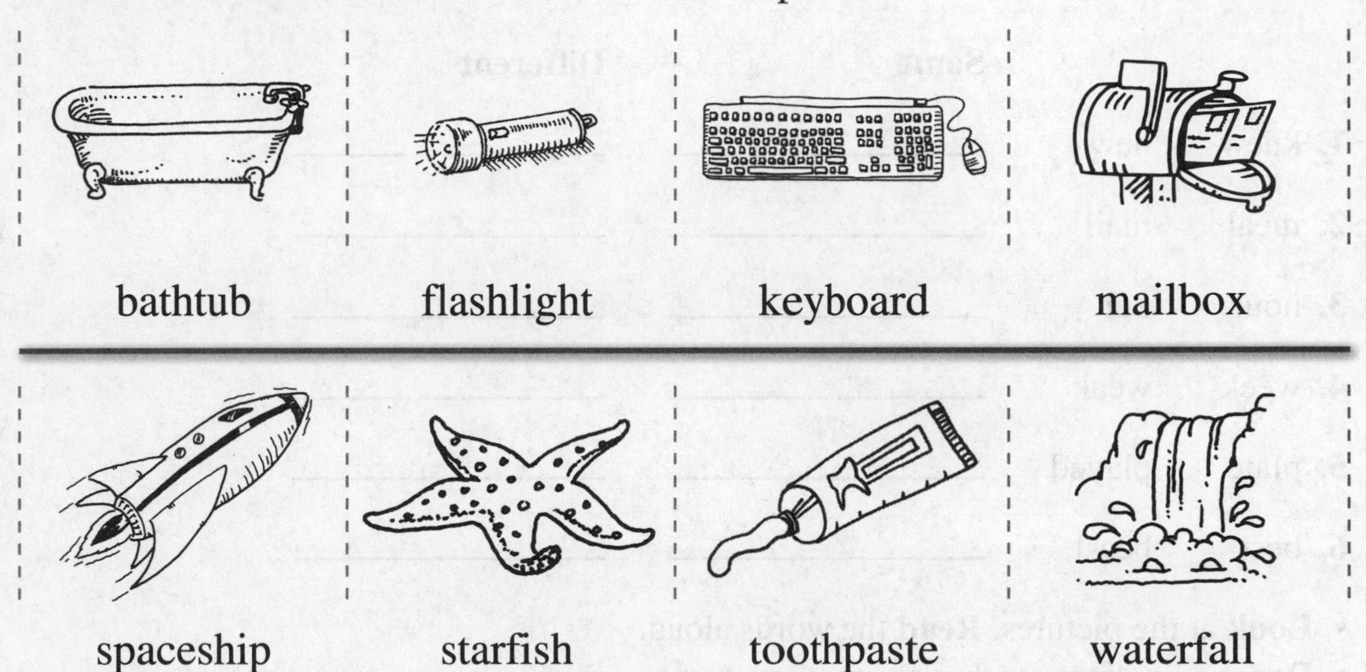

PART 2

- **Read** the two lists of words.
- **Connect** words from each list to make compounds.

back	boat
book	bow
class	brush
finger	mark
hair	nail
rain	pack
sail	room
side	walk

Name ______________________________

Homophones

- **Read** each pair of words aloud.
- Do the words sound the same? **Check** "Same."
- Do the words sound different? **Check** "Different."

		Same	Different
1. knew	new	____________	____________
2. meal	mail	____________	____________
3. hour	our	____________	____________
4. week	weak	____________	____________
5. plate	played	____________	____________
6. best	beast	____________	____________

- **Look** at the pictures. **Read** the words aloud.
- **Draw** a line from each word to its picture.

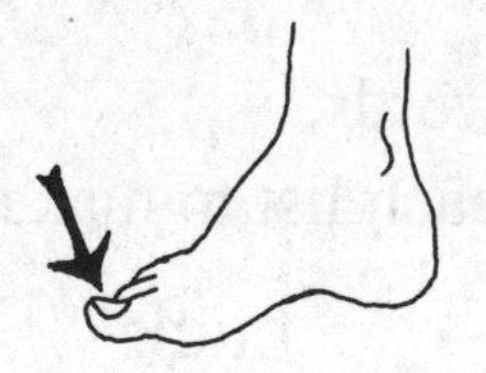

flour
flower

tow
toe

sun
son

through
threw

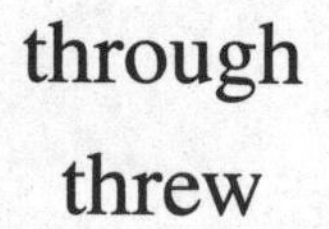

Name ______________________________

Contractions

- **Read** the dialogue.
- **Choose** the correct word from the box to complete each sentence.
- **Write** the correct word on the blank line.

didn't
doesn't
I'll
I'm
I've
isn't
it's
we're

Dad: Hi, Grace. Where are you going?

Grace: ______________ going to soccer practice.

Dad: ______________ soccer practice on Thursday night?

Grace: Yes, ______________ usually on Thursday, but tonight ______________ having a special practice because of the game on Saturday.

Dad: You finished your homework, ______________ you?

Grace: ______________ done my math and English. The science teacher ______________ give us homework.

Dad: OK. Have a good practice.

Grace: Thanks, Dad. ______________ be home by six o'clock.

Choose four contractions. **Write** the two words that make up each one.

______________ ______________ ______________ ______________

Transfer Skills

Some English prefixes and suffixes have equivalent forms in the Romance languages. For example, the prefix *dis-* in English *(disapprove)* corresponds to the Spanish *des- (desaprobar)*, the French *des- (desapprouver)*, and the Haitian Creole *dis-* or *dez- (dezaprouve)*. Students who are literate in these languages may be able to transfer their understanding of prefixes and suffixes by using parallel examples in the home language and in English. Some suggestions for Spanish are provided below. The following lessons provide additional practice with prefixes and suffixes.

Prefixes *un-* and *re-*

Use with page 291.

Preteach Write these word pairs on the board: *happy, unhappy; safe, unsafe; lucky, unlucky.* Read the words aloud with students, and discuss their meanings. Ask: *What do you notice about these words?* Guide students to see that each word pair is a set of opposites, and that one word in each pair begins with *un-*. Circle the prefix *un-* in each word and say: *This syllable,* un-, *is a prefix. A prefix is a word part that is added to the beginning of a word. Adding a prefix changes the meaning of a word. A new word is made.*

Teach/Model Present the prefixes *un-* and *re-*. Use these examples to explain how the prefixes can change the meanings of words.

Prefix	Meaning	Examples	Spanish Examples
un-	not	happy → unhappy safe → unsafe locked → unlocked	*feliz* → *infeliz* *seguro* → *inseguro*
re-	again	tell → retell do → redo write → rewrite	*contar* → *recontar* *hacer* → *rehacer*

Practice Copy and distribute page 291. Read the directions aloud, and read the first example together. Have volunteers say the words they wrote in each column of the chart. (See answers on page 310.)

Assess Have students write these prefixes and base words on cards: *un-, re-, afraid, lock, run, unite.* Have students use the cards in different combinations to make words that have prefixes. Have students show you a base word without a prefix, add a prefix, say the new word, and tell what it means.

Prefixes *im-, in-, mis-, over-*

Use with page 292.

Preteach Write these word pairs on the board: *patient, impatient; polite, impolite; proper, improper; pure, impure.* Read the words aloud with students, and discuss their meanings. Ask students what they notice about these words. Guide students to see that each word pair is a set of opposites, and that one word in each pair begins with *im-*. Circle the prefix *im-* in each word and explain: *This word part,* im-, *is a prefix. It usually changes the meaning of a word to its opposite.*

Teach/Model Present the prefixes *im-, in-, mis-,* and *over-*. Use these examples to explain how the prefixes can change the meanings of words. Tell Spanish speakers that the Spanish prefixes *im-* and *in-* have similar meanings *(impaciente, intolerante)*. The Spanish prefix *sobre-* is sometimes used like the English prefix *over- (sobrecarga)*.

Prefix	Meaning	Examples
im-	not	*impatient, imperfect, impossible*
in-	not	*insecure, intolerant, indestructible*
mis-	wrong	*misunderstood, misbehave, mismatch*
over-	beyond, more than	*overcook, overpay, overweight*

Practice Copy and distribute page 292. Read the directions aloud, and help students fill in the first blank line. After students complete the activity, have pairs of students practice the dialogue. (See answers on page 311.)

Assess Have students write these prefixes and base words on index cards: *im-, in-, mis-, over-, correct, interpret, load, coat, mature, take, use.* Tell students to use the cards to make words with prefixes. Circulate as they work, asking students to show you a base word and a prefix that goes with it. Ask advanced students to tell you what the word means and to use it in an oral sentence.

Transfer Skills

Point out to Spanish speakers that the prefix *mid-* is related in meaning to the Spanish word *medio,* which means *half* or *middle.* Display cognates such as *midnight/ medianoche* and *midday/mediodía* as examples.

Prefixes *pre-, mid-, over-, out-, bi-*

Use with page 293.

Preteach Write these word pairs on the board: *test, pretest; air, midair; time, overtime; run, outrun; monthly, bimonthly.* Read the words aloud with students and discuss their meanings. Ask: *What do you notice about these words?* Explain that the second word in each pair has a prefix that changes the meaning of the first word. Circle the prefix *pre-* and say: *This syllable,* pre-, *is a prefix. A prefix is a word part that is added to the beginning of a word to change its meaning. When you add a prefix, a new word is made. The prefix* pre- *means "before." So,* prepay *means "to pay before."*

Teach/Model Present the prefixes *pre-, mid-, over-, out-,* and *bi-.* Using the chart below, explain how adding prefixes to base words changes the meaning of the word.

Prefix	Meaning	Examples
pre-	before	paid → prepaid view → preview
mid-	in the middle of	day → midday night → midnight
over-	more than normal, too much	grown → overgrown cooked → overcooked
out-	outward; or to a greater degree	side → outside run → outrun
bi-	two	cycle → bicycle

Practice Copy and distribute page 293. Read the directions aloud, and complete the first example together. Have students choose a prefix to add to the base word and write a new word that makes sense in the blank. Then have them read the story aloud with a partner. (See answers on page 311.)

Assess Have students write these prefixes and base words on index cards: *pre-, mid-, over-, out-, bi-, paid, air, time, field, weekly.* Have them use the cards in different combinations to make words with prefixes. As an additional challenge, have students show a base word without a prefix, add a prefix, say the new word, and tell what it means.

Suffixes -ly, -ful, -less, -ness

Use with page 294.

Preteach Write the following words on the board: *careful, carefully, careless, carelessness.* Ask students what these words have in common and what makes them different from each other. They will notice that they all have the same base, *care.* But each successive word also has a different word part at the end. Explain that each of these word parts is a *suffix.* Say: *A suffix is a word part that is added to the end of a word. Adding a suffix changes the meaning of a word.*

Teach/Model Present the suffixes *-ly, -ful, -less,* and *-ness.* Write the following chart on the board, asking students to provide additional examples for the last column. Tell Spanish speakers that *-ly* is similar to the Spanish suffix *-mente.* The Spanish suffix *-dad (felicidad)* is similar to *-ness.*

Suffix	How and Why to Use It	Part of Speech	Examples
-ly	Add it to an adjective to tell how an action is done.	Adverb	*quickly* *calmly* *completely*
-ful	Add it to a noun to mean "full of" the noun.	Adjective	*thoughtful* *colorful* *helpful*
-less	Add it to a noun to mean "without" the noun.	Adjective	*spotless* *joyless* *flawless*
-ness	Add it to an adjective to describe a state of being.	Noun	*darkness* *happiness* *carelessness* *peacefulness*

Practice Copy and distribute page 294. Read the directions aloud, and have students look at the sample answer to help them get started. After students complete the activity, invite volunteers to take turns reading the passage aloud. (See answers on page 311.)

Assess Have students write these suffixes and base words on index cards: *-ly, -ful, -less, -ness, slow, quiet, perfect, fear, rude.* Tell students to use the cards to make words with suffixes. Circulate as they work, asking students to show you a base word and a suffix that goes with it. Ask advanced students to tell you what the word means and to use it in an oral sentence.

Prefixes and Suffixes

Suffixes -tion, -sion, -able, -ible

Use with page 295.

Introduce Write the following words on the board: *perfection, decision, walkable, sensible.* Tell students that each of these words is made up of a base word and a suffix. Circle the suffix *-tion* in the first word and explain: *This word part,* -tion, *is a suffix.* Ask volunteers to find the suffixes in the other three words. Point out that the base word might need a spelling change before the suffix is added. The word *decide,* for example, drops the final *-de* before adding *-sion.* The reason for these spelling changes has to do with pronunciation, and the rules are hard to generalize, as there are many exceptions to the rules. Students will learn the different spellings with practice.

Teach/Model Present the suffixes *-tion, -sion, -able,* and *-ible.* Explain that *-tion* and *-sion* have the same meaning, as do *-able* and *-ible.* Write the following chart on the board, asking students to provide additional examples for the last column. Spanish examples of these suffixes are *-ción (reacción), -sión (decisión), -able (confortable),* and *-ible (sensible).*

Suffix	How and Why to Use It	Part of Speech	Examples
-tion, -sion	Add it to a verb to describe an action or a state of being.	Noun	*perfection* *imagination* *reaction* *decision* *admission* *confusion*
-able, -ible	Add it to a verb to add the meaning "can be."	Adjective	*walkable* *comfortable* *dependable* *sensible* *reversible* *flexible*

Practice Copy and distribute page 295. Read the directions aloud, and do the first example together. Tell students that they can use the chart on the board to check spellings. After students complete the activity, review the answers together. (See answers on page 311.)

Assess Have students write these suffixes and base words on index cards: *-tion, -sion, -able, -ible, sense, comfort, confuse, react.* Tell students to use the cards to make words with suffixes. Circulate as they work, asking students to show you a base word and a suffix that goes with it. Ask advanced students to tell you what the word means and to use it in an oral sentence.

Suffixes -er, -or, -ess, -ist **Use with page 296.**

Preteach Write the following words on the board: *swimmer, actor, hostess, tourist.* Tell students that each of these words is made up of a base word and a suffix. Remind students that a suffix is a word part added to the end of a word to change its meaning. Circle the suffix *-er* in the first word and explain: *This word part, -er, is a suffix.* Ask individuals to find suffixes in the other three words. Explain that the base word may require a spelling change before a suffix is added. For example, the word *swimmer* adds an *m* before the suffix. Point out that some spelling changes are related to pronunciation. Explain to students that they will become familiar with different spellings as they practice using the words.

Teach/Model Present this chart to practice the suffixes *-er, -or, -ess,* and *-ist.* Ask students for additional examples of words with these suffixes.

Suffix	What It Means	Examples
-er *-or*	a person or thing that does something	*teacher* *opener* *editor* *tutor*
-ess	a female who does something as a job; a female	*actress* *lioness*
-ist	a person who has studied something or does something as a job	*artist* *dentist*

Practice Copy and distribute page 296. Read the directions to students, and complete the first example together. Tell students that they can use the chart on the board to check spellings. After students complete the activity, review the answers together. (See answers on page 311.)

Assess Have students write these suffixes and base words or word parts on index cards: *-er, -or, -ess, -ist, act, sell, host, dent, tour, teach, lion.* Have students use the cards in different combinations to make words that have suffixes. As an additional challenge, have students show a base word without a suffix, add a suffix, say the new word, and tell what it means.

Suffixes -y, -ish, -hood, -ment

Use with page 297.

Preteach Write the following words on the board: *rocky, foolish, parenthood, shipment.* Tell students that each of these words is made up of a base word and a suffix. Remind students that a suffix is a word part that is added to the end of a word to change its meaning. Circle the suffix *-y* in *rocky* and explain: *This word part, -y, is a suffix. The base word in* rocky *is* rock. Ask students to find base words in the other three words. Have them tell you what each base word means.

Teach/Model Present this chart to practice the suffixes *-y, -ish, -hood,* and *-ment.* Have students identify each base word and suffix in the examples. Ask students for additional examples of words with these suffixes.

Suffix	What It Means	Examples
-y	having the quality of	*cloudy* *rainy* *thirsty*
-ish	describing nationality or language; somewhat	*Spanish* *brownish* *foolish*
-hood	a state or condition of	*childhood* *fatherhood*
-ment	a state, action, or quality	*excitement* *movement*

Practice Copy and distribute page 297. Read the directions aloud, and have students look at the sample answer to help them get started. After students complete the activity, have individuals take turns reading the passage aloud. (See answers on page 311.)

Assess Have students write these suffixes and base words on index cards: *-y, -ish, -hood, -ment, smell, Brit, mother, excite, wind, brown, false, ship.* Have students use the cards in different combinations to make words that have suffixes. As an additional challenge, have students show you a base word without a suffix, add a suffix, say the new word, and tell what it means.

Name ___________________________

Prefixes *un-* and *re-*

- **Read** each group of words.
- **Use** *un-* or *re-* to make one new word.
- **Write** the new word.

1. read again ___reread___

2. appear again ______________

3. not believable ______________

4. not familiar ______________

5. heat again ______________

6. not interested ______________

7. not like ______________

8. start again ______________

9. use again ______________

10. not kind ______________

- **Write** all the new words in the chart.

un-	re-

Name ______________________________

Prefixes *im-, in-, mis-, over-*

- **Read** the conversation. **Finish** the sentences with words from the box.
- Then **practice** the conversation.

Alex: This game costs too much. It is ______________ (1).

Tanya: This ball doesn't cost too much. It is ______________ (2).

Alex: The price on that sign is wrong. It is not correct.

Tanya: You're right! The price must be ______________ (3).

Alex: Let's tell someone that the sign has a ______________ (4). Then they can fix the sign.

Tanya: OK, but let's hurry. I want to go.

Alex: Why are you so ______________ (5)? We have a lot of time!

impatient
incorrect
inexpensive
misprint
overpriced

Write one more word for each prefix. You may **use** a dictionary to **find** the words.

im-	in-	mis-	over-
______________	______________	______________	______________

Name ______________________________

Prefixes *pre-*, *mid-*, *over-*, *out-*, *bi-*

- **Read** the story.
- **Add** *pre-*, *mid-*, *over-*, *out-*, or *bi-* to the beginning of each word in parentheses.

Today is the worst day ever! Yesterday I took a ______________ (test) in
(1)
class. I did not do well. I have a hard time with ______________ (fixes). My
(2)
teacher said that I need to study hard for the next test. She said that I should make an
______________ (line) to help me study.
(3)

Last night I studied until ______________ (night). I also have a report that is
(4)
______________ (due). I am going to have to work ______________ (time) to
(5) (6)
finish all of my homework.

My friends are ______________ (side) having fun. But I am still in my room.
(7)
My mom and dad said that I could go outside and ride my ______________ (cycle)
(8)
when I finish. I hope I can finish all my work soon!

Name ______________________________

Suffixes *-ly, -ful, -less, -ness*

- **Read** the story.
- **Add** *-ly, -ful, -less,* or *-ness* to each word in parentheses.

Yesterday I took Domingo, my dog, to my grandmother's house. As usual, her house was ____spotless____ (spot). We had milk and cookies in the kitchen while Domingo sat ________________ (quiet) in the living room. In fact, he was *too* quiet.
(1)
I went to check on him. He had ________________ (complete) chewed a pillow into
(2)
bits and pieces. There were feathers everywhere!

My grandmother came in the room and said, "Oh my ________________!" (good)
(3)
"I'm sorry, Grandma," I said. "I should have been more ________________." (care)
(4)
________________ (lucky) for me, my grandmother laughed. She
(5)
________________ (playful) threw a pillow at me, and we had a pillow fight. We had
(6)
so much fun it was easy to forget Domingo's ________________. (frisky)
(7)

Name ______________________________

Suffixes *-tion, -sion, -able, -ible*

- **Read** the sentences. **Look** at the underlined word.
- **Add** *-tion, -sion, -able,* or *-ible* to make a new word. **Write** the word.

1.

Yasmin imagined being a princess.

She used her ________________.

2.

We can walk on this path.

The path is ________________.

3.

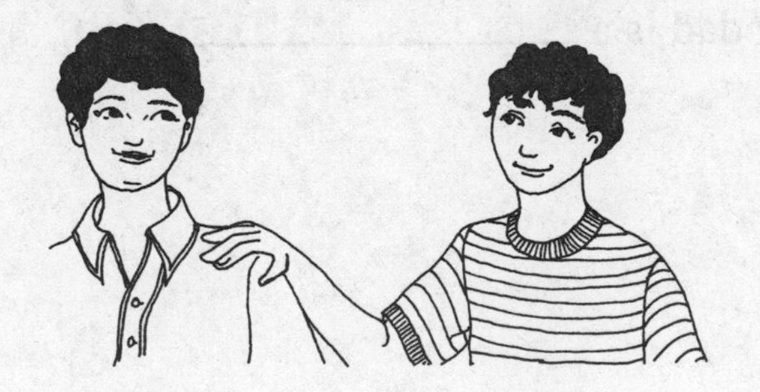

I can depend on Pablo.

Pablo is ________________.

4.

Aisha decided which book to read.

She made a ________________.

5.

I can reverse this shirt.

The shirt is ________________.

Name ________________________________

Suffixes -*er,* -*or,* -*ess,* -*ist*

- **Read** the sentences. **Look** at the underlined word.
- **Add** *-er, -or, -ess,* or *-ist* to make a new word. **Write** the word.

1.

Olivia and her mother went to the pharmacy.

They spoke to the ________________.

2.

It is a long commute to my dad's office.

My dad is a ________________.

3.

I like to invent things.

I am an ________________.

4.

We saw a male lion on our safari.

He was sitting next to a ________________.

Name ______________________________

Suffixes *-y, -ish, -hood, -ment*

- **Read** the story.
- **Add** *-y, -ish, -hood,* or *-ment* to the end of each word in parentheses.

Emma looked outside. She was happy because it was not a rainy (1) (rain) day. It was sunny. She liked to walk outside in her ______________ (2) (neighbor). She had a lot of energy. She did not feel ______________ (3) (sleep) at all.

Emma skipped happily down the sidewalk. She saw ______________ (4) (move) ahead of her. She wondered what it was. But then she felt ______________ (5) (fool). It was just her brother, John, trying to surprise her. He can be so ______________ (6) (child) sometimes!

Cognates and Word Roots

Cognates are words that share origins and appear in similar forms in different languages. For example, the English word *school* is of Greek origin, and it is similar to the Spanish *escuela,* the French *école,* the Polish *szkoła,* and the German *Schule.* For speakers of languages that share word origins with English, the study of cognates can be a powerful vocabulary-building tool. The following lessons provide practice for working with cognates and words with Greek and Latin roots.

Cognates

Use with page 303.

Preteach Present a chart like the one below. Read the words with students, and note the similarities across various languages. Tell students that when words look similar and have a similar meaning in different languages, they are called *cognates.* Invite students to suggest other cognates they know in English and another language. Tell students that cognates can help them understand more words in English.

English	Spanish	French	Haitian Creole	Polish
telephone	teléfono	téléphone	telefonn	telefon

Use this lesson with students who are literate in languages that have many cognates of English words, such as Spanish, Portuguese, French, and, to a lesser extent, Haitian Creole, Polish, and Russian.

Teach/Model Explain to students that cognates in different languages usually have the same origins. For example, the different words for *telephone* are all based on the Greek word parts *telē,* which means far off, and *phōnē,* which means sound or voice. Explain that because many scientific words have Greek or Latin origins, they often are cognates.

Then point out that sometimes words in different languages are "false friends"—they look almost the same, but they don't mean the same thing. For example, the Spanish word *sopa* looks and sounds similar to the English word *soap,* but it means *soup.* Ask students to give other examples of "false friends," words that are not cognates.

Practice Copy and distribute page 303. Have students look for English cognates of home-language words in an English text they are currently reading. (A nonfiction science or social studies text is likely to offer more examples.) Help them decide whether or not the words really are cognates. Suggest that students consult resources such as bilingual dictionaries, other students, or the Internet (with your guidance) to find translations and word meanings. Students might make a class chart showing words for *computer* in various languages. (See answers on page 311.)

Assess Ask students to say or write five examples of cognate pairs in English and their home language, and one example of "false friends."

Words with Greek Roots Use with page 304.

Preteach Write the following words on the board: *autograph, phonograph, photograph, paragraph.* Ask students what all these words have in common. Confirm for them that they all have the word part *graph.* Tell students that this word part comes from the Greek language. It means "written." Conclude by saying: *Many other words in English have Greek roots, too. Learning these roots can help you learn more words.*

Teach/Model Write the following chart on the board, asking students to provide additional examples for the last column.

Greek Root	Meaning	Sample Words
biblio	book	bibliography
bio	life	biography
crac, crat	rule, govern	democrat
demos	people	democracy
geo	earth	geology
graph, gram	written, drawn, describe, record	photograph
log	idea, word, speech, study	biology
meter	measure	perimeter
phono	sound	symphony
scope	to see	telescope

Show students how different word parts can be combined. The root *bio,* for example, can be combined with *graph* to form *biography,* and it can also be combined with *log* to form *biology.* Knowing this, students can conclude that any word with the root *bio* has to do with life. Tell Spanish speakers that many Spanish words have these same Greek roots. Ask them to provide translations for the sample words in the chart *(bibliografía, biografía, demócrata, democracia, geología, fotografía, biología, perímetro, sinfonía, telescopio).*

Practice Copy and distribute page 304. Read the directions aloud, and have students look at the sample answer to help them get started. After students complete the activity, invite volunteers to take turns forming other words with the Greek roots in the word box. (See answers on page 311.)

Assess Write the following words on the board: *autobiography, phonology, geography,* and *telescope.* Ask students to copy these words and to write their definitions, based on what they've learned. When they've finished, have a volunteer write his or her answers on the board, and model corrections as necessary. You can collect students' work for later assessment.

Cognates and Word Roots

Words with Latin Roots Use with page 305.

Preteach Write the following words on the board: *animal, animation, animated.* Ask students what all these words have in common. Confirm for them that they all have the word part *anima.* Tell students that this word part is from Latin, an ancient language that was originally spoken in Italy. *Anima* means "living." Conclude by saying: *Many other words in English have Latin roots, too. Learning these roots can help you learn more words.*

Teach/Model Write the following chart on the board, asking students to provide additional examples for the last column. Tell Spanish speakers that Spanish comes from Latin, so these roots should be familiar.

Latin Root	Meaning	Sample Words
aqua	water	aquarium
aud	to hear	auditorium
cent	one hundred	century
cert	sure, to trust	certificate
circ	around	circle
compute	to compute	computer
dic, dict	to say, to speak	dictionary
fin	to end	finish
grad	step, degree	graduate
scrib	to write	scribble

Practice Copy and distribute page 305. Read the directions aloud, and have students look at the sample answer to help them get started. After students complete the activity, invite volunteers to take turns forming other words with the Latin roots in the word box. (See answers on page 311.)

Assess Write the following words on the board: *certain, final, audition, gradual,* and *dictate.* Ask students to copy these words and to identify their Latin roots. To check comprehension, ask students to make a sentence with each of these words.

Related Words

Use with page 306.

Preteach On the board, write *breath, breathe,* and *breathless.* Ask students what these words have in common. Confirm for them that they all have the word *breath* as the base. The endings on the other two words change their part of speech and meaning. *Breathe* is a verb and *breathless* is an adjective. Many other words are closely related in the same way. Tell students that it will help them expand their vocabulary if they try to learn new words in groups with other related words.

Teach/Model Write the following chart on the board, asking students to provide additional examples for the last column. Spanish examples include *planeta/planetario, horizonte/ horizontal,* and *salud/saludable.*

Base Word	Related Words
jewel	jeweler, jewelry
planet	planetary, planetarium
paint	painter, painting
act	action, actor, active
sign	signature
compute	computer, computation
horizon	horizontal
pot	potter, pottery
bank	banker, banking
heal	health, healthy
relate	relative, relationship
produce	product, production
please	pleasant, pleasure

Practice Copy and distribute page 306. Read the directions aloud, and have students look at the sample answer to help them get started. (See answers on page 311.)

Assess Ask students to take turns thinking of other words that are related to the words in the word box on page 306 or the words in the above chart.

Reading Multisyllabic Words

Use with page 307.

Preteach On the board, write the word *dic/tion/ar/y,* dividing it into syllables, as indicated. Sound it out, pausing between each syllable, and then blend the syllables together. Ask students how many syllables it has (4). Follow the same procedure for *en/cy/clo/pe/di/a,* which has 6 syllables. Tell students: *Pay attention to the syllables in a word. This will help you spell the word, and it will help you pronounce it, too.*

Teach/Model Distribute multiple copies of a dictionary, and point out how each entry word is divided into syllables. Ask students to find the word *brontosaur,* for example. Ask: *How many syllables does this word have?* (3) *What's the first syllable?* (bron) *What are the other syllables?* (*to* and *saur*) Repeat the procedure with the following words: *mystery, parentheses, enthusiasm, personality.*

Practice Copy and distribute page 307. Read the directions aloud, and have students look at the sample answer to help them get started. Help students read the words if necessary. (See answers on page 311.)

Assess Write the following words on the board: *relative, warrior, mathematical, magnificent, principal.* Have students use a dictionary to find out how many syllables each word has. Tell students to write the words on a piece of paper, showing the syllable divisions.

Name ________________________________

Cognates

- **Read** a few pages of a book or article. **Find** English words that look like words in another language you know.
- **Write** the words in both languages on the chart.
- **Write** the meaning of each word, using dictionaries if necessary. Then **tell** if the two similar words are cognates.

English	______________ (language)	Cognates? (yes/no)
Word: Meaning:	Word: Meaning:	
Word: Meaning:	Word: Meaning:	
Word: Meaning:	Word: Meaning:	
Word: Meaning:	Word: Meaning:	
Word: Meaning:	Word: Meaning:	

- **Find out** how to say *computer* in at least two different languages. **Use** sources such as dictionaries, the Internet, and people you know. **Write** the words.
- **Decide** which words are cognates of *computer.*

Name ______________________________

Words with Greek Roots

- **Read** the word parts in the box.
- **Look** at the pictures. **Put** one word part from each box together to make a word.
- **Write** the correct word on each blank line.

auto = self **mega** = large **micro** = very small	**photo** = light **tele** = from a distance	**scope** = to see **phone/phono** = sound **graph** = written

1. megaphone = a tool used to make sound "larger"

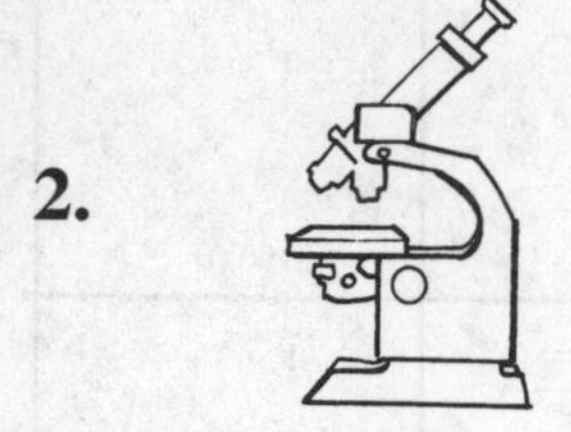

2. ______________________ = a tool for seeing very small things

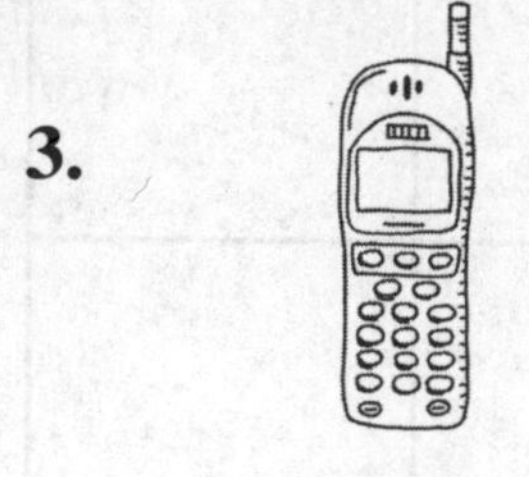

3. ______________________ = a machine that allows two people in different places to talk

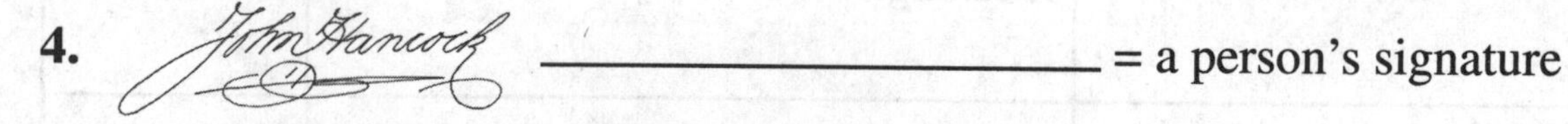

4. ______________________ = a person's signature

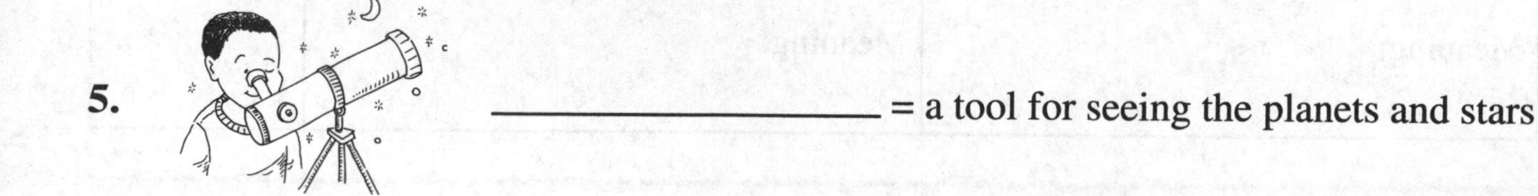

5. ______________________ = a tool for seeing the planets and stars

6. ______________________ = an image taken by a camera

Name ______________________________

Words with Latin Roots

- **Study** the word parts in the box.
- **Read** the sentences.
- **Complete** each sentence. **Write** the correct word in the blank space.

aqua = water	**herba** = plant	**terr** = earth
carn = meat	**mill** = thousand	**tract** = pull
cent = one hundred	**project** = throw	

1. A ____carnivore____ is an animal that eats meat, and an ______________ is an animal that eats plants. (herbivore, carnivore)

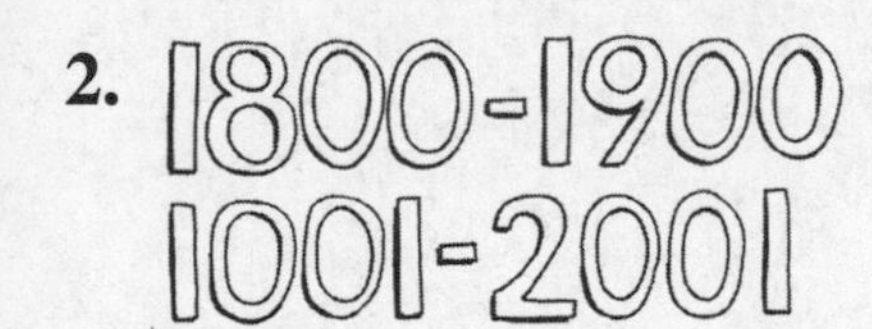

2. A ______________ is one hundred years, and a ______________ is one thousand years. (century, millenium)

3. A ______________ is a machine that "throws light," and a ______________ is a machine that pulls heavy loads. (tractor, projector)

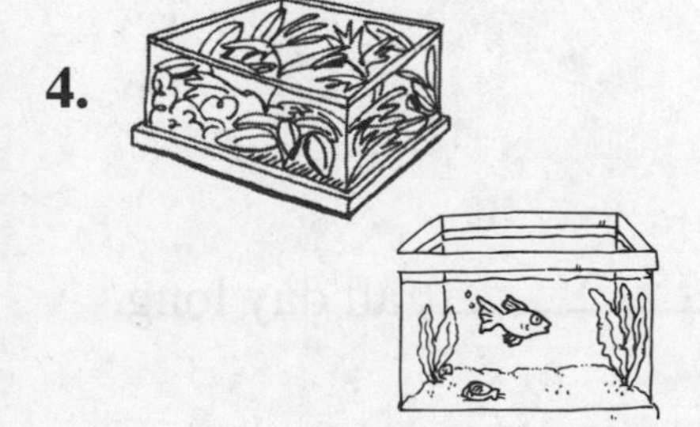

4. Small plants are grown in a ______________, and fish are kept in an ______________. (terrarium, aquarium)

Name ___________________________

Related Words

- **Look** at the words in the box.
- **Read** the sentences.
- **Complete** each sentence. **Write** the correct word in the blank space.

desert	dirt	mask	painter	volcanic
deserted	dirty	masquerade	painting	volcano

1. 

The ___volcano___ exploded with a huge blast. ________________ ash rose into the air and then settled on the ground.

2. 

The ________________ is finishing a pretty ________________.

3. 

This part of the ________________ is quiet and ________________.

4. 

Everybody at the ________________ wore a ________________.

5. 

After playing in the ________________ all day long, Cory's shirt was completely ________________.

Name ______________________________

Reading Multisyllabic Words

- **Read** the words. **Sound out** the number of syllables.
- **Write** each word in the correct column of the chart.

ROW 1

baseball

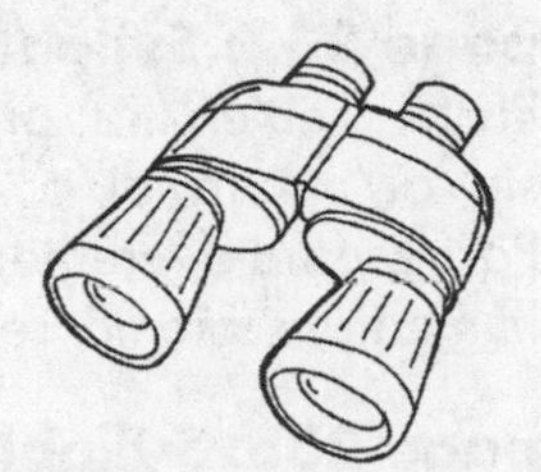

binoculars

champion

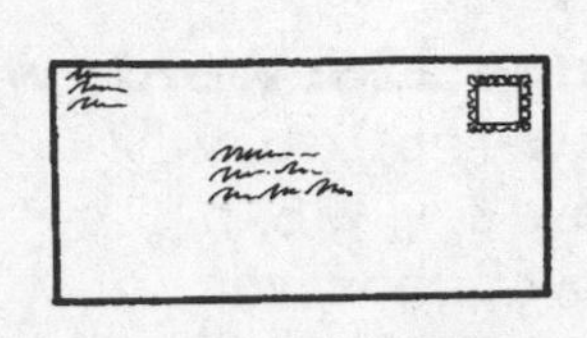

envelope

ROW 2

mushroom

pineapple

watermelon

meditation

ROW 3

barbecue

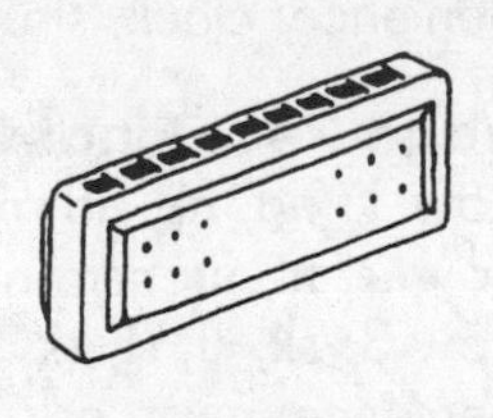

harmonica

telescope

zipper

Two Syllables	Three Syllables	Four Syllables
baseball		

pages 223–225: Confusing Consonants, Assess
b and *v:* b, v, b, v, v, b, v, b, b, v, b, v, v
ch and *sh:* ch, sh, ch, sh, ch, ch, sh, sh, ch, ch, sh
d and *th:* th, d, th, th, d, d, th, d, th, d
l and *r:* r, l, r, l, r, r, l, r, l, r, l, l
m and *n:* m, n, m, n, m, n, m, n, n, m, m, n
s and *th:* s, th, s, th, s, s, th, th, s, th

page 226: Words with *b* and *v*
Row 1: b, v, b, v
Row 2: v, v, b, b
Row 3: box, van
Sentence: Val, Billy, dove, wave

page 227: Words with *ch* and *sh*
Row 1: sh, ch, ch, sh
Row 2: sh, sh, ch, ch
Row 3: child, shop
Sentence: Sherry, Shark, chewed, shiny, shoe

page 228: Words with *d* and *th*
Row 1: d, th, th, d
Row 2: th, th, d, d
Row 3: third, desk
Sentence: Think, thought, daring, dog, through, thick

page 229: Words with *l* and *r*
Row 1: r, l, l, r
Row 2: r, l, l, r
Row 3: leg, ring
Sentence: red, river, runs, little, lake

page 230: Words with *m* and *n*
Row 1: n, n, m, m
Row 2: m, n, m, n
Row 3: mask, nest
Sentence: man, in, moon, cream, spoon

page 231: Words with *s* and *th*
Row 1: s, th, th, s
Row 2: s, s, th, th
Row 3: sun, thorn
Sentence: Sara, sipped, thick, soup

pages 232–235: Syllables, Assess
Syllables V/CV and VC/V: broken, silent, seven, female, rapid
Syllables CV/VC: stu/di/o; cre/ate; i/de/a; me/di/um; pi/o/neer; im/me/di/ate; bi/on/ic; re/li/ance
Syllables VCCCV: ad/dress; dis/trict; sub/stance; com/plete; con/troll C+ *-le:* thumbs up: purple, bubble, people, noodle; thumbs down: puppy, softball, broken

page 236: Syllables V/CV and VC/V
Circle: *broken, frozen, music, tulip;* Underline: *salad, lemon;* Write: *broken, salad, frozen, music, lemon, tulip*

page 237: Syllables CV/VC
Part 1: sci/en/tist; pi/an/o; vi/o/lin; vid/e/o; sta/di/um; ra/di/o; ro/de/o; me/te/or
Part 2: studio, create, idea, medium, pioneer, immediate, bionic, reliance

page 238: Syllables VCCCV
1. purchase; **2.** inspect; **3.** surprise; **4.** children; **5.** explode; **6.** address

page 239: C + *-le*
Part 1: bubble, puddle, eagle, candle
Part 2: mar/ble, mid/dle, dou/ble, lit/tle, ti/tle, han/dle

pages 240–241: Consonant Blends, Assess
Initial Consonant Blends: cr, pl, cl, pr, tr, str, dr, st
Final Consonant Blends: nk, nch, nk, nd, nch, nk, sk, st, nt, nd, nt, nd

page 242: Initial Consonant Blends
Row 1: cr, cr, cl, cl
Row 2: pr, pl, pr, pl
Row 3: str, str, st, st
Sentence: clock, struck, students, snapped

page 243: Final Consonant Blends
Row 1: nd, nk, nd, nk
Row 2: nt, nt, nch, nch
Row 3: sk, st, st, sk
Sentence: must, ask, band, paint, bench

page 244: Silent Consonants *wr, kn, gn, st, mb,* Assess
Silent Consonants: kn, kn, kn, wr, wr, wr, gn, gn, gn, st, st, st, mb, mb, mb

page 245: Silent Consonants *wr, kn, gn, st, mb*
Row 1: mb, wr, gn, kn, kn
Chart: write, knee, gnat, listen, thumb; wrench, knot, sign, castle, crumb

pages 246–247: Short Vowels, Assess
Short *a:* pat, hat, bad, man, tag

Short *e:* set, ten, net, sell
Short *i:* tin, six, pig, trip
Short *o:* hop, top, dog, lock
Short *u:* bug, tub, cup, cub

page 248: Words with Short *a*
Row 1: acrobat, bat, ant
Row 2: cap, man, map, can
Row 3: man, bat, ant, hat
Sentence: acrobat, an, apple, bat, act

page 249: Words with Short *e*
Row 1: vest, elephant, tent
Row 2: pen, web, bell, bed
Row 3: ten, bell, nest, web
Sentence: elephant, entered, tent, elegant, step

page 250: Words with Short *i*
Row 1: dinner, gift, inch
Row 2: pin, zip, dig, sit
Row 3: zip, gift, pig, six
Sentence: Six, pigs, with, bibs, grinned, did, jig, in, minute

page 251: Words with Short *o*
Row 1: dog, octopus, box
Row 2: lock, rock, fox, hop
Row 3: box, dog, lock, mop
Sentence: lock, fox, box

page 252: Words with Short *u*
Row 1: truck, puppy
Row 2: bus, duck, tub, rug
Row 3: bus, truck, duck, sun
Sentence: bug, rug, jumped, up, pup

pages 253–254:
Long Vowels, Assess
Long *a:* cage, rage; ate, late
Long *e:* leaf, lean; seen, seat
Long *i:* sky, sly; rice, price
Long *o:* globe, lobe; low, blow; hose, toes
Long *u:* rule, tool; glue, blue

page 255: Words with Long *a*
Row 1: rake, train, plate
Row 2: snake, chain, plane, hay
Row 3: grapes, tray, rake, rain
Sentence: came, (a), gate, cave, waited, Dave

page 256: Words with Long *e*
Row 1: eagle, teeth, feet
Row 2: he, wheel, thirty, leaf
Row 3: tree, leaf, me, bee
Sentence: See, leaves, trees, street

page 257: Words with Long *i*
Row 1: bike, night, mice
Row 2: ice, child, tie, light
Row 3: five, kite, light, sky
Sentence: Five, kites, sky, flying, high

page 258: Words with Long *o*
Row 1: rope, nose, bone
Row 2: robe, gold, bow, boat
Row 3: goat, rose, snow(man), gold
Sentence: Joan, wrote, note, rode, boat

page 259: Words with Long *u*
Row 1: boot, suitcase
Row 2: glue, stool, fruit, mule
Row 3: fruit, flute, moon, cube
Sentence: Sue, blue, drew, moon

page 260: Vowel Diphthongs, Assess
/ou/: plow, how, owl, south
/oi/: soy, enjoy, choice, toil, join

page 261: Vowel Diphthongs
Row 1: soil, boy, coin
Row 2: crowd, count, towel, plow
Row 3: cow, toy, voice, cloud
Sentence: boy, count, toy, cows

pages 262–263:
***r*-Controlled Vowels, Assess**
Words with *ar, are, air, or, ore:* thumbs up: chair, chore, far, stare, store, car, more; thumbs down: chew, feet, stand
Words with *er, ir, or, ur,* and *eer, ear:* cheer, steer, her, deer, fear

page 264:
Words with *ar, are, air, or, ore*
Row 1: air, ar, ar, air
Row 2: corn, horse, fork
Row 3: star, hair, store, porch
Sentence: Chairs, forks, corn, more, are, for, store

page 265:
Words with *er, ir, or, ur, eer, ear*
Row 1: ur, ear, ur, ear
Row 2: bird, butter, skirt
Row 3: worm, deer, purse, shirt
Sentence: dear, girl, tear, purse, near, here

page 266: The Schwa and Unstressed Syllables, Assess
asleep, final, panel, cradle, lesson, ribbon

page 267:
The Schwa and Unstressed Syllables
Row 1: circle: alarm, afraid; underline: bottle, dragon
Chart: medal, nickel, table, wagon; sandal, shovel, apple, button
Sentence: apples, bagels, alarm, (a), pretzel, table

pages 268–269:
Inflected Endings, Assess
Plurals and Possessives: Answers will vary, but will include possessives.
Verb Endings *-s, -ed, -ing:* Answers will vary.

page 270: Plurals and Possessives
1. pets; **2.** Martin's; **3.** birds'; **4.** Mia's; **5.** Carlos's; **6.** puppies

page 271: Verb Endings *-s, -ed, -ing*
Part 1: /s/: asks, helps, writes, walks; /z/: calls, plays, runs, sees
Part 2: /d/: called, opened, played, rubbed; /t/: fixed, helped, walked, washed
Part 3: calling, hoping, playing, running

Pages 272–274: Spellings, Assess
Spellings of /j/, /s/, /k/,: j: jet, cage, jam; k: coins, back, cat, knock; s: bus, dancing; not used: tree, photo, branch
Spellings of /[insert D12]/ in *a, au, aw, al: al, au, aw, al, al, au, aw, aw, aw*
Spellings of /[insert D12]/ in *augh, ough; ough, augh, augh, augh, augh, ough, ough*

page 275: /j/, /s/, /k/
Row 1: jet, cage, jam
Row 2: bus, dancing
Row 3: back, cat, knock(ing)
Sentence: Jessica, checks, crossing, bridge

page 276: /ȯ/ spelled *a, au, aw, al*
Row 1: saw, sausage, straw
Row 2: applause, lawn, walnut, salt
Chart: au: sausage, applause; aw: saw, straw, lawn; al: walnut, salt

page 277: /ȯ/ spelled *augh, ough*
1. brought; **2.** daughter; **3.** thought; **4.** fought; **5.** caught; **6.** taught

pages 278–280:
Compound Words, Homophones, and Contractions, Assess
Compound Words: Answers may include any of the words on page 281.
Homophones: Answers will vary.
Contractions: Answers will vary.

page 281: Compound Words
Part 1: bath/tub; flash/light; key/board; mail/box; space/ship; star/fish; tooth/paste; water/fall
Part 2: backpack, bookmark, classroom, fingernail, hairbrush, rainbow, sailboat, sidewalk

page 282: Homophones
1. same; **2.** different; **3.** same; **4.** same; **5.** different; **6.** different
Students will match pictures to words.

page 283: Contractions
I'm, Isn't, it's, we're, didn't, I've, doesn't, I'll
Answers will vary, but will be four of the following: *did not, does not, I will, I am, I have, is not, it is, we are.*

pages 284–290: Prefixes and Suffixes, Assess
Prefixes *un-* and *re-*: unafraid, not afraid; unlock, open the lock; rerun, run again; reunite, unite again
Prefixes *im-, in-, mis-, over-:* incorrect, misinterpret, overload, overcoat, intake, mistake, overtake, misuse, overuse
Prefixes *pre-, mid-, over-, out-, bi-:* prepaid, midair, overtime, outfield, biweekly
Suffixes *-ly, -ful, -less, -ness:* slowly, slowness, quietly, quietness, perfectly, fearful, fearless, rudely, rudeness
Suffixes *-tion, -sion, -able, -ible:* sensible, comfortable, confusion, reaction
Suffixes *-er, -or, -ess, -ist:* actor, seller, hostess, dentist, tourist, teacher, lioness
Suffixes *-y, -ish, -hood, -ment:* smelly, British, motherhood, excitement, windy, brownish, falsehood, shipment

page 291: Prefixes *un-* and *re-*
2. reappear; **3.** unbelievable; **4.** unfamiliar; **5.** reheat; **6.** uninterested; **7.** unlike; **8.** restart; **9.** reuse; **10.** unkind
un-: unbelievable, unfamiliar, uninterested, unlike, unkind; *re-*: reread, reappear, reheat, restart, reuse

page 292: Prefixes *im-, in-, mis-, over-*
1. overpriced; **2.** inexpensive; **3.** incorrect; **4.** misprint; **5.** impatient
Additional words: Answers will vary. Words may include *impolite, insecure, mismatch,* and *overcook.*

page 293: Prefixes *pre-, mid-, over-, out-, bi-*
1. pretest; **2.** prefixes; **3.** outline; **4.** midnight; **5.** overdue; **6.** overtime; **7.** outside; **8.** bicycle

page 294: Suffixes *-ly, -ful, -less, -ness*
1. quietly; **2.** completely; **3.** goodness; **4.** careful; **5.** Luckily; **6.** playfully; **7.** friskiness

page 295:
Suffixes *-tion, -sion, -able, -ible*
1. imagination; **2.** walkable; **3.** dependable; **4.** decision; **5.** reversible

page 296: Suffixes *-er, -or, -ess, -ist*
1. pharmacist; **2.** commuter; **3.** inventor; **4.** lioness

page 297: Suffixes *-y, -ish, -hood, -ment*
1. rainy; **2.** neighborhood; **3.** sleepy; **4.** movement; **5.** foolish; **6.** childish

pages 298–302: Cognates and Word Roots, Assess
Cognates: Answers will vary.
Words with Greek Roots: autobiography: a book about yourself; phonology: the study of sounds; geography: description of the Earth; telescope: something that lets you see far away
Words with Latin Roots: certain, cert; final, fin; audition, aud; gradual, grad; dictate, dict
Related Words: Answers will vary.
Reading Multisyllabic Words: Syllabication may vary among dictionaries. rel/a/tive; war/ri/or; math/e/mat/i/cal; mag/ni/fi/cent; prin/ci/pal

page 303: Cognates
Chart: Answers will vary. The Spanish word for *computer, computadora,* is a cognate.

page 304: Words with Greek Roots
2. microscope; **3.** telephone; **4.** autograph; **5.** telescope; **6.** photograph

page 305: Words with Latin Roots
1. carnivore, herbivore; **2.** century, millennium; **3.** projector, tractor; **4.** terrarium, aquarium

page 306: Related Words
1. volcano, Volcanic; **2.** painter, painting; **3.** desert, deserted; **4.** masquerade, mask; **5.** dirt, dirty

page 307: Reading Multisyllabic Words
Two Syllables: baseball, mushroom, zipper; Three Syllables: champion, envelope, pineapple, barbecue, telescope; Four Syllables: binoculars, watermelon, meditation, harmonica

Part 4
Grammar Instruction for English Language Learners

Contents

Introduction to the Grammar Transition Lessons

English language learners may have experience mainly with their home languages, and the grammars of different languages vary widely. As these students encounter English, keep in mind that their home languages may differ in aspects such as the following:

- The languages may use different word order than English does.
- They may not use the same parts of speech as English does.
- Their tense structures may be simpler or more complex than English tense structure.
- Nouns and adjectives that are neutral in English may be masculine or feminine in a child's home language.

For teachers, it is vitally helpful to remember that grammar is much more than a set of rules for saying and writing sentences correctly. Grammar primarily consists of the ways that speakers and writers of a language communicate ideas, mainly in sentences. As students learn the meanings of new words and how English sentences work, they become able to successfully communicate their ideas. They will gradually learn rules, read and write punctuation, and eventually become proficient in standard English usage.

The core grammar and writing lessons in *Scott Foresman Reading Street* provide the systematic instruction that students need to write. The following Grammar Transition Lessons and Practice Pages will supplement the core instruction with customized lessons that meet the particular needs of English learners.

Each group of grammar lessons covers a topic, such as Nouns, Verbs, or Sentences. Each lesson is supported by a reproducible Practice Page that provides strong context for the skill. Throughout the Grammar Transition Lessons, a **Transfer Skills** feature identifies challenges faced by English learners, based on the grammar of their home languages, as well as language knowledge that can transfer to English. Each lesson also includes a **Grammar in Action** feature to reinforce the skill through active learning.

In addition to the Grammar Transition Lessons and Practice Pages, you can further support grammar instruction with routines such as the following:

- **Emphasize sentence meaning.** Encourage children to try to understand and convey ideas rather than focusing only on separate words. Build their knowledge by presenting many examples that show how English sentences convey meaning. Include sentences that the children say or write.
- **Strengthen oral language skills.** Allow beginning English speakers to work with partners when completing grammar activities, talking about what English words and sentences mean. Encourage students to make up new phrases and sentences together.
- **Engage students as active learners.** Students who are acquiring English will make mistakes. They need encouragement rather than constant correction. Let students sing, chant, and play language games together. Allow them to communicate freely and have fun with English.
- **Relate to the home language.** Whenever possible, help students build on what they already know by making connections between a target grammar skill and the home language. Use available resources, such as bilingual staff members, language Web sites, and the students themselves, to gather information about the home language.

Transfer Skills

Common Nouns
In languages such as Spanish and French, nouns are masculine or feminine. You can point out that while some nouns in English refer to males or females *(boy, girl, uncle, aunt)*, English nouns do not have masculine and feminine endings.

Grammar *in Action*

Noun Hunt Have partners look through picture books and make a list of nouns they find in the pictures or texts.

Common Nouns

Preteach Point to objects in the room, and have students name them. Tell students: *We have names for the things around us. A noun is a word that names something or somebody.*

Teach/Model Present the concept and provide examples:
- A noun names a person, a place, an animal, or a thing.

person	place	animal	things
girl	yard	dog	box, music

Practice/Assess Copy and distribute page 318. Read the directions aloud, and name the items in the picture before students complete the page. (See answers on page 382.)

Transfer Skills

Proper Nouns
Students who are literate in nonalphabetic languages such as Chinese, Korean, and Japanese may not be familiar with capitalizing proper nouns.

Grammar *in Action*

Use capital letters On chart paper, have students draw pictures and write or dictate the names of people and places that are special to them. Remind them to use capital letters.

Proper Nouns

Special Names

Preteach Have students practice writing each other's names. Point out that each student's name begins with a capital letter. Tell students: *Each of us has our own special name. A proper noun is the special name of a person, place, animal, or thing. Proper nouns begin with capital letters.*

Teach/Model Present the concept and provide examples:
- A proper noun names a special person, place, animal, or thing.
- A proper noun begins with a capital letter.

special person	special place	special animal	special thing
Sandra	Africa	Fifi	Statue of Liberty

Practice/Assess Copy and distribute page 319. Read the directions aloud. Help students name the people and animals in the picture before they complete the page. (See answers on page 382.)

Titles and Abbreviations

Preteach Write the names of various school staff members on the board, including titles such as *Mr., Mrs.,* and *Dr.* Read the names aloud with students, and underline the titles as you say them. Point out the titles that are abbreviations, or shortened forms of words.

Teach/Model Present the concept and provide examples:
- Proper names may begin with a title such as *Mrs.* or *Dr.*
- A title begins with a capital letter. If a title is an abbreviation, it ends with a period.

Title	Example
Mr. *(mister)*	Mr. Garza
Ms. *(miz)*	Ms. Prince
Mrs. *(missus)*	Mrs. Dexter
Miss *(miss)*	Miss Wong
Dr. *(doctor)*	Dr. Marco

Practice/Assess Copy and distribute page 320. Read the directions aloud before students complete the page. (See answers on page 382.) Have students read their own answers aloud.

Transfer Skills

Titles
- Students may not realize that, in English, the title *Doctor* is used for both men and women.
- In some countries, the word *Teacher* is used as a title. Point out that in the U.S., teachers are addressed with a title such as *Mr., Ms., Mrs.,* or *Miss.*

Grammar *in Action*

Oral Language Have students practice introducing adult staff members to each other, using the correct titles.

Days, Months, and Holidays

Preteach Ask students to name today's day and date. Write them on the board, and point out that the day and month begin with capital letters.

Teach/Model Present the concept and provide examples:
- The names of the days of the week, months of the year, and holidays begin with capital letters.

Days of the Week	Months of the Year		Holidays (Examples)
Sunday	January	July	Memorial Day
Monday	February	August	Labor Day
Tuesday	March	September	Thanksgiving
Wednesday	April	October	
Thursday	May	November	
Friday	June	December	
Saturday			

Practice/Assess Copy and distribute page 321. Read the directions aloud. Go through the sample calendar with students before they complete the page. (See answers on page 382.)

Transfer Skills

Days and Months
- In languages including Spanish, French, Polish, and Vietnamese, the names of days and months are not usually capitalized.
- In languages such as Chinese, Vietnamese, and Portuguese, the names of the days are formed by counting from the first day of the week.

Grammar *in Action*

Word Origins Have students use dictionaries that show etymologies to find out the origins of the English names for days of the week.

Transfer Skills

Plural Nouns

- Spanish speakers use *-s* and *-es* endings for nouns.
- In some languages, including Chinese, Hmong, and Vietnamese, nouns do not have plural forms. Instead, the plural is indicated with an adjective.

Grammar *in Action*

Noun Sort Have students make a 3-column chart with the headings *"add -s," "add -es,"* and *"change* y *to* i *and add -es."* Invite students to look through magazines to find nouns that fit each category.

Singular and Plural Nouns

Preteach Point to one book and say: *book.* Point to two books and say: *books.* Repeat with *(lunch)box* and *(lunch)boxes.* Have students name other singular and plural nouns as you point to them. Say: *A singular noun names one thing. A plural noun names more than one thing.* Plural *means "more than one."*

Teach/Model Present the concept and provide examples:

- Add *-s* to most nouns to form the plural.
- If the noun ends in *-ch, -sh, -s, -ss,* or *-x,* add *-es.*
- If the noun ends in a consonant + *y,* change the *y* to *i* and add *-es.*

Add -s	Add -es	Change y → i and add -es
girl/girls	box/boxes	berry/berries

Practice/Assess Copy and distribute page 322 after teaching *Irregular Plural Nouns.*

Transfer Skills

Irregular Plurals

English learners may add -s to irregular nouns in sentences or to nouns for which English uses the singular for a quantity: *sheeps, mens, clothings.*

Grammar *in Action*

Concentration Have partners create "singular noun" word cards: *child, tooth, leaf, foot, man,* and "irregular plural noun" cards, including incorrect forms: *childs, children, teeth, tooths, leafs, leaves, feet, feets, men, mans.* Partners place the "singular" and "plural" cards face down in two separate groups, then take turns drawing correct pairs.

Irregular Plural Nouns

Preteach Write this sentence on the board: The children brushed their teeth. Ask a volunteer to name the singular of the underlined nouns *(child, tooth).* Tell students: *Most nouns add* -s *or* -es *to form the plural. Some nouns form the plural in a special way. They are called* irregular plural nouns.

Teach/Model Present the concept and provide examples:

- Most nouns add *-s* or *-es: books, girls, boxes, brushes.*
- Irregular plural nouns have special forms. Here are some examples:

Irregular Plural Nouns			
child/ children	foot/feet	life/lives	man/men
ox/oxen	tooth/teeth	leaf/leaves	woman/ women

Practice/Assess Copy and distribute page 322. Help students name the singular and plural nouns in the picture. (See answers on page 382.) Have students name the irregular plural nouns. As an extension, have students list the singular of the plural nouns.

Singular Possessive Nouns

Preteach Display these sentences, gesturing as appropriate: *This is Maya. This is Maya's desk.* Explain: *The first sentence is about Maya. The second sentence says that Maya has something. To show that a person, place, or thing has or owns something, add an apostrophe* (point to apostrophe) *and the letter* s. *The word* Maya's *is called a* singular possessive noun.

Teach/Model Present the concept and provide examples:
- A singular possessive noun ends in *'s.*

Singular Nouns	Singular Possessive Nouns	Examples
Sam	Sam's	Sam's mom
friend	friend's	friend's house
class	class's	class's pet
child	child's	child's jacket

Practice/Assess Copy and distribute page 323 after teaching *Plural Possessive Nouns.*

Transfer Skills

Possessive Nouns
In many languages, speakers show possession in phrases rather than noun endings. Show students how to change phrases such as *the tail of the cat* and *the nest of the bird* to *the cat's tail* and *the bird's nest,* in order to show possession in English.

Grammar *in Action*

Oral Language Have students place school supplies on their desks. Then have students point to and name a friend's things. For example: *This is Lin's book. This is Lin's calculator.*

Plural Possessive Nouns

Preteach Display these sentences: *All my students have desks. These are my students' desks.* Encourage students to discuss the meanings of the two sentences. Explain: *To show that two or more people, places, or things have or own something, use a plural possessive noun.*

Teach/Model Present the concept and provide examples:
- If the plural noun ends in *-s, -es,* or *-ies,* add an apostrophe (') to make it possessive.
- If the plural noun does **not** end in *-s, -es,* or *-ies,* add *'s* to make it possessive.

Plural Nouns	Plural Possessive	Examples
friends	friends'	friends' houses
classes	classes'	classes' teachers
puppies	puppies'	puppies' tails
children	children's	children's jackets

Practice/Assess Copy and distribute page 323. Make sure students understand the directions. Have students read their completed sentences aloud. (See answers on page 382.)

Transfer Skills

Plural Possessive Nouns
An apostrophe after the letter *s* may seem incorrect to many students. Explain the difference between clear examples such as *a cat's tail* and *cats' tails* or *a bird's nest* and *birds' nests.* Use pictures or simple drawings to help students understand.

Grammar *in Action*

Use Plural Possessive Nouns Provide sentences such as these, and ask students to rewrite or rephrase them using plural possessive nouns: *This cake belongs to the students. (This is the students' cake.) These chairs belong to the children. (These are the children's chairs.)*

Name ___________________________

Common Nouns

Practice

- **Look** at the picture.
- **Name** the people, places, animals, and things in the picture.

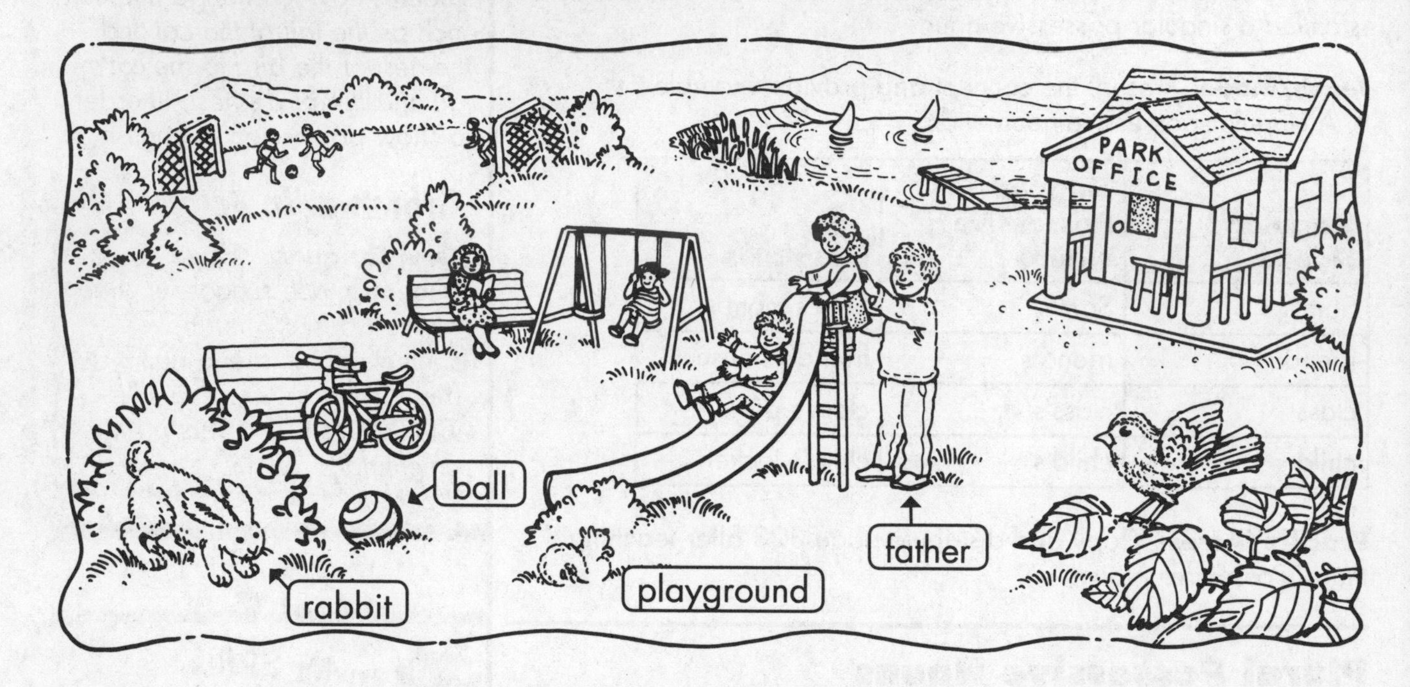

People	Places	Animals	Things
girl	pond	bird	slide

Assess

- **Look** around the room. What do you **see**?
- **Write** six nouns. **Name** things that you see.

____

____

Name ______________________________

Special Names

Practice

- **Look** at the picture.
- **Find** the children, animals, and places that have special names.
- **Write** the names. Remember to **begin** the names with a capital letter.

Names of Children	Names of Animals	Names of Places
Maya		

Assess

- **Write** the names of two people you know.

____

- **Write** the names of two special places you know.

____

Name ______________________________

Titles and Abbreviations

Practice

- **Look** at the pictures.
- **Write** the name of each person.
- **Include** a title for each person.

Title	Use with:
Mr.	a man
Ms.	a woman
Mrs.	a married woman
Miss	an unmarried girl or woman
Dr.	a doctor (male or female)

Mark Tanaka

Mr. Turner

Eva Santos

Lisa Johnson

1. Who is the teacher? ______________________________

2. Who is the doctor? ______________________________

3. Who is the dancer? ______________________________

4. Who is the carpenter? ______________________________

Assess

- **Write** the names of four adults you know. **Include** their titles.

____

____

Name ______________________________

Days, Months, and Holidays

Practice

- Use this class calendar to **answer** the questions.
- Remember to **begin** the names of days, months, and holidays with capital letters.

November						
Sunday	Monday	Tuesday	Wednesday	Thursday	Friday	Saturday
				1	2	3
4	5	6 Election Day	7 LIBRARY VISIT	8	9	10
11 Veterans Day	12	13	14 LIBRARY VISIT	15	16	17
18	19	20	21 LIBRARY VISIT	22 Thanksgiving	23	24
25	26	27	28 LIBRARY VISIT	29	30 BOOK FAIR	

1. What holiday is on Thursday, November 22? ______________________

2. What holiday is on Sunday, November 11? ______________________

3. When is the Book Fair? ______________________

4. When is Election Day? ______________________

5. When does the class visit the library? ______________________

Assess

- **Write** the names of the seven days of the week.

____

- **Write** the name of a holiday or another day that is important to you. **Tell** the date of the holiday, or when it takes place.

______________________ ______________________

Name of the holiday Date of the holiday

Name ______________________________

Singular and Plural Nouns

Practice

- **Look** at the picture.
- **Write** three singular nouns. **Write** three plural nouns.

Singular Nouns	Plural Nouns
tree	flowers

Assess

- **Look** around the room. What do you **see**?
- **Write** three singular nouns and three plural nouns.

____

____

Name ______________________________

Singular and Plural Possessive Nouns

Practice

- **Look** at the picture. **Read** the sentences.
- **Circle** the correct possessive noun to complete each sentence.

1. (Today, Today's) date is May 19.
2. It is time for the (childrens', children's) story hour.
3. The (reader's, readers) name is Ed.
4. The (lady's, ladies') book club chooses a book.

Assess

- **Choose** a singular possessive noun from the sentences above. **Use** it in another sentence here.

____

- **Choose** a plural possessive noun from the sentences above. **Use** it in another sentence here.

____

Transfer Skills

Present Tense
English verb endings differ from verb endings in languages such as Spanish and Polish, which use different endings for person and number. However, students may need practice adding *-s* or *-es* to present-tense verbs with third-person singular subjects.

Grammar *in Action*

Present Tense Practice
Write these subjects on index cards: *The baby, The girls, Sam, My brother, I.* Write these verbs on another set: *work, sleep, jump, run, play.* Have students draw a card from each set and create a sentence.

Verbs in Present Tense

Preteach Perform these actions as you narrate: *I walk to the front of the room. I point to the board. The words* walk *and* point *are verbs. The tense of a verb tells when something happens. A verb in present tense, like* walk *or* point, *tells what happens now. To talk about one other person or thing, add* -s: *He walks. She points.*

Teach/Model Present the concept and provide examples:
- Verbs in present tense tell what happens now.

	Verb	Example
I, you, we, they	see	I see my sister.
he, she, it	sees	She sees me.

Practice/Assess Copy and distribute page 330. Help students describe the picture. (See answers on page 382.)

Transfer Skills

Past Tense
- Explain that regular past-tense verbs in English always have an *-ed* ending.
- In Chinese, Hmong, and Vietnamese, verbs do not change to show the tense. Adverbs or expressions of time indicate when an action has taken place.

Grammar *in Action*

Oral Language Display a list of verbs: *walk, play, jump, call, move, push, listen, watch.* Begin to tell a story: *Yesterday I walked to the park with my friend.* Have students add to the story, using the verbs from the list in the past tense.

Verbs in Past Tense

Preteach Display these sentences: *I walked to the front of the room. I pointed to the board.* Explain: *I did these things in the past. Many verbs in past tense end with* -ed. *If a verb ends in* e, *like* move, *drop the* e *and then add* -ed: moved. *If a verb has one syllable and ends with a vowel followed by a consonant, such as* shop, *double the consonant before adding* -ed: shopped.

Teach/Model Present the concept and provide examples:
- Verbs in past tense tell what happened in the past.

	Verbs in Past Tense
Add *-ed*	He jumped over the chair.
Drop the final *e* and add *-ed*	I moved the chair.
Double the consonant and add *-ed*	He slipped on the rug.

Practice/Assess Copy and distribute page 331 after teaching *Irregular Verbs,* page 325.

Irregular Verbs

Preteach Display these sentences: *I think about you. I write a note. I thought about you. I wrote a note.* Explain: *Usually, you add -ed to a verb to form the past tense. But here, I didn't use* thinked *or* writed. *Some verbs are not regular verbs. They are called* irregular verbs. *An irregular verb has a different spelling in the past tense.*

Teach/Model Present the concept and provide examples:
- Irregular verbs do not add *-ed* to form the past tense.
- Irregular verbs have different spellings in the past tense.

Irregular Verbs	Past Tense
write	I wrote a poem yesterday.
sing	I sang a song last night.
eat	I ate an apple earlier today.

Practice/Assess Copy and distribute page 331. Explain that some answers will be irregular verbs. (See answers on page 382.)

Transfer Skills

Irregular Verbs
Many English learners need extra practice with the variety of irregular verbs that also feature unfamiliar phonics elements, such as *catch/caught, buy/bought,* and *can/could.*

Grammar *in Action*

Oral Language
Prepare index cards with irregular verbs. On one side, write the present tense. On the other side, write the past tense: *write/wrote; sing/sang; make/made; give/gave; eat/ate; have/had.* Have partners dictate sentences to each other using the words on both sides.

Verbs in Future Tense

Preteach Say: *What will I do after school today? I will go home. I will eat a snack. I will read my e-mail.* Explain: *To talk about the future, we use verbs in future tense. The future may be later today, next week, or even next year.* Write one of the statements and point out the word *will*. Say: *Use the helping verb* will *to form the future tense.*

Teach/Model Present the concept and provide examples:
- Verbs in future tense tell what will happen in the future.

Verbs in Future Tense
I will go home. I will eat a snack. I will do my homework.

Practice/Assess Copy and distribute page 332. Help students describe the picture. Review the meanings of the verbs. (See answers on page 382.)

Transfer Skills

Future Tense
Spanish, Haitian Creole, and Hmong speakers may use present tense in places where English calls for future tense. Help students practice verbs in statements such as *I will read later* and *After we hear the story, we will write a new story.*

Grammar *in Action*

Oral Language Have partners tell each other what they will do when they get home from school or at some other time. If students can pantomime the action, have them act out the verb.

Transfer Skills

Verb Tenses
Speakers of several languages, including Arabic, may find the English distinction between the past and present perfect tenses unfamiliar. Show contrasting examples, and explain how the sense of time differs.

Grammar *in Action*

Present Participle Practice
Say and display these verbs: *jump, walk, talk, wave, laugh.* Have students give the present participle of each verb, with the subjects *I, you, she,* and *they.* Have them pantomime the actions and point to the corresponding subject.

Principal Parts of Regular Verbs

Preteach Display these sentences: *I talk to you. I am talking to you. I talked to you. I have talked to you many times.* Explain: *A verb's tenses are made from four basic forms: Present, Present Participle, Past, and Past Participle. These are called the verb's principal parts. The present form is used in the first sentence. The second sentence uses the present participle form. The third sentence uses the past form, which is the -ed form of the regular verb. The fourth sentence uses the past participle.*

Teach/Model Present the concept and provide examples:
- The four basic forms are called the principal parts.
- The present participle can use *am, is,* or *are* and the *-ing* form.
- The past participle uses *has, have,* or *had* and the *-ed* form.

	Principal Parts: Regular Verbs
Present	The baby plays all day.
Present Participle	The baby is playing now.
Past	You helped me yesterday.
Past Participle	You have helped me before.

Practice/Assess Copy and distribute page 333. Have students share their sentences. (See answers on page 382.)

Transfer Skills

Learning Verb Forms
Spanish, like English, has irregular verbs (such as *ser,* which means "to be," and *ir,* "to go"). Challenge students who are literate in Spanish to identify irregular Spanish verbs, and see whether English verbs with the same meanings are irregular.

Grammar *in Action*

Find the Parts Write the principal parts of *go, sing, take,* and *write* on index cards. Give each student a card. Students circulate to find others with principal parts of the same verb.

Principal Parts of Irregular Verbs

Preteach Display these sentences: *You grow every day. You are growing so much! You grew an inch last year. You have grown an inch every year.* Point out the past and past participle: *Irregular verbs change spelling in these forms.*

Teach/Model Present the concept and provide examples:
- The principal parts of irregular verbs are the same four kinds as the principal parts of regular verbs. The *-ing* form is made the same way, such as *growing* or *going.*
- But irregular verbs do not use the *-ed* ending for the past and the past participle. For example, we do not say "growed"; we say "grew." We do not say "have growed"; we say "have grown."

I go. I am going. I went. I have gone.
He sees it. He is seeing it. He saw it. He has seen it.

Practice/Assess Copy and distribute page 334. Remind students that irregular verbs have their own spellings of the past and past participle. (See answers on page 383.)

Helping Verbs

Preteach Display these sentences: *I am planting seeds. They will grow fast. I have planted seeds before.* Explain: *The underlined parts are called* verb phrases. *The main verbs*—planting, grow, *and* planted—*show action. The helping verbs*—am, will, *and* have—*tell more about the action. The helping verb* am *tells what I am doing now.* Will *tells what the seeds will do in the future.* Have *tells what I have done that started in the past.*

Teach/Model Present the concept and provide examples:
- Helping verbs can tell the time of the action.

	Helping Verbs
Present	The dog **is** wagging his tail.
Past	He **was** barking last night.
Future	He **will** stay inside tonight.
Started in the Past	You **have** helped me before.

Practice/Assess Copy and distribute page 335. Have students read their sentences aloud. (See answers on page 383.)

Transfer Skills

Helping Verbs
The uses of *have* and *had* as helping verbs may be familiar to Spanish-speaking students once they learn the English words. The Spanish verb *haber* is used similarly.

Grammar *in Action*

Time to Listen Have each student create three index cards labeled *present, past,* and *future.* Say these sentences and have students hold up the corresponding card: *You were playing basketball yesterday. You are listening to me now. You will go to the library later.* Encourage students to say other sentences with helping verbs.

Linking Verbs

Preteach Display these sentences: *I am tired. I feel sick. She seems sad. He is the leader. The car was new.* Explain: *In these sentences, the underlined words are called* linking verbs. *They tell what the subject is or what the subject is like.*

Teach/Model Present the concept and provide examples:
- Linking verbs do not show actions.
- They tell what the subject is or what the subject is like.

Linking Verbs	Examples
is	Summer is here.
are	The days are longer.
feels	The sun feels warmer.

Practice/Assess Copy and distribute page 336. Help students describe what is happening in the picture. (See answers on page 383.)

Transfer Skills

Linking Verbs
- In languages such as Chinese and Korean, linking verbs often are not required: *She tired. They sad.* Help students practice English sentences with linking verbs.
- Vietnamese speakers may use the English verb *have* in place of *there are* or *is,* as in "Inside the box have a gift." Help students practice with sentences using forms of *be.*

Grammar *in Action*

Oral Language Have partners tell each other three nice things they observe about each other: *You seem happy. You are smart. You are funny.*

Transfer Skills

Contractions
Ask students if there are contractions in their home languages. (In Spanish, *a* + *el* = *al* and *de* + *el* = *del;* in Portuguese, *de* + *as* = *das.)* Explain that an English contraction uses an apostrophe to replace the missing letters.

Grammar *in Action*

Contraction Substitution
Say these sentences, and have students rephrase them using contractions: *You are hiding. I do not see you. I am going to find you. I will not stop looking.* If necessary, help students learn *you're, don't, I'm,* and *won't.*

Contractions

Preteach Display these sentences: *You're calling me. I'm far away. I can't hear you.* Explain: *The underlined words are contractions. A contraction is a shortened form of two words. An apostrophe* (point to an apostrophe) *takes the place of one or more letters. Look at these contractions:* you *and* are *become* you're, I *and* am *become* I'm, can *and* not *become* can't.

Teach/Model Present the concept and provide examples:
- A contraction is a shortened form of two words.
- An apostrophe takes the place of a letter or letters that are removed when you write a contraction.

	Contractions
I *and* have	I've eaten breakfast.
Should *and* not	You shouldn't run in the hall.
Can *and* not	She can't come to my party.

Practice/Assess Copy and distribute page 337 after teaching *Negatives.*

Transfer Skills

Negatives
In Spanish, Haitian Creole, and some other languages, double negatives (similar to *We did not do nothing)* are correct. Tell students that standard English does not use double negatives.

Grammar *in Action*

Double Negatives Write these sentences on the board: *I can't never tell you. I won't say nothing. I don't want nobody to hear.* Invite students to come up and show how they would fix the double negative. Ask them to read the new sentence.

Negatives

Preteach Display these sentences: *I never eat fish. I don't ever eat fish.* Explain: *The underlined words are negatives. They mean "no" or "not." Contractions with* n't *are negatives. In English, we use only one negative with one verb.* I don't never eat fish *has a double negative. Take away one negative.* (See the first two examples.)

Teach/Model Present the concept and provide examples:
- Use only one negative with one verb.
- Use a positive word in a sentence with *not.*

	Examples
Negative	Nothing is on the table.
Positive	I don't see anything there.
Negative	They went nowhere.
Positive	We didn't go anywhere.

Practice/Assess Copy and distribute page 337. Remind students to watch for double negatives. (See answers on page 383.)

Troublesome Verbs Lie/Lay, Sit/Set

Preteach Write and say: *The boy lays his book on the table. Then he lies down on his bed to take a nap.* Explain that in the first sentence, the boy puts his book down on a table. In the second sentence, he goes to bed to rest. Write and say: *Miguel sets the plates on the table. Then he sits at the table.* Show the difference between *set* and *sit* in these sentences by pantomiming the actions.

Teach/Model Present the concept and provide examples:
- Some verbs look similar or have similar meanings.
- Think of the meanings and the main parts of verbs.

Troublesome Verb	Past	Past Participle
Lie: "rest" or "recline"	lay	*(has, have, had) lain*
Lay: "put" or "place"	laid	*(has, have, had) laid*
Sit: "sit down"	sat	*(has, have, had) sat*
Set: "put something somewhere"	set	*(has, have, had) set*

Practice/Assess Copy and distribute page 338. Read the directions aloud and discuss the picture with students before they complete the activity. Then ask students to read their original sentence aloud. (See answers on page 383.)

Transfer Skills

Troublesome Verbs
Tell students that the verbs *set* and *lay* usually take a direct object. Display the sentences: *She set her keys on the counter. He lays his wallet on the table.* Use the sentences to show students that a direct object (keys, wallet) is a noun or pronoun that receives the action of a verb (set, lays) or shows the result of the action.

Grammar *in Action*

My Turn, Your Turn
In pairs, have students take turns creating sentences that include troublesome verbs. The partner accepts a correct example and offers a new example.

Troublesome Verbs Leave/Let, Rise/Raise

Preteach Write and say: *The girl will leave with her friends. Her mother let her go.* Explain that first the girl is going away. Her mother allows, or permits, her to go. Write and say: *The sun will rise every day. The children raise their hands in class.* Use pantomime or pictures to discuss the differences between *rise* and *raise* in these sentences.

Teach/Model Present the concept and provide examples:
- Some verbs look similar or have similar meanings.
- Think of the meanings and the principal parts of the verbs to use them correctly.

Practice/Assess Copy and distribute page 339. Read the directions aloud. Discuss the picture. Have students complete page 339. Then ask them to read their original sentence aloud. (See answers on page 383.)

Transfer Skills

Troublesome Verbs
Have English learners study the meanings and principal parts of troublesome verbs. Then provide additional examples of the verbs used correctly.

Grammar *in Action*

Incomplete Sentences
Display several incomplete sentences, asking students to complete each sentence with a troublesome verb. For example, say: *The teacher ______ (let) the children go home. The children ______ (left) quickly.*

Name ___________________________

Verbs in Present Tense

Practice

- **Look** at the picture. **Read** the sentences.
- **Write** the correct verb in present tense to complete each sentence.

1. At 8:00, we ____________________ (wait, waits) for the bus.

2. Liz ____________________ (talk, talks) to her mom.

3. Adam ____________________ (sit, sits) on the bench.

4. I ____________________ (see, sees) the bus!

Assess

- **Look** at the picture. **Write** a sentence about the dog. **Use** a verb in present tense.

____

Name ______________________________

Verbs in Past Tense

Practice

- **Look** at the picture. **Read** the sentences.
- **Circle** the correct verb in past tense.

Yesterday was my little sister's first day of school. We (celebrated, celebrates) with a picnic. I (gived, gave) her a soccer ball. She (play, played) with it all day. My mom (maked, made) snacks. We (haved, had) a good time!

Assess

- **Look** at the picture again. **Write** another sentence about the picnic. **Use** the verb *ate*.

____

Name ______________________________

Verbs in Future Tense

Practice

- **Look** at the picture. **Read** the story. **Read** the verbs in the box.
- **Write** the correct verb in future tense to complete each sentence.

The mother bird ______________________________ food for the babies.

In a few days, she ______________________________ them to fly. Soon,

the baby birds ______________________________ big and strong. They

______________________________ away from the nest.

will find	will fly	will teach	will grow

Assess

- What do you think the mother bird will do when the baby birds fly away? **Write** a sentence about it.

____

Name ____________________________

Principal Parts of Regular Verbs

Practice

- **Look** at the picture. **Read** the sentences.
- **Circle** the verb in each sentence. **Write** *present, present participle, past,* or *past participle* to name the principal part of the verb.

1. The concert has started. ____________________

2. We listen to Sofia, Ben, and Ray. ____________________

3. Sofia and Ben are playing violins. ____________________

4. Sofia has played the violin for three years. ____________________

5. Ray plays the flute well. ____________________

Assess

- **Write** a sentence about the concert. **Use** the present participle *playing.*

____

Name ______________________________

Principal Parts of Irregular Verbs

Practice

- **Look** at the picture. **Read** the sentences.
- **Circle** the verb in each sentence. **Write** *present, present participle, past,* or *past participle* to name the principal part of each irregular verb.

1. Yesterday I went to the doctor's office. ______________________

2. I go every year. ______________________

3. I have grown two inches this year. ______________________

4. I am growing very fast. ______________________

Assess

- **Write** a sentence to say what the doctor did. **Use** the past tense verb *wrote.*

____

Name ______________________________

Helping Verbs

Practice

- **Look** at the picture. **Read** the sentences.
- **Circle** the verb phrase in each sentence. **Underline** the helping verb.

1. We are learning about dolphins in class.

2. We have seen dolphins at the zoo.

3. I am using the Internet now.

4. I will give my report tomorrow.

Assess

- **Write** a sentence about the girl's report. **Use** the verb phrase *will tell.*

____

Name ______________________________

Linking Verbs

Practice

- **Look** at the picture. **Read** the sentences.
- **Circle** the linking verb in each sentence.

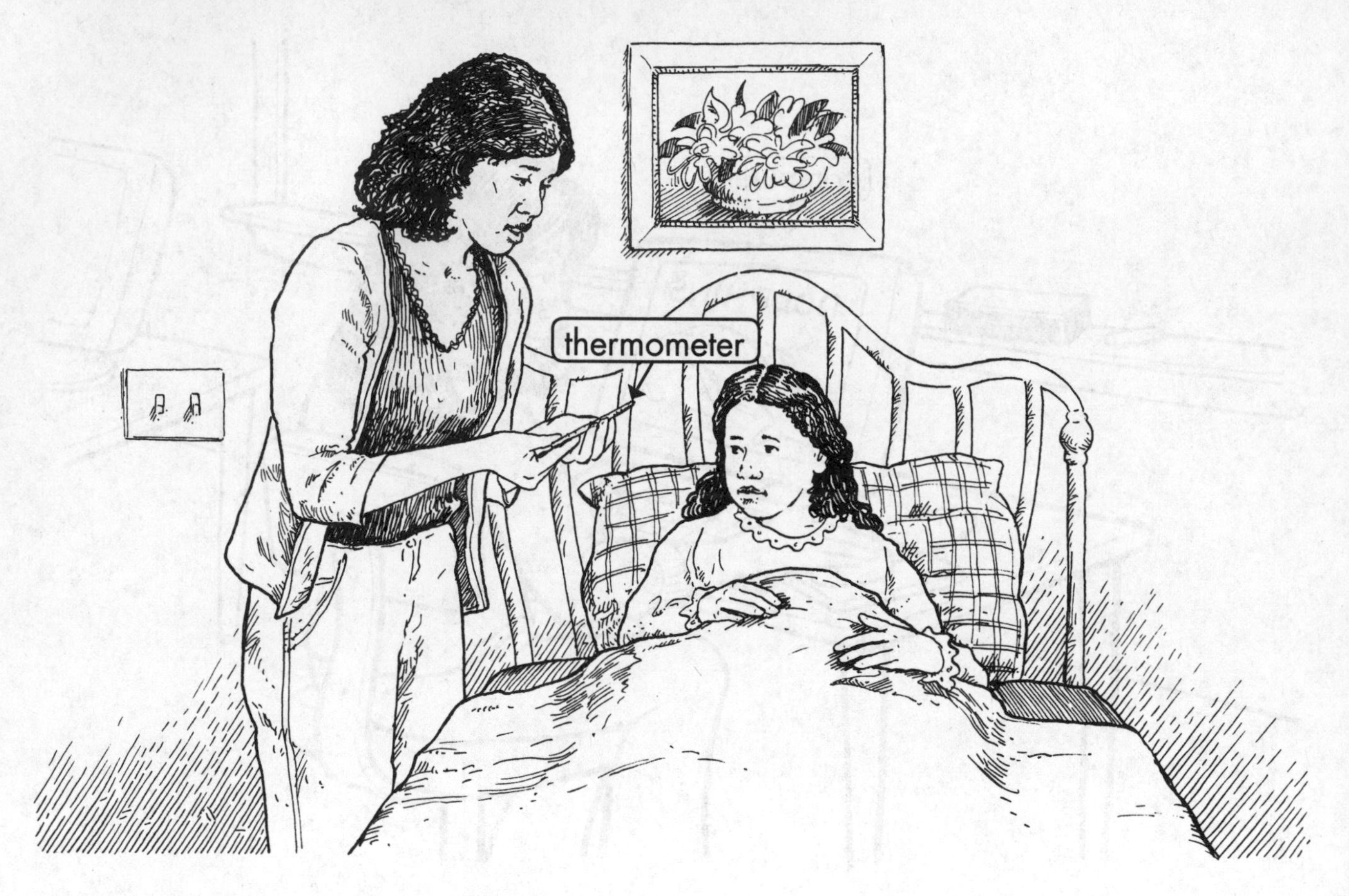

1. I am sick today.

2. I feel tired and cold.

3. Mom seems worried.

4. My temperature is 102°F.

Assess

- **Write** a sentence about the girl. **Use** the linking verb *is*.

____

Name ______________________________

Contractions and Negatives

Practice

- **Look** at the picture. **Read** the sentences.
- **Circle** the correct word to complete each sentence.

1. Dad, (I'm, I'll) going out to play baseball.

2. (Shouldn't, Should'nt) you do your homework first?

3. Oh, (I've, I'm) already done it.

4. (You're, Your) such a good student!

5. I won't (ever, never) forget to do my schoolwork.

Assess

- **Write** a sentence about the girl's dad. **Use** a contraction with *not*.

____

Name ______________________________

Troublesome Verbs Lie/Lay, Sit/Set

Practice

- **Look** at the picture. **Read** the sentences.
- **Circle** the correct verb in each sentence.

1. Judy (lays / lies) on the chair by the pool.

2. She likes to (set / sit) on the edge of the pool.

3. The little girl (set / sit) her goggles on the table.

4. My mom (lays / lies) her towel on the chair.

Assess

- **Look** at the picture again. **Write** and then **say** a sentence about it. **Use** the verbs *lie, lay, sit,* or *set.*

____

Name ______________________________

Troublesome Verbs Leave/Let, Rise/Raise

Practice

- **Look** at the picture. **Read** the sentences.
- **Circle** the correct verb in each sentence.

1. Marcos, do not (let / leave) class without your music!

2. (Leave / Let) me play this song for you.

3. The teacher told us to (raise / rise) our hand when we have a question.

4. We want to (let / leave) a gift for our teacher.

5. We watched the balloons (raise / rise) into the air.

Assess

- **Look** at the picture again. **Write** and then **say** a sentence about it. **Use** the verbs *leave, let, rise,* or *raise.*

____

Subjects and Predicates

Preteach Display this sentence: *The girl walks to school.* Explain that "The girl" is the subject of the sentence. The sentence is about the girl. A sentence is about its subject. Explain that "walks to school" is the predicate. What does the girl do? (walks to school) A predicate tells something about the subject.

Teach/Model Present the concept and provide examples:
- The subject of a sentence tells whom or what the sentence is about.
- The predicate of a sentence tells what the subject is or what the subject does.

Subject	Predicate
Sam	went to the store.
The students	write a paper.
The vegetables	are fresh.
My dog	had puppies.

Practice/Assess Copy and distribute page 348. Look at the picture after students complete the page. Have students contribute other sentences and identify the subjects and predicates. (See answers on page 383.)

Transfer Skills

Subjects and Predicates
The typical English sequence of subject then predicate is not standard in some languages. For example, in Spanish the verb often appears before the subject, while in Korean and Hindi the verb typically appears at the end of a sentence.

Grammar *in Action*

Sentence Scramble Write these sentences onto strips: *My friend rides a bike. My dog barks at cats. The fish smells good. The clown is funny.* Cut each strip into subject and predicate. Have students scramble the sentence parts to form new sentences such as *The fish rides a bike.*

Subject-Verb Agreement

Preteach Display these sentences: *The bird sings a song. The birds sing a song.* Encourage students to discuss the differences between the underlined parts. Explain: *The first sentence has a singular subject:* bird. *The second sentence has a plural subject:* birds. *The subject and the verb must work together, or agree. That's why the first sentence uses* sings *and the second sentence uses* sing.

Teach/Model Present the general concept and provide examples:
- If the subject is singular, add -*s* to the verb.
- If the subject is plural, do not add -*s* to the verb.

Subject	Verb
man	dances
Mom	works
friends	play
both feet	hurt

Practice/Assess Copy and distribute page 349. Help students describe the picture, emphasizing subject-verb agreement. (See answers on page 383.)

Transfer Skills

Verbs and Subjects
Students of various language backgrounds may add -*s* to both the nouns and verbs in sentences: *The robots walks.* Point out that, in English, verbs add -*s* for singular nouns *(A robot walks)*, not for verbs with plural nouns *(The robots walk)*.

Grammar *in Action*

Subject-Verb Agreement
Encourage students to scour the day's headlines for examples of subject-verb agreement. For example: *Schools Close; Teams Win; Gas Prices Rise; Dog Saves Girl.*

Word Order

Preteach Display these sentences and read them aloud, gesturing: *The bird flies. Flies the bird.* Ask: *What is the subject of the first sentence? (The bird) The second sentence does not sound right. The words are not in the right order to make a statement. In an English statement, the subject usually comes first. The predicate usually follows.*

Teach/Model Present the concept and provide examples:
- Sentences need to have words in the right order.
- In a statement, the subject usually comes first. The predicate usually follows.

In the right order:	Pablo is my friend.
Not in the right order:	Is friend my Pablo.

Practice/Assess Copy and distribute page 350. Help students describe what is happening in the picture. (See answers on page 383.)

Transfer Skills

Word Order
- Help students see that word order strongly affects meaning in English. *Lee thanked Tony* has a different meaning from *Tony thanked Lee*.
- See the Transfer note about the sequence of subjects and predicates on page 340.

Grammar *in Action*

Oral Language Say these groups of words: *The food is good. Is good the food. My friend rides a bike. Rides a bike my friend. Plays the dog. The dog plays.* Have students say which sentences are in correct word order.

Complete Sentences and Sentence Fragments

Preteach Write this sentence and fragment on the board: *Tom went to the library. Went to the library.* Ask: *Who went to the library?* (Tom) *Which sentence tells you this? The first sentence tells a complete idea. It says who did something. The second set of words* (went to the library) *is called a* sentence fragment. *It does not tell a complete idea. It does not say who went to the library. How would you make this fragment a complete sentence?* (Add a subject.)

Teach/Model Present the concept and provide examples:
- A sentence tells a complete idea.
- A fragment is a piece of a sentence. It does not tell a complete idea.

Sentence	Cheny eats her lunch.
Fragment	Her lunch in a bag.

Practice/Assess Copy and distribute page 351. As an extension, have students choose a fragment from the Practice and create a sentence from it. (See answers on page 383.)

Transfer Skills

Sentence Fragments
Spanish- and Chinese-speaking students may omit some pronouns as sentence subjects because in their home languages the pronoun may be unnecessary. For example, the Spanish equivalent of *Am reading* is a complete sentence.

Grammar *in Action*

Time to Listen Say these groups of words. Have students call out *sentence* or *fragment* after each one: *My brother. We walk to school. We ride on the bus. In the car. After school.* Invite students to contribute other sentences.

Transfer Skills

Statements
Children who have begun to read in Spanish and other alphabetic languages may recognize that sentences begin with capital letters and end with periods.

Grammar *in Action*

Fix the Statements Write groups of words such as these on the board, including the mistakes: *my friends are funny. / They tell me jokes / I laugh every day* Have volunteers come up and fix the statements by adding correct punctuation and a capital letter at the beginning.

Types of Sentences

Statements

Preteach Display these sentences: *I went to the library. My brother went too. We both found good books.* Say: *Let's look at these sentences. Each one starts with a capital letter and ends with a period. Each one tells something. A sentence that tells something is called a* statement.

Teach/Model Present the concept and provide examples:
- A sentence that tells something is called a *statement.*
- It begins with a capital letter and ends with a period.

Statements
I had a party yesterday.
All of my friends came to my house.
You ate pizza.

Practice/Assess Copy and distribute page 352 after teaching *Questions.*

Transfer Skills

Questions
Speakers of Chinese, Vietnamese, and other Asian languages often form questions by adding words to statements, comparable to *The food is hot, no?* or *You see or not see the bird?* Provide model English questions for students to understand and to follow the patterns.

Grammar *in Action*

Oral Language Have pairs of students ask each other questions about what they did yesterday. For example, *What did we do in school yesterday? What is your favorite subject?*

Questions

Preteach Display these sentences: *What is your name? Where do you live? How old are you? Do you have any brothers?* Ask: *How are these sentences different from statements? They each ask something, and they end with question marks. A sentence that asks something is called a* question. Model the difference in intonation between these two sentences: *That is your dog. Is that your dog?*

Teach/Model Present the general concept and provide examples:
- A sentence that asks something is called a *question.*
- It starts with a capital letter and ends with a question mark.

Questions
How are you?
Did you go to Sam's party?
Does Ami like pizza?

Practice/Assess Copy and distribute page 352. Help students describe the picture. (See answers on page 383.)

Exclamations and Interjections

Preteach Write and say in an excited voice: *I am so happy!* Have students repeat, and then ask: *What feeling does that sentence express?* (excitement; happiness) *Whenever you say something with strong feeling, you are saying an exclamation. A written exclamation ends with an exclamation mark.* Next, write and say: *Hooray!* Explain: *This word also shows strong feeling and ends in an exclamation mark. However, it is* <u>*not*</u> *a complete sentence. It is called an* interjection.

Teach/Model Present the concept and provide examples:

- An exclamation is a sentence that shows strong feeling. It ends with an exclamation mark.
- An interjection is a word or group of words that shows strong feeling. It ends with an exclamation mark, but it is not a complete sentence.

Exclamation	I have a new baby brother!
Interjection	Wow!

Practice/Assess Copy and distribute page 353. Remind students that exclamations are complete sentences. (See answers on page 384.)

Exclamations

Speakers of Russian, Polish, and other languages may need to practice correct word order in exclamations. Have students make and use sentence strips, correcting exclamations such as *We enjoy very much movies!*

Grammar *in Action*

Interjection Charades
Write these interjections on index cards: *Ouch! Wow! Oh, no! Hooray!* Display them. Have a volunteer secretly choose an interjection and pantomime a scene that would elicit that interjection. Whoever guesses correctly takes the next turn.

Commands

Preteach Give students various commands such as these: *Please stand up. Walk to the front of the class. Say hello. Sit down.* Ask: *How are these sentences the same? Sentences that tell someone to do something are called* commands.

Teach/Model Present the concept and provide examples:

- A command is a sentence that tells someone to do something.
- It begins with a capital letter and ends with a period.

Commands

Open the door. Turn on the light. Sweep the floor.

Practice/Assess Copy and distribute page 354. Have students use it as a model for writing another recipe. (See answers on page 384.)

Transfer Skills

Commands

Vietnamese speakers may recognize commands when they include an adverb or another clue word: *Go to school now. Take this to the office; go now.*

Grammar *in Action*

Oral Language Teach students the jump rope chant "Teddy Bear," in which the jumper obeys these commands while jumping rope: *Teddy Bear, Teddy Bear, turn around. Teddy Bear, Teddy Bear, touch the ground. Teddy Bear, Teddy Bear, stomp your feet. Teddy Bear, Teddy Bear, show your teeth.* Invite students to play.

Transfer Skills

Compound Sentences Students may have difficulty distinguishing the clauses in a compound sentence in English. Give them additional practice finding the subject and verb within each independent clause.

Grammar *in Action*

Oral Language Say several pairs of simple sentences. Have students say compound sentences, keeping in mind the differences among *and, but,* and *or: I want to buy juice. I do not have a dollar. / I can drink water. I can borrow a dollar. / Tom is my friend. He gave me a dollar.*

Simple and Compound Sentences

Preteach Display these sentences: *I went to Sal's house. We watched a movie.* Ask students to tell the subjects and predicates. Explain: *A simple sentence has one subject and one predicate. You can join the two simple sentences this way: I went to Sal's house, and we watched a movie. The new sentence is called a* compound sentence. *The two simple sentences are joined with the word* and.

Teach/Model Present the concept and provide examples:
- A simple sentence has one subject and one predicate.
- A compound sentence has two simple sentences joined by a comma and one of these words: *and, but,* or *or.*

Simple Sentences	Lena is my sister. I love her. I like peanuts. They make me sick. You can walk to school. I can drive you.
Compound Sentences	Lena is my sister, and I love her. I like peanuts, but they make me sick. You can walk to school, or I can drive you.

Practice/Assess Copy and distribute page 355. In the first compound sentence, help students see the two simple sentences. (See answers on page 384.)

Transfer Skills

Combining Sentences Speakers of Indonesian and some other Asian languages may need practice combining sentences.

Grammar *in Action*

Form Sentences Make a set of sentence cards: *Mari wrote a poem. David sings. Rita went home.* Make a second set and distribute: *Mari read it to the class. David plays the guitar. Simón went home.* Read a sentence from the first set. The student holding a sentence with the same subject or predicate reads it. Have a volunteer form a combined sentence.

Combining Sentences

Preteach Display these sentences: *I ate a sandwich. I drank some milk.* Ask: *What is the subject of both sentences? You can combine two sentences that have the same subject: I ate a sandwich and drank some milk.* Display these sentences: *Max went to the beach. I went to the beach.* Ask: *What is the predicate of both sentences? You can combine two sentences that have the same predicate: Max and I went to the beach.*

Teach/Model Present the concept and provide examples:
- Combine two sentences that have the same subject.
- Combine two sentences that have the same predicate.

Same Subject	Dan sat down. Dan did his homework. Dan sat down and did his homework.
Same Predicate	Miguel walked to school. I walked to school. Miguel and I walked to school.

Practice/Assess Copy and distribute page 356. Help students describe the picture. (See answers on page 384.)

Complex Sentences

Preteach Review compound sentences. Then present these complex sentences: *When I run, I feel good. I feel good when I run.* Explain: *This type of sentence is called a* complex sentence. *It has two parts, called* clauses. *The underlined part cannot stand alone as a sentence. If it comes first in the sentence, use a comma. The other part* (I feel good) *can stand alone as a complete sentence.*

Teach/Model Present the concept and provide examples:
- A complex sentence is made of two clauses.
- The two clauses are joined together with words such as *because, when, since, if,* or *until.*

Complex Sentences	When I grow up, I will be a teacher. I will be a teacher when I grow up.

Practice/Assess Copy and distribute page 357. Remind students that a complex sentence has two clauses. (See answers on page 384.)

Complex Sentences
Functional words such as *if, that, so,* and *because* are often used somewhat differently in English than how their equivalents are used in other languages. Help students practice and understand usages of these words.

Grammar *in Action*

Identify Complex Sentences Have students write these sentences and tell whether they are complex or not: *My sister's name is Lupe. (no) Since she is little, I help her with homework. (yes) I also tie her shoes. (no) When I was little, my mom helped me. (yes)*

Independent and Dependent Clauses

Preteach Present this complex sentence: *We cross the street when the light is green.* Explain: *The underlined part cannot stand alone as a sentence. It is a dependent clause. It depends on another part. The other part* (we cross the street) *can stand alone. It is an independent clause.*

Teach/Model Present the concept and provide examples:
- A complex sentence is made of an independent clause and a dependent clause.
- The dependent clause cannot stand alone.
- The independent clause can stand alone.

Independent Clause	Dependent Clause
I am happy	because I passed the test.

Practice/Assess Copy and distribute page 358. Remind students that dependent clauses often start with words such as *since, although, when, if,* or *until.* (See answers on page 384.)

Transfer Skills

Dependent Clauses
Provide models of dependent clauses that begin with words such as *after, although, as, because, before, if, since, then, until, when,* and *while.* These words may have uses that are unfamiliar to students of many language backgrounds.

Grammar *in Action*

Write Complex Sentences Say these dependent clauses. Have students add independent clauses to form complex sentences: *Since I was little / When I grow up / Because it was raining / If you help me / Until my alarm clock rings.* Have students write the complex sentences.

Transfer Skills

Commas
Some students may use commas in places where periods are used in the United States, such as in decimals (*1,5* for *1.5*). Determine the intended meaning, and clarify the standard usage in American English.

Grammar *in Action*

Oral Language On the board, write menu items such as *soup, salad, sandwich, milk, tea,* and *juice.* Have pairs play the roles of server and customer at a café. The server starts with *"May I take your order?"* The customer names three items, such as: *"I want soup, salad, and milk."* The server says and writes the order: *"He wants soup, salad, and milk."* Have students switch roles.

Commas

In a Series and in Direct Address

Preteach Display this sentence: *My favorite colors are red, blue, and yellow.* Point out the commas. Say: *Commas help you understand a sentence. They tell you when to pause, or rest. Put commas after items in a series of words such as red, blue, and yellow.* Display these sentences: *Kim, may I use your pen? Yes, Lucas, you may.* Say: *When we write a sentence in which a person is directly addressed by name, we use a comma.*

Teach/Model Present the concept and provide examples:
- Use commas to separate items in a series.
- Use commas with direct address.

Commas in a Series	I like baseball, basketball, and soccer. I play Monday, Wednesday, and Friday.
Commas in Direct Address	Lori, would you come here? Yes, Mom, I'm coming. I need your help, Lori.

Practice/Assess Copy and distribute page 359 after the lesson on commas with appositives and introductory phrases.

Transfer Skills

Commas
Commas can be challenging for any student. English language learners may need help distinguishing needs for commas from uses of other kinds of punctuation.

Grammar *in Action*

Comma Practice
Brainstorm names of school staff. Write their names and job titles, such as *Mrs. Olson, the bus driver.* Have students use this information to write sentences with appositives.

With Appositives and Introductory Phrases

Preteach Display these sentences: *Mr. Hays, my teacher, speaks Spanish. Yes, I know.* Explain: *The underlined part of the first sentence is called* an appositive. *It is a noun phrase that describes another noun. Use a comma before and after an appositive. The underlined part of the second sentence is called an introductory* word. *Put a comma after an introductory word or phrase such as* well, no, oh, *and* "in other words."

Teach/Model Present the concept and provide examples:
- Use a comma before and after an appositive.
- Use a comma after an introductory word or phrase.

Appositives	Mr. Sims, my neighbor, has a dog. The dog, a poodle, barks all night.
Introductory Words or Phrases	Oh, I am very sorry. In other words, you cannot sleep.

Practice/Assess Copy and distribute page 359. Read the sentences, pausing where commas belong. (See answers on page 384.)

Quotations

Preteach Display and read the following dialogue: *"Do you have homework?" my mother asked. "Yes, I have to read a book," I said. "What is the name of the book?" my mother wanted to know.* Point out the position of the quotation marks in the dialogue.

Teach/Model Present the concept and provide examples:

- A quotation shows the exact words of a speaker.
- Quotation marks enclose a quotation.
- Use a comma to separate the speaker's exact words from the rest of the sentence. When the quotation doesn't end with a question mark or exclamation mark.
- Quotation marks are also used for poetry, song titles, and story titles.

Quotation	Story Title
"Mr. Chung is my favorite teacher," said Joy.	"The Cat Has a Hat"

Practice/Assess Copy and distribute page 360. Have students add quotation marks in the sentences where appropriate. (See answers on page 384.)

Parentheses

Preteach Write and say the following sentence: *Jin has several pets (dog, bird, fish), but he is allergic to cats.* Ask: *What information is provided in the parentheses of this sentence?* Explain: *The information in the parentheses tells us more about Jin's pets.*

Teach/Model Present the concept and provide examples:

- Words in parentheses give an explanation or a comment in an already complete sentence.
- The information in parentheses is not necessary but adds detail to the sentence.

Sentence Without Parentheses	Sentence With Parentheses
Some subjects are very hard for me.	Some subjects (especially math and science) are very hard for me.

Practice/Assess Copy and distribute page 361. Have students add parentheses in the sentences where appropriate. (See answers on page 385.)

Quotation Marks
Help students use quotation marks by having them complete the following sentence frame in English: *My favorite song is "______."* Model an answer and write it with for quotation marks. Have students repeat. Ask about writing song titles in home languages.

Grammar *in Action*

Correct or Incorrect?
Display correct and incorrect examples of quotation use within a sentence. Write the sentences *"He plays soccer"* (incorrect) and *He said, "I am going to play soccer."* (correct). Offer several examples and ask students to identify correct and incorrect usage.

Transfer Skills

Parentheses
The writing systems of students' home languages may have different conventions for parentheses. Have students practice finding parentheses in classroom texts.

Grammar *in Action*

Oral Language Have students give extra details about a friend by completing the following sentence: *My friend likes to do many things after school (such as ______).*

Name ______________________________

Subjects and Predicates

Practice

- **Look** at the picture. **Read** the sentences.
- **Circle** the complete subject of each sentence. **Underline** the complete predicate of each sentence.

1. The farmer's market is a busy place.

2. The sun shines brightly today.

3. A man sells big, red tomatoes.

4. A woman puts carrots into her bag.

Assess

- **Look** at the picture again. **Write** a subject to begin this sentence.

______________________ sells flowers at the market.

Name ___________________________________

Subject-Verb Agreement

Practice

- **Look** at the picture. **Read** the sentences.
- **Circle** the correct verb to complete each sentence.

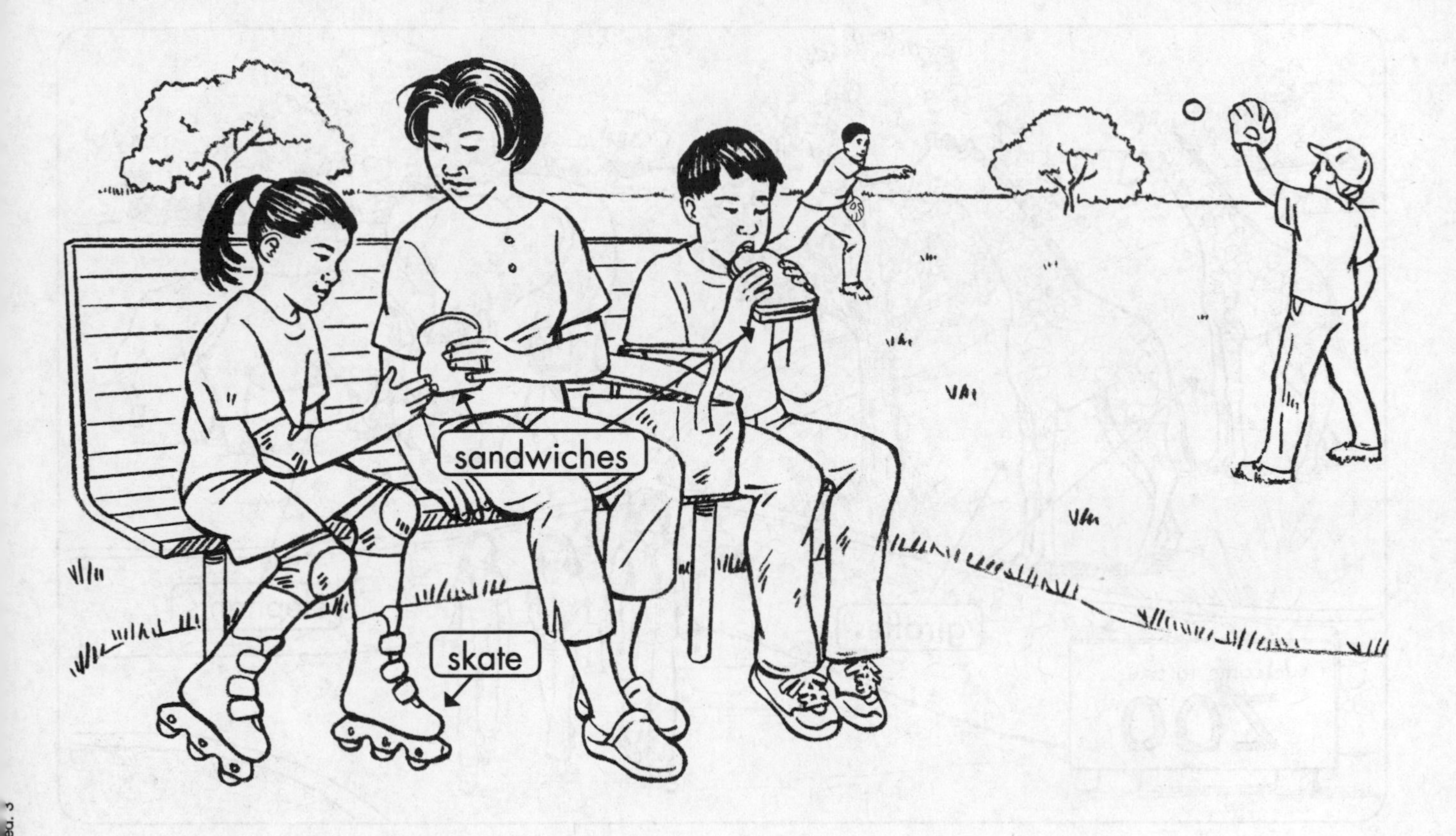

1. Mom (give, gives) the children sandwiches.

2. The children (enjoy, enjoys) a day at the park.

3. The boys (throw, throws) a ball.

4. The girl (like, likes) to skate.

Assess

- **Write** a sentence about one person or two people doing something at the park. Make sure that the subject and the verb work together.

____

Name ___________________________

Word Order

Practice

- **Look** at the picture. **Read** the sentences.
- **Circle** the sentences with the words in the right order.

1. We went to the zoo.
Went to the zoo we.

2. Elephants I saw the.
I saw the elephants.

3. Were tall the giraffes.
The giraffes were tall.

Assess

- **Look** at the picture again. **Write** another sentence about it.

____

Name ______________________________

Complete Sentences and Sentence Fragments

Practice

- **Look** at the picture. **Read** the groups of words.
- **Write** each group of words that is a complete sentence.

1. How the baker bakes. The baker bakes bread.

____

2. He puts the bread into the oven. Many different breads.

____

3. Makes delicious bread. He makes delicious bread.

____

Assess

- **Choose** one of the fragments. **Add** more words and **make** a complete sentence.

____

Name ______________________________

Statements and Questions

Practice

- **Look** at the picture. **Read** the sentences.
- **Write** each sentence correctly. If it is a statement, **end** it with a period. If it is a question, **end** it with a question mark.

1. This is Raquel's party

____

2. Do you like to dance

____

3. Raquel's mom takes pictures

____

4. Len eats pizza

____

5. What time is it

____

Assess

- **Look** at the picture again. **Write** another question about Raquel's party. **Start** with one of these words: *did, was, when, how.*

____

Name ______________________________

Exclamations and Interjections

Practice

- **Look** at the picture. **Read** the sentences.
- **Write** the exclamation or interjection that each person says.

I am running fast!

Hooray! You will win!

I want to go home!

Assess

- What would you say if you won a contest? **Write** it here.

____

Name ______________________________

Commands

Practice

- **Look** at the pictures. **Read** the sentences.
- **Circle** the sentences that are commands.

1. Lemonade is easy to make.

2. Squeeze lemon juice into the pitcher.

3. Add water, sugar, and ice.

4. This lemonade is so good!

Assess

- **Write** how to make lemonade. **Use** only commands. **Use** these words: *find, cut, squeeze, add.*

____

____

Name ___________________________

Simple and Compound Sentences

Practice

- **Look** at the picture. **Read** the compound sentences.
- **Write** the two simple sentences in each compound sentence.

1. Mom needs to go to work, but Jon is still eating his cereal.

____

____

2. Jon needs to hurry, or Mom will be late for work.

____

____

3. Jon finishes his cereal, and they both run out the door.

____

____

Assess

- Do you think Jon's mom will be late for work? **Write** a compound sentence about it.

____

____

Name ______________________________

Combining Sentences

Practice

- **Look** at the picture. **Read** the sentences.
- **Combine** each pair of sentences. **Use** the underlined words only once in the new sentence.

1. Dad <u>went to the park</u>. I <u>went to the park</u>.

____

2. <u>Dad</u> sat on a bench. <u>Dad</u> read his book.

____

3. <u>I</u> found a stick. <u>I</u> threw it.

____

4. <u>My dog</u> ran far. <u>My dog</u> got the stick.

____

Assess

- **Write** another sentence using one of the underlined parts.

____

____

Name ___________________________

Complex Sentences

Practice

- **Look** at the picture.
- **Read** the sentences. **Check** the circle next to the ones that are complex sentences.

1. ◯ I watch Tran because she is a good painter.
◯ She is making a big, beautiful painting!

2. ◯ I want a painting for my room.
◯ Since this painting is big, Tran will put it in Mom's room.

3. ◯ Tran will make a smaller painting.
◯ She will start it when she finishes this one.

Assess

- **Write** another complex sentence about the girl who is painting.

____

____

Name ____________________________

Independent and Dependent Clauses

Practice

- **Look** at the picture. **Read** the sentences.
- **Circle** the dependent clause in each sentence.

1. After I do my homework, I play basketball.

2. When David is there, he plays with me.

3. We play until we are very tired.

4. David goes home because he has homework.

Assess

- **Write** a sentence that starts with *When David goes home.*

____

____

Name ______________________________

Commas

Practice

- **Look** at the picture.
- **Read** the sentences. **Add** commas where they are needed.

1. Gino's the new Italian restaurant has great food.

2. Mom thank you for buying us dinner.

3. I want soup salad pizza and lemonade.

4. Well I hope you can eat all that!

Assess

- **Write** three things you would order at your favorite restaurant. Then **read** your sentence to a partner. Remember to **pause** after each comma.

____

____

Name ______________________________

Quotations

Practice

- **Read** the sentences.
- **Add** quotation marks.

1. I am excited about our skating lesson, said Aunt Beverly.

2. David said, I think you will be great.

3. What if I fall down on the ice? Aunt Beverly asked.

4. I fell down the first time too, David said. But you should keep trying.

5. I will feel better if you stay close to me, Aunt Beverly said.

6. Don't worry, David said, I will.

Name ________________________________

Parentheses

Practice

- **Read** the sentences.
- **Add** parentheses.

1. Anita and her father are making dinner. They need different cooking utensils pan, spoons, cups, knife for their dish.

2. Anita put the food eggs, sausage, cheese, bread on the counter.

3. Her father showed her how to prepare cutting, pouring, stirring the dish.

4. When they were finished, Anita and her father put the rest of the meal vegetables, potatoes on the table.

5. Anita told the rest of her family mother, sister, brother that dinner was ready.

Assess

- **Write** another sentence with parentheses about the picture.

____

____

Transfer Skills

Subject Pronouns

- In Spanish, unlike English, speakers may omit subject pronouns because Spanish verbs can indicate the subjects.
- Korean speakers may add a subject pronoun after the noun, reflecting a pattern in Korean: *Nathan, he is my brother.*

Grammar *in Action*

Oral Language Say these sentences, and have students rephrase them using subject pronouns: *Ana sits in the third row. Max sits here. Ana and Max are cousins. The sandwich is the teacher's lunch.*

Subject Pronouns

Preteach Point to yourself and say *I am a teacher.* Point to the students and say *You are students.* Point to a boy and say *He is a student.* Point to a girl and say *She is a student.* Indicate everyone in the room and say *We are at school.* Explain: *Pronouns such as* I, you, he, she, we, *and* they *are used in place of nouns or noun phrases such as people's names. These pronouns are used for subjects of sentences. We do not say "Me am a teacher" or "Him is a student."*

Teach/Model Present the concept and provide examples:
- A subject pronoun is used as the subject of a sentence.

	Subject Pronouns
Singular	I, you, he, she, it
Plural	we, you, they

Practice/Assess Copy and distribute page 365. Review gender and number of subject pronouns. (See answers on page 385.)

Transfer Skills

Object Pronouns

Spanish, Chinese, and Vietnamese speakers and other English learners may use subject pronouns as objects *(Give the book to she.)* until practice in English clarifies the different pronoun forms.

Grammar *in Action*

Oral Language Pose open-ended sentences, cueing object pronoun endings by gesturing to different people in the room: *I will help....* [gesture toward a girl]. Students should finish the sentence: *her.*

Object Pronouns

Preteach Display these sentences: *Give the book to me. Mom made us a snack. They talked with Tom and her.* Explain: *Pronouns such as* me, you, him, her, us, *and* them *are used after verbs, or after words such as* for, at, with, *or* to. *We do not say "Give the book to I" or "Mom made we a snack."*

Teach/Model Present the concept and provide examples:
- An object pronoun is used in the predicate, after an action verb or preposition.

	Object Pronouns
Singular	me, you, him, her, it
Plural	us, you, them

Practice/Assess Copy and distribute page 366. Help students describe the picture. (See answers on page 385.)

Possessive Pronouns

Preteach Hold a book and say: *This is my book. This book is mine.* Explain: *The words* my *and* mine *are possessive pronouns. They show that I have this book. Possessive pronouns show who or what has or owns something.*

Teach/Model Present the concept and provide examples:
- Use *my, your, her, our,* and *their* before nouns.
- Use *mine, yours, hers, ours,* and *theirs* alone.
- *His* and *its* can be used before nouns and alone.

Possessive Pronouns
Before nouns: This is your pen. It is her doll.
Alone: The shoes are mine. The doll is hers.
Both: The pen is his. This is his home.

Practice/Assess Copy and distribute page 367. Have students read their sentences aloud. (See answers on page 385.)

Transfer Skills

Possessive Pronouns
Students who speak Asian languages may try various forms for possessive pronouns—*the hat of her, you hat*—or may not always state the pronoun *(Mo Yun took off hat)*. Provide practice with possessive pronouns.

Grammar *in Action*

Oral Language Have students look around the room and identify objects that belong to them or to someone else. Have them use each item in a sentence with a possessive pronoun: *Here is my pencil. This calculator is yours.*

Pronouns and Antecedents

Preteach Display this sentence: *Sam says he will go.* Explain: *In this sentence, the pronoun* he *replaces the name* Sam. *The sentence does not have to say, "Sam says Sam will go."* Sam, *the noun being replaced, is called the* antecedent. *A pronoun must agree in number and gender with the noun or noun phrase it replaces. Sam is one person, a boy. So we use the pronoun he, which is singular and masculine. The pronoun for a girl is feminine: she. Lisa says she will go.*

Teach/Model Present the concept and provide examples:
- A pronoun and its antecedent must agree in number and gender.

Pronouns and Antecedents
Laura knows what she wants. Bobi and Ben call me when they get home. The parrot repeats what it hears.

Practice/Assess Copy and distribute page 368. Remind students that singular antecedents are either masculine, feminine, or neuter. (See answers on page 385.)

Transfer Skills

Third-Person Pronouns
Some Asian languages emphasize distinctions such as older and younger people rather than gender pronouns. At first, students may use pronouns that do not match the antecedents—*Joanne and his family; throw the ball to it* (rather than *him*).

Grammar *in Action*

Antecedent Agreement
Display this sentence: *The cat eats what it likes.* Write the following on cards and distribute to students: *The girl; My brother; The children; The teacher; she; he; they.* Invite students to substitute antecedents and pronouns in the sentence using the cards.

Transfer Skills

Indefinite Pronouns
In some languages, the words *everyone* and *everybody* take a plural verb. Students may try using verbs such as "Everyone are" or "Everybody say. . . ."

Grammar *in Action*

Oral Language Show students a picture of a concert. Have them describe it, using these or similar starter sentences: *Everyone is in the concert. Some are singers.*

Indefinite Pronouns

Preteach Display this sentence: *Someone wrote you a note.* Ask: *Who is this someone? If we don't know, then we can use an indefinite pronoun:* someone. *Other singular indefinite pronouns are:* anybody, everyone, everything, either, each. *Some plural indefinite pronouns are:* few, several, both, others, many, all, some.

Teach/Model Present the concept and provide examples:
- Indefinite pronouns may not refer to specific nouns.
- Use the correct verb forms with singular indefinite pronouns and with plural indefinite pronouns.

	Indefinite Pronouns
Singular	Everyone is clapping. Somebody has sung very well.
Plural	Some are standing. Others are sitting.

Practice/Assess Copy and distribute page 369 after teaching *Reflexive Pronouns.*

Transfer Skills

Reflexive Pronouns
Chinese speakers learning English may omit a second reference to one person in a sentence. Rather than "I enjoyed myself," a student may feel that "I enjoyed" is complete.

Grammar *in Action*

Pronoun Match Write these subject pronouns on index cards: *I, you, he, she, it, we, they.* Make another set with reflexive pronouns. Have students draw a card from the reflexive set and match it to its subject pronoun.

Reflexive Pronouns

Preteach Display these sentences: *I will write a note to myself. She will buy herself a snack. Explain:* Myself *and* herself *are reflexive pronouns.*

Teach/Model Present the concept and provide examples:
- Reflexive pronouns reflect the action back on the subject: *They gave themselves a chance to rest.*
- Reflexive pronouns end in *-self* or *-selves.*

	Reflexive Pronouns
Singular	himself, herself, myself, itself, yourself
Plural	ourselves, yourselves, themselves

Practice/Assess Copy and distribute page 369. Have students read the completed sentences aloud. (See answers on page 385.)

Name ______________________________

Subject Pronouns

Practice

- **Look** at the picture. **Read** each sentence.
- **Circle** the correct pronoun in parentheses.

1. David and (I, me) are good friends.

2. (Us, We) ride the bus together every morning.

3. Today there were many cars. (Them, They) moved very slowly.

4. David had a phone, so (he, him) called the school.

Assess

- **Write** a sentence about the students on the bus. **Start** with the subject pronoun *They.*

____

Name ______________________________

Object Pronouns

Practice

- **Look** at the picture. **Read** the sentences.
- **Circle** the correct pronoun to complete each sentence.

The Spanish Club is having a book sale. Mrs. Ruiz asked Jen and (me, I) to collect books. Many students bought books from (we, us). I had fun selling (them, they). How many books are left? I will count (it, them).

Assess

- **Write** another sentence about the book sale. **Use** *him* or *her.*

____

Name ______________________________

Possessive Pronouns

Practice

- **Look** at the picture. **Read** the sentences.
- **Circle** the correct possessive pronoun in parentheses.

1. Mr. Sims is (our, ours) neighbor.

2. (His, Her) bird flew out of (it's, its) cage.

3. Did you find a yellow bird in (yours, your) tree?

4. That bird is (his, theirs).

Assess

- **Write** a sentence about the yellow bird. **Use** the possessive pronoun *its*.

____

Name ______________________________

Pronouns and Antecedents

Practice

- **Look** at the picture. **Read** the sentences.
- **Circle** the correct pronoun in each sentence. The antecedent is underlined for you.

1. Cecilia wanted to surprise <u>Ali</u> in (her, their) new home.

2. Cecilia bought <u>balloons</u> and gave (they, them) to Ali.

3. <u>Ali</u> said, "(I, We) am so surprised!"

4. <u>Balloons</u> are fun, and (them, they) make people happy.

Assess

- **Look** at the picture again. **Write** another sentence about the balloons. **Use** the word *they* or *them.*

____

Name ______________________________

Indefinite and Reflexive Pronouns

Practice

- **Look** at the picture. **Read** the sentences.
- **Circle** the correct pronoun in parentheses to complete each sentence.

1. (Other, Someone) left a note on my desk.

2. I read it out loud to (myself, itself).

3. It said that (everyone, either) thinks I am a good writer.

4. (Somethings, No one) heard me read the note.

5. Maybe the writer of the note will identify (himself, ourselves).

Assess

- **Write** a sentence about yourself. **Use** a reflexive pronoun.

____

Articles, Adjectives, and Adverbs

Transfer Skills

Articles

- Spanish speakers may use the word *one* in place of the article *a* (or *an*), just as *un/una* is used in Spanish. Students may use *ones* as a plural article.
- English learners may use (or omit) the article *the* differently from native English speakers—*I like the science; my cousin is nurse.*

Grammar *in Action*

Time to Listen Copy and distribute a simple newspaper article. Read it aloud and have students follow along, highlighting the articles they encounter.

Articles

Preteach Say: *I need a pencil.* Hold up a pencil and say: *Here is a pencil with an eraser. The pencil is yellow.* Show some pencils: *The pencils are new.* Explain that *a, an,* and *the* are called *articles: Articles are these words that come before nouns: A pencil, the paper, an ink pen. Use* a *or* an *before a singular noun. You can use* the *before singular nouns or plural nouns.*

Teach/Model Present the concept and provide examples:

- *A, an,* and *the* are articles.
- Use *a* before a singular noun that begins with a consonant sound; use *an* before a singular noun that begins with a vowel sound.

Articles
I want a banana. Sue wants an apple.
The fruit salad was good. The girls ate it all.

Practice/Assess Copy and distribute page 373. Explain that *an* is used before a word beginning with silent *h*. (See answers on page 385.)

Transfer Skills

Adjectives

- Spanish adjectives have endings that match the gender and number of nouns they modify. Assure students that English adjectives do not have these endings.
- In Spanish and Vietnamese, adjectives often follow nouns.

Grammar *in Action*

Oral Language Have a student describe a classmate: *She is smart. She is quiet. She is wearing a blue sweater.* Whoever correctly guesses the classmate gives the next clues.

Adjectives

Size, What Kind, How Many

Preteach Say: *You know that nouns are words that name people, places, animals, or things—for example,* girls *and* house. *Adjectives are words that tell more about the nouns: small house, four girls, blue car, long hair. Which words are the adjectives?* (small, four, blue, long)

Teach/Model Present the concept and provide examples:

- An adjective tells more about a noun or pronoun.

	Adjectives
What Kind?	a good friend; The food is spicy.
How Many?	two men; many apples
Size	a big hat; The school was small.

Practice/Assess Copy and distribute page 374. Explain the chart to students. (See answers on page 385.)

Comparative and Superlative Adjectives

Preteach Draw three long lines of different lengths on the board. Point to the different lines and say: *This line is long. This line is longer. This line is the longest.* Say: Long *is an adjective.* Longer *compares two nouns, like two lines. To compare two nouns, add* -er *to most adjectives.* Longest *compares three or more nouns. To make a superlative adjective, add* -est *to most adjectives.*

Teach/Model Present the concept and provide examples:

- Many comparative adjectives end in *-er: faster, thinner, tinier.* Change the spelling of some adjectives, like *tiny,* when you add *-er.*
- Many longer adjectives use the word *more* instead of *-er: more exciting, more beautiful.*
- Many superlative adjectives end in *-est: brightest, loudest, tallest.* Use *most* with longer adjectives: *most beautiful.*
- Some adjectives have irregular forms, such as *good, better, best.*

Comparative	Superlative
bigger; more important	fastest; most difficult

Practice/Assess Copy and distribute page 375. Discuss the completed sentences. (See answers on page 385.)

Demonstrative Adjectives

Preteach Present three girls and three boys, with the boys farther away. Ask: *Which students are girls? These students are girls. Those students are boys. Which girl is Tina? This girl is Tina. That boy is Ben.* These, those, this, *and* that *are called* demonstrative adjectives. *They help you demonstrate, or show, which one or which ones. Use* this *and* these *when things are close. Use* that *and* those *when things are far.*

Teach/Model Present the concept and provide examples:

- Demonstrative adjectives: *this, that, these, those*

	Demonstrative Adjectives
Singular	This book is longer than that book.
Plural	These shoes are bigger than those shoes.

Practice/Assess Copy and distribute page 376. Remind students that *this* and *that* are used with singular nouns. (See answers on page 385.)

Transfer Skills

Comparative and Superlative Adjectives
Speakers of African and Asian languages may use English adjectives in patterns from their first languages: *She was the most fastest runner. My story is less longer than yours.*

Grammar *in Action*

Classroom Comparisons
Have pairs of students find pairs or sets of objects in the classroom to compare. For example, one pencil might be longer than another, while one book might be the heaviest of three. Have pairs present their findings.

Transfer Skills

This and That
In certain languages, including Korean, the relationship between expressing *this* and *that* and *here* and *there* does not correspond exactly to the way these terms are used in English. Clarify that the words *this* and *that* can modify nouns.

Grammar *in Action*

Oral Language Provide two sets of word cards for a game of Concentration. Place both sets face down, and have students find matching pairs. As they play, they should say: *I want this card, I want that card,* or *These cards match.*

Adverbs

Adverbs for When, Where, and How

Preteach Say and act out this chant: *Slowly I turn. Loudly I clap! I walk here and there. I end with a tap.* Say: Slowly, loudly, here, *and* there *are adverbs. They tell how, when, or where something happens.*

Teach/Model Present the concept and provide examples:
- Adverbs tell more about the actions of verbs.
- Adverbs that tell *how* something happens often end in *-ly*.

	Adverbs
When?	I always walk to school.
Where?	I like to walk outside.
How?	I walk quickly.

Practice/Assess Copy and distribute page 377. Explain that an adverb can come before or after the verb. (See answers on page 386.)

Comparative and Superlative Adverbs

Preteach Say each sentence: *I speak quietly. Katya speaks more quietly. Raúl speaks most quietly.* More quietly *is a comparative adverb. It compares two actions: I speak, Katya speaks.* Most quietly *is a superlative adverb. It compares three or more actions. If an adverb does not end in* -ly, *add* -er *or* -est *to compare.*

Teach/Model Present the concept and provide examples:
- A comparative adverb compares two actions.
- A superlative adverb compares three or more actions.
- Some adverbs are irregular: *well, better, best*

Comparative and Superlative Adverbs
Julia runs fast. Anil sings beautifully.
Pat runs faster. Kenji sings more beautifully.
Tere runs the fastest. Ivan sings most beautifully.

Practice/Assess Copy and distribute page 378. Remind students that *more* or *most* are not added to an adverb that already has an *-er* or *-est* ending. (See answers on page 386.)

Transfer Skills

Adverbs
- English learners may use adjectives as adverbs. Help students use adverbs.
- Point out to Spanish speakers that the adverb suffix *-ly* is like the ending *-mente* in Spanish. Give examples with cognates such as *rapidly/rápidamente*.

Grammar *in Action*

Time to Listen Write adverbs on slips of paper: *slowly, quickly, loudly, sleepily.* Display them. Have a volunteer choose one. Give a command, such as *Walk to the door.* The volunteer must walk in the manner of the adverb. The student who guesses the adverb takes the next turn.

Transfer Skills

Comparative Adverbs
English phrases can be challenging for students whose home languages use different phrasing, and students may say or write: *running quickly more than you* or *studying more hard than you.* Model sentences with comparative adverbs.

Grammar *in Action*

Oral Language Display 3 pictures of athletes. Have students compare them, using *well, better, best* or *fast, faster, fastest* with verbs *run, play,* or *swim.*

Name ________________________________

Articles

Practice

- **Look** at the picture. **Read** the sentences.
- **Circle** the article in parentheses that completes each sentence.

1. Cali, Beth, and Lyn found (an, a) rope in their garage.

2. (An, The) rope was six feet long.

3. Beth knew (a, an) song for jumping rope.

4. (The, A) girls jumped rope for (a, an) hour.

Assess

- What can you do for an hour? **Write** about it here. **Use** articles.

____

Name ________________________________

Adjectives for Size, What Kind, How Many

Practice

- **Look** at the picture. **Read** the story.
- **Circle** the adjectives in the story.

My two brothers and I have a small garden. We have three plants. The plants have many tomatoes that are big and red. They are delicious!

Assess

- **Write** the adjectives from the story in the chart.

Size	What Kind	How Many

Name ___________________________

Comparative and Superlative Adjectives

Practice

- **Look** at the picture. **Read** the sentences.
- **Write** the correct adjective to complete each sentence.

1. Buffy is ____________________ than Chico. (smaller, smallest)

2. Chico is the ____________________ of the three dogs. (largest, larger)

3. Max is ____________________ than Buffy. (more beautiful, beautifulest)

4. The big dog should have a ____________________ name. (gooder, better)

5. Buffy has the ____________________ name of all. (funniest, funnier)

Assess

- **Write** your own sentence that compares one of the dogs to another dog.

____

Name ______________________________

Demonstrative Adjectives

Practice

- **Look** at the picture. **Read** the sentences.
- **Circle** the correct adjective to complete each sentence.

1. (These, This) flowers are called poppies.

2. Each spring, (this, these) field is full of poppies.

3. (That, Those) tree on the hill looks like a person.

4. People ride their bikes in (those, this) hills.

5. Many people take pictures of (this, these) place.

Assess

- **Look** at the picture again. **Write** another sentence about the field. **Use** *this, that, these,* or *those.*

____

Name ___________________________

Adverbs for When, Where, and How

Practice

- **Look** at the picture. **Read** the sentences.
- **Circle** the correct adverb for each sentence.

1. My sister sings (loudly, neatly).

2. I stand (outside, below) and listen.

3. She sings (beautifully, safely)!

4. I (always, yesterday) like listening to my sister sing.

Assess

- **Write** a sentence that tells how, when, or where you do something. **Use** an adverb.

____

Name ______________________________

Comparative and Superlative Adverbs

Practice

- **Look** at the picture. **Read** the sentences.
- **Circle** the correct adverb to complete each sentence.

1. The stars shine (more brightly, brightly) in the country than in the city.

2. The dogs bark (louder, more louder) here.

3. I sleep (better, goodly) with the window closed.

4. People walk (more faster, faster) in the city.

5. This is the place I like to visit the (later, most).

Assess

- Do you like the city or the country better? **Write** a sentence about it. **Include** an adverb.

____

Prepositions and Prepositional Phrases

Preteach Stand behind a chair, and have students do the same. Say: *Behind the chair,* and have students repeat. Continue moving and speaking with *beside, around,* and *on* (sit). Explain: Behind, beside, around, *and* on *are prepositions.* Behind the chair *and* on it *are prepositional phrases.* Behind *is a preposition, and* chair *is a noun.* On *is a preposition, and* it *is a pronoun.*

Teach/Model Present the concept and provide examples:

- A prepositional phrase can tell where, when, how, or which one.
- A prepositional phrase begins with a preposition (*above, across, at, behind, for, from, in, near, with,* and so on).
- A prepositional phrase ends with a noun or pronoun.

Preposition	around
Prepositional Phrase	around the chair

Practice/Assess Copy and distribute page 380. Help students describe the picture. (See answers on page 386.)

Transfer Skills

Prepositional Phrases
Prepositional phrases will be familiar to speakers of various languages, but students may choose prepositions based on home-language usage or meanings: *in Friday; on April; until there.*

Grammar *in Action*

Following Directions
Model as you give students directions to follow: *Walk to this side of the room. Walk across the room. Stand by a desk. Look under the desk.* Have volunteers take turns giving directions that include prepositional phrases.

Conjunctions

Preteach Use colored pens or markers to illustrate: *I have a red pen and a green pen. The word* and *joins two similar things: two colors of pens. Do you like red or green better? The word* or *gives a choice: red or green. You can use the green pen, but don't use the red pen right now. The word* but *joins two different ideas:* use *and* don't use. Or, but, *and* and *are called* conjunctions.

Teach/Model Present the concept and provide examples:

- A conjunction joins words, phrases, and sentences.

Related ideas: *Pak and I are friends.*
Different ideas: *We live far apart, but we talk often.*
Choice: *We talk on the phone or we send e-mail.*

Practice/Assess Copy and distribute page 381. Help students name the items in the picture. (See answers on page 386.)

Transfer Skills

Conjunctions
Speakers of Chinese and some other languages may build sentences using two conjunctions where English typically uses one: *Because the sun came up, so I could see the clock.* Help students practice English patterns.

Grammar *in Action*

Common Phrases Share these common phrases with conjunctions: *salt and pepper; thanks, but no thanks; stop-and-go traffic; left or right; boy or girl.* Invite students to say them while using gestures to help show the meanings.

Name ___________________________

Prepositions and Prepositional Phrases

Practice

- **Look** at the picture. **Read** the sentences.
- **Circle** the correct preposition to complete each sentence.

1. We are (behind, at) the lake.

2. I play a game called "catch" (with, over) my dad.

3. Jeff walks (after, near) the water.

4. Mom sits (under, on) a chair and reads.

5. Ducks swim (in, from) the water.

Assess

- **Write** a sentence about the lake. **Use** a prepositional phrase.

____

Name ______________________________

Conjunctions

Practice

- **Look** at the picture. **Read** the sentences.
- **Circle** the correct conjunction to complete each sentence.

1. Are you ready to order, (but, or) do you want me to come back later?

2. I want a tuna sandwich, (and, or) the young lady wants soup.

3. Do you want a roll, (or, but) do you want a salad with your lunch?

4. I would like a salad, (or, but) please do not put salad dressing on it.

Assess

- What do you think the waiter said next? **Write** a sentence that has one of these words: *and, but, or.*

____

page 318: Common Nouns

Practice
People: father, boys, woman; **Places:** soccer field, playground, park office; **Animals:** rabbit; **Things:** swing, ball, bike

Assess
Answers will vary. Students should write the names of items found in the classroom.

page 319: Special Names

Practice
Names of Children: Alex, Karen, Tuan; **Names of Animals:** Spot, Lulu, Speedy, Goldie; **Names of Places:** Greenview School, Hope Garden, Barton Library

Assess
Answers will vary. Students should write the names of specific places and people, beginning each name with a capital letter.

page 320: Titles and Abbreviations

Practice
1. Mr. Turner; **2.** Dr. Lisa Johnson; **3.** Miss Eva Santos; **4.** Mr. Mark Tanaka

Assess
Answers will vary. Verify that students include a title such as Mr., Ms., Mrs., Miss, and Dr. when writing each names of adults they know.

page 321: Days, Months, and Holidays

Practice
1. Thanksgiving; **2.** Veterans Day; **3.** Friday, November 30; **4.** Tuesday, November 6; **5.** on Wednesdays

Assess
Sunday, Monday, Tuesday, Wednesday, Thursday, Friday, Saturday; Answers will vary. Students should begin the name of each holiday and each month with a capital letter.

page 322: Singular and Plural Nouns

Practice
Singular Nouns: nest, bird, sun; **Plural Nouns:** men, butterflies, feet, leaves, benches

Assess
Answers will vary but should include three singular and three plural nouns. Students should write the names of items found in the classroom.

page 323: Singular and Plural Possessive Nouns

Practice
1. Today's; **2.** children's; **3.** reader's; **4.** ladies'

Assess
Answers will vary. For sentences using singular possessive nouns, students may choose *reader's* or *today's*. For sentences using plural possessive nouns, students may choose *children's* or *ladies'*.

page 330: Verbs in Present Tense

Practice
1. wait; **2.** talks; **3.** sits; **4.** see

Assess
Answers will vary, but students may write a sentence such as *The dog barks.*

page 331: Verbs in Past Tense

Practice
celebrated; gave; played; made; had

Assess
Answers will vary, but students may write *We ate apples at the picnic.*

page 332: Verbs in Future Tense

Practice
The mother bird will find food for the babies. In a few days, she will teach them to fly. Soon, the baby birds will grow big and strong. They will fly away from the nest.

Assess
Answers will vary, but students may write a sentence such as *The mother bird will go too.*

page 333: Principal Parts of Regular Verbs

Practice
1. *has started*, past participle; **2.** *listen*, present; **3.** *are playing*, present participle; **4.** *has played*, past participle; **5.** *plays*, present

Assess
Answers will vary, but students may write a sentence such as *Ray is playing the flute.*

page 334: Principal Parts of Irregular Verbs

Practice

1. *went*, past; **2.** *go*, present; **3.** *have grown*, past participle; **4.** *am growing*, present participle

Assess

Answers will vary, but students may write a sentence such as *The doctor wrote on the chart.*

page 335: Helping Verbs

Practice

1. *are* learning; **2.** *have* seen; **3.** *am* using; **4.** *will* give

Assess

Answers will vary, but students may write a sentence such as *She will tell her friends about dolphins.*

page 336: Linking Verbs

Practice

1. *am*; **2.** *feel*; **3.** *seems*; **4.** *is*

Assess

Answers will vary, but students may write *The girl is sick.*

page 337: Contractions and Negatives

Practice

1. *I'm*; **2.** *Shouldn't*; **3.** *I've*; **4.** *You're*; **5.** *ever*

Assess

Answers will vary, but students may write *The dad didn't know she already did her homework.*

page 338: Troublesome Verbs Lie/Lay, Sit/Set

Practice

1. lies; **2.** sit; **3.** set; **4.** lays

Assess

Answers will vary, but students may write *The cat lies on the bed.*

page 339: Troublesome Verbs Leave/Let, Rise/Raise

Practice

1. leave; **2.** Let; **3.** raise; **4.** leave; **5.** rise

Assess

Answers will vary, but should include *leave, let, rise,* or *raise.*

page 348: Subjects and Predicates

Practice

1. The farmer's market / is a busy place;
2. The sun / shines brightly today;
3. A man / sells big, red tomatoes;
4. A woman / puts carrots into her bag.

Assess

Answers will vary, but students may begin the sentence with *A woman.*

page 349: Subject-Verb Agreement

Practice

1. gives; **2.** enjoy; **3.** throw; **4.** likes

Assess

Answers will vary. Check for subject-verb agreement.

page 350: Word Order

Practice

1. We went to the zoo. **2.** I saw the elephants. **3.** The giraffes were tall.

Assess

Answers will vary, but make sure students start sentences with the subject or use another word order that makes sense.

page 351: Complete Sentences and Sentence Fragments

Practice

1. The baker bakes bread. **2.** He puts the bread into the oven. **3.** He makes delicious bread.

Assess

Answers will vary but should be complete sentences.

page 352: Statements and Questions

Practice

1. This is Raquel's party. **2.** Do you like to dance? **3.** Raquel's mom takes pictures. **4.** Len eats pizza. **5.** What time is it?

Assess

Answers will vary; possible questions: *Did you go to Raquel's party? Was it fun? When did people dance?*

page 353: Exclamations and Interjections

Practice
Runner would think: "I am running fast!"
Friend would say: "Hooray! You will win!"
Crying boy would say: "I want to go home!"

Assess
Answers will vary. Encourage students to imagine themselves winning at a school or sports competition. Some suggestions: *Hooray! Wow! I worked so hard!*

page 354: Commands

Practice
Sentences 2 and 3 are commands.

Assess
Answers will vary, but students may write *First, find a pitcher and some lemons. Cut the lemons. Squeeze the lemons. Add water, sugar, and ice.*

page 355: Simple and Compound Sentences

Practice
1. Mom needs to go to work. Jon is still eating his cereal. **2.** Jon needs to hurry. Mom will be late for work. **3.** Jon finishes his cereal. They both run out the door.

Assess
Answers will vary, but students may write *Jon will not be late for school, and Mom will not be late for work.*

page 356: Combining Sentences

Practice
1. Dad and I went to the park. **2.** Dad sat on a bench and read his book. **3.** I found a stick and threw it. **4.** My dog ran far and got the stick.

Assess
Answers will vary, but sample answers include: *My friend and I went to the park. Dad drove us there and read his book. I played with my friend and with my dog. My dog was happy and playful.*

page 357: Complex Sentences

Practice
1. I watch Tran because she is a good painter; **2.** Since this painting is big, Tran will put it in Mom's room; **3.** She will start it when she finishes this one.

Assess
Answers will vary, but students may write sentences such as *When Tran finishes this painting, she will make another one. Since Tran's sister wants a painting, Tran will make one.*

page 358: Independent and Dependent Clauses

Practice
1. After I do my homework; **2.** When David is there; **3.** until we are very tired; **4.** because he has homework

Assess
Answers will vary, but sample answers include: *When David goes home, I go home also. When David goes home, he does his homework.*

page 359: Commas

Practice
1. Gino's, the new Italian restaurant, has great food. **2.** Mom, thank you for buying us dinner. **3.** I want soup, salad, pizza, and lemonade. **4.** Well, I hope you can eat all that!

Assess
Answers will vary, but make sure students use a comma after each menu item in the series.

page 360: Quotations

Practice
1. "I am excited about our skating lesson," said Aunt Beverly. **2.** David said, "I think you will be great." **3.** "What if I fall down on the ice?" Aunt Beverly asked. **4.** "I fell down the first time too," David said. "But you should keep trying." **5.** "I will feel better if you stay close to me," Aunt Beverly said. **6.** "Don't worry," David said, "I will."

page 361: Parentheses

Practice
1. They need different cooking utensils (pan, spoons, cups, knife) for their dish. **2.** Anita put the food (eggs, sausage, cheese, bread) on the counter. **3.** Her father showed her how to prepare (cutting, pouring, stirring) the dish. **4.** When they were finished, Anita and her father put the rest of the meal (vegetables, potatoes) on the table. **5.** Anita told the rest of her family (mother, sister, brother) that dinner was ready.

Assess
Answers will vary, but make sure students use parentheses correctly.

page 365: Subject Pronouns

Practice
1. I; **2.** We; **3.** They; **4.** he

Assess
Answers will vary, but students may write a sentence such as *They were late for school.*

page 366: Object Pronouns

Practice
me; us; them; them

Assess
Answers will vary, but students may write a sentence such as *Jen gave the book to him.*

page 367: Possessive Pronouns

Practice
1. our; **2.** His, its; **3.** your; **4.** his

Assess
Answers will vary, but students may write a sentence such as *The bird will fly to its cage.*

page 368: Pronouns and Antecedents

Practice
1. her; **2.** them; **3.** I; **4.** they

Assess
Answers will vary, but students may write a sentence such as *Ali loved the balloons because they were from her friend.*

page 369: Indefinite and Reflexive Pronouns

Practice
1. Someone; **2.** myself; **3.** everyone; **4.** No one; **5.** himself

Assess
Answers will vary, but students may write a sentence such as *I like to teach myself English words.*

page 373: Articles

Practice
1. a; **2.** The; **3.** a; **4.** The, an

Assess
Answers will vary, but students may write a sentence such as *I can play baseball for an hour.*

page 374: Adjectives for Size, What Kind, How Many

Practice
two; small; three; many; big; red; delicious

Assess
Size: small, big; **What Kind:** red, delicious; **How Many:** two, three, many

page 375: Comparative and Superlative Adjectives

Practice
1. smaller; **2.** largest; **3.** more beautiful; **4.** better; **5.** funniest

Assess
Answers will vary, but students may write a sentence such as *Max is larger than Buffy.*

page 376: Demonstrative Adjectives

Practice
1. These; **2.** this; **3.** That; **4.** those; **5.** this

Assess
Answers will vary, but students may write a sentence such as *This field is beautiful.*

page 377: Adverbs for When, Where, and How

Practice
1. loudly; **2.** outside; **3.** beautifully; **4.** always

Assess
Answers will vary, but students may write a sentence such as *I run quickly.*

page 378: Comparative and Superlative Adverbs

Practice
1. more brightly; **2.** louder; **3.** better; **4.** faster; **5.** most

Assess
Answers will vary, but students may write a sentence such as *I like the city better.*

page 380: Prepositions and Prepositional Phrases

Practice
1. at; **2.** with; **3.** near; **4.** on; **5.** in

Assess
Answers will vary, but students may write a sentence such as *Ducks live near the lake.*

page 381: Conjunctions

Practice
1. or; **2.** and; **3.** or; **4.** but

Assess
Answers will vary, but students may write a sentence such as *Thank you for your order, and I will be back soon.*

Part 5
Workshops for English Language Learners

Contents

Introduction to English Language Learner Workshops

To develop their skills in English, English language learners need instruction that integrates speaking, listening, reading, and writing. While core lesson content encourages the development of these skills, English language learners need targeted instruction to navigate listening and speaking in situations that, for native speakers, come naturally. Students who are first using spoken English may have difficulty in areas such as the following:

- knowing appropriate times to use formal and informal English
- using the correct syntax patterns for sentences, including placement of nouns, verbs, adjectives, and prepositions
- expressing opinions and feelings
- using the transactional language of the classroom
- retelling or summarizing a message in English

In addition, students who are newcomers or who have not interacted with instructional materials in English may have difficulty with the following:

- interacting with environmental print and understanding what information they can get from reading the words around them
- using classroom resources
- expanding their knowledge and use of academic vocabulary words
- using graphic organizers to record ideas and organize information

Each one of these lessons covers a particular topic with a lesson for the teacher and a reproducible blackline master for students. The lessons are designed to be fluid and needs-based. Some of the lessons will correspond to your teaching with the core program, while others can be introduced when students have a need for the instruction. The workshop on group discussion, for example, can be introduced when you notice that students are struggling to use the transactional give-and-take language in group discussions.

All Workshops follow the same format:

- A **Preteach** section provides simple scripted language that allows you to introduce the strategy or skill.
- The **Teach/Model** section involves students while you carefully scaffold instruction in the skill or strategy.
- In the **Practice** section, students begin to take ownership of the skill, sometimes through practice with a blackline master, and sometimes through interaction with peers.
- Each workshop includes an **Assess** section, with ideas for both assessment and corrective feedback.
- **Leveled Support** suggestions allow students to practice the skills at their individual levels of proficiency and progress from level to level.
- An accompanying **blackline master** allows for practice with the skill. The master often includes a rubric for self-assessment or a word bank to which students can add their ideas throughout the year.

Many of the blackline masters can be used multiple times. Based on students' needs, consider how to integrate the workshops into your instruction and use them multiple times to measure students' growth as users of classroom and conversational English.

In addition to the workshops, support students' development of spoken English with activities such as the following:

- **Answering questions**. Have students answer questions that you pose, first with yes/no questions and then with longer answers. Supply sentence frames and models as necessary.
- **Have dialogues**. Use various scenarios to have dialogues with students before having them pair up to have conversations of their own.
- **Picture the conversation**. Show students a photograph of people immersed in conversation in a familiar setting. Have them talk about what the people in the picture might be saying. Encourage them to role-play.

Use Informal English

Preteach Model informal language for students and explain: *The words I use depend on who I am talking to and why I am speaking. When I am talking with my friends in casual situations, I use informal language. I might use slang words. I might speak in sentences that are not complete. I usually don't organize my ideas before I speak. It's more like having a conversation.*

Teach/Model With a volunteer, act out the scene on the right side of the page. Model using informal language, such as sentence fragments. Then model rating your knowledge using the rubric.

Practice Direct students to look at the second picture. Explain that in the picture, two teammates are talking about a soccer game. *Why would their language be informal?* (They are teammates in a game. They do not need to speak formally.) *What phrases might the friend say?* (Hey! Let's go! Good job!) For additional practice, students can draw another scenario that calls for informal English and use that drawing as the basis for role play. As students role-play, work with them to create a bank of words and phrases that they use when they speak informally with their friends or family.

Assess Assess students' conversations to clear up any misconceptions about informal English. Review students' ratings. Revisit the workshop so that students can reevaluate their progress in recognizing speaking situations in which informal language is acceptable and using appropriate language.

Beginning Have students do a simple role-play activity in which one student acts as a student in class and the other acts as a new student who is trying to find a certain room in the building. The students may use informal English.

Intermediate Ask students to work with partners to role-play a conversation with a sibling that would use informal English. Remind students that informal English is "relaxed," but it should also be appropriate.

Advanced/Advanced High Have students create new scenarios where they might use informal language and model appropriate language they might use and hear.

Name ____

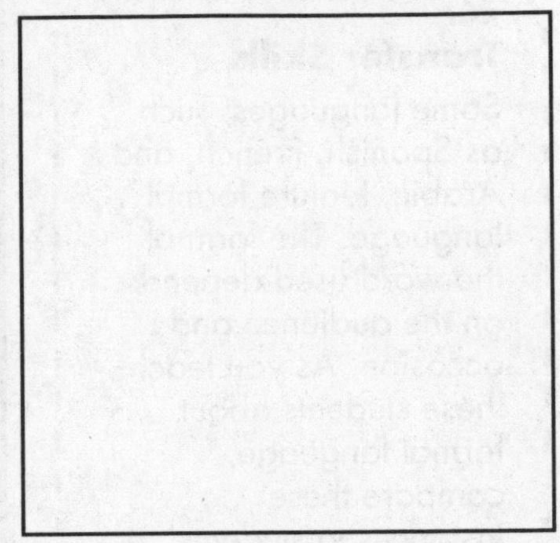

Act out what is happening in each picture. **Say** what the people would be saying.

Draw a situation in which you could use informal English.

Circle the rating for each sentence. **Tell** how you use informal English.

1 I need help to do this better.

2 I do this sometimes.

3 I know how to do this.

I understand when to use informal English.	1	2	3
I am respectful of others when I use informal English.	1	2	3
I use slang that is appropriate.	1	2	3
I listen to others before I speak.	1	2	3

Use Formal English

Transfer Skills

Some languages, such as Spanish, French, and Arabic, feature formal language. The form of the word used depends on the audience and occasion. As you teach these students about formal language, compare these instances to students' experiences with their home languages.

Preteach Model formal language for students and explain: *The words I use depend on who I am talking to and why I am speaking. When I am talking with older people or to bigger groups, I use formal language. For example, I use titles for people, like* Mrs. *or* Mr. *I don't use slang in formal language. I might say* Hello *instead of* Hey. *My speech may be slower. I might take more time to organize my thoughts before I speak.*

Teach/Model With a volunteer, act out the scene on the right side of the page. Model using formal language, such as titles. Then model rating your knowledge using the rubric. *When I speak to a teacher or other adult, I use titles such as* Miss, Mr., *and* Mrs. *I ask questions using more formal words, such as* please.

Practice Direct students to look at the second picture. Explain that in the picture, a girl is introducing a friend to her grandparents. *Why would she use formal language?* (to show respect for her grandparents) *What phrases might the friend say?* (Pleased to meet you.) For additional practice, students can draw another scenario that calls for formal English and use that drawing as the basis for role play. As students role-play, work with them to create a bank of words and phrases used in formal English for their reference.

Assess Assess students' conversations to clear up any misconceptions about formal language. Review students' ratings. Revisit the workshop so that students can reevaluate their progress in recognizing formal speaking situations and using appropriate language.

Beginning Have students do a simple role-play activity in which one student acts as a student and the other as the principal. The student should use formal language in greeting the principal.

Intermediate Ask students to work with partners to role-play introducing themselves in a formal situation, such as a club meeting. Write out the students' introductions and have them read them back to you. Identify phrases that make the speech formal, such as *It's nice to meet you.*

Advanced/Advanced High Have students create new scenarios where they might use formal language and model appropriate language they might use and hear.

Name ____

Act out what is happening in each picture. **Say** what the people would be saying.

Circle the rating for each sentence. **Tell** how you use formal language.

1 I need help to do this better.

2 I do this sometimes.

3 I know how to do this.

When speaking formally with adults:

I do not use slang.	1	2	3
I use titles and formal names such as *Mr., Mrs., Ms.,* and *Miss.*	1	2	3
I use polite words such as *please* and *thank you.*	1	2	3

When speaking formally to a big group:

I think about and organize what I will say.	1	2	3
I slow down my speech.	1	2	3

Distinguish Between Formal and Informal English

Teaching Tip
The use of formal and informal language depends on social context. Help students understand that the type of language is dependent on who they are speaking to, their familiarity with the speaker, the purpose for speaking, and the larger audience. Give paired examples and ask students which example would require more formal English, such as: *You are playing a board game with your friend. His mom asks if you would like a snack.*

Preteach *Informal language is casual or relaxed. Formal language does not use casual language, such as slang.* Have students name differences between formal and informal language. Then write these examples of informal English on the board. Have students say the same phrases in more formal English. Examples: *Hi, teach! How are ya'? What's up?*

Teach/Model With a volunteer, act out the first scene of the child shaking hands with an adult. Ask students to identify if they would use formal or informal English. Why would they use that type of English? What words or phrases would they use? *When I speak to a teacher or other adult, I use titles such as* Miss, Mr., *and* Mrs. *If I am meeting them for the first time, I might say things like* How do you do? *or* It is nice to meet you.

Practice Direct students to look at the second picture. Have them identify if this is a formal or informal speaking situation. With partners, have them take turns telling what the friends might say to each other when skating. Model using informal language or slang, such as referring to a friend as *dude* or talking about *grinding* on their skateboards.

Assess Have students use the T-chart to record situations in which they would use formal or informal English in the correct columns. Assess their placements of the situations to see if they need more support in distinguishing between when to use formal and informal English. Have them choose situations to role-play and add other situations to the chart.

Beginning Show students magazine pictures of various settings (e.g., a business meeting, family watching television). Ask the students to indicate whether the people in the situation would use formal or informal English.

Intermediate Write an informal conversation on the board. (Sample: *Hey John. Wanna play a game?*) Have the students work with partners to repeat the conversation. Then have them role-play the conversation again, this time substituting formal language for the informal.

Advanced/Advanced High Have students work with partners to talk about a soccer game. The first conversation should be telling a friend about a game. The second conversation should be a recap of the game for the school announcements.

Name ______________________________

Act out what is happening in each picture. **Say** what the people would be saying.

Decide if the language you used was formal or informal.

Read each situation below. **Write** each situation in the chart under Formal English or Informal English.

Write and **share** your own situations. Have others decide if they are formal or informal.

a family dinner
playing a game with friends
giving a speech at school
meeting a new teacher
asking for help at the store
helping a younger brother

Formal English	Informal English

Give Directions

Teaching Tip
Have students collect examples of directions such as recipes, lab notes from science class, or directions for putting something together. Discuss their common attributes, such as clear steps and sequence words to keep steps in order. Display examples for students to use as models.

Preteach *I am going to give you directions for making a cheese sandwich: Last, eat the sandwich. Next, put the bread slices together. Second, put the cheese on the bread. First, take out two pieces of bread and some cheese. Did those directions make sense? What was wrong? They did not make sense because they are out of order! When we give directions, we need to be sure the steps are clear. The steps need to be in order.*

Teach/Model Provide a simple scenario for students, such as *I want to give directions for getting from our classroom to the lunchroom.* Ask students to provide steps as you write them on the board. Help them to use sequence words and clear directions. Read the directions back. Can students use the directions to find the lunchroom? As students form the directions with you, write order words on the board for students' reference.

Practice Place students in groups and ask them to give directions orally for a simple task, such as sharpening a pencil or folding a sheet of paper. One student can give directions while the others complete the task. Do the directions make sense? Guide practice as needed. Have volunteers share the best examples with the class.

Assess Listen in as students give directions. Assess their abilities to provide clear steps and use sequence words.

Beginning On index cards, write steps or draw simple pictures for a simple process. Write one step per card. Give the cards to groups of students and have them work together to place the cards in order. Then students can say or read the directions aloud.

Intermediate/Advanced Provide out-of-order directions without order words. Have students place the directions in order and say them aloud, inserting sequence words to add organization.

Advanced High Have students work with partners to create a list of sequence words they can use in giving directions. Then have them give directions for a simple task, using words from their list.

Name ______________________________

Use the sentence starters to give directions for a task, such as tying your shoe.

First, you should . . .

Second, . . .

Next, . . .

After that, . . .

Finally, . . .

Ask a friend to follow your directions. Were the directions clear? How could you improve them?

Circle the rating for each sentence. **Tell** how you give directions.

1 I need help to do this better.

2 I do this sometimes.

3 I know how to do this.

I can give directions with more than one or two steps.	1	2	3
I use order words when I give directions.	1	2	3
My directions are clear. People can follow them.	1	2	3

Follow Directions

Teaching Tip
As students are able, make directions more complex. Start with simple one- or two-step directions for students to follow, both oral and written. Then gradually increase the complexity of the directions you give and have them restate the directions to clarify meaning.

Preteach *I have to follow directions every day. This morning, I followed directions for making breakfast in the microwave. I follow directions when I drive to school. I had to read the directions for using the DVD player when I showed you a video. And my teacher books have directions for teaching lessons. It is important to look at the steps in directions and read them (or listen) carefully to follow them.*

Teach/Model *Listen as I give you directions.* Give students directions for drawing things on sheets of paper, such as *First, draw a star in the upper right corner. Next, draw a circle in the middle.* After students have followed your directions, have them compare their drawings to the "answer." Point out important features of directions: time-order words that organize directions, and steps that need to be completed in order. If students had trouble following the directions, what made them difficult?

Practice Have students work in pairs to answer the questions on the student worksheet. Discuss and identify what makes the directions easy to follow (details in the steps and the numbers in order). Then have pairs read the directions for making a healthy snack to each other. One student can listen and the other student can gesture to show understanding.

Assess Assess students' oral and written work to check their ability to follow directions. Be sure that students understand they need to look for important details in directions and follow steps in order. Help them to understand that restating directions helps to clarify understanding.

Beginning Give simple one- or two-step directions for students to follow. Ask them to restate the most important details of each step before they follow it.

Intermediate Gather directions for students, such as recipes or directions for making or building simple things at home. Have them look for sequence words or other clues to order as well as the important details in the steps. Discuss in small groups, and then practice giving each other directions.

Advanced/Advanced High Provide directions for making or doing something. Have students work in small groups to discuss the directions and complete the tasks.

Name ______________________________

Read the directions.
Answer the questions.
Make a healthy snack!
You will need: one red or green pepper, carrot sticks, celery sticks, salad dressing, a sharp knife, an adult helper

1. Have an adult cut the pepper in half across the middle.
2. Scoop out the seeds and material from inside the pepper.
3. Wash the inside and outside of each pepper. Each half of the pepper is a bowl!
4. Put salad dressing in each bowl.
5. Dip carrots and celery into the salad dressing. Eat them.
6. When you finish eating the celery and carrots, you can eat the bowl!

How many pepper bowls does this recipe make?

____

What do you do with the salad dressing in step 5?

____

____

What does the adult helper do? Why do you need an adult helper? ______________________________

____

Draw the steps on the back of this sheet.

Use Classroom Language

Teaching Tip
While some classroom language is straightforward transactional language that students need to practice in order to learn, other classroom language is idiomatic and may be confusing for students. When you tell students to "line up," for example, they may think of drawing a line or putting up a line like a clothesline. Tell students the meanings of the idiomatic phrases used in the classroom in language they can understand.

Preteach *Every day in class, we communicate with each other. We ask questions and give directions. We work in groups. Students listen and ask for help from classmates and from the teacher. We have some words and sentences that we use often in the classroom. It's important for us to know how to use classroom language to get help, work with others, and understand what is happening around us in class.*

Teach/Model Ask several students to assist you in a role play. *Please take out your books. Open your books to page 15.* Assist students as needed to open their books to the correct page. *I used classroom language. You hear your teacher ask all the time to open your books to a certain page. That means that you can see that page in front of you.* Pairs can role-play, taking turns saying the classroom language and opening their books to the correct page.

Practice Help students gather examples of classroom language to record in the chart on the student worksheet. Some examples are already included on the chart. Have students role-play using the language. As students think of more examples of classroom language, add the examples to a large chart displayed on the wall.

Assess As students role-play and use classroom language, listen to the conversations and clear up any misconceptions. Continue to have students add examples to the worksheet and the chart in the classroom.

Beginning Give simple examples of classroom language for students to use, role-playing a scenario such as a student asking another student or the teacher to repeat what he or she said.

Intermediate/Advanced Have students role-play a scenario in which they are trying to understand a new word. They can use classroom language such as *What does ________________ mean? How do you say ________________ in English?*

Advanced High Have students create reference sheets or posters to use in the classroom that capture various examples of classroom language. Students can illustrate the posters to show the situations in which they use the classroom language and teach those words and phrases to others.

Name ______________________________

Read the examples of classroom language.
Use them in conversations with classmates.

Is this right?
What are we supposed to do?
Put this in your own words.
Can you say it again, please?
How do you say it in English?
How do you spell it in English?
What does . . . . mean?
What do you think?
I agree with you.
I disagree. Here's why.
Let's ask the teacher about this.
Open your book to page . . .
Copy this into your notes.
Listen and repeat.
The homework is . . .
Work in pairs.
Work in groups.

Circle the rating for each sentence. **Tell** how you use classroom language.

1 I need help to do this better.
2 I do this sometimes.
3 I know how to do this.

I ask for help in English.	1	2	3
I use classroom language with classmates.	1	2	3
I use classroom language with the teacher.	1	2	3
I understand the directions my teacher gives me.	1	2	3

Learn New Words

Teaching Tip
Make multiple copies of the student master. As you introduce words tied to the reading selections, as well as words from content areas, students can add to their own dictionaries of new words. Challenge students to refer to their dictionaries and use the new words twelve times in their writing and speaking to internalize meaning.

Preteach Copy the student blackline master on chart paper or display on an overhead. *When I read or hear a word I don't know, I think about what I do know about the word. Does it have a cognate I know to give a clue to meaning? Then I try to describe what the word means in a way that makes sense to me. I think about how the word relates to something in my own life. I try to remember where I've seen this word before. Sometimes I even draw a picture to help me remember what the word means. Then I use the word many times so I don't forget the meaning.*

Teach/Model Model how to use the chart with a word from a reading selection or from content-area studies, such as *weather.* Write the word on the line. Then model rating your knowledge: *A 1 means that I don't know this word at all. A 4 means I know it well enough to explain it to someone else. I understand what weather is, but I'm not sure I could define it. I'll give it a* 3. Then explain or describe weather and write a description. Be sure that your description uses simple language that all students understand.

Practice Write a word for students to copy on the chart. Pronounce the word, and then have students say it three times. Ask students to rate their knowledge of the word. Then guide students to describe the word to build understanding. Give an example of how the word relates to a class experience, tell a story that includes the word, or show a picture that defines the word. After you have defined the word, students should create their own descriptions of the word on their charts. Students can work in pairs or small groups.

Assess Assess students' word descriptions to clear up any misconceptions about the words. Look over word understanding ratings and periodically have students reevaluate their understandings of the words. Give students multiple opportunities to listen, speak, read and write with the new words, to internalize meaning.

Beginning Rather than write word meanings, students can draw and label pictures of the words.

Intermediate Have students use the words in simple spoken sentences that they share with partners. Listen in for correct word use.

Advanced/Advanced High Students can use a dictionary or glossary to reinforce their understandings of the words.

Name ______________________________

Write the word on the line.

Rate how well you understand the word.

1 I don't know the word.

2 I think I know what the word means.

3 I know the word. I can use it in a sentence.

4 I can teach this word to someone else.

Describe the word in a way that helps you understand it.

Word: __________ My Understanding 1 2 3 4

Describe the word: ______________________________

____

Word: __________ My Understanding 1 2 3 4

Describe the word: ______________________________

____

Word: __________ My Understanding 1 2 3 4

Describe the word: ______________________________

____

Ask Clarifying Questions

> **Teaching Tip**
> Write the list of the question starters on chart paper for students to use as a reference for speaking and writing. Be sure to pause often during teaching or giving directions. Students need time to process the language. Give multiple opportunities to ask questions if students need clarification.

Preteach *If I don't understand something, I need to ask the person speaking to repeat what they said. Then I can understand it. That is called* clarifying. *I ask questions to clarify, or be sure I understand. I also ask questions when I am reading. I ask questions before I read, while I read, and after I read. That helps me understand what I am reading.*

Teach/Model Work with a student to role-play a situation in which you would ask a clarifying question. Have the student give you simple directions for doing something. As the student speaks, find an opportunity to ask a question such as *What does that mean? Can you repeat that, please?* or *How do you do that?*

Practice Share the worksheet with students and talk about situations in which students would use each of the clarifying questions. Then point out the question starters. Have students use the question starters to ask questions about a selection you have recently read.

Assess As students role-play asking clarifying questions, assess their abilities to ask the questions in appropriate situations. Provide multiple opportunities to practice using question starters. Assess students' abilities to use those question words to form questions that make sense.

Beginning Have students role-play situations with you in which they ask for assistance for completing a math problem or other classroom task.

Intermediate/Advanced Have students work in small groups to identify questions they would ask the teacher, their parents, other students in a group, and so on to clarify their understanding.

Advanced High Have student use the "5Ws and an H" to ask and answer questions about a reading selection.

Name ____

Read the examples of clarifying questions.

Use them in conversations with classmates and your teachers.

Use the question starters to ask questions about what you read or hear.

Is this right?
Can you say it again, please?
Can you speak slower, please?
How do you say it in English?
How do you spell it in English?
What does . . . mean?
What do I need to do?
What should I do next?

Use these sentence frames to ask questions. **Use** the sentence frames to answer questions, too.

Who is ________? That person is ________.

What is ________? That is ________.

When did ________ happen? It happened ________.

Where is ________? The ________ is ________.

Why did ________ happen? It happened because ________.

Use Classroom Resources

Teaching Tip
Place labels on various classroom resources (maps, dictionaries, thesauruses, and others you may have in the room) to help students remember the names of the resources. Model using various resources as you read, write, and look for locations. Think aloud to demonstrate how to use these resources.

Preteach *I was reading a story, and I found a word I didn't know. I tried to figure out what the word meant from reading the words around it, but I still needed help. I asked my friend, but she didn't know either. So I used this.* (Show a dictionary.) *A dictionary is a classroom resource. It's a tool that I can use to find out word meanings.* Model how to use a dictionary and its features: guide words, pronunciations, and so on.

Teach/Model Draw attention to the student worksheet with the list of classroom resources. Start with the first one. *A map shows the locations of things. I'll write that in the chart. Why would I use a map? I'd use a map to find the capital of our state. I'd use a map to figure out how to get somewhere. I'd use a map to locate natural features. I'll write one of these uses in the chart.*

Practice As you use various resources with students, have students consider how and why to use the resources. The worksheet can be completed as an ongoing activity. Be sure to think aloud as you use various resources and demonstrate how and why to use them. Students can add resources that are particular to your classroom.

Assess Assess students' abilities to choose appropriate resources. They would use a thesaurus, for example, to make writing more interesting. Other examples would be to use a DVD to get information in a visual way and to use a computer to find out information for presentations.

Beginning Have students work in pairs to use a picture dictionary to find a word from a reading selection. Help them restate the definition in their own words.

Intermediate/Advanced Have small groups of students use a classroom resource such as a map to locate directions, cities, and physical features.

Advanced High Ask students to add more classroom resources to the chart and explain to other students how to use those resources.

Name ____________________________

Read the name of the resource.
Explain what the resource is like.
Tell why you would use it.
Add more resources to the chart.

Classroom Resources

Resource	What's it like?	Why would I use it?
Dictionary	a book of words and definitions; words are in alphabetical order	to find out the meaning of a word; to find out how to say a word
Map		
Thesaurus		
Almanac		
Encyclopedia		
Computer		

Retell or Summarize

Teaching Tip
Remind students that a summary does not contain all of the ideas, just the important ones. Help students sort details into categories: *need to know* and *nice to know*. Help students summarize both written material and spoken messages.

Preteach *I saw a movie yesterday. When my friends asked me about it, I didn't tell every detail from the beginning to end. Instead, I told the most important things. This is called summarizing. I summarize things I see, things I read, and things I hear. When I summarize, I know that I have sorted out the most important details. A summary includes important things, not everything. Retelling is a little different. When you retell something, you listen to or read the message, and then say it in your own words to show you understand it.*

Teach/Model Ask students to listen carefully as you read a short passage aloud. After you read, ask students to contribute to a summary of the passage. Help frame their thinking as you list their ideas to create a summary. Have pairs of students read the complete summary together. Then reread the passage. Have pairs decide if the summary lists the most important details. What should be added or changed? Discuss and clarify answers.

Practice Have students use the graphic organizer on the student worksheet to list details from a written or spoken passage. In the box at the bottom, students can write their summaries. Encourage them to keep their summaries short and to the point. Ask them to read their summaries aloud and compare them with classmates' summaries.

Assess Assess students' summaries to be sure that students have included only important details. Ask questions to guide their thinking, (e.g., *Why is this detail important? Does your summary match what the author wanted us to remember?*).

Beginning Have students orally summarize a simple spoken message or a simple text, such as a comic strip. They can work in pairs to practice, then share oral summaries with the group.

Intermediate Provide a simple text and a sample summary that is missing some information and provides too many details about the text. Ask students to read and discuss the summary in pairs. *What details are missing? What details don't need to be included?*

Advanced/Advanced High Ask students to work in pairs to create directions for summarizing. Have them share their directions and sample summaries with other students.

Name ____

Use the graphic organizer to list important details.

Write a summary in the box.

Say the summary aloud.

Use the summary starters if you need to.

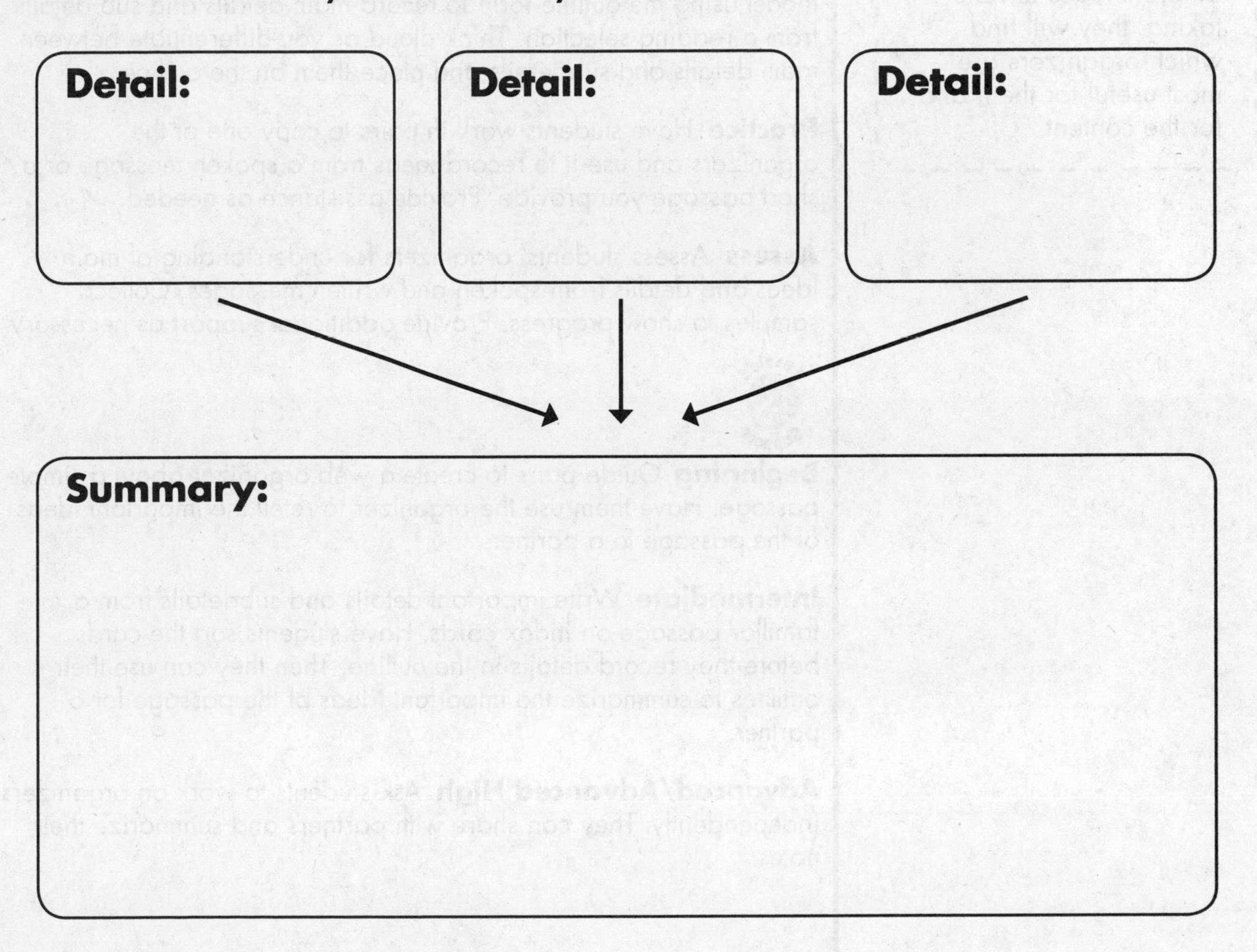

Summary language:

In summary, . . .

The most important ideas are . . .

What we need to remember is . . .

Take Notes/ Create an Outline

Teaching Tip

Provide graphic organizers for taking notes, such as concept webs, T-charts, and others you plan to use with students. As students work with different types of note taking, they will find which organizers are most useful for them and for the content.

Preteach *When I am in a meeting, I listen for important ideas and take notes. You do the same thing in class. When you listen, you write down important ideas. When you read, you write down important ideas too. Writing down ideas, or taking notes, helps you remember them later.*

Teach/Model Model using the web graphic organizer and the outline on the student worksheet. Tell students that the web organizer is great for writing down details about one idea. Then model using the outline form to record main details and sub details from a reading selection. Think aloud as you differentiate between main details and subdetails and place them on the outline.

Practice Have students work in pairs to copy one of the organizers and use it to record ideas from a spoken message or a short passage you provide. Provide assistance as needed.

Assess Assess students' organizers for understanding of main ideas and details from spoken and written messages. Collect samples to show progress. Provide additional support as necessary.

Beginning Guide pairs to create a web organizer about a simple passage. Have them use the organizer to retell the important ideas of the passage to a partner.

Intermediate Write important details and subdetails from a familiar passage on index cards. Have students sort the cards before they record details in the outline. Then they can use their outlines to summarize the important ideas of the passage for a partner.

Advanced/Advanced High Ask students to work on organizers independently. They can share with partners and summarize their notes.

Name ______________________________

Choose a graphic organizer to take notes.

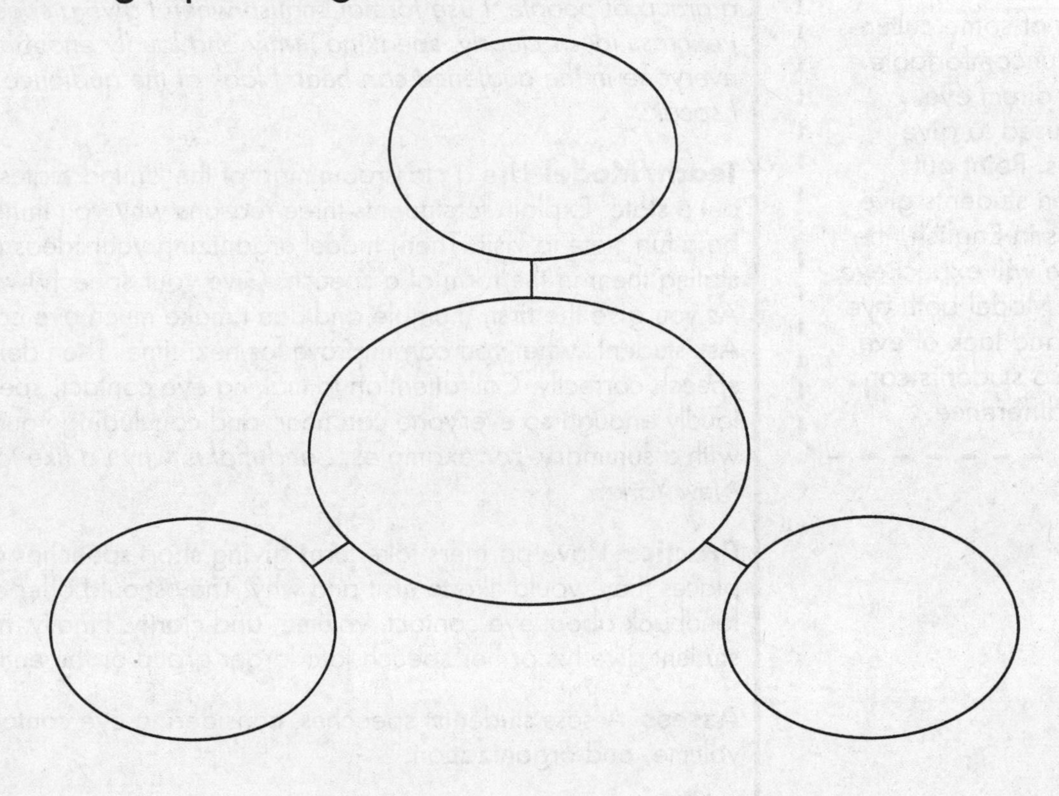

Outline

I. ______________________________

A. ______________________________

B. ______________________________

II. ______________________________

A. ______________________________

B. ______________________________

III. ______________________________

A. ______________________________

B. ______________________________

Give a Speech

Teaching Tip
Students of some cultures may be uncomfortable with the direct eye contact used to give speeches. Point out that when students give speeches in English, the audience will expect eye contact. Model both eye contact and lack of eye contact so students can see the difference.

Preteach *A speech is a planned talk that you give in front of a group of people. I use formal English when I give a speech. I express ideas clearly, speaking firmly and loudly enough so everyone in the audience can hear. I look at the audience when I speak.*

Teach/Model Use a classroom map of the United States to pick out a state. Explain to students three reasons why you think it would be a fun state to visit. Then, model organizing your ideas and stating them in the form of a speech. Give your speech two times. As you give the first, mumble and don't make much eye contact. Ask students what you can improve for next time. Then deliver the speech correctly. Call attention to making eye contact, speaking loudly enough so everyone can hear, and concluding your speech with a summary. For example: *...and that is why I'd like to visit New York.*

Practice Have partners take turns giving short speeches about places they would like to visit and why. They should offer corrective feedback about eye contact, volume, and clarity. Finally, have each student give his or her speech to a larger group or the entire class.

Assess Assess students' speeches, considering eye contact, volume, and organization.

Beginning Have students work on delivering speeches by answering simple questions, speaking aloud. Because speeches are planned, give students a chance to plan what they will say. Tell them the questions first so they can think through their answers.

Intermediate Have students work on elaborating. Lead them by explaining that sentences that add more details include words such as *because, as a result,* etc.

Advanced/Advanced High Give students time to plan, then have them speak on a topic for two minutes. Speakers should elaborate with details and avoid using *um, uh,* and *you know.*

Name ____________________

Use the planner to organize ideas for your speech.
Write your topic.
Explain how you will introduce your speech.
List details to include in the speech.
End with a conclusion, or a final thought for your audience to remember.

Topic:

____

To **introduce** my topic, I will:

____

____

Details I will include:

____

____

I will **end** my speech by:

____

Evaluate your speech.
1 I need to practice more to do this.
2 I did this sometimes.
3 I did this during my whole speech.

I spoke loudly enough for my audience to hear.	1	2	3
I looked at the audience when I spoke.	1	2	3
I spoke clearly.	1	2	3
I used formal English.	1	2	3
I organized my ideas with a clear beginning and end.	1	2	3

Express Opinions

Teaching Tip

Students may think of facts as "true" and opinions as "false." Locate statements of opinions that are supported by facts and discuss them with students. Point out that people trust opinions when they are supported with facts.

Preteach *We express opinions to show what we think or believe. We cannot prove if an opinion is true or false. If I say,* It is raining outside, *that's a fact. I can look outside and see rain falling. If I say,* Rainy weather is the best weather, *that's an opinion. I like rainy weather because it helps my flowers grow in the garden. But some people don't like rain. They have a different opinion.*

Teach/Model Display the words and phrases from the student page. *We use these words to give our opinions. These words tell what we think or believe.* Model creating an opinion using one of the words or phrases.

Practice Have students work with partners to state opinions about sports, food, television shows, books, or movies. Have them use the words in the box on the student page. Refer them to the sentence frames as needed. Point out that these frames will help them correctly express opinions in English. For additional practice, have students write statements of opinion and then say them aloud with partners. Have students elaborate by giving reasons for their opinions.

Assess As students state opinions, assess understanding. Do students state ideas that cannot be proven true or false and express feelings or beliefs? Do students use words or phrases from the box? Correct students as necessary.

Beginning Write sentence frames on index cards and distribute them to students. Have them work in pairs to state opinions using the frames.

Intermediate When calling on students to give oral opinions, have them use phrases such as *I like* or *I do not like* rather than single words. Have pairs ask each other why they have that opinion. Report answers to the class.

Advanced/Advanced High Challenge students to add other opinion words or phrases to the box and write additional sentence frames. They can use the frames to state opinions.

Name ______________________________

Opinion Words

I think	I believe	my opinion is	I agree
I disagree	I like	I do not like	
best	worst	good	bad

Complete opinions using these sentence frames:

I like ______________________________.

I think ______________________________.

I believe ______________________________.

I do not like ______________________________.

My opinion is ______________________________.

Statements of opinion:

____

____

____

Challenge! Add more details to your sentence.

I like ______________ because ______________.

Her opinion is ______________ because ______________.

Express Feelings

Teaching Tip
All people experience feelings, yet the "correctness" of expressing those feelings varies from culture to culture. Work with students to understand the appropriate times to openly express feelings and the social norms associated with the process.

Preteach *If you see someone with a frown on his or her face* (demonstrate for students), *you know that person might be sad or angry. Anger and sadness are feelings. We often express our feelings with our facial expressions and our actions, but we can also use words to express feelings. Finding the right words isn't always easy!*

Teach/Model Use exaggerated facial expressions and body language to express a feeling, such as happiness or confusion. Model by speaking: *I am happy. I feel happy.* Model another feeling and have students use the frames after you model:

You feel ________________. *You are* ________________.

Practice Explain a situation to students that would elicit a feeling, such as *Your favorite cousin is coming to a family party. You haven't seen your cousin in a long time. How do you feel?* (excited, happy) *You came to school without your homework. You know your teacher is going to ask for it.* (worried, guilty) Have students gesture to show the emotion and then work with partners to express that feeling in words. As students suggest more feeling words, write them on a chart for reference so that students can include them on their worksheets.

Assess As students express their feelings, assess the sentences they use as well as their ability to identify feelings. Correct any misconceptions as students use sentence frames to express feelings.

Beginning Have students draw or make faces to show a facial expression that expresses a feeling. Partners can identify the feeling and create a sentence: *He/she feels* ________________.

Intermediate Have students look for pictures in magazines or newspapers that show a situation that would elicit feelings. Have them speak about the picture.

Advanced/Advanced High Challenge students to think of specific words for feelings, such as *joyful, ecstatic, lively, overjoyed, pleased, thrilled,* or *upbeat* instead of *happy.*

Name ______________________________

Record words that express feelings in the box. A few words are already in the box. **Add** more.

Feeling Words

glad   afraid   proud   angry

lonely   confused   surprised

Speak a sentence using one of the frames below. **Choose** words from the box.

I feel ______________________________.

I am ______________________________.

He/She is ______________________________.

They felt ______________________________.

They are ______________________________.

He/She was ______________________________.

They were ______________________________.

Challenge! Add more details to your sentence.

I feel ______________ because ______________.

They felt ______________ when ______________.

Discuss with Classmates

Teaching Tip

Consider setting roles for class discussions, such as a timekeeper, a leader (keeps the group on track), a note taker, and a summarizer. Model how to do each of these roles and provide guided practice before assigning these roles for students to do independently.

Preteach *When do we have discussions? I discuss work with students. I talk with my family at the dinner table. I discuss ideas with other teachers at school. In a discussion, we speak and we listen. We respect other people's ideas.*

Teach/Model Create a fishbowl, in which you and a few students are in the center while others are around you watching. Introduce an easy discussion topic such as a question about a selection you have just read. Model the discussion behaviors from the rubric on the next page. As you model these behaviors, pause to think aloud. You might say *I repeated back what Tommy said to me. He knows that I have understood him. He also knows I was listening. Now it is my turn to speak. It is important to take turns being a good listener and a good speaker.*

Practice Have students work in small groups. Introduce a topic such as: *What is your favorite thing to do after school?* As students discuss, monitor and encourage the positive behaviors you observe. Share these positive behaviors with the class and have students identify others they know.

Assess Use the rubric on the student page to have students assess their discussion skills. Follow up with your own observations of student discussions.

Beginning Offer students examples of nonverbal communication skills that a good listener uses: nodding, making eye contact, and making appropriate expressions. Have them mimic you as you model them.

Intermediate Offer students an example of a conversation that could occur at the lunch table. Have the students mimic you, each partner playing another role. Stress the importance of active listening and behaviors that go with it.

Advanced/Advanced High Have students model discussion scenarios and demonstrate behaviors of listening and speaking for other groups.

Name ______________________

Rate what you do during discussions with your classmates.

1 I need to practice this skill.
2 I do this sometimes.
3 I almost always do this.

I share my ideas with others.	1	2	3
I answer questions when classmates ask.	1	2	3
I give a lot of facts or details when I speak.	1	2	3
I respect other people in the group.	1	2	3
I listen to other people's ideas.	1	2	3
I look at the person speaking.	1	2	3
I repeat back what other people say to show I understand.	1	2	3
I support other people's ideas.	1	2	3

What topics would you like to discuss with classmates? **List** them here. Then **discuss!**

____

____

____

____

____

____

Act Out or Draw Meaning

Teaching Tip

Drawing a word helps etch the meaning of that word into the brain, making it a part of our active vocabularies. Students may think they cannot draw pictures because they are not artistic. Help them devise symbols or other ways to illustrate meaning when they are "stuck" for picture ideas.

Preteach Choose a content-area or lesson word that students recently learned. *When I learn new words, I want to remember them. Drawing a picture of a word's meaning or acting out the meaning of a word helps me remember a word, what it means, and how it is used. I just learned a new word in science: fault. A fault is a place in the earth where an earthquake takes place. I drew a picture of a circle to show the Earth and draw a line on it. I put arrows to show how the Earth shifts at the fault line.* (Show picture.) *I can also act out the meaning by taking two blocks and rubbing them together to show what happens at a fault to make an earthquake.*

Teach/Model Introduce words from a recent story or from content-area studies. Place students in small groups, and give each group a word. Have students work together to create a picture and/or gestures to demonstrate meanings of the words. Groups can share with other groups as you monitor for understanding.

Practice Play a guessing game with students. Distribute words on index cards that students have learned in class. Students can take turns drawing pictures or acting out word meanings for other classmates to guess. Use the student worksheet for students to create "dictionaries" of word meanings. Distribute copies of the drawing frames when students learn new words. Have students keep and add to their own personal word books.

Assess Assess students' drawings to clear up any misconceptions about the words. Discuss with students how drawing words may help them remember word meanings.

Beginning Ask students to follow up their drawings or gestures by explaining word meanings orally.

Intermediate Ask students to use each word in a sentence to describe what they drew or acted out.

Advanced/Advanced High Have students look up the definitions of words in a dictionary to supplement their understanding of the words. They can write definitions in their own words to show understanding.

Name ____________________

Word: ____________________

Drawing

This word means ____________________

Word: ____________________

Drawing

This word means ____________________

Read the Words Around You

Teaching Tip

Engage students by asking them each to bring in something from home with words on it that they can read: a cereal box, a milk carton, or a flyer from a store, for example. Create a display. Ask students what information they get from reading the words on each of these items.

Preteach Before starting, draw a stop sign on the board and ask what it means. Students may answer *stop. We are surrounded by words and signs that can be useful. We need to learn what these signs tell us.* Point out that the name of the school is on the front of the building. *The sign tells people what this building is. It helps people find the school.* Then, point out that the classrooms have numbers. *These help students find their way around the school.*

Teach/Model Walk around the classroom until you find an example of instructional environmental print. Model reading the word, and figuring out what it means: *A sign on this door reads P-U-L-L. I know that word is* pull. *This sign tells me how to open the door.* Then, model opening the door.

Practice Tell students that their task is to keep a log of the signs they notice and can read throughout the school day. They must keep track of the words in the table on their worksheets. At the end of the day, have students share one word they recognized in a sign, and one they did not. Discuss as a class. Help them understand the meanings of words they did not recognize. As you discuss students' examples, talk about the information they get from reading the signs or other environmental print. Students can keep a running log of environmental print they see and learn. Discuss the words regularly.

Assess Assess students' understandings of environmental print by questioning them as they share their results, for example: *Why do you think the sign "gymnasium" was placed in that spot?* (The sign tells us where the gym is.) Explain the meanings of unknown words to students.

Beginning Have beginning students only keep track of words they recognize and know.

Intermediate Have students organize their words by category, such as *foods, signs, rooms, clubs,* and so on.

Advanced/Advanced High Provide environmental print for students, such as store advertisements, posters, and additional signs. Students can discuss with partners what they learn from reading the signs and texts.

Name ______________________________

Write the words you see around you.

Practice saying each word aloud.

Date	Words I Know	Words I Do Not Know Yet

Use Nouns in Your Speaking

Teaching Tip

In some languages, there is no difference between count and noncount nouns. For students who speak these languages, provide sentence frames and models to help them understand the difference.

Preteach *Nouns are words that name people, places, or things. Nouns can name one thing, or they can name more than one thing. I can count these pencils: one, two, three, four. But the word* weather *is a noun, too. I can't count weather, though: one weather, two weathers, three weathers? That doesn't make sense! There must be different kinds of nouns, with different rules for how we say them and write them.*

Teach/Model Write *desks* and *furniture* on the board and draw a quick sketch under each: three desks under *desks* and a desk, chair, and couch under *furniture. Let's make sentences with these words. I see three desks. I can count them: one, two, three. I see that furniture. I used the word* that *because I cannot count furniture and say* one furniture, two furnitures, three furnitures. *Nouns that you can count, such as* desk, *are called* count nouns. *Nouns that you cannot count, such as* furniture, weather, *or* anger, *are called* noncount nouns.

Practice Have students complete the student worksheet. Focus on the ability to count some nouns and ask questions to frame as necessary. For the first sentence, for example, you might say: *You can count the apples. One, two, three, four. Write the word* four *on the line*. For the second sentence: *When I drink the water, I can't count how many waters. So I'll complete the sentence with* the. As students complete the exercise, point out that some noncount nouns might have the word *a* or *an* in front of them.

Assess As students complete their worksheets, circulate to assess their work and clear up any misconceptions.

Beginning Say a count noun, such as *bird*. Ask students to use the word in a sentence. Then say a noncount noun, such as *music*. Have students use the word in a sentence. Check for understanding.

Intermediate Write words on index cards, one word per card. Have students work together to sort the words into count and noncount nouns. They can choose one count noun and one noncount noun to use in a sentence.

Advanced/Advanced High Challenge students to find sentences in magazines or newspapers and underline the nouns. Have them work in pairs to classify nouns as count or noncount nouns. Then have them speak using those nouns as you check for understanding.

Name ______________________________

Look at the picture.

Read the sentence.

Complete the sentence by writing a number OR by writing the word *the*.

Say the sentences aloud.

1. We need ________ apples for our pie.

2. Hold up ________ fingers.

3. ________ weather is hot.

4. We heard ________ music.

5. There are ________ houses on this block.

6. Please put those ________ books on the shelf.

Circle the count nouns in the sentences above.

Explain the difference between a count and a noncount noun to a partner.

Listen for other count and noncount nouns you hear in conversations.

Use Prepositions and Adjectives in Your Speaking

Teaching Tip
Follow a similar routine for teaching adjectives. Focus on adjectives that are troublesome for your students. You might, for example, focus on position of adjectives (before the nouns they describe or as predicate adjectives). You might also focus on comparative and superlative adjectives to help students avoid speaking sentences like *This is more better* or *That was most crunchiest.*

Preteach Demonstrate as you describe prepositions. *I push the chair under the table. I put my coat on the hook. When I was describing where I put things, I used special words to tell where. These words,* on *and* under, *are called prepositions. We can use prepositions to tell locations. We can also use prepositions to tell when things happen. We eat lunch after our math class. In that sentence,* after *is a preposition that helps us tell time.*

Teach/Model Use a preposition in a sentence that shows location, such as *I walk between the rows of desks.* Demonstrate by walking between the desks. Say the sentence again and ask students to raise their hands when they hear the preposition. Then pair students. Assign each a preposition. Have students say and demonstrate a sentence using the preposition.

Practice Have students use the space on the bottom of the worksheet to draw a picture. They can write about the picture using prepositions. Model if necessary: *I drew a picture of myself riding my bicycle. I put my helmet on my head. I was careful when I rode across the street.* Students can also use this sheet to work with adjectives. Have them list adjectives in the second column. They can use adjectives to describe the picture they drew.

Assess Assess students' pictures and sentences for understanding of how to use prepositions. Provide extra support as necessary.

Beginning Write prepositions on index cards, one preposition per card. Demonstrate putting books *on* the table or putting your pencil *into* a desk. As you model and say the prepositional phrases, students can repeat the prepositions and hold up the cards with the corresponding prepositions. Then have students use gestures to demonstrate prepositions, while other students guess the prepositions they are demonstrating.

Intermediate/Advanced Share photographs from magazines. Ask students to describe locations of items in the photographs using prepositions. They can use adjectives to describe the photos as well.

Advanced High Challenge students to find prepositions and adjectives from their reading or from other sources. They can add them to the worksheet and to a chart for class reference. Have them practice using prepositions that tell time in addition to location.

Name ______________________________

Write prepositions in the first column.

Write adjectives in the second column.

Prepositions	Adjectives

Draw a picture.

Write about it. **Use** prepositions and adjectives.

Use Verbs in Your Speaking

Teaching Tip

Phrasal verbs may prove difficult for students, because they are idiomatic expressions. Use the worksheet as a basis for a chart to which you can add phrasal verbs as students encounter them in their reading and listening. As you add phrasal verbs to the chart, have students discuss their meanings and use them in sentences.

Preteach *Verbs are words that show action. I look before I cross the street.* (Model turning your head to look both ways before crossing the street.) *The word* look *is a verb. It describes something I do. If I said, Please look up a word in the dictionary, does that mean that you would really look up?* (Model looking up toward the ceiling.) Look up *is a group of words that has a different meaning as a group of words than if you say each word individually. The phrase* Look up *is called a phrasal verb. It's a verb with a preposition or an adverb. The phrase makes a meaning different from the verb's meaning.*

Teach/Model Choose a phrasal verb from the chart for modeling. *Let's focus on the phrase* go over. *A car can* go over *a hill. But* go over *can have a different meaning. What does it mean if I say* Let's go over your homework? *That means that we are going to review and check your answers.* Guide students by choosing another phrasal verb and explaining and modeling its meaning.

Practice Have students work in pairs to complete the worksheet by choosing the correct phrase to complete each sentence.

Assess Assess students' answers on the worksheet. Correct any errors, and explain misconceptions students may have.

Beginning Assist students by reading the sentence and inserting the meaning of the correct answer. After students use the chart to choose the correct answer, they can reread the sentence to reinforce their understanding of the concept in English.

Intermediate/Advanced Ask students to choose a phrase and work in pairs to write a sentence that includes the phrase. They can illustrate their sentences to show meaning.

Advanced High Have students search for phrasal verbs in their reading selections or other printed material, share them in small groups, and discuss their meanings.

Name ______________________________

Read each phrasal verb in the chart.

Phrasal Verb	Meaning
show up	arrive
make up	create or invent something
run into	meet
look up	find
back up	support an idea
come across	find something
come up with	think of an idea
do over	do something again
give up	stop doing something
go over	check something; review
hold on	wait for a short time
keep up	go at the same speed
make up one's mind	decide something
turn in	give something to someone

Circle the verbal phrase that fits the sentence.

1. Let's ____________ the correct answers.
go over   give up

2. I want to make a better drawing. I'll ____________.
give up   do it over

3. Did you ____________ that story?
keep up   make up

4. Please ____________. I am almost ready to go.
hold on   back up

5. I cannot ____________ my mind about lunch.
make up   give up

Role-play conversations with phrasal verbs. **Share** them.

Part 6
Multilingual Vocabulary

Introduction to Multilingual Vocabulary

The lesson words are arranged by unit and week to coincide with the reading selections. Each lesson word is translated into Spanish, Chinese, Vietnamese, Korean, and Hmong. Use the translated lesson words to build students' background knowledge before reading a selection. Frontloading the vocabulary will allow students to access the content and will aid their comprehension of the text.

The multilingual thinking words, also translated into the same languages, are process words, such as *analyze, compare, describe, illustrate, list*, and *predict*. Students can use these words to discuss the strategies they use as they read various selections, including content-area texts.

Table of Contents

Multilingual Vocabulary
Unit 1

English	Spanish	Chinese	Vietnamese	Korean	Hmong
Week 1: Charlie McButton					
bat	murciélago	蝙蝠	Con dơi	박쥐	puav
battery	batería	電池	bình điện/pin	건전지	lub roj
blew	cayó	燒斷	thổi	불었다	tshuab
fuel	combustible	燃料	dầu	연료	roj
plug	enchufe	插頭	gắn	접속하다	ntxig
term	tiempo	期限	thời kỳ	기간	tib
vision	visión	畫面	tầm nhìn	통찰력	pom
Week 2: What About Me?					
carpenter	carpintero	木匠	thợ mộc	목수	tus neeg ua tsev
carpetmaker	alfombrista	做地毯的工匠	thợ làm thảm	카펫 만드는 사람	tu neeg ua kas plev (carpet)
knowledge	conocimiento	知識	kiến thức	지식	paub ntaub paub ntawv
marketplace	mercado	市場	nơi họp chợ	시장	kiab kw
merchant	comerciante	商人	thương gia	상인	tus neeg ua lag ua luam (suav los pav)
plenty	mucho	許多	nhiều	많은	ntau heev
straying	descarriando	迷路	đi lạc	헤매는	yuam kev
thread	hilo	線	sợi chỉ	실	xov
Week 3: Kumak's Fish					
gear	equipo	裝備	thiết bị	장치	Cia
parka	abrigo parka	毛皮外套	parka	파카	paj kas
splendid	espléndido	美好的	tráng lệ	근사한	zoo

English	Spanish	Chinese	Vietnamese	Korean	Hmong
twitch	sacudirse	猛烈拉扯	giựt giựt	홱 잡아채다	Tig
willow	sauce	木棒	cây liễu	버드나무	ntoos qis
yanked	haló a	用力拉	kéo	홱 잡아당겼다	chua
Week 4: Supermarket					
laundry	artículos para la lavandería	洗衣用品	giặt giũ	세탁물	ntxua khaub ncaw
section	sección	分區	đoạn	구역	kab
shelves	despensas	貨架	cái kệ	선반	txee
spoiled	se echaba a perder	腐敗的	hư hỏng	상한	lwj lawm
store	tienda	商店	tiệm	가게	lub khw
thousands	miles	上千的	hàng ngàn	대량	Phav
traded	negocian	交易	trao đổi	교환했다	Pauv
variety	variedad	多樣	khác nhau	갖가지	ntau yam
Week 5: My Rows and Piles of Coins					
arranged	ordené	安排	được sắp	정리하다	kho
bundles	paquetes	捆	gói, cuộn, bó	꾸러미	ib plawg
dangerously	peligrosamente	危險	nguy hiểm	위험하게	phom sij
errands	recados	差使	việc vặt	심부름	me ntsis hauj lwm laug sij hawm
excitedly	con emoción	激動	hào hứng	흥분하여	zoo siab
steady	estable	穩定	vững vàng	꾸준한	mus ncaj, mus zoo
unwrapped	desenvolví	打開	mở ra	포장을 풀다	nthuav
wobbled	me tambaleé	搖晃	bị lung lay, lảo đảo	흔들흔들하다, 비틀거리다	tshee

Unit 2

English	Spanish	Chinese	Vietnamese	Korean	Hmong
Week 1: Penguin Chick					
cuddles	se arrima a	擁抱	nép mình vào, ôm ấp	껴안다	sib puag
flippers	aletas	鬭鰭	cánh chim như cái chèo gạt nước	(펭귄의) 날개	tis
frozen	congelada	結冰	bị đông	얼음이 언	khov
hatch	salir del cascarón	孵化	nở	부화하다	daug
pecks	picotea	啄	mổ	쪼다	thos
preen	atusa	用嘴或舌舔整理	rỉa lông	날개, 털 등을 다듬다	kaus ncauj plhwg kom ntxheev
snuggles	se acurruca	舒適地蜷伏	rúc vào, quấn quít	다가붙다	sib puag sib qawg
Week 2: I Wanna Iguana					
adorable	adorable	可爱	đáng yêu	사랑스러운	ntxim nyiam
compassionate	compasivo	有同情心	động lòng thương	인정 많은	hlub tshua
exactly	exactamente	刚好	chính xác	정확하게	sib thooj kiag
iguana	iguana	鬣蜥	con cự đà	이구아나	nab qa dev
mature	maduro	成年	trưởng thành	성숙한	tiav hlob
mention	mencionar	说到	nêu lên	언급하다	piav
trophies	trofeos	锦标	cúp	상패	khoomplig ua muaj yeej

English	Spanish	Chinese	Vietnamese	Korean	Hmong
Week 3: Prudy's Problem and How She Solved It					
butterflies	mariposas	蝴蝶	bươm bướm	나비들	npauj npaim
collection	colección	收藏品	bộ sưu tầm	수집	kaws cia
enormous	enorme	巨大	to lớn	거대한	loj heev
scattered	desparramadas	散佈	rải rác	흐트러뜨리다, 없애다	zeeg txhua qhov
shoelaces	cordones de los zapatos	鞋帶	dây giày	신발끈	hluas khau
strain	doblarse	伸長	kéo căng, ráng sức	얼룩	ntxeev
Week 4: Tops & Bottoms					
bottom	parte de abajo	下面	cái đáy	밑바닥	hauv qab
cheated	engañaste	詐騙	gian lận	속이다	kib lav
clever	listo	聰明	khôn ngoan	영리한	ntse
crops	cosechas	莊稼	mùa màng, hoa màu	곡물	qoob loo
lazy	perezoso	懶惰	lười biếng	게으른	tub nkeeg
partners	socios	夥伴	những người cộng sự	동료	cov khub
wealth	riqueza	財富	sự giàu có	재산	nyaij txiag
Week 5: Amazing Bird Nests					
bill	pico	鳥嘴	cái mỏ chim	부리	kaus ncauj
goo	pelotitas de saliva	黏液	cục nhớt	끈적거리는 것	aub ncaug
hunters	cazadores	獵人	người đi săn	사냥꾼들	neeg yos nqaij
material	material	材料	vật liệu	재료	Qhov qho
platform	plataforma	平台	nền	연단	sam thiaj
tons	toneladas	大量	hàng tấn	톤(무게의 단위)	too
twigs	ramitas	嫩枝	cọng cây	작은 가지	Tig

Unit 3

English	Spanish	Chinese	Vietnamese	Korean	Hmong
Week 1: How Do You Raise a Raisin?					
area	área	地方	vùng	지역	thaj chaw
artificial	artificial	人工	nhân tạo	인공, 인위적인	neeg tsim
grapevine	vid	葡萄藤	cây nho	포도 덩굴	mab txiv quav ntswg
preservative	preservativo, conservador	防腐剂	chất bảo quản	방부제	tshuaj txuag cia
proof	prueba	证据	chứng cớ	증명, 증거	pov thawj
raise	criar	栽种	nuôi lớn	기르다	tu loj hlob
raisin	pasa	葡萄干	nho khô	건포도	txiv quav ntswg qhuav
Week 2: Pushing Up the Sky					
antlers	cuernos	鹿角	gạc, sừng nai	(사슴 따위의)가 지진 뿔	kub
imagined	imaginar	想像	tưởng tượng	상상하다	xav tau
languages	idiomas	語言	ngôn ngữ	언어	yam lus
narrator	narrador	敘事人	người kể chuyện	이야기하는 사람/내레이터	tus piav zaj dab neeg
overhead	por arriba	高出地面的	phía trên đầu	머리 위에	suam taub hau
poked	(agujeros) hechos	戳破的洞	chọc thủng	찌르다	tho
Week 3: Seeing Stars					
dim	opacas	暗淡的	mờ	희미한	qauj qauj
gas	gas	氣體	hơi	기체	pa roj
gigantic	gigantesca	巨大的	to lớn	거대한	loj loj kawg
ladle	cucharón	杓子	cái vá	국자	yawm fo
patterns	patrones	圖案	kiểu mẫu	모양	muaj qauv
shine	brillante	發亮	sáng	빛나다	ci ci

English	Spanish	Chinese	Vietnamese	Korean	Hmong
temperature	temperatura	溫度	nhiệt độ	온다	txawj kub txawj txia
Week 4: A Symphony of Whales					
anxiously	ansiosamente	焦慮	nôn nóng	걱정하여	txawj
bay	bahía	海灣	vịnh	(바다, 호수의)만	pas dej
blizzards	ventiscas	暴風雪	bão tuyết	눈보라	los daus hlob hlob thiab cua ntsawj ntsawj
channel	canal	水道	eo biển	해협	ib tshooj
chipped	picaron	切為小片	bị mẻ	짹짹거리다	ntais
melody	melodía	旋律	âm điệu	선율	suab nkauj
supplies	suministros	東西	đồ dự trữ	공급하다	khoom siv
surrounded	rodeada	四周	bị bao quanh	둘러싸다	ib puag cig
symphony	sinfonía	交響曲	nhạc giao hưởng	교향곡	zaj nkauj
Week 5: Around One Cactus					
incredible	increíble	难以置信	khó tin	믿을 수 없는, 상상을 초월하는	tshaj lij kawg
lofty	elevado	崇高	cao quý	고상한	tsa siab
noble	noble	高贵	cao cả	훌륭한	hwm
search	buscar	寻找	tìm kiếm	찾다	nrhiav
stinging	doler, molestar	刺伤	chích	찌르는, 쏘는	chob chob
survivors	sobrevivientes	幸存者	sống sót	생존자	neeg dim tshuav txoj sia
topic	tema	题目	đề tài	화제, 주제	zaj lus
unseen	inadvertido	看不见	không ai thấy	보이지 않는	tsi pom
waterless	seco, árido, sin agua	缺水	không có nước	물이 없는	tsi muaj dej

Unit 4

English	Spanish	Chinese	Vietnamese	Korean	Hmong
Week 1: The Man Who Invented Basketball					
basketball	baloncesto	篮球	bóng rổ	농구	ntaus npas basketball
disease	enfermedad	病	chứng bệnh	병	kab mob
freeze	congelarse	冷藏	đông đá	얼다	nkoog
guard	ala	后卫	cầu thủ	(농구의) 가드	zov npas
popular	popular	普及	bình dân	인기가 많은	nto npe
sports	deportes	运动	thể thao	스포츠	leeb ua si
study	examinar	考察	chú trọng	공부하다	kawm
terrible	terrible	可怕	kinh khủng	무서운, 끔찍한	phem heev
Week 2: Hottest, Coldest, Highest, Deepest					
average	promedio	平均	trung bình	평균	nyob nruab nrab
depth	profundidad	深度	chiều sâu	깊이	tob li cas
deserts	desiertos	沙漠	sa mạc	사막	av suab puam
erupted	hizo erupción	噴出的	nổ tung/phun ra	폭발했다	tawg
outrun	correr más rápido que	超過	chạy nhanh hơn	앞지르다	khiav tshaj
peak	cima	尖端	đỉnh	산봉우리	nco roob, nyiag ntsia
tides	mareas	潮汐	nước thủy triều	조수	dej ua tej kwb kab
waterfalls	cataratas	瀑布	thác nước	폭포	dej tsaws tsag
Week 3: Rocks in His Head					
attic	ático	阁楼	căn gác xếp	다락방	nthab
board	consejo	板	bảng	판자	daim txiag (ntoo)

English	Spanish	Chinese	Vietnamese	Korean	Hmong
chores	quehaceres	家庭雜務	công việc	허드렛일	hauj lwm
customer	cliente	顧客	khách hàng	고객	tus neeg yuav khoom
labeled	rotuló	標記	dãn nhán	분류된	los npe
spare	de repuesto	備用品	dư	예비의	tseg cia
stamps	estampillas	郵票	các con tem	도장	ntaus thwj
Week 4: America's Champion Swimmer: Gertrude Ederle					
celebrate	celebrarán	慶祝	ăn mừng	축하하다	ua kev zoo siab
continued	siguió	繼續	đã tiếp tục	계속된	txuas ntxiv
current	corriente	水流	dòng nước	현재의	lub sij hawm no
drowned	se ahogó	淹死	bị chìm	익사하다	poob deg
medals	medallas	獎牌	huân chương	메달	cov puav pheej
stirred	revolvió	攪動	đã khuấy động	휘젓다	do
strokes	brazadas	拍擊	động tác bơi	수영법	strokes
Week 5: Fly, Eagle, Fly!					
clutched	agarraron	夾住	đã nắm chặt	꽉 쥐다	tuav ruaj ruaj
echoed	hicieron eco	反射	đã dội lại	울리다	suab echoed
gully	barranco	小峽谷	đường nước chảy mòn trên sườn đồi	작은 협곡	kwj deg
reeds	juncos	蘆葦	đám sậy	갈대	nyom los ua lev les
scrambled	luchó por salir	緊急起飛	leo trèo, tranh lấy	기어오르다	ua sw niab, kos dog dig
thatch	techo de paja	茅草屋頂	thảm cỏ	이엉(지붕을 이는 재료)	daug
valley	valle	山谷	thung lũng	골짜기	hav

Unit 5

English	Spanish	Chinese	Vietnamese	Korean	Hmong
Week 1: Suki's Kimono					
cotton	algodón	棉質	cô tông	면직물	paj rwb
festival	festival	節慶	hội chợ	축제	koom txoo lom zem
graceful	elegante	優雅	biết ơn	우아한	zoo siab heev
handkerchief	pañuelo	手帕	khăn tay	손수건	phuam so ntswg
paces	pasearse (de un lado al otro)	步調	rảo bước	걸음걸이	Tsis xav kom muaj teeb meem liv
pale	pálido	蒼白	tái nhợt	창백한	phooj ywg
rhythm	ritmo	旋律	nhịp	리듬	plaim
snug	ajustado	舒適合身	ấm áp	아담한	rub tu
Week 2: I Love Saturdays y domingos					
bouquet	ramo	花束	bó	꽃다발	lub tais paj
circus	circo	馬戲團	gánh xiệc	서커스	Tsiaj ua si
difficult	difícil	困難的	khó khăn	어려운	nyuaj nyuaj
nibbling	mordisqueando	輕咬	gặm	(물고기가) 입질 하는	xaw
pier	muelle	碼頭	cầu tàu	방파제	chaw tos nkoj
soars	vuela alto	高飛	bay lượng	높이 치솟다	qaub
swallow	tragarlos	燕子	nuốt	삼기다	nqos
Week 3: Good-Bye, 382 Shin Dang Dong					
airport	aeropuerto	機場	phi trường	공항	tshav dav hlau
cellar	sótano	地窖	cái hầm	지하실	chav
curious	curiosa	好奇	tò mò	호기심이 강한	xav paub
delicious	deliciosa	美味	ngon	맛있는	qab heev

English	Spanish	Chinese	Vietnamese	Korean	Hmong
described	descrito	描述	miêu tả	묘사하다	piav txog
farewell	despedida	告別	từ giã	작별 인사	mus zoo
homesick	nostálgico	思鄉病	nhớ nhà	고향을 그리워 하는	nco tsev
memories	memorias	記憶	hồi ức, kỷ niệm	기억	kev cim xeeb
raindrops	gotas de lluvia	雨點	những giọt mưa	빗방울	dej nag
Week 4: Jalapeño Bagels					
bakery	panadería	麵包店	tiệm bánh, lò bánh	빵집	tsev ua thiab muag qhob noom
batch	hornada	一批	đợt, lô	한 가마분	ib pawg
boils	hierva	煮沸	nấu sôi, luộc	끓다	npau
braided	trenzado	麻花辮一樣的	thắt thành bím	꼬아 만들다	ntxias, qhaib
dough	masa	生麵團	bột	가루 반죽	cuav
ingredients	ingredientes	材料	vật liệu	재료	khoom rau
mixture	mezcla	混合物	hỗn hợp	혼합물	si xyaws
Week 5: Me and Uncle Romie					
cardboard	cartón	紙板	giấy cac-tông/ bìa cứng	판지	ntawv
feast	festín	筵席	bữa ăn thịnh soạn	축제	npluag mov noj
fierce	feroz	劇烈	dữ dằn	사나운	npau taws
flights	tramos (de escalera)	飛行	các chuyến bay	비행	ya
pitcher	lanzador	大水罐	bình nước	투수	tus txawb, tais rau dej
ruined	arruinado	破壞	bị hư hỏng	파괴된	phiav tag
stoops	pórticos	向前彎身	cúi thấp người, hạ mình	구부리다	taw ntaiv yuav mus rau hauv tsev
treasure	tesoro	珍寶	bảo vật	보물	khoom muaj nuj nqis khaws zais cia

Unit 6

English	Spanish	Chinese	Vietnamese	Korean	Hmong
Week 1: The Story of the Statue of Liberty					
crown	corona	冠	vương miện	왕관	nkauj mom
liberty	libertad	自由	tự do	자유	ywj pheej, ywj siab
models	maquetas	模擬	mô hình kiểu	본보기	yam khoom me me sawv cev ntawm yam khoom loj
symbol	símbolo	象徵	biểu tượng	상징	duab cim
tablet	lápida	片劑	bài vị	평판	ntawv
torch	antorcha	火炬	ngọn đuốc	횃불	ib zes ntaws
unforgettable	inolvidable	令人難忘	không thể quên	잊을 수 없는	tsis hnov qab li
unveiled	descubrió	揭幕	tháo bỏ vải che để làm lễ khánh thành	베일을 벗기다	tsis qhia ntawm
Week 2: Happy Birthday Mr. Kang					
bows	inclina	鞠躬	cúi chào	절하다	tais
chilly	frío	番椒	se lạnh	으슬으슬한	txhais
foolish	tonto	愚蠢	rồ dại	어리석은	ua ruam ntsuav
foreign	extranjero	外國	ngoại quốc	외국의	txawv teb chaws
narrow	estrechas	窄	hẹp	폭이 좁은	nqaim
perches	se posa	鱸	đậu trên cành	앉다, 자리잡다	tus pas uas noog zaum sov
recipe	receta	食譜	công thức nấu một món ăn	방법, 수단	lus qhia
Week 3: Talking Walls: Art for the People					
encourages	anima	鼓勵	khuyến khích	용기를 북돋워 주다	cuab zog
expression	expresión	表示	sự diễn đạt	표현	hais qhia ntawm

English	Spanish	Chinese	Vietnamese	Korean	Hmong
local	locales	當地	địa phương	지역의	hauv zos
native	natales	本土	bản xứ	태어난 땅의, 타고난	cov ib txwm nyob thaum ub los
settled	se asentaron	安定	đã định cư	정착하다	sov
social	sociales	社會	về xã hội	사회의	nyob ua ib zog
support	apoyar	支持	ủng hộ	(떠)받치다	sib pab
Week 4: Two Bad Ants					
crystal	cristal	水晶	tinh thể	수정	pob zem dawb
disappeared	desapareció	消失	biến mất	사라지다	nploj lawm
discovery	descubrimiento	發現	sự khám phá	발견	nrhiav tau
goal	meta	目標	mục tiêu	목표	hom phiaj
journey	viaje	旅行	cuộc hành trình	여행	txoj kev, lub neej
joyful	alegres	快樂	vui vẻ	즐거운	zoo siab
scoop	cucharilla	匙	múc	퍼내다	diav
unaware	no se dieron cuenta	不知道	không hay biết	모르는	tsis nco ceev faj
Week 5: Atlantis					
aqueducts	acueductos	渡槽	cống dẫn nước	물길, 수도	kwj dej
content	contento	满足	mãn nguyện	만족한, 행복한	txaus siab
crouched	agachado	蹲	co mình lại	쭈그렸다	khoov
guidance	guía	指导	sự hướng dẫn	안내, 지도	cob qhia kev
honor	honor	荣誉	vinh dự	명예	hwm
pillar	columna	柱子	cột nhà	기둥	ncej txheem
thermal	termal	热的	nhiệt	열의, 열에 의한	ceev cua sov

Multilingual Thinking Words

English	Spanish	Chinese	Vietnamese	Korean	Hmong
Analyze	Analizar	分析	Phân tích	분석하다	Xam pom
Apply	Aplicar	应用	Áp dụng	응용하다	Tso rau
Assess	Calcular	估值	Lượng định	평가하다, 감정하다	Ntsuam xyuas
Categorize	Categorizar	分类	Phân loại	분류하다	Teev uake tej pawg
Clarify Information	Clarificar la información	阐明信息	Nói rõ thông tin	정보를 분명히 하다	Ntaub ntawv meej zog ntxiv
Classify	Clasificar	分类	Xếp loại	분류하다	Xaiv uake tej pawg
Combine Information	Combinar la información	拼合信息	Kết hợp thông tin	정보를 합치다	Ntaub ntawv sis dhos
Compare	Comparar	比较	So sánh	비교하다	Sis piv
Conclude	Concluir	归纳	Kết luận	마무리짓다	Xaus
Connect	Conectar	联系	Kết nối	연결하다	Txuas
Construct	Construir	建构	Xây dựng	건축하다, 구성하다	Ua txuas
Contrast	Contrastar	对比	Đối chiếu	대조하다	Tsi sib thooj
Define	Definir	限定	Định nghĩa	정의하다	Txhais
Demonstrate	Demostrar	示范	Chứng minh	증명하다	Nthauv tawm
Describe	Describir	描述	Mô tả	묘사하다	Piav
Determine Importance	Determinar la importancia	判断重要性	Thẩm định tầm quan trọng	중요성을 결정하다	Xam tseem ceeb
Determine Main Idea	Determinar la idea principal	判断要旨	Thẩm định Ý Chính	주제를 정하다	Xam ntsiab lus
Diagram	Diagrama	图表	Lập biểu đồ	그림, 도표	Kos duab
Differentiate	Diferenciar	辨别	Phân biệt	구별하다	Qhia qhov txawv
Elaborate	Abundar	阐述	Tạo lập	상세히 말하다	Piav meej zog
Evaluate	Evaluar	评估	Lượng giá	평가하다	Soj ntsuam
Examine	Examinar	核查	Khảo sát	조사하다	Tshuaj xyuas

English	Spanish	Chinese	Vietnamese	Korean	Hmong
Explain	Explicar	辩解	Giải thích	설명하다	Piav
Generalize	Generalizar	概括	Tổng quát hóa	일반화하다	Hais dav dav
Identify Characteristics	Identificar características	辨认特征	Nhận diện các Đặc tính	특징을 밝히다	Qhia yam ntxwv
Identify Pattern	Identificar patrones	辨认规律	Nhận diện Khuôn mẫu	형태를 밝히다	Qhia tus qauv
Identify Relationships	Identificar relaciones	辨认关系	Nhận diện Tương quan	관계를 밝히다	Qhia kev txheeb ze
Illustrate	Ilustrar	说明	Minh họa	설명하다	Taw qhia
Infer	Inferir	推论	Luận ra	추론하다	Txhais
Judge	Juzgar	判定	Xét thấy	판단하다	Txiav txim
Label	Etiquetar	命名	Dán nhãn	(-라는) 딱지를 붙이다	Lo ntawv
List	Hacer una lista	列表	Liệt kê	열거하다	Teev
Match	Igualar	相配	Tương xứng	-에 어울리다, 필적하다, 대등하다	Sib phim
Observe	Observar	观察	Quan sát	관찰하다	Saib
Organize	Organizar	组织	Tổ chức	정리, 조직구성하다	Sis sau
Outline	Esbozar	概述	Phác thảo	윤곽을 그리다	Teev cov ntsiab
Predict	Predecir	预计	Đoán trước	예측하다	Kwv yees
Recall	Recordar	回想	Nhớ lại	기억하다	Xam txog
Record	Grabar	纪录	Ghi lại	기록, 녹음하다	Teev tseg
Restructure	Reestructurar	重构	Tái cấu trúc	재구성, 구조조정하다	Teeb dua
Sequence	Secuenciar	次序	Xếp thứ tự	순서대로 나열하다	Teev cov ntsiab sis dhos
Show	Mostrar	展示	Chỉra	보여주다	Qhia
Solve a Problem	Resolver un problema	解决一个问题	Giải quyết	문제를 풀다, 해결하다	Kho teeb meem
Summarize	Resumir	概括	Tóm tắt	요점정리하다	Piav zuaj zog uake
Verify	Verificar	查证	Kiểm lại	확인하다, 입증하다	Kuaj kos meej

Part 7
High-Frequency Words, Linguistic Contrastive Analysis, ELL Teaching Routines, and Graphic Organizers

Contents

High-Frequency Words

The high-frequency words section includes activities and word cards that allow students to use these words in speaking and writing to build their competency and fluency.

Linguistic Contrastive Analysis

Use these pages to find out more about challenges in pronunciation and grammar that your English language learners may face as they produce spoken English. The linguistic contrastive analysis chart equates sounds in English with sounds in Spanish, Vietnamese, Cantonese, Hmong, Filipino, Korean, and Mandarin.

English Language Learner Teaching Routines

These routines support systematic and scaffolded instruction in using core lesson materials.

Graphic Organizers

Graphic organizers provide visual support important to English language learners' comprehension.

High-Frequency Words

The high-frequency words are words that appear most often in written English, words of the greatest general service to English language learners. Many of the words are part of word families that are useful for students to know as they learn English.

Each week, provide the list of high-frequency words for students' reference for speaking and writing. Choose strategies from this bank of activities to ensure students' mastery.

Cloze Activity

Create a passage that includes high-frequency words. Display the passage covering high-frequency words with sticky notes. Ask students to read the passage with you, substituting the missing words. Have them explain how they figured out which words to use.

Play Bingo

After students have learned at least 25 words, provide a 5 x 5 grid with a high-frequency word written in each square. Read aloud high-frequency words as you draw them randomly. Students cover words they hear with markers to create a row. When a student has created a row, have him or her read the words aloud.

Semantic Map

For words with richer meanings, create semantic maps. Place the word in the middle of a web and ask students to supply related words for the "arms." Discuss word relationships.

High-Frequency Scavenger Hunt

Have students keep the word lists on their desks for the week. Ask them to tally how many times they see each word in their reading selections, science or social studies books, magazine articles, and so on. They can tally how often they say the word.

Realia and Visuals

Use both hands-on experiences and visuals to reinforce meanings of the words.

- Provide realia that evokes meanings of high-frequency words. For *year,* for example, you might show a calendar. For *see,* you might show a pair of eyeglasses. Discuss the items, using the high-frequency words.
- Use visuals to teach abstract high-frequency words. For *of,* for example, you could show pictures: a basket of laundry, a slice of bread, a glass of water.

Word Sorts

Have students sort the words. Provide index cards with words, one word per card. Students can sort them into categories you provide (*words that show action, words that name things, words in the same family,* and so on) or sort them and explain the rationale behind their categories.

Flashcard Activities

- Post high-frequency words on a word wall as you introduce them. From time to time, hand students flashcards with the words on them, one word per card. Students match the card to the word on the wall and then use the word in a sentence.
- Hand out flashcards, one word to each pair of students. Students work together to create two sentences using the word.
- Make up simple sentences using the high-frequency words. Write the sentences on cards, one word per card. Hand the cards out to students. Have them unscramble the words to make a sentence and read it aloud chorally.
- Pair students and give one student in each pair a card. The student with the card gives clues about the word for the other student to guess.

Unit 1 Week 1	Unit 1 Week 2	Unit 1 Week 3
1 the	11 that	21 by
2 be	12 for	22 this
3 of	13 they	23 we
4 and	14 I	24 you
5 a	15 with	25 do
6 to	16 as	26 but
7 in	17 not	27 from
8 he	18 on	28 or
9 have	19 she	29 which
10 it	20 at	30 one

Unit 1 Week 4	Unit 1 Week 5	Unit 2 Week 1
31 would	41 if	51 about
32 all	42 no	52 than
33 will	43 man	53 into
34 there	44 out	54 could
35 say	45 other	55 state
36 who	46 so	56 only
37 make	47 what	57 new
38 when	48 time	58 year
39 can	49 up	59 some
40 more	50 go	60 take

Unit 2 Week 2	Unit 2 Week 3	Unit 2 Week 4
61 come	71 work	81 day
62 these	72 now	82 also
63 know	73 may	83 after
64 see	74 such	84 way
65 use	75 give	85 many
66 get	76 over	86 must
67 like	77 think	87 look
68 then	78 most	88 before
69 first	79 even	89 great
70 any	80 find	90 back

Unit 2 Week 5	Unit 3 Week 1	Unit 3 Week 2
91 through	101 because	111 little
92 long	102 good	112 world
93 where	103 each	113 very
94 much	104 those	114 still
95 should	105 feel	115 nation
96 well	106 seem	116 hand
97 people	107 how	117 old
98 down	108 high	118 life
99 own	109 too	119 tell
100 just	110 place	120 write

Unit 3 Week 3	Unit 3 Week 4	Unit 3 Week 5
121 become	131 under	141 begin
122 here	132 last	142 while
123 show	133 right	143 number
124 house	134 move	144 part
125 both	135 thing	145 turn
126 between	136 general	146 real
127 need	137 school	147 leave
128 mean	138 never	148 might
129 call	139 same	149 want
130 develop	140 another	150 point

Unit 4 Week 1	Unit 4 Week 2	Unit 4 Week 3
151 form	161 interest	171 again
152 off	162 large	172 hold
153 child	163 person	173 govern
154 few	164 end	174 around
155 small	165 open	175 possible
156 since	166 public	176 head
157 against	167 follow	177 consider
158 ask	168 during	178 word
159 late	169 present	179 program
160 home	170 without	180 problem

Unit 4 Week 4	Unit 4 Week 5	Unit 5 Week 1
181 however	191 fact	201 city
182 lead	192 group	202 put
183 system	193 play	203 close
184 set	194 stand	204 case
185 order	195 increase	205 force
186 eye	196 early	206 meet
187 plan	197 course	207 once
188 run	198 change	208 water
189 keep	199 help	209 upon
190 face	200 line	210 war

Unit 5 Week 2	Unit 5 Week 3	Unit 5 Week 4
211 build	221 side	231 study
212 hear	222 try	232 woman
213 light	223 provide	233 member
214 unite	224 continue	234 until
215 live	225 name	235 far
216 every	226 certain	236 night
217 country	227 power	237 always
218 bring	228 pay	238 service
219 center	229 result	239 away
220 let	230 question	240 report

Unit 5 Week 5	Unit 6 Week 1	Unit 6 Week 2
241 something	251 though	261 better
242 company	252 young	262 big
243 week	253 less	263 boy
244 church	254 enough	264 cost
245 toward	255 almost	265 business
246 start	256 read	266 value
247 social	257 include	267 second
248 room	258 president	268 why
249 figure	259 nothing	269 clear
250 nature	260 yet	270 expect

Unit 6 Week 3	Unit 6 Week 4	Unit 6 Week 5
271 family	281 car	291 per
272 complete	282 law	292 often
273 act	283 industry	293 kind
274 sense	284 important	294 among
275 mind	285 girl	295 white
276 experience	286 food	296 reason
277 art	287 several	297 action
278 next	288 matter	298 return
279 near	289 usual	299 foot
280 direct	290 rather	300 care

Introduction to Linguistics

How People Speak

All languages have consonant and vowel sounds. Consonants are made with some obstruction of the vocal tract, either a complete stoppage of air or enough constriction to create friction. Vowels are produced with a more open vocal tract; there is no constriction that might cause friction.

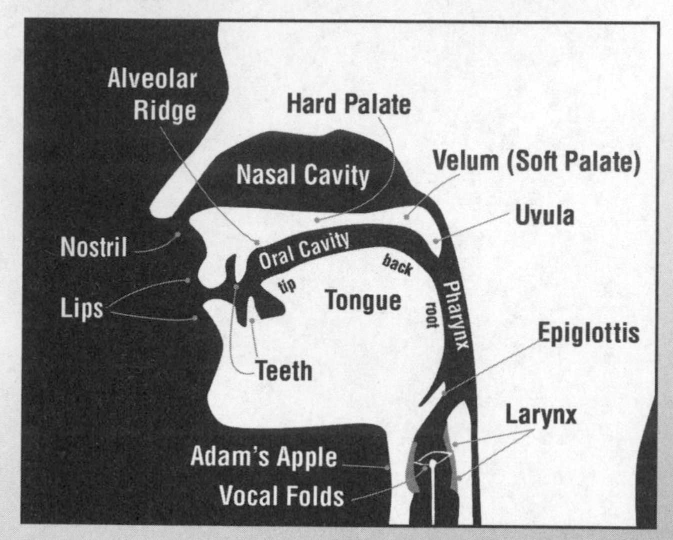

Figure 1: The human vocal tract makes the sounds of speech.

Consonants

Every consonant can be described by noting three characteristics: voicing, place of articulation, and manner of articulation.

Voicing

Many sounds of language, including all vowels, employ vibration of the vocal folds in the larynx. This creates more resonance and energy for the sound. All speech sounds are characterized as either voiced (with vocal fold vibration) or voiceless (with no vocal fold vibration). Feeling the vibration around the Adam's apple can help you understand this difference. If you say "sssss" and then "zzzzz," you can feel the distinction: /s/ is voiceless and /z/ is voiced.

Place of Articulation

This is the location in the vocal tract where the air stream may be constricted. The /s/ sound, for example, is made with the tongue tip close to the alveolar ridge (see Figure 1).

Place of Articulation Terms

Alveolar: tongue tip and ridge behind teeth

Bilabial: using both lips

Glottal: produced at the larynx

Interdental: tongue tip between upper and lower teeth

Labio-dental: upper teeth and lower lip

Labio-velar: rounding of lips; tongue body raised toward velum

Palatal: body of tongue and high part of palate

Palato-alveolar: tongue tip and palate behind alveolar ridge

Velar: body of tongue and velum (soft palate)

Manner of Articulation

This is the type or degree of constriction that occurs in an articulation. For example, the /t/ sound completely stops the airflow with the tongue tip at the alveolar ridge, but /s/ allows air to pass noisily through a small opening.

Manner of Articulation Terms

Affricate: complete constriction followed by slow separation of the articulators resulting in friction

Approximant: close constriction, but not enough for friction

Fricative: narrow constriction; turbulent airflow causing friction

Glottal: produced at the larynx

Lateral: air passes over sides of tongue

Nasal: lowered velum to let air escape through the nose

Stop: complete constriction, closure so that air cannot escape through the oral cavity

Tap: brief contact between tongue tip and alveolar ridge

Vowels

Vowels are open, sonorous sounds. Each vowel can be uniquely described by noting the position of the tongue, the tension of the vocal tract, and the position of the lips. Vowels are described by ***height,*** where the tongue is relative to the roof of the mouth. They can be high, mid, or low. Tongue backness tells if the tongue articulation is in the front or back of the mouth.

Tense vowels are more common around the world. In English, they are longer and include an expansion of the throat at the pharynx. Lax vowels are shorter with a more neutral pharynx. An example is the tense long *e* as in *meet*

Speaking English

versus the lax short *i* as in *mitt.* The lips either can be in a spread or neutral position, or they can be rounded and protrude slightly.

English is the third most widely spoken native language in the world, after Mandarin and Spanish. There are about 330 million native speakers of English and 600 million who speak it as a foreign language.

English Consonant Sounds

The following chart gives the International Phonetic Alphabet (IPA) symbol for each English consonant along with its voicing, place, and manner of articulation. This information can be used to understand and help identify problems that non-native speakers may encounter when learning to speak English.

CONSONANTS OF ENGLISH		
IPA	Articulation	Example
p	voiceless bilabial stop	**p**it
b	voiced bilabial stop	**b**it
m	voiced bilabial nasal stop	**m**an
w	voiced labio-velar approximant	**w**in
f	voiceless labio-dental fricative	**f**un
v	voiced labio-dental fricative	**v**ery
θ	voiceless interdental fricative	**th**ing
ð	voiced interdental fricative	**th**ere
t	voiceless alveolar stop	**t**ime
d	voiced alveolar stop	**d**ime
n	voiced alveolar nasal stop	**n**ame
s	voiceless alveolar fricative	**s**oy
z	voiced alveolar fricative	**z**eal
ɾ	voiced alveolar tap	bu**tt**er
l	voiced alveolar central approximant	**l**oop
ɹ	voiced palato-alveolar affricate	**r**ed
ʃ	voiceless palato-alveolar fricative	**sh**allow
ʒ	voiced palato-alveolar affricate	vi**s**ion
ʧ	voiceless palato-alveolar affricate	**ch**irp
ʤ	voiced palato-alveolar affricate	**j**oy
j	voiced palatal approximant	**y**ou
k	voiceless velar stop	**k**ite
g	voiced velar stop	**g**oat
ŋ	voiced velar nasal stop	ki**ng**
h	voiceless glottal fricative	**h**ope

English Vowel Sounds

Most languages in the world have around five vowel sounds. English has 13 common vowel sounds, which means that many students of English must learn more vowel distinctions than there are in their native language. The lax vowels are most difficult. Some vowels are diphthongs, meaning the tongue is in one position at the beginning of the sound, and it moves to another position by the end of it.

VOWELS OF ENGLISH		
IPA	Sound	Example
i	ē	b**ea**t
ɪ	ĭ	b**i**t
e	ā	b**ai**t
ɛ	ĕ	b**e**t
æ	ă	b**a**t
u	o͞o	b**oo**t
ʊ	o͝o	c**ou**ld
o	ō	b**oa**t
ɔ	aw	l**aw**
ɑ	ŏ	h**o**t
ə	ə	**a**bout
ʌ	ŭ	c**u**t
ɝ	er	b**ir**d
ɑʊ	ow	h**ou**se
ɔɪ	oy	b**oy**
ɑɪ	ī	bite

Figure 2 is a schematic of the mouth. The left is the front of the mouth; the right is the back. The top is the roof of the mouth and the bottom is the floor. Placement of the vowel shows where the tongue reaches its maximum in the English articulation.

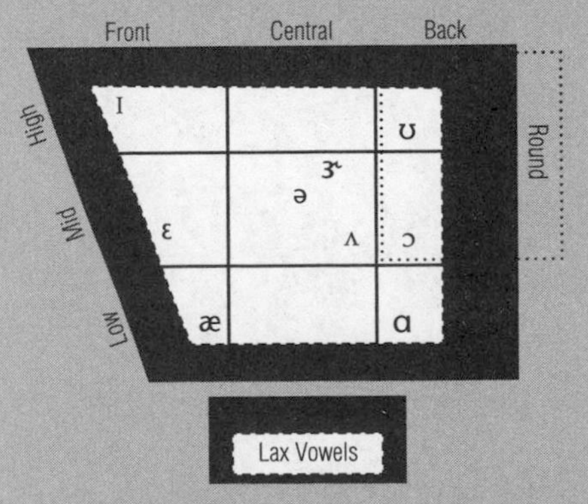

Figure 2: English vowel sounds

Transference

Pronunciation

All languages build on the same fundamentals. All languages contrast voiced and voiceless sound and have stops and fricatives. Many languages use the same places of articulation for consonants as well. The majority of sounds will easily transfer from another language to English.

However, there will always be some sounds that are not found in a person's native language that can pose a challenge to the English language learner. English has a few relatively rare sounds, such as the interdental sounds spelled with *th,* /θ/ and /ð/. The /r/ sound in English is also a very rare type of sound. Most other languages use a tap or trill articulation for an /r/ sound.

In some languages, the /l/ and /r/ sounds belong to one psychological category. This means that they count as the same sound in that language. In this case, it is not the articulation that is difficult, but the perception of the difference and consistent use of one versus the other in any word context. This type of psychological category is called a *phoneme,* and multiple speech sounds all can be categorized as the same phoneme in that language.

This is true for English as well, where, for example, the alveolar lateral /l/ as in *lob* and the velarized lateral /ɫ/ as in *ball* are both counted as the same sound—an *l*—to native speakers of English. It is important to keep in mind that both the phonetic articulation of a sound and its psychological, phonemic category factor into the learning of a new language.

Grammar

Pronouncing English is not the only stumbling block for English learners. The grammar and usage, or syntax, of English may present distinctions that are unique to the language. For example, English syntax requires adjectives to precede the nouns they modify, as in *the tall girl.* In other languages, such as Spanish, Hmong, and Vietnamese, adjectives follow nouns, as in *la chica alta* (literally *the girl tall* in Spanish). This may cause word-order problems, particularly for less advanced English learners.

Other syntactic differences are less obvious and may cause problems even for advanced learners. For example, many East Asian languages (such as Mandarin, Cantonese, and Korean) do not mark agreement between subject and verb. Speakers of these languages may therefore leave out agreement markers, such as the *-s* in *The girl like cats.*

The use of articles varies across languages. For instance, Spanish uses the definite article more often than English, while Mandarin and Cantonese do not have articles. A Spanish-speaking English learner might say *The girl likes the cats* instead of *The girl likes cats,* and a Mandarin or Cantonese speaker might say *Girl like cat.*

Plural marking is another potential trouble spot: Vietnamese, Filipino, Cantonese, and Mandarin do not add plural markers to nouns. Learners speaking these languages may have difficulty with English plurals, saying *cat* instead of *cats.*

Grammar Hot Spots

Look for Grammar Hot Spots on the following pages for tips on the most common syntax errors by speakers of languages other than English.

Common First Languages

In the Common First Languages section, you will find details of some common non-English languages spoken in the United States. They are:

- Spanish
- Vietnamese
- Cantonese
- Hmong
- Filipino
- Korean
- Mandarin

You can use the fundamentals of speech articulation already covered to help you understand where the languages differ from English. Differences in the spoken language and in the writing systems are explored as well. These sections pinpoint common trouble spots specific to learners of English.

Culture Clues

Look to Culture Clues for insights into the cultural differences of each language learner as well as ideas for ways to embrace students' diversity.

Linguistic Contrastive Analysis

The Linguistic Contrastive Analysis Charts provide a quick reference for comparing English sounds with those of other languages. The charts allow you to check at a glance which sounds have equivalents in other languages. For those sounds that don't have equivalents, you can find the closest sound used as a substitute and suggestions for helping someone gain a native English articulation.

In these charts, the sounds are notated using the International Phonetic Alphabet (IPA). This is the most widely recognized and used standard for representing speech sounds in any language. A guiding principle of the IPA across all languages is that each sound is uniquely represented by one symbol, and each symbol represents only one sound.

The chart has columns for each native language with rows corresponding to each English phoneme. Each cell in the chart gives an example word using that sound in the native language, a definition in parenthesis, and transference tips below. If there is no sound equivalent to English, a common substitution used by speakers of that language may be provided.

Transference Tips

Transference tips give you ideas of how the sound will be produced by the learner. Cells in bold print indicate where the English learner may have particular difficulty with the English sound.

Spanish

Background

Spanish is the second most widely spoken language in the world. There are more than 400 million native Spanish speakers in 20-plus countries on three continents. Spanish vocabulary and pronunciation differ from country to country. While most dialect differences in English are in vowel sounds, Spanish dialects differ in their consonants.

Spoken

Spanish sounds are similar to those found in English, so there is a strong foundation for the native Spanish speaker learning English. However, there are three key differences between English and Spanish consonants:

1. Most of the alveolar sounds in English, such as /t/, /d/, and /n/, are produced farther forward in the mouth in Spanish. Instead of the tongue touching the alveolar ridge as in English, in Spanish it touches the back of the teeth.
2. Another difference is that the /r/ sound in English is not found in Spanish. There are two /r/ sounds in Spanish. One is the tap /ɾ/, which occurs in English as the quick sound in the middle of the name *Betty*. Psychologically, this tap sound is a kind of /t/ or /d/ sound in English, while in Spanish it is perceived as an /r/. The other /r/ sound in Spanish is a trill, or series of tongue taps on the alveolar ridge. This does not occur in English.
3. The third key difference between English and Spanish can be found in the English production of the voiceless stops /p/, /t/, and /k/. In English these sounds are aspirated, with an extra puff of air at the end, when the sound occurs at the beginning of a word or stressed syllable. So, /p/ is aspirated in *pit.* Learners can add a puff of air to such sounds to sound more like native English speakers.

There are five vowels in Spanish, which are a subset of the English vowels. Spanish vowels include tense vowel sounds *a, e, i, o, u.* Lax vowel sounds in English are the problematic ones for native Spanish speakers.

Written

Like English, written Spanish uses the Roman alphabet, so both writing systems are similar. There are a few orthographic differences to note, however:

- The letter *h* in Spanish is silent, but the sound /h/ is written as *j* or *g.*
- A single letter *r* in Spanish represents a tap, while the double *rr* represents a trill.
- Accents are used to show the stress on a syllable when the stress is different from the usual rules. In some cases, words change meaning according to the accents. For example, *el* means *the* while *él* means *he.*

Written Spanish vowels are pronounced like the symbols in the IPA. So, the Spanish *i* is pronounced with the long *e* as in the word *beat.* The IPA and Spanish symbol for this letter is the same: *i.*

Culture Clues

The Spanish language covers many countries, dialects, and cultures. Always encourage students to share special things about their culture, such as foods, festivals, or social customs.

Grammar Hot Spots

- Double negatives are part of standard grammar in Spanish. Stress the single negative construction in English.
- English prepositions are a common stumbling point for Spanish speakers.

Vietnamese

Background

Approximately 80 million people in Vietnam speak Vietnamese. The northern dialect is the standard, though central and southern dialects also exist. Most Vietnamese speakers in the United States are from southern Vietnam and speak the southern dialect.

Spoken

Vietnamese is a tonal language, so each syllable is pronounced with a distinctive tone that affects meaning. Vietnamese has a complex vowel system of 12 vowels and 26 diphthongs. Its consonants are simpler, but Vietnamese syllable structure allows few possibilities for final consonants.

Students may need help noticing and learning to reproduce final consonant sounds in English words and syllables. Vietnamese syllable structure allows for limited combinations of initial consonants. Students also may need help with the more complex initial consonant clusters of English words and syllables.

Culture Clues

In traditional Vietnamese education, there is a strict division between the roles of student and teacher. Students may be confused if asked to direct a part of their own study, so encourage group work.

Written

Since the 1600s, Vietnamese has used a Romanized alphabet. Many characters written in Vietnamese have sounds different from their English counterparts, such as *d, x, ch, nh, kh, g, tr, r,* and *e.*

Grammar Hot Spots

- Like English, Vietnamese uses Subject-Verb-Object (SVO) syntax, or word order.
- Vietnamese does not use affixes; instead, syntax expresses number, case, and tense.

Cantonese

Background

Cantonese is one of the seven major Chinese languages, not all of which are mutually intelligible. Cantonese is mostly spoken in China's southern provinces, Hong Kong, and Macau by about 66 million people. It is a tonal language, and the same sequence of letters can have different meanings depending on their pitch.

Spoken

Cantonese has six stops, aspirated and non-aspirated /p/, /t/, /k/; three fricatives /f/, /s/, /h/, and two affricates /ts/, /ts^h/. Some that do not exist in Cantonese can be difficult for the English language learner. The /v/ often gets pronounced as /f/ or /w/; the /z/ is often said as /s/; the sounds spelled with *th* are often said as /t/, /d/, or /f/. Cantonese speakers have difficulty distinguishing between /l/ and /r/, since /r/ is not present in their language. They tend to produce an /l/-like sound for both English sounds in words such as *ride* and *lied.*

Cantonese has 11 vowels and 10 diphthongs. One of the major problems for Cantonese speakers is distinguishing between English tense and lax vowels because the distribution of Cantonese short and long vowels is determined by the sound context.

Syllables in Cantonese don't have consonant clusters. English consonant clusters are often deleted or broken up by vowel insertion (e.g., *list* becomes *lis*). This may be especially problematic when producing English past tense (e.g., *baked*).

Written

Cantonese is written with standard Chinese characters known as *Hànzi* where each character represents a syllable and has a meaning. Additional Cantonese-specific characters were also added. Cantonese speakers may have difficulty with sound-letter correspondences in English.

Grammar Hot Spots

- English articles and prepositions are difficult for Cantonese speakers. *In, on,* and *at*, for instance, can be translated as the same preposition in Cantonese.
- Plurals, tenses, and gerund endings are difficult for Cantonese speakers to transfer to English.

Hmong

Background
Hmong is a group of approximately 18 languages within the Hmong-Mien family. There are roughly four million speakers of Hmong, including 200,000 in the United States. They are mainly from two groups with mutually intelligible dialects—Hmong Daw and Mong Leng.

Spoken
Hmong vowels are few and simple, but its consonants are complex and differ from those of English. Notable features of Hmong phonology absent from English include consonantal pre-nasalization (the /m/n/ŋ/ sound before a consonant) and the contrast between nasalized and non-nasalized vowels. Hmong is tonal. Each syllable is pronounced with a distinctive pitch.

Culture Clues
In traditional Hmong culture, learning takes place through hands-on experience. Students may find it difficult to adjust to the use of graphics or print media. Competition, personal achievement, and self-directed instruction may be unfamiliar concepts, so students may prefer group work.

Written
The Romanized Popular Alphabet (RPA), developed in the 1950s, is the usual way of transcribing Hmong. Syllable-final consonants are absent in pronunciation but are used to orthographically represent the tonal value of a given syllable. Students may need particular help in identifying and learning to reproduce the final consonant sounds of English words and syllables.

Grammar Hot Spots
- Like English, Hmong is an SVO language. Personal pronouns are marked for number, including inflection for singular, dual, and plural, though they are not marked for case.
- Because Hmong and English prepositions often have different semantic qualities, students may need help mastering uses of English prepositions. For example, it is correct to say "think <u>about</u> [something]" rather than "think <u>on</u> [something]."

Filipino

Background
Filipino and English are the official languages of the Philippines, where 175 languages are spoken. There are about 24 million native speakers of Filipino, and more than 50 million people speak Filipino as a second language. You may hear the terms *Filipino* and *Tagalog* being used interchangeably. Another term is *Pilipino.*

Spoken
Filipino has many similar speech sounds to English. The notable exceptions are the lack of the consonant sounds /f/, /v/, and those spelled with *th.* Of these, the English /f/ and /v/ cause the most difficulty for learners. For /f/, they may substitute /p/. The distinction between long *e* (as in *beat*) and short *i* (as in *bit*) is also a trouble spot. Filipino does not allow consonant clusters at the end of syllables, so *detect* may be simplified to just one final consonant *(detec).*

Culture Clues
Most people from the Philippines can speak Filipino, but for many it is not their first language. Ask Filipino students about other languages they speak. Because English is used alongside Filipino as the language of instruction in the Philippines, most Filipinos are familiar with English.

Written
The Filipino alphabet has 28 letters and is based on the Spanish alphabet, so the English writing system poses little problem.

Grammar Hot Spots
- Filipino word order is Verb-Subject-Object (VSO), which does not transfer well to English.
- Inflectional verb endings, such as *-s, -en, -ed,* and *-ing* do not exist in Filipino, so it is common to leave out the third person singular verb marker (*"He walk,"* not *"He walks"*).

Korean

Background

Korean is spoken by 71 million people in North and South Korea. Standard Korean is based on the speech in and around Seoul.

Spoken

Korean does not have corresponding sounds for English /f/, /v/, /ɵ/, /ð/, and /ʤ/. In word-initial position, all Korean stops are voiceless. Voiced stops /b/, /d/, and /g/ are only produced between two vowels. Korean speakers may have difficulty producing /s/, /ʃ/, and /z/ in some contexts, in addition to English /r/ and /l/ sounds (e.g., *rock* and *lock*). They may have problems in producing English consonant clusters (e.g., *str-*, *sk-*). These problems can often be eliminated by vowel insertion or consonant deletion. In addition, the distinction between English tense and lax vowels (e.g., long *e* as in *beat* vs. /ɪ/ as in *bit*) may be problematic for Korean speakers.

Culture Clues

Korean uses a complex system of honorifics, so it is unusual for Korean students to use the pronoun *you* or call their teachers by their first name.

Written

Modern Korean uses the Korean alphabet *(Hangul)* or a mixed script of *Hangul* and Chinese. *Hangul* is an alphabetic script organized into syllabic blocks.

Grammar Hot Spots

- In contrast to English, Korean word order is Subject-Object-Verb (SOV). The verb always comes at the end of a sentence.
- Korean syllable stress is different, so learners may have difficulties with the rhythm of English.

Mandarin

Background

Mandarin Chinese encompasses a wide range of dialects and is the native language of two-thirds of China. There are approximately 870 million Mandarin speakers worldwide. North Mandarin, as found in Beijing, is the basis of the modern standard language.

Spoken

Mandarin Chinese and English differ substantially in their sound structure. Mandarin lacks voiced obstruent consonants (/b/, /d/, /g/, /ʤ/), causing difficulty for speakers in perceiving and producing English voiced consonants (e.g., *buy* may be pronounced and perceived as *pie*). The sounds spelled with *th* are not present in Mandarin, so they are often substituted with /s/ or /t/ causing, for example, *fourth* to be pronounced as *fours.* Mandarin Chinese has five vowels. Due to the relatively small vowel inventory and contextual effects on vowels in Mandarin, many English vowels and tense/lax distinctions present problems for speakers of Mandarin Chinese. Mandarin allows only a very simple syllable structure, causing problems in producing consonant clusters in English. Speakers may drop consonants or insert vowels between them (e.g., *film* may become /filəm/). The use of tones in Mandarin may result in the rising and falling of pitch when speaking English.

Written

Chinese is written with characters known as *Hànzi.* Each character represents a syllable and also has a meaning. A Romanized alphabet called *Pinyin* marks pronunciation of characters. Chinese speakers may have problems mastering letter-sound correspondences in written English, especially for sounds that are not present in Mandarin.

Grammar Hot Spots

- The non-inflected nature of Chinese causes Mandarin speakers to have problems with plurals, past tense markers, and gerund forms *(-s, -ed, -ing).*
- Mastering English tenses and passive voice is difficult. Students should be familiarized with correct lexical and syntactic features as well as appropriate situations for the use of various tenses and passives.

Linguistic Contrastive Analysis Chart

The Consonants of English

IPA	ENGLISH	SPANISH	VIETNAMESE	CANTONESE
p	*pit* Aspirated at the start of a word or stressed syllable	*pato* (duck) Never aspirated	*pin* (battery)	*pʰa (to lie prone)* Always aspirated
b	*bit*	*barco* (boat) Substitute voiced bilabial fricative/ɞ/ in between vowels	*ba* (three) Implosive (air moves into the mouth during articulation)	**NO EQUIVALENT** **Substitute /p/**
m	*man*	*mundo* (world)	*mot* (one)	*ma* (mother)
w	*win*	*agua* (water)	**NO EQUIVALENT** **Substitute word-initial /u/**	*wa* (frog)
f	*fun*	*flor* (flower)	*phu'o'ng* (phoenix) Substitute sound made with both lips, rather than with the lower lip and the teeth like English /f/	*fa* (flower) Only occurs at the beginning of syllables
v	*very*	**NO EQUIVALENT** Learners can use correct sound	*Việt Nam* (Vietnam)	**NO EQUIVALENT** **Substitute /f/**
ө	*thing* Rare in other languages. When done correctly, the tongue will stick out between the teeth.	**NO EQUIVALENT** Learners can use correct sound	**NO EQUIVALENT** **Substitute /th/ or /f/**	**NO EQUIVALENT** **Substitute /th/ or /f/**
ð	*there* Rare in other languages. When done correctly, the tongue will stick out between the teeth.	*cada* (every) Sound exists in Spanish only between vowels; sometimes substitute voiceless ө.	**NO EQUIVALENT** **Substitute /d/**	**NO EQUIVALENT** **Substitute /t/ or /f/**
t	*time* Aspirated at the start of a word or stressed syllable English tongue-touch. Is a little farther back in the mouth than the other languages.	*tocar* (touch) Never aspirated	*tám* (eight) Distinguishes aspirated and non-aspirated	*tʰa* (he/she) Distinguishes aspirated and non-aspirated
d	*dime* English tongue-touch is a little farther back in the mouth than the other languages.	*dos* (two)	*Đồng* (Dong = unit of currency) Vietnamese /d/ is implosive (air moves into the mouth during articulation)	**NO EQUIVALENT** **Substitute /t/**
n	*name* English tongue-touch is a little farther back in the mouth than the other languages.	*nube* (cloud)	*nam* (south)	*na* (take)
s	*soy*	*seco* (dry)	*xem* (to see)	*sa* (sand) Substitute *sh–* sound before /u/ Difficult at ends of syllables and words
z	*zeal*	**NO EQUIVALENT** Learners can use correct sound	*rồi* (already) In northern dialect only Southern dialect, substitute /y/	**NO EQUIVALENT** **Substitute /s/**
ɾ	*butter* Written 't' and 'd' are pronounced with a quick tongue-tip tap.	*rana* (toad) Written as single *r* and thought of as a /r/ sound.	**NO EQUIVALENT** **Substitute /t/**	**NO EQUIVALENT** **Substitute /t/**
l	*loop* English tongue-touch is a little farther back in the mouth than the other languages. At the ends of syllables, the /l/ bunches up the back of the tongue, becoming velarized /ɫ/ or dark-l as in the word *ball*.	*libro* (book)	*cú lao* (island) /l/ does not occur at the ends of syllables	*lau* (angry) /l/ does not occur at the ends of syllables

HMONG	FILIPINO	KOREAN	MANDARIN
peb (we/us/our) Distinguishes aspirated and non-aspirated	*paalam* (goodbye) Never aspirated	*pal* (sucking)	*p^hei* (cape) Always aspirated
NO EQUIVALENT **Substitute /p/**	*baka* (beef)	**NO EQUIVALENT** **/b/ said between vowels** **Substitute /p/ elsewhere**	**NO EQUIVALENT**
mus (to go)	*mabuti* (good)	*mal* (horse)	*mei* (rose)
NO EQUIVALENT **Substitute word-initial /u/**	*walo* (eight)	*gwe* (box)	*wen* (mosquito)
faib (to divide)	**NO EQUIVALENT** **Substitute /p/**	**NO EQUIVALENT** **Substitute /p/**	*fa* (issue)
Vaj ('Vang' clan name)	**NO EQUIVALENT** **Substitute /b/**	**NO EQUIVALENT** **Substitute /b/**	**NO EQUIVALENT** **Substitute /w/ or /f/**
NO EQUIVALENT **Substitute /th/ or /f/**	**NO EQUIVALENT** Learners can use correct sound, but sometimes mispronounce voiced /ð/.	**NO EQUIVALENT** **Substitute /t/**	**NO EQUIVALENT** **Substitute /t/ or /s/**
NO EQUIVALENT **Substitute /d/**	**NO EQUIVALENT** Learners can use correct sound	**NO EQUIVALENT** **Substitute /d/**	**NO EQUIVALENT** **Substitute /t/ or /s/**
them (to pay) Distinguishes aspirated and non-aspirated	*takbo* (run) Never aspirated	*tal* (daughter)	*ta* (wet) Distinguishes aspirated and non-aspirated
dev (dog)	*deretso* (straight)	**NO EQUIVALENT** **Substitute /d/ when said between vowels and /t/ elsewhere.**	**NO EQUIVALENT** **Substitute /t/**
noj (to eat)	*naman* (too)	*nal* (day)	*ni* (you) May be confused with /l/
xa (to send)	*sila* (they)	*sal* (rice) Substitute *shi*– sound before /i/ and /z/ after a nasal consonant	*san* (three)
NO EQUIVALENT Learners can use correct sound	**NO EQUIVALENT** Learners can use correct sound	**NO EQUIVALENT** Learners can use correct sound	**NO EQUIVALENT** **Substitute /ts/ or /ts^h/**
NO EQUIVALENT **Substitute /t/**	*rin/din* (too) Variant of the /d/ sound	Only occurs between two vowels Considered a /l/ sound	**NO EQUIVALENT**
los (to come) /l/ does not occur at the ends of syllables	*salamat* (thank you)	*balam* (wind)	*lan* (blue) Can be confused and substituted with /r/

The Consonants of English (continued)

IPA	ENGLISH	SPANISH	VIETNAMESE	CANTONESE
ɹ	*red* Rare sound in the world Includes lip-rounding	**NO EQUIVALENT** **Substitute /r/ sound such as the tap /ɾ/ or the trilled /r/**	**NO EQUIVALENT** **Substitute /l/**	**NO EQUIVALENT** **Substitute /l/**
ʃ	*shallow* Often said with lip-rounding	**NO EQUIVALENT** **Substitute /s/ or /ʧ/**	*sieu thị* (supermarket) southern dialect only	**NO EQUIVALENT** **Substitute /s/**
ʒ	*vision* Rare sound in English	**NO EQUIVALENT** **Substitute /z/ or /ʤ/**	**NO EQUIVALENT** **Substitute /s/**	**NO EQUIVALENT** **Substitute /ts/**
ʧ	*chirp*	*chico* (boy)	*chính phủ* (government) Pronounced harder than English *ch*	**NO EQUIVALENT** **Substitute /ts/**
ʤ	*joy*	**NO EQUIVALENT** **Sometimes substituted with /ʃ/ sound** **Some dialects have this sound for the ll spelling as in llamar**	**NO EQUIVALENT** **Substitute /ch/, the equivalent sound, but voiceless**	**NO EQUIVALENT** **Substitute /ts/** **Only occurs at beginnings of syllables**
j	*you*	*cielo* (sky) Often substitute /ʤ/	*yeu* (to love)	*jau* (worry)
k	*kite* Aspirated at the start of a word or stressed syllable	*casa* (house) Never aspirated	*com* (rice) Never aspirated	*kʰa* (family) Distinguishes aspirated and non-aspirated
g	*goat*	*gato* (cat)	**NO EQUIVALENT** **Substitute /k/**	**NO EQUIVALENT** **Substitute /k/**
ŋ	*king*	*mango* (mango)	*Ngũyen* (proper last name)	*phaŋ* (to cook)
h	*hope*	*gente* (people) Sometimes substitute sound with friction higher in the vocal tract as velar /x/ or uvular /χ/	*hoa* (flower)	*ha* (shrimp)

HMONG	FILIPINO	KOREAN	MANDARIN
NO EQUIVALENT **Substitute /l/**	**NO EQUIVALENT** **Substitute the tap /ɾ/**	**NO EQUIVALENT** **Substitute the tap or /ɾ/ confused with /l/**	*ran* (caterpillar) Tongue tip curled farther backward than for English /r/
sau (to write)	*siya* (s/he)	Only occurs before /i/; Considered a /s/ sound	*shi* (wet)
zos (village)	**NO EQUIVALENT** Learners can use correct sound	**NO EQUIVALENT**	**NO EQUIVALENT** **Substitute palatal affricate /tɸ/**
cheb (to sweep)	*tsa* (tea)	*cʰal* (kicking)	*cheng* (red)
NO EQUIVALENT **Substitute *ch* sound**	*Dios* (God)	**NO EQUIVALENT** **Substitute *ch* sound**	**NO EQUIVALENT** **Substitute /ts/**
Yaj (Yang, clan name)	*tayo* (we)	*je:zan* (budget)	*yan* (eye)
Koo (Kong, clan name) Distinguishes aspirated and non-aspirated	*kalian* (when) Never aspirated	*kal* (spreading)	*ke* (nest) Distinguishes aspirated and non-aspirated
NO EQUIVALENT **Substitute /k/**	*gulay* (vegetable)	**NO EQUIVALENT** **Substitute /k/** **Learners use correct sound between two vowels**	**NO EQUIVALENT** **Substitute /k/**
gus (goose)	*angaw* (one million)	*baŋ* (room)	*tang* (gong) Sometimes add /k/ sound to the end
hais (to speak)	*hindi* (no)	*hal* (doing)	**NO EQUIVALENT** **Substitute velar fricative /x/**

Linguistic Contrastive Analysis Chart

The Vowels of English

IPA	ENGLISH	SPANISH	VIETNAMESE	CANTONESE
i	*beat*	*hijo* (son)	*di* (to go)	*si* (silk)
ɪ	*bit* Rare in other languages Usually confused with /i/ (*meat* vs. *mitt*)	**NO EQUIVALENT** **Substitute /ē/**	**NO EQUIVALENT** **Substitute /ē/**	*sik* (color) Only occurs before velars Substitute /ē/
e	*bait* End of vowel diphthongized—tongue moves up to /ē/ or short *e* postions	*eco* (echo)	*kê* (millet)	*se* (to lend)
ɛ	*bet* Rare in other languages. Learners may have difficulty distinguishing /ā/ and /e/ (short e): *pain* vs. *pen*	**NO EQUIVALENT** **Substitute /ā/**	**NO EQUIVALENT** **Substitute /ā/**	*seŋ* (sound) Only occurs before velars; difficult to distinguish from /ā/ in all positions
æ	*bat* Rare in other languages Learners may have trouble getting the tongue farther forward in the mouth	**NO EQUIVALENT** **Substitute mid central /u/ (short u) or low front tense /o/ (short o)**	*ghe* (boat)	**NO EQUIVALENT** **Hard to distinguish between long *a* and /æ/**
u	*boot*	*uva* (grape)	*mua* (to buy)	*fu* (husband)
ʊ	*could* Rare in other languages. Learners may have difficulty distinguishing the vowel sounds in *wooed* vs. *wood*	**NO EQUIVALENT** **Substitute long *u***	**NO EQUIVALENT** **Substitute long *u* (high back unrounded)**	*suk* (uncle) Only occurs before velars Difficult to distinguish from long *u* in all positions
o	*boat* End of vowel diphthongized – tongue moves up to long *u* or ʊ position	*ojo* (eye)	*cô* (aunt)	*so* (comb)
ɔ	*law*	**NO EQUIVALENT** Substitute long *o* or short *o* Substituting long *o* will cause confusion (*low* vs. *law*); substituting short *o* will not	*cá* (fish)	*hok* (shell) Only occurs before velars Difficult to distinguish from long *o* in all positions
ɑ	*hot*	*mal* (bad)	*con* (child)	*sa* (sand)
ɑ ʊ	*house* Diphthong	*pauta*	*dao* (knife)	*sau* (basket)
ɔ ɪ	*boy* Diphthong	*hoy* (today)	*rồi* (already)	*soi* (grill)
ɑ ɪ	*bite* Diphthong	*baile* (dance)	*hai* (two)	*sai* (to waste)
ə	*about* Most common vowel in English; only in unstressed syllables. Learners may have difficulty keeping it very short	**NO EQUIVALENT** **Substitute short *u* or the full vowel from the word's spelling**	*mua* (to buy)	**NO EQUIVALENT**
ʌ	*cut* Similar to schwa /ə/	**NO EQUIVALENT** **Substitute short *o***	*giờ'* (time)	*san* (new)
ɝ	*bird* Difficult articulation, unusual in the world but common in American English Learners must bunch the tongue and constrict the throat	**NO EQUIVALENT** **Substitute short *u* or /er/ with trill**	**NO EQUIVALENT** **Substitute /ɨ/**	*hæ* (boot)

HMONG	FILIPINO	KOREAN	MANDARIN
ib (one)	*ikaw (you)* This vowel is interchangeable with /ɪ/; hard for speakers to distinguish these	zɪ:ʃaŋ (market)	*ti* (ladder) Sometimes English /i/ can be produced shorter
NO EQUIVALENT **Substitute long *e***	*limampu* (fifty) This vowel is interchangeable with /i/; hard for speakers to distinguish these	**NO EQUIVALENT** **Substitute long *e***	**NO EQUIVALENT**
tes (hand)	*sero* (zero)	*be:da* (to cut)	*te* (nervous) Sometimes substitute English schwa /ə/
NO EQUIVALENT **Substitute long *a***	*sero* (zero) This vowel interchanges with /ā/ like *bait;* not difficult for speakers to learn	*thɛ:do* (attitude)	**NO EQUIVALENT**
NO EQUIVALENT **Substitute short *e***	**NO EQUIVALENT** **Substitute short *o* as in *hot***	**NO EQUIVALENT**	**NO EQUIVALENT** **Substitute /ə/ or short *u***
kub (hot or gold)	*tunay* (actual) This vowel interchanges with vowel in *could;* not difficult for speakers to learn	*zu:bag* (watermelon)	*lu* (hut) Sometimes English long *u* can be produced shorter
NO EQUIVALENT **Substitute a sound like long *e* (mid central with lips slightly rounded)**	*gumawa* (act) This vowel interchanges with long *u* like *boot;* not difficult for speakers to learn	**NO EQUIVALENT**	**NO EQUIVALENT**
NO EQUIVALENT	*ubo* (cough)	*bo:zu* (salary)	*mo* (sword) This vowel is a little lower than English vowel
Yaj (Yang, clan name)	**NO EQUIVALENT** ***Spoken as short o, as in hot***	**NO EQUIVALENT**	**NO EQUIVALENT** **Substitute long *o***
mov (cooked rice)	*talim* (blade)	*ma:l* (speech)	*ta* (he/she) Sometimes substitute back long *o* or *u*
plaub (four)	*ikaw* (you)	**NO EQUIVALENT**	**NO EQUIVALENT**
NO EQUIVALENT	*apoy* (fire)	**NO EQUIVALENT**	**NO EQUIVALENT**
qaib (chicken)	*himatay* (faint)	**NO EQUIVALENT**	**NO EQUIVALENT**
NO EQUIVALENT	**NO EQUIVALENT** ***Spoken as short o, as in hot***	**NO EQUIVALENT** **Difficult sound for learners**	**NO EQUIVALENT**
NO EQUIVALENT	**NO EQUIVALENT** ***Spoken as short o as in hot***	**NO EQUIVALENT**	**NO EQUIVALENT**
NO EQUIVALENT **Substitute diphthong /əɨ/**	**NO EQUIVALENT** **Spoken as many different vowels (depending on English spelling) plus tongue tap /ɾ/**	**NO EQUIVALENT**	**NO EQUIVALENT**

ROUTINE 1 • ELL VOCABULARY ROUTINE

1. **Introduce the Word** Point to the word and say it slowly. Supply a student-friendly definition and relate the word to students' prior knowledge and experience. When possible, also relate the word to the weekly concept. Have students say the word.

   Example: A place is an area. Your home is a place. Your school is a place. Today we will learn about other places. Say place.

2. **Demonstrate** Provide examples to show meaning. When possible, use gestures, pictures, realia, or other visuals to help convey the meaning.

   Example: Look at the picture. This is a park. A park is a place. This is a building. A building is a place too.

3. **Apply** Have students demonstrate understanding of the word. Include opportunities for both verbal and nonverbal responses, such as using the word in a sentence, drawing, or physical gestures to show understanding.

   Example: Draw a place you know. What is this place, a house or a park?

4. **Display the Word** Display the word in the classroom. Use a word wall or a graphic organizer to show meaning.

   Example: Write the word *place* at the top of a chart. Have students write or draw examples below. When possible, have students include examples from the weekly concept.

ROUTINE 2 • WHOLE-WORD BLENDING

1. **Introduce Whole-Word Blending** Write the word. When possible, use visuals or gestures to help convey the meaning.

2. **Connect Sounds to Spelling**

   MODEL Point to each spelling and say its sound. Remind students to watch how you move your mouth and emphasize any letter combinations.

   Example: Show how the letters *s* and *h* make one sound, /sh/. Say /f/ /i/ /sh/ as you touch under *f*, *i*, and *sh*.

   GUIDE PRACTICE Have students say the sounds as you touch under the letter(s). *When I touch under the letter(s), you say the sound.*

   CORRECTIVE FEEDBACK If students say an incorrect sound, refer them to the appropriate Sound-Spelling Card. Provide examples of other words with this sound spelling and have them pronounce the words. Point out any sounds that may be different or new to students' native languages.

3. **Blend Sounds**

   MODEL Blend the word by saying the sound for each spelling, with no pause between sounds, as you move your hand in a continuous motion from one letter to the next. Stretch continuous sounds.

   Example: Blend /f/ /i/ /sh/.

   GUIDE PRACTICE Run your hand below the word as students blend the sounds with you and without you.

   Example: Students blend /f/ /i/ /sh/ as you run your hand under the word *fish*.

   CORRECTIVE FEEDBACK If students stop between sounds, then model how to say the sounds without stopping between them.

4. **Read the Word** Display the word.

   MODEL Blend the word by pronouncing it normally as you smoothly, but quickly, run your hand beneath it.

   GUIDE PRACTICE Have students say the sounds quickly to read the word.

   CORRECTIVE FEEDBACK If students have difficulty saying the sounds quickly, then model how to say the words first slowly and then quickly.

ROUTINE 3 • SOUND-BY-SOUND BLENDING

1 Introduce Blending Write and say the word and use visuals and gestures to convey its meaning.

2 Connect Sounds to Spelling

MODEL Say the first sound in the word and write the letter(s) that spell that sound. Tell students to watch your mouth and emphasize any letter combinations. Touch under the letter(s) as you say the sounds.

GUIDE PRACTICE Have students say the sound as you touch under the letter(s).

CORRECTIVE FEEDBACK If students say an incorrect sound, refer them to the appropriate Sound-Spelling Card.

3 Add a Sound-Spelling

MODEL Say the next sound in the word and add the letter(s) for that sound. Touch under the letter(s) as you say the sound.

GUIDE PRACTICE Have students say the sound as you touch under the letter(s).

CORRECTIVE FEEDBACK Use corrective feedback as shown above.

4 Blend Sounds

MODEL Run your hand from letter to letter as you say the sounds without pausing. Repeat until all sounds have been blended.

Example: Blend /sssaaaa/, /sssaaannn/, and /sssaaannnd/.

GUIDE PRACTICE Have students repeat each sound. Then have students blend the sounds with you and then without you.

CORRECTIVE FEEDBACK If students stop between sounds, then model how to say the sounds without stopping between them.

5 Read the Word

MODEL Blend the whole word. Run your hand under the letters as you say the sounds quickly to read the word.

GUIDE PRACTICE Have students blend the sounds quickly to read the word.

CORRECTIVE FEEDBACK If students have difficulty saying the sounds quickly, then model how to say the sounds first slowly and then quickly.

ROUTINE 4 • NONDECODABLE WORDS

1 Introduce Nondecodable Words
Some English words do not sound like their spellings. We learn how to say them by remembering the letters. We will say and spell the words together.

Example: Write *we.*

2 Connect Letters to Words

MODEL Point to and say the word. Use visuals, gestures, or examples to demonstrate the meaning of the word. Identify the letters in the word and indicate the number of letters in the word.

Example:
This is the word we.
It has two letters.
The letters are w *and* e.

GUIDE PRACTICE Have students repeat with you the word, the letters of the word, and the number of letters in the word. Then, have the students do this with a partner and then on their own.

CORRECTIVE FEEDBACK If students pronounce the word incorrectly, model again the sounds in the word. Remind students to watch how you move your mouth. Point out any letters that do not follow the standard rules or may be different from their native language patterns.

3 Demonstrate Usage

MODEL Use the nondecodable word in a sentence to demonstrate usage of the word. Provide an example that relates to their experience and uses the word in the same context as the text.

Example: Listen to this sentence: We go to school together.

GUIDE PRACTICE Have students use the word in a sentence. Provide a sentence frame if necessary.

CORRECTIVE FEEDBACK If students are not using the word correctly, model the correct usage again.

ROUTINE 5 • MULTISYLLABIC WORD STRATEGY

Use this routine for multisyllabic words that do not have prefixes, suffixes, or roots.

1. **Introduce the Strategy** *We can break some words into parts. Word parts, or chunks, help us read longer words.*

   Example: Write *rabbit.*

   When possible, use visuals or gestures to demonstrate the meaning of the word.

2. **Connect to Sound-Spellings** Explain that the parts of a word are called *syllables*. Break the word into syllables.

   Example: Rabbit *has two syllables:* rab *and* bit.

   MODEL *The syllables help me say the word.* Say each syllable as you run your hand from one syllable to the next. Then read the syllables together as you say the word.

   GUIDE PRACTICE Have students say each syllable as you run your hand underneath the letters in that syllable. Point out any letters or syllables that may be different from the students' native language.

   CORRECTIVE FEEDBACK If students have difficulty understanding syllables, have them place their hands underneath their chin. Then have the students repeat the word. Explain that each time their chin touches their hands, it indicates a syllable. Then write the words to show them how the words are divided into syllables.

3. **Read the Word**

   MODEL Read the syllables as you run your hand beneath them, and then read the syllables together as you say the word.

   Example: This is how I read this word. First I read each syllable, and then I read the syllables together: rab/bit—rabbit.

   GUIDE PRACTICE Have students read the syllables, and then read the word as you run your hand beneath the parts.

   CORRECTIVE FEEDBACK If students have difficulty using sound-spellings and syllabication to read word parts, then read one part at a time as you cover the remaining parts.

ROUTINE 6 • WORD PARTS STRATEGY

Use this routine to teach word structure skills: base words and inflected endings, prefixes, suffixes, contractions, compound words, syllables.

1. **Introduce the Strategy** *We will break longer words into smaller parts. Some word parts help us understand what a word means.*

   Example: Write *shorten.*

   When possible, use visuals, gestures, or examples to demonstrate the meaning of the word.

2. **Introduce the Word Parts** Discuss the word part that is the focus of the lesson, and, if appropriate, describe its relationship to the base word. Help students make any connections between suffixes or prefixes in English and their native language.

   Example: A word part added at the end of a word is called a suffix. *This word has two parts—*short *and* -en. Short *is the base word, and* -en *is the suffix.*

3. **Use Word Parts for Meaning** Explain the meanings of prefixes, suffixes, and inflected endings when introducing them. For compound words, demonstrate how you can sometimes, but not always, tell the meaning from its parts. Provide examples. Then check students' understanding.

   Example: The suffix -en *means "to make." When you add* -en *to the end of* short, *it changes the word. What does* shorten *mean?*

4. **Read the Word**

   MODEL Read the word parts as you run your hand beneath them, and then read the parts together to say the word.

   Example: First, I read the base word, short; *next, I read the suffix,* -en. *Then I read the two parts together:* short, en—shorten.

   GUIDE PRACTICE Have students identify the word parts and then read the word as you run your hand beneath the parts.

   CORRECTIVE FEEDBACK If students have difficulty reading word parts, then have them identify one part at a time as you cover the remaining parts. It may be necessary to have them blend the base word or individual syllables before reading the whole word.

ROUTINE 7 • FLUENCY: PAIRED READING

1. **Select the Text** Select a text or passage that is at students' reading level. If possible, pair the ELL with a student who reads fluently.
2. **First Reading** Students read the selected text, switching readers at a logical breaking place—for example, at the end of a sentence, paragraph, or page. Choose a smaller segment of text for students needing more support. Reader 1 begins while Reader 2 follows along, tracking the print with his or her fingers or eyes when the partner is reading.
3. **Second Reading** Partners reread, but Reader 2 begins so that each child is reading different text.
4. **Reread** For optimal fluency, students should reread the text three or four times.
5. **Provide Corrective Feedback** Listen to students read and provide corrective feedback regarding their oral reading (stress, rhythm, and intonation) and use of blending strategies. Keep in mind that ELLs can read fluently in English with an accent.

ROUTINE 8 • FLUENCY: CHORAL READING

1. **Select a Passage** Select a grade-level passage.
2. **Model** Have students track the print as you read. While you read, pay attention to the elements of fluency. Read at an appropriate rate and rhythm. Emphasize the correct stress and intonation for each sentence, such as phrasing a question and stressing the important words in the sentence.
3. **Guide Practice** Have students read along with you.
4. **On Their Own**
   - Have the class read aloud with you.
   - For optimal fluency, students should reread three or four times.

ROUTINE 9 • FLUENCY: TIMED READING

1 Select a Passage
- Select a passage at the student's reading level.
- Have two copies of the passage. Allow the student to read the text to him or herself before beginning.

2 Timed Reading
- Have the student read the text aloud.
- On your copy, mark any errors the student makes.
- Mark where the student is after one minute.

3 Figure Words Correct per Minute (WCPM) To figure WCPM, subtract the number of mistakes from the number of words the student read in one minute. Tell the student his or her WCPM, and explain that by practicing, he or she will try to exceed it.

4 Review Review with the student mistakes he or she made. Help the student reread unknown words until he or she can do so without errors.

5 Timed Reading
- Have the student reread the passage now that he or she is comfortable with the difficult words.
- Figure out his or her WCPM during the second round. Let the student know how much he or she has improved. Point out the importance of practicing.

6 Provide Corrective Feedback Remind students that the goal is not to read as quickly as possible, but to read accurately and quickly.

7 Extra Time Invite students to set their own WCPM goal for another section. Help them to reach that goal.

ROUTINE 10 • RETELLING/SUMMARIZING: NARRATIVE

1 Introduce Retelling *When we retell a story, we tell the story in our own words. Before we can retell a story, we need to know the parts of the story.*

2 Identify Setting and Character

MODEL *First, I think about the setting and characters. The setting is where the story takes place. The characters are the people or animals in the story.* Give an example from a familiar story. You may choose a story the student knows from his or her native culture.

> *Example:* In this story, there is a little girl named Goldilocks and three bears. The three bears live in the forest.

GUIDE PRACTICE Help students list the characters and setting of the story. *The three bears live in the forest. What is the setting? The three bears are characters. Who is another character in the story?*

CORRECTIVE FEEDBACK If students have difficulty identifying the setting and characters, have them use the illustrations or Retelling Cards as clues.

3 Identify Plot Help students create a three-part story map to list what happens at the beginning, middle, and end of the story. *When I retell a story, I think about the plot. The plot is what happens in a story. A plot has a beginning, a middle, and an end.*

MODEL *In the first part of the story, Goldilocks was walking in the forest when she saw an empty house.*

GUIDE PRACTICE *What happens at the middle of the story? What happens at the end?* Help students draw or write their answers in each section.

4 Retell the Story

MODEL *My story map will help me retell the story.* Model retelling the story, emphasizing the characters, the setting, and the plot.

GUIDE PRACTICE Have partners take turns retelling the story using their own story maps.

CORRECTIVE FEEDBACK If a student has difficulty retelling the story, have him or her reread the story or use the illustrations in their retelling.

ROUTINE 11 • RETELLING/SUMMARIZING: NONFICTION

1 Introduce Summarizing Explain to students that summarizing a passage means telling what it was about. Summarizing does not include details. It just includes the most important parts.

2 What Happened?

MODEL *When I summarize, I ask myself, what is the passage mostly about? Sometimes, I use pictures or graphic sources to remind me.*

Example: This selection is mostly about wild animals because most of the selection tells about animals that can be found in the wild. I also see a picture of a bear in a forest.

GUIDE PRACTICE Help students make a concept web. In the center, write a few words about the selection. Then have students write or draw the most important parts in the outer circles.

CORRECTIVE FEEDBACK If students have difficulty telling the important parts, model how to find them by pointing to pictures and talking about what you see.

3 When Did It Happen?

MODEL *I can also summarize important events that happen over a period of time. I tell what happened first, next, and last. Knowing when the events happened helps me understand what I read.*

Example: First, the bird collects twigs. Next, it builds a nest. Last, the bird lays its eggs.

GUIDE PRACTICE Help students fill out a sequence chart. Write the words *first, next,* and *last* and fill in the first event. Have students write or draw to fill in the chart.

CORRECTIVE FEEDBACK If students have difficulty tracking the sequence, have them use the pictures and point to what happens first, next, and last.

ROUTINE 12 • SPELLING

1 Introduce Spelling *We will use the sounds and letters we know to spell words. First, listen to the word. Then say its sounds and write the letters.*

2 Dictate the Word Say the word, use it in a sentence, and then repeat the word.

Example: clog. *The sink has a* clog. clog.

3 Segment the Sounds

MODEL Sound out the word. The word is *clog*. The sounds in *clog* are /kl/ /ȯ/ /g/. Have students echo each sound.

GUIDE PRACTICE Repeat the word and have students segment the sounds.

CORRECTIVE FEEDBACK If students are having difficulty, drag each sound out: /cl/ /ȯ/ /g/. Remind students to watch how you move your mouth. Emphasize any sounds that may be different or new to the students' native languages.

4 Spell the Sounds

MODEL Say the first sound and write its spelling. Continue with each sound and spelling until the entire word has been written.

GUIDE PRACTICE Ask a volunteer what letter or letters make the first sound. Write the letter or letters. Repeat with the other sounds. Have students say each sound with you and then write its spelling after you.

CORRECTIVE FEEDBACK If students have difficulty spelling a sound, have them refer to the Sound-Spelling Card to identify the spelling.

5 Proofread Spelling Continue the dictation until all words have been spelled. Then display the correct spelling for each word. Help students proofread their work, circle any misspelled words, and write them correctly. Help them understand any common errors by asking their reasoning for the mistake. Point out any spelling patterns that do not follow the standard rules or may be different from their native language.

ROUTINE 13 • CONCEPT TALK VIDEO

1. **Introduce Talk Video** Explain to students that they will be watching a video. Explain that the video will introduce the Question of the Week.
2. **Assess Understanding** Once the video ends, ask students, "What is the question of the week?" Have students write the answer. Then, replay the section of the video that answers this question. Pause it when done. Ask students if everyone got the answer right.
3. **Access Prior Knowledge** Invite students to discuss any prior knowledge they have about the weekly question or concept. Encourage them to share their experiences. Invite struggling speakers to draw a picture that illustrates their experience.
4. **Summarize** Begin the video again. Pause it at critical points, such as when new information is taught. Confirm that students understand what they have seen by asking them to summarize the section they just watched.

   CORRECTIVE FEEDBACK If students are unable to summarize sections, rewind and watch that section again. Before they attempt to summarize, ask questions that will guide them to understand the main idea of the section.
5. **Graphic Organizer** Draw a two-columned graphic organizer. Title one column *What I Knew* and the next *What I Learned*. Have students fill in the columns using information about the weekly question that they already knew, and information they learned while watching the video.

   CORRECTIVE FEEDBACK If students struggle when filling in the second column, allow them to watch the video again.

ROUTINE 14 • AUDIOTEXT CD

1. **Before Listening** Have students open their Student Edition to the selection. Explain to students that they are going to read along while listening to the selection on a CD.
2. **During Listening** Ask students to keep pace with the CD by moving their finger along the text of their Student Edition. Encourage students to raise their hand if they get lost or hear a phrase or word they do not understand. Pause the CD and write the problem words and phrases. Allow the selection to finish.
3. **Model** Replay the CD, allowing students to watch you choral read along with it. Make sure you imitate not only the words but the expression with which they are read.
4. **After Listening** Review any misunderstood words or phrases. For words, sound each out, calling special attention to blends before putting them all together. Have students choral read the words with you. If a phrase is an idiom, explain its meaning.
5. **On Their Own** Place students in pairs. Instruct them to practice reading sections of the text until they are comfortable reading them at the same pace as the CD. Encourage partners to help each other through passages they may find difficult.

   CORRECTIVE FEEDBACK Make sure students do not sacrifice accuracy for speed. If there is a difficult section in the reading, replay it so students can practice.

ROUTINE 15 • GRAMMAR JAMMER

1 Introduce Grammar Jammer Tell students that you will play a song about the weekly convention. Describe what the song is about and how it relates to the lesson.

Example: The song is about adjectives. It tells how to use adjectives to compare nouns.

2 Display the Concept Review the concept before playing the song. Write one or more key parts from the song that is supported by the text on the screen.

Example: You can use an adjective to compare two nouns. Just add an -er.

short + er = short<u>er</u>

tall + er = tall<u>er</u>

loud + er = loud<u>er</u>

quiet + er = quiet<u>er</u>

MODEL Play the song for students. Pause the song at key points to review concepts. Write the text on screen and point to the visuals that support the concept. Replay these parts and model using them to understand the concept.

GUIDE PRACTICE Have students read aloud the text on screen. Prompt students to apply the grammar concepts. Ask questions, provide sentence frames, or have students give more examples.

Example: Shorter, taller, louder, quieter. *These are comparative adjectives. Can you give another example?*

CORRECTIVE FEEDBACK Replay any parts that students do not understand. Pause to review the text on screen and visuals. Have a volunteer explain how the song relates to the concept.

ROUTINE 16 • MODELED PRONUNCIATION AUDIO CD

1 Before Listening Tell students that they will be listening to a CD to help with sound pronunciation. Advise them to keep their Sound-Spelling Cards ready.

2 During Listening After each pronunciation, hit pause. Repeat the sound, exaggerating your mouth movements. Then, have students repeat the sound after you. Rewind and play the sound again. Write the letters that make the sound. Repeat it and have students do the same.

Example: The sound is /mp/. The letters that make the sound are m *and* p. *Listen as I say the sound again: /mp/.*

3 After Listening Guide students to look at the letters you wrote. Then have them match their Sound-Spelling Cards to the sounds they learned. Once again, go through each sound, this time allowing the student to look at his or her card as you do so.

4 Guided Practice Hold up a Sound-Spelling Card and call on a volunteer to pronounce the sound. Continue to do so until they have all been pronounced in the order they were learned. Finally, challenge students by rearranging the cards and have them repeat the exercise.

5 On Their Own Pair students with partners. Challenge them to pronounce the sound on each card without referring to the CD.

CORRECTIVE FEEDBACK If students have difficulty recalling the sound, replay the CD and point out each example as it plays.

Graphic Organizers

Table of Contents

K-W-L Chart

Topic ______________________

What Do I **K** now?	What Do I **W** ant to Learn?	What Did I **L** earn?

Word Rating Chart

Word	Know	Have Seen	Don't Know

Story Predictions Chart

Title______________________________

What might happen?	What clues do I have?	What did happen?

Story Map A

Title ______________________________

Beginning

↓

Middle

↓

End

Story Map B

Title

Characters

Who is in the story?

Setting

Where does the story happen?

When does the story happen?

Events

What happens in the story?

Story Comparison

Title A ______________________

____

Characters

Who is in the story?

Setting

Where and **when** does it happen?

Events

What happens in the story?

Title B ______________________

____

Characters

Who is in the story?

Setting

Where and **when** does it happen?

Events

What happens in the story?

Web

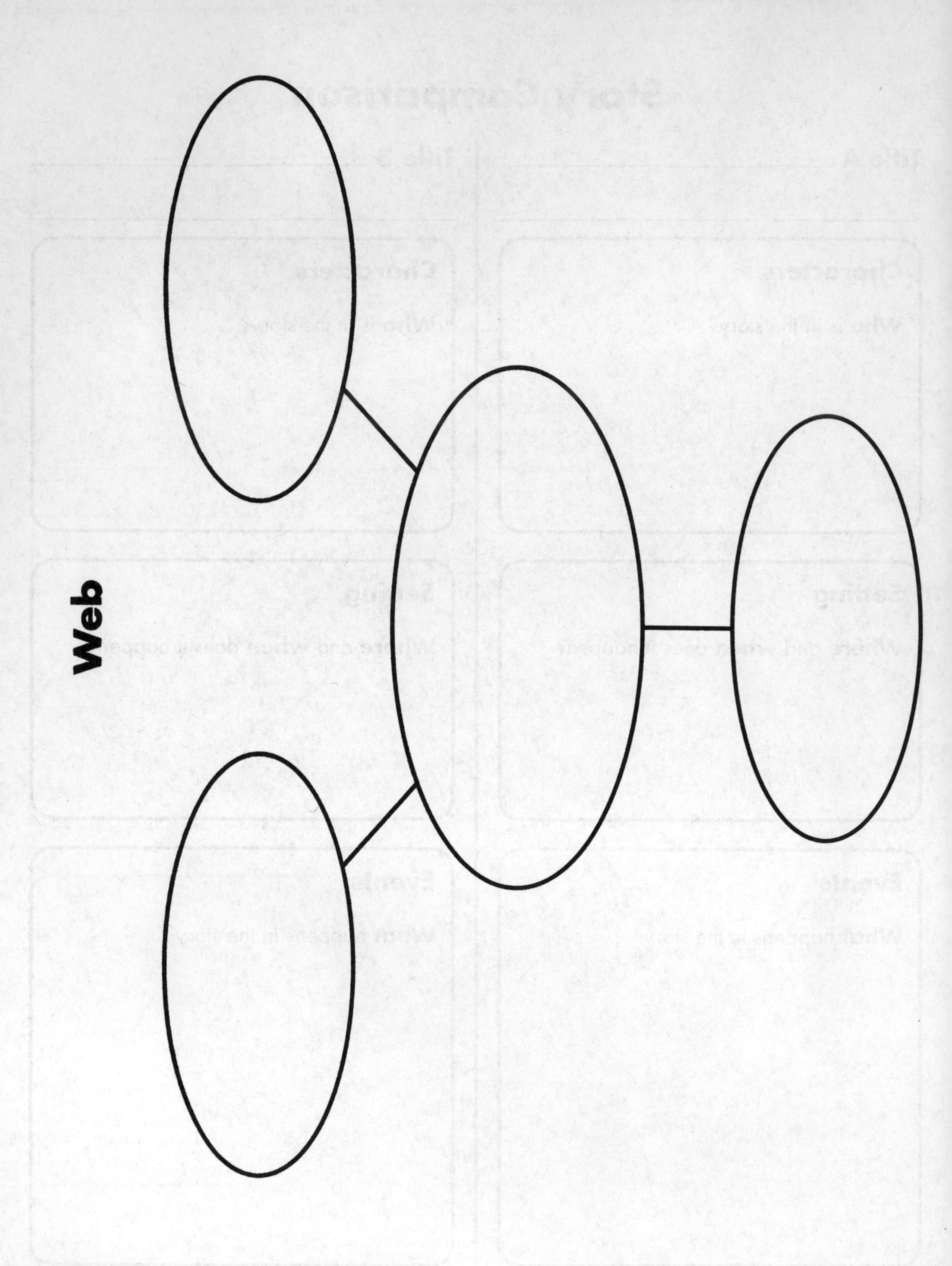

Main Idea

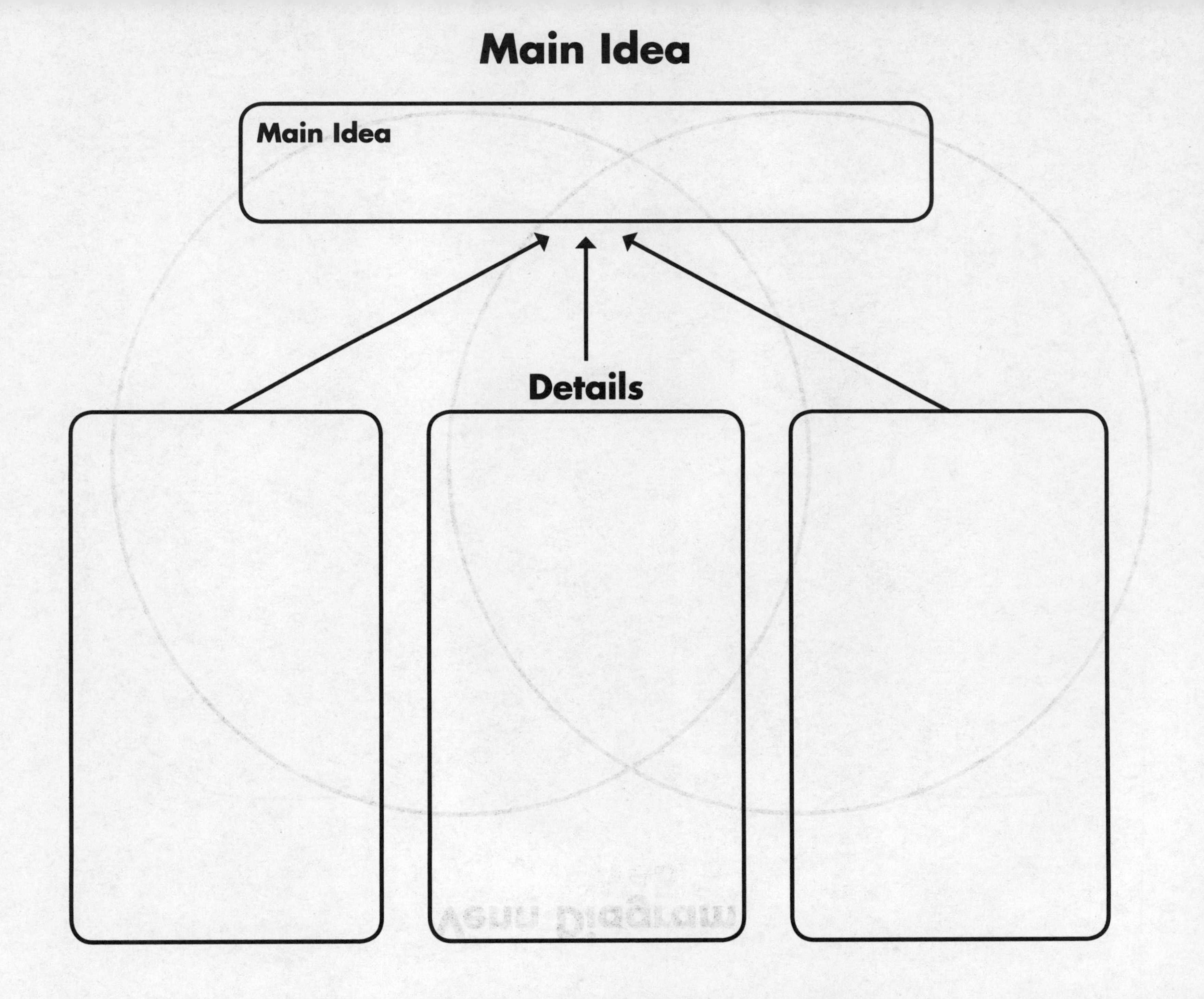

Venn Diagram

Cause and Effect

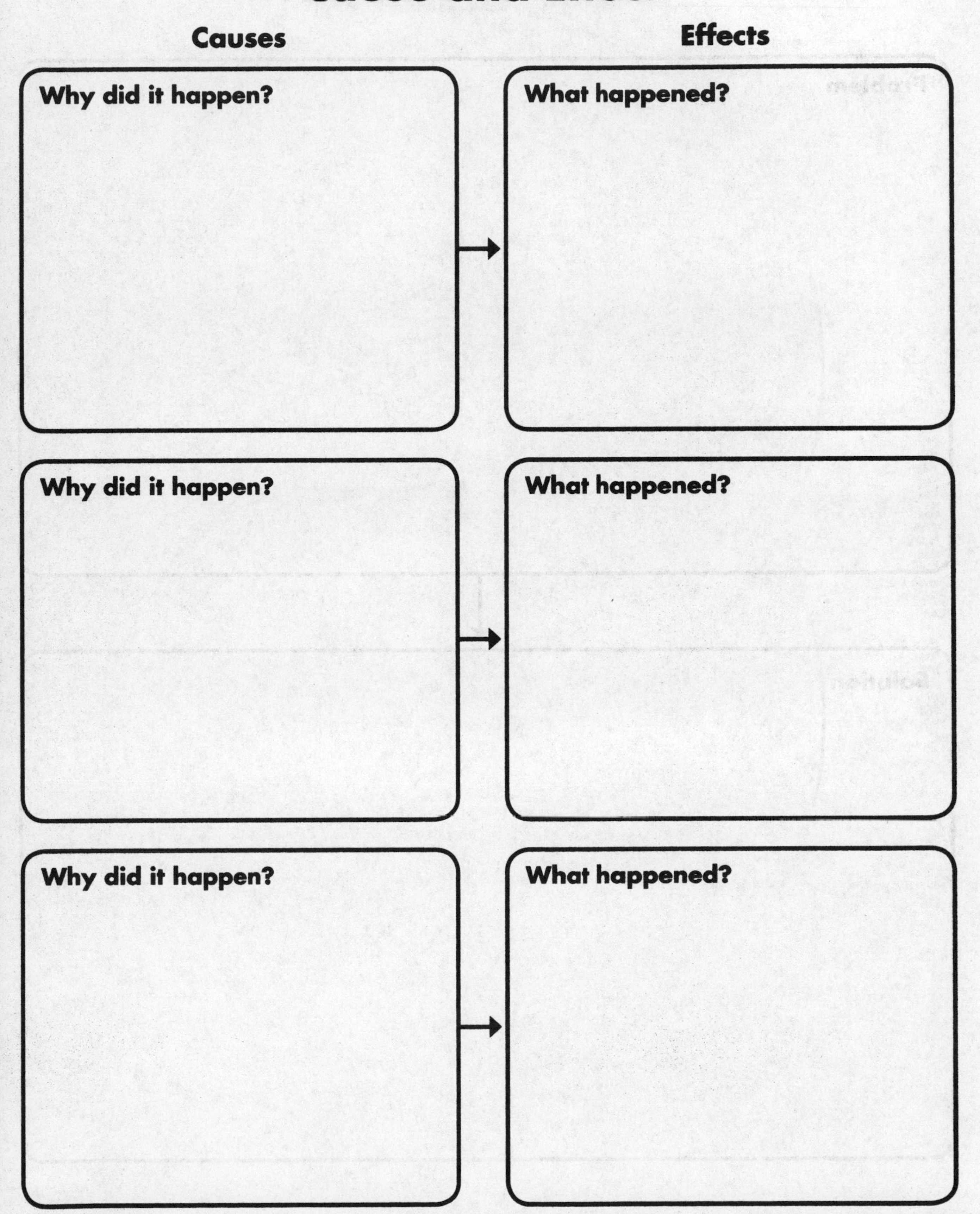

Problem and Solution

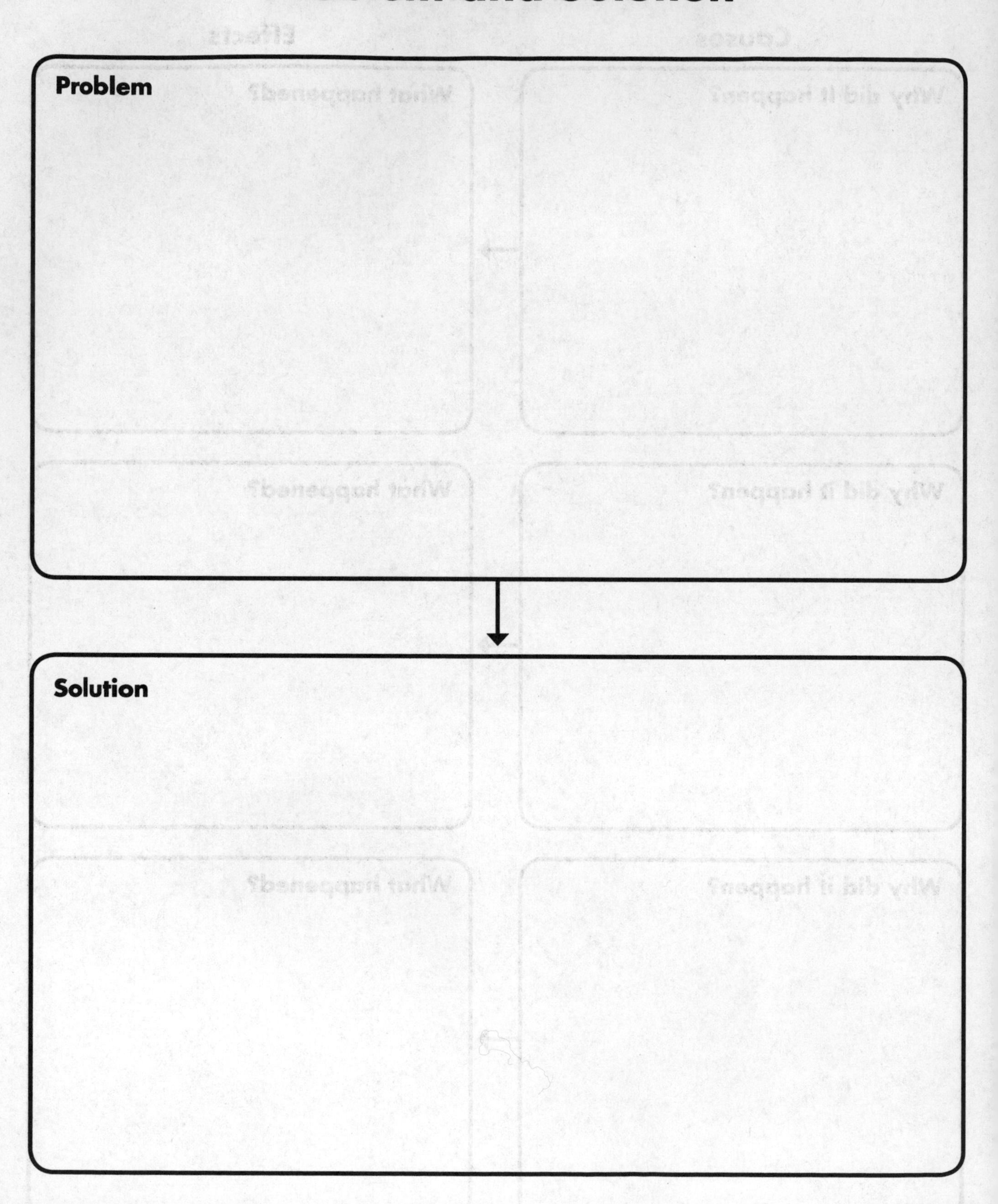

Time Line

Date

Steps in a Process

Process ________________________________

Step 1

Step 2

Step 3

T-Chart

Three-Column Chart

Outline Form

Title ______________________________

A ______________________________

1. ______________________________

2. ______________________________

3. ______________________________

B ______________________________

1. ______________________________

2. ______________________________

3. ______________________________

C ______________________________

1. ______________________________

2. ______________________________

3. ______________________________

K-W-L CHART

About the Graphic Organizer

Students use what they know to explore prior knowledge about a selection, set purposes for reading, and record what they learn as they read.

Instructional Routine

The K-W-L chart works well with expository text. Display the chart for students.

- Write the word *Know* on the board. Underline the *K*. Tell students that the *K* stands for "What Do I Know?" Ask students what they know about the topic and model recording their responses.
- Write *Want* on the board and underline *W*. Tell students that the *W* stands for "What Do I Want to Learn?" Ask students what they want to know about the topic. Model recording their responses in the form of questions.
- Write *Learn* on the board. Underline the *L*. Tell students that the *L* stands for "What Did I Learn?" As you read, ask students what they are learning. Model recording their responses on the chart.

Teaching Tips

- After modeling, students can complete the K-W-L chart in pairs or small groups.
- Suggest that, if students are unclear about a topic they have recorded in the *K* column, they can turn it into a question for the *L* column.
- Modify the chart if necessary by changing the headings into sentence frames: *I know* __________ *I want to know* __________ *I learned* __________

Extensions

- Create K-W-L charts that you can post in the room as you learn about different topics in content areas, such as social studies and science. Students can add to the charts as they learn more.
- Have students work in pairs to read an article at their reading level. They can use K-W-L charts to organize their thinking.

Skill and Strategies

- Activate Prior Knowledge
- Set Purpose
- Summarize

WORD RATING CHART

About the Graphic Organizer

The word rating chart helps students explore what words they already know and what words are new to them.

Instructional Routine

You can use this chart with any list of words that students are studying.

- Display the chart for students and list words on the chart. Have students copy the chart.
- Explain that the word *Know* means that students know and can use the word. Model placing a check in the second column for words that students know.
- Explain that column 3, *Have Seen*, means that students have seen or heard the word, but they aren't sure what it means. Model placing a check in the third column.
- Explain that column 4, *Don't Know*, means that students don't know the word at all. Model placing a check in the fourth column.

Teaching Tips

- After modeling, students can complete a word rating chart on their own. You might write the words in the chart and copy before distributing.
- Use the chart as a diagnostic tool to determine which words you'll focus on in classroom studies.

Extensions

- Have students revisit their charts after they have read a selection or studied the words. They can adjust their ratings.
- Consider adding a column to the chart in which students can write sentences with words they know.
- Encourage students to state meanings of words in their own words. Explain what it means to tell a meaning in your own words.

Skill and Strategies

- Activate Prior Knowledge
- Recall and Retell
- Context Clues

STORY PREDICTIONS CHART

About the Graphic Organizer

Students preview the selection title and illustrations and then predict what might happen in the selection.

Instructional Routine

This graphic organizer works well with any selection in which the title and/or pictures suggest predictions about the events in a story. Consider using it for content-area selections as well.

- Preview the selection with students. Read the title and lead a picture walk. Ask students to predict what they think will happen in the selection. Remind them to use what they know about the topic of the story. Record their predictions in the chart.
- Ask students how they figured out what would happen. Tell them that they used *clues*. Ask what clues they used and record those clues in the chart.
- After reading, look back at the predictions. Write what actually happened in the third column. Ask students how their predictions were different. Why do they think their predictions were different from what really happened?

Teaching Tips

- Focus on clues in illustrations. What details in the illustrations help students make predictions?
- Provide sentence frames for predicting. *I think ________ will happen. I think this will happen because ________.*

Extensions

- After completing this activity as a class exercise, have students use the chart in pairs, small groups, or independently.
- Use the chart with content-area selections. Focus on the content, giving students a sentence frame to use: *I think I will learn about ________ because ________.*

Skill and Strategies

- Predict
- Activate Prior Knowledge
- Draw Conclusions

STORY MAP A

About the Graphic Organizer

Students use this chart to record the sequence of events in a selection.

Instructional Routine

This organizer works well with any selection with a clear sequence of events.

- Display the organizer. Write the title of the selection.
- Start reading. Ask students to tell you what events in the beginning of the story are important. Write them on the chart.
- Focus on events in the middle of the story, recording them in the chart.
- As you finish the selection, record important events from the end.

Teaching Tips

- Make a list of words that tell time order, such as *after, later, first,* or *next*. Provide sentence frames to help students use them.
- Encourage students to use story maps to retell the events to partners.

Extensions

- Have students draw pictures of events in the organizer. They can label the pictures.
- Use the story map with events in social studies or with steps in a sequence in other content-area reading.

Skill and Strategies

- Sequence/Plot
- Recall and Retell
- Text Structure
- Summarize

STORY MAP B

About the Graphic Organizer

Students record the characters and setting of a story and track a sequence of events.

Instructional Routine

This graphic organizer works well with any selection that has a clear series of events. It can help students understand the relationship between the sequence of events and the outcome of the story.

- Display the organizer. Write the title of the selection on the organizer.
- Read the selection. Ask students where and when the story takes place. Record those details in the *setting* section.
- As you read, record information about characters on the organizer.
- As you read, pause to record information about the sequence of events.

Teaching Tips

- Model sentence frames for talking about characters and setting: _____ *is a person/animal in this story. This story takes place in (the future/the past/today).*
- Help students look for clue words for sequence. Make a list of clue words to display for students' reference.
- Students may not need all the boxes, or they may need more. Help them modify the organizer depending on the story.

Extensions

- After completing this activity as a class exercise, have students use the chart in pairs, small groups, or independently.
- Students can draw events in the organizer and label those events.
- Help students think of words to use to describe characters. Make a list and have students add to it.

Skill and Strategies

- Story Elements: Character, Setting, Plot
- Recall and Retell
- Summarize

STORY COMPARISON

About the Graphic Organizer

Students use this chart to record how two selections are similar and different.

Instructional Routine

This organizer works well with selections that have something in common. It's a great tool for comparing texts by the same author or about the same topic.

- Choose two stories to compare. Write their titles on the organizer.
- Ask questions to elicit characters, setting, and plot events. Record details on the chart.

Teaching Tips

- After modeling how to use the organizer, students can work on the organizer with partners or in small groups.
- Provide sentence frames for comparison and model how to use them, such as: *The characters in this story are* _____, *but the characters in that story are* _____.
- Invite students to use the chart to retell stories.

Extensions

- Students can use the chart to compare a story and a nonfiction text about the same topic.
- Have students use one half the chart to plan the writing of their own story.

Skill and Strategies

- Story Elements: Character, Setting, Plot
- Text Structure
- Summarize
- Compare and Contrast

WEB

About the Graphic Organizer

Students explore their prior knowledge as they brainstorm related ideas, recognize concept relationships, and/or organize information. They can highlight a central concept and connect it to related words, ideas, or details.

Instructional Routine

This graphic organizer has multiple uses and is appropriate for all levels of learners. Use different approaches to the web as you develop the organizer with students.

- Display the organizer. Write a central idea or topic in the middle of the web.
- Ask students for ideas that are related to the central idea. Record those ideas in the circles attached to the middle circle.
- You can add ideas related to the "sub ideas" in additional ovals.

Teaching Tips

- Once you have modeled how to use the organizer, have students complete the organizer independently, in pairs, or in small groups.
- Encourage students to explain how the ideas on the web are related to the central ideas. Provide sentence frames to help students talk about the web. *The main idea is* ________ *One related idea is* ________
- Use this web to explore main ideas and details, character names along with their traits, vocabulary words and their synonyms, and so on.

Extensions

- Students can use the organizer to record ideas about a theme or about a topic in content-area reading.
- Have students use the web to record background knowledge about a topic. Use the webs to assess gaps in understanding as you plan instruction.
- Enlarge the graphic organizer so that students can draw in the circles. They can label or write sentences about their drawings.

Skill and Strategies

- Classify
- Summarize
- Main Idea and Details

MAIN IDEA

About the Graphic Organizer

Students recognize a main idea and distinguish between the main idea and the details.

Instructional Routine

This organizer works especially well with nonfiction selections that are organized around main ideas and details.

- Record a main idea in the top box. Define *main idea* as the most important idea.
- Model by recording a detail that supports, or tells more about, the main idea. Then have students supply additional details as you record them.

Teaching Tips

- Supply a sentence frame about main ideas: *The most important idea is* ________ Supply a sentence frame about details. *One detail about this idea is* ________
- Model how to tell a supporting detail from a detail that is not a supporting detail. Let students know that some ideas are important to know and other ideas are interesting to know. Display part of a selection and model highlighting important ideas.
- Extend or add additional boxes if necessary to add more details.

Extensions

- Have students use the organizer to record ideas for writing pieces of their own.
- Have students use the chart in pairs or small groups to record important ideas from content-area reading, such as in social studies or science.

Skill and Strategies

- Main Idea and Details
- Summarize

VENN DIAGRAM

About the Graphic Organizer

Students use this organizer to record similarities and differences between places, ideas, characters, or other elements of fiction or nonfiction.

Instructional Routine

A Venn diagram works well in any situation that lends itself to comparing and contrasting.

- Start by comparing and contrasting something simple and familiar, such as cats and dogs. Write the subjects you are comparing over the circles of the Venn diagram.
- Point to where the circles overlap. Let students know that in this section, you'll write similarities, or how the two things are alike. Ask how the two subjects are alike. Record students' responses.
- Point to an individual circle and let students know that, in this section, you'll write details that describe only what is labeled at the top of the circle. Ask students to list details as you record them.

Teaching Tips

- It might help students if you ask questions that lead to details to write in the diagram, such as *Are both of these objects blue? Do both of them have four legs?* and so on.
- Help students with sentence frames: *These two things are alike because* ________ *These two things are different because* ________
- List words that signal comparing and contrasting, such as *alike, different, but,* and so on. Students can point to those words in the text.

Extensions

- Students can create Venn diagrams to compare themselves to characters in fictional texts.
- Students can use Venn diagrams to compare topics in content areas, such as comparing two types of rock, two types of volcanoes, or two animals or plants.

Skill and Strategies

- Compare and Contrast
- Summarize

CAUSE AND EFFECT

About the Graphic Organizer

Students identify cause-and-effect relationships in either fiction or nonfiction.

Instructional Routine

This graphic organizer works well with any selection that has clear cause-and-effect relationships.

- Tell students that something that happens is an effect. Record an effect on the graphic organizer.
- Then ask students "Why did it happen?" Tell them the reason something happens is a cause. Record the cause on the graphic organizer.

Teaching Tips

- Remind students to ask themselves *What happened?* and *Why did it happen?* to identify effects and causes. It is usually easier to identify effects first, before the causes.
- List clue words that signal causes and effects, such as *because* and *so*. Look over the clue words with students, but remind them that not all causes and effects in selections have clue words.

Extensions

- Students can write causes and effects in their content-area classes. They could record, for example, causes of thunderstorms or of events in history.
- Once students are able to use this organizer, point out that, in some cases, there are many causes for one effect or many effects for one cause. Alter the organizer with students so they can use it with multiple causes and effects.
- If students need extra assistance, fill in either causes or effects before distributing the organizer. Ask students to work in pairs to find the corresponding causes or effects.

Skill and Strategies

- Cause and Effect
- Summarize
- Text Structure

PROBLEM AND SOLUTION

About the Graphic Organizer

Students identify problems and solutions presented in fiction or nonfiction.

Instructional Routine

This graphic organizer works well with any selection with clear problems and solutions.

- Tell students that a problem is something that needs to be solved. Give an example of a simple classroom problem. Record it in the organizer.
- Ask students what they might do to "fix" the problem. Tell students that fixing a problem is solving a problem. Ask students how they might solve the problem. Record their ideas in the solution section.

Teaching Tips

- Once students understand how to use the organizer, focus on a problem and solution from a piece of text.
- Point out that not all solutions are "good." Sometimes the way a character solves a problem might result in an unhappy ending for the story.
- Provide sentence frames to help students discuss problems and solutions. *One problem in the text is ______. One way to solve it is ______.*

Extensions

- Write a problem in the school, classroom, or community in the first box and distribute organizers to pairs or small groups. Students can brainstorm solutions.
- Students can draw problems and solutions in the organizer and then label them with words or phrases.

Skill and Strategies

- Plot
- Summarize
- Text Structure

TIME LINE

About the Graphic Organizer

Students organize events from fiction or nonfiction in sequential order along a continuum.

Instructional Routine

This organizer works well with any selection that presents events in sequential order. It can also help students organize events in order.

- After reading a short text, ask students what happened first. Record the first event on the chart.
- Continue asking students to name events in order, placing them on the continuum.

Teaching Tips

- Remind students to look for clues in the text to the order in which things happen. They might find dates or clue words such as *first, next, then,* and *last.*
- If students need extra support, write events from the text on sentence strips. Have students work in pairs or small groups to place the strips in order and then write the events on the time line.

Extensions

- Students can create time lines about events in history or even things that have happened in their school or community.
- Have students interview partners and create time lines based on important events in their partners' lives.
- Share time lines from social studies texts with students. Have them discuss what the time lines have in common and identify their features.

Skill and Strategies

- Summarize
- Text Structure
- Sequence/Plot

STEPS IN A PROCESS

About the Graphic Organizer

Students break down a process into simple steps or directions.

Instructional Routine

This graphic organizer works well with any procedure that has relatively few steps. If students need more or smaller steps, help students redesign the organizer.

- Display the organizer. Write the title on the organizer, such as *Making a Peanut Butter Sandwich.*
- Ask students what the first step is. Record the first step in the organizer.
- Write the remaining steps in the organizer in order as students supply them.

Teaching Tips

- Once students can contribute to a steps in a process chart, have them work in pairs or small groups to write the steps of a simple process.
- Tell students to look for clue words such as *first, next,* and *later* to help them sequence the steps.

Extensions

- Students may draw the steps in the organizer and label them with words or phrases.
- Have students use the organizer to show steps in a recipe, a science project, or in another content area.

Skill and Strategies

- Steps in a Process
- Sequence
- Visualize

T-CHART

About the Graphic Organizer

Students can explore and compare ideas, story elements, or vocabulary words. They can also chart ideas within and across texts, or between prior knowledge and new ideas.

Instructional Routine

This is a multipurpose graphic organizer that is helpful when exploring two concepts. It works well with all types of selections.

- Model using the chart. Display the chart and write two topics being studied on the chart, one topic per column.
- Elicit responses from students based on the topics chosen. Record responses in the chart.

Teaching Tips

- Students can write in the chart, but they can also draw and list or label.
- Students can use the T-chart to compare story elements, such as the traits of two characters.
- Use a T-chart to organize ideas gathered in a class brainstorming session.
- Use a T-chart to explore two vocabulary words. Write the words at the tops of the columns. Then under each word, list part of speech, a simple definition, and a sentence using the word in context.

Extensions

- Students can work with partners, each partner completing one half of the chart.
- Students can use T-charts to write the pros and cons of a topic for a debate or discussion.

Skill and Strategies

- Compare and Contrast
- Main Idea and Details
- Summarize
- Activate Prior Knowledge

THREE-COLUMN CHART

About the Graphic Organizer

The chart can be used to explore or classify ideas, story elements, genres, or vocabulary features. It can also help students recognize comparisons and contrasts, or chart ideas within and across texts.

Instructional Routine

This is a multi-purpose organizer that works well for exploring and organizing ideas for three concepts, words, or ideas. It works well with many selections.

- ○ Display the organizer. Choose three simple headings and write them on the chart, such as three different vocabulary words.
- ○ Ask students for details for each heading and record them on the chart. Point out that this chart helps organize information.

Teaching Tips

- Once you have modeled how to use the organizer, students can complete organizers independently or in pairs or small groups.
- Students can draw in the charts as well as list ideas.
- Students can use the three-column chart to explore story characteristics or characteristics of genre.
- Students can use the chart to organize ideas they generate during brainstorming.
- Students can use the chart to organize synonyms, antonyms, and multiple meanings of words. Create a class chart to model using the chart for vocabulary study.

Extensions

- Students can use the organizer to record ideas that follow the idea of *before, during,* and *after.*
- Students can use the chart to organize ideas in any curricular area. For example, students could organize odd numbers, even numbers, and prime numbers in math. In science, they could record details about categories of animals, such as birds, reptiles, and mammals.

Skill and Strategies

- Classify
- Summarize
- Main Idea and Details
- Activate Prior Knowledge

OUTLINE FORM

About the Graphic Organizer

Students use a simplified outline form to take notes on the organization of print materials or to organize their own thoughts before writing.

Instructional Routine

Writers can change the outline form to suit their own purposes, but this form gets students started with the basic outline organization.

- ○ Model using the outline form by outlining a simple text. Place the title on the top line.
- ○ Show students how to record the main ideas. You might display the text to point out where to find the main ideas in the text. Reread the main ideas as you record them on the form.
- ○ Break down the main ideas into smaller details on the secondary lines.
- ○ Model the same form as the basis for a class writing about something that you are currently studying.

Teaching Tips

- Depending on their English proficiency, students can use words, phrases, or sentences in their outlines. Encourage them to be consistent throughout the entire outline.
- If students use outlines for writing, point out that the outlines are tools that can be revised before and during writing if the organization will make more sense.

Extensions

- Create an outline by doing a class outline on a piece of content-area text, such as an article from a science book.
- Show students text features in a content-area book, such as titles, heads, subheads, labels, and captions. Ask how these features might help them create an outline.

Skill and Strategies

- Text Structure
- Summarize
- Main Idea and Details